ILLUSTRATED THEATRE PRODUCTION GUIDE

Illustrated Theatre Production Guide delivers a step-by-step approach to the most prevalent and established theatre production practices, focusing on essential issues related to the construction of wooden, fabric, plastic, and metal scenery used on the stage. A must-have resource for both the community theatre worker who must be a jack of all trades and the student who needs to learn the fundamentals on his or her own, it covers the necessities in great detail, without bogging you down. Offering techniques and best-practice methods from an experienced industry expert, it will allow you to create a foundation on which to build a successful and resourceful career behind the scenes in theatre production.

This third edition has been completely restructured to more effectively lead you through the basics of stagecraft. Through detailed lessons and hundreds of drawings, author John Holloway offers you solutions to the problems that you'll face every day in a production, from rigging to knot tying. New to this edition are guides to jobs in theatre, construction documentation, and video projection methods, with expanded information on Thrust Theatres, lighting, and audio and video practices.

John Holloway is a Full Professor in the Theatre Department of the University of Kentucky where he has taught for 31 years. He is an on-going freelancer involved in designing, engineering, and constructing stage scenery for television and theatre. He worked as stagehand and Technical Director for over 30 years, and has built scenery for over 300 plays, television shows, commercials, operas, and trade shows. He is a longstanding member of the professional stagehand's union, IATSE, and served as the president of Local 346 for many years. He toured with the national touring companies of *Grand Hotel* (Tony Award winner, 1989), *The Will Rogers Follies*, and *Camelot*. He also works as a rigger and spot operator for rock concerts.

ILLUSTRATED THEATRE PRODUCTION GUIDE

THIRD EDITION

JOHN HOLLOWAY

Focal Press
Taylor & Francis Group

NEW YORK AND LONDON

First published 2002 by Focal Press

This edition published 2014
by Focal Press
70 Blanchard Road, Suite 402, Burlington, MA 01803

and by Focal Press
2 Park Square, Milton Park, Abingdon, Oxon OX14 4RN

Focal Press is an imprint of the Taylor & Francis Group, an informa business

Library of Congress Cataloging in Publication Data
Holloway, John, 1954–
    Illustrated theatre production guide/John Holloway. — Third edition.
    pages cm
    1. Stage management. 2. Theaters—Stage-setting and scenery. I. Title.
    PN2085.H64 2014
    792.02′32—dc23
    2013050360

ISBN: 978-0-415-71752-6 (pbk)
ISBN: 978-1-138-78144-3 (hbk)
ISBN: 978-1-315-87129-5 (ebk)

Typeset in Adobe Garamond and Frutiger
by Florence Production Ltd, Stoodleigh, Devon, UK

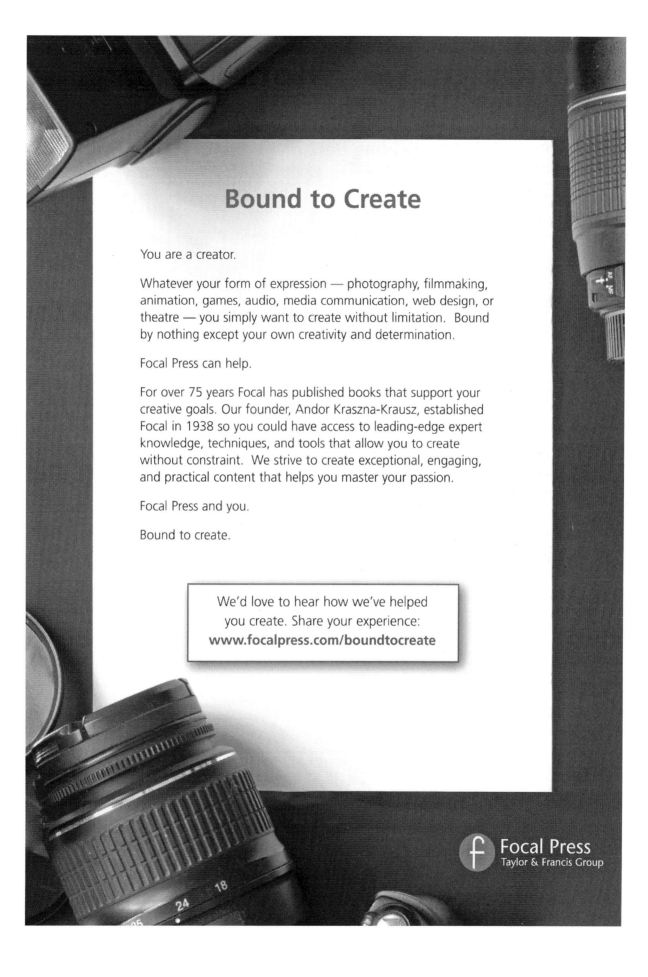

CONTENTS

Preface   ix

SECTION ONE—**WORKING IN A THEATRE**   **1**

 1 Jobs in Theatre   3
 2 Theatre Buildings   25
 3 Thrust Theatres   33
 4 Proscenium Theatres   37
 5 Curtains and Backdrops   45
 6 Ropes and Knots   60
 7 Theatre Rigging   68
 8 Arena Rigging   82

SECTION TWO—**THINGS IN A SCENE SHOP**   **91**

 9 Hand Tools   93
10 Wooden Joinery   111
11 Wood and Lumber   134
12 Essential Theatre Supplies   145

SECTION THREE—**BUILDING SCENERY**   **175**

13 Construction Documents   177
14 Flats   189
15 Stairs   220
16 Decking   232
17 Metal Working   249

SECTION FOUR—**STAGE LIGHTING**   **275**

18 Electrical Theory   277
19 Power Distribution   295

20   Lighting Control   308

21   Photometrics   325

22   Hanging and Focusing   347

SECTION FIVE—AUDIO AND VIDEO   **365**

23   Audio Theory   367

24   Sound Reinforcement   374

25   Digital Audio Files   386

26   Video Projection for the Stage   398

Appendix   *411*

Index   *419*

PREFACE TO THE THIRD EDITION

FIFTEEN YEARS AGO this book began life as a "shop cookbook" that had lots of information about the techniques for building wooden scenery that I'd learned over decades of doing just that. At the same time I worked as an IATSE stagehand. Sometimes I did that on tour with Broadway musicals, and sometimes through IATSE Local 346 in Lexington, Kentucky. Working in commercial theatre was quite a learning experience. If you want to know how to build scenery that functions well in the backstage environment, it really helps to spend some time "under the blue lights" backstage, and even more time moving scenery in and out of trucks. I had a great time doing all of that, it was so much fun.

Since then I've spent my time designing more, and learning about new technologies. The scope of the book has changed to something much more inclusive about theatre production in general, which the title always promised, and now fulfills. I still don't know all that much about building costumes, but have learned a huge amount about electronics and computers and projectors. I'm very proud of how inclusive the book has become. It is now divided into five sections that cover different aspects of working in theatre production. Check out the chapters "Jobs in Theatre" and "Construction Documents." They are brand new additions to this edition, although the need should have been obvious. Indeed it was to several reviewers who guided the process of planning this edition, and I'm glad to include those topics.

I need to thank several people who have helped with this edition. Charles Calvert of the University of Charleston who read many of the chapters and added his viewpoint as a former NYC designer. Charlie loaned me several drawings to use in the book. The very scholarly Michael O. Sanders of Transylvania University who was also a reader who had very intriguing comments. Jeromy Hopgood of Eastern Michigan University, who helped with a previous edition, and is an expert in using QLab. Daniel Brodie is a Broadway projections designer. His master classes at NYU gave me a much more formal view of projections. That area is really booming right now, and the technology is changing rapidly. I had been working with projected video for about ten years, but didn't get the "big picture" before attending his class. John Fergusson is a brother stagehand in IATSE Local 346, a member of the band *Apples in Stereo*, and sound mix guy extraordinaire. Of course I need to thank my colleagues Tony Hardin and Zak Stribling who contributed their ideas to the process. Last but not least, I would like to thank Patty Holloway for reading every word of the book from the viewpoint of an outsider, and letting me know when my explanations needed work.

THE STAGE CARPENTER.

WRITTEN FOR THE NEW YORK CLIPPER.
BY MONROE H. ROSENFELD.

He wanders up, he wanders down,
  A phantom on the scene;
He talks to none, he does his work
  With conntenance serene;
Although his purse is never fat,
  'Tis like his figure—lean.

What is there he cannot construct?
  An elephant to him
Is but a simple plight, or eke
  A dragon fierce and grim,
And golden goblets all begemmed,
  That never will grow dim.

He builds a ship, a paradise,
  Where angels music speak—
Bright angels with a salary
  Of just five bones a week;
And yet, in spite of genius,
  His actions are so meek.

Tanks are his special workmanship,
  And buzz saws meet his line;
And cottages and other things—
  At these he's very fine;
And he can make a thunder cloud,
  And moons that move and shine.

But who applauds his mystic art?
  The bass drum wouldn't nod
At him, while on his daily rounds
  The carpenter doth plod;
The manager? He knows him not—
  A stranger in the fold.

I wonder if he ever thinks
  Who cleverly will make
A little box for him, some day,
  That will not be a fake,
When Life's last scene on him shall close
  And Heaven's joy awake !

SECTION ONE

WORKING IN
A THEATRE

JOBS IN THEATRE

EARLY STAGEHANDS AT THE TECK THEATRE IN BUFFALO

THESE FELLOWS SEEM AWFULLY WELL DRESSED BY MODERN STANDARDS,
BUT PERHAPS THEY KNEW IT WAS PICTURE DAY.

WHAT KINDS OF theatre jobs are there? If you were to ask a person on the street that question you would probably get an answer like, "Well there are actors of course, and directors, and the authors who write the plays." A more detailed answer from someone who enjoys theatre might include choreographers and dancers and people who design scenery or lights. Those are all very visible occupations to the public, especially the actors, because they are what theatregoers actually experience when they go to see a show.

But we all know of course that there is much more to it than that. Actors might get together in a *storefront theatre* (one with very limited technical facilities) and put on their favorite play with a small budget, but finding a larger audience generally requires more advanced visual support with lighting, scenery, props, costumes, and the aural element of sound. That is where stage *production* comes in. Production is a catch-all term that means all of the elements of producing a play that are not acting, directing, and so forth. You might think of excluding designers as well because designers are involved in the creative process of imagineering a play, although many people would disagree with that. The term production as I use it in this book mostly refers to the work of carpenters, painters, electricians, stagehands, and the like as they find ways to bring the creative experience to life. The word *artisan* comes to mind. Artisans are people who use a creative approach to craft objects for everyday life. So they are both utilitarian and artistic at the same time. Scenery and props for a play should be wonderful and fun, but they also need to work for the action of the play, every night and without fail.

The production field is much wider than just theatre, especially when it comes to lighting, sound, and video. There are many other uses for the same skills, in what is often generically referred to as the entertainment business. A *stagehand* who sets up lighting for a play uses the same general skill set as one who installs the lighting for a concert. Theatre-type lights are also used in somewhat predictable places such as TV studios, library lecture halls, churches, and schools, but also in venues that you might not suspect like museums and shopping malls. Someone has to install and maintain that equipment, which means more jobs for theatre production. Most of the people who do this type of work have a theatre school background.

WORK ENVIRONMENTS

Generally speaking there are three different types of legitimate theatre work environments: schools, not-for-profit/regional theatres, and commercial. They are organized in somewhat different ways. *Commercial theatre* is just that, a theatre engaged in commerce, or money making. Broadway shows and the tours that spin off from them make up the largest share of the commercial theatre business, although even some of those have become not-for-profits in recent years. You can also find commercial theatre ventures in Las Vegas, the few remaining dinner theatres, and the African American touring companies making up the "chitlin' circuit." The latter is a loose affiliation of producers who create tours of black themed shows that tour to various roadhouses, mostly in the south. It was most famously the home base of comedian and writer Tyler Perry.

In the commercial theatre model, and especially a Broadway show, a corporation is formed to produce a certain work, and only that work. That is a financial barrier that protects assets in case the show is not as big a hit as everyone hopes it will be. Commercial theatre groups last only as long as the show does, and when it ends so too does the corporation. Most of us consider this to be the "big time" of the theatre world, but in reality there are very few Broadway Houses, and even fewer tours out at any one time. There are many more people working in smaller venues. But Broadway gets most of the popular attention, and since lots of money is in play a system of paying workers fairly is required. That's where unions like *USA* (designers) *IATSE* (stagehands) and *Actor's Equity Association* are a must. A union of some sort covers every aspect of a Broadway show from the director to the ticket takers.

Regional theatres come in many different sizes and shapes; some of them exist under the *LORT* (League of Regional Theatres) contract with Actor's Equity and tend to be the larger ones. But there are many smaller regional theatres that do not have such a contract, undoubtedly the lion's share of the total number. Most exist as *not-for-profits*, meaning that they get tax breaks because they exist for the public good. Typically, a regional theatre exists as an ongoing enterprise, such that they have a new *season* of plays each year and a permanent facility. Some of them produce plays year round, some only in the summer and some only in the other months of the year. The head of the theatre may be called its *Managing Director* to distinguish the position from the director of an individual show. The title *Artistic Director* is also popular. Because they have a season of plays, regional theatres tend to have a *company* of actors who take turns being in the different shows. There are staff designers who do most of the design work, and shops that turn out the required scenery, costumes, and lighting.

One very important job in a regional theatre, that doesn't exist in commercial theatre, is the *Technical Director*. The job of "TD" generally requires the oversight of the shop where the scenery is built, but can include many other tasks such as scheduling and budgeting. In some theatre companies, the scheduling and budgeting are handled instead by a *Production Stage Manager* who is responsible for all the shows in a season rather than just one. There are lots of different titles for that position, other theatres might name it Production Manager or Managing Producer or some other combination of the words that means about the same thing. In a very small group with a limited staff, the TD may be the only other paid member other than the managing director, such as in a *community theatre*. The term "community theatre" is often used to describe a group that exists because people in the community want to act in plays and are willing to do themselves what it takes to make that happen. Although sometimes seen as a pejorative inside joke in the theatre world, many of them are actually quite good, some with lavish facilities and well-paid staff.

A regional theatre is sometimes called a *stock company*, which is related to the idea of keeping things in stock. Long ago this meant the roster of plays that a specific company could do on demand. These days you might think of it more in terms of physical things used in production, such as *stock scenery*. Regional companies tend to save scenery, props, costumes, etc., in order to reuse them for another production, or perhaps the same show will be run again if it was popular enough. Some theatres save and reuse lots of stuff. Some theatres save very little. Things like platforms, escape stairs, curtains, and so forth are so generic that it only makes sense to reuse them in order to keep costs down. Lighting, sound, and projection equipment are obvious things to save. In commercial theatre all of those things are instead rented. This book often discusses the pros and cons of what should constitute stock items.

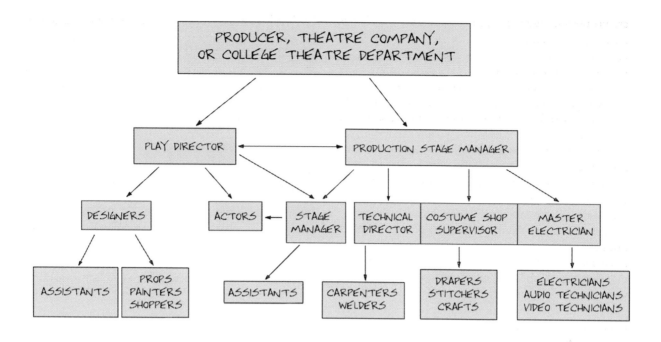

```
PRODUCER, THEATRE COMPANY,
OR COLLEGE THEATRE DEPARTMENT
```

PLAY DIRECTOR ⟷ PRODUCTION STAGE MANAGER

DESIGNERS | ACTORS ← STAGE MANAGER | TECHNICAL DIRECTOR | COSTUME SHOP SUPERVISOR | MASTER ELECTRICIAN

ASSISTANTS | PROPS PAINTERS SHOPPERS | ASSISTANTS | CARPENTERS WELDERS | DRAPERS STITCHERS CRAFTS | ELECTRICIANS AUDIO TECHNICIANS VIDEO TECHNICIANS

IT'S COMPLICATED! NOT ALL THEATRES HAVE ALL OF THESE POSITIONS, BUT SOME HAVE MANY MORE.

MOST SCHOOLS HAVE SHOPS THAT THE TD AND/OR COSTUME SHOP SUPERVISOR OVERSEE, WHICH INCLUDES MAKING SCHEDULES, ORDERING SUPPLIES AND MANAGING THE WORKFORCE.

The school theatre environment is much more closely aligned with what you would expect from a regional theatre, rather than commercial theatre. Schools are the original not-for-profits, especially if you consider a state-owned institution. The faculty of the school is the producer of the plays, and generally has more say over governance than in a regional theatre. Most schools of a certain size have teachers who are themselves directors, designers, and TDs, and perhaps freelance on the side. Like a regional theatre, schools are in it for the long haul, so they tend to keep stock units like those suggested above. They have a season of plays each year, and shops to turn out the required production elements. Instead of a company of actors and technicians, a college or university has students who do most of the work of creating costumes, scenery, and props. That is the best way for students to learn those crafts.

In a commercial theatre model, the organization is much different. In a Broadway union environment stagehands are divided into different departments, and they tend to specialize. They are *electricians*, *carpenters*, *properties*, *wardrobe*, and *hair*. Audio and projections are considered to be a part of the electrics department. Each theatre is owned by a group that rents it to the company producing a show. By contract with IATSE Local One, the owner of each theatre owner employs a house carpenter, electrician, and prop guy. These are largely managerial positions, and the *house heads*, as they are

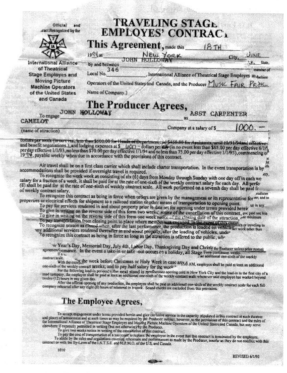

AUTHOR'S PINK CONTRACT FROM A TOUR OF CAMELOT
YOU ARE REQUIRED TO CARRY THIS WITH YOU - HENCE THE WRINKLES!

called, are responsible for hiring Local One stagehands on a *white contract* to actually run the shows. The show itself can hire an equal number of *pink contract* stagehands from other locals who owe their allegiance to the show producer rather than the theatre owner. It is a complex environment. The terms pink and white come from the literal colors of the paper the contracts are printed on.

In a commercial touring show environment, the *head carpenter* is charged with the day to day business of dealing with the stagehands. The author, director, and designers do not travel with the show, so the *stage manager* is the overall head of everything, with a *company manager* who takes care of the money aspects of the show, as well as getting folks from place to place. The head carpenter is a liaison with the *business agents* of local unions along the way. Each local union has a separate number; New York was the first so they are Local One. Chicago is Local Two. A *yellow card* (they have been printed on yellow cardstock since time began) is sent out telling how many hands will be required in each department for the *load-in*, *load-out*, and for the run of the show. The local business agent calls local stagehands to be at a venue for the show. Although the Broadway model is fairly limited to just NYC, with previews in Boston or Philadelphia possibly thrown in for good measure, there is a very long list of union roadhouses across the country that work the same way. So this collection of titles, departments, and work rules is more prevalent than the limited number of Broadway theatres would make us believe.

IATSE stands for International Alliance of Theatrical Stage Employees. Most IATSE locals have some sort of apprenticeship program for new workers. If you are interested in that type of work, go to the IATSE website and find out the name and contact information of the local that covers your area. After contacting their *business agent* you will probably be put on a list of those who are called when work is available. The list tends to be somewhat hierarchical, so don't expect to be given the sweet jobs right away. There are more concerts and sporting events than theatrical jobs, so that is where you will likely begin, where rolling boxes to and from the trucks is the logical place to start. Eventually you will have enough experience to ask to join the union as an apprentice.

In general, you should come prepared to work in a busy environment with sturdy clothes and shoes, gloves, hair tied back and generally ready to go. If you work a performance or *show call*, be sure to bring a small flashlight for the darkness of backstage. Wardrobe folks tend to prefer a *bite-light*, which they can put in their mouth leaving both hands free. Someone will probably tell you what else to have. I was told early on in my career that "You can't be a real stagehand without a knife" which is true and it seems like there is often something that needs to be cut.

A DRESSER WORKING BACKSTAGE

SHE IS HELPING THE ACTOR GET HIS COAT ON DURING A QUICK-CHANGE. NOTE THE BITE-LIGHT SHE USES TO SEE WITH.

Most stagehand work is built around the idea of a four- or five-hour call. The word *call* is used, indicating that you have literally been called there to work by the business agent. After that amount of time, it is generally necessary to have a dinner break, even when it is the

UNION "BUG" OR SYMBOL

TYPICAL IATSE STAGEHAND AT WORK

wrong time of day. Each local has its own idiosyncratic rules. Pay is by the hour, but frequently a show call is instead a set rate for any length of the show unless it runs longer than four hours. It may seem like that could never happen, but a concert with many opening acts, or perhaps a wrestling show may well exceed that time limit. You can see how diverse commercial live entertainment can be. Different venues may have different rates, and skill level may also be a factor. Certain specialties like rigging may pay more. Each IATSE local has its own set of rules, but the ones discussed above are generally true in most jurisdictions.

It is interesting how different the two worlds of the union stagehand and the college theatre student can be, and how little they sometimes seem to know about each other. In large cities, stagehands are mostly engaged in setting up shows and running them, so those are the important skills. The apprentice exam in my local is mostly about electrics, the rigging system, and followspot operation. These are things that stagehands are most frequently asked to do. Being a stagehand is often a family tradition. It is a craft learned by being an *apprentice* and then moving on to *journeyman*. Except for very specific union shops in New York and at larger regional theatres, most union stagehand work occurs in theatres or convention centers. Most IATSE stagehands know a great deal about load ins, load outs, and running shows, but probably not so much about building scenery, which is something college theatre students can spend a lot of time doing.

A GROUP OF IA STAGEHANDS
WAITING BY THE STAGE DOOR

In a college theatre environment, students are immersed in all phases of theatrical activity, from acting and directing to design and production. A student may hang lights for one show, act in another, and build costumes for a third. College theatres generally build all

their own scenery, and constructing scenery in the shop is an important activity, requiring a huge amount of effort. College is a place for young people to see what careers are available, learn something about them, and then decide which one is most appealing to them personally. In a larger sense, college is a place to learn about the huge complexity of the world at large and to discover your place in it.

COLLEGE STUDENTS
IN A SCENE SHOP

There are many different theatre jobs open to college students, especially in the summer months when most schools are not in session. There are many different places to search for these on the internet, but one of the most established is *Offstage Jobs*. ARTSEARCH is also good, but isn't free like Offstage Jobs. There are listings for all sorts of jobs, but you should plan on applying earlier on in the spring rather than waiting until the last minute. There are conferences too, such as the *South Eastern Theatre Conference* or *SETC*, and the *New England Theatre Conference* or *NETC*. These two have been holding auditions for actors and interviews for technicians for many years. Summer theatre work is something you should take very seriously as it will be a great learning experience in a practical situation that is different from your school. It is also an opportunity to network and compare notes with your fellow technicians and stagehands about how to find jobs in the future. There is a virtual ocean of summer theatre jobs out there that pay enough to get by on, and will build your skills and resume for future jobs that are better paying.

WORKING AS A SHOP CARPENTER

Working as a carpenter in a scene shop can take many different forms. You might eventually wind up in a union shop that provides scenery for a Broadway show or a large LORT theatre. Or you might work very happily at a children's theatre or a community theatre. The work you do at any of these is really very similar. A shop carpenter should be very skilled at using various woodworking tools. Two of the five sections in this book go into great detail about that. In addition, most shops in the modern era require some expertise with metal working, especially MIG welding for steel.

A shop carpenter should be able to look at plans and know how to make a cut list of parts for constructing what is there. Very frequently the drafted plans include overall sizes of the scenery, but do not show the individual lengths of the various 2×4s and other framing members. You will need to figure that out on your own. A bit of math is involved to add and subtract fractions, and you should be able to work such problems quickly and accurately.

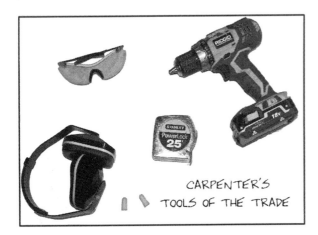

CARPENTER'S
TOOLS OF THE TRADE

A person who works as a shop carpenter for a living should invest in certain pieces of equipment. Everyone should have their own tape measure. You will use that more than any other tool. You should probably have your own cordless drill that also doubles as a screw gun. You should definitely have your own pair of safety glasses and hearing protectors, and should wear them whenever you are working in the shop.

If you are a competent worker, you will probably be given plans for a unit of scenery and be asked to complete it on your own. That is why reading plans, making cut lists, measuring and cutting the parts, and assembling them with tools like pneumatic staplers and screw guns are very important skills to have mastered. The job of shop carpenter is a very highly skilled position.

WORKING AS A STAGE CARPENTER

Stage carpenters who work a show are entirely different from those who work in a shop. Stage carpenters are involved in setting up the scenery when it arrives at the theatre, and also in running the show. Being a flyman is

a subspecialty, which is somewhat different from a deck carpenter who moves scenery around on stage. In the movies the term *grip* is used instead, and some theatres use that term as well. The scenery in a musical typically moves when there is a change from one scene to another, so much of your time being a deck carpenter is spent waiting for a cue light to come on. Then there is a flurry of activity when it goes off and the scenery changes.

DECKHAND WATCHING A CUE LIGHT

AS SOON AS IT GOES OUT HE WILL
USE THE PUSH STICK TO MOVE THE SCENERY
OUT ON STAGE

Much of the scenery is on wheels, and must hit a spike mark on stage. You should learn how to move wheeled scenery with ease. There are a few tricks to it depending on how the casters are arranged on the piece. Some scenery has all swivel casters and can move in any direction, but turning and going the opposite way requires the casters to spin around their offset. As a result it is very hard to get the piece started, and then much easier after the swivel has occurred. To avoid slowing down the scene change, you should stage the piece so that the casters are turned the right way before the change starts so that the piece moves easily and quickly. Some scenery has a mix of swivel and rigid casters and drives like a car, making it easier for one deckhand to move it. More information about how casters work can be found in the hardware chapter. There are lots of other little tricks to being a deck carpenter that you will learn over time.

WORKING AS A FLYMAN

Being a *flyman* requires some special skills that relate to the counterweight rigging system found in most modern proscenium houses. You would not usually have a flyman in a thrust or arena theatre because they typically don't have that sort of rigging in them. Several chapters in this book explain the workings of a counterweight system in detail, and you can refer to them for more information about how to operate the equipment. Like deckhands, flymen spend a lot of time waiting for a cue light to come on as a warning for a cue, and even more time waiting for it to go out as a signal to begin. All of that before actually moving any ropes.

It takes a strong person to effectively pull the ropes and move the rigging. Loading the weights also takes a

FLYMAN MEGAN JELLISON LOADS COUNTERWEIGHTS ON A SINGLE PURCHASE SYSTEM

certain amount of strength. A flyman must be physically fit enough to climb up to the load rail and do that. In addition, he or she cannot be afraid of heights. Flymen are not necessarily men, there are many fine women doing the job. The terms "flyperson" and "flier" never caught on.

You must be very aware of safety practices in order to be a flyman, because the process of flying scenery in to the stage can be very dangerous if a heavy piece comes in and no one on the deck knows it is coming. Rehearsing should make everyone aware of the movement during a show, but at other times it is very important to warn them when you fly something in.

The weight of scenery and lights on a pipe and the amount of counterweight in an arbor must be carefully matched, and flymen must be very knowledgeable about how to do that. In achieving that goal, there are many situations that require an imbalance in the system for a short time while scenery/lights are loaded or removed. A journeyman flyman should be very well experienced in those methods. Proficiency in rope handling and knot tying is a must.

The ropes can be rough on your hands, so a flyman should carry a good pair of close-fitting gloves.

WORKING AS AN ELECTRICIAN

Most of the work of an electrician will be in the theatre itself. Even so, you might find a job working for a company that rents stage lighting equipment, in which case you would work in their shop repairing equipment and assembling rental packages.

A stage electrician should be able to look at a light plot and understand where the various hanging positions are located throughout the theatre. The plot also tells what types of lights are hung on those positions and where they go. As a result you should be able to readily identify the different types. An electrician should be thoroughly familiar with how to securely hang the lights on pipes, and how to safely operate the rigging system to fly them out over the stage. Usually a flyman is present to actually run the counterweight system, or alternately fly the truss, but even so electricians must know how to complement that work, which is a matter of working safely. If you are an electrician you should also know how to rig a chain motor to a tower or truss.

A competent stage electrician should know how to move and set up ladders used in focusing lights, and how to use a stage lift. Ladders are often very tall, and must be *footed* and *walked up* in a safe manner. The same can be said for a lighting tower used from the wing. It is likely that lights will be installed in the tower before it is placed on the stage, and it will be very heavy as a result.

Stage electricians should be able to work with some fairly complex computer systems that are used to control the lights. They should be very familiar with how

WALKING DOWN A SPOT TOWER

"FOOT" THE END ON THE GROUND THAT SERVES
AS A PIVOT POINT. IF IT SLIDES THE TOWER
WILL FALL ON THE OTHER STAGEHANDS.
DON'T GET UNDER THE MIDDLE LIKE THE GUY
IN THE DARK PANTS.

COIL HEAVY MULTICABLE ON THE FLOOR
IT'S REALLY TOO HEAVY TO HOLD IN YOUR HANDS

THE TECHNIQUE SHOWN HERE IS CALLED
"OVER AND UNDER" AND IS A GOOD WAY TO AVOID
NEEDING TO TWIST ONCE FOR EACH LOOP

electricity works and have an intuitive sense about how to use equations such as $P = IE$ and $I = P/E$ to determine when an overload is eminent.

One of the most challenging aspects of working as a stage electrician is dealing with all of the cables and wires used in setting up the lighting rig. Many of them are used for power distribution, meaning that they carry enough current at 120VAC to make the lights come on. In addition, there are DMX lines that carry information to dimmers and intelligent lights, and four pin XLR cables that carry data and power to things like scrollers and rotators. Most modern systems also use category five cables as an Ethernet connection.

As a result of all of the above, electricians must be master cable coilers and have a very neat approach to installing the cables on various battens and trusses. Coiling involves many different types of cables from the tiny cat five to monstrously heavy feeder and multicable. Different coiling techniques are used for different types and you should know what they are.

When working as an electrician it is absolutely essential to bring a 6 inch *Crescent wrench*. Most bolts on lighting equipment can be manipulated with that size. An 8 inch might also be used as a matter of preference, but anything bigger is too clumsy.

An electrician who is employed to work a show might be a board operator who runs the cues when instructed to by the stage manager, or a person who runs a follow-spot, or a deck electrician who pages cable when the scenery moves. Electricians may also include stagehands involved with operating sound or video equipment.

Electricians are often tasked with setting up the intercom system, which is used to communicate backstage when words are important. Generally speaking, stagehands who must move around a lot like deckhands and flymen don't wear headsets, but those whose jobs are more stationary do. That would include spot and board operators as well as assistant stage managers.

The standard intercom headset has an earpiece and a microphone. The earpiece is called a muff, (as in earmuff) and the headset can be either the single or double muff type. *Double muff* headsets are frequently used when the show is very loud like a concert, but in a much quieter stage show a *single muff* headset allows the user to hear both the stage manager and the show that is going on around them. The headset mike on most models will turn itself off when rotated to the up position, which places it on top of the head.

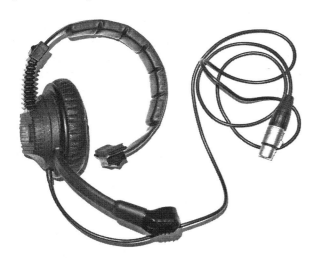

SINGLE MUFF HEADSET
WITH ATTACHED MICROPHONE

BELT PACK FUNCTIONS

PUSH THE SIGNAL BUTTON TO LIGHT THE LED, WHICH LETS OTHERS KNOW TO PUT ON THEIR HEADSET.

THE THUMBWHEEL ADJUSTS THE VOLUME OF YOUR EARPIECE (NOT YOUR MICROPHONE).

PUSH THE MIC BUTTON TO TURN YOUR MICROPHONE ON AND OFF. DON'T LEAVE YOURS ON UNATTENDED!

Intercom headsets are meant to be used in combination with a *belt pack*. The headset plugs into the belt pack, which has a couple of adjustment features. A switch turns the microphone on and off. A knob or thumbwheel adjusts the volume of the earpiece. Most types have an LED indicator *call light* that warns the user someone is asking them to pick up the headset.

Belt packs are powered by a main station, which generally lives at the stage manager's desk because it has switches the SM can manipulate to control the system. Three pin XLR cable runs to each of the belt packs, which have in and out parallel connections so that the cable can run from one belt pack to another, rather than each one needing a direct line to the main station.

Backstage protocol dictates that users be careful to turn the mike off when it is not in use, so as to keep down unwanted noise. This is especially true when laying your headset down and walking away. Make sure you switch the mike off so that a) it doesn't make a loud bang when you lay it down, and b) so that extraneous noise doesn't run through the system while you are away. Avoid standing too close to a stage light, because induction from the filament will create a 60 cycle hum in the entire system. Some intercom systems have more than one channel, so that the stage manager can select who can hear what she is saying. Switches turn various channels on and off.

THIS PARTICULAR INTERCOM HAS TWO CHANNELS, A & B. YOU CAN ROUTE INFORMATION TO SPECIFIC PERSONNEL BY SELECTING WHICH CHANNEL THEY CAN RECEIVE. "LINK" CONNECTS THE TWO CHANNELS TOGETHER. VARIOUS KNOBS ARE USED TO ADJUST VOLUME LEVELS.

WORKING AS A PROP GUY

Long ago, theatre people would use the terms "prop master" or "prop mistress" to describe this job, but those terms seem old-fashioned today. However the job hasn't changed all that much since that time. A stagehand working with props is almost always called a "prop guy" for some reason, even if that hand is a woman. Stagehands in general are called guys, regardless of their sex. I suppose that could be construed as sexist to some outsiders, but really it is just one of those quirky things that make theatre fun.

You may ask the question "What is the difference between props and scenery?" The line is often blurred. Very small things that you can hold in your hand such as a book or binoculars, or a pistol, are obviously props and are sometimes called a *hand prop*. Other things can be less well defined. A piece of furniture is almost always considered a prop, as would window curtains—but not the window itself. A table lamp would be a prop, but most likely not a wall sconce.

In Broadway theatre or a union roadhouse, the prop department is responsible for getting coffee and donuts together for the required break times. But most of the work has to do with setting up the props so that actors can get to them easily. Quite often props are arranged on a table that is marked with labels as to what goes where so that the prop guy can tell at a glance if anything is missing. Very often a *prop cabinet* is used instead so that the props can be secured at night, especially if some of them are expensive and worth stealing. If the prop cabinet has shelves you can mark them in the same way you would a table, and if it has wheels you can roll it around

backstage or into a truck. Prop guns should definitely be locked up, even if they are rubber and non-functioning. Never use a real gun that fires actual bullets on stage.

Generally speaking, actors can go to the table or cabinet and get their own props. If they have been well trained they can most often take them back to the same place, and most actors will do that instinctively. Sometimes though you will need to pick things up and replace them yourself because the action of the play requires it when the actor doesn't have time to get to the prop table before re-entering. Receiving a prop from an actor as they leave the stage is called a *hand-off* and the same term is used to describe the process of handing a prop to an actor as they are headed on stage.

It is hard to describe what tools a prop guy might need because the work entails so many different possibilities. You should for sure have a hot glue gun and other types of glue as well because props very often break in the process of their use. I would also recommend a screw gun, as well as pliers, a hammer, and other common tools close at hand. Prop guys definitely need a flashlight backstage because they often need to show actors where to go. The workers in the wardrobe and props departments have a much closer relationship with actors than most other departments.

Working as a Spot Operator

Being a spot operator is a very specialized category of stage electrician and requires more explanation, especially of the equipment, which is not discussed elsewhere in the book. *Followspots* are used in many productions. In some areas of the country they are known as a *front light*, or perhaps simply as a spotlight, or spot. As the name implies, a followspot is a lighting instrument used to follow the action of a play. The basic idea is to open up on an actor and then stay with them until the scene is over, no matter where they may move on the stage.

Followspots can range in size from tiny club instruments of 1000 watts to the giant behemoths used in sports arenas. IATSE stagehands are often called upon to run a spot for concerts, ice shows, wrestling bouts, and other entertainments, as well as for theatre shows.

Modern spots use a sealed-beam arc lamp like the Xenon or HMI. Xenon lamps contain a pair of electrodes sealed in a glass enclosure. The electrodes are made from a special alloy that, in conjunction with the xenon gas inside the tube, helps to re-plate burnt parts of the electrode so that they last longer. The lamps get very hot, the gas inside is under pressure, and thus there is a tendency for the lamp to explode if it is removed from the fixture without cooling down, so extreme caution must be used when changing one.

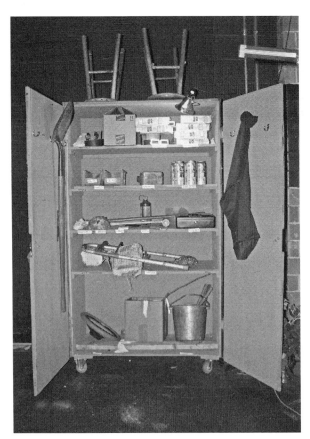

BACKSTAGE PROP BOX ON WHEELS

THE SHELVES ARE MARKED AS TO WHAT GOES WHERE. THE ADVANTAGE OVER A TABLE IS THAT THE BOX CAN BE LOCKED UP OVER NIGHT.

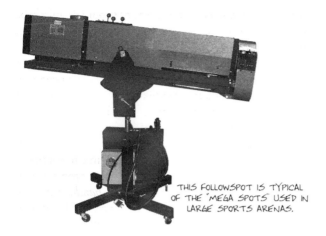

THIS FOLLOWSPOT IS TYPICAL OF THE "MEGA SPOTS" USED IN LARGE SPORTS ARENAS.

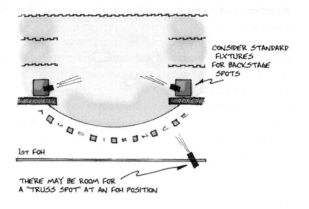

CONSIDER STANDARD FIXTURES FOR BACKSTAGE SPOTS

1st FOH

THERE MAY BE ROOM FOR A "TRUSS SPOT" AT AN FOH POSITION

Different followspot models have different mechanical parts, but almost all have the same basic ones. These include the dowser, iris, and boomerang.

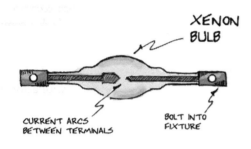

XENON BULB

CURRENT ARCS BETWEEN TERMINALS

BOLT INTO FIXTURE

XENON IS A RARE GAS THAT CAN CONDUCT ELECTRICITY, AND EMITS LIGHT WHEN EXCITED BY ELECTRONS.

THE GAS IS UNDER PRESSURE, AND THE LAMPS REQUIRE SPECIAL HANDLING.

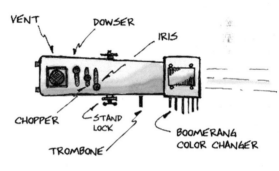

VENT   DOWSER   IRIS

CHOPPER   STAND LOCK   BOOMERANG COLOR CHANGER

TROMBONE

TYPICAL CONTROL PLACEMENT
P L A N   V I E W

Followspots are typically used from a position in the rear of the theatre and require a lamp much brighter than that used in a standard fixture, which is one reason arc lamps are preferred. But arc-type lamps are not dimmable. If the voltage pressure supplied to them decreases below a certain point, the arc won't be able to jump across the gap and will simply sputter out. Instead of dimming, most followspots use a mechanical device to vary the light intensity. Other mechanical devices can change the size/shape of the beam, and the color of the light.

Traditional followspots sit on stationary bases at the rear of the theatre where they command excellent sightlines to the stage. In more recent times much smaller conventional fixtures may be used from an area backstage. For a play, a high angle spot is often used when a subtle halo of diffuse light is required to highlight an actor, but it can also be used in a variety of other ways that would perhaps mimic concert lighting. In a theatre situation, spots like this may be used from a tower especially installed for the purpose. Spot towers, larger versions of a regular lighting tower, can be used as a lighting position.

A *dowser* is used both to vary the intensity of the light output, and to black out the spot so that no light gets to the stage. The dowser is a metal disc, or perhaps metal doors, that can be rotated into the light beam. This occurs very close to the lamp, and optically in a manner so that the apparent change is a dimming effect rather than seeing

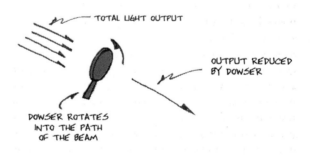

TOTAL LIGHT OUTPUT

OUTPUT REDUCED BY DOWSER

DOWSER ROTATES INTO THE PATH OF THE BEAM

THE SOLID METAL DOWSER BLOCKS PART OF THE LIGHT OUTPUT. SOME DOWSERS ARE CONSTRUCTED DIFFERENTLY, IN THE MANNER OF BARN DOORS, OR VENETIAN BLINDS.

an eclipse-like change to the light beam. The dowser is used because these are arc lights, which cannot be dimmed like a conventional fixture. Frequently regular ellipsoidals are used as spot tower lights and can be dimmed. They are usually controlled by the light board rather than the spot op.

You can use the dowser to make small adjustments in the amount of the light beam that is blacked out, but it is difficult to stop at precise points by marking them, which would cause you to take your eye off the stage. Running a followspot is somewhat more artistic than that, and the operator must often intuit what the show demands.

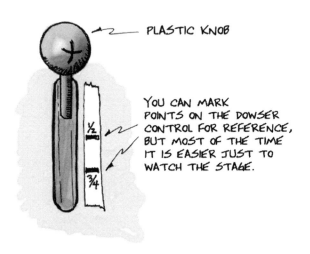

PLASTIC KNOB

YOU CAN MARK POINTS ON THE DOWSER CONTROL FOR REFERENCE, BUT MOST OF THE TIME IT IS EASIER JUST TO WATCH THE STAGE.

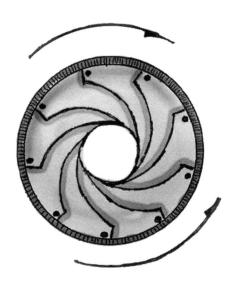

TURNING THE OUTER RING WILL MAKE THE CENTER OPENING LARGER OR SMALLER

IRIS

Dowsers absorb a lot of heat, especially if they are not opened up for a long period of time during the show. Even so, it is generally not a good idea to turn an arc light on and off. You may have a difficult and noisy time getting it to start back up. Virtually all spots have some sort of fan that cools both the power supply and the light itself. This fan should be allowed to run for a while, even after the spot is turned off, in order to avoid overheating the lamp.

The *iris* is another control found on virtually all follow spots. An iris is a system of thin, curved metal plates in a movable housing. The plates overlap one another, and when an outer retaining ring is rotated, the thin plates form a larger or smaller circle, and hence a larger/smaller pool of light on the stage. A fixture designed specifically as a followspot has a built-in iris, but a drop-in iris unit can be used in a conventional fixture to do the same thing.

It is sometimes possible to completely black out the light by closing the iris in all the way. Do not do this. The iris is a delicate device and it is very close to the light source, which is extremely hot. If you block all of the output with the iris, the thin metal plates will heat up very rapidly. They will warp out of shape and be ruined.

You can use the iris to create a variety of spot sizes. The largest is generally the *full-body* size, which is large enough to include the entire body of the actor. You may need to go larger than that to include two characters standing right next to one another. *Three-quarter* means from the knees up and including the head. It is very rare for a designer to ask for a shot that does NOT include the actor's head and face. You should always strive to keep the head in the light no matter what. The next smaller shot is the *waist*, and then finally the *head-shot*.

Traditional followspots have a color changing device known as a *boomerang*. Normally, six different colors are possible. The gel is loaded into round *frames* that are designed especially for each particular light. Add-on boomerang units are available for ellipsoidal fixtures used as a spot.

There are six levers on the outside of the housing that can be used to bring a particular frame up into the path of the light beam. Most lights have a button you can use to cancel out a gel frame and make it drop back out of the light beam. Alternatively, if you pull a different frame lever all the way down, the first color will be automatically cancelled. The term *no color* is used to indicate that no gel is to be used on a particular cue.

Running a followspot requires a lot of concentration. Professional stagehands are expected to come in and run a show cold, without ever having seen any of the action

FULL BODY   THREE-QUARTER

KNEE

WAIST   HEAD

COMMON SPOT SIZES

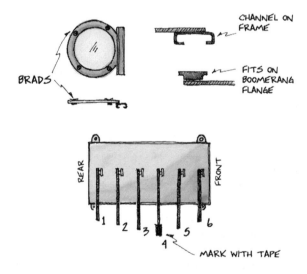

BRADS

CHANNEL ON FRAME

FITS ON BOOMERANG FLANGE

REAR   FRONT

1   2   3   4   5   6

MARK WITH TAPE

COLOR CHANGER OR "BOOMERANG"

of the piece. Generally, there is a *lighting director* to call the cues for a musical act, ice show, or circus, while in a theatre show, the cues are called by a stage manager, or possibly by a spot operator who travels with the show and is familiar with it. There are standard methods of setting up a show and of calling cues, which make it possible for an experienced operator to understand the cues with a minimum of explanation.

A typical spot cue might go something like this: "Stand by for spot one to pick up the woman in the red dress up left in a frame one, and spot two on the man in the black suit down right in a frame five. Spots standby and . . . Go." If you are spot one you should push down on the first lever on the boomerang to load frame one. Spot two should do the same with frame five. On the go, both spot ops should run their dowser levers to bring the light up on the target specified by the cue caller. From that point on it is just a matter of staying with the target until the next cue is called.

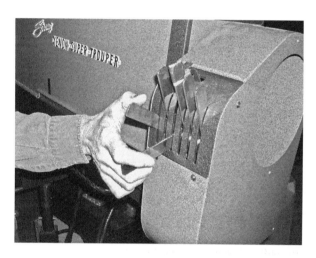

USE YOUR THUMB AND FINGERS TO ARTISTICALLY CHANGE FROM ONE FRAME TO ANOTHER

Most of the time, operators are asked to stay on one person until the light fades out, and then to fade back up on another subject. On occasion, the design calls for the light to move directly from one target to the next. The cue caller may express this by saying, "*slide* over to so and so." In this instance you simply move discretely from one place to the other. This often happens when two actors are close together and the idea is to trade one for the other. If you can time it so that this happens as they pass one another, the audience may never notice it.

It can be difficult to keep your light on the face of an actor, especially if the stage is bright and the difference in value is hard to see. It is generally easier to keep track of things by choosing to watch the shadow of the actor rather than the actor in the light. If there is a bit of light over the shadow of the head, you are properly on the target. As a general rule, you should avoid jerking the light around unnecessarily. Stay still even if you are slightly off target, wait for the actor to move some, and then readjust.

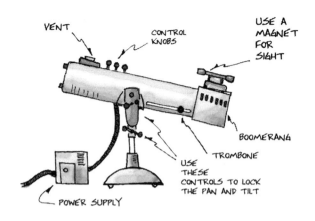

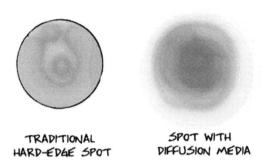

TRADITIONAL
HARD-EDGE SPOT

SPOT WITH
DIFFUSION MEDIA

It is often difficult to have your spot lined up on the actor when the light comes up. It is very distracting to have a light appear near center stage and then uncertainly wander around until it finds the woman in the red dress upstage left. You can avoid this by using some kind of targeting device. This can be as expensive as a high-powered *telescopic rifle sight*, or as low tech as a bent piece of wire. There are a number of proprietary devices that are made specifically for this purpose and new ones are developed from time to time. You should try different things and find one that works well for you personally. Using a sight of some sort is a really important step that can enhance the artistic qualities of your spotting work.

There are some rather quirky spot instructions that come up on a fairly regular basis, often enough so that they have actual names. One of these is the *ballyhoo*. This occurs when the spots criss-cross the audience area in a figure-eight pattern, or perhaps a swirl. This is generally done to excite the crowd, as though the lights are searching for someone. It is even more effective if you change speeds occasionally, as though you are slowly searching, then speed over to another possible target, then slowly search again. Another technique is to *pan* back and forth over a group that is too large for one or more spots to cover effectively. This works well for a line of actors at curtain call, or perhaps even a line of elephants on the back track near ring two.

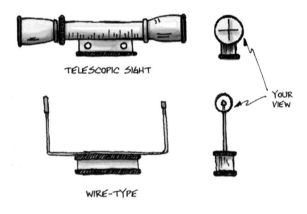

TELESCOPIC SIGHT

YOUR VIEW

WIRE-TYPE

USE A SIGHT TO IMPROVE YOUR AIM

The sight is a personal tool, and you will need to move it from one spot to another each time you work. It is common practice to attach the sight, of whatever type, to a powerful magnet so that it can be easily mounted on the steel housing of the spotlight. Then it is just a matter of adjusting the sight so that it is accurately centered on the light beam coming out of the spot. For best results, make your adjustments at maximum distance, with the iris as small as practical.

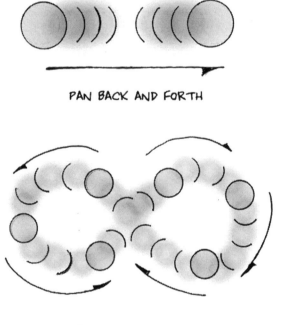

PAN BACK AND FORTH

BALLYHOO THRU THE AUDIENCE

WORKING AS A STAGE MANAGER

Stage managers have many responsibilities related to rehearsing and performing theatre. They are typically the first to arrive and the last to leave. It is a tough job, but also very rewarding. Throughout the process of producing a play, a stage manager should be the center of communications in sharing ideas and information, whether they are artistic, administrative, or technical in nature. That may be a simple statement, but the true challenge of the job is keeping up with the many ways this information is presented, and making sure that it gets disseminated in an accurate and timely fashion. Professional stage managers are members of Actors' Equity Association, the union for actors. It has been that way since the union was formed. At that time virtually all stage managers were people whose acting careers had gone awry. That is no longer true, and the position of stage manager is of course very respected. Even though stage managers are members of the actor's union rather than USA or IATSE, their work is discussed here because of the close relationship between the crew that runs a show and the SM who calls the show. Stagehands should be very familiar with how cues are called.

In a school setting where students serve as stage manager, the role of SM is generally limited to organizing rehearsals and calling cues for a show. Each theatre organization is somewhat different, and has its own rules. Equity stage managers must follow the rules set down in the AEA contract with their group. Equity has contracts with many different organizations, but in each case the contract is published as a booklet that contains all the *work rules* for that venue. You can find samples of that online. All unions have work rules, which are used to define responsibilities, duties, rights, and privileges.

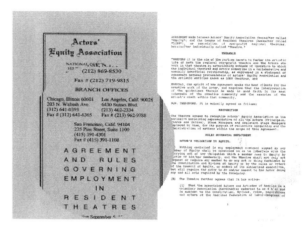

THE COVER AND FIRST PAGE OF THE EQUITY CONTRACT WITH LORT THEATRES BACK IN THE 1990s.

A UNION CONTRACT SPELLS OUT THE RULES AND OBLIGATIONS OF THE PARTIES, SO IN ESSENCE IT IS THE 'RULE BOOK' FOR THE RELATIONSHIP. SCHOOL THEATRES DON'T USUALLY HAVE A RULEBOOK, BUT THEY DO HAVE AGREED UPON DUTIES AND RESPONSIBILITIES.

MATTERS SUCH AS THESE ARE NOW POSTED ON THE AEA WEBSITE RATHER THAN BEING PRINTED ON PAPER. YOU CAN GO TO THEIR WEBSITE AND CHECK THE ENTIRE DOCUMENT.

AN EXAMPLE OF AN EQUITY CONTRACT FROM THE 1950s

THE CONTRACT MENTIONS THAT THIS IS A "LEGITIMATE" SHOW, WHICH MEANS IT IS NOT A VAUDEVILLE TYPE PERFORMANCE, BUT RATHER A SHOW WITH A SET SCRIPT AND PLOT.

STAGE MANAGERS ARE UNION MEMBERS OF ACTORS' EQUITY ASSOCIATION RATHER THAN IATSE, THE UNION FOR STAGEHANDS. EVEN SO, STAGE MANAGERS HAVE A LOT OF INTERACTION WITH THE CREW OF A SHOW, AND OFTEN IDENTIFY MORE WITH STAGEHANDS THAN WITH ACTORS.

The information in this section is presented in a roughly chronological order of the way things happen, beginning with design meetings, auditions, the rehearsal process, production meetings, tech rehearsals, dress rehearsals, and finally the running of the performances.

FIRST MEETING WITH THE DIRECTOR

At some point, you should have a first meeting with the director. It is best to do this as early as possible so that the two of you can discuss how to work together in putting together the play. You should get some idea of the director's artistic view of the piece, and find out how the director would like the process to develop. Some directors like to shape the production organically, or in a loose manner. Others are much more structured. Be sure to ask questions about this particular director's process. Be honest with the director, if you don't have any experience in a particular area, let them know so that they can help you learn.

DESIGN MEETINGS

Sometime early on, weeks or maybe months before rehearsals begin, designers will start working with the director to solidify the way the show will look and sound. The role of the stage manager in these meetings is to take notes of the ideas that are put forward, and to publish a record of the discussions. This will help the director and the designers stay on track with one another. A bit of efficiency on your part will greatly aid the process. Be sure to disseminate the notes as quickly as possible, they are of little use days or weeks later. Social networking sites have become a good way of doing that, but be careful because not everyone uses them.

AUDITIONS

There is a wide diversity of style in how directors like to hold auditions, and the only way for you to find out how your director works is to ask her. Find out when and where the auditions are to be held. Most theatre organizations have a place to post information known as the *call board*, which might be an online resource as well as a physical bulletin board. The director may want you to post a notice on the call board detailing how actors should prepare for the auditions. Some directors want actors to come with a prepared selection. Some choose to have the actors read from the script of the play that is being done. Sometimes it is both. There may be singing or dancing auditions. If actors must read from a script, make sure that copies are available. Often times, the scripts will have been ordered in advance, but if not, you will need to make copies of only the pertinent pages for use at the auditions. That should be OK under the fair use guidelines for copyright law.

It is usually best to set up a table in the theatre to use in processing the auditionees. This will give you a place to lay the scripts and the *audition forms*. Consult with the director about what information should be required on the audition form, but the most obvious data should be name, phone number, email address, sex, height, weight, hair color, as well as any activities that may conflict with the rehearsal schedule. Quite often, the theatre or the director may have a standard form already made up. You should expect to make announcements to the auditionees about who the director wants to see, and to perform other crowd control duties.

Actors' Equity Association requires two assistants for a musical, but only one for a straight play. This is because musicals are more complex and harder to run. Your theatre probably has its own rules about assistants, or perhaps they will leave those details up to you. You will find that off-book rehearsals run much better with at least one assistant *on-book* when actors *call for lines*. Stage managing is a skill best learned by observing others, so assisting is a way to move into stage managing on your

own. The abbreviation for stage manager is SM, and ASM for an assistant. *ASM* is a more frequently used term, as stage managers are not usually called SMs.

After auditions are completed, the director will make decisions regarding the cast list. On occasion, the director may ask for help with this, but for the most part they won't need you, and especially not your opinion as to whom should be cast. Even if the director asks your opinion about an artistic matter, it is best to be conservative in your answer to avoid over-sharing. They may wish instead to confer with an assistant director. Assistant director is a position that carries with it an expectation of artistic input, that is, the AD is often asked to do research, or to help rehearse scenes, take acting notes, and generally give opinions about how the work is progressing artistically. Some directors use the stage management staff to take notes, but they never really want your honest opinions on artistic matters.

Stage managing is a "people" job, and good managers have good people skills. A stage manager should be careful to avoid breaking any confidences that exist with the director. You may well have access to sensitive information that the director would not like the cast to know. If you gossip about such matters, the director will soon find out. You will not be an effective stage manager if the director must hesitate to tell you things. Acting in a consistently professional manner will build confidence in you as a person, and as a member of the production team.

THE FIRST READ THROUGH

The first read through, which often includes designers and other artistic/administrative staff, is an informal chance for the company to meet and hear the play for the first time as a group, especially if it is a new play. Optimally, the designers will be on hand to explain elements of their work to the acting company. The director will have comments to the group as a whole, and there may be introductions and other such "get to know each other" functions. Then the cast will read through the play.

You may be asked to read *stage directions*, or help in some other way. It is the director's rehearsal; you are there to make sure that things go smoothly. Quite often, it is best to have this meeting in a room with a large table where the participants can sit and face each other comfortably. You should ask about the director's preference in advance and make the necessary arrangements. Some people call this *table work*. It is a good idea to time this rehearsal so that there is some idea of how long the play will run. You should make it a practice to record the *run time* of any rehearsal that doesn't stop for a significant portion of the play. You probably don't need to time blocking rehearsals because they stop and start so frequently.

PRODUCTION MEETINGS

Most theatre organizations have some sort of *production meetings*, which are sometimes very informal, perhaps after a rehearsal or on the spur of the moment. For other theatres, production meetings are very well defined, happening each week (or even every day) at a specific time set aside expressly for them. This is a time when the nuts and bolts of a production are discussed. Things like schedules, how many crew people are needed, how to handle problems discovered in rehearsal, and so forth. Everyone is given a chance to review their work, and to comment on any problems they see on the horizon. Many times there is a discussion of how to integrate the work of different departments, such as when scenery will be ready for painting, how to paint the floor and focus lights on the same day, or where in a costume to hide a radio transmitter. Quite often it seems that an inordinate amount of time is spent discussing socks, or how many people it will take to pull a rope, but the meetings are very important tools in keeping the production running smoothly.

During the rehearsal process, the director may mention that an extra lamp is required in a certain scene, or that a costume needs a pocket, or that perhaps a door could open the opposite direction, or that thunder and lightning are required at a certain point. Be sure to take careful notes about those revelations, and to mention them at the next production meeting.

PREPARING FOR REHEARSALS

You must do a number of things before the standing rehearsal phase begins, in order to get ready for the process. The following things are always included, but there may be others that are specific to the production you are managing.

Tape out the set in the rehearsal area

The scenery designer will supply you with a *plan view* of the setting, and you must use tape to mark it out on the floor. This is to give the director and the actors an understanding of the spaces involved, and to aid in the blocking process. Use a *scale rule* to measure the drawing, and a regular tape measure to transfer the full size dimensions to the stage or rehearsal studio floor. If you don't know how to do this ask someone (perhaps an assistant) who does, or check out the chapter on construction documents which has a discussion of how to use a scale rule. It is important to do this work properly so that the actors get a true sense of how much space they have for certain scenes.

Use either vinyl electrical tape, or narrow strips of gaff tape, or cloth spike tape to mark the stage. The *electrical tape* is easy to find and comes in many colors.

TOOLS FOR MARKING OUT THE STAGE

You may wish to use that if your layout has multiple scenes and is very complicated. That will make it easier for the actors to orient themselves. Electrical tape has some quirks. The vinyl tape stretches a lot when you pull it off the roll, so let it draw back up some before sticking it to the floor or it will come back up later. Tape pulling up in the middle of the first rehearsal is a rookie mistake that you should avoid in order to save face.

If you use 2″ wide *gaff tape* instead, rip off narrow strips so that less tape is used. This not only saves on tape, but it is much kinder to the floor. Tape often pulls up the paint on the floor, and less tape equals less damage. White is good for a black stage floor and is readily accessible since it is used for many other purposes.

Spike tape is ½″ gaff tape that comes in different colors and is really the best type to use.

Find rehearsal props/costumes

You probably won't have the real props until just before tech rehearsals, so you need to find some stand-ins to use until that time. Your *rehearsal props* should be about the same size and weight of the real thing so that actors will have a chance to practice realistically. A block of wood with a rope on it can be a microphone, or a bundle of fabric can be a baby doll. A plastic soda bottle would not be a good substitute for a whiskey bottle, because the liquor bottle is much heavier. Find something closer to the actual size and weight.

You might need something heavy like a couch. Most of the time you can set up chairs in a row for a sofa, but other times you must improvise. You shouldn't automatically expect the designer or the shop to help you with this, other than offering advice as to whether your choices are appropriate. They are busy with their own chores.

The wardrobe department may have a supply of *rehearsal skirts* and other items that can be used to simulate costume pieces. If you need something specific, you should ask about it in the production meeting. You cannot expect wardrobe to supply your rehearsal with too many specific items, because that is really your job. Actors should be expected to wear appropriate clothing from home. For men that might include a suit jacket, or shoes with a leather sole. Women might be asked to wear low-heeled pumps, also known as *character shoes.*

The stage manager is often responsible for scheduling *costume fitting* appointments for the actors. Ask the wardrobe department for a list of who they would like to see, available times, and how long an appointment should last. You are responsible for scheduling because you have contact with actors at rehearsal that others do not have. You can discuss this process at production meetings.

Make a production/prompt book

Your *production book* should contain copies of all your paperwork. Things like a *contact sheet*, rehearsal schedule, crew list, and other things that are needed for your particular show. The main component is your *prompt script.* This is used to mark blocking, give lines to actors off-book, and to call cues during the run of the play.

The method of making a prompt script is largely a matter of personal preference, but there are some givens. If you received a small acting edition type script, make a photocopy of it to use in creating your book. Although

technically a copyright infringement issue, everyone does this to make a stage manager script, and it is expected. Make each page of the script its own single copy so there will be lots of space to make notes. You may wish to enlarge the print so that it is easier to read and so that there will be more space between the lines. By the end of technical rehearsals, the need for extra white space will be well understood.

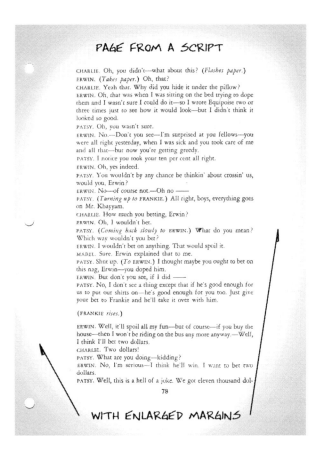

THE REHEARSAL PHASE

The first few rehearsals are typically blocking rehearsals, and you will need your prompt script from the get-go in order to write down the blocking notes. *Blocking* is a catch-all term for movement on the stage. If there is a very large cast, and the blocking is complex, you may wish to make a number of 8½×11 copies of the ground plan to go in your book so that you can mark the exact locations of actors on the stage. Writing down the blocking could be something you do yourself, or it could be an ASM chore. It is important to be accurate, because actors will definitely ask "Where do I enter?" many times before the show opens.

At some point the actors will be *off-book* meaning that they are no longer allowed to use their scripts on stage. They will however, have the option to *call for line* if they cannot remember one. An ASM should be located near the front of the stage to supply the lines as they are called for. This is often a delicate balance between saying too much and saying too little. Actors are taught not to break concentration when calling for a line. It is important for the person *on-book* to follow along very closely and to speak right up with the proper line the instant it is called for. Choose a person who is capable of focusing on that job without being distracted. *Feeding lines* means to offer them so that the actor can repeat them just after being prompted. If possible, you should rotate the duty of being on-book to keep one person from getting too bored. Having an ASM follow the book for you will keep you free to observe the overall process and to jump in where necessary. If there are starts and stops, you may need to move furniture around, or call "lights up" or something else that will keep the rehearsal moving and make everyone's work more efficient.

Usually, directors have a run through early on after the blocking is completed in order to see how the pieces fit together. Be sure to time this stumble through so that an idea of the running time can be determined. It is important to let the design staff know when this is happening so that they have an opportunity to observe the rehearsal. This is especially important for lighting designers who must know something about the blocking in order to complete their work.

Sometimes sound is an integral part of the performance, and you may need to provide music in order for certain scenes to be rehearsed effectively. Most of the time that is done with a jam box. You or an assistant should cue up the sound and play it at the appropriate moment. This process is much easier in the modern age of iPods.

You should familiarize yourself with the physical plant of the theatre, including where lights can be turned on and off, and which doors lead where. Lights used for general illumination at rehearsals are called *work lights*. Remember to have your electrician set out the *ghost light* at the end of the rehearsal.

TECH REHEARSALS

In commercial theatre, going through production means a long slog through the entire show with everyone in the theatre all the time. It can be exhausting, but all issues should be resolved by the end. Many schools use the Dry/Wet tech system instead. A *dry tech* rehearsal is used to set cues with no actors present, and a *wet tech* tries them out at a rehearsal where actors are present. The dry tech is often referred to as a cue setting rehearsal, because lighting, sound, and scenery cues are determined at that rehearsal. A *cue to cue* rehearsal skips over the dialog inside a scene, and jumps from one cue to the next.

Actors don't usually attend the dry tech because they would spend a lot of time waiting and becoming frustrated. Much of the action centers on a collaboration between the lighting designer and the director, looking at different lighting schemes and deciding which ones they want to use for the play. Sometimes the designer will arrive with a number of cues already worked out, or the whole thing may occur at the dry tech. Either way it is a time-consuming enterprise. The same thing happens with sound design, and with moving scenery around the stage. Each change in the lighting is distilled into a cue. Your job as stage manager is to write down in your book the exact moment each cue should happen, and what number has been assigned to that cue. Cues are given numbers in order to organize them, so you can call for them efficiently during the run of the show. Sometimes sound cues have letters, so that there is less confusion. You may work on just light cues, and then sound, and set cues, or they may be all done at once. Lighting cues are generally marked as electrics, sound as sound, and scenery as either fly or deck.

THEATRE GHOST LIGHT

ALTHOUGH THEATRE FOLKLORE SAYS THE LIGHT IS MEANT TO KEEP THE GHOSTS AWAY, ITS REAL PIURPOSE IS TO KEEP US FROM WALKING OFF INTO THE ORCHESTRA PIT WHEN THE THEATRE IS DARK

In your book you might begin with a cue sequence something like this:

Electrics 2, House to half GO
This cue asks for the house lights to dim ten to twenty seconds before the play begins. The audience knows the show is about to start, and they turn their attention to the stage.

Electrics 3, House out GO
This sequence asks for the house lights and preset lights to go out for the play to start. The theatre becomes dark.

Fly 1 GO
The curtain begins flying out in the dark.

Electrics 4 and Sound out GO
The pre-show music fades down as the lights fade up on the first moment of the play.

Electrics 1 is generally the *pre-show preset* that the audience sees as they enter the theatre. That could be lights on the curtain if one is used, or it could be an interesting look for the stage if it is not. At any rate, the first cue is called just before the *house opens*.

🌹 GREEN IDEAS TIP BOX

The pre-show lighting effect should be brought up before the audience comes into the theatre so that it sets the mood for what is about to happen. Before that, the work lights will have been on. Generally speaking, work lights use less electricity than the stage lights, especially if the theatre has energy-saving CFL fixtures. Don't bring up the pre-show preset until just as the house opens, and you will save on both electricity and expensive stage lamps.

It is very important for you to be well organized when writing down the cues in your book. There may easily be hundreds of cues in a single show, and you are the only person who is taking notes on their placement, everyone else is looking at other things.

Your assistants will probably be asked to move around the stage as ersatz actors, and/or to help move props around the stage. Because they have been in rehearsals, and know how the show works, they can instruct the deckhands and prop guys as to where things go.

Quite often it is necessary to mark where something should go when it is brought on stage. Spike two legs of a chair or two corners of a box. You can use colored tape to separate out spikes that overlap one another. *Glow tape* is sometimes used if the stage will be very dark when the prop is brought out.

At the end of every rehearsal, you should remind the crew of their next call time. It is common for call times

to change during this period, because so many things are still being worked out. Tell the crew not to leave the theatre without checking in first.

After the cues have been set, but before the next rehearsal, you need to mark your prompt script so that you can *call the show*. Calling the show means listening to and watching the actors on stage, and alerting the crew when to take their cues. In order to call the show you need to have the cue WARNs and GOs marked in your prompt script. The exact method of marking them is governed by personal preference, but some techniques are fairly standard.

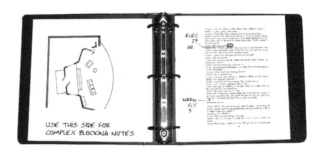

PROMPT BOOK

IT IS HELPFUL TO HAVE LOTS OF EXTRA WHITE SPACE AROUND THE SCRIPT SO THAT YOU HAVE ROOM TO MARK THE CUES, AND TO MAKE NOTES ABOUT OTHER THINGS THAT MUST HAPPEN DURING THE SHOW.

Cues must often happen on a particular line, or perhaps one particular word within that line. So the marking must be done with some precision. Most stage managers mark the word placement in the text and draw a pencil line off to the margins of the script. Pencil is important, because cues are very frequently changed between tech rehearsal and opening night. Mark the cue type and number in the margin so that the pencil line connects the cue number and the correct word in the script. It should read something like ELEC 23 GO, or SOUND 7 GO; depending on the actual placement.

Notice that the GO word is placed last. When you actually make the call, the crewperson involved should take the cue exactly on the word go. That is one way that a high degree of precision in cuing can be achieved. Stagehands are taught to be very meticulous about taking cues exactly on the word go, and not before or after. You should reinforce that standard.

Most stage managers give *warnings* for cues, and those should be written down in the book as well. Quite often a number of cues can all be warned at the same time when they are in close proximity to one another. Warns or *standbys* (either term is appropriate) should be announced in the opposite manner to a GO. The correct phrasing is "Standby electrics 23 and sound 7." Announcing the call as a standby first will avoid confusion as to the nature of the call. Warnings should be marked in your script in the same manner as the GOs, with pencil lines and marginal notations.

Cue calling is typically done via *intercom headset*, which is especially true when speaking to assistant stage managers, the light board operator and spot operators. If you assign one assistant to SL and the other to SR, they can be your eyes and ears as to what is going on backstage. You should position your desk to get the best view of the actors on stage, and/or use any video monitoring equipment available.

Another means of communication is via *cue lights*, which are controlled by switches on the stage manager's desk. When the switch is turned on, a cue light is lit. This is a warning for action to take place, so the switch should be turned on a reasonable amount of time before the cue is to occur. If the time span is too short there won't be enough time to get ready. If the time span is too long, the stagehands will get bored and look away just as the light goes off. Cue lights are a good way to communicate with the fly rail, or with deckhands, because many of them can see the light all at once, and because it doesn't unnecessarily burden them with equipment. When the cue light is switched off, it is the same as if the stage manager has said "GO."

The stage manager really begins to take over the show during this period. Most directors avoid stopping during a *dress rehearsal* because it disrupts the artistic flow of the actors. The last dress rehearsal before opening is called the *final dress*. In some theatres tickets are sold for the last few rehearsals which are billed as *preview performances*.

The wet tech is generally the most chaotic period of any show. Everyone is dashing about, preparing for their individual tasks. For this rehearsal the actors are called as well as the crew, and they will be excited about the new elements being added. Try your best not be overwhelmed by the hubbub going on around you, but rather learn to enjoy it instead. Everyone will be happier that way.

Frequently a *tech table* is set up in the auditorium of the theatre for you to use during the tech rehearsals. Lighting and sound control may be located nearby. This is because a large amount of cross-talk must occur between the designers, the director, and the SM. A close-knit grouping makes it easier to communicate. Position an assistant at the stage manager's desk backstage in order to operate the cue lights.

Tech week is the time between the dry tech and opening night. It is a busy period full of last-minute changes and phrases like "Oh, just one more thing. . ."

THE STAGE DOOR TYPICALLY LEADS TO THE DRESSING ROOM AREA.

IT IS BAD MANNERS TO ADMIT PEOPLE WHO ARE NOT INVOLVED WITH THE SHOW.

It is customary to have a *sign-in sheet* posted on the callboard near the *stage door* for actors to sign, showing that they are in the theatre. This is good practice to follow, because it will let you know right away if someone is missing. You must telephone them immediately if they are. Stage managers alert the actors and stagehands when *half-hour* has been reached. In commercial theatre, IATSE show calls are measured from the half-hour call, and it is very important to the stage hands. Most stage managers also make 15 minute and 5 minute calls. *Places* means that the show is about to start, and that cast and crew alike should make their way to their opening positions without delay.

TERMS USED IN THIS CHAPTER

Actor's Equity Association
apprentice stagehand
artisan
Artistic Director
audition form
bite-light
blocking
Business Agent (IATSE)
call board
call for line
call light
call the show: warn, standby, go
carpenter, head
commercial theatre
community theatre
Company Manager
company of actors
contact sheet
costume fitting
Crescent wrench
cue light
cue to cue rehearsal
deckhand
dress rehearsal
dry tech
electrician
feeding lines
final dress
followspot: boomerang, color
    frame, dowser, iris, sight
followspot spot size: full body,
    three-quarters, waist,
    head
followspot terms: ballyhoo, pan,
    slide

foot (a ladder)
ghost light
grip
half-hour
headset: belt pack, double or
    single muff, channel, call
    light
house heads; carpentry, electrics,
    fly, sound
house open
IATSE: International Alliance
    of Theatrical Stage
    Employees
journeyman stagehand
Lighting Director (LD)
load-in
load-out
LORT: League of Regional
    Theatres
Managing Director
NETC: New England Theatre
    Conference
no color
not-for-profit theatre
Offstage Jobs website
on- or off-book
pink contract
places call
plan view
pre-show preset
preview performance
production
production book
production meeting
Production Stage Manager

prompt script
prop: cabinet, hand prop, hand-
    off
prop guy
property department
regional theatre
rehearsal: prop, skirt, run time,
    character shoes
scale rule
SETC: Southeastern Theatre
    Conference
show call
sign-in sheet
spike tape
spot op
stage directions
stage door
Stage Manager or SM
stagehand
stock scenery
storefront theatre
table work
tape: electrical, gaff, glow,
    spike
tape out the set
tech or technical rehearsal
tech table
Technical Director
truss spot
USA or United Scenic Artists
walk up (a ladder)
wet tech
white contract
work lights
yellow card

CHAPTER 2

THEATRE BUILDINGS

THROUGHOUT HISTORY, the design of theatrical structures has been heavily influenced by the engineering and construction methods that were known to the people who built them. But just as important was the type of entertainment those people wanted to watch. The type of *venue* needed for a play based on words and ideas is entirely different from one needed for the spectacle of a Roman chariot race, or in modern times, a Taylor Swift concert. The Greeks were the first culture to build large theatres specifically for entertainment, and invented the *amphitheatre*, which is largely the same today as it was back then. Greek amphitheatres became the archetype for all subsequent venues, especially open air ones. But they didn't arbitrarily select that design for their structures because they liked being outdoors. They used the construction methods available in their time period to create the most useful and efficient space possible, to be used in producing the type of entertainment that was popular in their culture. Large, covered indoor structures were simply not possible until more modern engineering methods were developed.

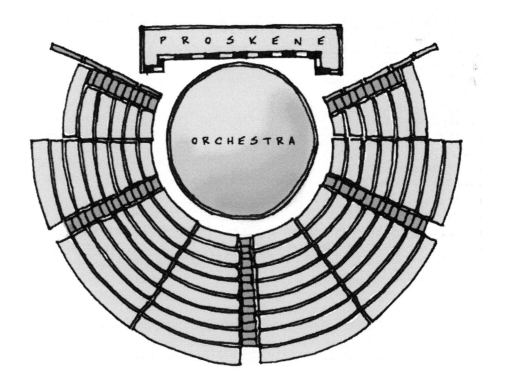

SYMMETRICAL GREEK THEATRE

Greek Amphitheatres

The earliest Greek-style theatres took advantage of existing hillsides to form a sloping audience area that curved around a circular performance area. Often-times large amphitheatres were somewhat asymmetrical as a result of following the existing terrain. That could invite a discussion of how that irregularity ran counter to Greek sensibilities about order and harmony in all things. Perhaps the practical concern of adding the most seats possible trumped their need for geometrical perfection. As a society the Greeks had a philosophical love of geometry, which was the basis for all their mathematical inventions.

CLASSICAL AMPHITHEATRE SPACE

THE ARCHITECTURE IS GREEK REVIVAL, AND SO IS THE SMALL OUTDOOR THEATRE SPACE ATTACHED TO THE BUILDING. NOTE THE BALCONY FOR ORATORY.

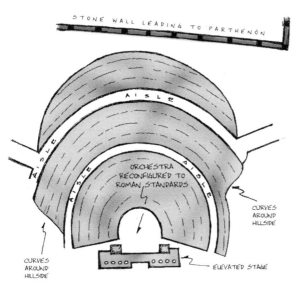

STONE WALL LEADING TO PARTHENON

AISLE

ORCHESTRA RECONFIGURED TO ROMAN STANDARDS

CURVES AROUND HILLSIDE

CURVES AROUND HILLSIDE

ELEVATED STAGE

SHAPE MODIFIED TO FIT EXISTING HILLSIDE

THE ROMANS CONVERTED THE ORCHESTRA AT THE THEATRE OF DIONYSUS TO MEET THEIR SPECIFICATIONS

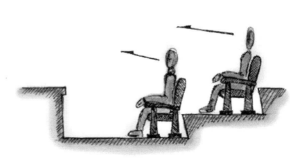

RAKED SEATING IMPROVES SIGHTLINES

Modern outdoor theatres are generically known as amphitheatres, especially if they resemble the original Greek model. Modified versions are very popular for outdoor historical dramas that run only in the summertime when the weather permits it. There is also an astounding number of small, Greek inspired modern-day performance venues which are often more of an aesthetic addition to some other building or landscape than a real performance space.

Greek theatres are an excellent example of the science of *sightlines* as used in designing a performance space. The study of sightlines is a notion whereby the proper arrangement of a seating area can greatly enhance (or detract from in a bad space) the ability of the audience to see the performance. This term can also be used to indicate which portions of a stage space are visible to the audience. Obviously, the head of another person sitting directly in front of you makes it difficult to view the stage.

Raking the seating rows and staggering the seats can vastly improve sightlines.

Greek theatres were designed around a circular performance area or *orchestra*, and as a result the seating rows in their theatres curved around that shape both to be in harmony with it, and to keep the seats as close to the stage as possible. This creates a traditional fan shape that is often associated with Greek amphitheatres. Classical architects were very interested in graceful geometrical shapes and symmetry. Greek mathematicians were rather exclusively concerned with geometry rather than numbers and formulae that make up math as we know it today.

Keeping the audience and actor close to one another is an important factor in creating a sense of intimacy between them. Most Greek theatres were quite large in relation to a modern indoor theatre, creating an immense gulf between performer and viewer. To counterbalance that loss of intimacy, a *chorus* of performers was used, all making the same movements and reciting the same lines, and as a group had more impact on the audience than a single actor would. The chorus in a modern musical is used in the same way, in essence amplifying their contribution by using a large number of performers together.

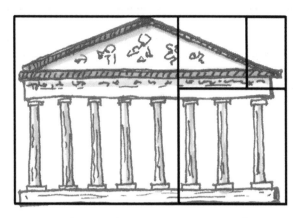

THE PARTHENON WAS CONSTRUCTED
WITH PROPORTIONS CHOSEN FROM THE GOLDEN MEAN

THE WIDTH OF A RECTANGLE SHOULD BE 1.6 TIMES ITS HEIGHT.

PLACING A SQUARE IN A RECTANGLE THUS PROPORTIONED
CREATES ANOTHER RECTANGLE OF THE SAME PROPORTIONS.

It is hard to say now whether having a chorus called them to use the circular orchestra, or if the orchestra called for a chorus. Whichever it was, when the Greek choral form of entertainment eventually began to give way to individual actors speaking lines of dialog, a raised platform area was provided to give them added prominence. This area was called the *skene* by the Greeks, and is the root of our word *proscenium,* meaning in front of the skene or scene/scenery.

ACTOR ON SKENE
GAINS HEIGHT ADVANTAGE
OVER ACTOR STANDING
IN ORCHESTRA

THIS ACTOR GAINS FOCUS
EVEN THOUGH HE IS
FARTHER AWAY

ROMAN ADVANCES

Many historians have pointed out that Greek philosophers concentrated on ideas, but their Roman counterparts dwelt on developing ideas into something more practical. As a simplification it has been said that the Greeks asked "why" and the Romans asked "how."

Taking an idea from pure science and making it useful is at the heart of the engineering ideal and engineering was very important to the Romans. That's possibly because the Roman army conquered most of Europe and needed excellent civil engineers to design the roads and bridges that tied the empire together. They also used their talents to create civic improvements like aqueducts and public buildings. Most of these achievements involved the use of arches. A stone arch holds together because the downward force of gravity acting on the segments of a curved structure is balanced by its shape, with the force being redirected outward at the base of the arch. In a structure created by several arches placed side by side, the outward pressure from one arch is counterbalanced by one or more adjacent arches. The result is a lightweight structure that has been left open on the inside.

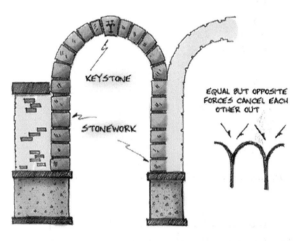

KEYSTONE

STONEWORK

EQUAL BUT OPPOSITE
FORCES CANCEL EACH
OTHER OUT

HOW ARCHES WORK

Egyptian pyramids were instead solid structures that required a vast amount of stone to construct. That was hugely expensive and thus not practical in other cultures where wealth is more dispersed. A Greek building such as the Parthenon depended on the strength of stone beams to span the distance between columns and to carry the weight of the roof, but stone is not well suited to that purpose because it lacks tensile strength. Arches, when made into domes and barrel vault roofs, can be used to create open interiors, and don't require nearly so much stone material. Arches that are rounded at the top are today called *Romanesque,* as is a style of architecture that uses them.

The Romans used a series of arches to build the *Colosseum*, a freestanding oval structure best suited to the games, races, and physical contests that were popular types of entertainment in that period. The Colosseum was an architectural marvel of its day, not only because of its size, but also because of its clever high-tech features like stage elevators and trap doors that allowed performers to enter the space suddenly. These same devices are often used in modern arena rock concerts, and for the same reason, because they present the audience with a surprise that excites them.

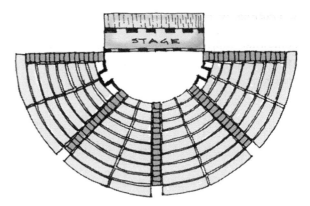

TYPICAL ROMAN THEATRE

THE COLOSSEUM IN ROME IS CONSTRUCTED FROM MANY SMALL ARCHES

THAT APPROACH USES FEWER MATERIALS AND CREATES A MORE OPEN SPACE THAN IF THE WALLS WERE SOLID

Roman theatres for plays were constructed in much the same manner as the Greek ones were, with the major differences being that the elevated stage area was greatly enlarged and elaborated upon, and the circular choral area was cut in half to form a semicircle. That brought the stage closer to the audience. Individual actors had become more important. As with the Colosseum, the Romans were able to build freestanding banks of tiered seats for their urban theatres rather than depending entirely upon the geography of hillsides, although many of the still existing examples were built more in the Greek style. Their solid earth foundations have proved to be sturdier and longer lasting than the arched type. The free-standing theatres were smaller in scope than their Greek counterparts, perhaps due to more urban settings, but also it seems judging from the few surviving examples, the plays themselves had a more modern structure requiring greater intimacy between performer and audience. They are less a series of public speeches, and more a dialog between characters. The archetypical Roman theatre seems to have had a lot in common with a more modern type, the thrust theatre. The Theatre of Pompey was the first permanent theatre structure in Rome itself.

Roman theatres often had shade awnings covering at least some portions of the audience from the sun, which could be pulled back and forth using ropes and pulleys. Of course all performances were held during daylight hours. The Colosseum had a complex, retractable awning system known as the *vela* that could be adjusted to provide maximum comfort for the spectators. Care was taken to heighten the sense of pleasure that patrons felt in a public spectacle. Theatres were often a part of a complex of gardens and other public spaces, much the same as in today's environment.

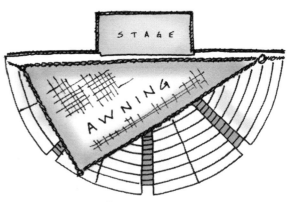

HOW ROMANS MIGHT HAVE USED ROPES AND FABRIC TO MAKE A SUN AWNING

THE ROMANS COULDN'T BUILD LARGE, UNSUPPORTED ROOF SPANS BECAUSE THEY DIDN'T HAVE THE TECHNOLOGY. BUT EVEN IN MODERN TIMES, MANY OUTDOOR VENUES USE ROPES AND NETTING TO PROVIDE A PARTIAL SUN SHADE FOR THE AUDIENCE.

Proscenium Theatres

Somewhat capriciously skipping past the religious performances of the Middle Ages, Asian drama, and commedia (all of which had less effect on modern theatre architecture) the next period to greatly influence the progress of theatrical design came during the Renaissance. The Renaissance was a rebirth of interest in the classical societies of Greece and Rome, as well as a time when ideas flowed more easily than they had during the darker past. The development of theories pertaining to illusionist painting and perspective rendering were adapted to theatre use, and created the need for much more advanced production methods. The type of scenery utilized during the Renaissance period was often based on the methods used in *one-point perspective* drawing, where a single *vanishing point* is located somewhere near the bottom center of the viewing plane.

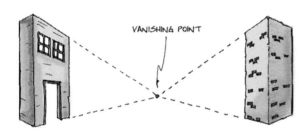

FORCED PERSPECTIVE DRAWING

Objects in the foreground are shown in a larger scale than those objects in the distance. This technique creates an illusion of depth and three-dimensionality. The effect was further realized by using a series of viewing planes spaced at intervals, moving away from the audience. Objects further upstage were rendered in a smaller size than those downstage. For a city scene, this would require a number of building images painted on flat panels, with each successive building being rendered in a scale somewhat smaller than the one preceding it. This style of design is known generically as *wing and drop* scenery. The "wings" were the panels off to the side of the stage, and the "drop" was a painted cloth dropping down in the rear from the ceiling of the stage.

Because the vanishing point in this *forced perspective* style of design must be elevated from the stage floor in order for the lines to appear realistic, the stage floor behind the acting area was *raked* upward, away from the audience to achieve the desired effect. This was of course the origination of the terms upstage and downstage. An actor who traveled toward the back wall would literally be walking *upstage*, and on the return trip would be treading *downstage*. The concepts embraced by wing and drop scenery are still very much alive in the twenty-first century.

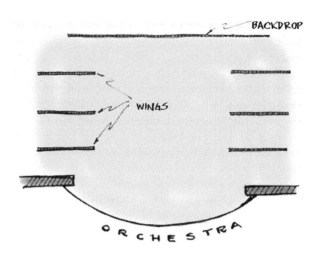

WING AND DROP SCENERY

Historians are fortunate to have several written records of how theatre was staged during the Renaissance period. Books by *Sebastiano Serlio* and *Nicola Sabbatini* have survived to the present day and each has a wealth of descriptions and illustrations. The staging of Greek and Roman dramas is not nearly so well known, and most of the information about that has been deduced from the surviving play scripts. The writings of Serlio and Sabbatini are first-hand accounts of theatre in the sixteenth and seventeenth centuries, and have detailed information about wing and drop staging methods. Scenery designed

A PAGE FROM SABBATINI'S BOOK

NOTICE HOW THE BUILDINGS ARE GROUPED ON PLANES TO THE STAGE LEFT AND RIGHT. THEY ARE THE WINGS. THE BUILDING TO THE REAR IS MEANT TO BE A BACKDROP.

for proscenium theatres today has many parallels to this early style of design, based primarily upon wings, drops, and forced perspective painting.

The question arises of how to easily change from one set to another when the show is in progress if one needs to change location. Today of course we fly scenery in and out using a counterweight system, but they didn't have that technology. In a small theatre, it could be done in a manner similar to sliding closet doors. One set of panels could be pulled offstage, revealing another set behind them. Hence the term *stage set*, or a set of stage wings. Some much larger sixteenth-century theatres used the *chariot and pole* system of shifting scenery. This consisted of a series of slots cut into the stage floor running left to right, and a number of symmetrically arranged poles that rose up through them. These upright poles were mounted on carts in a basement. Moving the carts, or chariots, back and forth moved the poles, and thus the scenery. This was of course in an age before the creation of modern rigging from overhead and seems to be a very clumsy arrangement to modern eyes.

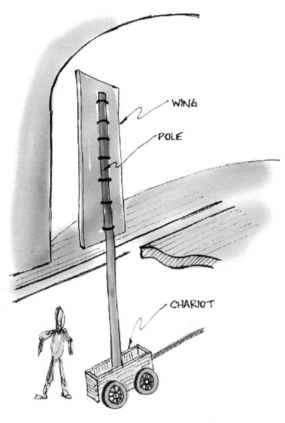

CHARIOT AND POLE SYSTEM

The late Renaissance saw the development of the proscenium theatre as we know it today. The farthermost downstage set of flats or wings became a permanent architectural feature of the building. When supplemented by an overhead masking piece they together became the proscenium we know today. The proscenium not only serves as a frame for the setting, but also separates the audience from the stage, allowing the use of intricate mechanical devices that are completely hidden from patrons in the auditorium.

By the late nineteenth century it became possible to construct an overhead fly house of the sort in use today. The advent of realism and *box sets* in the early twentieth century eventually did away with the practice of raking the stage for forced perspective settings.

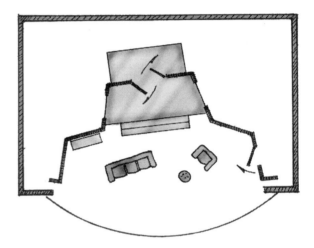

EARLY TYPE OF BOX SET

THE ADVENT OF REALISM IN DRAMA
MOVED DESIGN AWAY FROM
FORCED PERSPECTIVE SCENERY AND
TOWARD THE MORE "REALISTIC" BOX SET

The proscenium house is a very common type of theatre, and is used throughout the world. Its mechanics are most useful when *spectacle* is an important element of the production because it contains such a large collection of mechanical devices used for stage effects. Professional touring companies of commercial Broadway shows play only in proscenium theatres because they allow for a large audience capacity and also because of the similarity of stage equipment available in all proscenium houses. Although the lobbies and auditoriums of various road houses throughout the country are vastly different in style and size, equipment available upstage of the plaster line is more or less standard. An in-depth discussion of the proscenium theatre can be found in the chapter devoted to them.

MODERN DEVELOPMENTS

Thrust theatres began a surge in popularity in the 1960s and 1970s in an effort to break through to a more "actor friendly" type of space. It is interesting to note that this sort of theatre was also popular in Elizabethan times, and the reasons for its success now and then are largely the same. Thrust theatres are best suited to the production of intimate dramas. Plays that depend on the accurate understanding of words and/or the transmission of small emotional moments are well served by the close proximity of audience and actor found in thrust theatres.

The *Globe* theatre was truly for the masses, at least the middle-class people of the day. The theatre of Serlio and Sabbatini was reserved for the elite of society. The Globe and its London counterparts provided a standing room only area for groundlings on the dirt floor in front of the stage. The stage itself was raised about head high over the ground, and audience seating was arranged in a circle around the space and completely enclosed it. At the painstakingly researched historical recreation of the Globe in London, there is a thatched roof over the heads of the higher-paying seated patrons and over the stage, but the groundlings in the center were/are unprotected.

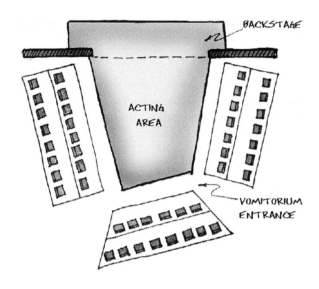

THRUST THEATRE

GLOBE THEATRE

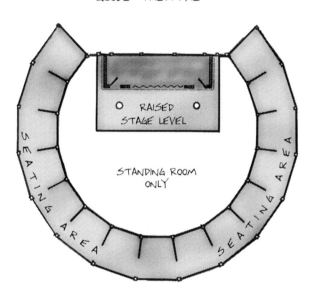

THE GLOBE WAS AN EARLY EXAMPLE OF TODAY'S THRUST THEATRES

Generally, in a thrust theatre, the audience seating wraps around three-fourths of the stage area, giving the stage the appearance of "thrusting out" into the spectators. This in effect makes the front of the stage longer/wider, making it possible to fit a larger number of seats into a small number of rows. A smaller number of rows going away from the stage results in more audience members being closer to the stage. Designers need to be careful not to place bulky scenery and props too far downstage, as this can be problematic for sightlines.

Arena, or *theatre in the round* is another popular modern form. As the name suggests, the audience seating wraps entirely around the stage, eliminating the upstage

opening found in thrust theatres. Other than the loss of the upstage facade, the sightline rules are primarily the same for arena theatres as they are for thrust theatres. Almost all arena theatres have a grid of lighting pipes over the stage, and lighting is very important to them because view-blocking scenery must be kept at a minimum.

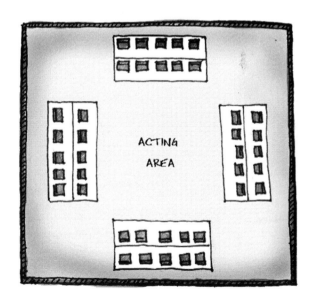

THEATRE IN THE ROUND

At this point you might well wonder how actors are able to enter the acting space of a theatre in the round, as they don't have a backstage area to enter from. Arena theatres almost always use one or more *vomitorium* entrances to bring the actors and props on stage. A vomitorium is a passageway under the audience seating from the backstage space to the stage itself. They are also popular in thrust theatres, where they provide a more direct route to the downstage area. "Voms" are also used to provide entrance to audience seating in stadiums, sports arenas, and very large proscenium houses.

Another form of theatre space is the *black box* or *flexible* seating theatre. Either of these names is actually quite descriptive. This type of theatre is generally housed in a large, black, rectilinear room. Audience seating chairs may be moved around and set up in whatever configuration is desired. *Risers* are often used to facilitate better sightlines. Some theatres actually have bleacher seats like those in an athletic stadium that can be moved around the space.

The black box style of theatre is especially popular with off-off-Broadway theatre groups because of its low cost, extreme intimacy, and its ability to conform to more experimental genres of performance. The seating may be set up to resemble virtually any style of theatre: proscenium, thrust, in the round; as well as more offbeat arrangements such as *stadium.* (In which the performance area is flanked on two sides by seating, as in a football stadium.) Or it may be truly flexible, allowing the performance area to flow in and around the seating (or standing) area. Audience members in this latter concept may move from place to place during the performance, becoming a part of the action, and blurring the dividing line into performance art. Scenic elements become less important in black box theatres, although lighting, props, and sound retain a great deal of influence.

BLACK BOX THEATRE SPACE

THE LUCILLE LITTLE THEATRE AT TRANSYLVANIA UNIVERSITY IS TYPICAL OF MANY BLACK BOX THEATRES; WITH MOVEABLE SEATING RISERS AND AN OPEN WIRE LIGHTING GRID.

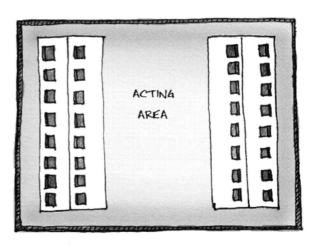

STADIUM SEATING

TERMS USED IN THIS CHAPTER

amphitheatre	one-point perspective	stadium seating
arena theatre	orchestra	stage set
black box theatre	proscenium	theatre in the round
box set	raked stage	thrust theatre
chariot and pole	riser for seating	upstage
chorus	Romanesque arches	vanishing point
Colosseum	Sabbatini, Nicola	vela
downstage	Serlio, Sebastiano	venue
flexible seating	sightlines	vomitorium
forced perspective	skene	wing and drop
Globe theatre	spectacle	

CHAPTER 3

THRUST THEATRES

THE MODERN INTEREST in thrust theatres might well trace its origins back to the 1950s when theatres like those at the *Stratford Festival* in Ontario, and the *Guthrie Theatre* in Minneapolis emerged. These theatres were two of the first, but were among many others formed by companies of actors who were interested in creating a new type of emotional realism on the stage. They became the first large *regional theatres*, ones not in New York, but rather in other regions of the country. Before that most theatre outside the city was in the form of touring companies, many of which had origins and/or bookings that came from New York. Most theatre venues in cities across America were owned by theatre *syndicates*, which had complete control over what shows would be staged. Actors often had little or no control over how they were treated by large monopolies.

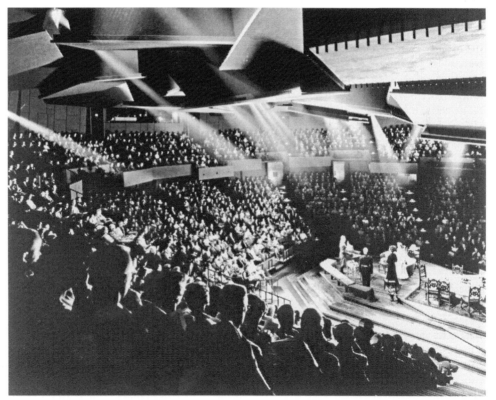

Photo by Marty Nordstrum

THE GUTHRIE THEATER IN MINNEAPOLIS

1963 PRODUCTION OF CHEKHOV'S "THE THREE SISTERS"
DIRECTED BY TYRONE GUTHRIE.

In the 1920s the *New Stagecraft* movement began when artists like playwright *Eugene O'Neill* felt that control of the theatre should shift away from theatre owners and be given to the artists themselves. These theatres would later become what we now know as not-for-profits, which are funded in part by donations from their patrons and not just ticket sales. Theatre intellectuals promoted the idea of the *Little Theatre*, in which small, independent theatres were formed by artists who lived and performed in that area rather than by bringing in outsiders via touring. A couple of decades later *Constantine Stanislavsky's* ideas about *method acting* were made popular in the USA by *Lee Strasberg* and the *Actor's Studio*, which completed a cycle that brought out the need for a type of theatre architecture that celebrates the connection between actor and audience rather than serving as a facility for spectacle, which proscenium theatres had long provided.

The thrust theatre became very popular because it brought audience and actor together in a way that was quite astounding for the day. Modern theatregoers have become so accustomed to this form of seating arrangement that they probably don't appreciate how novel it all was in the beginning for an audience accustomed to a proscenium picture-frame stage. With audience wrapping around three sides, the number of seats in the front row is doubled or perhaps even tripled. The number of seats in each row going back is larger than the one in front of it. Thus relatively few rows are needed, and even the back row is closer to the stage than the middle of a large proscenium house. With such a close association, audiences can easily hear small intonations in the actor's voices, and feel much more connected to them than in a larger house.

Thrust theatres have remained popular, or perhaps even gained in popularity, possibly because the type of drama (other than musicals) Americans prefer has shifted in the direction of what can be staged in a thrust theatre. Many modern plays are often said to be written "like a movie script" where notions of time and place are blurred, and they shift back and forth quickly from one location to another. It is generally not possible to create scenery for each new location in such a script, and instead designers often use a *unit set* that serves all locations in an abstract way. The thrust theatre is perfect for that, and has been used for such purposes going back to the Elizabethan stage of Shakespeare's era, where the audience was asked to imagine vast palaces and battle scenes. Instead of literal, physical scenery the audience is asked to use their imaginations.

You might also consider that the type of play performed in a thrust theatre is a reaction against the faux realism of gritty movie scripts. It isn't possible for any type of theatre to compete with movies shot on exotic locations, no scenery will compare with that. But movies are a recorded art form, and don't have the excitement

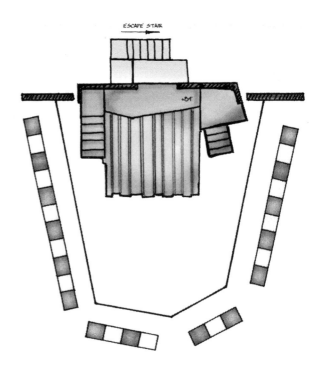

UNIT SET ON A THRUST STAGE

ONE SET CAN BE USED FOR MANY LOCATIONS

of live actors on stage. Perhaps thrust and arena theatre performances have surged in popularity because they do the best job of utilizing the live aspect of theatre rather than attempting to compete with a movie in creating spectacle. The transformation started by actors in the 1950s and 1960s, who were attracted to emotional realism and to a close connection of actor and audience, is now complete.

THE THEATRE ITSELF

In a proscenium house, the audience view of the stage is more or less constant throughout the theatre, and although some seats on the extreme sides have a slanted view of the action, the stage retains a kind of movie-screen quality that is familiar to viewers. In a thrust theatre, the audience view from the far left is completely the opposite of that from the far right, much the same as in stadium seating. Patrons seated at the downstage edge of the stage see the action from straight ahead, and more like a proscenium. This variation in *sightlines* requires that special techniques be used by both directors and designers so that everyone in the audience enjoys the same quality experience.

Most thrust theatres have either a modified proscenium opening, or some type of architectural staging at the upstage end of the playing area. (Architectural features are those built into the theatre by the architect, and are permanent constraints for the set designer.) Some theatres have semi-permanent Shakespearean inner/above inner/ below balcony type features which are very much like Shakespeare's Globe stage. For a few, the thrust is really just an extraordinarily large proscenium apron. For most there is an open proscenium arch with a backstage area that allows the set designer to concentrate larger scenic units there. Designers must carefully plan these so that they do not stick out so far downstage that they block the audience view from the extreme sides. Likewise, care must be taken not to use visual elements in the far downstage space that might block the view of persons sitting there. A wall, or a refrigerator, or even a large wingback chair is certain to annoy anyone who cannot see past it to the action of the play.

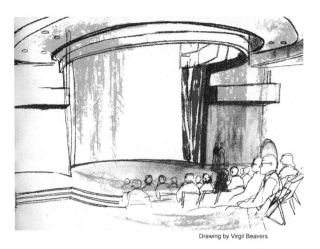

Drawing by Virgil Beavers

A LOVELY HAND SKETCH FROM THE DALLAS THEATER CENTER'S OPENING IN 1959

NOTE THE TWO SIDE STAGES, WITH OVERHANGING BALCONIES. ARCHITECT FRANK LLOYD WRIGHT MAY HAVE IMAGINED THEM BEING USED BY JULIET.

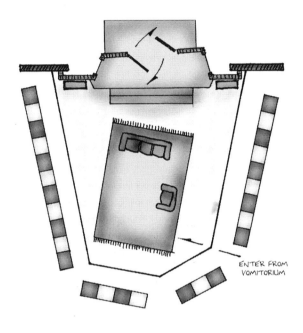

ENTER FROM VOMITORIUM

REALISTIC INTERIOR IN A THRUST THEATRE FLATTENED OUT AGAINST THE BACK WALL

Seats in a thrust theatre are generally quite steeply raked to help alleviate this issue, and as a result the appearance of the stage floor assumes a much greater focus than in a proscenium theatre where the audience view of the floor is extremely oblique, other than from the balcony. Low platforms and other intricate floor treatments are popular choices in a thrust theatre. Low-mass scenic elements like lamp posts, bentwood chairs, and small props are often used in downstage areas.

Some thrust theatres have a completely unique aspect such as an elevated performance area that is not connected to the main part of the stage. Perhaps this is an homage by the architect to the Shakespearean concept of staging that included balconies for important speeches such as Juliet's famous words to Romeo. Each theatre seems to have its own unique name for such a space, and although not found in all thrust theatres it is a frequent addition.

Many thrust theatres have one or more entrances from under the stage, or between seating areas known as a *vomitorium* or vom, just like in an arena theatre. The purpose is clear, to provide an alternate entrance to the stage other than just the one upstage. It can be really exciting to have an actor enter right next to you when seated near a vom. Scenery and props can move on from there as well, but this is often complicated by ramps and steps used to reach the stage floor.

Because thrust theatre scenery is often a unit set, or completely open staging, lighting takes on even greater importance here than in a proscenium space. If the setting is abstract, or perhaps merely a group of different platform levels, lighting must take over the job of establishing time and place. To add yet another level of complexity, just illuminating the faces of the actors becomes more difficult when the audience is seated on three sides of the stage and views of the performance are from three different angles. As a result the lighting positions in a thrust theatre are often treated in a substantially different way than what you would expect in a proscenium theatre. Whereas proscenium stages have front of house positions and on stage electrics, thrust theatres generally have a set of *catwalks* over the stage to provide positions for lights hung over the acting area, and often more catwalks over the audience areas to provide pipes for fixtures that allow light to enter the space at an angle. Steel beams create an open appearance to the grid over the stage so that there is more opportunity to hang lights pointing different directions. Rather than running drop boxes to the positions as in a proscenium, dimmer circuits are spread throughout, reducing the need for an excessive number of jumpers.

Some theatres may have an altogether different approach to creating a grid over the stage and audience,

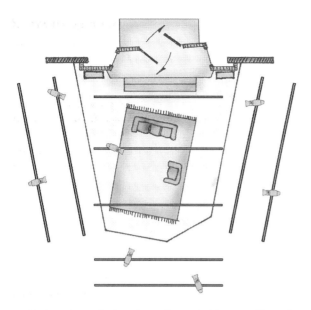

LIGHTING POSITIONS IN A THRUST THEATRE

THEY MAY VARY WIDELY FROM THEATRE TO THEATRE, BUT MOST THRUST SPACES HAVE EXCELLENT ACCESS TO LIGHTING POSITIONS

TENSION CABLE GRID

THE GRID IS MADE FROM 1/8TH INCH AIRCRAFT CABLES WOVEN TOGETHER, AND THE EFFECT IS VERY MUCH LIKE WALKING ON A CIRCUS NET.

using a woven mat of aircraft cable instead. The individual cables are small, perhaps ⅛″ or so in diameter, and are several inches apart. They cover the entire space so that catwalks are not needed. As a result, the floor space is quite open and allows for much more freedom in focusing lights in multiple directions. That is not always possible when a grid made of steel beams and catwalks is used. The *cable grid* is weight bearing, so that the electricians can walk around on it with no need for individual catwalks. The effect is somewhat like walking on a circus net and takes some getting used to, but it is actually quite fun once you get your sea legs. You might think that the steel cables would cast shadows on the stage when light passes through them, but that does not happen. The cables and lights are so close together that the shadow effect is blurred and not visible on the stage.

In general, thrust theatres tend to have a more modern look than most proscenium theatres because they have an open ceiling and often make no attempt to hide mechanical systems used for heating and cooling, a design choice that has become quite popular in public spaces everywhere. Many modern buildings take the same approach in celebrating the look of their mechanical workings rather than hiding them. In a traditional proscenium house, care is often taken to attempt to hide the mechanics of lighting, but the more modern thrust type tends to lean in the direction of the adage "form follows function" and lighting equipment is exposed to the audience in a constructivist manner. This allows for much wider latitude concerning fixture placement, and thus leads to superior lighting design possibilities.

TERMS USED IN THIS CHAPTER

Actor's Studio	method acting	Strasberg, Lee
cable grid	New Stagecraft	Stratford Festival
catwalk	O'Neill, Eugene	Syndicate (theatre owners)
Guthrie Theatre	Sightlines	unit set
Little Theatre	Stanislavsky, Constantine	vomitorium

CHAPTER 4

PROSCENIUM THEATRES

I F YOU ARE STAGING a Broadway musical, this is the theatre for you. Proscenium theatres were developed for just that sort of spectacle. Plays are written with specific ways of staging them in mind, and any show more than 40, but less than 400 years old was probably written with a proscenium theatre in mind. They have lots of equipment to "make the magic happen" and it is important for any aspiring stagehand or shop carpenter to know as much as possible about this type of theatre.

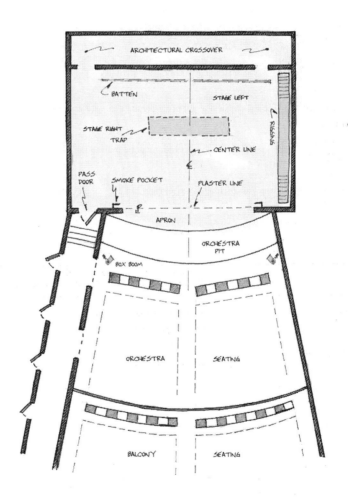

PLAN VIEW OF A PROSCENIUM THEATRE

The Auditorium

In any *plan view* drawing of a theatre, the stage is always shown at the top of the paper and the auditorium at the bottom. Downstage is down the page toward the audience, and upstage is up toward the back wall. Stage left is to your left if you are facing the audience, and stage right is to your right. Audience left and right are just the opposite, and are the way the drawing looks on the page. I always have to stop and think about that for a second when out in the house of the theatre, even after all this time. The proscenium frames the stage for the audience, just like the frame on a painting. The area to the side of the stage, upstage past the edge of the proscenium opening is called a *wing*. Some theatres have very little wing space, and some have a great deal. The Metropolitan Opera in New York has the same amount of wing space on each side as there is on the stage itself, but that is very rare.

Wings are quite important as a storage space for moving scenery that must be carried or rolled offstage. The *rail*, which comprises the rigging equipment used to fly scenery over the stage, can be on one side or the other, but whichever side that is probably has less wing space than the opposite one. In an older theatre like those on Broadway but found in many other places, the dressing rooms are likely on the non-rail side, and go up several floors.

In a newer theatre, the architects may have created a hallway directly behind the stage that is used to travel from one side to the other, and this passageway is known as a *crossover*. Road houses used for touring shows probably have a *loading door* on the back wall that leads to an alley or street, making that impossible. An alternate style of crossover runs under the stage and is accessed by a set of stairs on either side. You are more likely to find that in an older building, especially one in an urban setting. Quite frequently the staging of a particular show requires that actors exit from one side of the stage and immediately reappear on the other, and there may not be time for a quick run through the basement. A temporary crossover is often created by hanging drapes across the upstage part of the stage. A space is left between the drapes and the back wall, allowing actors and stagehands easy passage from one side to the other.

You may find a door on the back of the proscenium wall, down left or right, which leads to the *front-of-house* areas. This passage is often referred to as the "passage" or *pass door*.

An imaginary line that runs across the stage from one side to the other directly upstage of the proscenium opening is known as the *plaster line* and is used as a point

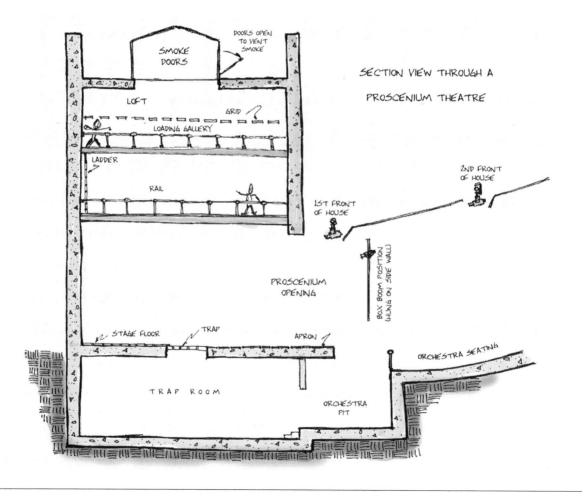

of reference for locating scenery on the stage. The center of the stage is marked by the *center line*. You might consider them to be the x and y axes of a graph, because they are used for measurements in the same way. The stage area downstage of the plaster line is referred to as the *apron*. The *main drape* is usually located just along the plaster line. Off the front edge of the stage, and sometimes partially underneath, is the *orchestra pit*. Most theatres have an entrance to the pit from underneath the stage, possibly from the trap or dressing rooms. In some theatres the pit can be lifted on hydraulic jacks to become part of the apron for a straight play when no orchestra is needed.

Seats on the lower level of the auditorium are known as *orchestra seats*, being near the orchestra pit. Sometimes the term *dress circle* is used as well. In many theatres additional seating is provided through the use of *balconies*. If there are multiple balconies, the lowest one may be called the *mezzanine,* and the very front of that the *loge* seats. Balconies are stacked up on top of a portion of the orchestra seats in order to reduce the average distance from any one seat to the front of the stage. Otherwise, the auditorium would be extremely deep and the very back seats would be an incredible distance from the stage. *Box seats* are on the side very near the stage, you might picture where Lincoln was sitting in Ford's theatre. The idea in years past was for those seats to be taken by very high profile viewers, so that the audience could see them at the same time as the show. Paradoxically, these were generally the worst seats in the house because of their bad sightlines. Nowadays they are the cheap seats.

LIGHTING AND SOUND

Many mid-century theatres have a room for lighting and sound in the rear of the auditorium called the booth. It is interesting to note that many of those sound booths are enclosed in glass to provide a sound barrier from the auditorium, which was an idea that pre-dated modern sound reinforcement methods. In modern times that just won't work. In one of those theatres the sound console is usually set up in an area cleared of seats in the rear of the auditorium. Some newer theatres have a permanent *house mix position*, which is by far the best option. Somewhere near that booth position may be a place to operate followspots.

Overhead lighting pipes located in the auditorium of a theatre are known as front-of-house or *FOH positions*. These positions may be laid out in many ways, depending mostly on how the theatre was constructed. FOH pipes may be concealed in soffits, rigged on trusses lowered by chain motors, or may simply be exposed pipes reachable only by a ladder. Front-of-house positions in a newer space are often numbered in relation to their proximity to the stage. The pipe that is closest to the stage is the first FOH. The next closest will be the second, and

so forth. In some theatres one or more of the FOH positions may be called a *beam position*.

Another popular place for lights in the house of a theatre is the *box boom position*. A boom is any vertical pipe used to hang lights. Box booms are located in the place where theatre box seats were traditionally placed, on the side of the auditorium and close to the front of the stage. This is an excellent lighting angle for cross lights across the front of the stage and is a favorite with lighting designers.

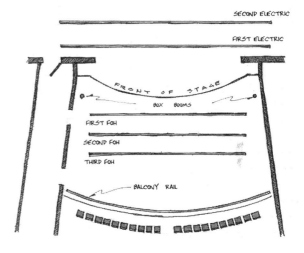

PLAN VIEW OF LIGHTING POSITIONS

There are as many different arrangements of FOH positions as there are theatres that house them. Touring companies that travel with a lighting package usually designate two front-of-house locations, box boom and *balcony rail*. Once in a particular theatre, the design is modified somewhat to accommodate the existing road house positions. Sometimes there is an actual balcony rail, which is a pipe that has been secured to the front edge of the first balcony and is found in virtually every Broadway theatre.

Pipes used to hang lights over the stage are called *electrics*. Electrics are also numbered from the front of the stage, and hence the numbers run backward from those used for the FOH positions. The first electric is the one most downstage, and the second is just upstage of that. You could also consider that all lighting positions are numbered with the plaster line as a beginning point, just like an x/y graph where the electrics are on the y axis.

Some theatres have permanent lighting electrics, which is to say that the same battens are always used for that purpose. Consequently these pipes have a permanently attached *plugging strip* running along the batten to provide power to the lighting instruments. They are generally found in theatres that have their own lighting equipment. Some houses that are strictly for rental purposes may not have any sort of lighting circuits, but

PLUGGING STRIP WITH PIGTAILS

THE NUMBERS REPRESENT BOTH CIRCUITS AND
DIMMERS IN A DIMMER PER CIRCUIT SYSTEM

rather depend upon the touring company to bring everything in themselves. Many Broadway theatres are of this type.

Other theatres may use a system of *drop boxes* that are moved from one batten to another in order to make any pipe available into an electric. Drop boxes consist of a large diameter multicable containing a number of conductors that feed a junction box with several connectors on it. Many lighting cables may be plugged into one box. Drop boxes are lowered from above and clamped to any batten being used as an electric. This second type of powering system is much more flexible than the dedicated electric type but also requires more effort to set up and use.

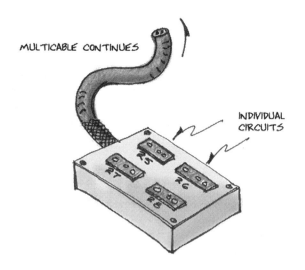

MULTICABLE CONTINUES

INDIVIDUAL CIRCUITS

Quite often you may find that the second or third lineset upstage of the plaster line is dedicated strictly for use as an electric even if movable drop boxes are used for all the other electrics. This position is the traditional location of the *first electric*, which is required for virtually

all lighting designs. Often this batten is rigged with some kind of *motorized winch* system. The first electric is always loaded down with fixtures, and they can be very heavy. A winch system helps avoid the necessity of loading and unloading what can become a large number of stage weights needed to counterbalance the heavy load. Electrics are typically the heaviest pipes in any show, and the first electric is often the weightiest of them all.

Tours of Broadway shows carry their own lighting packages of dimmers, cables, lights, and control equipment. Electrics are formed by running multicable from the lights, off whichever side of the electric the dimmers are located, and down to the floor. It is necessary to swag the cables offstage and out of the way of the fly system, actors, scenery, and other such stuff. That is done with a cable pick-up line, or *cable pick*. The line is tied to the cable with a clove hitch, and the bundle is raised into the air. Then the pick line is tied off at some convenient offstage spot. Some theatres have a specific area known as a jump that is used for this purpose, or pick lines can be hung from the pin rail, if the rail is an elevated one and on the proper side of the stage.

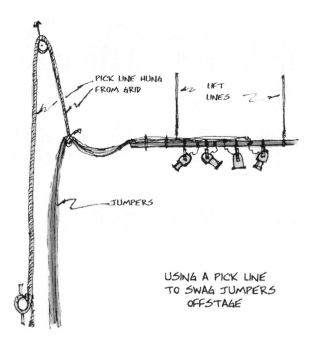

PICK LINE HUNG FROM GRID

LIFT LINES

JUMPERS

USING A PICK LINE TO SWAG JUMPERS OFFSTAGE

THE STAGE

Many theatres have holes in the stage floor equipped with removable covers. These passages are known as *traps*. Traps are useful for productions that require actors or props to disappear into the floor. If a theatre doesn't have a trapped floor, but you need the effect anyway, you can use temporary decking to raise the floor level of the setting in order to "invent" the required space. Many modern facilities are constructed with large basements under the stage. This area is also used as a dressing room, green room, and/or passageway to the orchestra pit. Broadway theatres have trap rooms, and they are often used to install *automation*, mechanical devices used to move scenery.

The major architectural element of any proscenium theatre is the *fly house*, or tower. Theatre buildings are quite often easy to spot on a college campus because the tower is a large, square, unattractive building with no windows. Older urban theatres were quite often built so that the fly house is off the street in the middle of the block, and were covered on at least one side by another structure. Many of the original Broadway theatres have an entrance on the street that leads backward to the theatre, which is actually at a 90 degree angle to the entrance, so they take up very little street frontage. They are not so easy to spot. Fire laws prevented architects from building offices over a theatre, but that has changed now.

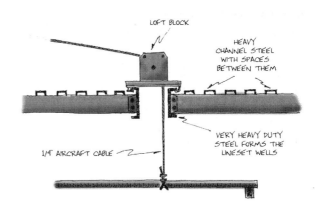

ARRANGEMENT OF STANDARD-STYLE RIGGING IN THE LOFT OF A PROSCENIUM THEATRE

THE FLY TOWER ON THIS NINETEENTH CENTURY THEATRE WAS EXPANDED UPWARD WITH A METAL-CLAD ADDITION

On the interior, a fly tower is a large open space, very tall, with a *loft* space above. The floor of the loft is a series of beams with spaces in between and is known as a *grid*. The loft space is used for rigging equipment. That equipment is covered in detail in the chapter on theatre rigging. In some theatres the rigging is *under-hung* from beams in the ceiling in order to save on cost, but this can lead to some serious problems in reaching the equipment when servicing is required.

Ideally, a fly house should be tall enough so that scenery can fly up entirely out of site. Newer theatres tend to be taller, but sometimes multiple-use facilities in schools may not have an actual tower and rigging system, but rather curtains fastened to the ceiling of the stage. It isn't possible to fly scenery up out of sight in that type of venue, but they do at least allow curtains to be hung.

 GREEN IDEAS TIP BOX

The loft of a proscenium house is just one of many areas in a theatre that need some type of work lights, so that stagehands can do their work safely. Unfortunately, the grid is also just the sort of place where one finds that the work lights are burned out *after* climbing all the way up there. Also, it is the type of place where workers often forget to turn off the lights when they are finished. (Which may be the reason they so often seem to have burned out . . .) Try using compact fluorescent or CFL bulbs in spaces like that. The bulbs use a lot less electricity, and last several times longer than conventional bulbs. But be sure to dispose of them properly, the fluorescent powder coating the inside of the glass tube is very unhealthy.

Very stringent *fire code* restrictions are placed on theatres because of the large crowds involved, and also due to the many catastrophic accidents which occurred in the days before electric lighting came into vogue. The use of open flame candles, and later gaslights, spawned some spectacular and deadly fires. Electric lights are no guarantee against disaster, and theatres today are required to have fire prevention, detection, and extinguishing devices. Code requirements vary from city to city and state to state, but theatres are generally required to be equipped with smoke detectors, heat detectors, automatic alarms, sprinkler systems, and emergency lighting systems. Local *fire marshals* are the sole arbiters of how to interpret the fire code for any particular theatre. Many municipalities require that scenery be *flame-proofed* and prohibit the use of open flames onstage. Large cloth draperies and wooden scenery can provide ample fuel for voracious fires.

On a Wednesday afternoon, December 30, 1903 the Iroquois theatre in Chicago was showing a matinee of the play *Mr. Bluebeard* when a fire broke out, possibly caused by a calcium spotlight igniting a muslin drop. Stagehands immediately attempted to put the small fire out with their hands, but it grew too fast for them and was soon out of control. Other stagehands attempted to lower the asbestos fire curtain, but it became fouled, possibly from a strong draft from outside or perhaps on a border light framing the proscenium opening. Hundreds died in the auditorium because the exits were inadequate, and a loss of power turned off all the newly installed incandescent lights. Had the painted drop been flame-proofed, the entire tragedy might have been avoided.

The term "flame-proofing" has a specific meaning. Technically, the definition is that the treated material will not support flames, but will merely smolder and go out if ignited. Often the test is performed by holding a match against the material until it burns itself out. Sometimes a lighter is used for one minute instead. "Fireproof" is a misleading term as it indicates an inability to burn at all, and virtually anything will oxidize if heated to a high enough temperature. Flame-proofing is intended to prevent a large, self-sustaining blaze from becoming established. Once that has happened, only a well-trained fire company will be able to extinguish the flames.

Many theatres have a *sprinkler system*, which sprays water outward over a specific area, much like a lawn sprinkler does. Never do anything to block the spray heads, because they won't work properly if you do.

The sprinkler system supply pipes often run on or around the rigging grid, and you should be especially careful not to disturb them when working in that area. Never tie off a rope to a sprinkler pipe, it isn't meant to hold any weight, and you may well break it as a result. A huge amount of nasty water will spray out if you do.

Most people who die in fires are not necessarily burned, but rather succumb to *smoke inhalation*. This is especially true when modern petrochemical materials such as those used for carpeting and seat padding are considered. For that reason, theatres are generally required to have equipment designed specifically to remove smoke from the building and to separate the audience from any smoke and/or fire which may emanate from the stage. The most easily visible of these is the *fire curtain*.

Fire curtains are traditionally made of *asbestos*, a fibrous mineral that can be stranded and woven into a fabric. Being a mineral (or rock), it is highly resistant to fire. However, virtually everyone is aware by this time that asbestos can be a very dangerous substance, especially when it becomes frayed and gets into the air. Even so, it is still in use in many theatres because it does such a great job of preventing fires from spreading. Sealers are applied to lessen the possibility that flaking of the material into the air will occur. Curtains of this type should be used with care and be left alone as much as possible. There are some substitute materials for fire curtains, but they are not permitted in all jurisdictions. One of them is a very large steel door that slides down into place when a fire is detected. Other theatres are equipped with a deluge system that dumps an incredible amount of water, which forms a sheet across the proscenium opening. (Just imagine that going off by accident!) Whatever method is used, the purpose of the system is to seal off the auditorium from the stage house.

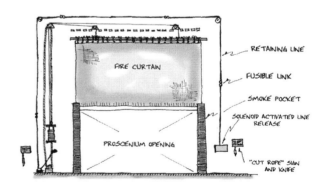

WHEN THE HEAT FROM A FIRE TRIPS THE CONTROL MECHANISM, A FIRE SUPPRESSION SPRINKLER SPRAYS WATER IN ALL DIRECTIONS

FIRE CURTAIN

PROSCENIUM OPENING

RETAINING LINE

FUSIBLE LINK

SMOKE POCKET

SOLENOID ACTIVATED LINE RELEASE

"CUT ROPE" SIGN AND KNIFE

Fire curtains are hung directly upstage of the proscenium wall and are rigged to fall automatically in case of an emergency. There are a variety of ways to rig an asbestos fire curtain, but the most popular uses a self-governing counterweight system. Ropes and pulleys connect the curtain to a balancing counterweight that weighs slightly less than the curtain itself. When a restraining line is released, the fire curtain will drop into place by virtue of its own weight. That also works for the steel door types. The curtain can be released in one of several ways, all of which depend on the use of a lightweight rope that is stretched from one side of the proscenium opening to the other. This line restrains the fire curtain from falling. When slack appears in the line, a special knot tied to the counterweight operating line releases the weight, and the curtain falls.

SASH CORD

TWO "LINKS" SOLDERED TOGETHER

FUSIBLE LINKS ARE CONSTRUCTED SO THAT THE TWO HALVES WILL PULL APART IN THE HEAT OF A FIRE

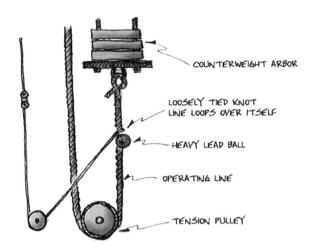

COUNTERWEIGHT ARBOR

LOOSELY TIED KNOT LINE LOOPS OVER ITSELF

HEAVY LEAD BALL

OPERATING LINE

TENSION PULLEY

THIS TYPE OF MECHANISM IS OFTEN USED TO RIG A FIRE CURTAIN FOR QUICK RELEASE

There are several ways of severing the line. Many theatres have a knife fastened to the back of the proscenium. (An oft-sighted article: "In case of fire, cut rope.") This seems like the method *least* likely to work, because the knives are rarely sharp enough to cut through the line with enough speed to match the urgency of the situation.

Another method of releasing the line is through the use of *fusible links*. These links are two small pieces of metal (originally chain links) that have been soldered

together with a material that will melt at a temperature of 160 degrees. The high temperature of a fire will soon cause the solder to melt, the links to pull apart, the line to sever, and the fire curtain to drop. Fusible links are very frequently used in industrial buildings where roll-up fire doors must lower automatically in a fire.

A final method of operating the fire curtain is through the use of electronic fire detection devices such as heat detectors, smoke detectors, and sprinkler water pressure detectors. These electronic devices can be used to trigger a solenoid hook that releases the line. Some combination of these various methods is almost certain to bring the curtain in as planned, but if all other methods fail, a good hard yank on the restraining line will break apart one of the fusible links and release the system. Bear that fragility in mind when you are working around them and *not* trying to trip the curtain. Fire curtains are sealed at the edges by heavy steel flanges that wrap around the curtain and help to prevent smoke from entering the auditorium. These flanges are called *smoke pockets*.

KNIFE

IN CASE OF FIRE CUT ROPE

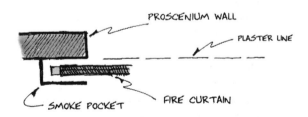

PROSCENIUM WALL

PLASTER LINE

SMOKE POCKET

FIRE CURTAIN

PLAN VIEW OF CURTAIN AND SMOKE POCKET

It is important to keep the fire curtain and all other safety equipment in good working order. Any problems should be taken care of as soon as they arise. If you have tied off the fire curtain counterweights to circumvent a problem with the system, the curtain will not work in the event of an emergency.

A fire curtain does a great job of protecting the audience from fire and smoke, but will also seal everyone on the stage in a smoke filled box. To avoid this, exhaust fans are located on the roof of the fly tower to draw smoke from a fire upward. In older buildings, *smoke doors* are used in place of the fans. Smoke doors are a passive system based on the same principle as a chimney. A shed type structure entirely surrounded by doors is constructed on the roof. The doors are hinged at the bottom so that they will open down and out by force of gravity alone. The same type of fusible links that are used to rig a fire curtain hold them in place. In the heat of a fire, the links melt, fall apart, and release the doors, which then flop open on their own.

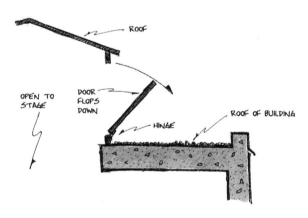

SMOKE DOOR OPERATION

Most fire marshals will agree that the best thing for you to do in a serious fire is to get yourself and others out of the theatre as quickly as possible.

 GREEN IDEAS TIP BOX

Safety is important in a theatre, which can be a dangerous place to work what with all the stuff hanging overhead, and the vast number of electrical devices, but also because of more subtle things like falling into an orchestra pit. Falling into the pit is more likely to happen than you would think, and is especially likely if you consider the danger of walking into a dark theatre space where it is very difficult to tell where the apron ends and the pit begins. For this reason, most theatres like to leave a light on at all times, even when the space is not in use. Theatre work lights are often very high wattage bulbs because of the size of the space they must light and the same switch often turns on several of them. High wattage bulbs consume a lot of electricity. Consider instead using a theatre *ghost light* to illuminate the front of the stage when the theatre is not in use. A ghost light is a single bulb (compact fluorescent or LED if you like) on a rolling stand that can be moved down to the apron of the stage and plugged in to illuminate the front of it. When someone enters the space in the dark, the ghost light will help them to see the line between stage and pit. Ghost lights are a theatre tradition, and are said to keep the ghosts away when the theatre is dark.

TERMS USED IN THIS CHAPTER

apron	fire marshal	orchestra pit
asbestos	first electric	orchestra seats
automation	flame-proofed	pass door
balcony	fly house	plan view
balcony rail lighting position	front-of-house or FOH lighting	plaster line
beam lighting position	position	plugging strip
box boom position	fusible link	rail
box seats	ghost light	smoke doors
cable pick	grid	smoke inhalation
center line	house mix position	smoke pocket
crossover	loading door	sprinkler system
dress circle	loft	trap
drop box	loge seats	under hung rigging
electric lighting position	main drape	wing
fire code	mezzanine	
fire curtain	motorized winch	

CHAPTER 5

CURTAINS AND BACKDROPS

EVERY STAGE CARPENTER should have a good working knowledge of stage draperies. Curtains are used for just about any show that you can think of, because without them the audience would see all of the magic happening backstage. The term *soft goods* is often used to indicate scenery made from fabric, as opposed to wood or steel. Different types of curtains are intended for use in specific situations. This chapter is a discussion of those different types, as well as construction methods, and the working practices used to hang stage curtains and other fabric scenery. The terms *curtains* and *drapes* are used interchangeably.

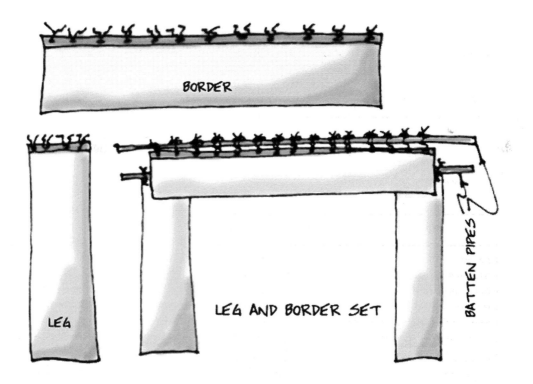

DRAPES AND DROPS

Drapes and *drops* are different things. Drapes are usually made from an opulent fabric like *velour*. They tend to have a generic quality and can be used in many different ways, whereas drops are painted or printed backgrounds designed for a specific purpose. Drops are usually rendered on scenic *muslin* and are essentially large paintings. They are flat with no folds or pleats. Most of the time we think of drops as covering the entire stage picture as a background.

THIS AREA IS OPEN

NOTICE HOW THE CONTOUR IS DESIGNED
SO THAT THE FREE ENDS WILL STILL HANG STRAIGHT

— PAJAMA GAME CUT DROP —

CUT DROP WITH A BACKING DROP BEHIND IT

THE FOLIAGE DROP FORMS A FRAME FOR THE ONE
THAT HANGS BEHIND IT

But they can also have an edge that has been trimmed to some interesting profile as in a cut drop that forms a portal, or opening to the upstage. They may have some other unusual shape, and/or have textural materials stuck to them. But they are always painted representations of something. You can find a lot more information about painting drops in the book *Scenic Art for the Theatre*, by Susan Crabtree.

Drapes, on the other hand, are generally unpainted and are most often used as masking. Drapes are often constructed of a heavier fabric that has a thick sound and light absorbing pile. *Duvetyn* is a less expensive substitute. Duvetyn has a nappy, textural surface but no actual pile. The nappy surface helps to trap light, making the drapes non-reflective and less obtrusive. Black is the most popular color for all stage drapes, because that color absorbs the most light. Drapes that belong to a certain theatre are sometimes called the house *rags*.

MASKING

Masking is a term used to identify curtains that block the audience view of the backstage area. Curtains that mask the overhead space of a stage are called *borders*. Borders are really wide but not very tall. Ideally, they should be the same width as the battens that they are hung on, so that they run all the way from one side of the stage to the other. *Legs* mask the offstage space or wings. Legs are tall, but usually not very wide. They should be at least

several feet taller than the proscenium opening, but not so tall that the bottoms do not clear sightlines when they are flown all the way out. In a theatre with a very short fly tower, that may not be possible.

A standard method exists for using legs and borders to mask the stage. It is customary to hang one border in front of a set of two legs in order to create a frame for the stage picture. These *leg and border sets* are used from downstage to upstage in repetition. The legs should be wide enough left/right stage and close enough together up/down stage so that the audience cannot see around them into the wings. Sometimes that's not possible if there is very little offstage space, and/or if the auditorium is especially wide. Leg and border sets create the *sightlines* for the stage, defining where the audience can and cannot see. It is important for borders to be on separate linesets from the legs so that they are independently adjustable. Be sure to hang the border downstage of the two legs so that it will cover the leg pipe.

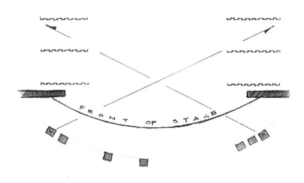

SIGHTLINES

The spaces between the border and leg sets are often referred to as *in one*, *in two*, *in three*, etc. This terminology refers to the spaces in-between the legs and is often used to indicate the place where an actor or a piece of scenery should enter. Example: "Enter through the stage left in one with the chair and place it on the red spike marks downstage." Leg and border sets are a direct descendent of the wing and drop scenery used in early proscenium theatres. Setting up the stage that way was so efficient that it remains in use to this very day.

A *blackout* is a piece of masking with a very specific use. It is a large black drape that covers the entire width of the stage, about halfway back. This curtain can be flown in to cover stagehands who are shifting scenery upstage while actors are playing a scene downstage. It is most often constructed as two solid panels that are hung side by side on the batten, or perhaps hung on a traveler track instead. In that case the travelling curtains automatically form a pair of legs when they are open, saving the space of one batten. A blackout can also be put

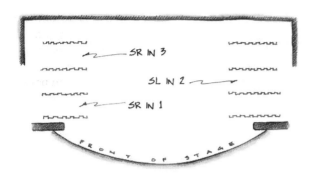

THE "IN BETWEENS"

together from multiple sets of legs hung on one batten to create a similar effect, but from smaller curtains. Be sure to overlap the edges by at least a foot (also equal to one tie) to prevent a split from showing.

SPECIALTY CURTAINS

Some theatres are equipped with a batten that curves around the entire stage area rather than merely from side to side. This type of batten is known as a *cyclorama* or *cyc* pipe. The two arms of the cyc run up/down stage at the offstage ends of a regular pipe. If the cyc is meant to be lighted in order to create a sky effect (which it usually is), it is known as a sky cyc.

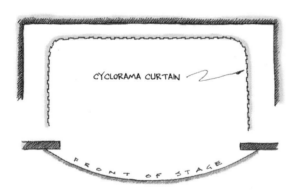

AN OLD-STYLE CYCLORAMA

As you could well imagine, it is almost impossible to arrange for entrances and exits if the sides of the stage have been closed off by using a wrap-around cyc. To avoid that problem, a sky cyc can also be used on an ordinary straight batten. It is still called a cyc even though it only goes from side to side. This latter method is so prevalent that most stage workers will assume this is what you mean when a cyc is mentioned. The wrap around type of cyc is much more popular in a television studio where

different colors of fabric are used for special effects. This difference in terminology can be confusing to a person who has crossed over from TV to stage or vice versa.

Scrim is the most popular of a variety of net-type fabrics that are used in the theatre. Years ago it was called sharkstooth scrim because of its open weave structure made up of tiny triangular shapes, but it seems like most scrims these days have a rectangular weave instead. Scrims are used in a variety of ways. They can be painted in much the same manner as muslin, or can be used as a toner for cycs or other drops. Sometimes scrim may be used as a low-tech (but quite effective) method of materializing a person or object, such as the ghost of Hamlet's father.

Scrims have a common operating principle however they are used. Variations in light intensity are used to create variations in the opacity of the scrim fabric. An analogy can be found in observing the way window

SEE-THROUGH QUALITIES OF A SCRIM

A SCRIM LOOKS SOLID WHEN LIT FROM THE FRONT. BUT WHEN A PERSON BEHIND IS LIT, YOU CAN SEE RIGHT THROUGH IT. THIS PARTICULAR SCRIM STILL HAS QUITE A BIT OF LIGHT HITTING THE FRONT TO MAKE IT SHOW. IF YOU TOOK AWAY ALL OF THE FRONT LIGHT IT WOULD BE ALMOST INVISIBLE.

screens reflect light. You may have noticed that a window screen restricts your ability to see into a house from the outside when there is bright sunshine lighting it, yet at night when the only light source is inside the room, a person outside can quite easily see through the screen to the room. When light strikes the surface of the screen, the screen itself reflects this light and appears as a solid object. At night when no light reflects off the screen it tends to disappear, and anything that is lit inside the house becomes visible. Theatrical scrim curtains work in exactly the same manner.

This principle is put to good use in a process known as a *bleed-through*. A bleed-through is used to change from one scene to another by means of a lighting effect. A painted backdrop scrim is lit from the front so that the painting on it is visible, as well as the actors who are standing in front of it. The bleed-through effect is created by fading light down on the front of the scrim while simultaneously fading light up on the scene behind it. One picture fades out as the other fades in, much the same way that movie editing cross-fades from one scene to another. As the lighting change is completed, the scrim is flown out for an unobscured view. The dreamy quality of bleeding from one scene to another is quite stunning. The recent production of *Trip to Bountiful* on Broadway used this effect at the top of the show, and never failed to get a murmur of appreciation from the audience.

Black scrims are often used in front of a sky cyc to create darker, more vivid colors. As an added bonus, the scrim leaves a black background when the cyc lights fade all the way down. This is much like a bleed-through in reverse. More information about scrims and other theatrical fabrics can be found in the chapter on shop supplies.

Grand drape or *main* refers to a curtain hung in front of the stage to separate it from the auditorium. It is often a decorative, very plush curtain, since it may be all the audience has to look at while waiting for the show to begin. A matching decorative *valance* is often used to finish off the top of the main rag, as it is known in stagehand slang. Grand drapes are almost always sewn with a large amount of *fullness* to give them a more opulent appearance. Fullness is the technique of gathering the fabric at the top to form folds or pleats in the curtain. The greater the amount of pleating, the richer and heavier the curtain appears to be. The amount of fullness is usually given as a percentage. As an example, 100% fullness requires a velour panel 80 feet wide to produce a drape 40 feet wide. After a backing is added, the curtain will be quite heavy. Regular legs and borders don't usually have fullness, because the folds catch sidelight in an unattractive way.

On occasion, scenic designers opt to paint a special drop that is used in place of a front curtain. It is almost always related stylistically to the design of the production, and may indeed include a logo or the name of the play

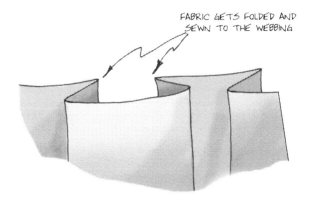

HOW PLEATS ARE MADE IN A CURTAIN

IF THE EDGES OF THE FOLDS MEET EACH OTHER THE AMOUNT OF FULLNESS WILL BE 100%

FABRIC GETS FOLDED AND SEWN TO THE WEBBING

PROSCENIUM PORTAL AND SHOW CURTAIN

A PORTAL TELLS THE AUDIENCE SOMETHING ABOUT THE SHOW AND PROVIDES A FRAME FOR IT. THIS ONE REPRESENTS A HELLMOUTH. A "SHOW CURTAIN" IS ACTUALLY A PAINTED DROP RATHER THAN A CURTAIN. THE DROP IS BEHIND THE PORTAL AND FLIES OUT TO REVEAL THE STAGE.

being presented. This practice is often used for musicals. A drop of this sort is generally referred to as a *show drop*.

A grand drape may be rigged to operate with a *traveler* when there is no room for it to fly in and out. Travelers open a curtain sideways across the stage on a track, usually parting in the center. This is a good way to overcome a lack of overhead space, when the stage house isn't tall enough to fly curtains all the way out.

Small auditoriums and some older movie palaces may be rigged with one of several other types of systems that require only limited overhead space. One of those is the *Austrian* curtain. This type of drape has a series of small nylon lift lines evenly spaced across the back of the curtain. Each lift line feeds through a number of small rings that are sewn to the back of the Austrian. As the lift lines are pulled upward, the drape gathers itself up from the bottom creating small swags as it rises. An Austrian curtain is sewn with many small horizontal pleats to enhance the effect. The fabric is usually some sort of thin satin material, because that fabric bunches up better. This curtain is popular with older movie theatres from the mid-twentieth century, but is the sort of thing you

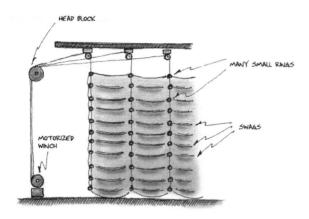

AUSTRIAN CURTAIN

can still see at Radio City Music Hall where spectacle is king.

Another method of dealing with a low overhead is to use an *oleo* curtain, which was quite popular in the days of vaudeville. An oleo is actually a painted drop like a show curtain. A large round tube is attached to the bottom. Ropes at either side of the tube are used to pull it up and roll it at the same time.

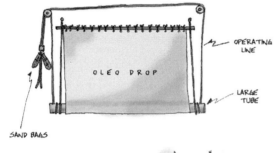

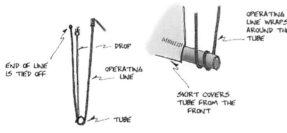

The drop rolls up on the tube as it rotates. A full stage oleo requires a very large diameter bottom tube for two reasons. First, because of the distance the tube must span without sagging, and also because the large diameter of the tube makes it possible for the drop to roll easily even if it is relatively stiff from being repainted several times. A large oleo is difficult and expensive to construct, although this type of curtain may easily be shop built in smaller versions and put to good use for window treatments and other smaller openings. Sabbatini, the designer from the Renaissance period, included drawings for an oleo drop in his book.

RIGGING TRAVELER TRACKS

A traveler track is the most popular type of low overhead curtain-moving device. Stage travelers are similar to ones that you might see in a house, but they are much larger and able to hold more weight. A *traveler track* consists of a metal *channel* and the rollers that fit into it. The curtain is tied to chains that extend downward from the rollers. A pull rope is used to drag the rollers, and thus the curtain, from side to side. Travelers can be rigged to part in the middle, or to extend all the way from one side of the stage to the other. There are several different brands of traveler track made by different companies, and the parts from one won't necessarily work with parts from another. You can also buy tracks that don't have pull ropes, in which case actors move the curtain themselves.

Rigging a traveler is one of those jobs that looks to be very complicated because travelers have a large number of moving parts, but in reality the process is fairly straightforward and quite logical once you get the hang of it. The shape of the metal channel is such that the rollers or *carriers* fit into grooves in the bottom that act as guides, allowing the wheels to roll freely back and forth. Carriers "carry" the weight of the curtain. Each carrier has a rounded opening just below the wheels for the operating line to fit through. Below this opening is a chain used to attach the curtain to the carrier.

The traveler channel is hung on a batten using a series of *hanging clamps*. They come in two parts and bolt together around the outside of the channel, and then chain is used to secure the entire rig to a batten. Chain is used because altering the links of the chain is an excellent way of adjusting the trim so that the traveler can be made level to the stage floor, even if the batten is not.

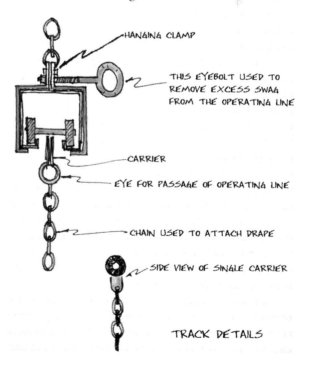

TRACK DETAILS

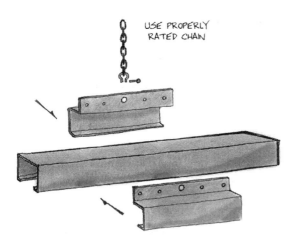

USE PROPERLY
RATED CHAIN

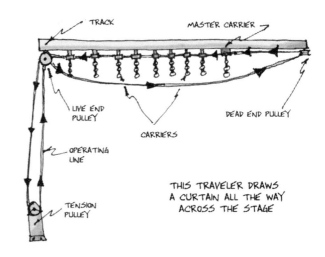

TRACK   MASTER CARRIER

LIVE END
PULLEY

DEAD END PULLEY

CARRIERS

OPERATING
LINE

TENSION
PULLEY

THIS TRAVELER DRAWS
A CURTAIN ALL THE WAY
ACROSS THE STAGE

THE HANGING CLAMP FITS AROUND
THE OUTSIDE OF THE TRACK
SO THE BOTTOM CHANNEL STAYS OPEN

The hanging clamps come in two pieces so that they can be bolted-on around the sides only. It is very important not to obstruct the bottom of the traveler track, because that would prevent the carriers from rolling back and forth.

A curtain that moves all to one side of the stage rather than splitting in the middle just needs one long track on the batten.

Many times a main drape is hung on a batten that can fly in and out, but is also on a traveler track so that it can work either way. You would probably have very little need to move that track, but it might be necessary to install a new operating line rope from time to time. The traveler tracks used for a blackout are much more likely to be moved from one pipe to another for different productions. It is helpful to know how the track is rigged in case you must repair or move one.

The onstage leading edge of the curtain is attached to a *master carrier* that has four wheels rather than two and is substantially larger than the single carrier. The master carrier has a clamp on the side so that the operating line can be securely connected to it. When the operating line moves the master carrier, it pulls everything else along with it. The illustration shows how to rig the line to make the curtain travel *all the way across the stage* from one side to another.

Clamp the operating line to the side of the master carrier, and pass it through the center of each of the single carriers. There should be as many single carriers as there are grommets on the drape, except for the first and last ones. The first grommet on the drop is attached to the master carrier. The last grommet gets fastened to the offstage end of the channel so that end of the curtain stays in place. The *end stop* is used to keep the carriers from running off the end of the track, and it is a handy place to secure the offstage edge of the curtain.

The *live end pulley* has two sheaves on it, one to change the direction of the rope when it goes down to the floor, and another to do the same when it passes back up to the track.

The operating line connects with a *tension pulley* when it gets to the stage floor. As the name implies, this pulley helps to keep the line taut and prevents it from becoming twisted and tangled. If the traveler track stays in one position, it may be possible to permanently attach the tension pulley to the deck. If it is occasionally necessary to fly the traveler out, then it is best to use a temporary method of securing the pulley, and several different types are produced by different manufacturers. A commonly used *shop-built* method is to secure the pulley to a small section of plywood that can be weighted with counterweights when the traveler is in its down position.

When the operating line passes back over the second sheave in the live end pulley, it shoots straight down to the *dead end pulley* at the opposite end of the track not touching any of the carriers. Here the line reverses direction back to the master carrier where it is held fast by the clamp. If the track is very wide, it may be necessary

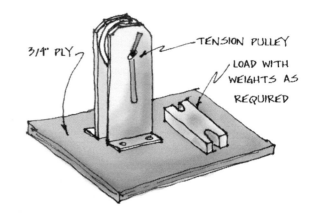

3/4" PLY

TENSION PULLEY

LOAD WITH
WEIGHTS AS
REQUIRED

SHOP-BUILT TENSION PULLEY BASE

to provide some support to the operating line as it crosses the stage from the live end pulley to the dead end pulley. Unless the line is exceptionally taut, it will tend to sag in the middle and may become visible to the audience. An *eyebolt* attached to the side of one of the hanging clamps can be used to avoid that.

A traveler that parts in the center is rigged a bit differently, but the basic concept remains the same. The fabric curtain must be in two sections in order to split. Hang the track in two sections connected by a *lap splice* so that they overlap one another by a foot or more. The two halves of the traveler operate exactly the same way as the side-to-side type, but one half is the slave of the other.

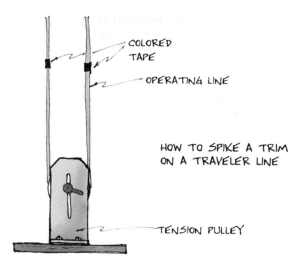

HOW TO SPIKE A TRIM
ON A TRAVELER LINE

COLORED TAPE
OPERATING LINE
TENSION PULLEY

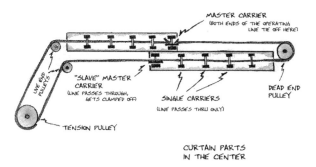

CURTAIN PARTS
IN THE CENTER

MASTER CARRIER
(BOTH ENDS OF THE OPERATING LINE TIE OFF HERE)

"SLAVE" MASTER CARRIER
(LINE PASSES THROUGH, GETS CLAMPED OFF)

LINE END PULLEYS

DEAD END PULLEY

SINGLE CARRIERS
(LINE PASSES THRU ONLY)

TENSION PULLEY

Attach the operating line to the master carrier on the tension pulley side of the stage. Feed it through the single carriers, and then pass it through one sheave of the live end pulley. The line should go down to the floor, through the tension pulley and then back up through the live end pulley. So far this process is exactly the same as before, but now the method differs. The line passes through the clamp on the second master carrier, the one in the channel of the track which services the opposite side of the stage. The line passes through the clamp and continues without being cut, which is the secret to making this rig work.

To operate properly, the placement of the "slave" carrier must be calibrated with its master. While the slave carrier is still loose, arrange both halves of the curtain so they are in their normal closed position and all of the slack is out of the operating line. Then tighten the clamp to secure it in place. The two master carriers now move symmetrically, but opposite of one another.

Sometimes cueing requires that a traveler open partially rather than all the way. For that you need trim marks on the operating line. Open the traveler the desired amount and use tape to mark both sides of the rope with *spike marks* that are right together at a comfortable height for the operator to see. The exact distance from the floor doesn't affect how the spike marks work. When the stagehand opens the traveler she should stop pulling on the rope when the two spike marks line up with one another. Use different colors of tape to spike multiple positions.

Sightlines can be improved by hanging *tab curtains* on the sides of the stage so that the audience cannot see into the wings. This is especially common in theatres where the seating is very wide and that width creates problematic sightlines. The name tab is used for several different types of curtains, but in this case it refers to a short traveler that runs up and down stage between two leg and border sets. Tabs are most commonly used across the in one position, because that's where sightlines are usually at their worst.

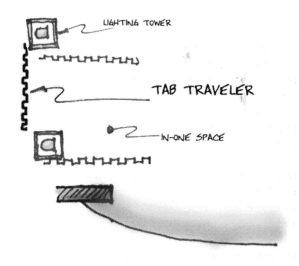

LIGHTING TOWER

TAB TRAVELER

IN-ONE SPACE

Hang the track at a slight angle and gravity will close it for you automatically. The track itself need be no more than 6 to 8 feet long, because the distance between the first set of legs and the second is only about that far. The track should hang at about a five-degree angle, but that is somewhat dependent on the type of curtain, its height and weight, how well the carriers roll, etc., and some experimentation will be required. You will most likely have to dead hang the track from the grid or some other structure, because it runs up- and downstage rather than across the stage like a regular batten.

Touring shows often use towers for side lighting because the lights can travel inside the truss, and also because towers keep the lights from being hit and being de-focused during the show. Towers are an excellent place to hang the side tabs, especially if the tabs are considered when the placement of the towers is planned. Tie pulleys to the tower tops before they are raised to make it easy to hoist the track into position with ropes. Pulleys also make it easy to adjust the trim of the track's angle to give the proper amount of closing force.

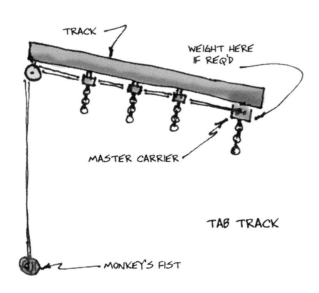

Pulling on the rope causes the tab to open, and gravity closes it for you when the rope is released. If the curtain does not close well, try a slightly greater angle to the traveler track. That will cause the curtain to hang somewhat askew, but considering its position and use, that shouldn't matter. If the curtain is very light, fasten a small weight of some sort to the top of the curtain where it attaches to the master carrier. The added mass should help the rig to overcome the friction of the carrier wheels inside the traveler track.

HANGING THE GOODS

Drops and drapes are often called "goods" by stagehands. They have jute or nylon webbing at the top to reinforce them, and brass grommets placed 12″ apart. Tie line or cloth tape ties go through the grommets and are used to tie the fabric onto a batten. You should secure the goods to the pipe using bow knots (like your shoe) so that they are easy to remove. You can tell which lineset the curtains should be on by looking at the plan view or hanging schedule. If you are hanging legs, the designer's ground plan should show the distance of the onstage side of the legs from the *centerline* of the stage. You will probably need to measure the distance with a scale rule. In most theatres the center of the battens is marked with tape or

paint. Measure along the batten from the center to the appropriate point and mark the pipe with chalk. Always measure distances from the center of the batten, never from the end. Plans are notoriously inaccurate about the length of battens. If you are moving from theatre to theatre, there is no way to draw a plan that is accurate for all of them, but the center of the stage is always an easily defined starting point. The intersection of the centerline and the *plaster line* is often considered to be something like the origin of a graph when it comes to laying out points on the stage.

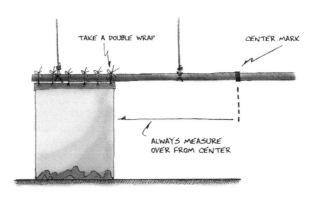

Tie the onstage edge of the leg beginning at the point you measured, and then work your way toward the offstage end of the pipe. It is helpful to begin the first tie with a double wrap around the pipe and then a regular bow knot so that the tie line is choked onto the pipe. This keeps the onstage edge from creeping offstage along the batten as you stretch the goods out tight. Only double the first tie, not all of them. An extra wrap on all of them won't help anything and will be problematic at the load out. Frequently legs are too wide for the length of the pipe and must be tied back by folding to the rear and continuing to tie. Most legs are sewn flat, with no fullness. Folding them back is a better choice than bunching up the fabric at the end of the pipe because it keeps everything flat.

Most drops are hung with the center of the drop aligned with the center of the batten pipe, so there is no need to measure anything. The drop should have a center line marked on the webbing and/or have a different colored tie that marks the center.

When a folded drop comes out of a hamper and is laid out on the stage, it may not be obvious which way to turn it before unfolding. Quite often there is a lot of confusion with ten stagehands arguing about which way the thing should go, but I have found that this strategy always works: Lay it out on the floor with the webbing facing up, and pointing upstage. The goods will always be in the proper position to face toward the audience. If it has been properly folded, you can tie the drop to the pipe without needing to unfold it all the way. That will happen as it flies out.

Begin at the center tie on the center of the pipe. If the drop is heavy, it is often best to skip along and tie every fifth or sixth tie, stretching the goods each time. Then come back and fill in the open spots. This technique prevents having to pick up the full weight of the drop with every tie. If a group is working together be sure to reach over the pipe each time or your arm will be in the way of the others. It is important to stretch the drop as you tie it on the batten to remove the wrinkles.

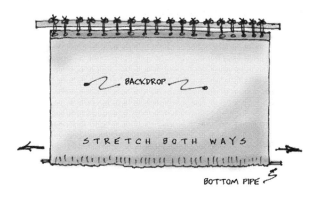

REMOVING WRINKLES WITH A
BOTTOM PIPE

Curtains with fullness often have a chain sewn into the hem, which adds a bit of weight to the bottom and encourages the goods to hang straight. A *bottom pipe* works well on any drop or curtain that is sewn flat instead. The weight of the pipe does a great job of straightening out any horizontal wrinkles. Drops or masking curtains must be sewn with a *pipe pocket* along the bottom for the pipe to run through. The pipe itself is usually ⅜″ black steel water pipe, cut into ~10′ lengths that are connected together with threaded couplings.

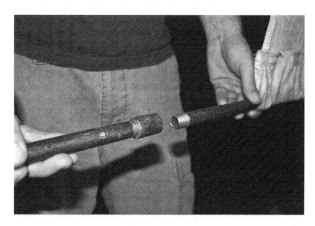

⅜″ BLACK STEEL BOTTOM PIPE

ALTHOUGH IT COMES FROM THE FACTORY IN 21′ PIECES, MOST PEOPLE CUT THOSE IN HALF TO MAKE THEM EASIER TO WORK WITH BACKSTAGE. IF YOU THREAD THE ENDS, YOU CAN USE A COUPLING TO JOIN THE PIECES BACK TOGETHER.

Bottom pipe should be installed after the drop has been flown out, with the pipe pocket about waist high off the floor. The reason for short sections (the pipe is originally made in 21 foot lengths) is because wing space is often at a premium and longer ones might not fit. One stagehand holds the pocket open while two others slide in a length of pipe and attach a second section to the first. Repeat until the pocket is full, but don't leave too much bare pipe sticking out the end as a hazard. It is often helpful for one or more stagehands to hold up the weight of the pipe as it works its way through the pocket and across the stage. Sometimes lightly bouncing the pipe will help it pass. Special care should be taken when the pocket is old and torn, which unfortunately is a common occurrence. When the pipe is in place, the bottom of the drop can be stretched by gently but firmly pulling on the extreme sides to remove the wrinkles. That is known as "stretching the goods."

Accomodating Drops that Are too Large for the Theatre

Rental drops are often painted with the largest possible theatre in mind. If you are touring, or if you have occasion to rent painted backdrops, you may well have a problem fitting them into a theatre that is too small. If the drop is too wide you can fold it back on the batten like the legs in an earlier part of this chapter, an easy fix. For a scrim, tie the ends back and forth several times offstage instead, or the difference in opacity will show.

If a drop is too tall you won't be able to fly it out far enough to clear the sightlines and things are a bit trickier. There are two possible solutions: tripping the bottom or rolling the top. *Tripping* involves using a second batten to fly out the bottom of the drop. On rare occasions a drop will be sewn with a special pipe pocket halfway down that is intended from the get-go to be used for tripping. This is done when the design of the show calls for a drop that is extraordinarily tall and unlikely to fit anywhere. More commonly, a second method is employed when it suddenly becomes apparent that the drop "just won't fit."

Use a batten directly upstage of the drop to pick up the bottom pipe of the too-tall drop. The easiest way to attach the second batten is to connect a number of small lines that run from that batten pipe to the bottom pipe of the drop. You need these *tail-down* lines to connect things because the tripping batten cannot fly in all the way to the deck to meet the bottom pipe when it's on the floor. Something must bridge the gap. A variety of different small line types are workable, but make sure that whatever you use will indeed bear the weight of the drop and bottom pipe safely. Use a number of lines, one every 8 feet or so, and not just one on either end, which would

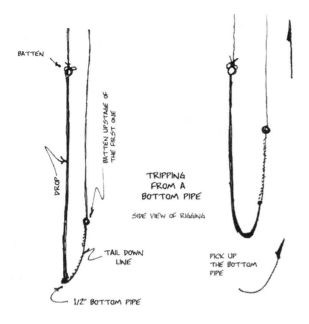

BATTEN

DROP

BATTEN UPSTAGE OF THE FIRST ONE

TRIPPING
FROM A
BOTTOM PIPE

SIDE VIEW OF RIGGING

TAIL DOWN
LINE

1/2" BOTTOM PIPE

PICK UP
THE BOTTOM
PIPE

The tripping method works by flying out the tripping pipe at the same time the original one does. That will pick up the bottom and make the out trim height of the bottom almost twice as high as it was when you began. Obviously the two flymen must work well together in a coordinated effort. The linesets will be out of weight most of the time so this technique will only work if the drop is relatively light.

A second method of shortening a drop is by *rolling*. Rolling the top of the goods reduces the height of the drop but also gets rid of its top. The top where it ties to the pipe shouldn't show anyway, so the bunched up fabric and clamps won't show either. A note of caution though, the design may be adversely affected when a significant portion of the image is lost. But sometimes there is no extra batten to make tripping possible, and rolling is the only solution. Whether tripping or rolling is appropriate must be decided on a case-by-case basis taking aesthetic factors into consideration.

cause a huge bow in the bottom pipe. This means, of course, that you will need to poke several holes in the pipe pocket in order to pass the line around the bottom pipe. (This is just one of the reasons that the pocket gets so torn up.) Make sure that all of the tail-downs are the same length so that the pipe will be picked up evenly.

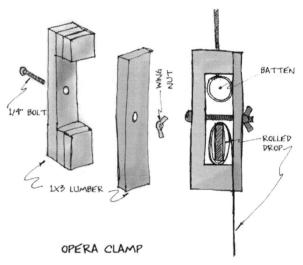

1/4" BOLT

WING
NUT

1X3 LUMBER

BATTEN

ROLLED
DROP

OPERA CLAMP

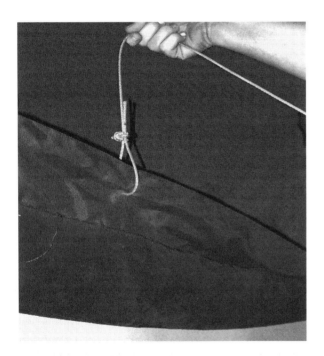

PICK LINE THRU THE PIPE POCKET

NOTICE THAT THE FLAP IS STILL HANGING DOWN, SO THE PICK LINE WON'T SHOW FROM THE FRONT. YOU NEED SEVERAL PICK LINES ACROSS THE BOTTOM OF THE DROP

It takes a few extra parts to roll a drop. You'll need several lengths of *1×4 lumber* and a number of *opera clamps* as described in the accompanying diagram. To do the actual rolling, lay the drop out on the floor face up and as straight and square as possible. Perhaps the top can be lined up with a long straight joint on the stage floor. Take several very straight 1×4s and lay them out evenly with the top of the goods. These boards should go all the way from side to side. Gather a number of stagehands to hold the boards, and to rotate them, rolling the fabric onto the boards. It is important to roll together, and to keep everything nice and neat.

Continue to roll until the desired height is reached. Pick up the rolled top and secure it to the batten with the opera clamps. Attach the clamps by rotating the flat part, and make use of the u-shaped part by hanging one end on the pipe and using the other to hold onto the rolled part of the drop. Rotate the flat part to seal in the pipe and drop, and then tighten the wing nut to secure it.

Storing Drops And Curtains

Folding curtains and drops is one of the oldest stagehand skills, handed down from the time when stagehands were dry-land sailors. You can just imagine how early stagehands may have equated drop folding with sail folding.

A few basic concepts govern the folding of any type of hanging goods. One of these is to remember to leave the webbing and ties in an accessible position. This makes it possible to see whatever markings are written on the webbing and also makes it possible to hang the goods without completely unfolding them. Second, you should be as neat as possible when folding any soft goods. Proper folding will reduce the amount of wrinkling that occurs, and generally keep the goods in better condition. It is not possible to clean or iron most drops and curtains. Beautifully painted backdrops are works of art in and of themselves, so take great care to ensure that they are well kept. Lastly, you should do your best not to walk on the goods unless it is really necessary.

Begin any type of folding with the goods laying flat on the floor with the "pretty" side up. It is customary that the back side be touching the floor to save the face from damage. A stagehand should be at each of the four corners to pull the goods out and stretch them. Try to get them as flat and smooth as possible. Flopping the corners up and down while pulling makes that job easier, because a small amount of air underneath allows the fabric to float with less drag.

The stagehands on the bottom two corners should lift up, pull against one another to keep sideways tension on the drop, and then quickly move up to the top two corners. The two stagehands at the top grab those corners and match them with their own. Again, a bit of air captured in the curtain makes it easier to *float* the bottom to the top. Too much will cause you to overshoot, so don't go too far. If you are drastically off it might be best to start over. The same two stagehands who carried the bottom to the top the first time return to the middle of the drop, which has now become the bottom by virtue of the folding. Straighten everything out, let the air escape from the inside, and repeat the procedure as many times as necessary until a 2 or 3 foot wide strip has been created.

Bring both ends to the center rather than one end to the other end because that will leave the center tie line exposed and in the middle when you hang the drop next time. It also makes a neater fold. Leave a space about 1 foot wide so that there will be enough slack for the final fold when the fabric has many layers. Repeat bringing the ends to the middle until a 2 or 3 foot bundle is left on either side. Fold one side over the other, and folding is completed.

Some words of advice: A large number of stagehands are on deck at most load outs and the natural inclination is for everyone to want to help. That is a good thing, but

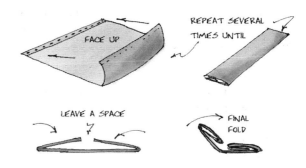

FOLDING A DROP

doesn't usually work out well when drop folding unless the material is really heavy and doesn't want to float. Most of the time you should avoid stepping on the goods at all cost, but if the curtain is really heavy, someone will need to carry the middle to the top.

Folding most often happens at the end of the load out when the floor has been cleared of other set materials. Be sure to sweep first. Also, if you are folding a light-colored drop it is a good idea to have everyone wash their hands before they start. This is especially true at the end of a long and dirty load out.

SOFT GOODS HAMPER

Soft goods are traditionally stored in large laundry *hampers*. If you have carefully folded an expensive drop, it only makes sense to exercise the same amount of care when easing it into the hamper. Lift it by the four corners and gently place it down into the container. (The instruction "four corners" is commonly used to mean a piece of scenery is heavy and needs extra hands.) On occasion you may encounter a drape that is so large and heavy it is impractical to consider lifting it up and into the hamper. When that happens roll the goods into the hamper instead. Use the normal folding procedure until

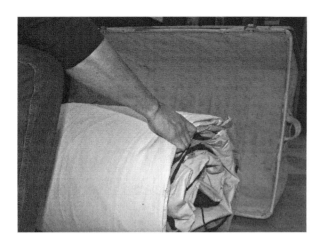

IF A DROP IS TOO HEAVY TO LIFT,
ROLL INTO THE HAMPER INSTEAD

you have a narrow strip of fabric, narrower than the hamper. Begin rolling the drop from one end to the other. Place a hamper on its side at the far end and simply roll the goods into the hamper like a huge snowball. Since this is a technique for very large pieces, the one curtain will most likely fill the hamper completely.

Drops, borders, and blackout drapes are wider than they are tall, and should be folded as just described. But there is another method. Legs and other goods that are taller than they are wide are folded side to side first. Repeat that fold until a workable size is reached. Finish the folding by bringing the bottom to the top, rather than both ends to the middle like a full stage drop. This will leave the webbing exposed. The bottom part tends to curl up a bit with every fold, so you will need to straighten it out each time. Repeat the process until a pleasing size is reached.

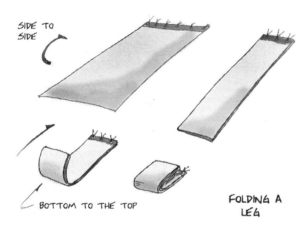

SIDE TO SIDE

BOTTOM TO THE TOP

FOLDING A LEG

Curtains sewn with fullness are a real bear to fold. In all honesty there is no really good method, and you must do the best you can. Sometimes legs are simply lowered into a hamper when the lineset is brought in, and there is no attempt at all made to fold them. If the drapes are velour, and will be taken back out relatively soon, then this is a fine solution. The wrinkles in velour tend to fall out when it is re-hung, but I wouldn't try this with a finely woven fabric with no pile or nap. The problem in folding goods with fullness is of course that the webbing is so much smaller than the body of the curtain, and when stretched out the curtain makes a fan shape.

Scrims and other very lightweight drops are sometimes *west-coasted*. In this procedure, many stagehands are positioned under the drop as it is flown into the deck, the bottom pipe having been removed earlier. The stagehands should position themselves with arms extended so that the scrim furls up on their arms and creates a bundle rather than hitting the floor. Untie about every fifth tie from the batten and retie it, but this time around the bundled scrim so that a kind of tube is created. Untie the remaining ties from the batten and feed the bundle into its hamper. Never drag a scrim on the floor as it will rip on every splinter.

WEST-COASTING A SCRIM

SCRIMS NEED SPECIAL HANDLING WHEN IT COMES TO FOLDING AND STORING. HOLD YOUR ARMS OUT TO CATCH THE FABRIC AS THE SCRIM FLIES IN. THEN TIE EVERY ~6TH TIE AROUND THE GOODS TO SECURE IT TO ITSELF.

CONSTRUCTION TECHNIQUES

The construction of stage draperies is quite a difficult chore, and unless you are very experienced at sewing it is a practice best left to professionals who have a shop devoted to that work. It is not easy to get curtains to hang straight, especially large ones, and the velour makes them very heavy. On the other hand, sewing drops is not nearly such a problem. The fabric is much lighter, it comes in wider widths, and methods of preparing for painting give you a bit of latitude in sewing it to a precise size. This margin for error is not found in sewing drapes that must hang straight from the outset.

A good fabric choice for drop construction is 120″ wide, heavyweight, muslin. *Muslin* is a good choice because the 100% cotton type sizes well, meaning that cotton fabrics shrink when treated with starch or glue. Heavyweight muslin is strong enough to hold up over a period of time.

Imagine a stage with a proscenium opening 18 feet tall. The design calls for a drop 20 feet tall to fit in the space. If 120″ (10′) wide muslin is used, you can create a 20 foot tall drop connecting two horizontal pieces of fabric. Muslin comes in a variety of widths, so you can pick one that works well for the drop you actually need.

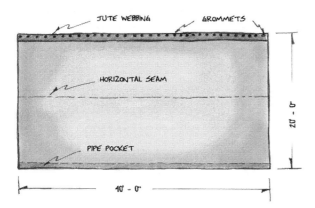

PARTS OF A MUSLIN DROP

A large open space is helpful when sewing drops. A dance studio during off-peak hours works really well because the floor is clean and smooth. Most scene shops are a poor choice because they are so dusty from sawdust and crusted with spattered paint.

Not much equipment is required; a sewing machine that can make a straight stitch through fairly heavy fabric, a large tape measure (like a construction tape, not a sewing tape), some scissors, thread, pins, and grommeting equipment. If you are good with a sewing machine you may not need the pins. An industrial-type sewing machine works really well.

Scenic muslin is usually sold in a ~60 yard bale, and many shops buy it that way. Traditional jute *webbing* is 3½″ wide and comes on a roll that is 72 yards long and is quite cheap. A newer type of webbing is made from polypropylene, and although only 3″ wide, it is really stronger and superior in all respects. The standard size of *grommet* to use is the #2. You will need a #2 grommet hole cutter and setter for the purpose. The same #4 tie line used for electrics can be used for the ties, or you can buy cloth tape that has flatter appearance. It is important to use a substance that is easy to tie and durable.

Unless you are working on some really odd shape of cut drop, the seams in a drop should run horizontally. The drop will hang better that way, with the weight of the pipe pulling on the seams. The webbing is sewn to the top of the drop, and becomes a stable and sturdy strip for the grommets.

The pipe pocket is made from separate pieces of muslin, and sewn to the bottom of the drop. That will add several inches to the finished height, but a couple of inches will be taken away by seams, so the finished product will most likely be only an inch or two larger than the ideal.

Lay out the bundle of muslin on the floor and measure off 40 feet in length. Use scissors to cut through the thick *selvage edge*, and then rip the muslin straight across the warp. Ripping actually makes a much straighter cut than the scissors would, because the rip follows one thread straight across the fabric. It is also much faster than trying to establish a right angle to use as a guide.

It is best to begin construction by making the pipe pocket. A professionally sewn drop has added features like a nylon interior to the pocket that makes it last much longer. You may not need that if you are using the drop for a short period of time. And they usually have a flap sewn in front to hide the pocket. These instructions are for a more easily constructed drop.

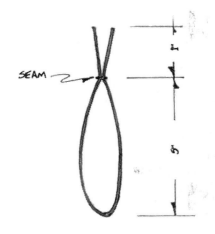

PIPE POCKET

Rip some 12″ wide strips of cloth from scrap, and sew enough of them together end to end to form a strip that is at least as long as the width of the drop, in our case 40′-0″. Fold the strip in half lengthwise and sew it together creating a tube 6″ wide. Make sure that any seams previously made by sewing together the smaller strips go to the inside where they will not be seen.

Do not turn the tube inside out; the top seam will wind up on the back of the drop and won't show. Sew the completed pocket to the bottom piece of muslin. Make sure that your seam allowance is large enough to include the entire selvage, which on scenic muslin is sometimes quite large. Usually about a 1″ allowance is enough.

Another step is sewing the webbing to the top section of the muslin. Cut a section of webbing that is about 6″ longer than the width of the drop so that you can turn under 3″ at each end. Pin the webbing to the muslin every foot or so to make it easier to get the drop through the sewing machine. Fold over and pin down the last 3″ of the webbing just like you did the first 3″. Extra material folded over at the ends creates more strength in the corner areas, which get the most intense use. The webbing in the illustration is the older, jute type, which has a colored stripe on the back. The newer type does not, and is usually solid black. The older type shows up better in a drawing, but really the poly type is much stronger and longer lasting.

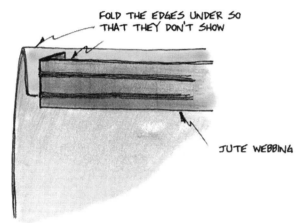

FOLD THE EDGES UNDER SO THAT THEY DON'T SHOW

JUTE WEBBING

ATTACHING THE WEBBING

Sew down the webbing with a straight stitch ¼″ from each edge, and also down the middle. A setting of eight or ten stitches per inch is good. An industrial machine is by far the best to use, because of the thickness of the webbing and the extreme length of the seams.

The top and bottom subassemblies get sewn together last. Make sure that the middle seam, webbing, and pipe pocket seam all fall on what will become the upstage side of the drop. Joining the big parts was saved until the very last because that way you only have to deal with the weight of the whole drop once.

Grommets protect the fabric and webbing from tearing when you pull on a tie line. Lay the drop out face up, and use a tape measure to find the center. Put marks at 1 foot intervals all across the top in either direction. Make sure that the center mark is dead center, because that will make it easier to properly tie the drop onto the batten when it gets to the theatre. The grommets should be placed 1 inch from the top of the webbing, any closer to the edge and they tend to tear out. Placing the grommets in the center of the webbing leaves too much fabric at the top.

Use a grommet-hole cutter to punch holes in the webbing. It is best to place the drop on top of a block of wood and/or some thick scrap leather when punching the holes to prevent damage to your floor and tool.

GROMMETS SHOULD GO CLOSER TO THE TOP

PUTTING THEM IN THE MIDDLE DEFORMS THE TOP WHEN YOU HANG THE DROP

The leather seems to help keep the punch from dulling so quickly.

Follow the instructions that come with your grommet setter to attach the #2 brass grommets. Basically, this involves threading the male side through the hole, placing it on the base, slipping the female side over the male, and then using the setter and a hammer to curl the male side flange down so that it secures the female side. The instructions will most likely say something about not trying to do the job with one hard blow, but rather with many small taps. That is good advice.

GROMMETING SUPPLIES AND TOOLS

Grommeting is one of those processes that sounds really easy but takes considerable practice to master well. Expect to ruin a few grommets in learning how. A much better alternative to the hammer is a grommet setting tool, which resembles a huge nutcracker. Pressure on the handle smoothly and easily turns down the edge of the male grommet.

Cut some tie line to a length of 30″ and then tie one to each grommet using a square knot. It is traditional to use a contrasting color of tie to mark the center of the drop.

The Susan Crabtree painting book has very good instructions on how to prepare a drop for painting.

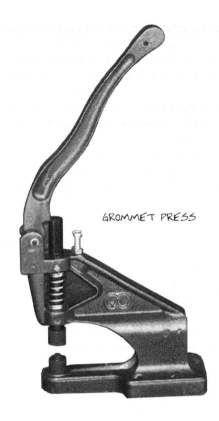

GROMMET PRESS

TERMS USED IN THIS CHAPTER

1×4 lumber	grommet	spike mark
bleed-through	hamper	tab curtain
bottom pipe	in one	tail-down lines
center line	leg and border set	tension pulley
curtains: Austrian, blackout, border,	masking	traveler track: carrier, channel,
cyclorama/cyc, grand	muslin	dead end pulley, end stop,
drape/main, leg, oleo, scrim,	opera clamps	eyebolt, hanging clamp,
show, traveler, valence	pipe pocket	lap splice, live end pulley,
drape	rags	master carrier
drops	rolling	tripping
duvetyn fabric	selvage edge	velour fabric
floating fabric with air while	shop built	webbing
folding	sightlines	west coasting
fullness	soft goods	

CHAPTER 6

ROPES AND KNOTS

I T ISN'T SURPRISING that rope handling skills are very important to stagehand work, considering that sailors were the originators of our craft. Knowledge about rope selection, coiling, and accurate knot tying are skills you should learn early on in your training. You can avoid the adage that "If you aren't sure you are tying a knot properly, tie lots of them." Poorly executed knots can lead to serious injury for anyone unfortunate enough to be underneath a falling piece of scenery. Not every rope or line will work for every purpose, and you should know how to make a proper selection. Knots should be tied with the same understanding. In addition to working well for its purpose, a good knot should be both easy to tie and easy to untie. There are literally hundreds of different kinds of knots. It is best to begin with a few of the most common, and this chapter will help you with that.

THIS TWO-COLOR NYLON ROPE HAS A BRAIDED EXTERIOR WOVEN OVER LINEAR INTERIOR STRANDS. THE END HAS BEEN MELTED TO KEEP IT FROM FRAYING.

TRADITIONAL HEMP ROPE IS MADE BY TWISTING FIBERS TOGETHER. THE END OF THIS LINE HAS BEEN INTENTIONALLY FRAYED TO EXPOSE THE INDIVIDUAL YARNS.

TWO METHODS OF ROPE CONSTRUCTION

ROPES

Some types of knots, especially if misused, may dangerously reduce the load limit of a rope. When overstressed, ropes almost always break at the point where a knot has been tied or some other kink has disturbed the straight passage of the line. Ropes are said to be *de-rated* when knots, bends, or kinks have made them more likely to break.

A SIMPLE OVERHAND KNOT CAN DERATE THE BREAKING STRENGTH OF A LINE BY AS MUCH AS 50%

Two basic types of cordage are used in the theatre, those made of stranded fibers that are *twisted* together, and those that are *woven* or *braided* together. Twisted ropes are made from fibers that are spun into loose strands known as *yarns*, that are then twisted together to form the line. The size and weight rating of the rope depends upon the number and size of the yarns, as well as the material used in making the rope. The rating of a line is usually its *breaking strength* but may instead be its *working limit*. These are not the same thing, but are literally what they say. It's common to use a safety factor of four with a line's breaking strength, so divide that number by four to get a safe working limit. The working limit is how much weight you should actually put on the rope.

Yarns are usually twisted together in a right-handed orientation (clockwise as you look toward the end), making it easier to coil ropes in a clockwise direction. Twisting is the oldest form of rope making, and has existed for thousands of years. It requires only a moderate amount of technology to manufacture twisted ropes. Rope fibers of this type may consist of *sisal*, *hemp*, or synthetics like *polypropylene* or *polyester*.

Hemp was commonly used as a rope fiber for centuries, but has been mostly replaced by polypropylene and/or polyester ropes in recent years. These synthetics start as very long strands and are more easily manufactured into rope than the shorter hemp strands.

They are somewhat stronger and rot resistant in most situations except where UV radiation is an issue. Hemp is rapidly losing favor for rigging applications but a lot of it is still around. Sisal is a poorer quality fiber than hemp and should not be used for lifting overhead items.

Braided lines are formed by weaving together many very small yarns to form a cover, or sheath, that fits over an interior group of strands. Since they are not twisted together, these ropes are easier to work with and less likely to become kinked than a twisted one. Cotton fibers were historically used for this type of rope because they are soft and bendable. Hemp fibers come from the stalks of that plant, which are pulverized into individual strands. The long fibers are easy to twist together which is why they were used for twisted lines. Although the fibers are long, they are also very stiff, so rope made from them is stiff as well. It is much easier to tie knots with a more flexible line, which is why cotton sash cord became popular in the theatre. It is harder to twist the short cotton fibers into yarns, so rather than make traditional rope from it, the braided exterior concept was developed. Nylon rigging ropes are also made in this way, and so is cotton tie line. Tie line is really just very small diameter sash cord.

Sash cord gets its name from its original intended use as a line meant to connect the counter-balancing weights used in old-style windows. The sash is the part of a window that moves up and down when it opens and closes. The same properties that make sash cord bend well around a small diameter window pulley also make it an excellent choice for tying knots. It is very supple and is often used where great strength in a line is not required, but tie line is not strong enough.

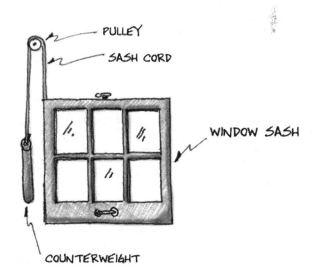

Number 4 black *tie line* is the most popular choice for securing cable to an electric, or for the ties on top of a curtain. Jute tie line was used in the past, but it is so loosely put together that it does not last very long and has fallen into disfavor. It is not at all suitable for use on drapes or other goods that must be frequently tied and

BRAIDED TIE LINE COMES ON
A 3,000 FOOT SPOOL

You should learn some basic terms used for tying knots in order to better understand the descriptions in this chapter.

- The free end of a line is called the *tail*. It is the part that you actually manipulate to tie the knot.
- The *standing part* is the long length of a rope that may be formed into a coil, or be tied to the grid, or laid out in some other fashion.
- Most knots begin with a *loop* of some sort which is a rounded turn of the line.
- To *double-over* means to bend the line over itself, thus creating an artificial tail in the middle of the line.

The Bow Knot

You probably already know how to tie your shoe, and it seems that it would require no explanation. But if you start off with an easy knot, it will build confidence for the harder ones ahead. The same actions are used to tie all knots, so working with the bow first will give you an understanding of the terminology in an environment where you are sure to be successful. The *bow* is actually the most often used knot in theatre because it is used to hang drops and curtains. Drapes are traditionally manufactured with a tie every 12 inches, so a 40 foot long border has 41 knots to tie. Multiply this number by however many curtains are in a show, and the importance of the bow knot becomes clear.

The bow contains the same basic building blocks that are used in all knots. It is essentially a square knot in which the two tails are doubled-over before making the final half hitch. Pulling on the very end of the tails slides the two "double-overs" through the knot and the bow is untied. If you can visualize that process, it will make it much easier for you to understand more complex knots.

untied. The #4 designation comes from an older way of determining the size of a braided line with a gauge number, much like with electrical wires. The #4 is ⅛″ in diameter.

Sash cord has become increasingly hard to find in recent years, as the windows it was designed to rig have been mostly replaced by more energy efficient ones. It is still available from some theatrical suppliers. Newer versions of this same basic type of line, but made from synthetic materials, are readily available from local hardware stores.

More information about ropes, aircraft cable, and chains can be found in the chapter, "Essential Theatre Supplies."

KNOTS

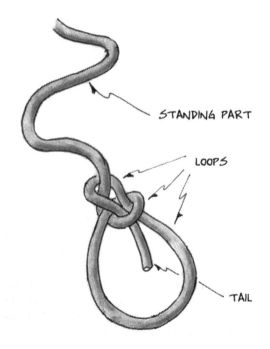

STANDING PART

LOOPS

TAIL

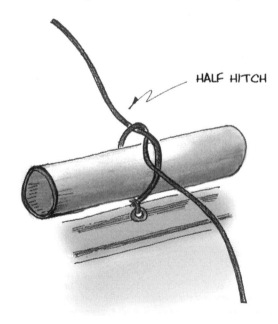

HALF HITCH

The bow knot requires two tails, or ends. The first part of the knot involves tying a *half-hitch*, which is simply wrapping the two tails around one another, and tightening. The friction of the two lines rubbing against one another tends to make them stay together. But a half-hitch will not stay tied on its own; the friction is not great enough.

Double-over the two tails so that they are about half of their original length. Now tie a second half hitch using the doubled over tails. This completes the knot. It is very easy to untie by pulling on one of the tails. The bow is an excellent example of the adage that a good knot is easy to tie and easy to untie. When you are untying curtains from a batten, pull one tail all the way straight up, and then down to the side; it will loosen the entire knot in one easy motion without having to loosen the half-hitch separately.

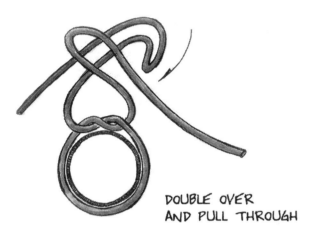

DOUBLE OVER
AND PULL THROUGH

The Choke

This very simple knot is quite useful for attaching a piece of tie line to a pipe or lighting cable so that it grips with holding force and will not slide down. The *choke* is one

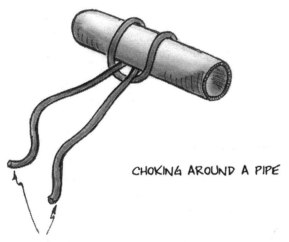

CHOKING AROUND A PIPE

THESE TAILS CAN BE SEPARATE,
OR CONNECTED TOGETHER LIKE
A SPANSET.

member of a family of knots that uses a double wrap around a pipe for extra gripping power. It is also the most common manner of attaching a sling, as discussed in the chapter on rigging. Slings are often used in arena rigging.

As an example, a choke works well if you want to tie up some lighting cable onto a boom so that it is up off the deck. Apply the choke so that it is about chest high off the floor. Then coil the cable and secure it with a bow knot.

The greater the force exerted on the choke, the tighter its grip becomes, preventing it from sliding down the pipe and lowering the coil to the deck. This method also works for tying cable (or any other reasonable object) to a truss, handrail, rope, or other tubular form.

The Slip Knot

The *slip knot* can be used to make a loop in the end of a line that will tighten when force is exerted. It has many useful applications for attaching tie line when speed is essential. The slip knot is also used in tying another knot, the trucker's hitch. Knitters may recognize it as the same knot that is used to start yarn onto a knitting needle.

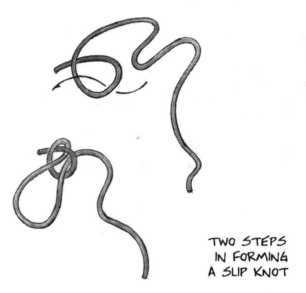

TWO STEPS
IN FORMING
A SLIP KNOT

Make a small loop in the tail near its end. Double-over the standing part and draw it through the loop. (Remember that the standing-part is the long end.) Hold the doubled-over loop and pull on the tail to secure the knot. If the knot has been properly tied, pulling on the standing-part makes the loop smaller, while pulling on the loop itself makes it larger. If you tug on the loop and the tail pulls through and you are left with a half-hitch, you have tied the knot backward and it will not work properly. An easy way to avoid this problem is to make sure that your first loop is formed very close to the end of the tail. Then there will not be enough of the tail sticking out to make the mistake of pulling it, rather than the standing-part, through the loop.

The Clove Hitch

The *clove hitch* is used to fasten a line around a pipe, handrail, or other rounded object. It's another important theatrical knot that every stagehand should know and be able to tie without thinking. Like the choke we looked at earlier, this knot grips more tightly when force is applied. Unlike the choke, the clove is meant for use with a long line, and especially one that is under load while the knot is tied. One example of that would be dead hanging a drape or a piece of scenery. In that situation, weight is on the line as you haul it up into the air, and a clove hitch is easy to tie under those circumstances because you can take a *wrap* around the pipe to safety the line while you tie the knot. Wrap means to pass the line around a pipe and hold it there. Wrapping around a pipe makes the weight much easier to hold because the friction of the rope on the pipe is helping.

The clove hitch is a very simple knot to tie. Drape the line over the pipe, and wrap it around the right side of itself. Bring the line around the pipe and wrap it to the left side. Slip it under the first wrap that you took. That's all there is to the clove hitch. However, the clove will hold better if you take an extra half hitch around the standing part to ensure that the line will not accidentally untie itself under stress, especially when the load is repeatedly shifted.

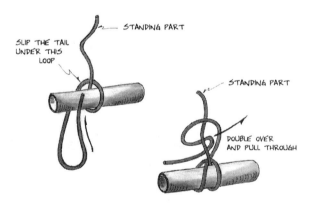

TYING THE CLOVE HITCH

Quite often there is a great deal of excess rope on the floor after hauling something into the air for a dead hang. When this happens, the clove hitch can be tied in the center of the rope by doubling-over a few feet of the line and using this doubled-over part as though it were the end. That avoids pulling a huge amount of excess line through the knot. Doubling-over to create an end in the middle of a line is a common practice with many different kinds of knots, which you have already experienced with the bow and slip knots.

The Bowline

This knot is pronounced "Boleyn" and not "bow line." If you mispronounce it, you run the risk of becoming an object of ridicule by your fellow stagehands and/or climbing enthusiasts. The *bowline* is used to create a fixed loop in the end of a rope. It is yet another of the quintessential stagehand knots that everyone must know. It is the basic knot used by rock and roll riggers to hang chain motors in an arena. The bowline's popularity stems from the fact that it is easy to tie, it is very safe, and it is also easy to untie, which are all essential elements of a good knot. It will be much easier to tie the bowline if you keep these two ideas in mind: Make the first loop small. Make the second loop (the one you want to keep) much larger.

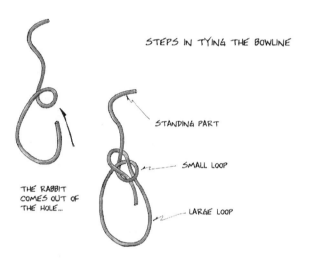

STEPS IN TYING THE BOWLINE

STANDING PART

SMALL LOOP

LARGE LOOP

THE RABBIT COMES OUT OF THE HOLE...

The following method of tying a bowline is probably the easiest, although there are others. These instructions are intended for a right-handed person. If you are left-handed it is probably best to try the right-handed method first, and then adapt it to your own style later. Basically, the left-handed approach is a mirror image of the right and will work just as well.

Hold the line across your left palm so that the long, standing part is lying away from you. The length of the rope making up the tail dictates the size of the loop in the finished knot. For some rigging jobs, the size of the loop is critical. If you need a 2 foot loop in the bowline, start with a bit over 4 feet of tail.

Coil the rope counterclockwise so that one small loop is in your hand. Pass the tail through the loop from back to front, then around the back of the standing part and again through the small loop, so that the line passes back along itself. Tighten the knot by pulling on the tail in opposition to the standing part.

A story is often told to make it easier to remember the steps in tying the bowline. "There is a hole in the ground (the small loop). A rabbit (the tail) comes up out of the hole and runs behind a tree (the standing part). The rabbit circles the tree and runs back down into the

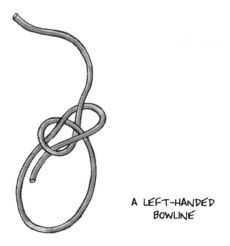

A LEFT-HANDED
BOWLINE

hole." This is a silly story, but I didn't make it up, and it is the traditional method of teaching the bowline. Feel free to embellish it, and adapt it to any animals and/or objects you feel are appropriate.

The left-handed approach is really just a mirror image of the instructions that were given for a regular bowline. Notice that in either version, the tail should wind up to the inside of the large loop rather than to the outside. If you are a left-handed person, you are already aware that lefties are generally shafted by tool manufacturers, so enjoy something technical that works just as well left-handed as it does right-handed.

The Square Knot

The *square knot* is another very basic knot used in a variety of different situations such as tying two lines together, tying a bundle, or in combination with other knots.

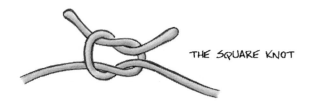

THE SQUARE KNOT

Tying the square knot requires two tails. Holding one tail in either hand, lay the right tail over the left and twist it around to make a half hitch. Then take the left tail and pass it over the right making another half hitch. Right over left, left over right, as the saying goes. Tighten this up and you will have a square knot. Right over left twice, or left over right twice will make a granny knot that is harder to untie and is prone to slipping. A true square knot appears as two loops choked over one another and is easily recognizable.

A GRANNY KNOT

The Trucker's Hitch or Snub and Loop

The most complicated has been saved for last. The *trucker's hitch* is a popular knot to use when you need to put a great deal of tension on a line. It is often used to tie down loads for trucking, hence its name. Of course in a modern trailer used for touring, straps and load bars are the preferred method, but there are still plenty of other uses for the trucker's hitch. This knot is excellent for stretching a cyclorama, holding scenery tight to a wall, or for making small changes in the trim of a dead hung piece. I have included two methods of tying the trucker's hitch, using either one piece of rope or two, depending on the situation at hand.

It is easier to learn the two-rope method first. A practical illustration may make it easier to understand how the trucker's hitch is used. Visualize a cyclorama that needs to be stretched to remove its wrinkles. Fasten clamps to the edges of the cyc so that lines can be tied between the clamps and the offstage wall of the theatre. You can stretch out the wrinkles in the fabric by adding tension to the line.

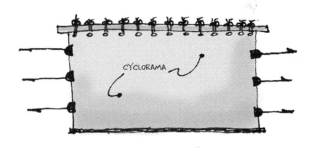

CYCLORAMA

STRETCHING CLAMPS AND LINES
ON A CYCLORAMA

Attach a piece of tie line to the clamp with a bowline. At a convenient distance from the clamp, tie another bowline in the other end of the line. That second bowline creates an eye for the other section of line to pass through. Tie a second piece of tie line to a structure to the side of the stage. Bring the two lines together and pass the tail of the second line through the loop of the first. If you then pull this tail back in the direction of the wall, tension will be placed on the line, and the friction of the tie line doubling-over through the loop will keep it from slipping as long as tension is kept on the tail you are holding.

BOWLINE — DOUBLE OVER AND PULL THROUGH

USING TWO LINES FOR A TRUCKER'S HITCH

Finish the knot by tying off to the loop. Hold the doubled-over line with two fingers where it is kinked through the bowline loop. The friction of the lines and the pressure from just your two fingers should be plenty to keep the line from slipping. If you try to hold it with more than that, your hand will be in the way of tying the rest of the knot. Double-back a small portion of the tail and wrap it through just as you would if tying a bow. It will take some practice to get this to work without losing tension on the line. That is the part that most people struggle with, but after a few practice attempts you should get the hang of it.

Untie the knot by pulling on the tail. The doubled-over section will pull through just as it does when untying your shoe. On the other hand, if you pull the doubled-over tail all the way through you won't be able to get it to come loose so easily.

To tie the one-line trucker's hitch, fasten the line at one end with a suitable knot and then tie a slip knot in the middle of the line an easy distance away from the second tie-off point. The slip knot should be tied so that the loop size is dependent on the tail rather than the standing part. If you do this backward, the loop will shrink to nothing when tension is applied, and it will be obvious that something is wrong. The line should be able to pass easily around the second tie-off point without jamming, or the one-line method won't work. To finish the knot, pass the line around the second tie-off point and run it back through the loop, making it fast in the same manner as used in method one.

ONE-LINE METHOD OF TYING
THE TRUCKER'S HITCH

It is possible to make the first small loop by doubling-over the line and making a half-hitch rather than using a slip knot, but it is very hard to remove this alternate knot later on down the road. If your plan is to keep the line in place permanently, you might prefer the half-hitch loop to a slip knot one.

Using the trucker's hitch to tension the line provides a two-to-one mechanical advantage and will allow you to pull the line really tight. This is to say that for every pound of force on the tail, the standing part will be two pounds tighter. But it also doubles the load on the line and increases the possibility that it will break.

ROPE COILING AND STORAGE

Coiling a rope for storage can be more complex than amateurs would think. It is fairly easy to roll a rope up into some sort of clump, but not so easy to play it back out in a straight line without a lot of tangles. One thing is for sure, you will NEVER see a professional stagehand wind a rope up around her elbow, because that means she has no control over how twisted it becomes. This is especially problematic when using a twisted rope like hemp, or when coiling an electrical cable.

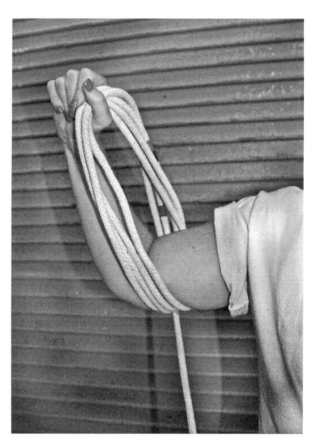

DON'T COIL THIS WAY

Here is the issue: When a rope is coiled into a circle, it must spin one time for each turn in the coil. If you wind the rope around your elbow, you won't be able to put the proper twist into it, and the rope will come out with some of the loops making a figure-eight shape, while others are a circle. The figure-eight shape comes from a turn of the rope that did not get twisted. The arm method also produces a very small size coil that will most likely be hard to play back out.

Instead of using the distance between thumb and elbow to set the size of the turns in the coil, let it be a natural function of the length of your arm as it moves in

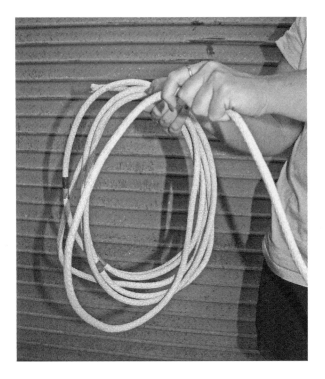

DO THIS INSTEAD

THIS ROPE IS TOO BIG AND HEAVY TO HOLD, SO COIL IT ON THE FLOOR INSTEAD.

an arc back and forth. Hold the tail of the rope in your right hand and swing your left out to grasp the standing part of the rope a comfortable distance away. As you bring that part of the rope over to the right hand, rotate it once with your fingers so that it makes a flat coil. Repeat the procedure, but remember to rotate each time you bring the rope back to your right hand to make a new turn of the coil. Sometimes you will find that the rope is actually twisted too many times, so that you must turn the opposite way. Let the feel of the rope tell you which way it needs to twist in order to coil properly. You should finish up with a coil about 2 feet in diameter, which is appropriate for a line that is about ½ inch thick, the most common kind.

If the line is really thick, or hugely long, you might try coiling it onto the floor instead of into your hand, but use the same twisting technique. If the line is all kinky from being improperly coiled by someone else, it may take some stretching and massaging to get it back into shape. It may need to spin an incredible amount. Make sure that the far end of the rope is free to spin, because each twist that you make will need to work its way along the standing part, and out of the free end.

TERMS USED IN THIS CHAPTER

bow	hemp	tail
bowline	loop	tie line
braided/woven	polyester	trucker's hitch
breaking strength	polypropylene	twisted
choke	sash cord	working limit
clove hitch	sisal	wrap
de-rated	slip knot	yarns
double-over	square knot	
half-hitch	standing part	

CHAPTER 7

THEATRE RIGGING

RIGGING CAN MEAN a variety of things in the entertainment business. A shirt may be "rigged" with Velcro when a quick change happens too fast for buttons. Flats may be "rigged" with stiffeners when they are too floppy to stand on their own. Chain motors in an arena are "rigged" with wire rope and shackles. In this chapter though, rigging will cover the techniques and equipment used in hanging scenery and lighting over the stage.

Photograph Courtesy of the National Archives

DEPRESSION ERA
STAGEHANDS

WORKING WITH
HEMP STYLE RIGGING

TRADITIONAL RIGGING SYSTEMS

There are two main types of theatre rigging systems. The first and oldest type is known as the hemp system, and a second, newer type is known as a counterweight system. The word "system" is used to denote that there are many parts to each type and that these parts work together in concert to form a method of flying scenery. Some theatre buildings also use various types of electric and/or hydraulic winches to fly scenery. In those, wire rope cable is wound/unwound from a drum, something like a winch that you might find on the front of an off road vehicle. *Winches* can be very helpful in certain situations when the weight of a load, like a first electric, is very heavy and using a counterweight system is problematic.

MOTOR

CABLE DRUM

GEAR CASE

THIS CABLE WINCH IS RATED AT 3000 POUNDS

A CABLE WINCH DOESN'T NEED COUNTERWEIGHTS LIKE OTHER THEATRE SYSTEMS, BUT ALSO DOESN'T HAVE THE DELICATE TOUCH OF A HUMAN FLYMAN.

The problem with winches in general though is that precise control of automated equipment can be difficult to achieve. These machines have no ability to "feel" when something is going wrong. A good flyman can slip a batten past a crowd of others in a graceful way that a machine cannot possibly mimic. The flyman gets feedback from eyes, touch, and ears that a machine does not. This is an example of how the art of theatre sometimes wins out over the science of technology.

Chain motors have become very popular in recent years as scenery has gotten heavier and more complex. Most of the time motors are used for items that are dead hung, and consequently do not move during the normal course of a performance. Chain motors are quite noisy when they operate. That is not so much a problem in the concert business where performances are very loud, but they are problematic in a quiet theatre. A separate chapter, "Arena Rigging," is devoted to rigging with hoists.

HEMP SYSTEM

The *hemp system* was developed in the mid-nineteenth century by stagehands who were recruited from the ranks of the merchant marine. As sailors, these stagehands were familiar with methods of using *hemp rope* to lift heavy objects. As a result, many stagehand terms are derived from nautical sources. On a sailing ship, the ropes and pulleys used to manipulate the sails are known collectively as "the rigging" of the ship. More about ropes and knots can be found in the related chapter.

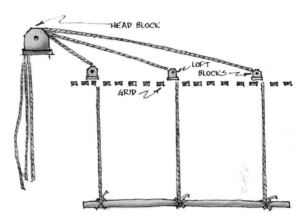

HEAD BLOCK

LOFT BLOCKS

GRID

HEMP SYSTEM RIGGING

In studying the hemp system it is helpful to imagine a practical rigging problem. In the following example, imagine that a curtain needs to be hung across the stage, parallel with the plaster line, and that at some point the curtain needs to be flown up and out of sight.

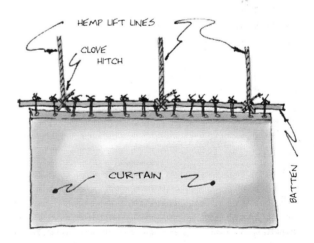

HEMP LIFT LINES

CLOVE HITCH

CURTAIN

BATTEN

BATTEN SUSPENDED WITH HEMP LIFT LINES

If you lay the curtain out on the stage floor or *deck*, you'll notice that the first thing you need is a horizontal *pipe*, or *batten* to tie the drapes on, like a curtain rod, only

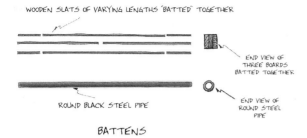

WOODEN SLATS OF VARYING LENGTHS "BATTED" TOGETHER

END VIEW OF THREE BOARDS BATTED TOGETHER

ROUND BLACK STEEL PIPE

END VIEW OF ROUND STEEL PIPE

BATTENS

BACK IN THE DAY, BATTENS WERE MADE BY CONNECTING PIECES OF WOOD TOGETHER, BUT NOW STEEL PIPE IS USED. AT THAT TIME, STEEL PIPE WAS NOT AVAILABLE, AND INDIVIDUAL WOODEN SLATS WERE NOT LONG ENOUGH.

sturdier. You'll also need some method of hoisting the batten into the air and leaving it suspended. You can do the latter by tying hemp lines to the batten and pulling it up toward the grid. At one time, battens were made by splicing together pieces of wood, but modern battens are made of steel pipe instead. The terms batten and pipe are now interchangeable. "Batting" is a carpenter's term for making a larger piece of wood from several smaller ones.

In the curtain hanging example it takes three stagehands to haul the piece into position and tie it off at its designated trim. The word *trim* is used to indicate the proper position of a flown piece. *Setting a trim* means to adjust a piece to its proper location and then mark that spot so that it can easily be found again.

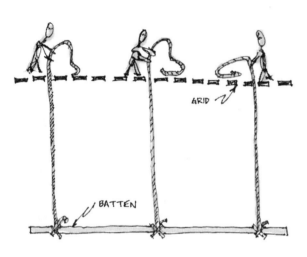

GRID

BATTEN

DEAD HANGING

A curtain that has been tied off in one position and cannot be easily moved is said to be *dead hung*. In general practice, dead hanging is a last resort situation because it is a difficult and time-consuming procedure. It is hard to get all the lines tied off so the pipe is level and at the right height. Our rigging example dictated that this drape would need to move on cue, and dead hanging won't work for that.

There are other problems as well. It seems like using three stagehands is an inefficient use of labor and it would

be better if one could do the job instead. Also it would be difficult for the three of them to move at a synchronized speed, keeping the curtain level. Lastly, there needs to be a method of balancing the weight of our load rather than using brute force. A hemp rigging system uses pulleys and weights to address these issues.

The various parts associated with one of the rigging pipes over the stage are collectively known as a *lineset*. *Pulleys* and *blocks* are used to change the direction a rope travels. The wheel inside a pulley that touches the rope and spins is called a *sheave* (usually pronounced "shiv"). Technically, pulleys are free to swivel and blocks are held fast in one place. Most of the pulleys in a lineset are actually blocks because the only part that moves is the sheave.

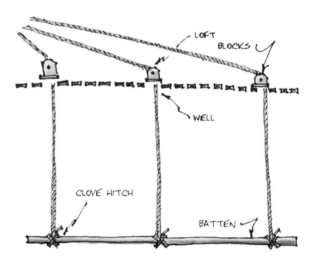

LOFT BLOCKS

WELL

CLOVE HITCH

BATTEN

LOFT BLOCKS

A *loft block* changes the direction of rope travel from vertical to horizontal when the rope meets the grid and turns toward the wing. In this example three hemp lines change direction and are bundled together when they reach the side of the stage. The *head block* is located directly over the pin rail. In this example the head block

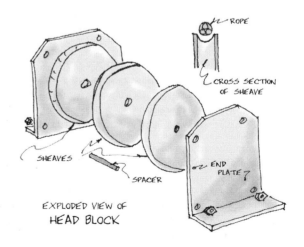

ROPE

CROSS SECTION OF SHEAVE

SHEAVES

SPACER

END PLATE

EXPLODED VIEW OF HEAD BLOCK

has three sheaves because there are three lines used to lift the batten. The block is constructed so that the three sheaves are side by side in the same housing, but turn feely and independently.

Our hemp lines are now hanging downward in the direction of the pin rail. You get better leverage that way because it is physically much easier to pull down on a rope than it is to pull sideways. The rope and the pipe are inversely proportional to one another. When you pull the ropes down a foot, the batten moves up a foot. If the ropes were released, gravity would cause the batten to move down.

SANDBAGS, CLEWS, AND ROPES IN A HEMP SYSTEM

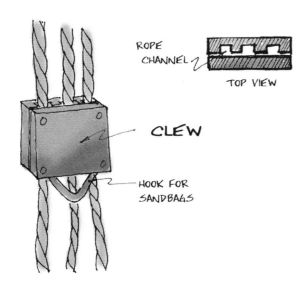

In a hemp house, *sandbags* are used to balance out the weight of the battens and the loads on them. A *clew*, which is a rope clamp with an individual channel for each rope, is used to attach them. The clew makes it easy to take small adjustments in the lengths of the different lift lines, and thus you can adjust the trim of the batten so that it will hang level and parallel to the stage floor. Otherwise the pipe might be bowed or slanted, and the curtain would not hang straight. A hook at the bottom of the clew is used to attach sandbags. Remember that the curtain is raised when you pull down on the rope, but there is no way to reverse the process by pushing up on the rope. As a result the weight of the bags should be slightly less than the weight of the load on the batten. This condition is referred to as *batten heavy*. If the lineset is batten heavy, its own weight will cause it to fly in (down) when the ropes are loosened.

The final step in operating a hemp system is to secure the group of lines to the *pin rail* when the batten is not in use. The rail itself is a large diameter horizontal pipe that runs up and down stage. Holes are drilled through the rail from top to bottom and are used in conjunction with *belaying pins*. In nautical terms, belay means to stop, or hold fast. When inserted through the rail a belaying

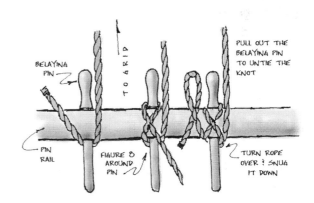

TYING OFF TO A BELAYING PIN

pin forms a *cleat*. The hemp lift lines are figure-eighted around the cleat into a special knot that will come completely untied whenever the belaying pin is removed from the rail. This method of tying off makes it easier to deal with several ropes at once.

There are a number of shortcomings associated with the hemp system of rigging. The largest of these is the difficulty of attaching sandbags to the line sets. It is at best a cumbersome task, and when the added weight is over two or three hundred pounds, the sheer size of the bags is a test of anyone's strength and endurance. Also, since there are many such linesets arranged side by side, it becomes quite a trial to maneuver the bags past one another as several linesets are being simultaneously worked. In addition, there is the problem of the hemp lines stretching. Hemp rope tends to stretch when a load is placed on it, and to shorten in humid conditions.

Lastly, it is difficult to tie off the hemp lines at the rail, and to deal neatly with the massive amount of line that ends up on the floor. Several years of apprenticeship are required to develop the necessary skills. As you will see, the invention of the counterweight system was a giant step forward.

Even so, it is good to understand how this early system of rigging worked, because stagehands are often called upon to rig lines for temporary lifting jobs, and understanding the basic principles of hemp-style rigging will make such tasks much easier. Although it would not seem possible there are still a number of road houses using a hemp system.

Counterweight System

The *counterweight system* of rigging works on the same basic principles as the hemp system, but with a number of important refinements. *Aircraft cable*, a very high-strength stranded steel cable, is used in the place of hemp for the lift lines. This product was originally developed for use in linking the control surfaces of early airplanes, hence the odd name.

Most rigging installations use ¼″ cable generally rated at around 7,000 pounds *breaking strength*. This far exceeds the breaking strength of any reasonably sized hemp rope. It is important to realize that breaking strength is just that, the point at which the cable will break. Most riggers use a safety factor of four, meaning that the load placed on a component should be only one-fourth of the breaking strength.

Instead of tying off to a pin rail, the counterweight system uses an *arbor* that holds steel or lead weights rather than sandbags. The metal used in manufacturing counterweights is dense, and these weights take up much less space than sandbags do. Aircraft cable lift lines are attached to the batten, run upward through the loft blocks, across the grid to the head block, and down to the top of the arbor. A large diagram of that is at the end of the chapter. Counterweights are added to the arbor to exactly balance out the weight of the batten and its load.

The cable may be fastened to the pipe with a clove hitch and *wire rope clamp*, or it may have a *trim chain* that can be used to adjust the exact length of the cable.

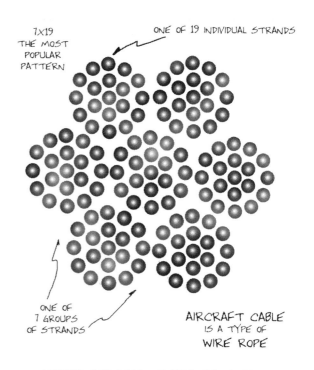

7X19 THE MOST POPULAR PATTERN

ONE OF 19 INDIVIDUAL STRANDS

ONE OF 7 GROUPS OF STRANDS

AIRCRAFT CABLE IS A TYPE OF WIRE ROPE

INDIVIDUAL STAINLESS, OR GALVANIZED STEEL WIRES ARE TWISTED TOGETHER TO FORM A ROPE, JUST LIKE HEMP IS. AIRCRAFT CABLE IS AN ESPECIALLY STRONG AND DURABLE TYPE.

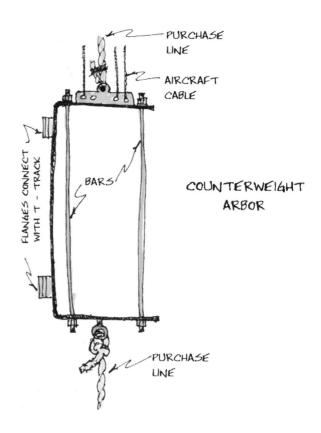

PURCHASE LINE

AIRCRAFT CABLE

FLANGES CONNECT WITH T-TRACK

BARS

COUNTERWEIGHT ARBOR

PURCHASE LINE

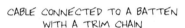
CABLE CONNECTED TO A BATTEN
WITH A TRIM CHAIN

CABLE CONNECTED TO A BATTEN
WITH A CLOVE HITCH

It is not necessary to leave the lineset batten heavy because there is a positive way to haul the arbor both up and down. You do that with a large diameter hemp line known as the *purchase* or *operating line*. A ¾″ line is standard because the large size is easy to grip. Although some purchase lines may still be hemp, most modern systems use a synthetic rope instead.

The purchase line is attached to the top of the arbor, passes over the head block, down to a tension pulley and back up to the bottom of the arbor where it is again secured. Pulling down on the rope causes the arbor to move upward. As the arbor travels up, the batten travels down. So pulling down on the purchase line causes the batten to go down. Pulling up sends it upward. That is easier to remember than what happens in a hemp system, where the motions are reversed.

A hemp or synthetic purchase line tends to change length over a period of time. The bottom *tension pulley* (remember pulleys move) serves to keep the line taut at all times. It is set into special guides known as *T-tracks* that allow it to move downward by force of gravity, but cause it to jam rather than slide back up. The same tracks

COUNTERWEIGHT RAIL

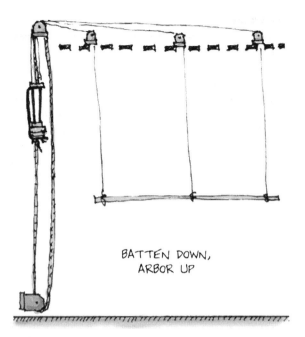

BATTEN DOWN,
ARBOR UP

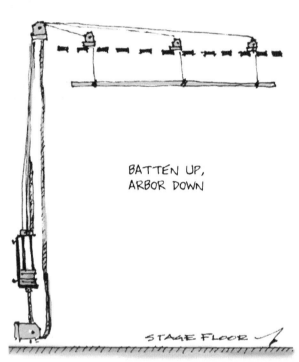

BATTEN UP,
ARBOR DOWN

STAGE FLOOR

purchase system, cable length is increased by passing the aircraft cable lift lines around a pulley on top of the arbor, and then tying them off at the grid.

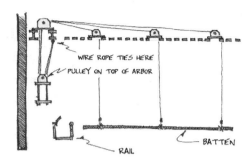

WIRE ROPE TIES HERE

PULLEY ON TOP OF ARBOR

RAIL

BATTEN

A 2 TO 1 OR "DOUBLE PURCHASE" SYSTEM ALLOWS SCENERY TO MOVE OFF STAGE UNDER THE RAIL

What this means is that for every foot the arbor rises, about 2 feet of lift line pass over the head block, and as a consequence, the batten drops 2 feet. You can clearly see how the names "2 to 1" and/or double purchase originated. One drawback of this system is that it also requires twice the amount of weight in the arbor. If your scenery weighs 150 pounds, then it takes 300 pounds of stage weights to balance it. When hanging a heavy load, these arbors tend to fill up in a hurry. Theatres with a double purchase system sometimes use lead weights rather than the standard steel ones, since a same-size lead weight is about twice as heavy as a steel weight.

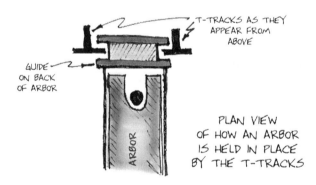

T-TRACKS AS THEY APPEAR FROM ABOVE

GUIDE ON BACK OF ARBOR

ARBOR

PLAN VIEW OF HOW AN ARBOR IS HELD IN PLACE BY THE T-TRACKS

guide the arbor as it moves up and down. Older systems use a cable-guiding device that is not nearly as effective, especially in a tall house.

In some theatres a lack of wing space means that the floor space under the rail must remain unobstructed, so that scenery and actors can pass back and forth. This is made possible with a 2 to 1, or *double purchase* counter-weight system. In this case, the rail is located approx-imately halfway between the deck and the grid. With that ratio, if the same type of cable system were used as in the standard counterweight system just discussed, battens would only move halfway up and down. In a double

When a batten is lowered all the way down, its corresponding arbor stops when it reaches a *barrier* at the top of the T-track. This barrier is usually a piece of angle iron with a rubber or wooden cushion bolted to it. It is bolted at a 90 degree angle across all of the T-tracks. When an arbor is snug against the top barrier, it is physically unable to move any higher. If the arbor cannot move any higher, the batten cannot sink any lower; at least until the weight limit of the various component parts is reached. This limit should be several thousand pounds

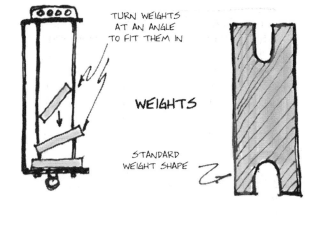

should be stacked in the arbor so that their weight equals the weight of the load on the batten. Bricks most commonly have rounded indentations at either end that are intended to fit around the upright bars found on an arbor. Tilt a brick at an angle to fit it into the arbor and then lay it flat. The weights will not fall out of the arbor when they have been properly placed between the bars.

Most arbors have one or more flat pieces of metal connecting the two upright bars. These *spreader plates* slide up and down on the rods, and are intended to prevent the bars from warping out of shape from the weight of the bricks. Spreader plates should be distributed more or less evenly throughout the stack of weights in the arbor.

at least, but in any case more than the largest amount of weight the arbor can hold. When the batten is flown out, the arbor is stopped by a similar barrier at the bottom of its travel, preventing it from colliding with the tension pulley.

When the batten is flown all the way in and the arbor is snug against its top barrier, it is safe to load any reasonable weight of scenery or lighting equipment onto the batten. Of course this presupposes that you securely fasten that load. Be careful though, to *completely* lower the batten all the way in before adding anything to the pipe. If you stop a few inches short, and a large amount of weight is put on the pipe, it will suddenly slip down until the arbor reaches its fully out position at the T-track barrier. That can be very dangerous to anyone working around the pipe.

You should add weights to the arbor AFTER you've put your entire load on the pipe, and not before. If you reversed that, the arbor and weights could fall if the locking mechanism fails. It probably would fail under those circumstances, because the lock isn't meant to carry that kind of a load.

Counterweights are generally stored on the *loading gallery* or *loading rail*. The loading gallery is positioned near the grid where it is possible to reach the arbors when they are at their highest point of travel. *Counterweights*, which are often referred to as *bricks* because of their shape,

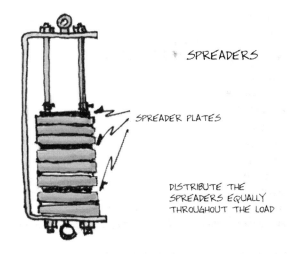

Counterweights are manufactured in a variety of different poundages, but the 20 and/or 25 pound weights seem to be the most popular. Theatres often have a small number of half-sized bricks so that a more exact balance can be reached than is possible with the standard types.

Remember to load the batten first and the arbor second. This avoids a situation where a heavily weighted arbor can fall. If the arbor were loaded first instead, the only thing holding it up would be the rope lock on the rail. The batten is always loaded first because it has nowhere else to go. It has no potential for movement.

Conversely, when removing a load from a batten, always unload the arbor first to avoid the same unsafe situation from occurring in reverse. If a batten gets unloaded before its corresponding arbor, the system will be very far out of balance. Again, the weight of the arbor would be held in check from falling only by the pressure of the rope lock on the purchase line, which won't be able to hold it. When the process is done properly, linesets should be safe to load and unload even with the rope lock open.

STEPS FOR SAFELY LOADING AND UNLOADING STAGE WEIGHTS

<u>When loading:</u>

- Fly the pipe all the way in.
- Place the load on the pipe, taking care to properly secure it.
- Load the proper amount of stage weights into the arbor.
- Fly the lineset out to its proper trim.

<u>When unloading:</u>

- Fly the pipe in to its extreme bottom position.
- Unload the arbor.
- Remove the load from the batten.

ADVANCED TECHNIQUES

There are a number of added complexities to operating a stage counterweight rigging system. One of them is that the weight of the pipe itself must be balanced out by one or two weights in the arbor that need never be removed. This is often referred to as *pipe weight*. It is helpful to strap these weights down, or to paint them a safety color, or otherwise mark them in some way so that they are not accidentally removed. It is customary that when the *loaders*, as they are called, are finished unloading an arbor they yell down "*pipe weight*" so that flymen on the rail below know that it is safe to unload the pipe, and can announce this to the stagehands on the deck.

Unless you have hung the same show a number of times, it is often difficult to know exactly how much weight should be loaded on a batten. There is a danger of greatly overloading the arbor so that it is vastly heavier than the pipe and thus creating a safety hazard. When an exact weight total is not known, it is best to load the arbor with the purchase line unlocked. When you reach the correct weight the lineset will shift a bit, signaling that you are finished. You can test the balance by attempting to fly the pipe out, judging if it is in balance. It is very important not to greatly overload the arbor.

Unfortunately, scenery or drapes hung on a pipe may be too large to hang without at least some portion of the load resting on the floor and not on the pipe. This would obviously affect your ability to judge the weight of the load by the process just described. In this event you'll need to determine the weight by some other means to within a couple of bricks of the actual number of pounds. You might try setting a scale under one end, and then doubling that amount.

After the load has been secured to the batten, a *bull line* is used to safely get the piece into the air. A bull line is a stout length of rope that you can use to take the place of the weight of scenery that is still on the ground. The larger the diameter of the line, the easier it is for the stagehands to grip. The rope should be lengthy enough so that it reaches the floor even after it's been doubled over the batten, and the pipe has been flown out far enough for the entire weight of the load to be resting on it. Don't tie it to the batten because you won't be able to get it loose after the piece is in the air.

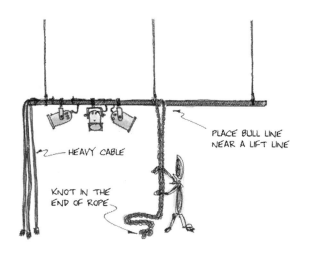

USING A BULL LINE

Stagehands take the place of the eventual load by keeping tension on the bull line as the batten is flown out. After you've manhandled it all the way out, the arbor will be in far enough to fine-tune from the rail. It is very important that a knowledgeable flyman be on hand when using a bull line.

On occasion, and especially with a double purchase system, a need arises to hang a piece that is heavier than the amount of counterweight that can be fitted into one arbor. When this happens, it is possible to use a second lineset as a helper.

This is known as *marrying* the two pipes. It is good to keep a number of short chains and shackles on hand to use for this procedure. Make sure the hardware has a capacity rating high enough to hold the weight involved. Shackles are the best connectors because they have a

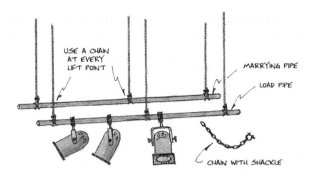

USE A CHAIN AT EVERY LIFT POINT

MARRYING PIPE

LOAD PIPE

CHAIN WITH SHACKLE

MARRYING PIPES TOGETHER

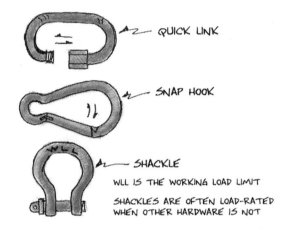

QUICK LINK

SNAP HOOK

WLL

SHACKLE

WLL IS THE WORKING LOAD LIMIT

SHACKLES ARE OFTEN LOAD-RATED WHEN OTHER HARDWARE IS NOT

HANGING HARDWARE

known *working load limit,* or WLL stamped on their sides. You don't need to use a safety factor when the WLL is known; it is OK to use the entire limit.

Fly in a pipe that is either just upstage or downstage from the one which is being loaded, and wrap chains around the two pipes so that they are tightly bound together. It is best to put the chains next to the lift lines. Use one marrying chain for each of the lift lines in your particular system. This will ensure that they are evenly spread out along the length of the pipe.

As a matter of physics, it really doesn't matter how the weight is distributed between the two arbors so far as its effect on the load. As a practical consequence though, it is easier to load and unload the arbors if a majority of the weight is in the primary arbor. This also places less stress on the marrying hardware. If the piece must *work,* or move during the show, both linesets must be unlocked and moved together when the piece flies. It takes more physical strength to overcome the inertia of a heavy weight, but it is still possible for one person to fly the piece, because when one purchase line is pulled, the other will automatically follow as a slave.

The aircraft cable making up the lift lines has a certain weight itself. This weight can really add up in a

large system. If the arbor and batten are visualized as opposite ends of a set of balance scales, the passage of the aircraft cable from one side of the scales to the other can be seen to make a measurable difference in the balance of the system. Therefore, when the batten is very far in, the lineset will seem a bit batten heavy, and when it is all the way out it may seem quite *arbor heavy.* This is a natural occurrence and there is not much that can be done about it.

There are times (such as those calling for a bull line) when loading and unloading weights require that the system be very arbor heavy for a short while. When this situation occurs special steps can be taken to insure that the lineset does not become a "runaway," meaning that the arbor is falling and out of control.

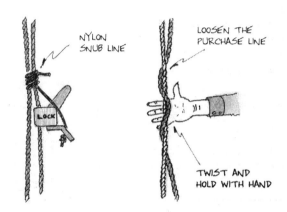

NYLON SNUB LINE

LOOSEN THE PURCHASE LINE

LOCK

TWIST AND HOLD WITH HAND

THREE WAYS TO SAFETY A LINESET

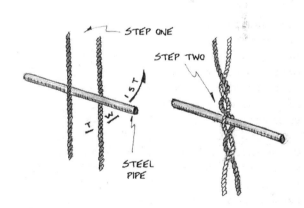

STEP ONE

STEP TWO

1ST

STEEL PIPE

One method is to tie the front and back parts of the purchase line together with a timber hitch or other suitable choking knot. The friction between the two ropes lashed together will keep them from slipping. It is imperative that the two ropes be very tightly bound.

Another method is to take a short length of pipe and twist the front and back portions of the purchase line together several times until enough friction is created to prevent the line from slipping. If you wish to leave the lineset unattended for a moment, it is possible to jam one end of the pipe in-between two of the T-track rails so that it will stay put. (Just make sure that it does.)

The last method is to create slack in the purchase line by pushing down on the front of the tension pulley. Not all systems work this way. If yours does, the pulley will become unjammed and jump up several inches, creating slack in the line. You can then twist the front and rear portions of the purchase line around one another and hold them together tightly with a gloved hand. This last method has the added advantage of allowing the flyman to slowly let the two lines slide through his or her hands while flying the piece out. For loads that are not too greatly out of balance, this technique can take the place of a bull line, but be careful, as it takes a great deal of experience to know the difference. Do not exceed your limitations, and as they say, better safe than sorry.

RUNNING THE SHOW

Running a show from the rail involves marking trims (the limits a purchase line should move), clearly labeling the linesets you are using, making up a cue sheet, and establishing a means of communication from the stage manager. Flymen should exercise a great deal of caution when flying scenery. The inertia of a heavily laden batten can cause severe damage to scenery or props on the deck, as well as to humans. If it is not possible to see the stage while running a cue, it is best to have someone else watch for you. During work calls, a flyman should always announce a batten moving in or out. The most common way is to call "Pipe number so and so, coming in. Heads up!" Remember to speak loudly. The responsibility is yours to make sure that everyone hears your warning.

Although the term fly*man* is used here in an effort to respect tradition, the rail is by no means an exclusively male domain. There are many fine women flymen, and the term is not intended to exclude them.

Before running a show, you need to mark in trims for all of the pipes used in the show, and out trims for

the working pipes. *Working* means that the pipe moves during the show. Electrics and borders are usually static, but drops fly in and out. The basic concept is to fly the batten to its desired trim and mark the purchase line where it lines up with a stationary point on the rail. In this way the pieces to be flown in can be stopped at a precise, predetermined point without hesitation. The trim of a lineset is generally marked with colored tape wrapped around the purchase line.

The best practice is to mark the *in trim* with a contrasting color of tape so that the mark is even with the top of the rope lock when the low trim is reached. As the scenery is flying in, the front part of the purchase line will be moving down. When you see the trim mark come into view, cover the mark with your hand and gently stop the momentum of the lineset as the mark reaches the top of the rope lock. It is important not to run past the mark, as the scenery may well hit the deck with some force and make an unpleasant noise.

Not seeing your trim mark, running a curtain in too far and piling it up on the deck is known as *overhauling*. Frequently the bottom pipe in a drop makes quite a thunk when that happens. The error is particularly brutal if it extends to a point where the batten pipe shows to the audience. When that occurs, you should expect a stern reprimand from the stage manager. With a bit of experience though, you should be able to touch in the curtain to the deck without making a sound. If you are flying in a hard piece, snugging it against the deck will keep it from drifting back and forth during the scene. Slow way down as the trim mark approaches the lock, let the piece just touch the floor, and then give a small tug on the line to settle it against the floor. You should be able to tell a definite difference in the feel of the purchase line when the piece reaches the deck. With some of the weight on the floor, the arbor will seem heavier.

An *out trim* is used when a piece goes out. It is best NOT to mark the out trim so that it matches up with the top of the rope lock as before because the purchase

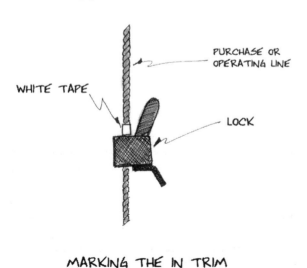

MARKING THE IN TRIM

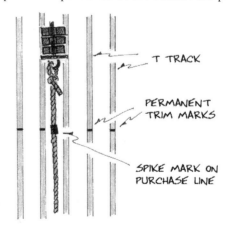

MARKING THE OUT TRIM

line is moving upward when the piece flies out, and a mark in that position would be coming from the wrong direction to be easily seen. The tape would be invisible until it suddenly popped up past the lock and had already passed its stopping point.

It is far better to mark an out trim on the rear part of the rope. It will be passing downward as the scenery flies up. In this way you can see the mark approach and more easily stop at the proper trim. With this method both trim marks will be coming down toward you. Usually there is some horizontal framing member that is a part of the T-track system that can be used as a visual reference for the stopping point. If not, one can easily be established using marker or paint to create a line across the tracks themselves. You might consider marking the out trim with an alternate color of tape on the purchase line.

On occasion, you may need to mark an intermediate trim. That is a point for scenery to stop somewhere between the high/out and low/in trims. You should mark this trim at the rope lock as you would the low trim, but find some means of differentiating the two either by color or size of the trim mark.

Some people like to add warning tape to the purchase line of a particularly problematic piece to ensure that the trim mark is seen.

All linesets should be clearly marked by name on the locking rail. Often there is a card holder or marker board on which to write. I personally prefer to use white gaff tape and a black Sharpie marker. The tape is less likely to fall off at some crucial moment. Marking in the clearest possible manner can prevent some fairly embarrassing, though perhaps memorable moments in the theatre. Clearly marking everything backstage that must be found in the dark is always a good idea. White tape with black writing is perfect for that.

A fly rail *cue sheet* should be made in a large enough format that several people can look at it at the same time. It is not at all unusual for three or four lines to move on

RAIL CUE SHEET SOUND OF MUSIC ACT I				
CUE #	MAN	PIECE	DIRECTION	LIGHT
1	1	MAIN	↑	RED
1A	2	SCRIM	↑	BLUE
2	1	PORTAL	↓	RED
3	1	LEGS	↑	BLUE
	2	BORDER	↑	BLUE
4	2	SCRIM	↓	RED

USE THE CLOTHESPIN TO MARK WHICH CUE IS NEXT

one cue, meaning that the same number of flymen will need to review their cues, or *pulls*, all at once. Most often, each flyman is given a number to use as a reference when reading the cue sheet. Sometimes there is a change in personnel, and rather than changing the cue sheet, simply tell the new person their number.

The sheet should list the number of the rail cue, the numbers of the flymen involved, the name of the piece each will be pulling, its speed and direction, and the color of cue light on which the pull is to occur. *Cue lights* are double sets of small colored bulbs controlled by the stage

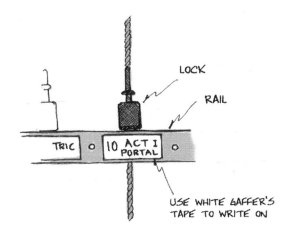

MARKING THE NAME OF A LINESET

LOCK

RAIL

TRIC 10 ACT I PORTAL

USE WHITE GAFFER'S TAPE TO WRITE ON

WAITING FOR THE CUE LIGHT TO GO OUT

manager. You may wish to use a red clothespin or some other small clamp to mark your place on the cue sheet. After a cue is taken, the pin is moved down to the next reference. When the cue light comes on, and the hands gather to check their next pull, the red pin marks the appropriate spot.

The cue light coming on is a warning to get ready for the cue. When the light goes out, the cue should be taken immediately. This method allows any number of flymen to see the command at one time, and synchronizes their moves. Trying to run a headset to each person would involve far too many pesky wires and would unnecessarily burden the stage manager with too many verbal commands. When there are a series of cues going in a close time period, it is best to use a different color of light for each section of the cue to reduce confusion. Switches at the stage manager's desk are used to control the cue lights, which are often used on the deck as well as the fly floor.

Running a fly cue involves knowing which lineset you are to use, the direction of travel (in or out), the speed, and the color of cue light. If your pull is downward so that the scenery flies into the view of the audience, you should unlock the lineset when the cue light comes on and stand ready. Watch the light carefully until it goes out. On that command, pull down on the rope until the trim mark is seen. Cover the mark with your hand, slow down the line as the trim mark approaches the lock, and stop it gently in the right spot. Remove your hand, and after checking to see that you are indeed correct, replace the lock and ring.

A *knuckle buster* is essentially a small clamp which may be attached to the purchase line at the low trim mark. It is too large to fit through the lock and is a certain means of assuring that the line cannot travel through the lock any farther than is intended. Even limited experience with a knuckle buster will well acquaint a novice flyman with the origins of its colorful name. They are a last resort and should be avoided in most situations.

Flying a piece out to its high trim is essentially the same as flying one in, but there are several important

KNUCKLE BUSTER

differences. Some pieces of scenery are quite heavy, and as a result, the amount of inertia to overcome in starting to move the lineset can be rather large and difficult to handle. Bear in mind that it is much easier to pull down on a rope than to pull up. You can use the back part of the purchase line (which runs opposite to the front part) to get a better start. Pull down on the back line, at least until the pipe is up to speed. As the trim mark comes down into view, you can stop by using downward force on the front line at the appropriate point.

Another difference about flying out is the position of the scenery just before the cue is taken. A piece ready to be flown out is in view of the audience. Often when a lock is pulled open the lines will tend to creep a bit, and this might be seen by the audience, or worse yet, by the stage manager. Grasp both the front and back lines together before the lock is opened and hold them together to prevent the scenery from moving visibly.

Many small nuances make a really experienced flyman an expert in the field, and I've listed just the basic methods in this chapter. Other methods are just as good, but I have found the practices outlined here to be the most easily understood and universally practiced. Perhaps the best advice is to simply watch carefully at all times and pay attention to what is happening around you. There will be many occasions when lines will foul, wrong lines will be pulled, or pieces will move in the wrong direction. If you are watchful, these mistakes can be caught when they are still relatively minor and corrected.

TERMS USED IN THIS CHAPTER

aircraft cable	double purchase system	purchase line
arbor	hemp rigging	rigging
batten	hemp rope	sandbag
batten heavy	in/out trim	sheave
belaying pin	knuckle buster	spreader plate
block: head, loft	lineset	tension pulley
bricks	loaders	trim
bull line	loading gallery or rail	trim chain
chain motor	marry battens together	T-track
cleat	operating line	T-track barrier
clew	overhauling	winch
counterweight system	pin rail	wire rope clamp
cue light	pipe	working load limit (WLL)
cue sheet	pipe weight	working piece
dead hung	pull	
deck	pulley	

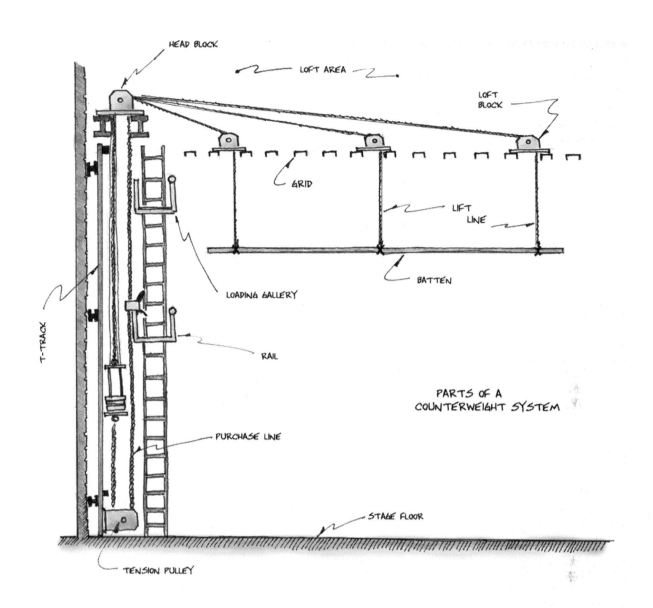

HEAD BLOCK

LOFT AREA

LOFT BLOCK

GRID

LIFT LINE

BATTEN

T-TRACK

LOADING GALLERY

RAIL

PARTS OF A COUNTERWEIGHT SYSTEM

PURCHASE LINE

STAGE FLOOR

TENSION PULLEY

CHAPTER 8

ARENA RIGGING

*A**RENA RIGGING* WAS developed to set up lights and sound in multi-purpose indoor arenas that are often used for things like ice shows and rock concerts. Wire rope similar to the aircraft cable in theatre rigging is used to suspend industrial-type *chain hoists* from the roof trusses. The chain hoists are then used to lift aluminum trusses, which have scenery and/or lights attached to them. The terms chain hoist and *chain motor* are interchangeable.

CHAIN MOTORS HAVE BEEN USED EXTENSIVELY
IN ARENA RIGGING FOR DECADES. THEY HAVE BECOME
INCREASINGLY IMPORTANT IN THEATRES IN RECENT YEARS.

CM Lodestar motors are by far the most common, although there are a couple of other types. The initials CM stand for Columbus McKinnon, the company that makes them. Lodestar is their premier model. Insurance companies feel better about lifting heavy loads over thousands of people in an audience if you use the best equipment available. An *inverted* type of hoist is made for use in the entertainment field. In a normal factory setting, hoists are

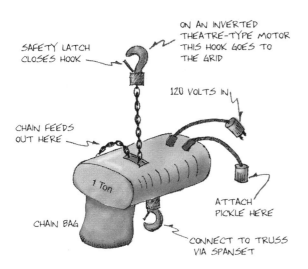

SAFETY LATCH CLOSES HOOK

ON AN INVERTED THEATRE-TYPE MOTOR THIS HOOK GOES TO THE GRID

120 VOLTS IN

CHAIN FEEDS OUT HERE

1 Ton

ATTACH PICKLE HERE

CHAIN BAG

CONNECT TO TRUSS VIA SPANSET

PARTS OF A CM CHAIN MOTOR/HOIST

THE CHAIN COMES OUT OF THE MOTOR AND INTO THE BAG. CONNECT THE FREE END OF THE CHAIN TO THE MOTOR TO HELP PREVENT IT FROM RUNNING.

semi-permanently attached to the ceiling by a swivel hook on the top of the motor. The chain hangs down, and a hook at the end of it is used to lift heavy loads in the same way a crane would do. In an arena, lifting the motor itself to the high ceiling is problematic because of its weight, so the hoists are reconfigured to operate upside down, with the chain hook in the air and the motor hook on the floor. When the hoist operates it lifts itself along with the load. These motors are designed to lift the full amount they are rated for, with a safety factor already considered.

Inside the hoist a sprocket connects with the chain, and as the motor turns the sprocket it also drives the chain. A very heavy-duty clutch inside the housing keeps the sprocket from slipping when the motor is turned off. The speed is not adjustable, but different motors are designed to run the chain at 16, 32, and 64 feet per minute. The 16 feet per minute type is standard, faster speeds are usually for some type of effect.

Chain motors are rated by how much weight they can lift. The *1 ton* size is by far the most common for entertainment purposes, but *2 ton* and *½ ton* are also available. Half ton motors are physically smaller and also use a smaller gauge chain, but the 2 ton variety is the same exact size as the 1 ton. The difference is made up by using an alternate chain hook that has a pulley connected to it. The chain is fed through the hook and back to the motor so that a 2 to 1 mechanical advantage is achieved. Columbus McKinnon makes many other types of hoists, but they aren't commonly used in the entertainment industry.

No matter what the type, the chain runs through the motor and is fed back out. As the motor lifts a load, the chain is gathered into a *chain bag* attached to the side. There are several different types, and some are better than others at preventing the chain from falling out of the bag on its own or *running*. That happens when enough chain misfeeds for its weight to pull all the rest of the chain out of the bag. The chains are heavy, and can cause serious damage when they run and hit some other part of the rigging, so you should take great care to arrange the bag so that doesn't happen. Usually, the free end of the chain is tethered to the motor itself so that if the chain were to run, it would only fall half its length.

Chains generally come in 60 or 80 foot lengths, meaning that the distance from the hook to the motor is about that long. Rigging the hook with wire rope from the ceiling increases the distance, so even if the ceiling of an arena is 85 feet tall, an 80 foot chain will probably still be long enough. Theatres are generally not that tall, and chain length is not usually an issue. Before rigging, stagehands must run the chain all the way out of the motor so that the hook to motor distance is at its maximum length. That is called *running the chain out*. The motors have a limiting device inside them that will (if it has been set) prevent the chain from coming all the

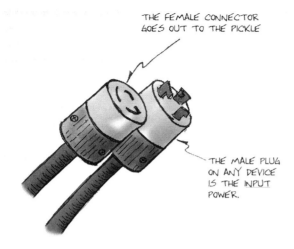

THE FEMALE CONNECTOR GOES OUT TO THE PICKLE

THE MALE PLUG ON ANY DEVICE IS THE INPUT POWER.

IF POWER WERE FED TO THE MALE CONNECTOR IT WOULD BE A CONSTANT SOURCE OF ELECTRICAL SHOCK

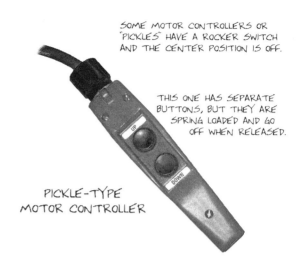

SOME MOTOR CONTROLLERS OR "PICKLES" HAVE A ROCKER SWITCH AND THE CENTER POSITION IS OFF.

THIS ONE HAS SEPARATE BUTTONS, BUT THEY ARE SPRING LOADED AND GO OFF WHEN RELEASED.

PICKLE-TYPE MOTOR CONTROLLER

IT IS IMPORTANT FOR THE SWITCH TO DISENGAGE THE POWER IF THE OPERATOR BECOMES DISTRACTED.

way out of the motor at the free end, or from hitting the hook at the hook end. The motor will stop on its own when the *limit* is reached. It is considered good practice to run the motor back a *bump* after reaching its limit so as to protect the inner workings of the motor during transport. To bump a motor means to turn it on and off rapidly. Additionally, the term is used to describe moving just a bit. You may be asked to "go up a bump" when setting the trim of a piece of truss.

Two, 1, and ½ ton entertainment motors generally work from a 120VAC 60 Hz power supply, which is the common North American line voltage. Two connectors are located on the motor. One is for the 120VAC input power, and the other is a lower voltage control circuit. In order to operate the motor you must connect it to a suitable power source, and then use a control mechanism to switch it on and off. The most common type of controller is called a *pickle*, and has a rocker switch on it with three positions. A spring inside automatically selects the center or off position, unless the operator intentionally presses and holds another setting. As a safety precaution, when the operator lets go of the button, the switch automatically shuts off the motor. The two other switch positions are up and down. That is achieved by having the motor run forward or backward so that the chain feeds either in or out. More complex switching mechanisms may run numerous motors all at the same time. Three-position toggle switches on a central panel are used to select up/off/down for the various motors in the system, and a GO button engages them all at once. Like the pickle, the GO button is spring loaded so that releasing it turns everything off automatically. This arrangement is sometimes known as a *dead-man switch*.

Most of the time in an arena, motors are used to hoist a system of trusses into the air. Scenery and lights are connected to the truss and fly out with it. That is a means of reducing the number of motors that would be needed

if each light were suspended from its own motor. The truss also keeps everything aligned and in the proper position. Aluminum *box truss* is the preferred type. Box truss is four-sided, while *delta truss* is three-sided and often made from steel. Box trusses are more heavy duty, and easier to connect together at angles, so they are the most commonly used. Motors in a theatre are most often used to hang lighting trusses, lighting towers, and speaker clusters. These units are designed with motor hoisting in mind. But motors may also be used to hoist scenic units in place, and care should be taken to find a safe hook up location on the piece so that lifting does not pull it apart. Sometimes there are built-in hard points in the scenery when lifting with a motor is foreseen during the construction process. Motors are an excellent way to lift heavy scenery parts that must be assembled on top

THIS ALUMINUM BOX TRUSS IS 12" SQUARE AND 10 FEET LONG. THE HARDWARE ON THE ENDPLATE CONNECTS WITH ANOTHER SECTION

BOX TRUSS

of some other unit, and can be thought of as a sort of impromptu crane.

Trusses were traditionally joined to the motors using *slings*, often called by the trade name *Spanset*. But in recent years the rules have changed because of a problem that can arise if there should be a fire in the theatre. In a fire, the synthetic Spansets can melt and fall apart, dropping their loads. Instead, metal cables are used, but the resulting slings are similar in outward appearance to the old ones. They are formed into a loop like a rubber band, so that there is no discernible end. They come in many different sizes. Typically, a sling is *choked* to the bottom horizontal member of the box truss, and then again around the top member. Identical slings are used on either side of the truss so that the ends of two loops are left at the top. These two loops are fitted into a shackle, and then into the hook that is on the motor. Just to be clear, in an inverted motor the chain hook is pulled up with the steel cables used to rig to the ceiling. That hook would already be connected to the overhead support structure, and the motor would be floating in the air by the time the trusses are connected. Thus the only hook available would be the motor hook.

THEN CHOKE SPANSET ON THE TOP OF THE TRUSS

FIRST CHOKE SPANSET ON THE BOTTOM OF THE TRUSS

CLIP SPANSETS FROM BOTH SIDES INTO MOTOR HOOK

When the motor is activated, and the hoist pulls the truss upward, the slings pick the truss up from the bottom, which is an arrangement that is less likely to pull it apart under load.

Excess chain should be fed into the chain bag from the free end first, so that the part nearest the motor outfeed goes in last. This will help keep the chain from becoming fouled when it feeds back out of the bag, and perhaps avoid its running out entirely. The free end of the chain is generally semi-permanently connected to the motor, but if not, you should at least tie it to the bag.

In an arena, steel cables are used to connect the motor's chain to the roof's support structure. In a theatre, the chains are often simply rigged to the grid itself using a pipe. This is especially true if the grid is the standard type constructed from heavy steel channels with spaces between them forming a slotted floor.

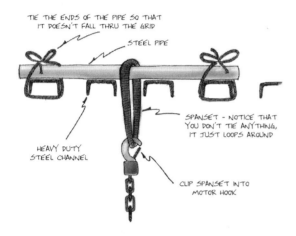

TIE THE ENDS OF THE PIPE SO THAT IT DOESN'T FALL THRU THE GRID

STEEL PIPE

SPANSET - NOTICE THAT YOU DON'T TIE ANYTHING, IT JUST LOOPS AROUND

HEAVY DUTY STEEL CHANNEL

CLIP SPANSET INTO MOTOR HOOK

THIS METHOD ONLY WORKS WITH A HEAVY DUTY STEEL GRID

If the chain is long enough to reach the grid all on its own, clip a sling through the hook on the chain and pull it up through a space in the grid at the desired location using a bowline. Slide a piece of *schedule 40*, 1.5″ ID or larger pipe through the sling and set the rig down across the grid channels with the pipe at a 90 degree angle to them. The channels should be no more than 4 inches apart, so the pipe is spanning a very small distance. Use some small line to tie off the ends of the pipe to the channel steel so that it does not accidentally turn sideways and fall through the slot. That is really just a safety against it being kicked while rigging, because under load the pipe will be pressed very firmly against the grid. The tie line has no real load on it. This method will only work in a theatre with an old-style, heavy-duty steel channel grid. It would be very dangerous to try this on an expanded metal, or cable style of grid; so don't do that! If you are not sure, then rig your load from the loft block wells instead.

If you do not have a standard grid with channel steel, you may be able to hang from the *wells* that support the loft blocks, a pair of large beams. Since they run up and down stage, you can pick a spot that has the proper up/down location. Wells are formed with much larger steel than the rest of the grid. The wells must support the weight of the batten loads, plus the weight of the bricks

USING ROPES TO RAISE THE RIGGING

Chapter 6 discusses ropes and knot tying, and has a thorough description of how to tie the most important rigging knot, the *bowline*. A bowline is used to create a fixed loop in the end of the rope, and is very useful for raising and lowering the steel cables used to hang chain motors. Tie the bowline so that the line of the loop goes through the sling if you are rigging to a channel steel theatre grid, or through the center shackle of the rig, if you are doing a bridle or dead hang with wire rope. The bowline knot will be easy to untie after the rig is secure. A large diameter, woven exterior nylon fiber rope is best for this work, because it is very supple and bends well—making the knots easier to tie. A larger rope is easier to grip, which is important when pulling up the heavy chain by hand.

USE A THICK, 3/4″ LINE FOR RIGGING.

THE THICKER THE ROPE, THE EASIER IT IS TO GRIP AND PULL UP.

TIE A BOWLINE THRU THE SPANSET AND USE THAT TO PULL THE RIG UP TO THE GRID

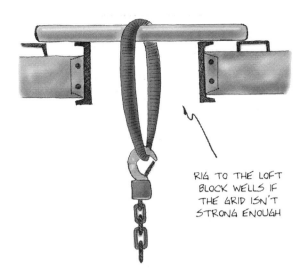

RIG TO THE LOFT
BLOCK WELLS IF
THE GRID ISN'T
STRONG ENOUGH

common diameter for the wire rope is ⅜″ because its load rating matches the load capacity of a 1 ton motor. Half inch diameter steel is used for a 2 ton motor. The end of the steel is made into a loop by passing it around a *thimble*. The resulting *eye* is used together with a *shackle*, in connecting pieces together. Steel comes in standard lengths of 2, 5, 10, 20, and 30 feet. They can be shackled together to form different lengths.

Shackles are used to connect the different parts of the rig together. When ⅜″ steel cable is used, a ⅝″ shackle is considered standard. Larger or smaller shackles might not properly fit through the eye of the thimble. A shackle has three distinct parts, the *pin*, the *bell*, and the *hubs*.

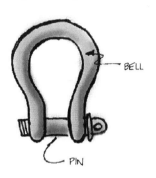

BELL

PIN

PARTS OF A SHACKLE

in the arbor, so they are usually very strong. Inch and a half schedule 40 steel pipe should be large enough to bridge the gap between the beams and hold the weight of a 1 ton motor and its load. If the span of the opening is more than a foot, you may want to use a larger piece of pipe, perhaps two or 3 inch in diameter, but otherwise the method of hanging the motor from the well is pretty much the same as hanging from the grid.

When rigging from the channel steel grid, correct placement is easy, because the channels fall every few inches left to right, and the open slot runs continuously up and down stage. So the rig can go most anywhere. If you must rig from the wells, you can still locate the rig at any point up and down stage (as long as you go between two loft blocks) but placement left and right can be a problem. If the well is not in the proper left to right location, you can use a *bridle* to adjust the rigging.

Bridles require the use of wire rope. In stagehand lingo, this wire rope is simply called *steel*. The most

When connecting two pieces of steel, the eye of one rests on the bell, and the pin is inserted through the eye of the other. Never use a shackle when the load rests only on the two sides because that tends to deform the bell, and places stress on the pin threads. You can buy shackles with cotter pins that hold the shackle pin in place, but they aren't intended for this type of rigging. The pins should have machine threads on them.

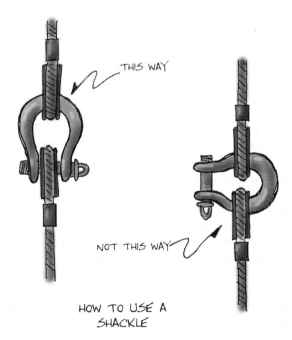

3/8″ STEEL CABLE

THIMBLE IS USED TO
FORM THE EYE

SWAGE

EYE
AT THE END OF A
STEEL CABLE

THIS WAY

NOT THIS WAY

HOW TO USE A
SHACKLE

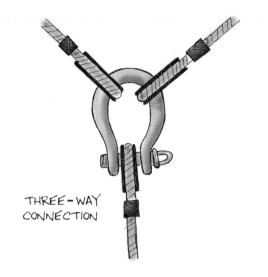

THREE-WAY
CONNECTION

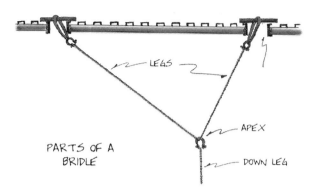

PARTS OF A
BRIDLE

LEGS

APEX

DOWN LEG

Shackles can also connect three points in a Y shape by using the bell for two of them, and the pin for the third. This type of configuration is used when forming the apex of a bridle.

Deck chain can be used to create a longer length by using a specific number of the 4 inch links, in the same way trim chains are used in standard theatrical rigging. Chains of this sort come from modern cargo ships, and are very heavy.

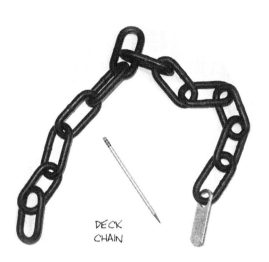

DECK
CHAIN

A simple rig that hangs straight down is call a *dead hang*, but when two pieces of steel are used in conjunction with the motor chain to form a "Y" shape, the result is known as a *bridle*. The parts of a bridle include the two *legs*, which are the two uppermost sections, and the *downleg*, which forms the vertical, lower part of the Y. The downleg could be simply the motor chain, or it could be another piece of steel if the chain isn't long enough. The intersection of the three parts of the Y is called the *apex*. A shackle forms the center of the apex and connects all the parts together.

An even bridle from two wells will make the rig hang dead center between the two points, and is formed by

using the same length steel on each leg. Uneven bridles are formed by using different lengths of steel rope on the two sides. If one of the legs is made up of a standard length piece of steel, you can design a length for the other that will make the rig fall in the exact spot you wish to hang your load. A bit of geometry is involved, having to do with congruent triangles and the *Pythagorean Theorem* of $a^2 + b^2 = c^2$. You can buy a computer program, or even an app to do the math for you, but it is good to know how to find the numbers the old-fashioned way.

A Practical Example

Imagine that the wells in the theatre are 15 feet apart. You would like to hang the rig so that it is 5 feet from one and 10 feet from the other. A diagram looks like this:

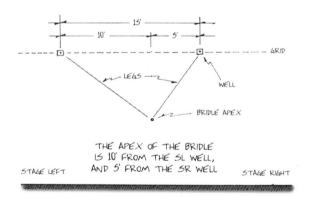

15'

10'   5'

GRID

LEGS

WELL

BRIDLE APEX

THE APEX OF THE BRIDLE
IS 10' FROM THE SL WELL,
AND 5' FROM THE SR WELL

STAGE LEFT   STAGE RIGHT

Arbitrarily select a reasonable length for one of the legs. Bear in mind that a bridle that hangs down more is easier to hang, and puts less stress on the equipment. But a bridle that hangs down too far may place the apex so low that the motor will not be able to fly out far enough. For our example let's pick a 15 foot bridle leg. Now our diagram looks like this:

You know the dimensions of two sides of one right triangle, because the apex hangs 10 feet over from the well, and the angular hypotenuse distance is 15 feet. Solve the equation $a^2 + 10^2 = 15^2$ to determine the distance from

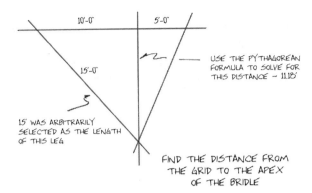

15' WAS ARBITRARILY SELECTED AS THE LENGTH OF THIS LEG

USE THE PYTHAGOREAN FORMULA TO SOLVE FOR THIS DISTANCE ~ 11.18'

FIND THE DISTANCE FROM THE GRID TO THE APEX OF THE BRIDLE

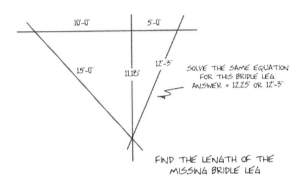

SOLVE THE SAME EQUATION FOR THIS BRIDLE LEG. ANSWER = 12.25' OR 12'-3"

FIND THE LENGTH OF THE MISSING BRIDLE LEG

connect the rig, and others. Since so many shackles are used to connect the example above, the chain link could probably be left out, or you could add an extra shackle. The standard tolerance for this type of rigging is usually 1 foot, and so close is close enough.

You may need to attach the two legs of the bridle to something other than a pipe on the grid. If you want to hook the bridle up to one side of the well or some other steel beam instead, use a *basket* to make the connection. A basket is a loop made from a 5' (or 10' if the beam is large) piece of steel. You should make the loop using two shackles so that one holds both the thimble of the 5' steel, and the other is used to make the connection.

5' STEEL

HOOKUP SHACKLE

USE THE HOOK UP SHACKLE TO ATTACH THE BRIDLE

PARTS OF A BASKET

the grid, down to the apex. The answer is ~11.18 feet. So now our diagram looks like this:

The base and altitude of the second congruent right triangle are already known and the same formula can be used to determine the missing bridle leg length. $11.18^2 + 5^2 = c^2$. The answer is 12.25 feet or 12'-3". Taking into consideration the standard parts available, this length can be made up from adding 10' + 2' + one 4" link from a deck chain. Shackles are used to connect the parts together.

In reality, there are a few more variables like the length of the sling used, the number of shackles used to

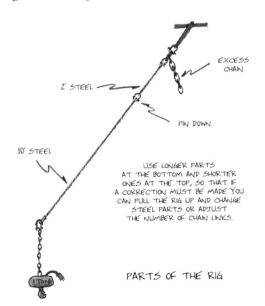

EXCESS CHAIN

2' STEEL

PIN DOWN

10' STEEL

USE LONGER PARTS AT THE BOTTOM AND SHORTER ONES AT THE TOP, SO THAT IF A CORRECTION MUST BE MADE YOU CAN PULL THE RIG UP AND CHANGE STEEL PARTS OR ADJUST THE NUMBER OF CHAIN LINKS.

PARTS OF THE RIG

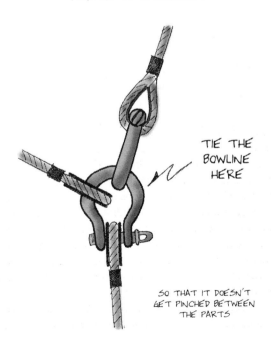

TIE THE BOWLINE HERE

SO THAT IT DOESN'T GET PINCHED BETWEEN THE PARTS

The large diameter rope is used to pull the rig up to the grid. Tie your bowline through the bell of the connecting shackle, to the outside of the 5′ steel. If you tie it between the steel and the hook-up shackle, there is a tendency for the two of them to pinch in on the rope, making it difficult to remove.

Pull the basket up to the beam and wrap the 5′ steel around the beam. Remove the pin from the shackle and use it to connect the free end of the steel. Frequently, a burlap bag, or perhaps a rubber pad are used to lessen the kink that forms when the steel meets the sharp corner of the beam.

TERMS USED IN THIS CHAPTER

1 ton motor	chain motor	running
2 ton motor	choke	schedule 40 pipe
apex	CM Lodestar	shackle bell
arbor	dead-man switch	shackle hub
arena rigging	deck chain	shackle pin
basket	downleg	sling
bowline	inverted motor	Spanset
box truss delta truss	limit	steel-wire rope
bridle	pickle	tension pulley
bump	pipe	thimble/eye
chain bag	Pythagorean Theorem	trim
chain hoist	run the chain out	wells

THINGS IN A SCENE SHOP

CHAPTER 9

HAND TOOLS

ONCE UPON A TIME, when speaking to my class about tools, I would begin my remarks with the statement that tools are really just an extension of our own bodies. And then continue with how our fingers can grasp things but a wrench or a pair of pliers can do it with more force, which is a normal humanistic approach to the subject. One year as I was standing before the class prepared to say just that, a student remarked, "You're not going to tell us that tools are an extension of our own bodies, are you?" and of course I said no. At least until now. I guess I wasn't the first person to think of that. Even so, it is good to approach a technical subject like tools by seeing how they relate to human beings.

CABINET FOR HAND TOOLS
IN A UNIVERSITY SCENE SHOP

MEASURING AND MARKING TOOLS

Undoubtedly, the most commonly used measuring tool is the measuring tape. It's a tool that seems obvious and self-explanatory at first glance, but it is actually much more complex than you might think. Physically, the standard type consists of a thin metal strip rolled up inside a plastic or metal housing. This strip is called the *blade*, and it is connected to a wind-up spring that retracts it into the housing. The blade is curved from side to side so that it has a certain rigidity when extended. That is to say that it stiffens and can be played out to a distant point. The width of the blade (the best are 1 inch wide) governs how far it can reach, and narrow blades will not go as far. Generally, there is a button or catch of some sort that locks the blade in an extended position.

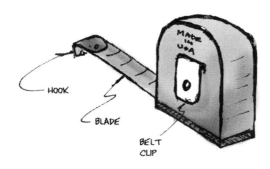

TAPE MEASURE

A bent metal piece on the end of the blade is used to snag on the end of a board that you are measuring. On close inspection, the *hook* appears to be quite loose, and the casual observer might attribute this looseness to shoddy workmanship on the part of the manufacturer.

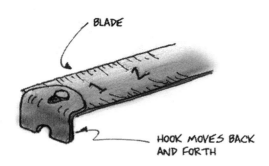

HOOK MOVES BACK AND FORTH

There is, however, a reason for the hook's looseness. It is intended to shift position in order to accommodate both inside and outside measurements. The hook does that by moving back and forth to account for its own thickness. When used to measure the inside of a space (such as the inside of a cabinet) the hook slides toward the user, making its outside the point of absolute zero. When hooked over the end of a board it extends outward, making its inside the point of absolute zero.

You can adjust the accuracy of a tape measure by bending the hook. Using a pair of pliers, bend the hook until the tape reads accurately when tested against an object of known size. If the hook has been flattened out by stepping on it or some other misadventure, it should be readjusted before further use.

The blade is marked with a series of numbers and lines used to reference measurements. Most tapes can measure an object down to the closest sixteenth of an inch, which is the distance between the smallest marks on the blade.

The fractional sizes used in woodworking may seem quite odd at first when compared to the metric system, but they are actually derived in a very logical way that comes from dividing distances in half. Notice that the fractional marks between inches are differing lengths. The longest mark is used to indicate one half of an inch. The two next-longest marks indicate one-half of that distance, either one-quarter or three-quarters of an inch. Next is one-eighth inch difference, and finally the smallest lines are used to measure one-sixteenth of an inch. One-sixteenth is equal to half of a half of a half of a half of an inch. If you are unsure which lines represent which fraction, simply look in the middle of the inch to find the half, the middle of the half to find the quarter, the middle of the quarter to find the eighth, and the middle of the eighth to find the sixteenth. Or count how many of a particular size space are between two inch marks. If there are eight of them, then those are the ⅛" spaces and/or marks.

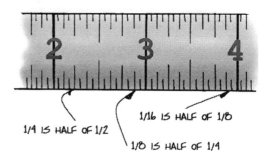

1/4 IS HALF OF 1/2
1/16 IS HALF OF 1/8
1/8 IS HALF OF 1/4

Notice that the numbering system on a tape measure has two different sets of numbers, one along either edge of the blade. The first consists of numbers that are all inches. Twenty-five feet, a common tape measure length, is equal to 300 inches. On the other side both feet and inches are shown, so that you have measurements such as 10 feet 2 inches. That could also be expressed as 122 inches. Look from side to side on the blade to convert systems. Dimensions listed on a plan sometimes use one method and sometimes the other, so the tape is manufactured to accommodate either one. If you are ever looking at a plan, and would like to convert feet and inches to just inches, you can look up the answer by cross referencing it on the tape rather than by multiplying.

Another series of numbers is marked in red ink or in some other special way. They start at 16 and continue onward to include 32, 48, 64, 80, 96, and so forth. These numbers are, of course, multiples of 16. They are printed red to make them easier to locate. Sixteen inches is the normal center spacing for framing members, like studs in the wall of a house. Most tools are designed for the home construction market rather than for scenery building. This can sometimes leave us with extraneous information, but in this case you may find occasions to also frame scenery on 16 inch centers.

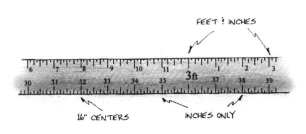

TAPE MEASURE MARKINGS

Another type of tape measure is more often used in the theatre itself rather than in the shop. A 50 or 100 foot cloth or *steel tape* that can be reeled in like a fishing rod is helpful for laying out the locations of large units of scenery. This kind of tape is also used for measuring the trim heights of battens by lightly attaching the end of the measuring tape to the batten with adhesive gaffer's tape and then flying the batten out. Hold the correct distance marking to the floor with your foot, and when the tape becomes taut, the proper height has been reached. It is fine to step on this kind of a tape measure because

STEEL TAPES ARE DIFFERENT, BECAUSE THEY ARE MEANT TO MEASURE LARGER DISTANCES. THE BLADE DOESN'T RETRACT ON ITS OWN.

it is already flat. Repeatedly stepping on a tape with a curved blade will eventually ruin it.

A *framing square* can be used for both measuring and marking. There are many different types of squares, but this one gets its name because it is often used in laying out the framing (or structure—studs, joists, and rafters) of a house. The best framing squares are made of aluminum because that makes them lightweight and rustproof. There are inch markings along all the sides.

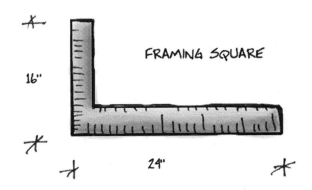

FRAMING SQUARE

Because this tool is often used to compute roof pitches, some of the markings may be in twelfths of an inch rather than in sixteenths of an inch. Roof pitches are expressed by stating a rise and a run in twelfths of an inch, such as $9/12$ or $12/12$. Twelfths of an inch will not work if you are measuring sixteenths or eighths. Be aware of that when using this square as a measuring tool. The framing square is most often used to check or create 90 degree angle corners, and to mark stair carriages.

A relative of the framing square is the *Speed Square* which is used in much the same manner. Speed Squares are smaller and sturdier than their larger cousins and also have a lip along one edge to make it easier to line them up with a board. They are very commonly used to mark the alignment of framing members. Speed Square is

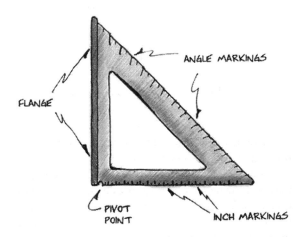

SPEED SQUARE

capitalized because it is a name of a specific brand. There are knock-off brands with names like "fast square."

Drywall squares look like a large metal version of the T-square that was once used for drafting. They are not terribly accurate, but they make excellent straight edges and are also useful for jobs such as laying out where nails should go in order to run into hidden framing when you are building hard-cover flats or platforms.

BLUE CHALK

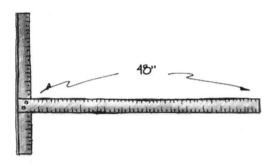

DRYWALL SQUARE

The *chalk line* is excellent for marking long straight lines. This tool consists of a fishing-type reel housed in a box filled with chalk dust. String on the reel becomes coated with the chalk. If the string is stretched between two points it will form a straight line, and snapping (pulling the string up slightly and letting it go) the string will leave chalk dust on the surface of whatever you are marking. Be sure to stretch the string tautly, in order to assure that the line is really straight.

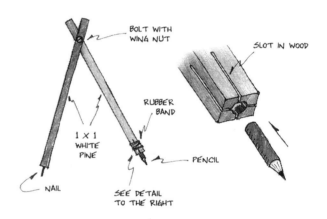

LARGE SHOP-BUILT COMPASS

A large wooden *compass* is essential for marking circles. You can easily construct this one from scrap lumber and a bolt.

For even larger circles, *trammel points* are used. These are essentially small clamps that can be attached to a wooden slat. One of the clamps forms a pivot point while the other holds a pencil. Two slats can be joined together if necessary. This type of rig is much more accurate than the old "string and a pencil" method. If trammel points are not available, a very satisfactory shop-built compass can be put together with slats of wood, a nail, and a hole drilled for the pencil. This alternative method is not quite as easy to use, but it can give excellent results.

Levels are used to check objects to see if they are level to the horizon, or *plumb* with a line that is perpendicular to the horizon. Those are the proper terms, level being flat, and plumb being upright. Most levels have several small vials with air bubbles inside of them. The vials are placed so that they are either in line with the length of the tool or perpendicular to it. That facilitates using the level either horizontally or vertically. A level with a

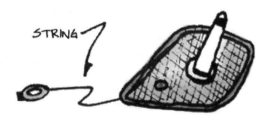

CHALK LINE

It is often easier to run the string past the two marks so that the line is longer than you really need. If the points are extremely far apart, have a third person hold the center of the string, and snap the line twice, once from either side.

Shake the box and hold it with the pointy end down to get extra chalk on the string as it comes out of the tool. Chalk is usually blue, but other colors are available. The red is meant to make semi-permanent lines in concrete, so you may have trouble getting that color off if you use it for woodworking. Painters like to use powdered charcoal instead of chalk.

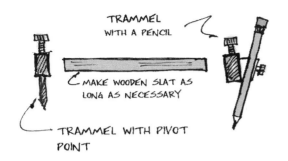

TRAMMEL WITH A PENCIL

MAKE WOODEN SLAT AS LONG AS NECESSARY

TRAMMEL WITH PIVOT POINT

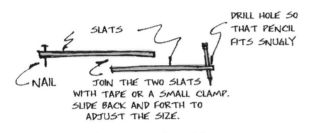

SLATS

DRILL HOLE SO THAT PENCIL FITS SNUGLY

NAIL

JOIN THE TWO SLATS WITH TAPE OR A SMALL CLAMP. SLIDE BACK AND FORTH TO ADJUST THE SIZE.

USING TWO STICKS

TWO METHODS OF MARKING LARGE CIRCLES

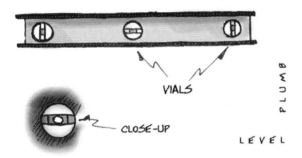

VIALS

PLUMB

CLOSE-UP

LEVEL

WHEN THE BUBBLE IS CENTERED THE OBJECT IS LEVEL OR PLUMB

longer body is generally more accurate. Short levels with magnets on them are very nice when working with steel tubing. Each vial has two marks toward its center. The middle of the vial bulges slightly to help steady the bubble inside. When the bubble is directly between the two marks, the level is in proper alignment.

Wrenches, Pliers, etc.

These tools are used for gripping and turning and come in a multitude of varieties for special purposes. A choice should be made as to which tool is the most appropriate for a particular task. Using the wrong tool can be very frustrating, while using the right one will make any job easier.

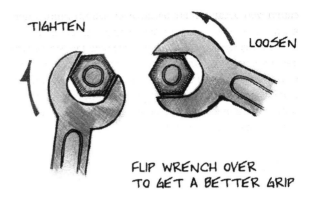

TIGHTEN

LOOSEN

FLIP WRENCH OVER TO GET A BETTER GRIP

The most commonly used wrench in most theatres is the *Crescent* or *adjustable wrench*. The Crescent tool company invented this type of wrench, and in modern usage any brand of adjustable wrench is often referred to as a Crescent or "C" wrench. A Crescent by any name is identifiable by its peculiar half-moon shape. The jaws of the wrench can be adjusted to different sizes by turning a screw-threaded device with your thumb. A C wrench is essential when hanging or focusing lights, since lighting equipment uses so many different sizes and types of bolts.

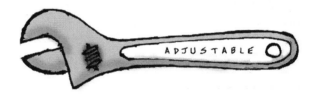

ADJUSTABLE

CRESCENT WRENCH

An *open-end wrench* is similar in appearance to a Crescent wrench except that it is not adjustable. A set of these wrenches is required in order to possess the different sizes. Quite often there are actually two different sizes incorporated into the same wrench, one at either end. Notice that the ends are fixed at an angle to the body of the tool. This allows you to get a wider range of motion when using the wrench in a small space. You can get a better angle to start from in tight quarters if you flip the wrench over each time you reposition it.

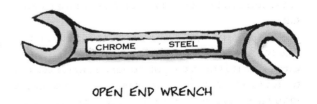

CHROME   STEEL

OPEN END WRENCH

A *box-end wrench* wraps entirely around a hex-headed bolt and makes for the surest possible grip. When a C-wrench slips off while you are turning a bolt, the corners of the head are damaged. Sometimes they become so rounded off that a wrench will no longer work. Box-end wrenches are less prone to slipping and damaging the bolt. They generally come in sets that are double ended, just like the open-ended wrenches.

BOX END WRENCH

Socket wrenches are very similar to box-end wrenches in the way that they grip a bolt head. The difference lies in the method of attaching a handle.

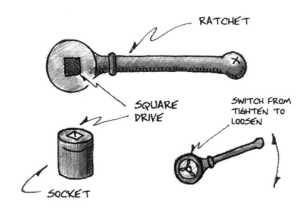

RATCHET

SQUARE DRIVE

SWITCH FROM TIGHTEN TO LOOSEN

SOCKET

SOCKET WRENCH

Sockets typically use a ratcheting handle that can be set to turn freely one way and grip in the other. This negates the need to remove the wrench from the bolt head in order to gain fresh purchase, and makes for especially speedy tightening and loosening. Deep sockets are useful when the end of the bolt protrudes a good distance through the nut and might cause the wrench to bottom out with a normal shallow socket.

The *drive* of the ratchet refers to the size of the square nub that fits into the top of the socket. The most common drive size is ⅜″.

Screwdrivers are relatively self-explanatory, other than to say that the tips must correspond to the *drive* of the screw. The most popular types of drive are slotted and Phillips, which everyone is familiar with from everyday life. Square drive and Torx are also available. Torx drives and screws have an asterisk shape to them. Screwdrivers

METRIC VS. AMERICAN SAE

Metric wrenches are made in millimeter sizes for metric bolts. They have numbers like 10 or 12 on them. 12mm is fairly close to ½ inch, but still the wrenches aren't interchangeable. Any product manufactured in a country other than the USA most likely uses metric bolts. In recent years, any product made in America, but likely to be exported also uses metric bolts.

In the USA, wrenches are made to the SAE standard, the Society of Automotive Engineers. They are fractional sizes like ⅜ or ⁹⁄₁₆. Virtually all fasteners for woodworking still use the SAE standard, so those wrenches are needed for stage carpentry work.

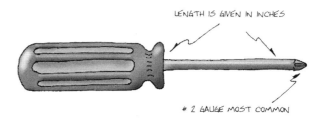

LENGTH IS GIVEN IN INCHES

\# 2 GAUGE MOST COMMON

PHILLIPS HEAD SCREWDRIVER

come in different sizes, both in length and diameter. The diameter is a gauge size, and the #2 is appropriate for a #8 wood screw of the sort that is used to attach hinges to a flat. In modern times, a battery powered screw gun is often used to install screws, and they use special tips with the same drive shapes. The hardware chapter has more to say about screw drives.

Pliers are the most quintessential gripping tool, and the most likely to be considered an "extension of the human body." Most pliers are *not* designed to be used on bolt heads, and indeed will often scar a bolt or nut and make it difficult to deal with later on. So don't use them in that way. Some types of pliers are really meant to be used as cutting tools and not with any type of fastener at all.

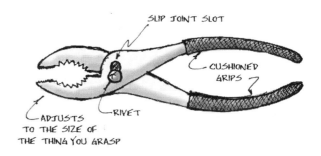

SLIP JOINT SLOT

CUSHIONED GRIPS

ADJUSTS TO THE SIZE OF THE THING YOU GRASP

RIVET

SLIP-JOINT PLIERS

Slip-joint pliers are the most common type. They can be used for gripping and holding different-sized objects when fingers are not strong enough. The slip-joint part comes from the fact that the rivet holding the two halves together can be adjusted, allowing the jaws to accommodate either very small pieces or very large pieces, depending on the placement of the rivet. This tool has a wide range of uses, such as gripping small wires or crimping together an S hook.

Needle-nose pliers are very similar, but have a long, pointy snout for small objects.

NEEDLE-NOSE PLIERS

Vise Grips (another brand name) are specialized pliers that can clamp and lock into place with great force. They are adjustable for a wide range of sizes. Vise Grips have an amazingly large variety of uses when you need a tool that can be clamped in place. They are particularly handy for removing stripped-out screws when there is enough of the head or body sticking out to get a grip on it.

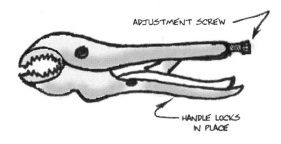

VISE GRIPS

Diagonal pliers or "dikes" are actually intended to cut pieces of wire or small metal hardware like pins or nails. You may also find them to be an excellent tool for misapplied pneumatic nails or staples. Use them to grip, rather than cut through the nail, and then twist the dikes and pull the nail out. The twisting motion is meant to

DIAGONAL PLIERS

gain leverage, just like a claw hammer. Of course this won't work on larger sizes of hand driven nails because the amount of force you would need is too large.

Bolt cutters. These really aren't pliers at all, but they are kind of similar in appearance. As the name implies, this tool can be used to cut off bolts, but also chain, metal rods, and the occasional padlock.

BOLT CUTTERS

You can get much more leverage on the cut if you place the bolt as far as possible into the jaws of the cutters, close to the pivot point. Padlocks are made with hardened steel and will ruin your bolt cutters after a few cuts.

Pipe or "monkey" wrenches are intended to grip a round object, most often a pipe. They are adjustable to fit different pipe sizes. *Pipe wrenches* only grip in one direction at a time and thus must be flipped over in order to go from tightening to loosening. (So any monkey wrench can be left-handed if you just turn it over.) If you are connecting two pipes with a coupling, use two wrenches facing in opposite directions.

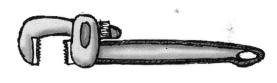

PIPE WRENCH

The Felco company invented this type of *cable cutting pliers*, which tend to be rather pricey. Felco cutters are meant to cut aircraft cable, and other types of wire rope. They are more delicate than you would think, and shouldn't be used to cut other ordinary objects. The jaws are angled so that the front part comes together first,

TIPS COME TOGETHER FIRST AND TRAP THE CABLE FOR A CLEAN CUT

CABLE CUTTER JAWS

which forces the cable inward and greatly reduces the amount of fraying that occurs when making the cut. An ordinary pair of dikes won't do that. The 7″ size cutters are big enough for ⅛″ aircraft cable used to hang most theatre scenery. You will need something larger for ¼″ cable used to rig battens.

HAMMERS AND MALLETS

There are two basic categories for hammers: those used for driving nails, and all others. Nail driving hammers are of course the most common in a woodworking shop. Other types include rubber mallets, sledge hammers, wooden mallets, and ball peen hammers. This second grouping is used for various tasks like demolition and metalworking.

The standard nail-driving hammer has a 16-ounce head, although they are also manufactured in lighter and heavier weights. There is a *curved claw* version and a *straight claw* type. The claw is the opposite side from the portion used to pound in nails. The curved claw is best for removing nails, as it allows the user to rock the hammer along the claw to gain leverage and more easily pry out the nail. A straight claw is easier to slip in between boards and pry them apart. Either one is about the same when it comes to driving nails.

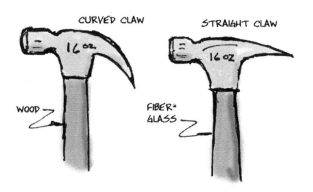

WOODWORKING HAMMERS

There is a definite difference in the quality of various hammers. The steel used in the head of the hammer should be hard enough not to wear away or be deformed by nails. You may have seen cheap hammers made from very soft steel whose claws have been bent and twisted from the force of removing nails. On the other end of the spectrum, if a hammer is made from steel that is too hard, it may be brittle as a result. Chips of the hammer head itself can shatter and fly away and are very dangerous. Some years ago, OSHA came up with guidelines for manufacturers about grinding some steel from the striking area of hammers to make them less likely to chip. You can see that the edges of a hammer are chamfered at a 45 degree angle.

The handle of a hammer is also important. It should be sturdy and unlikely to break. Steel handles are sturdiest, but they transmit a high degree of shock and vibration to the elbow. Prolonged use may result in tendonitis. Wooden or fiberglass handles are really the best. When using a hammer, try to keep in mind that it is intended for driving nails and not for pounding concrete or steel beams or other such items.

Using a hammer to drive nails takes a moderate amount of skill gained through practice. Holding the handle near its end increases the amount of leverage and hence force that is transmitted to the driving of the nail. However, the same statement can be applied to striking your thumb if your aim is not very good. Your thumbs will no doubt appreciate choking up a bit on the handle until your hand-eye coordination catches up with your enthusiasm. In this modern age of pneumatic nail guns

START OUT HOLDING THE HAMMER LIKE THIS

AND WORK YOUR WAY UP TO THIS AS YOUR SKILLS IMPROVE

and staplers, hammers have become somewhat outmoded, but skill with this basic tool is still important.

Rubber mallets are used when a soft, cushioned blow is required. The same is true of plastic or wooden types. Forcing together mortise and tenon joints and putting the lid on a can of paint are both examples of this concept. *Sledgehammers* are used primarily for demolition, although a large, rubber-coated Deadblow (trade name) is excellent for forcing decking pieces into place. *Ball peen hammers* are intended exclusively for the shaping of sheets of metal. You probably won't have much need for them unless you are crafting props or some other specialty item.

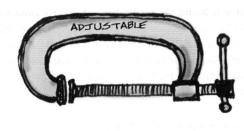

C-CLAMP

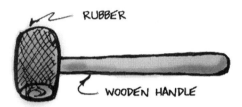

RUBBER MALLET

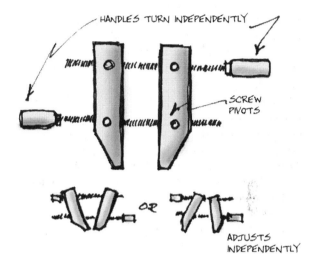

WOODEN CLAMP

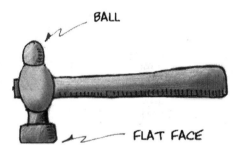

BALL PEEN HAMMER

Clamps

Clamps are used to hold things together. There are many various types, because there are many different kinds and shapes of things to hold together. The most common type is the *c-clamp*. The origin of the name should be obvious from its appearance. These clamps come in many sizes, but the 4 inch variety seems to be the most useful in a theatre shop because the jaw opens wide enough for two 2×4s and/or anything smaller. This type of clamp has very great holding power, but it may leave indentations on soft materials such as white pine lumber. If this is likely to be a problem, use some small blocks of scrap lumber as pads.

Wooden clamps are useful because they have very deep jaws and can clamp the interior of an item far from the edge of the piece. They are also the most adjustable for clamping at odd angles, but learning to operate the jaws

can take a bit of practice. This clamp is less likely to leave depression marks on your work.

Pipe and/or *bar clamps* are useful for clamping items that are very wide or long. They can be used for squeezing in or adjusting the framing of platforms or flats. A bit of room is required in order to turn the handle and tighten the clamp. Pipe clamps are made from a length of ¾" steel pipe and some commercially manufactured ends. You can make up virtually any length of clamp since this type uses pipe ordinarily found lying around the shop. Oftentimes it is handy to have a clamp longer than an 8 foot sheet of plywood, and a pipe clamp of that size is easily made up. When a less cumbersome size is required, you can exchange the long pipe for a shorter one. Bar clamps work the same way, but you are stuck with the length of flat bar that came with the clamp.

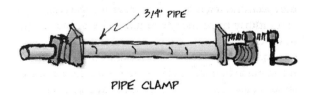

PIPE CLAMP

Vise Grip clamps are very easy to put on and have a great amount of holding power. The somewhat pointy ends of the clamp can be useful when the item being clamped is small. Once the size of the opening has been properly set, it is very easy to apply and/or remove this clamp. They are great for welding tabs and/or hinges onto square tubing. The mechanics of the handles are just like the pliers, but the jaws have been replaced with a clamp shape.

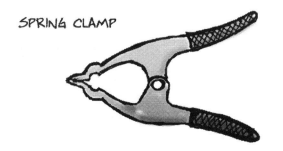

VISE GRIP CLAMP

Spring clamps are somewhat like giant clothes pins. They do not have a terrific amount of holding power but are very easy to attach. They are quite popular for pinning back stage draperies and other lightweight chores.

SPRING CLAMP

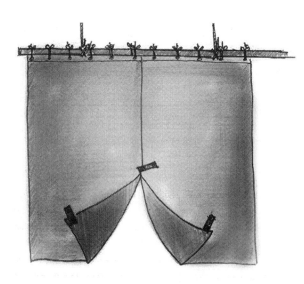

USE SPRING CLAMPS TO HOLD
THE CURTAINS OPEN

HAND-HELD POWER TOOLS

There are two basic types of small power tools. They are separated by the kind of power used to operate them. The most common and well-known power source is electricity, either from a wall outlet or a battery. Tools powered by compressed air are known as *pneumatic tools*, they are less well known to the public, but very important in a shop. There are pneumatic versions of virtually all tools. Some of them are not nearly as efficient as their electric counterparts, but pneumatic nail guns and staplers are much more efficient than electric ones. Of course you need an *air compressor* to use them. A compressor and its delivery system of pipes and hoses represents a sizable monetary investment, but one that is well worth the investment for a shop when compared to the resulting savings in time and labor.

A LARGE CAPACITY AIR COMPRESSOR

AN ELECTRIC MOTOR DRIVES A PISTON
THAT COMPRESSES AIR INTO THE TANK

BE SAFE!

A lot of safety is just plain old common sense. If something looks dangerous, then it probably is. But tools have hidden dangers that aren't so intuitive. Be sure to read, understand, and follow all of the safety rules that come with any power tool. Always wear safety glasses when using power tools.

ELECTRICAL TOOLS

Recent years have brought major breakthroughs in battery technology, especially ones used in a variety of power tools. Battery-powered drills and/or screw guns are the most popular, with the obvious advantage being a greater freedom of movement when the tool is free from a power cord that must be dragged about. Modern battery-powered drills are almost as powerful as their corded cousins, and the batteries last for hours even under heavy use. You may still need an older, corded drill for heavy jobs like using a paint mixer, or drilling large holes in concrete, but battery power is the best choice for day-to-day work.

The voltage rating of a battery makes a big difference in how well it works. The higher the voltage, the greater the *torque* it can produce. Torque in this case measures the rotating power of a motor, and on a tool this generally relates to how well it will drill, cut, or saw. There are different quality levels of most tools, and battery-operated drills and saws are no exception. The better batteries have a rating of 18 volts, which is enough to fully power a tool. Good batteries are somewhat expensive, and you may find that the cost of batteries is more than the cost of the tool itself.

Very recently lithium-ion batteries have begun to replace the older nickel-cadmium types. The Li-ion batteries don't necessarily work any better than the older types, but Ni-Cad batteries have been shown to be extremely toxic and are no longer allowed in some

GREEN IDEAS TIP BOX

Recycle Your Batteries!

Nickel-cadmium and lithium-ion battery technology is what makes the new cordless world spin. They can be recharged hundreds of times, but eventually they will wear out and no longer work. When that happens, it is important to recycle them because the chemicals inside are highly toxic. So putting them in the landfill is harmful to the environment. If the batteries are recycled, the toxic substances inside can be made into new products. Some batteries have this phone number printed on them, 800-8-BATTERY. It is a help line to find a recycler in your area, and is good for all makes and models.

countries. Li-ion batteries do generally have a longer life because you can recharge them more times before the chemicals inside don't work anymore. And they hold their peak voltage better than the Ni-Cad type. But they are not without quirks. A sensor in the battery shuts it off when the electrical charge becomes too low, so they tend to quit without warning. (You can tell when a Ni-Cad battery is low because the tool slows down near the end.) Also, Li-ion batteries are prone to overheating and will shut themselves down if they become hot. It is difficult

BATTERY - POWERED DRILL

THIS TOOL IS TYPICAL OF THE TYPE OF CORDLESS DRILL OFTEN USED AS A "SCREW GUN." IT HAS A PHILLIPS DRIVER TIP IN IT. THE POWER OF THE DRILL IS A FUNCTION OF THE VOLTAGE, AND AT 18 VOLTS THIS ONE HAS LOTS OF POWER. THE BATTERY CAN BE RECHARGED MANY TIMES AT THE CHARGING STATION.

CHUCK REQUIRES NO KEY

TORQUE SETTING

SET THIS FEATURE TO PROVIDE THE PROPER TORQUE FOR THE JOB YOU ARE DOING. WHEN THE DRILL REACHES THAT AMOUNT OF FORCE, THE CHUCK BEGINS TO RATCHET, AND DOESN'T TURN ANYMORE. USE A LOW SETTING FOR SCREWS GOING INTO SOFT MATERIALS. USE THE MAXIMUM SETTING (DRILL BIT) FOR TIMES WHEN YOU NEED THE MOST TURNING FORCE.

to predict what type of battery will be popular in five years, and perhaps something entirely new will come around.

Battery-powered drills often have a torque setting on the chuck that allows the user to select the exact amount of force that is applied. This will allow you to stop screws from damaging soft materials like sound-deadening insulation. All of the new types have a ratcheting chuck that works really well without a key, you simply tighten them with your bare hands.

At its most basic level, an electric hand drill consists of a motor, a trigger or switch that turns the motor on, and a *chuck* that is used to clamp a drill bit to the motor. The chuck rotates to move three jaws placed inside of it. They come together or apart, depending on the direction you rotate the chuck. When a drill bit is placed inside, the chuck is rotated until the jaws are firmly seated against it. Hand tightening is fine for newer drills, but some older types, and/or heavy duty ones use a *chuck key* to lock the bit in place. Gear teeth on the chuck correspond to teeth on the chuck key. These teeth make it possible to lock the chuck very tightly. A *drill press* is a large, stationary type of drill. They always use a chuck key.

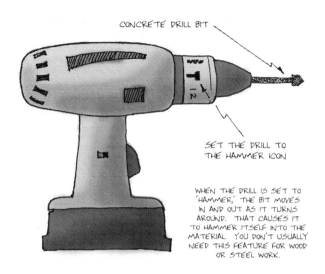

CONCRETE DRILL BIT

SET THE DRILL TO THE HAMMER ICON

WHEN THE DRILL IS SET TO "HAMMER," THE BIT MOVES IN AND OUT AS IT TURNS AROUND. THAT CAUSES IT TO HAMMER ITSELF INTO THE MATERIAL. YOU DON'T USUALLY NEED THIS FEATURE FOR WOOD OR STEEL WORK.

A HAMMER DRILL WORKS DIFFERENTLY

Most drills are of a type known as *variable speed reversible*. When you pull on the trigger, the amount of pressure dictates how fast the drill rotates. So a light pressure makes the drill spin very slowly, while pulling the trigger all the way back runs it at maximum speed. This feature is very important when using a drill as a *screw gun*. Slower speeds are essential when driving screws. Years ago, special types of drills were manufactured especially for driving drywall screws, but now just about any cordless drill will do that.

Driving screws is a common task, and of course it is much easier with a power tool. When using a drill to install screws, remember to "push hard, pull softly." If you pull the trigger switch in hard all the way, the drill will turn far too fast for you to control it. Use a soft touch on the trigger. But push hard against the screw with the

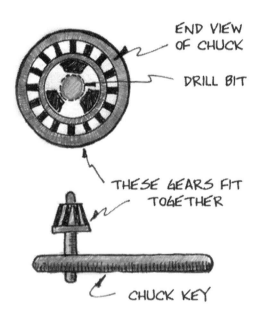

END VIEW OF CHUCK

DRILL BIT

THESE GEARS FIT TOGETHER

CHUCK KEY

Not all chucks are the same size. Some really small ones may only accommodate a ¼″ drill bit, but most modern cordless drills go up to ½″. A ½″ chuck will accommodate a bit shaft of up to that size.

Some more powerful drills are designed to bore large diameter holes into wood or steel, and have only one slow speed. They usually have a cord, and are physically much larger. Others are of a type called *hammer drills*, meaning that they not only spin, but that the bit oscillates forward and backward as well. This feature is especially helpful when drilling into concrete.

A COLLECTION OF DRIVER BITS

THERE ARE MANY DIFFERENT TYPES AND SIZES. GENERALLY SPEAKING, PHILLIPS BITS WORK MUCH BETTER THAN STANDARD.

drill so that the driver bit stays firmly seated in the screw head. It is also best to use a slower speed when drilling through steel in order to avoid overheating and damaging the bit.

It is important that the drill be reversible, because screws frequently need to be taken out as well as put in. Most drills have a switch near the trigger that selects forward or reverse.

Just like hand screwdrivers, driver bits for a drill come in different types. The old standard or slotted type isn't used very often because the driver bit tends to slip out as it rotates. Phillips bits were invented to avoid that problem. It is much easier to insert the tip into the screw head because it fits from any angle, and it tends to stay centered. There are different diameter/gauge sizes. The #2 diameter is best for most jobs, unless you are using very small screws. Some of the #2 bits have a special, narrower shape that makes them work especially well with drywall screws.

More recently two other types have become popular as well. The Robertson or square drive was also designed to be used with a power tool. The interior of the square hole is slightly slanted, which means the bit feeds into the hole easily.

Torx or star is another variety. This type grips more fully and is generally easier to drive without slipping. But it isn't available with a very wide array of fasteners.

The Phillips drive is by far the most popular and is used for all different sorts of screws and bolts.

There are a number of different types of drill bits. The most common are the twist drill, the spade bit, and the hole saw. It is important to know something about how the different types work so that you can choose the right bit for a particular job.

A *twist drill* has a spiral shape, as the name implies, and is intended for use in wood, metal, or plastic. (Only a special masonry bit should be used in concrete.) Twist drill bits are usually ½″ or smaller in diameter, because sizes larger than that tend to be quite expensive. The spiral flute is meant to carry the waste product away from the tip of the bit. These bits are somewhat difficult to sharpen once dull. With a bit of practice you can sharpen the tips with a bench grinder, but great care must be taken to maintain the original bevel. Twist drills come in a tremendous number of diameters, usually separated by ⅟₁₆″ difference, but the sizes corresponding to bolt sizes are the most useful.

A *spade bit* is a flat piece of metal with a round spindle that fits into the chuck of a drill. It is meant to be used in wood or other soft materials only, and will not work in steel. They somewhat resemble a garden shovel, hence the name. Spade bits are much easier to manufacture than twist drills are and as a result are much less expensive. Since the size of the cutting part of the bit is not in any way bounded by the size of the shank that fits into the drill chuck, it is easy to find quite large spade bits, all with ¼″ shanks. It is common to find this type of bit up to 1½″ diameter. For anything larger than that a hole saw should be used. Spade bits are also known as paddle bits.

SPADE BIT

As the name implies, the *hole saw* is actually a round-shaped saw blade that is rotated by the drill. Hole saws vary greatly in quality and price, and can be found in sizes up to 6″ in diameter. The larger sizes should be used with care, because the chances of the saw becoming jammed rise with an increase in diameter.

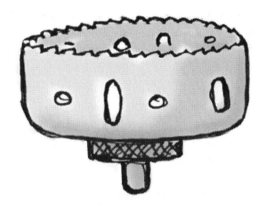

HOLE SAW

DRILL DIRECTON

Remember that drill bits are intended to cut only when the drill rotates in a forward, clockwise direction. If you notice that the drill bit you are using does not seem to be working at all well, check to see that the motor reversing switch is set properly. It is difficult to see which way the chuck is spinning when the drill is operating at full speed, and it is easy to reset the switch without knowing it.

SHANK REDUCED

TWIST DRILL BIT

Belt sanders are the most aggressive type of power sander and do the most work in the least amount of time. An endless belt of sandpaper moves along on two revolving drums. A mechanism allows you to shift the two drums closer together to allow for belt changing. An adjustment knob makes very small changes in the alignment of the front drum in order to make the belt "track" properly. This alignment prevents the belt from running to the edge of the drums and coming off, and/or from getting jammed against the other side. The sander must be running when the adjustment is made, and it is best to hold the tool upside down in order to see what effect the adjustments are making.

ROUNDED END

THE FLAT SIDE IS BEST FOR SMOOTHING

BELT SANDER

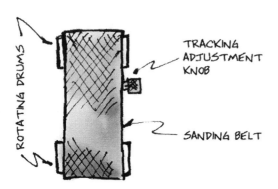

ROTATING DRUMS

TRACKING ADJUSTMENT KNOB

SANDING BELT

BOTTOM VIEW OF BELT SANDER

Sandpaper grits are an indication of how rough the paper is and how aggressively it will wear away any material you are sanding. A 40 grit belt is extremely rough and effective, while 100 grit is more suitable for sanding smooth to a paintable surface. When using a belt sander, it is important to remember this rule of thumb: if you want to sand something so that it becomes flat, be sure to use the flat, bottom part of the sander. Move the tool around a lot while you are sanding, much like you might move a steam iron around while removing the wrinkles from fabric. The front end is rounded where the belt curves around the roller, and sanding with that part makes the work go really fast, but it is difficult to get a smooth surface. Sometimes you may wish to have an uneven surface, perhaps when distressing wood to make it look older and more worn. The rounded front part of the sander is perfect for that type of work.

At first glance a *random orbit sander* looks like it just spins in a circle, but in fact this sander has a system of gears that moves the sanding pad along a random path. They work amazingly well, especially on curved surfaces. They are very aggressive, but because the sanding pad moves in a random orbit rather than just spinning it leaves no swirl marks behind. An ordinary orbital sander often leaves sanding marks that look a lot like the curved scrapes left behind by a circular saw blade. The random orbit sander is much easier to manipulate than a belt

RANDOM ORBIT SANDER

ORBITING PAD

sander and can be used in tight situations. It is great for smoothing rounded corners.

A good *jigsaw* is an essential tool in any theatre shop because of the preponderance of odd-shaped items that scenery work demands. Jigsaws use a "bayonet" type of blade. This is a flat piece of metal with saw teeth that is connected to the saw at one end. The jigsaw moves the blade up and down, thus creating the cutting action.

The best jigsaws have several features to look for that make them much easier to use than cheaper varieties. One of these is the *tang style blade* that can be inserted into its holder and held in place by a set-screw from the very top. Instead of that, some jigsaws use a set-screw that is placed through a hole in the blade itself. This hole in the blade is of course a weak spot that can cause premature blade breakage. The tang-style blades last longer and are much easier to change.

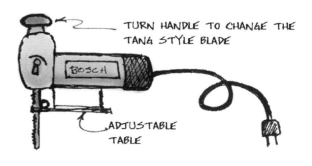

TURN HANDLE TO CHANGE THE TANG STYLE BLADE

BOSCH

ADJUSTABLE TABLE

JIGSAW

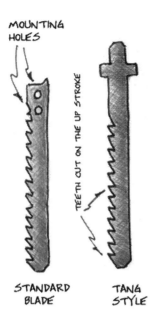

MOUNTING HOLES

TEETH CUT ON THE UP STROKE

STANDARD BLADE

TANG STYLE

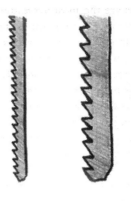

THE NARROW BLADE HAS A SMALLER TURNING RADIUS BUT IS MORE PRONE TO BREAKING THAN THE WIDER BLADE

JIGSAW BLADES

Another feature to look for is the ability to adjust the blade to kick outward as it travels up and down, leading to a much more aggressive cutting stroke. As with any saw blade, the more aggressive your cutting becomes, the more splintering or tearout will result. It is good to be able to adjust blade kick to a particular material and work situation.

Jigsaws can be used to cut out curved and otherwise odd-shaped pieces. Since the blade is free at one end, it can be inserted into a hole drilled in the interior of a piece and then used to cut out a shape in the middle of it. There are many kinds of blades for different types of materials, such as wood, plastic, and metal. The size of the blade from front to back makes a great difference in the turning radius of the blade. Some jigsaw blades are very small from front to back, and this allows them to cut very tight curves. Of course the smaller the blade, the more likely it is to break.

A *router* can be used in several different ways. You can create a decorative edge along a piece of wood by using a bit with a fancy shape. You can also trim off the outer edge of wood or plastic sheets, and in theatre, especially the thin plywood covering a hard cover flat. The basic moving parts are a very high-speed motor, a base that can be adjusted up and down, and a collet. The *collet* is similar to a drill chuck and is used to clamp router bits in position. Unlike drill bits, router bits are intended to

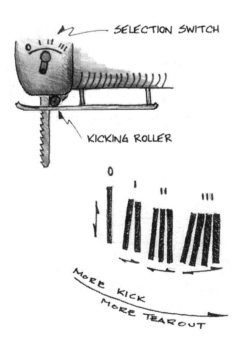

SELECTION SWITCH

KICKING ROLLER

0   I   II   III

MORE KICK

MORE TEAROUT

SELECT THE PROPER AMOUNT OF KICKING ACTION FOR YOUR JOB

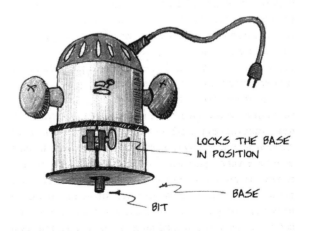

LOCKS THE BASE IN POSITION

BASE

BIT

PARTS OF A ROUTER

cut from the side of the bit rather than from the end, as when drilling a hole. There are many different types of router bits that may be used to cut profiles along the edge of a piece of wood.

Routers made for the USA have either a ¼″ or a ½″ collet. Some have two different interchangeable collets. Those sizes are meant to match up with the diameter of the shank portion of the router bit, which is the part that fits into the collet. Half inch bits are generally more stable and give a better cut. The horsepower rating of a router is relative to the strength of the motor.

A *flush trim bit* is used to trim the edges of hard cover flats, or other similar scenic elements. The roller on the bottom of the bit is the exact same size as the flutes that do the cutting. If you position the roller so that it runs along the framing of the unit, the flush trim bit will pare off anything sticking out past it, trimming the cover so that it is flush with the framing. This keeps you from needing to be hyper accurate when cutting the cover on the table saw, because any extra amount can be removed with the router.

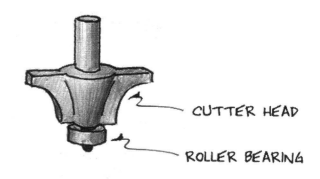

CUTTER HEAD

ROLLER BEARING

ROUND-OVER BIT

larger, shop saws. This blade is usually smaller, since the tool is intended to be guided by hand. The woodworking chapter has much more information about circular blades.

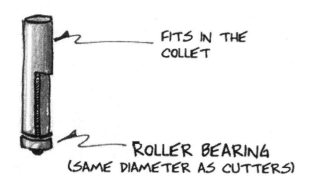

FITS IN THE COLLET

ROLLER BEARING
(SAME DIAMETER AS CUTTERS)

FLUSH TRIM BIT

The *router base* is adjustable up and down, allowing the operator to extend a variable amount of the bit below the surface of the base, which is the only portion that will actually cut anything. Varying the amount of bit will alter the profile that gets cut.

You can buy many different types of router bits to form decorative edges on wood trim. One of the simplest is the *round-over bit*, which is very popular in a scene shop. It is used to give wooden structures a finished appearance and to remove unwanted, sharp, and splinter-prone edges. The very similar *chamfer bit* does the same thing, but at a 45 degree angle instead. Remember that the bit represents the negative shape of the profile that will actually be created.

A hand-held *circular saw* is commonly called a Skil saw because the Skil tool company was an early manufacturer. Many other companies now manufacture what is generically called a circular saw, which does, in fact, use a circular blade very similar to that used on other,

THIS CIRCULAR SAW HAS A TABLE ON THE BOTTOM. THE GUARD RAISES UP AS YOU ENTER THE WORK

Most of the cutting in home building is done with a circular saw. In a theatre shop that is equipped with stationary cutting tools, this saw is not used as much, but it can still be very handy for cuts that are difficult to make on the larger tools. That most commonly occurs when making straight cuts in plywood that are not at a right angle to the edges, and/or when the sheet cannot be fed into the table saw for some other reason. Many times it

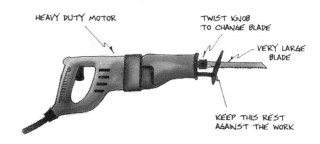

HEAVY DUTY MOTOR

TWIST KNOB TO CHANGE BLADE

VERY LARGE BLADE

KEEP THIS REST AGAINST THE WORK

RECIPROCATING SAW

is much easier to maneuver this saw through a large piece of work than to maneuver the work through a table saw. You can find instructions for using a circular saw guide in other chapters. The guide is very useful for making accurate long cuts in plywood.

The Sawzall tool was named by the Milwaukee tool company. It is generically known as a *reciprocating saw*. It is often used to tear scenery apart after the show is over with. The blade on a reciprocating saw is very much like a larger version of the jigsaw. A reciprocating saw is in its element when there are large, oddly shaped pieces to be dismembered in a hurry without much regard for accuracy. You can buy different types of blades to use on either metal or wood. The metal blades are especially nice for tearing apart scenery made from steel square tube.

PNEUMATICS

Some tools work more efficiently when they are powered by compressed gas, and nail guns/staplers definitely fit into this category. The pistons inside them are driven by the sudden release of air pressure from an outside source. They are connected to that source with a flexible hose. *Pneumatic* (meaning powered by air) tools require an air compressor. It is dangerous to use bottles of other compressed gasses, especially the oxygen type used in some types of welding, but really any kind of compressed gas bottle.

Several different companies make pneumatic guns, and each one produces equipment in its own style. Although the guns are somewhat different in their specific mechanics, the basic concept of how they propel a fastener is the same.

A piston inside the gun drives a shaft, which in turn forces a nail or staple down into the wood. Most guns are not intended to be used in metal or concrete. The fasteners are connected together either with glue, tape,

or plastic retainers. There is generally some sort of *magazine* to fit the nails into, and that feeds them up to the driving piston.

The fasteners are fed through the magazine toward the drive shaft by means of a spring mechanism that creates a semi-automatic type of firing sequence. Both staplers and nail guns are equipped with a *safety* at the point where the nail or staple fires out of the gun. The safety must be pressed against a solid object in order to fire, preventing the user from accidentally shooting a nail into the air and possibly hitting another person. The safety is not entirely foolproof, and if it becomes bent or coated with glue it may stick in the fire position. So be careful not to leave your finger on the trigger when moving the gun around the shop. Of course, you should never stick anything into the linkage to purposely circumvent the safety.

IT'S NOT LIKE THE MOVIES

You may have seen certain movies where a nail gun is used to shoot through steel walls, and or to pin victims against a wall from 20 feet away. It doesn't really work like that. Most nails and staples are very lightweight in comparison to bullets from a gun. They are also slower, and have much less force. And a nail gun doesn't have a rifled barrel like a pistol, so the nail would tumble through the air and be unlikely to stick into anything. Knowing that, you don't really have to try it yourself. Even though it isn't like the movies, shooting nails across the shop is incredibly dangerous.

A major cause of nail gun accidents is a nail that comes out the side of a board and strikes a finger. This can be a common problem if you are holding two boards together and fail to shoot the nail in straight. Sometimes a nail will curve out the side when it strikes a dense area inside the board, and there is really no way to predict when that will happen. It is a good practice to avoid putting your fingers anywhere a nail could conceivably shoot out the side of your work. Since it is also common for carpenters to use their fingers to judge when joints are lined up properly, you should make it a habit to line up the joint, and then move your finger before firing.

Some staplers have a wide crown or top, and are meant to ride on the surface of the material you shoot them into. Some narrow crown staples and/or nails are set below the surface of the board, with the theory being that filler will later be used to make the point of entry invisible. Some staplers have an adjustment feature that allows you to select the depth. Staples and nails come in a variety of different lengths. For neater work, make sure that the length staple you choose is short enough not to

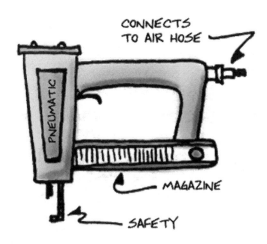

CONNECTS TO AIR HOSE

PNEUMATIC

MAGAZINE

SAFETY

TYPICAL STAPLER

exit the wood on the far side. If your hand or leg or some other body part is in contact with the backside of the wood, a too-long nail will come through into your flesh. So it is a good idea to avoid putting any part of your body under the board.

Numerous other tips for the use of nail guns can be found in the chapters on construction.

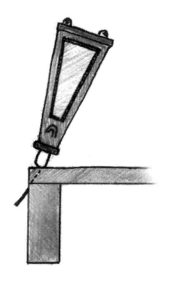

NAILS CAN COME OUT THE SIDE OF THE LUMBER

OUCH! BE CAREFUL!

TERMS USED IN THIS CHAPTER

air compressor	framing square	screw gun
belt sander	hammer drill	sledge hammer
bolt cutters	hole saw	slip joint pliers
box-end wrench	jigsaw	socket wrench
c-clamp	level/plumb	spade bit
chalk line	nail gun magazine	Speed Square
chamfer bit	needle nose pliers	spring clamp
chuck	Ni-Cad battery	steel tape
circular saw	open-end wrench	straight claw hammer
collet	pipe clamp	tang style blade
compass	pipe wrench	tape measure blade/hook
Crescent/adjustable wrench	pliers	torque
curved claw hammer	pneumatic tools	trammel points
diagonal pliers	random orbit sander	twist drill bit
drill press	reciprocating saw	variable speed reversible drill
drive size (rachet)	round-over bit	Vise Grip clamp
drywall square	router	Vise Grip pliers
Felco/cable cutters	rubber mallet	wooden clamp
flush trim bit	screw driver	

CHAPTER 10

WOODEN JOINERY

IT'S DIFFICULT TO explain exactly what scenery construction is like in contrast to other areas of carpentry. You might think that woodworking in the theatre has more in common with cabinet making than it does with most home construction jobs. Cabinet work is very exacting, and it results in freestanding units that are transported to the work site for installation. The cabinets are assembled inside an already existing structure, and have many moving parts. Scenery is also very exacting, and must be movable at least from the shop to the theatre and quite often, from one theatre to another.

STUDENTS RIPPING 1X
ON A TABLE SAW WITH A GUARD AND A DUST COLLECTION SYSTEM

In truth, building scenery is not like any other type of construction work. Stage carpenters are called upon to build very complicated units within a very short time span. There are often requirements for "magic" tricks, like an actor who gets sucked into the floor, walls that fly out on cue, or a bed that folds up into a table. If you were to ask a house carpenter for a bridge that flies out of the way for Act II, you might just get a blank stare in return. A theatre carpenter will ask how fast and how high.

Scenery is built in parts, or units, that are later assembled in the theatre. Many times scenery must also be moved during a show, either hand carried, rolled, or flown out on a rigging system. Moving the scenery around puts extra stress on its structure and that must be taken into account when the units are engineered. If scenery is flown, the pickup points must be determined and built in at the shop. It is really important that the person engineering such things have a good working knowledge of rigging, and also about how shows are run when they are in performance.

Being a proficient carpenter requires the mastery of many different techniques used in woodworking. It would be difficult to jump right into carpentry work after just reading through this material. An apprentice period of working in a shop will help you to work safely and efficiently. This chapter covers some general woodworking terms and practices that should give your learning period a place to start. There are dozens of different woodworking tools in most theatre shops. Many of them were mentioned in the last chapter. The tools in this chapter are so commonly used and so complex that they deserve some special attention. Of special interest are the table saw, the radial arm saw, the power miter saw, and the band saw.

Marking lumber and cutting it to size are essential skills in any woodworking shop. Three types of basic cuts make up the lion's share of woodworking. *Ripping* wood means cutting it along or with the grain. Since the grain in a piece of lumber generally runs along the length of the board, rip cuts tend to be very long. You might rip down some pieces of 1×12 lumber so that they become 1×3s instead. *Cross cutting* is done across the grain, at a 90 degree angle. It is often associated with trimming boards to length. You might cross cut some random lengths of 1×3 you've just ripped down to a specific length like 3'-0". The third type of cut is used to create odd angles. *Miter cuts* are used to trim the ends of boards or molding to some angle other than 90 degrees. The most common of these would be a 45 degree angle cut, such as might be used to make a picture frame.

There are many, many combinations and permutations of these types of cuts, but it seems helpful to begin with some way of organizing these different concepts to make them easier to remember.

TYPES OF JOINTS

There are some special names for the way that wooden parts fit together. When the end of one board hits directly upon another one they are said to be butting into one another, and if you nail them together like that, a *butt joint* is created.

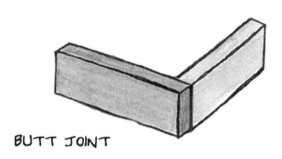

BUTT JOINT

If you connect two boards together so that they overlap one another, this creates a *lap joint*. If you cut away half of the material from each board so that they overlap one another without creating a bump you have made a *half lap*.

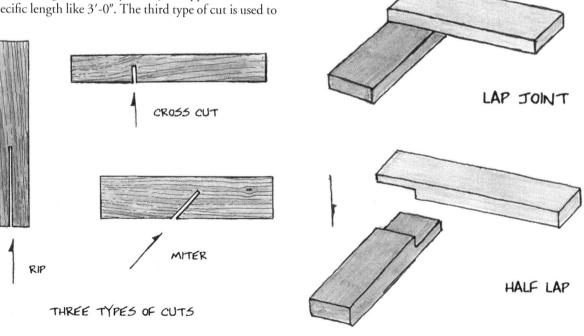

CROSS CUT

MITER

RIP

THREE TYPES OF CUTS

LAP JOINT

HALF LAP

Connecting two boards using a thin piece of plywood creates a *covered joint*.

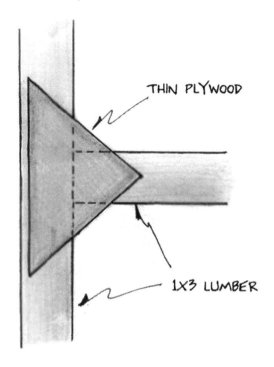

THIN PLYWOOD

1X3 LUMBER

COVERED JOINT

If you lengthen a board by using another piece of the same material, and then join the two sections with a third piece, the covering piece is called a *scab*.

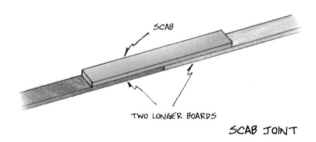

SCAB

TWO LONGER BOARDS

SCAB JOINT

A *dado* is a slot cut into a piece of wood large enough so that another piece of wood can fit into it.

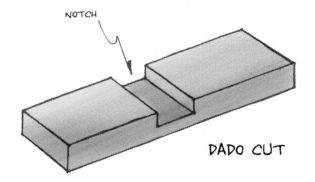

NOTCH

DADO CUT

There are lots of other joining techniques, such as mortise and tenon, dovetail, doweling, and finger joining. These joints are much more difficult to produce, and are typically reserved for furniture where the beauty of the joinery is meant to show. That doesn't happen so often with scenery where fancy joinery would be painted over later. *Joiner* is an archaic term for a carpenter. One of the mechanicals in Shakespeare's *Midsummer Night's Dream* is Snug the Joiner.

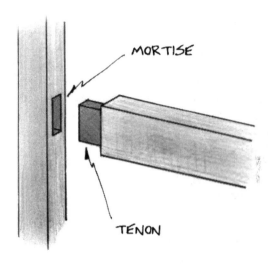

MORTISE

TENON

MORTISE AND TENON

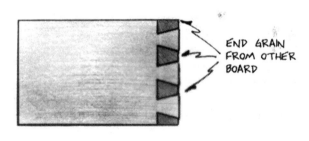

END GRAIN FROM OTHER BOARD

DOVETAIL

CIRCULAR SAW BLADES

Just to be clear, it is the blade that is circular and not the saw. As the name indicates, a *circular saw blade* has a round shape with teeth located around the outside edge. This type of blade cuts when it is rotated at a high speed and the teeth are pressed against the wood you are cutting. They are used in many different types of saws. Circular saw blades are sized according to their diameter in inches, so a 10 inch blade is therefore 10 inches across. A hole in the center is used to connect the blade to a saw. The post on the saw is called an *arbor*, and the hole an *arbor hole*. Most blades have either a ⅝″ or a 1″ arbor hole that corresponds to a specific saw, which has an arbor one of those sizes. It is not possible to install a ⅝″ blade on a 1 inch arbor because the hole is too small. The reverse is possible, but would be very dangerous because the blade would be unbalanced with more weight on one side than the other. This could have disastrous consequences.

Small teeth on a circular saw blade result in a finer cut with less *tearout*. Tearout is the splintering that occurs in wood as the blade passes through it. Blades with large teeth are commonly referred to as *ripping blades*, and those with smaller teeth as *cross cutting blades*. Larger teeth are fine when ripping lumber, because the wood is less likely to splinter when it is cut with the grain. Larger teeth are more aggressive and better suited to making the long cuts that are associated with rip sawing. Saw teeth are either the traditional type that are an integral part of the blade, or are built with tips made from carbide steel.

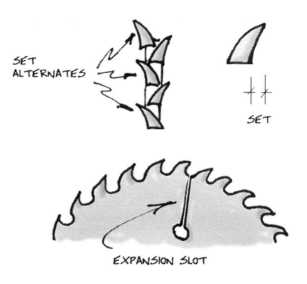

EXPANSION SLOT

SET IN A SAWTOOTH

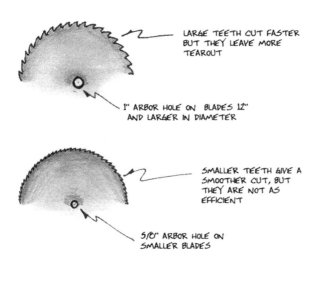

LARGE TEETH CUT FASTER BUT THEY LEAVE MORE TEAROUT

1″ ARBOR HOLE ON BLADES 12″ AND LARGER IN DIAMETER

SMALLER TEETH GIVE A SMOOTHER CUT, BUT THEY ARE NOT AS EFFICIENT

5/8″ ARBOR HOLE ON SMALLER BLADES

CIRCULAR SAW BLADES

Traditional blades require that the saw teeth be slightly bent over at the tip. This is known as *set* in the blade and is a very important part of how the blade works. Saw teeth are bent to the side in an alternating pattern, first to one side and then to the other. This is true of all blades, not just circular ones. We are all aware that friction causes heat, and if there is any doubt, rubbing your hands together rapidly will prove the point. When a circular saw blade is spinning at high speed (which it must do in order to cut) a great deal of heat could be generated by the blade rubbing against the piece of wood that it is cutting. Set in the blade teeth are used to minimize friction and thus heat by separating the wood from the body of the blade by a slight amount. Since it is really the tips of the teeth that do all of the cutting, setting the

teeth will ensure that the pathway that they cut through the board is a small amount larger than the body of the blade. This reduces friction and heat.

If the body of the blade gets too hot, it tends to warp out of shape. This happens because the circumference of the outside part of the blade is much larger than the circumference of the interior part of the blade. As the blade expands and warps, more friction is created and the heat build-up gets worse. Some blades have slots cut into them in several places around the outside circumference so that the blade can heat up and expand a bit without deforming.

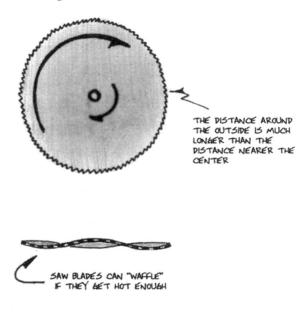

THE DISTANCE AROUND THE OUTSIDE IS MUCH LONGER THAN THE DISTANCE NEARER THE CENTER

SAW BLADES CAN "WAFFLE" IF THEY GET HOT ENOUGH

HEAT CAUSES EXPANSION
OF THE BLADE

The pathway cut through the wood by the blade is called the *kerf*, and that part of the wood is reduced to sawdust in the cutting process. If you were to cut halfway through a plank and then stop, the kerf is the leftover slot in the wood. The kerf disappears when you have finished cutting, and can seem somewhat ephemeral.

KERF

In recent years circular saw blades have become increasingly high tech as advances in technology have made it possible to manufacture them with ever increasing precision. Computer-controlled lasers and water jets can cut very complex shapes in tool steel that were not possible with older stamping methods. Also, you may have noticed that some blades have teeth that are not bent at the tips, but rather seem to have an entirely different piece of metal attached at that point. These blades are known as *carbide blades*, because the metal used to make the blade tips is comprised of tungsten carbide. Most modern circular saw blades have carbide teeth on them rather than teeth that are set to the side.

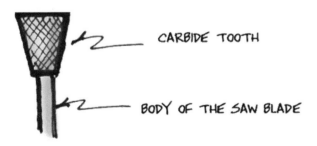

CARBIDE TOOTH

BODY OF THE SAW BLADE

The Rockwell Scale lists the density or hardness of a variety of different types of steel alloys. Alloys are not all the same, but rather have been created specifically because they have different properties. It is axiomatic that the harder something is, the more brittle it is. Tungsten carbide, being very dense and hard, can be honed to an incredible sharpness and can retain that edge for a very long time. Those are excellent qualities for a saw tooth. Conversely, this material is brittle and quite easy to shatter, which is not a quality you would ask for in a large chunk of metal spinning at high speed. As a result, manufacturers design blades with the carbide steel used only in small amounts that are welded onto the tips of the teeth, like caps.

THIS TOOL MEASURES HARDNESS BY PRESSING A POINT INTO THE STEEL AT A CERTAIN PRESSURE, AND THEN MEASURING THE SIZE OF THE INDENTATION

THE RELATIVE HARDNESS OF TUNGSTEN CARBIDE IS A ROCKWELL C SCALE NUMBER OF ABOUT 72, WHICH IS NOT MUCH LOWER THAN A DIAMOND. THE HARDNESS OF TOOL STEEL LIKE YOU WOULD FIND IN THE BODY OF A SAW BLADE IS IN THE 50S, AND MILD STEEL LIKE THAT FOUND IN SQUARE TUBE FOR SCENERY BUILDING IS IN THE 10 TO 20 RANGE.

The body of the blade is comprised of traditional *tool steel* that is also hard but more malleable. In this way, each part of the blade is made from the ideal material for that part. Carbide teeth are often ground into very advanced shapes at the factory, and these enhance their cutting abilities. They do not have set in the traditional sense, but rather each of the carbide tips projects to both the left and right sides creating the same effect.

One drawback to carbide blades is that they are often impossible to re-sharpen effectively because of the intricate nature of the shape of the teeth. So when the teeth are dull you must often replace the entire blade rather than take it in for a less expensive sharpening, like in the old days. The greatly increased efficiency of these blades more than offsets the added expense. They stay sharp much longer than an ordinary blade.

Although circular saw blades have been mentioned specifically, the concept of set in the teeth and the way a kerf is formed is true of all types of blades. Blades for jig, band, and reciprocating saws are almost exclusively of the bent-set type rather than the carbide type.

THE TABLE SAW

The *table saw* gets its name from its basic shape, which does indeed resemble a small table. The horizontal metal surface is referred to as "the table," and is the most easily recognized feature. Another important part is the *rip fence* or guide. This is the metal and/or plastic structure that runs from front to back on the saw. You can adjust the distance between it and the saw blade. The blade on a table saw is meant to be exactly parallel to the rip fence.

Probably by now you have realized that because it has a rip fence the table saw is most commonly used to rip lumber or plywood to a specific width. Basically, this involves taking long boards or sheets of plywood and feeding them through the saw to create long, thin strips of material, such as a 1×3.

There are several adjustable features on any table saw. These are: the rip fence, the angle of the blade as it intersects the table, and the height of the blade above the top of the table. There are wheels or knobs of some sort on the front and/or side of the saw that operate the blade moving mechanisms. The specific workings of a table saw differ from one manufacturer to another, but these features are a standard requirement of any table saw.

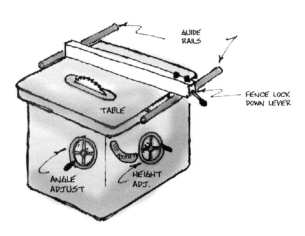

PARTS OF A TABLE SAW

It is important to be able to raise and lower the blade so that materials of varying thicknesses may be cut. It would be quite dangerous to leave the blade extended to its full height at all times. The normal rule of thumb is to set the blade to rise above the work about half an inch or so, enough to cut efficiently, but not so much as to be an undue hazard.

ONLY LEAVE ABOUT 1/2" OF BLADE EXPOSED ABOVE THE WORK

Some types of cuts will only work if the saw blade does *not* cut all the way through the work, and you must carefully measure how much is sticking up from the table.

The blade can be angled to produce a beveled edge along the side of a ripped board.

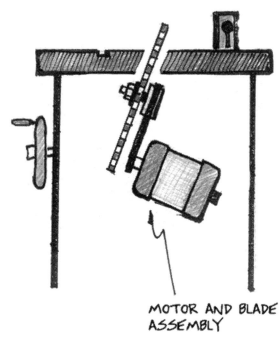

MOTOR AND BLADE ASSEMBLY

TILTING THE BLADE FOR AN ANGLED CUT

It is important to use a guard on your table saw. On newer equipment, the saw has been engineered so that the guard is attached to the motor rotation shaft, and a thin metal plate extends upward to the table. When wood is ripped on this type of saw, the metal plate holding the guard is aligned with the kerf coming out of the saw. Wood passes on either side of the plate. On older models, a guard extends from the back and fits on both sides of the blade. One problem with this type of guard is that it tends to obstruct the passage of large sheets of plywood when they are being ripped on the saw. Sometimes there is an arm that extends from the ceiling or wall, and the guard rests on that and is not so much in the way. No matter what type of guard is used, remember that it only makes the saw *safer*, not completely *safe*, and that you need to be very alert at all times when using power tools.

The rip fence is the most commonly adjusted feature of the table saw. The fence determines the size or width of the material being ripped. The distance is set by measuring between the face of the fence and the saw blade. Many shops add a better surface to the rip fence than was supplied by the manufacturer. Generally this involves some sort of plastic material that is slick, but will not wear away too soon. A low friction material makes it easier to feed the wood through the saw.

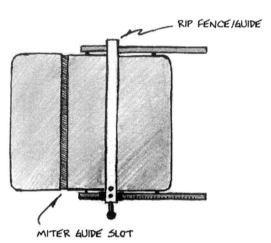

RIP FENCE/GUIDE

MITER GUIDE SLOT

SLOT AND FENCE SHOULD BE PARALLEL

The standard fence has an adjustment feature that allows you to realign it so that it remains perfectly parallel with the blade. If the blade and fence are not true to one another it is very difficult to feed work through the saw. A stable and secure rip fence is really important on a table saw. Aftermarket products are available to enhance the performance of most fences.

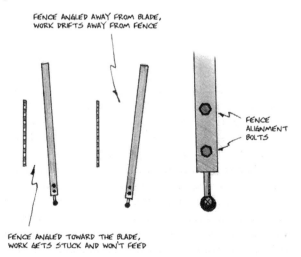

FENCE ANGLED AWAY FROM BLADE, WORK DRIFTS AWAY FROM FENCE

FENCE ALIGNMENT BOLTS

FENCE ANGLED TOWARD THE BLADE, WORK GETS STUCK AND WON'T FEED

RIP FENCE ADJUSTMENTS

With most types of woodworking equipment, the material being cut is marked in some way, and then the cutting tool is aligned with that mark in order to make the cut. The table saw is different. With it the fence is adjusted to a specific point. When the cut is made, the gap between the fence and the blade determines the size of the finished product. In order to be precise, you measure between the fence and the part of the blade that is closest to the fence. You can use an ordinary tape measure for this.

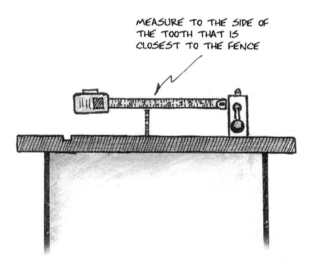

MEASURE TO THE SIDE OF THE TOOTH THAT IS CLOSEST TO THE FENCE

Put the hook up against the fence and move the fence and tape both until the correct distance reads against the blade tooth. If you check the discussion of blade tooth set, you will realize that the closest point will be either the extreme edge of one of the carbide teeth or one of the teeth that has its set bent in the direction of the rip fence. If you measure to the middle of the blade instead, the resulting rip will be too narrow by half the width of the saw kerf. If you measure to the far side of the blade, the rip will be too narrow by the width of the entire kerf, most likely about ⅛″. In woodworking, ⅛″ is quite a bit. You should strive for more accuracy than that.

Most saws have some sort of built-in measuring device, which will really speed up your work. If you aren't sure how well yours works, try setting it to a certain size and double checking with a tape measure. If you change the blade, you may need to recalibrate if the replacement blade has a significantly different set to its teeth. If heavy pieces of plywood have been slammed into the fence several times, the position of the fence will probably need to be reset to its original position.

When ripping material on the table saw, start by standing in front of the saw with your feet a comfortable distance apart. Most saws are set up for a right-handed person, and the fence is to the right of the blade. Stand to the left side of the board you are ripping. It is very important to keep the work firmly planted against the

fence as you pass it through the saw. If it drifts way, the result will be too narrow. Also, drifting away from the fence increases the chance of a kickback. When the board is fed through far enough to reach the far side of the table, your partner can pull it on through the saw. It is best to work with a partner until you have had enough experience and guidance to be safe and confident in your use of the saw.

It's a good practice to use a push stick to help feed the work through the saw, and this is always true when the piece you are cutting is small and brings you too close to the blade. Be sure to use any guards and/or hold downs that are required for your particular tool.

USING A PUSH STICK

You don't need a lot of strength to use the table saw, it's more of a balancing act, especially when the work is deftly fed through a well-maintained saw. If you meet a great deal of resistance you should check to see if the fence is properly aligned with the blade, that the blade is in good condition, and that you have properly held the board against the rip fence.

Most table saws have a slot milled into them to use with a *miter guide*. This guide is sometimes called a t-square. The miter guide slides back and forth in the slot and can be used to make cross and/or miter cuts. This is a somewhat cumbersome undertaking, and it will work for only relatively short boards. It's much better to cut long boards on the radial arm saw. Tool manufacturers like to make their products do as many different jobs as possible so that they are more attractive to buyers. Just because it is possible does not mean that it is particularly safe or efficient.

The saw motor should be aligned with the table at the factory or when you initially set up the tool, and it will rarely need adjustment. So the blade will always be parallel to the table. The rip fence is a different matter. You can use the miter guide slot to check the alignment between fence and blade by sliding the fence next to the slot and seeing if the two are parallel. If they are not, then adjust the fence so that it matches the slot using whatever

STAND ON THE LEFT, SO THAT YOU CAN SEE THE WORK AGAINST THE FENCE

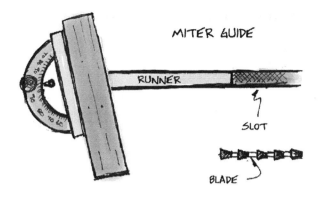

MITER GUIDE

RUNNER

SLOT

BLADE

features are on your particular saw. In reality, you may find that the saw is easier to use if there is just a tad more room at the back side of the saw than in the front. This allows the work to pass through more easily.

Some shops install an auxiliary table around the saw's own table so that it is easier to cut large pieces of plywood. In this way, you can cut through a section of plywood without worrying about the scrap part sagging and hitting the floor.

AUXILIARY TABLE

SAFETY ADVICE FOR THE TABLE SAW

Never try to cut anything on a table saw without using one of the guides. This is called *free handing*, and it is a good way to get injured by a *kickback*. A kickback occurs when the wood being cut gets jammed onto the blade, usually because the wood is turned a bit as it passes through the saw. When the blade becomes jammed in the kerf, it will shove the wood outward with tremendous force, and can cause serious injury. Never use the miter guide and the rip fence on the same cut, because a similar situation may develop. Be sure to wear safety glasses. Do not wear any clothes like a tie or gloves, or bulky sleeves that might get caught on some part of the saw. Keep long hair in a ponytail.

RADIAL ARM SAW

The *radial arm saw* is sometimes known as a bench saw or overhead arm saw. The three different names taken together are actually a good description of what this saw looks like. The radial arm saw is best suited to cross cutting long pieces of lumber such as 2×4s or 1×3s. Usually, the saw itself is fitted with a long table or bench that extends to either side of the saw. It is used to support the length of the boards being cut. The actual motor and saw blade are mounted on an overhead arm, which allows that assembly to roll back and forth when pulled over the bench and the piece you are cutting. The overhead arm can be pivoted radially from a point in the back of the saw in order to make miter cuts.

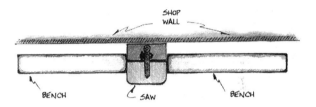

SHOP WALL

BENCH

SAW

BENCH

PLAN VIEW OF A RADIAL ARM SAW

The surface of the cutting table that comes with the saw is made from plywood or particle board because it is necessary for the blade to slightly penetrate this surface in order to cut all the way through your work. Toward the rear of the table is a fence that is used to align the

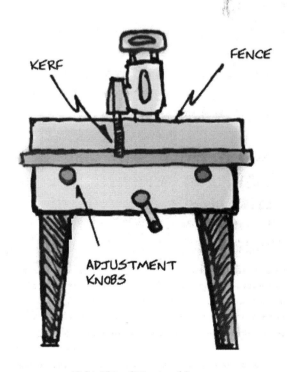

KERF

FENCE

ADJUSTMENT KNOBS

RADIAL ARM SAW

work (material being cut). The track of the saw blade is at a right angle to the fence. The wooden fence needs to be changed every so often because, like the table, the wooden fence erodes after a while. Changing the fence is an easy thing to do, and it will increase the accuracy of your cuts. A badly cut-up fence can also be a safety hazard.

A pair of clamps on the bottom of a radial arm saw are used to easily remove and replace the rear fence. Make a new fence from a section of 1×3 or 1×4, whose length is cut to the width of the saw table. It's an easy matter to remove the old fence and put in a new one using the clamps.

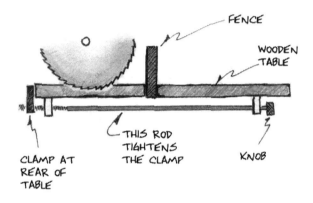

SIDE VIEW OF CLAMPING MECHANISM

A crank in front of the saw is used to raise and lower the blade. The blade should be lowered far enough into the table so that it cuts all the way through the wood, but not so far as to cut too deeply into the table. You must raise and lower the saw motor/blade assembly when changing blades, and also if you need to change the angle of the blade for a miter cut.

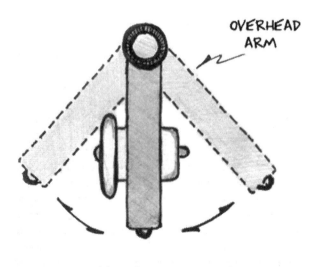

SAW ARM PIVOTS

The "radial" part of the saw name refers to the way this saw can be adjusted to rotate to an angle other than 90 degree. On most saws a locking mechanism disengages to allow the operator to turn the arm to any point up to 45 degree. This would by definition be a miter cut rather than a cross cut. The mechanism is different on various machines, but the basic principle is the same. There should be some kind of marking dial that will let you know the precise number of degrees you have pivoted.

Some saws allow the user to also turn the motor and blade assembly to an angle other than vertical. When both of the pivoting features are used in conjunction with one another, the resulting cut is known as a *double miter*. Naturally, these types of cuts take a toll on the wooden fence and table. Each new angle will leave a new cut mark in the fence and on the wooden surface of the table, and will require frequent replacement if you do it often.

The most common size radial arm saw is 10 inch, meaning that the blade is 10 inches in diameter, but it is possible to buy an industrial model that is 12, 14, or even 18 inches in diameter. The larger and heavier a saw is, the more stable it is. That is a good thing when you leave the arm set at 90 degrees to the fence, but readjusting a 14 inch saw to various angles can be a real bear—not to mention that the large table is somewhat difficult to replace. Rather than use this saw for making everyday miter cuts, you may consider a comparatively inexpensive power miter saw to cut small trim pieces. A miter saw is designed specifically for the purpose of cutting angles and is much more efficient at it, but is more limited with regard to size. If the pieces you have to cut are really wide, you may have no other choice than a radial arm saw.

The radial arm saw is at its best when there is a table or bench on both sides of the saw. The tables support the length of the lumber you are cutting. In an ideal situation, it is best to have an entire 16 feet on both sides of the saw. The longest commonly found lumber is 16 feet long, and a table that size on both sides will give you complete flexibility in cutting. Because that is frequently not possible, most right-handed carpenters like to have a longer bench on the left-hand side.

Some carpenters use a jig along the bench that has been marked with measurements back to the blade. That allows them to line the end of the board up with preset marks and avoid having to measure with a tape each time. If you are working in a shop with many other people with varying skill levels, it may be difficult to keep a jig like that properly calibrated. Your shop probably has its own policy set, and you can just follow those guidelines.

Before cutting a piece of dimension lumber to length you should trim one of the ends of the board a tiny amount so that it is perfectly square and even at that end. Most sawmill lumber is cut to only an approximate length, and the mill workers are not known for using the utmost care in trimming the ends.

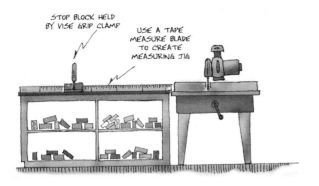

MEASURING JIG ON A RADIAL ARM SAW

DON'T MEASURE AT AN ANGLE, OR THE BOARD
WILL BE SHORTER THAN YOU THOUGHT

Typically, boards are about ½″ longer than the stated amount and cut at a small angle. There are often cracks at one end of a piece of lumber that are caused by the board drying out more at the end while banded together with others in a unit. This very common defect is known as *checking*. Trimming the end will get rid of this also. Since each board is different, the only way to know how to treat the end is to look at it.

CHECKS

TRIM THE END OF A BOARD
TO STRAIGHTEN IT AND
REMOVE CHECKING

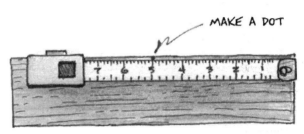

THE SMALLER THE DOT, THE MORE EXACT
THE MEASUREMENT WILL BE

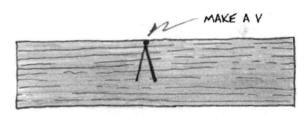

MAKE A V

MEASURING A BOARD

After trimming one end, you might need to flip the board over so that it fits well on the bench. Use a tape measure to mark the length of the cut. Take care to measure the board along one side rather than diagonally. This is all the more important on wider boards where the diagonal will cause your measurement to be much shorter than it should be.

Mark the cutting spot as close to the edge of the board as possible so that the mark will be easy to align with the blade. For the utmost in accuracy, make a tiny pencil dot on the very corner of the board, and then enlarge the mark by making a "V" with the dot being the apex. This V mark is sometimes called a *crow's foot*, and it is used by all types of carpenters to mark the exact placement of a cut. The dot alone would be difficult to find. A line on the board can be misleading if it is not exactly straight, and you are unsure which part is the true length. The point of a V mark is unambiguous.

A new fence on the saw makes it easy to line your crow's foot up with the blade, because the slot in the fence is exactly the same size as the blade. This means that the edges of the slot reference the edges of the blade. It is important to line your V mark up with the proper side of the kerf. Once you have had occasion to cut several hundred flat framing parts from a giant cut list, you will appreciate how easy it is to line the mark with the fence when there is a clean set-up. Over time, vibration from the saw motor, and just general wear and tear will cause the kerf in the fence to become larger and less accurate.

One of the most commonly made errors in using the radial arm saw is lining the board up with the wrong part of the kerf. Let us say that you have marked a board to be cut to 1′-0″. You have made your tiny dot close to the edge, and then made the dot into a V. Everything is going well. You have marked the board measuring from the

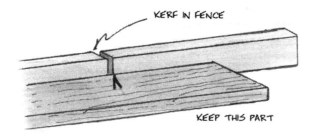

KERF IN FENCE

KEEP THIS PART

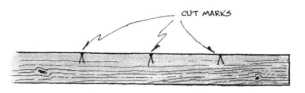

CUT MARKS

IF YOU MAKE A SERIES OF CUT MARKS
ALL AT THE SAME TIME
EACH PIECE WILL BE TOO SMALL

LINE THE V UP WITH THE PROPER SIDE OF THE KERF

right-hand side, and as a result the portion of the board you want to keep is to your right. To which part of the fence kerf should you align the cut mark, the left side, the center, or the right side?

The answer is found by considering what happens when the blade cuts through the wood. The blade is not like a knife, which would merely part the two sections without a reduction in the overall amount of material. The blade cutting through the wood creates a kerf and reduces a portion of it to sawdust. For all practical purposes it simply ceases to exist. Don't let any part of the kerf take away from the board you want to keep. After all, you have gone to great lengths to ensure that the measurement you made was very exact. If your measurement is exact and you shorten the piece with the saw blade it won't be the right size.

Align the crow's foot with the kerf so that none of the "keeper" is lost. If your keeper board is to the right side of the fence kerf, then you should line the V mark up with the right side of that kerf. If, on the other hand, the keeper piece were on the left-hand side, then you would need to line the V mark up with the left side of the fence kerf. The center of the kerf is never an option.

It is often necessary to cut a number of short pieces from the same board. It would be tempting to simply measure all of the pieces at one time down the length of the board, and cut them all at once. *This method does not work* because it does not allow for the passage of the saw blade and the creation of the kerf. Measuring that way will cause each section to be just a little bit smaller than it should be, about the same amount as the width of the blade.

A better method of cutting a large number of same size multiples is to use a *stop block*. This is a small block of wood clamped to the fence of the radial arm saw. To set that up, mark a board in the usual manner and place it against the fence as you normally would, but don't cut it yet. Instead, clamp a scrap piece of lumber to the fence so that it is just at the end of the board. You can cut your first piece and a virtually unlimited number of others without measuring again. Simply slide the raw stock over

against the stop block and cut each piece in turn. Be gentle when you do that. If the stock you are cutting from is large and you bang it hard into the stop block, the block will move over a slight bit each time and will soon be noticeably off. A Vise Grip clamp is excellent for holding the stop block because it is so easy to operate. It's a good idea to spot check the size of the completed parts with a tape measure. The only thing worse than cutting a board to the wrong length is cutting a hundred of them to the wrong length.

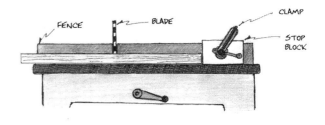

FENCE   BLADE   CLAMP

STOP
BLOCK

USING A STOP BLOCK

Be careful when using a stop block not to let parts get trapped between the blade and the block and get kicked back. This can happen when the already cut piece gets loose and turns at an angle. Of course, when the piece is at an angle, the length is increased on the diagonal, and it will tend to become jammed at first and then thrown clear by the spinning blade. This tends to be more of a problem with very small pieces. You can lessen the problem by cutting the stop block at an angle to the work, so that only the point is touching. But if your board is wide, and the pieces you cut are short, don't use a stop block.

However you have measured your cut, the method of actually sawing the board is the same. Make sure that none of your fingers are in the path of the blade as it crosses the table, firmly press the board against the fence, and steadily draw the saw across the board until it is cut through completely. The speed at which the blade moves through the wood is known as the *feed rate*. It will take a bit of practice to learn the exact feed rate for any particular saw, but here is a rule of thumb: If the motor slows, or worse yet becomes bogged down, you are

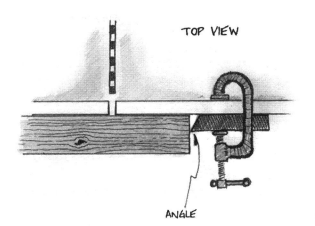

TOP VIEW

ANGLE

LEAVE AN ANGLE ON THE STOP BLOCK
TO MAKE IT WORK BETTER

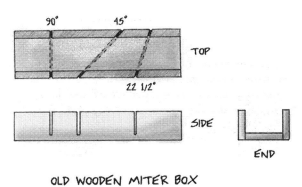

OLD WOODEN MITER BOX

cutting too fast. If there is smoking from the blade, you are most likely going too slowly, and the rubbing of the blade in the same location is resulting in excessive heat buildup. (Of course the latter might also be an indication that the blade is dull and should be changed and/or sharpened.) Do not pull the blade much farther toward you than is necessary to cut the board, as doing so will greatly increase the possibility of a kickback. Most saws have an automatic return spring that pulls the blade and motor rearward to its resting position. It is much kinder to the equipment to gently return the saw to its starting position than to allow the spring to slam it back there on its own.

There are several different types of anti-kickback devices manufactured for radial arm saws. Be sure to read the manufacturer's safety instructions for the particular saw you are using. Don't use a saw if the guard is removed.

THE POWER MITER SAW

Sometimes this tool is known as a power miter box. That's because it was developed from an earlier, non-powered tool. Like many names, this one came about over a period of time and has been expanded to reflect changes in technology. *Miter boxes* have been around for thousands of years and were originally intended to be used with a handsaw. They consist of a wooden box with saw kerfs at common miter angles.

A section of wood trim is placed inside the box, and a saw is used to cut the trim along the same lines as the preexisting kerf. The saw blade is held true to the desired angle by the wood surrounding the kerf.

While this type of low-tech solution is inexpensive and straightforward, it is also not terribly efficient. It is difficult to secure the trim inside the box. Using a handsaw is, of course, slow and difficult when compared to a modern power saw. The miter box is limited to a

small number of predetermined angles, and as such is not very flexible. Theatre work requires many odd angles, much more so than ordinary home construction where right angles are generally interrupted only by the occasional 45 degree angle. Theatre settings abound with odd shapes, raked stages, and other such interesting looking, but difficult to build structures.

Even so there are uses for shop-built miter boxes. You might be called upon to cut large pieces of Styrofoam trim for a cornice, which will not easily fit into a regular woodworking saw. Instead, construct a miter box to the size and angles you need to do the job. The difficulty of

POWER MITER SAW

cutting with a hand saw won't matter when cutting foam.

The *miter saw* is easily and quickly adjustable to any angle up to 45+ degrees. It has a fence in the back to hold the material in place. Naturally the electric motor makes the actual cutting quite easy to do. Most saws are capable of adjusting not only to one side or the other, but also on the opposing axis making it possible to double miter.

A power miter saw usually operates by pivoting from the rear. The blade goes through a slot in the table's surface when cutting, and the entire table, motor, and blade assembly rotates when changing the angle, making a consumable wooden top unnecessary. Most have a degree marker in front to use in adjusting the saw. The rotation mechanism itself has automatic stops at 90, 45, and 22½ degrees, because these are the most commonly used angles. When aligning a cut mark, you must bring the blade down so that it is almost touching the wood, as there is no kerf in the fence to use as a reference point. Since there is no kerf in the fence to line up the cut, and since the blade comes down in the middle of the work, it is really better to mark the wood in the middle rather than on the edge. Some newer saws have a laser light that comes on to illuminate a line along which the blade will cut and makes it much easier to line things up.

Rather than having a hinge point, some miter saws slide along two bars when they are making a cut. The method for aligning one of these saws is more like you would expect on a radial arm saw. This type is known as a *sliding miter saw*. A sliding miter saw can cut much wider material than the traditional hinged type, and some shops have replaced their radial arm saw with one of these.

Be very careful when using a power miter saw. There is a great temptation to hold on to pieces that are too small. Don't do that. Instead, use a large section of trim

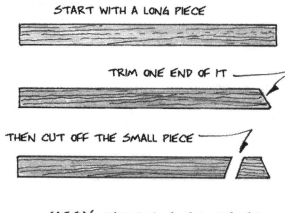

SAFELY CUTTING SMALL PIECES
ON A POWER MITER SAW

and cut the desired angle while holding onto the large leftover section. This way your hand will not come so near the blade.

HELPFUL HINTS FOR CUTTING ANGLES

When joining two angled pieces together so that the mitered ends match, the two ends must be cut to the same number of degrees in order for them to fit together properly. If the overall angle is 90 degrees, the angle of each member should be 45 degrees. If the overall angle is 60 degrees, each individual piece should have an angle of 30 degrees. If the angles of the two boards are not the same, the beveled ends will be different sizes and the mismatch will be noticeable.

Cutting angles confuses many people. You may find it difficult to decide how to measure an angle, and from which point. In reality, there are a few simple rules to follow that will make the entire process clear, or at least translucent.

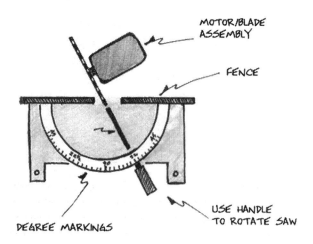

CHANGING THE ANGLE ON A
MITER SAW

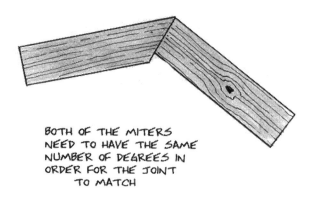

BOTH OF THE MITERS
NEED TO HAVE THE SAME
NUMBER OF DEGREES IN
ORDER FOR THE JOINT
TO MATCH

First a bit of geometry review to understand how *complementary* and *supplementary* angles interact. Many of the angles in common shapes are actually the same.

Look at the trapezoidal structure. Assume that the shape is regular, and that the left side is the mirror image of the right side. The top and bottom lines are parallel to one another. If you are given the number of degrees in just one angle, you can determine all the others by using simple geometry.

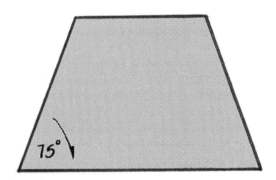

TRAPEZOID WITH EQUAL SIDES AND A PARALLEL TOP AND BOTTOM

The next drawing shows how adjacent angles are derived from the original one.

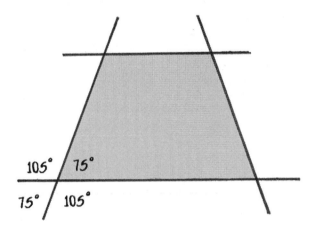

The angles at the bottom can be extended to the top left. Remember that the top and bottom sides of the trapezoid are parallel to one another.

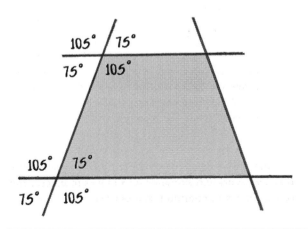

If the left and right sides are mirror images, you can infer that the angles for both sides are the same.

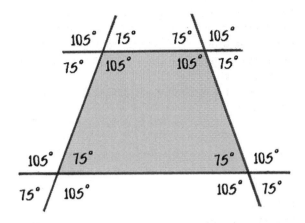

All of the angles in the trapezoid have been described from a starting point of just one. A traditional box set is shaped like a trapezoid with the fourth wall removed, so this example often plays out in real life.

You may notice that some of the angles in the example are greater than 45 degrees. But miter saws won't cut an angle greater than 45 degrees. (Some will do a couple of degrees extra for problem corners.) So how can you cut the larger than 45 degree angles? The secret is that you are not really cutting that angle, but rather its smaller complement.

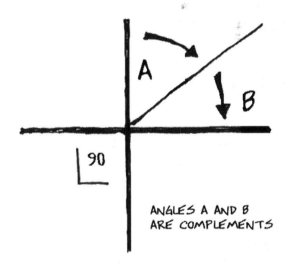

ANGLES A AND B ARE COMPLEMENTS

The complement of an angle used in woodworking is the angle that, when *added* to the original angle, totals 90 degrees. One angle completes the other to make a right angle. In the accompanying drawing the angle of 75 degrees is not used on the saw, but rather its complementary angle, 15 degrees. The complementary angle is used because the trapezoid drawing shows an angle measured from one *side*, whereas the degree

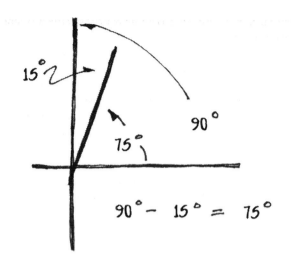

$$90° - 15° = 75°$$

markings on your miter saw are measured from the *end* of the board. The saw is set up so that it is operating from a starting point that is already at a right angle to the length of the section of lumber you are about to cut.

If you have determined an angle and it does not fit, the simplest thing to try next is to subtract the angle you have from 90 degrees and try again. This trick quite often works when you become confused; at least it works for me when I do. Subtracting from 90 degrees will give you the number of degrees in the complementary angle.

It is not unusual to receive drawings that have no degree markings at all, but rather size dimensions only. There is an easy method of marking angles without knowing what the angle degrees actually are.

First lay out a pattern of the perimeter of the shape. This may well occur as a natural consequence of laying out the platform top or some other construction. If not, you can draw the shape on a large piece of paper, or on the floor. This is sometimes known as a full-scale pattern.

Lay a length of lumber along the edge of one of the lines of the full-scale pattern you have drawn. Mark the end of it with a pencil by holding a section of scrap along the intersecting line. Take this marked piece to the miter saw and align the saw blade with the pencil mark you've made. If you cut the board and save both parts, you can lay them in place on your pattern and see if they fit. This is a very expedient method of working with angles, and much faster than using a protractor or bevel gauge. You may never need to know the number of degrees for any of the angles, but if you do, you can read them off the gauge on the saw itself. This method is very accurate because it uses a proportionally large scale to figure the angles. A full-scale pattern is 24 times larger than a ½" scale drawing.

CUTTING CROWN MOLDING

One of the most common jobs for a miter saw is cutting moldings. The most challenging of these is *crown molding*, because of the way that type fits in the corner of the ceiling at an angle.

IN A HOUSE, CROWN MOLDING GOES IN THE CORNER BETWEEN THE WALLS AND CEILING. ON A STAGE SET THERE GENERALLY ISN'T A CEILING, SO THE MOLDING IS ATTACHED ONLY TO THE WALL. IN THIS PICTURE, THE CROWN MOLDING HAS BEEN INSTALLED AND FILLED WITH LATEX CAULK - READY FOR PAINTING. A SEPARATE TRIM PIECE LIES BELOW THE CROWN.

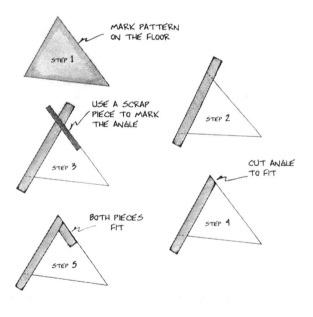

MARK PATTERN ON THE FLOOR

STEP 1

USE A SCRAP PIECE TO MARK THE ANGLE

STEP 2

STEP 3

CUT ANGLE TO FIT

BOTH PIECES FIT

STEP 4

STEP 5

HOW TO MARK AN ANGLE WITHOUT KNOWING THE DEGREES

If crown molding were solid, it would be much easier to visualize how to make it fit on the wall. But to save material and avoid uneven places on the wall, the molding is milled so that there is an open space in the corner where no one can see it. On the back of the crown there are two small flat surfaces, one that touches the wall, and one that touches the ceiling. Between them is a larger flat surface that connects the two smaller ones. The larger flat surface is the edge of the part that has been removed.

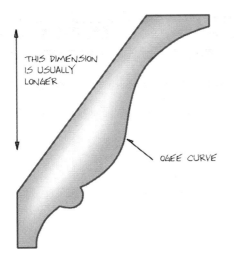

THIS DIMENSION IS USUALLY LONGER

OGEE CURVE

COMMON SHAPE FOR A CROWN MOLDING

GENERALLY SPEAKING, THE BULGE IN AN OGEE CURVE GOES TOWARD THE BOTTOM OF THE MOLDING. THE BOTTOM HANGS DOWN MORE THAN THE TOP PROJECTS OUT ONTO THE CEILING.

Most stage settings don't have a ceiling, and the crown molding is only attached to a wall, which is not a very stable arrangement. You can improve the stability by adding a nailing strip across the top of the wall.

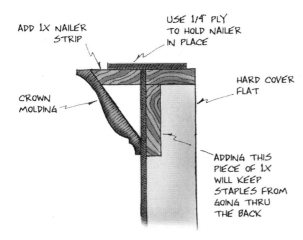

ADD 1X NAILER STRIP

USE 1/4" PLY TO HOLD NAILER IN PLACE

CROWN MOLDING

HARD COVER FLAT

ADDING THIS PIECE OF 1X WILL KEEP STAPLES FROM GOING THRU THE BACK

IT'S POSSIBLE TO SIMPLY STAPLE THE TRIM TO THE TOP OF A GROUP OF FLATS, BUT THE CONNECTION ISN'T VERY STRONG. THIS METHOD SUPPORTS THE CROWN MOLDING BETTER.

Crown moldings don't fit at a 45 degree angle like you might think they would. Instead, the lower part extends farther down onto the wall than the top part does onto the ceiling. The bottom of the molding has the outward sticking part of the ogee curve, and often has an extra detail as well and needs to be longer for aesthetic

reasons. It is important to know which way the molding should hang.

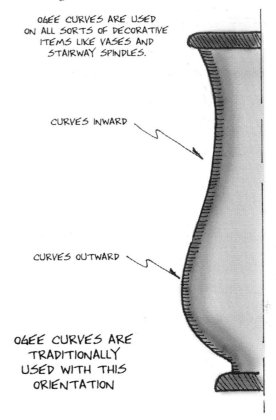

OGEE CURVES ARE USED ON ALL SORTS OF DECORATIVE ITEMS LIKE VASES AND STAIRWAY SPINDLES.

CURVES INWARD

CURVES OUTWARD

OGEE CURVES ARE TRADITIONALLY USED WITH THIS ORIENTATION

The molding fits together one of two basic ways, an inside corner or an outside corner. On an inside corner, the bottom of the trim meets the corner, but on the outside the top projects outward farther than the corner itself, to a point where it meets another piece of trim on the continuing wall.

INSIDE AND OUTSIDE CORNERS FIT DIFFERENTLY

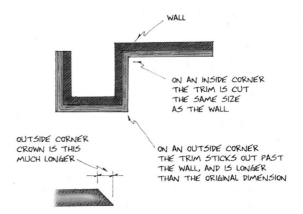

WALL

ON AN INSIDE CORNER THE TRIM IS CUT THE SAME SIZE AS THE WALL.

OUTSIDE CORNER CROWN IS THIS MUCH LONGER

ON AN OUTSIDE CORNER THE TRIM STICKS OUT PAST THE WALL, AND IS LONGER THAN THE ORIGINAL DIMENSION

IT IS MUCH EASIER TO MARK THE SECTIONS OF MOLDING BY HOLDING THEM UP TO THE WALL AND MARKING THEM, THAN BY MEASURING THE WALL AND THEN MARKING THE TRIM.

CUT AN INSIDE CORNER FIRST SO THAT THE TRIM WILL FIT AGAINST THE WALL, AND THEN MARK YOUR CUT FOR THE OUTSIDE CORNER.

It is best to cut the inside corner angle first, and then measure the length of the trim by holding it up to the wall. Carefully place the molding on the miter saw so that it is at the same angle it will later take on the wall. Pretend that the saw fence is the wall, and that the table is the ceiling. *The trim is upside down from where it will go on the wall.* Set the saw for a 45 degree angle and make your cut. You may wish to mark the location of the top and bottom of the crown on the saw by drawing a line with a pencil. That will make it easier to line things up the next time. Or, if you are using a nailing strip, lay a section of it on the saw to hold the crown in place at the correct angle.

Hold the molding up to the wall and mark where the corner meets up with the bottom side of it. The cut you make will angle away from your mark making the overall length longer than the point where the pencil mark is.

USE A PENCIL TO MARK THE SIZE ON THE MOLDING DIRECTLY FROM THE WALL, RATHER THAN USING A TAPE MEASURE. THIS METHOD IS MUCH LESS PRONE TO MISTAKES. THE WALL IN THE PHOTO IS ON ITS BACK, AND A NAILING STRIP ATTACHED.

Put the molding back on the saw in just the same way you had it before, and line the mark up with the blade. Notice that the two cut lines, the first you made and this second one, are actually parallel with one another on the piece of crown molding. This is much more noticeable on a small section. Hold the piece you've just cut back up on the wall to make sure that it fits, and then nail it on with a nail gun or narrow crown stapler. This is one of those jobs that is exponentially easier with a pneumatic tool.

It is easiest to mark the pieces of trim on the wall. It is certainly possible to measure and cut to length, but it is much harder for a beginner to visualize how the parts fit together. When you cut the next section, you will need to rotate the miter saw table 90 degrees in order to get the correct 45 degree angle.

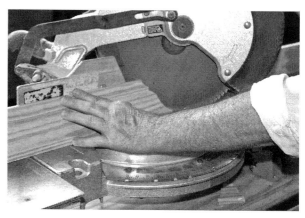

SWING THE SAW 90 DEGREES AROUND
TO CUT THE OPPOSITE ANGLE

IT LOOKS LIKE THE BLADE IS ABOUT TO CUT OFF THIS FELLOW'S ARM, BUT IN REALITY THE BLADE IS SEVERAL INCHES AWAY FROM IT. IT IS IMPORTANT TO KEEP A VERY STEADY GRIP ON THE TRIM, AND TO NOT GET YOUR FINGERS TOO CLOSE TO THE SAW BLADE.

A COMPLETED OUTSIDE CORNER

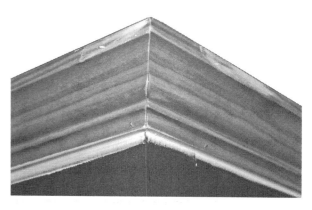

You can twist the trim a little bit this way or that to get a better fit when you attach it to the wall. If one of the sides runs past the other a small amount, sand that off to improve the fit. Use a bit of painter's caulk if there is a small gap that needs filling.

Homebuilders often use a method called *coping* to install crown moldings because it maintains a better fit when the wood dries and shrinks a bit over a long period of time. It is done by cutting the trim off at a 45 degrees angle, and then using a coping saw to remove all of the wood up to the face. That method is somewhat more complex and probably doesn't pay off on stage. Coping only works for inside corners.

Another method of cutting crown molding uses a *double miter* system instead. Notice that the molding cut with the previous method does in fact have a double miter to it, which comes from holding the trim at an angle while cutting it at another angle. If you cut a piece of crown the way I've described, you can set up for a double miter by laying it flat on the saw table and adjusting the blade in both directions so that it lines up with the end of the molding. Use this setting to recreate the same angle without having to hold the trim at a precarious tilt while cutting. The degree settings you discovered will work for any corner the same angle. In addition, you can download tables off the internet that give the number of degrees for corners of varying angles, without having to discover them on your own. The numbers for most crown moldings are approximately 32 and 34 degrees. The 34 is the blade tilt.

THE BAND SAW

Band saws are at their best cutting curves and other odd shapes, although they often have rip fences and miter guides as well. However, unlike the table saw and the radial arm saw, the band saw can be used *freehand*. This means that the piece you are cutting does not need to be guided by a fence, but rather may be manipulated by hand. It is possible to rotate the work through the saw in ways that would be extremely dangerous with a circular saw blade.

The name *band saw* is derived from the type of blade used. Band saw blades are exactly what the name implies, a thin metal strip that has been welded together to form an endless metal band with teeth on it. There are many different styles of blades for various cutting situations. The two main variables in band saw blade manufacture are the number of teeth per inch and the width of the blade from front to back. As with any saw, the larger the teeth (and the fewer per inch) the more aggressively the blade will cut, and also the rougher that cut will be. Six teeth per inch (*TPI*) is a blade with very large teeth, while 32 TPI is very fine. You may find that 10 or 12 TPI is the best for general-purpose work. Large teeth create a higher degree of tear out (splintering), and the sides of the wood that have been cut by the blade will have a rougher texture to them. Smaller teeth will of course result in a much finer cut, but the cutting will be slower and more difficult.

Band saw teeth need to have a fair amount of set to them in order to make cutting curves easier. The extra set allows the blade to cut to the side better. Another factor in cutting curves is the width of the blade from front to back. The smallest size is usually ⅛", and the largest ¾" or so. The thinner the blade, the tighter the possible cutting radius will be.

The best size of blade for general work is probably ⅜" on most saws. That size allows you to cut a reasonably small radius, but is large enough to stand up to some fairly hard use without breaking prematurely. Band saw blades are made by cutting a strip of blade material to a specific length and welding the two ends together to form the band. The weakest point in this structure is the weld, and

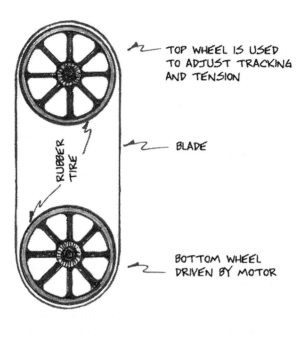

TOP WHEEL IS USED TO ADJUST TRACKING AND TENSION

BLADE

RUBBER TIRE

BOTTOM WHEEL DRIVEN BY MOTOR

BAND SAW WHEELS

if it is not executed properly, the blade will break at that point.

The length of the strip is determined by the size of the saw itself and must be known when new blades are ordered. The easiest way to measure the blade length is from a broken blade, but you can also measure the inside of the saw itself.

A band saw operates by spinning the blade over two (sometimes three) wheels inside the housing of the saw. The wheels have rubber tires on them to cushion the blade as it rotates. The tires have a slight crown in the middle, which causes the blade to center itself there. Outwardly focused inertia, sometimes called centrifugal force, causes the blade to seek the largest possible orbit around the wheel, causing the blade to center itself in the middle of the tire.

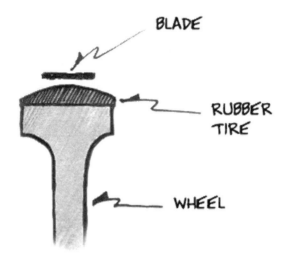

THE CURVATURE OF THE TIRE CAUSES THE BLADE TO CENTER ITSELF ON THE LARGEST DIAMETER

The bottom wheel is usually the drive wheel and is connected to the motor via a belt. The top wheel has a pair of adjustment knobs to keep the blade tracking properly. One knob tightens the blade by increasing the distance between the two wheels. The other is used to tilt the top wheel so that it is in proper alignment with the bottom one. This process is similar to the one used to adjust the belt on a belt sander. These adjustments are amazingly forgiving, but a saw too far out of whack will result in excessive vibration and blade wear, in much the same way that improper front end alignment will affect a car.

The band saw has a table to support the work. This table is generally similar to that on a table saw. There may be a means of attaching a rip fence, and you will most likely find a slot for a miter guide. The rip fence comes

TOP OF A BAND SAW

in handy when cutting foam. Most band saw tables rotate to an angle, making it possible to cut bevels on the machine. On a band saw the table rotates, rather than the blade as on a table saw. It is not practical to angle the two large wheels.

Just below the surface of the table is a *blade guide*. There is a similar guide on the guard that slides up and down to cover the blade. These guides are very important to the proper operation of the saw, and without them it is not possible to use the saw with much accuracy. The function of the guides is to prevent the blade from flaring to the side when a piece of work is fed through the saw. They are especially important for cutting curves. The pressure of cutting curves will bend the blade way out of alignment and make precise work impossible if the guides are not in good working order.

The guides should fit close to the blade to hold it steady, but they should not touch enough to deflect the blade at rest, as this would create a high degree of friction and heat. There are most likely some type of removable leaves that make it possible to alter the thickness of the guides from front to back in order to accommodate the thickness of the blade. Obviously, the guide will need to be thicker for a ¾″ blade than for a ⅛″ blade. There should be some kind of roller bearing to the rear of the guide that the back of the blade can press against when

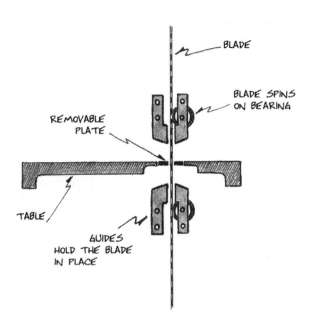

BAND SAW BLADE GUIDES

resistance is met in cutting wood. A roller bearing is used, so that it spins rather than allowing the rear of the blade to cut into its surface.

Installing a band saw blade is a matter of threading the blade through the machine and into its proper position. Of course you should disconnect the saw from power before opening it up. Use the top wheel adjustment knob to move the two wheels closer together. After the blade has been put into position around the wheels, use the same knob to increase the distance and tighten the blade. Most likely there is some sort of gauge to tell you when there is sufficient tension on the blade. If not, tighten the blade and pluck one side like a string on an upright bass. It should be taut enough to make a musical note. Trial and error will teach you the tone to listen for as an indication that the proper tension has been reached. If the blade is too tight, the saw will often make a squealing noise when you start it. If it is too loose, it may slip on the tire and slow down when cutting thick material.

It is possible to install the blade inside out, so that the teeth are pointed up rather than down. It makes sense that the saw cuts downward because that presses the work against the table. If the teeth are pointing up, flip the blade inside out to reverse their orientation.

The band saw is one of my favorite saws to use because it is so much quieter than any other and because most of the sawdust comes out at the bottom of the saw rather than hitting you in the face. There is hardly any danger of kickback, as may be a problem with a circular saw. It is often fun and relaxing to cut odd shapes on the saw. Do not be lulled into a false sense of security, as the band saw can be just as dangerous as any other saw. They

are often used as a meat cutting saw in a butcher's shop. Remember to wear safety glasses and to observe all the safety tips for your particular saw. One of the most important rules is appropriate use of the guard that covers the upper portion of the blade. It is adjustable up and down. Never leave more than an inch of blade exposed above the material you are cutting. Actually, this is a matter of craftsmanship as well, because the closer the blade guide is to your work, the more accurate your cuts will be.

The band saw is an excellent choice for cutting lightweight materials such as polystyrene foam. Foam is so light that it tends to vibrate too much in a table saw, and on occasion the vibration will create a kickback. This will not happen on a band saw.

There are a few techniques for cutting curves that will make your work more accurate. One of these is to start a curved cut with the "soft" side of the cut. If you have a curve that must gently begin at one straight side; that is the soft side. Begin with the edge of the work parallel to the blade and gently turn the wood into the blade. If you do not cut enough material off the first time, go back and try again. It is much better to cut too little than too much.

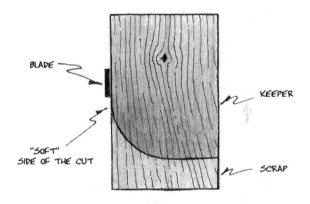

START YOUR CUT FROM THE SOFT SIDE

It is very common to cut circles on the band saw. Most of the time you can simply mark out the curve with a compass and freehand the circle on the saw. But sometimes more precision is required, and a jig can be used to align all the parts perfectly. A jig is a shop built tool that helps a carpenter in doing a specific job. A stop block used on the radial arm saw is a jig. This particular jig allows you to make really exacting curves. It takes a bit of time to get the saw set up for the first circle, but from then on they go really quickly.

A wooden top on the band saw table is required to make this jig work. If your band saw has rails for a rip fence, you can easily make something that slides on and off of the table. If not, you may need something that covers the entire saw table or fits into the miter guide slot.

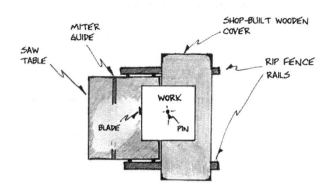

MAKE A WOODEN INSERT THAT YOU CAN NAIL INTO.
PUT A PIN THROUGH THE CENTER OF THE WORK, AND
ROTATE THE WOOD THROUGH THE SAW.

MAKING MANY PERFECT CIRCLES

Cut some squares to the same size as the diameter of the circles you want to make. Find the centers by marking across the corners diagonally. Put a pin through the center where the two marks cross each other. This can be as simple as driving a nail through the wood, if having a small hole in the middle is not problematic. Place the work on the saw table and press the pin down into the surface of the added-on wooden cover. Make sure that the pin is directly across from the blade, and that the edge of the plywood square is touching the edge of the band saw blade. Start the saw, and rotate the work 360 degrees to make a circle. To cut multiples, place the squares on the table one at a time and cut.

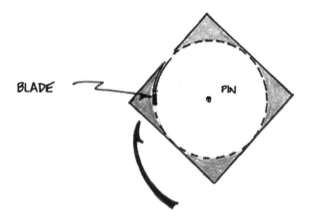

ROTATE THE WORK THROUGH THE SAW
ALL THE WAY AROUND

Another common task is to cut a slot, or notch in a piece of wood. To do that, cut one side, pull the work out, and then cut the other side. Use the blade straight in to *nibble* away at the bottom of the notch.

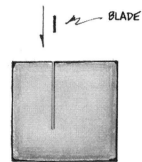

MAKE THE FIRST CUT
STRAIGHT IN, THEN PULL
THE WORK OUT

MAKE THE SECOND
CUT IN

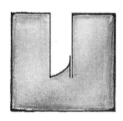

PULL BACK JUST A BIT,
AND THEN CUT OVER TO
THE FIRST CUT

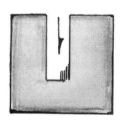

CUT STRAIGHT INTO THE
SLOT AS MANY TIMES AS
NECESSARY TO CLEAR
THE NOTCH

CUTTING A NOTCH WHEN
THE BLADE IS TOO LARGE
TO TURN

Sometimes you need to cut a curve that is very close to the turning limits of the blade. It may be that the saw comes close to cutting a particular curve but binds just a little too much to be workable. In this case you can cut a curve near the one you need, but leaving about ⅛" or so along the outside. If you then come back and cut the original curve, the blade will bind less because the small strip of wood is more easily deflected than the solid piece that was there. Leaving the small ⅛" strip makes the finish cutting more stable. If the curve is way too tight for the blade, you can try cutting many small lines that are tangent to the curve. These methods only work on outside curves and not on inside curves.

If you are cutting a small or lightweight piece, put your thumbs and forefingers on the work, and your other fingers on the saw table. This will help keep the piece steady and decrease vibration as you rotate it through the saw. It also keeps your fingers farther from the blade. There are limits to this. If the piece is too small, the danger of cutting your finger is too great to risk it. If you are not sure if the piece is too small, it probably is.

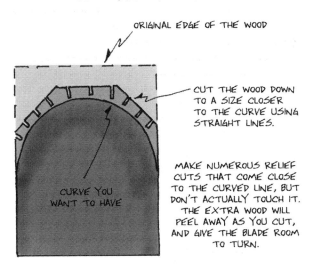

CUTTING SHARP CURVES

ORIGINAL EDGE OF THE WOOD

CUT THE WOOD DOWN TO A SIZE CLOSER TO THE CURVE USING STRAIGHT LINES.

MAKE NUMEROUS RELIEF CUTS THAT COME CLOSE TO THE CURVED LINE, BUT DON'T ACTUALLY TOUCH IT. THE EXTRA WOOD WILL PEEL AWAY AS YOU CUT, AND GIVE THE BLADE ROOM TO TURN.

CURVE YOU WANT TO HAVE

TERMS USED IN THIS CHAPTER

arbor	dado cuts	radial arm saw
band saw	double miter joint	rip cut
blade set	feed rate	rip fence
butt joints	freehand	ripping blades
carbide steel	half lap joint	scab joint
checking	joiner	sliding miter saw
circular saw blade	kerf	stop block
complementary angle	kickback	supplementary angle
coping	lap joint	table saw
covered joint	miter box	tearout
cross cut	miter cut	tool steel
cross cutting blades	miter guide	TPI
crow's foot	miter saw	work
crown molding	nibble	

CHAPTER 11

WOOD AND LUMBER

WOOD AND *LUMBER* are not interchangeable terms, although there is a direct relationship between the two of them. Wood refers to the species of tree that lumber comes from. Lumber is a product that is manufactured from wood. Lumber has a uniform size and fits into certain categories, so theoretically all 2×4s that are 10 feet long are exactly the same size. All lumber is made of wood, but not all wood is made into lumber. Plywood panels are made from logs, just like lumber is, but they are a manufactured product that often uses parts of many different trees sliced up and glued back together.

A BUNDLE OF ONE BUILDING MATERIAL, IN THIS CASE 2×4S,
IS KNOWN AS A UNIT. THE BOARDS LYING OFF TO THE SIDE
OF THE MAIN STACK ARE "CULLS." THE BOARDS NOBODY WANTED
BECAUSE OF A DEFECT—IN THIS CASE SEVERAL ARE QUITE BOWED.

TREES AND WOOD

Trees are divided into two different categories, *hardwoods* and *softwoods*. So is the wood that comes from them. You would naturally assume that the wood from a hardwood is denser than that from a softwood, and for the most part this is true, although the two divisions are actually defined in a way that has nothing to do with how dense they are. The technical definition is that hardwoods are broad-leafed trees, and softwoods are not. They are generally deciduous, losing their leaves in the winter and growing a new set in the spring. Hardwoods as a group are usually denser than softwoods, hence the obvious names, but this is not always the case. Well-seasoned yellow pine varieties can be much denser than some species of mahogany.

Softwoods are coniferous trees that have a needle-like leaf structure. *Spruce*, *pine*, and *fir* are the three types of wood most often used to produce lumber. Together they are sometimes known as SPF or species group one. There are many different varieties of pine trees, but they can be separated into two main types, *yellow* and *white*. Stage scenery has traditionally been constructed of white pine. White pine is an extremely workable wood for building scenery as it is soft and easy to cut, it has a straight grain pattern, and it is widely available in a 1 inch thickness.

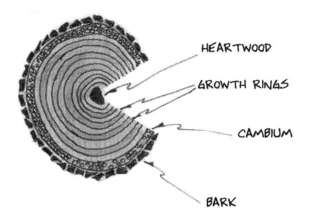

CROSS SECTION THRU
A TREE TRUNK

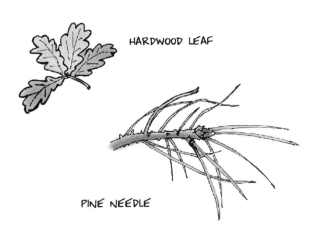

HARDWOOD LEAF

PINE NEEDLE

Understanding the mechanics of tree growth is important in understanding how wood reacts when you build things with it. There is a misconception that trees grow upward out of the ground, but this is not the case. In reality, they grow from the top up and from the outside out and not from the center or bottom. Just under the bark of a tree is a layer of fibers known as the *cambium* or sapwood. The cambium layer of a tree is the area where growth rings originate. Everyone has seen growth rings, which are evident when looking at a cross section of a tree trunk. Each year's growth ring, provided by the cambium layer, is added to the outside of the tree trunk, just under the bark, and not from the middle of the tree. Bark is very much like skin for a tree and protects the cambium layer

from weather and disease. Bark is rough because it must constantly expand as the tree grows.

The cambium is responsible for transporting water and nutrients from the ground to the leaves. It's really a mass of tiny tubes much like blood vessels. These fibers are very strong and pliable along their length, but they aren't bound together all that well. It's possible to strip the fibers from some trees into long strings. This works with other plants as well. Hemp fibers are stripped from the stalk of that plant and then twisted into rope. You might think of celery as being indicative of the fibers in the cambium layer of a tree. When you break celery the stringy fibers that make up the stalk are plainly visible.

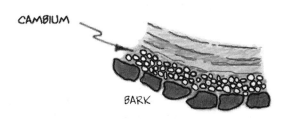

THE CAMBIUM LAYER IS MADE UP
OF MANY SMALL TUBES THAT
RUN FROM THE ROOTS UPWARD

Celery grows to its full size in one season, so there is no division of growth rings. A tree can grow over hundreds of seasons and the *heartwood*, or interior of the trunk, is the remaining evidence of many years' cambium layers. The heartwood is the rigid material that gives the tree its strength and ability to remain erect.

The way a tree grows means that objects on the outside of the tree trunk will eventually be enveloped by it. If a sign is nailed to the exterior of a tree trunk, some years later the tree will have grown around it, causing the sign to eventually disappear. The same thing can happen to wire fences and other man-made objects in the forest.

THIS OAK
HAS GROWN AROUND A SIGN

When a tree limb dies it eventually rots and falls off, leaving a small protuberance or stump. In time this stump is covered over by the natural growth of the trunk. When a tree is harvested and sawn into boards, the dead limb will show up as a *knot*.

Trees grow taller and straighter if other trees surround them, like you would expect in a forest. This forces the tree to grow upward to get to the sun, and causes the lower limbs to fall off. As a result the trunk of the tree, which is the source of lumber, is longer and taller and has smaller knots.

HOW THE CAMBIUM
GROWS AROUND A
DEAD LIMB

The grain is straighter in a forest tree, and lumber from it is less likely to warp out of shape. Most lumber today comes from farm grown trees which are planted just the right distance apart to get maximum production, and the highest quality grain structure.

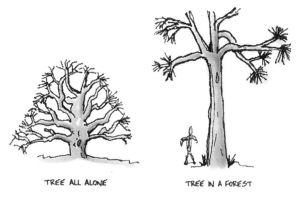

TREE ALL ALONE   TREE IN A FOREST

LUMBER

Lumber refers to wood from a tree that has been cut to a specific dimensional size for use in construction. Lumber is called by its *nominal* or name size, and not the actual dimensions of the board. It can be somewhat confusing, but there is a reason why things are done this way. When logs are harvested to be used as lumber, they are sawn into planks using a very large circular blade. The logs themselves are quite large in cross section and require a blade several feet in diameter in order to get through the entire log. The teeth on such a blade are very big and aggressive. The resulting cut is rough, and because of the difficulty in making precise cuts in so large and heavy an object, the size of the planks is not very uniform.

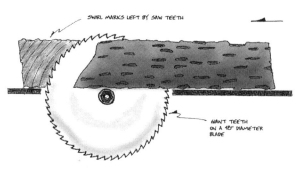

SWIRL MARKS LEFT BY SAW TEETH

GIANT TEETH ON A 48" DIAMETER BLADE

THE SAWMILL PRODUCES VERY ROUGH PLANKS
THAT MUST BE MILLED SMOOTH

In the late nineteenth and early twentieth centuries, buildings were constructed in a rougher way than they now are. Lath-and-plaster construction was much more forgiving of uneven walls and rooms that were not exceptionally square, and rough-cut lumber straight from the saw was good enough. But modern home builders require a more accurate dimension size. Most lumber is really cut for the home construction industry, which is a very large market, and not for the scenery construction business, which is very small by comparison. To accommodate the need for more accurate lumber, rough-sawn planks are today sent through a thickness planer to smooth and shape them to an exact size. This milling process reduces the size of the lumber by a certain amount and is what causes the *milled size* to be somewhat smaller than the nominal size. The milled size is the actual size of a piece of lumber.

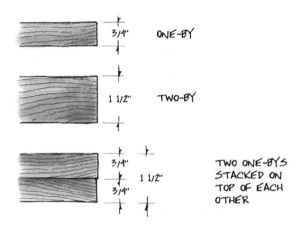

Light construction lumber comes in two main thicknesses. These are most often called by the names *one-by* (1×) and *two-by* (2×), referring to 1 inch thick by some variable width, or 2 inches thick by some width. This is of course a nominal size. Inch symbols (″) are used to represent the word inches. The milled or actual sizes are ¾″ for a one-by and 1½″ thick for a two-by.

The nominal widths of construction lumber are in even numbers of inches beginning with four. The chart shows the thickness and width of common lumber sizes in both the nominal and milled categories.

LUMBER SIZES CHART
NOMINAL TO MILLED

	4	6	8	12
1X	¾ x 3 ½	¾ x 5 ½*	¾ x 7 ¼	¾ x 11 ¼
2X	1 ½ x 3 ½	1 ½ x 5 ½	1 ½ x 7 ¼	1 ½ x 11 ¼

* SOME MILLS MAKE THAT 5 ¼ - THERE ARE SOME REGIONAL DIFFERENCES

There are some similarities in the milled sizes, making it quite easy to remember all of them. As mentioned earlier, all of the 1× thicknesses are actually ¾″ thick, and the 2× thicknesses are really 1½″ thick. All of the milled widths are ½″ narrower than the nominal size except for the 8″, 10″, and 12″ boards, which are ¾″ smaller. Lumber sizes have not always followed this pattern. Milled sizes have gotten smaller several times over the years, and perhaps will again.

Larger sizes of lumber such as 4×4 and 4×6 are available, but they are not commonly used in the construction of lightweight stage scenery.

Dimension lumber is cut to evenly numbered lengths starting at 8 feet long and running through 16 feet (8′, 10′, 12′, 14′, and 16′). (The symbol ′ is used to indicate feet.) The written description of specific lumber sizes is given using the formula: thickness × width × length, and the feet and inch marks are left off. Thus a 1×4 that is 10 feet long would be expressed as a 1×4×10. If this standard form is used, then anyone familiar with the industry should understand what you mean.

Quite often, and especially when building traditional soft covered flats, the need arises for a one-by material that is slightly narrower than a 1×4. It is common practice to rip down 1×12 lumber in order to get a theatrical size called the 1×3. These 1×3s are not available at the lumberyard. The width of 1×3 boards is determined by the largest practical width that can be gotten when dividing a 1×12 into four equal sections. Allowing for the width of the saw blade, this ripped down size is 2⅝″, so the actual, milled size of a 1×3 is ¾″ × 2⅝″. It is an important size to remember when figuring lumber cut lists for flats. Many people use the size 2½″ instead, because the math is easier to compute, but it does loose a bit of the wood.

Since lumber is formed from a natural source rather than being manufactured, the quality of individual pieces varies, and lumber is divided into grades based on how good it is. The major factors used in lumber grading are: grain structure, dryness, and the type and quantity of knots. Lumber with a straight grain structure is the best for construction. Grain that curves and swirls, or that varies greatly in size and consistency, indicates a tree that grew under stress of some type. These boards are more prone to splitting, breaking, and warping.

Lumber is generally dried in a *kiln* to remove excess *sap*, which naturally occurs in the wood. Sap is the nutrient rich fluid that flows up the fibers of the cambium layer, and allows the tree to grow. But after it is cut, an overabundant amount of moisture left in the wood can cause boards to warp and shrink. Lumber that is not thoroughly dried before construction begins will tend to shrink after the structure has been completed.

Even thoroughly dried wood expands and contracts in accordance with the amount of moisture in the air. In humid conditions wood grain absorbs water from the air and swells across its width, but the length of a board is not affected in the same way. The absorption of moisture causes the tiny tubes to swell like a sponge, but they only grow fatter, not longer. As a result, only the width of wood is affected and not the length. This factor is very important in furniture making, but doesn't seem to cause so much trouble with scenery. Even so it explains why doors are made from smaller panels where the grain runs different directions, and not one slab of wood.

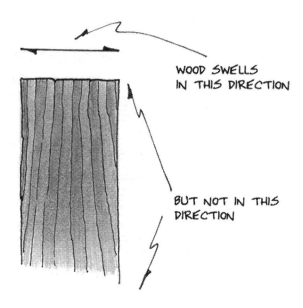

WOOD SWELLS
IN THIS DIRECTION

BUT NOT IN THIS
DIRECTION

WOOD SWELLS
ACROSS THE GRAIN

Knots are formed by limbs that dropped off the trunk as the tree grew. If the knots are small and solid, they have little effect on the structural soundness of the piece of lumber, but if they are large and loose, quality is greatly reduced. *Loose knots* are just that; the wood in the center of the knot is easily moved with your fingers, or is missing entirely.

A grading system has been established in order to differentiate between various grades of lumber.

Obviously, higher grades are more expensive because they are more desirable. In *construction grade* lumber, the grades are #1, #2, and #3. Number-three grade is sometimes known as utility. Number-one grade lumber is of a very high quality, having a straight grain pattern and a minimal number of small knots. Number-two has more knots that tend to be larger and more pronounced. Number-three lumber contains loose knots that fall out and leave a hole.

One of the issues with the grading of construction materials has to do with building codes which specify which materials are suitable for which uses. Codes in most parts of the country specify that #2 is appropriate for most work, so that is what is produced. Some lumber stamped number two is actually better than that stamp would indicate, and some is worse. It pays to be selective when it is possible.

Another grading system is used for *finish grade lumber*. Finish lumber is usually meant to be used in the construction of moldings, cabinets, windows, doors, and other such very exacting work. Finish lumber is much more expensive and is of a much higher quality. Finish lumber is often sold in its rough-cut state, with the customer being expected to plane the boards to a smooth finish. The grades of finish lumber are A, B, C, and D.

Finish lumber that is sold without the benefit of having been milled is generally known as *rough cut lumber*. Rough cut lumber of this type has no standard dimensional size like regular construction lumber. In order to make the most efficient use of the tree, the lumber is left as wide and as long as it is possible, and there are no sizes given other than thickness. The thickness of rough cut lumber is given in quarters. A rough-cut board 2 inches thick is called an 8-quarter board. A 1 inch thick board would be a 4-quarter board.

Finish lumber is priced by a volume measurement known as the *board foot*. One board foot is equal to a

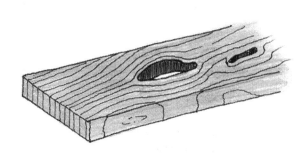

A LOOSE KNOT

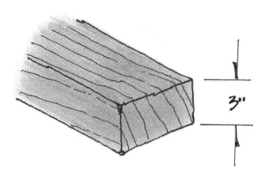

IN THE QUARTER SYSTEM,
A 3-INCH THICK BOARD WOULD
BE DESCRIBED AS 12 QUARTERS

volume that is 1 inch thick by 12 inches square. Another term is the *running foot*, which refers to the total length of all boards involved without regard to their width or thickness. If you have five 1×4s and each one is 12 feet long, then you have 60 running feet of 1×4.

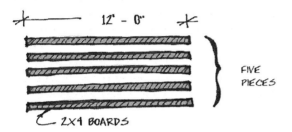

FIVE PIECES OF 2X4 LUMBER

EACH ONE IS 12'-0" LONG.

5 X 12 = 60

THAT IS A TOTAL OF 60 RUNNING FEET.

HOW MANY RUNNING FEET?

Back in the day, it was quite common for lumber yards to list their prices by the board foot, but *stick pricing* is much more common today. A "stick" is one piece of lumber. A price is given for each length of each type of board. Most do-it-yourself, chain-store lumberyards have only #2 lumber priced by the stick.

Because lumber is derived from natural sources, it has a tendency to bend into odd shapes after it has been cut into pieces and milled to an exact size. There are three main ways for this to happen. It is helpful to be able to tell them apart. Each one of these defects can be overcome during the construction process, but the approaches to doing that are different.

The first of these defects is cup. *Cupping* is most pronounced when a board is harvested just to one side of the center of the trunk. Unfortunately, this is the most common location for cutting 1×12s used in building scenery. As a result, the growth rings appear with a preponderance of the softer, lighter colored wood on one side of the board. That side will shrink a bit more in the drying process and the board will curl some to that side as a result.

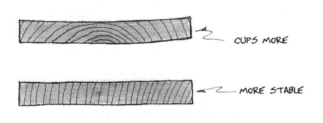

CUPS MORE

MORE STABLE

END GRAIN DIFFERENCES

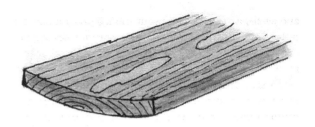

THIS BOARD IS CUPPED

The effect of cupping is reduced when lumber is cut into narrow strips. When the amount of the curve is divided between the boards it becomes proportionally smaller and may virtually disappear.

The second defect is known as *bow*, which occurs along the length of the grain. It is seen as either a turn to one of the flat sides, or to one of the edges. If the bow is a gentle curve along the entire length of the piece, then it can often be worked out as a consequence of internal bracing as in a soft cover flat with toggles. If the bow is the result of a large knot, causing the board to take a sudden turn, it is usually better to try to cut around the knot, and use the board for two shorter pieces.

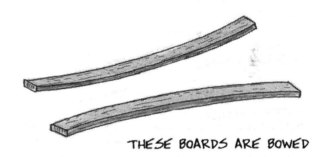

THESE BOARDS ARE BOWED

Warp is used to describe the twisting of a board from one end to the other like a piece of Twizzler candy. It is very difficult to remove this defect with internal bracing. It is best to use this sort of board for very short pieces of stock where the proportional amount of warp is reduced.

THIS BOARD IS REALLY WARPED

PLYWOOD

Plywood differs from dimension lumber in that it is a product *manufactured* from wood rather than being wood simply cut into strips. The main advantages of plywood are that it comes in large sheets, it is very strong, and it is less prone to splitting. Remember that the wood of a tree is formed by the slender tubes of the cambium layer. They run up and down the length of the trunk. The fibers themselves are very strong from end to end, but the bonds that hold them together are much weaker, and as a result wood tends to tear or split along its length. So although you can bend a *long* piece of lumber quite a bit, a *wide* one will snap if you cut a short piece of it and apply pressure.

The standard size of a sheet of plywood, and most other sheet goods, is 4'-0" by 8'-0". By comparison, the widest commonly available lumber is only 12" wide. However, lumber comes in much longer lengths than plywood. So the choice between using plywood or lumber can often be made on the basis of what size pieces you need for a particular project.

Plywood is made by peeling layers of wood off of a large log in much the same way that a hand-held pencil sharpener shaves tiny layers of wood off the end of a pencil. This method of forming plies is known as *rotary cutting*. Sometimes the individual plies are called *veneers*. The layers of wood are glued together to form large sheets.

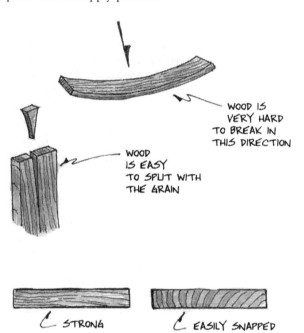

WOOD IS VERY HARD TO BREAK IN THIS DIRECTION

WOOD IS EASY TO SPLIT WITH THE GRAIN

STRONG

EASILY SNAPPED

GRAIN DIRECTION INFLUENCES WOOD STRENGTH

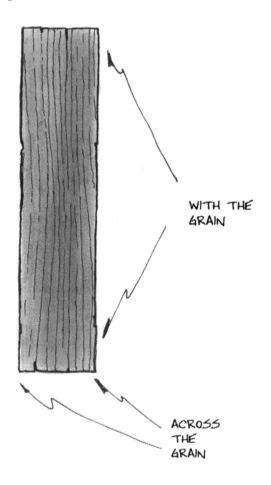

WITH THE GRAIN

ACROSS THE GRAIN

DEFINITION OF TERMS
WITH AND ACROSS THE GRAIN

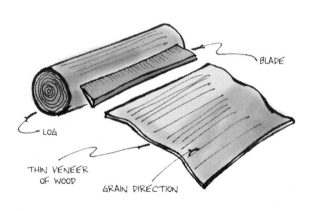

BLADE

LOG

THIN VENEER OF WOOD

GRAIN DIRECTION

PEELING VENEER FROM A LOG BY

Plywood develops its great strength from the way that the grain of various layers is oriented. You have seen that the strength of wood lies along the length of the fibers. The fibers are much stronger and more pliable along their length than are the bonds that hold them together. It is fairly easy to split the fibers apart from one another, but it is much more difficult to break them lengthwise.

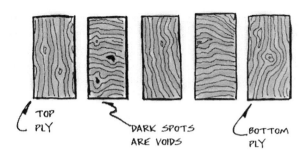

TOP PLY

DARK SPOTS ARE VOIDS

BOTTOM PLY

ALTERNATING WOOD GRAIN IN PLYWOOD

THE B SIDE OF A SHEET OF B/C PLY

ANY KNOTHOLES ARE FILLED AND SANDED SMOOTH

YELLOW PINE PLYWOOD SIDES

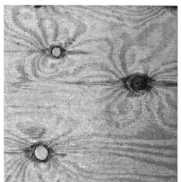

THE D SIDE OF A SHEET OF C/D PLY

KNOTS ARE LEFT OPEN, AND THE TEXTURE OF THE ENTIRE SIDE IS MUCH ROUGHER

If the grains of the various sheets of veneer that make up the plywood are oriented at right angles to one another, the resulting structure will have extraordinary strength in both directions.

That is how plywood is formed, by gluing together the layers of shaved wood with the grain of adjoining plies running in alternating directions. Both of the exterior top and bottom plies on any one sheet are oriented so that the grain of the wood runs along the 8 foot length of the sheet. This means that there are normally an odd number of plies, no matter what the exact number is. A larger number of plies is usually considered to be better. The grain pattern of rotary cut veneers is always rather extreme because the cutters are constantly weaving in and out of the various growth rings. On occasion this is called a "flame" pattern. Sometimes this makes it difficult to determine exactly which way the grain runs, but if you look at the entire sheet you will be able to see it.

The plies are stacked up with a layer of glue sprayed between each one. The adhesive sets up quickly in the presence of heat and great pressure. A press is used to squeeze the assembly together until the glue bonds. After the plies are securely joined together, the sheet is cut to its 4×8 size, and if the grade of plywood calls for it, the surface is sanded smooth to an exact thickness.

Plywood is made from many different types of trees, both hardwood and softwood. Common construction-grade plywood is manufactured from either yellow pine or fir. The type and quality of wood used to make plywood is reflected in its grade.

Plywood is graded with the letters A, B, C, and D. Since there are two distinct sides to a sheet of plywood, two letters separated by a slash mark are used to describe the sheet. For example, A/C or C/D. Statistically you would think that there could be 16 grades of plywood (4 × 4 = 16), but in reality there are many less because not all of the possible combinations of letters exist as grades of plywood. The most common grade of yellow pine plywood is C/D, which is frequently used as an underlayment in home building where the building code specifies it will be strong enough for the purpose. It is minimally sanded on the outside and is therefore very

rough. Knot holes are abundant on both sides. Yellow pine is also used to make B/C ply, which is a much better quality.

Fir plywood is much lighter than yellow pine and tends to warp less. Back in the day, A/C fir plywood was a fraction of the cost it is now, and was used extensively. At the time, mills were not able to effectively peel wild grown yellow pine logs into suitably smooth veneers. Plantation grown hybrid trees are different, and yellow pine plywood is now the norm. B/C yellow pine ply has been plugged and sanded on one side and is a bit rougher on the other. It is very commonly used in building scenery. A/C fir has one excellent side that is very smooth, but the good side of B/C yellow pine is almost as fine. However, fir plywood warps much less and is not nearly so heavy.

When a very good grade of plywood is needed, A2 cabinet grade ply may be the answer. This type of plywood has two sides graded A. It is usually made from birch or some other similar wood. Sometimes, A2 plywood has an inner core of birch veneers and an outer skin of a more exotic wood.

A2 is often touted as being very solid and having no voids. A *void* is an empty space on one of the interior plies of a sheet of plywood. They are quite common in construction grade plywood and usually show up as a slot on the edge of a sheet after it has been cut. They are most often caused by a knothole or some other defect in one of the plies. A2 is generally sanded very smooth on both sides.

GREEN IDEAS TIP BOX

According to the American Panel Association—the governing body for plywood manufacturers—the forest products industry plants about a billion trees every year, and there is more forest cover in the US now than there was in 1920. Yellow pine tree farms dot the southern states, and are often used to manufacture B/C and C/D plywood used to construct scenery as described in this book. You may notice that there are many tips on how to use plywood to create laminated structures that were at one time more likely to be constructed from dimension lumber. Yellow pine plywood is cheaper by comparison, and very abundant. On the other hand, lauan products are generally *not* made from sustainable forests, so you may wish to consider that when selecting materials.

Fir plywood sheets come in a variety of thicknesses from ¼″ to ¾″ in ⅛″ increments (¼, ⅜, ½, ⅝, ¾). The actual thickness of a sheet of yellow pine plywood is a bit smaller than the nominal size. Generally, ¾ is actually ²³⁄₃₂ and other thicknesses are also ¹⁄₃₂ smaller. This slight difference will most likely not matter in what you are building. You can generally depend on plywood to be exactly 4 feet by 8 feet and exactly square. It is often useful as a squaring-up device in constructing scenery.

Lauan is a mahogany plywood variety imported from the Pacific Rim and/or South America. Lauan is a specific variety of mahogany tree, and in today's market many substitutes are used in the same way but are technically not lauan, although the name has stuck. As one variety is exhausted another takes its place. The major advantage of lauan is that it has a very smooth finish that takes paint well. It is, however, not nearly as dense as domestic plywood, and that makes lauan not as sound structurally. It is not rated as to strength by building codes. Lauan is frequently used to make things like hollow core doors.

This material is most commonly available in a ¼″ thickness, but may also be found in ½″ and ¾″ varieties. The ¼″ variety is especially good for small profile pieces that must be cut out with a jigsaw. Since this material is made in countries where the metric system is used, the sizing can be a bit off, but the sheets are generally just as square as any other type of plywood. The actual thicknesses of the various sizes are 6, 12, and 16 millimeters respectively, which is a bit thinner than ¼″, ½″, and ¾″.

Several other engineered wood products come in sheets, but are not technically considered to be plywood. Most of the time that has to do with the way the grain structure of the wood is arranged.

OTHER MATERIALS SOLD IN LARGE SHEETS

A number of other building materials are sold in sheet form. These include hardboard, particleboard, MDF, OSB, foam insulation, and acrylic sheet.

Hardboard is often called by its trade name *Masonite*. It is made from finely ground wood particles that are glued together into a very dense cardboard-like material. The tempered version is semi-waterproof. Hardboard comes in ⅛″, ³⁄₁₆″, and ¼″ thicknesses. Sometimes there are two slick sides, and sometimes one side has a burlap-like texture. The lack of a grain structure greatly reduces the strength of this material and is a serious drawback. It is also very heavy, but it is quite often used as floor covering where those shortcomings are not as problematic. Hardboard can stand up to the punishment of casters, and weight is not so much of a problem once it is on the floor. Hardboard is also used to make pegboards of the sort used in retail stores and closets. You might already be familiar with it in that form.

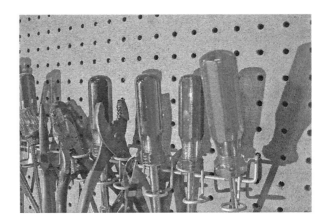

TOOLS ON PEGBOARD

Oriented-strand board (OSB) is made from wood chips arranged so that they overlap one another. The overlapping nature of the wood fibers gives OSB a structural integrity not found in hardboard. It develops a great deal of tearout when cut, but has the advantage of maintaining a flat stability that is not usually found in B/C yellow pine plywood. Plywood tends to keep a great deal of its strength when cut into narrow strips, but OSB does not.

Particleboard is similar to hardboard in that it is made from sawdust that has been glued together into sheets. The particles are larger, and the sheets are much thicker. It is often used for countertops or speaker enclosures where a very dense material is actually a plus. Particleboard is usually not suitable for scenic use because it is extremely heavy, and because it is completely lacking in strength due to the absence of any sort of grain structure.

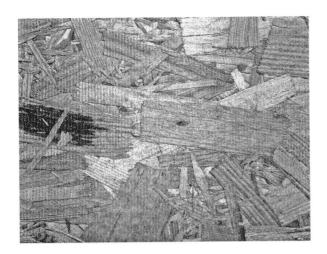

ORIENTED STRANDBOARD

As finding quality lumber has become more difficult, ¾" plywood has become a replacement for one-by lumber. As a result it is often cut into thin strips that are laminated back together. Plywood works fairly well in that application, but particleboard is generally a very poor choice.

MDF, or *Medium Density Fiberboard*, is made in a similar manner as hardboard, but is not nearly so dense. It is frequently used when a dimensionally thick material is required that is smooth and takes paint well. MDF can be very successfully shaped with a router, and is often used to make inexpensive cabinets and furniture. It comes in thicknesses similar to plywood.

PLASTICS

Foam insulation can be found in two main types. *Expanded polystyrene* is made from tiny plastic beads that are expanded and fused together to form large hunks of foam, which are then sliced into sheets. It is white in color, and when carved with a Surform or wood rasp, will

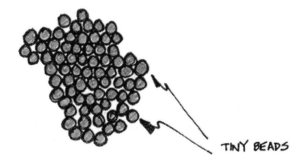

TINY BEADS

EXPANDED POLYSTYRENE IS MADE UP OF MANY TINY BEADS

come apart into small beads. It comes in a variety of thicknesses and widths.

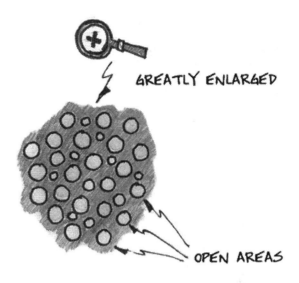

GREATLY ENLARGED

OPEN AREAS

EXTRUDED POLYSTYRENE HAS A VERY FINE SPONGE-LIKE TEXTURE

Extruded polystyrene was originally manufactured only by the Dow Chemical Company under the name Styrofoam. It does not flake off in beads, but has a more homogenous texture that is something like a sponge. It is more difficult to carve, but is better at maintaining sharp edges. Actual Styrofoam is always blue or gray. A competitor's very similar product is pink.

Acrylic sheet is often referred to by the trade name Plexiglas. It comes in clear, mirrored, white, black, and a variety of colors. It's rather expensive, but is much safer than using real glass on stage. Acrylic sheet will break, but does not shatter like glass, and the resulting pieces are not nearly as sharp or dangerous as glass is. Acrylic sheet can be found in a wide range of thicknesses from ¹⁄₁₆" to several inches, but the ¹⁄₁₆", ⅛", and ¼" sizes are by far the most common and usable.

Acrylic sheet bends quite easily, up to a point, and automatically returns to its original state when released. Past that point it will snap. But if acrylic sheet is heated to near its melting point with a heat gun, it can be bent at a sharp angle, and that angle will be retained when the plastic cools. It can be cut and drilled with ordinary woodworking tools, but care must be taken, as the material is very brittle. The main drawback to acrylic sheet is that it scratches so easily.

TERMS USED IN THIS CHAPTER

acrylic sheet
board foot
bow
cambium
construction grade lumber
cup
expanded polystyrene
extruded polystyrene
finish grade lumber
fir
hardboard/Masonite
hardwood
heartwood

kiln
knot
lauan
loose knot
lumber
Medium Density Fiberboard (MDF)
milled size
nominal size
one-by
Oriented-Strand Board (OSB)
particle board
pine
plywood

rotary cut veneer
rough-cut lumber
running foot
sap
softwood
spruce
stick pricing
two-by
void
warp
white pine
wood
yellow pine

CHAPTER 12

ESSENTIAL THEATRE SUPPLIES

WHEN THE WORD *hardware* was coined several centuries ago, it literally meant things made from metal, which was harder than the wood that carpenters used to build most things. Many hardware items that were once made of steel or brass are now plastic instead, but the vast majority of hardware is still metallic in nature. Thousands of different pieces of hardware are available for use in dozens of different construction crafts. Some of the hardware in this section was developed especially to build and rig scenery, but most of it is primarily used to build things other than theatre scenery. Stage carpenters have found creative ways to use hardware to suit their needs.

A trip to a hardware store can reveal many products that aren't made of metal or plastic. Glue certainly isn't, and yet it is often the best way to assemble wooden structures instead of nails or screws which are iconic hardware items. There are many different types of adhesives, for wood, plastics, and even metal. This chapter also includes things like wire, sandpaper, and fabrics that are used so frequently in a theatre scene shop that they are often kept "in stock" and ready to use at any moment. It isn't really practical to make a separate trip to the hardware store every time you need some hot melt glue.

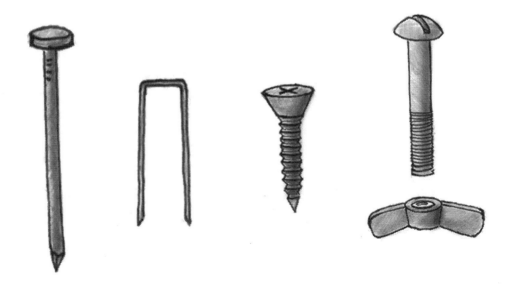

FASTENER TYPES

FASTENERS

Fasteners are used to connect building materials. It is the preferred modern term for the hardware group containing *nails*, *staples*, *screws*, and *bolts*. Each one of these fastener types has different qualities that separate it from the others. A nail is different than a staple, and a screw is not the same as a bolt. It is important to know the names and definitions of things not simply to be able to ask for them, but also because knowing how something works can help a technician to understand why it might be important to choose one piece of hardware over another.

NAILS

Nails were some of the earliest fasteners in common use, at least in part because they require very little technology to produce. The Industrial Revolution introduced machines that could easily manufacture all sorts of things in mass quantities, including metallic hardware. Before that, all metalworking was done by hand, one piece at a time. Early nails were made by cutting across bars of flat stock at a slight angle, and this type of nail is known today as a cut nail. Cut nails are triangular in shape, and if laid head to toe and side by side, it is easy to visualize how they were made. These nails are still manufactured in small quantities for historical restorations.

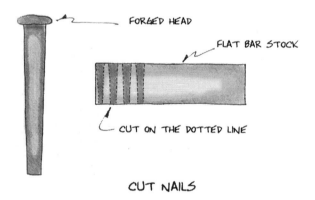

CUT NAILS

The method of categorizing nail sizes was developed during that time, and is related to how they were priced. Larger nails were harder to produce, took more materials, and hence were more expensive. In the US we use the ¢ symbol to indicate cents, but in England a lowercase d is used instead. When the penny system of sizing nails originated, one hundred 3 inch nails cost 16 cents, which was a great deal of money at that time. Smaller nails might have cost 8d or 6d per hundred instead. Of course, we've had quite a bit of inflation since then. The important thing to remember is that the larger the nail, the higher the penny number, and the smaller the nail, the lower the penny number.

In modern times, a two-penny is the smallest size nail available. The 16d nail is the largest commonly used in

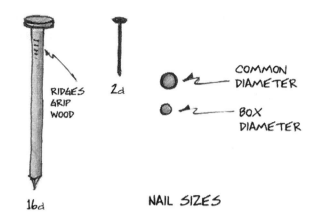

NAIL SIZES

woodworking. A 2d nail is about 1 inch long, while a 16d nail is about 3½ inches long, which should give you some indication of the relative sizes. Smaller nails are usually called *brads*, and larger ones are called *spikes*.

Constructing a home requires a considerable number of fasteners. Modern nails are made from round wire rather than flat bars of steel. They are quickly and easily manufactured by large machines that can turn out thousands in a minute. The prices of today's nails are mostly related to the cost of the steel wire and distribution of the finished product. Allowing for inflation, they are quite inexpensive by comparison to the earlier version.

Modern, machine-made nails are more precise than old cut nails, yet even so it is not really necessary to be terribly exact in making them. If a 16d nail is said to be about 3½" long, it might well be 3¼" or 3⅝". The work that they do does not require an exact tolerance.

The diameter of the nails is related to the length and is an arbitrary but standard gauge. The longer a nail is, the larger its diameter. Even so, there are two classifications of diameter, box and common. *Box nails* are thinner than *common nails*. A 16d box nail is skinnier than a 16d common nail, but a 4d common nail is smaller in diameter than a 16d box nail because the whole nail is smaller. Box nails are usually best for scenery because they are thinner and tend to split lumber less easily.

USUALLY A 20d FOR BACKFLAP HINGES

BENT NAIL FOR HINGE PIN

Most fastener outlets stock nails in even penny sizes from 2d to 16d. Larger than 16d, nails tend to come in even multiples of 10, like 20d, 30d, 40d, and so forth. These larger sizes are not of much use to the scenic technician as a nail per se, but if you bend the head at a 90 degree angle, a nail can become a replacement hinge pin. Bent 20d and bent 40d nails fit two commonly used sizes of hinges.

Nails today are typically sold in small boxes of arbitrary amounts, or possibly by the pound. Traditionally though, a larger, standard sized box of nails weighed 50 pounds. That is a very large number of 4d box nails, but not so many 16d common.

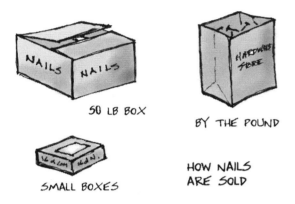

50 LB BOX

BY THE POUND

SMALL BOXES

HOW NAILS
ARE SOLD

There are several different types of nail heads. The most recognizable is the standard flat head. This kind of head is used for most nailing, especially when the heads will not show in the final product. The head of this type of nail is easy to grasp and remove with a claw hammer whenever that is necessary. However, the nail head serves another purpose that is not so obvious, but is the real reason it exists. The head prevents the nail from going entirely through a piece of lumber. In most construction scenarios, a thin piece of wooden material is being nailed to a thicker piece, such as a sheet of ¾″ plywood being

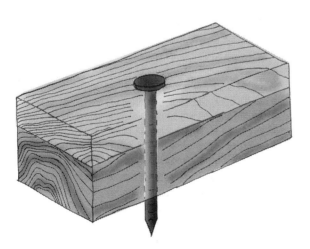

THE HEAD OF A NAIL KEEPS THIN PIECES OF WOOD
FROM SLIDING OFF THE NAIL SHAFT.

nailed to a 2×4. If the nail had no head, movement in the wood could easily work the nail all the way through the plywood, and the two pieces would come apart. The head keeps that from happening. It is important to drive nails all the way down so that the heads are snug in order to get the greatest holding power from them.

The *finish nail* is another type. Many people mistakenly think that a finish nail has no head, but in reality it has a very small head that is intended to be driven completely beneath the surface of the wood it is holding down. The small head is large enough to get a grip on the wood, but tiny enough to leave only a very small entrance hole on the surface of the wood. A close inspection reveals a small dimple on the finish nail head that may be used in conjunction with a *nail set* to "set" or drive the head just below the surface of the work. The resulting hole may later be filled and sanded so that it does not show. This technique is how the finish nail got its name, because it is meant to be used in "finishing" work, such as applying trim to doors and windows.

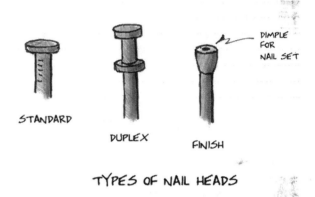

STANDARD

DUPLEX

FINISH

DIMPLE
FOR
NAIL SET

TYPES OF NAIL HEADS

A duplex or double-headed nail looks much the same as a standard nail, except that there are two heads on the shaft about ½ inch apart. The double head approach is meant to secure the wood with one head, and to leave the other head standing up so that you can pull the nail out at some future date.

Another category of nails is meant to be used in a *nail gun*. Most nail guns in a shop are pneumatic, meaning that they run on air pressure. They are covered in the chapter on tools. Nails of this type must be manufactured to a much closer tolerance than ordinary nails because they need to precisely move through the gun without jamming. Most often these nails come in some sort of strip, which is glued or taped together as a means of organizing them. Each company has its own patented method of producing nails that is different from everyone else's, so that the nails are usually not interchangeable. In recent years, competing nail manufacturers have sprung up to make generic "brand x" type nails for some of the guns. There are many different sizes, from those that shoot nails comparable to a 16d, down to those that shoot much smaller finish nails.

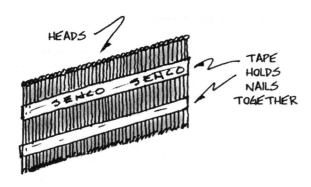

NAILS FOR A PNEUMATIC GUN

The holding power of small finish nails is not very great. Many of the construction methods depicted in this book require that wooden joints be glued together as well. Glue joints are very strong, but the parts must be closely held together until the glue has a chance to bond. In some types of construction, clamps are used for that purpose, but putting them on is a very slow and tedious process. Pneumatic finish nails are a great way of pinning the joinery together until the glue sets. Even though the tiny pneumatic nails don't have much holding power, they are easy to put in, and they hold well enough for the short time they are needed.

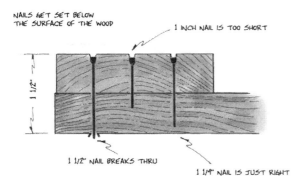

NAILS GET SET BELOW
THE SURFACE OF THE WOOD

1 INCH NAIL IS TOO SHORT

1 1/2"

1 1/2" NAIL BREAKS THRU

1 1/4" NAIL IS JUST RIGHT

MAKING A NAIL SELECTION

One thing to remember about these nails is that like all finish nails they are meant to be set into the surface of the work about ⅛″. If you are using them to join two pieces of one-by stock (that are really ¾″ thick), care must be taken to select a nail that will not go all the way through and out the far side of the work. The two pieces of wood are 1 ½″ thick when placed together. If a 1½″ nail is used, the setting of the nail will send it ⅛″ through the wood. A nail 1 ¼″ long would be a better choice in this application.

Some nail guns are meant to be used with much larger nails, and in general construction they are meant

to assemble the wooden skeleton or *framing* of a house. They are ideal for construction that involves 2×4 lumber, and can really speed things up if you are building scenery from that type of material. Large nail guns of this sort may be called framing guns, because of the type of work they are used for.

STAPLES

Staples are used in a very similar manner to nails, but there are some important differences. A nail is one metallic shaft, whereas a staple has two *legs* connected by a top section known as the *crown*. The physical manner in which staples connect materials together is different from a nail in a very important way.

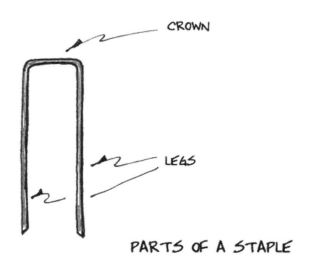

PARTS OF A STAPLE

Everyone is familiar with a desk stapler that uses very small staples to batch together loose sheets of paper. This kind of stapler uses a small metal plate to bend over the ends, or legs of the staple after they have passed through the last sheet, trapping the pieces of paper together. You can imagine what would happen if you drove a nail into the papers instead, the sheets would fall right off. Construction staples are different in that they are not intended to be bent over; instead the legs go all the way into a piece of wood. But construction staples are similar in that they are great at connecting very thin materials to a thicker frame.

As a result, staples are a better choice for certain applications than nails are. The most obvious example is attaching ¼ inch plywood or lauan to 1×3 framing. The crown of the staple tends to catch a certain amount of the wood fibers under itself and uses them to hold the thin ply to the framing underneath. Nails from a gun don't work well because they tend to shoot all the way through the thin plywood.

Construction staples come glued together in a strip just as desk staples do. They are generally classified by the

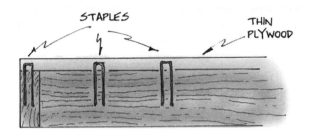

When using a thin covering material, staples grab some of the wood and hold it down rather than shooting right through

length of the leg in inches, ¾″, 1½″, etc, and by the width of the crown. Most staples have a crown that is either ¼″ or ½″ wide. One-quarter ″ wide staples will not fit into a gun intended for ½″ crowns. The narrow crown staples are generally set into wood like a finish nail, while wide crown ones are not.

Staples are also best suited to other thin materials, such as fabric or cardboard or paper, but a large construction stapler may be too powerful for them, and shoot the staple right through. Hand-operated, manually powered staplers are useful for stapling smaller objects. A fabric stapler is a pneumatic gun that shoots very small gauge staples that are often used in upholstery work.

Some staples are not intended to be used in a gun. There are fencing staples, which are essentially U-shaped bent nails with two sharp ends, and also insulated staples designed for electrical work. Modern insulated staples are made of two small 2d nails that are connected by a piece of plastic. Plastic is used in this application because it does not conduct electricity. It is not a good idea to use a metal crown staple on electric wires because of the chance that the staple will be driven too far and cut through the wiring insulation. That would cause a short circuit. Only the insulated staples are approved by the National Electric Code.

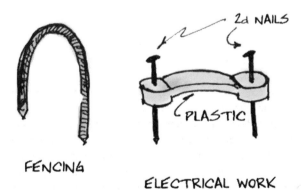

FENCING

ELECTRICAL WORK

SCREWS AND BOLTS

Screws and bolts are fasteners that use *threads* to hold themselves in position. Threads are the ridges found on the side of the shaft of a screw or bolt. A close inspection will reveal that a thread is really one long ridge that curves round and round, spiraling from one end to the other.

Sometimes it is easy to become confused about the difference between screws and bolts. Generally speaking though, bolts are used with a *nut* that holds the bolt in place. The nut has female threads that match the male threads on the bolt. On occasion, female threads are tapped into a hole drilled into a metal structure or housing. Then a bolt can be screwed into that pre-threaded opening rather than using a nut. The threads on a bolt are sometimes called *machine threads*. Bolts have a blunt end.

Screws have a pointy end and make their own pathway into wood, plastic, or sheet metal. They compress the material on either side in order to form that hole. The male threads of the screw grip the walls of the hole with much more holding power than a nail does. Screws form their own female threads in the work material.

Even though these descriptions hold true most of the time, some smaller bolts are referred to as *machine screws*. Many people think this is a plot hatched by manufacturers, just to make the whole thing more confusing. But if you remember that bolt threads are called "machine" threads, it is a bit easier to understand.

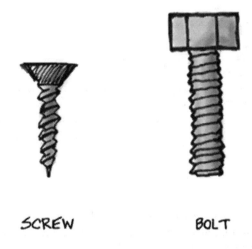

SCREW   BOLT

Screws and bolts come in a variety of different head shapes so that you can select a style that works well for the particular job at hand. Perhaps the most common type in theatre work is the *flat head*. The flat head is used when it is necessary to maintain a flat surface, with none of the screw head protruding above the surface of the work. This kind of head is often used to attach certain types of hardware, such as hinges, picture hangers, hanging irons, and so forth. The cone-shaped flat head is manufactured to fit into *countersunk* holes in the hardware just mentioned. Some screws and bolts have a *round head*. It is intended to show above the surface.

Older-style sheet metal screws have a head similar to the round head, but with a flattened top. This kind is called a *pan head* because it is the same basic shape as the interior of a cast iron skillet. Sheet metal screws are not intended to sink in flush because the material they are used on will not allow it. The pointy ends of these screws are used to connect pieces of thin sheet metal, and as a result the screws themselves are made from very hard steel. This theoretically allows them to work their way through the metal without dulling or breaking. Pan head screws are difficult to install with a power tool, so other types are more popular now, especially the hex head.

SCREW HEADS

Several very popular *drives* are used for screw heads, the *standard slot*, the *Phillips*, and the *square*. The drive is the part of the screw that is used to force, or drive it into the work. When screws were made by hand, slotted heads were the only type feasible to manufacture, but in the machine age the Phillips drive has all but totally replaced it. The Phillips drive is much easier to use with a power screwdriver, which is the only logical way to drive the thousands of screws it takes to put together a stage setting. In recent years there has been a move toward even more functional shapes, with the most successful being the square drive.

The major problem encountered in using a power screwdriver (such as a variable speed drill) is that the driver bit tends to slip out of the screw head. This can lead to deforming the head in such a way as to make it impossible

TYPES OF DRIVES

to get the screw in or out. The Phillips head handles this problem much better than the slotted head, and the square drive is better than the Phillips. The only problem with square drive screws is that they are more difficult to find in all sizes. As a result you might wind up with a mixture of half square and half Phillips drive screws in the shop. Obviously, production will be streamlined if only one kind of fastener is used, and there is no need to change bits back and forth. Perhaps in the future square drive will overwhelm the Phillips drive in much the same manner as Phillips replaced slotted.

The diameter of a screw is determined by a gauge number that is fairly arbitrary in nature. A common gauge screw for attaching hinges is the #8. To give some basis for comparison, #2 screws are teeny tiny, whereas a #12 screw is about the largest commonly found. The practically microscopic screws used on things like eyeglasses have numbers like 00 or 0000. The length of screws is described in inches or fractions thereof.

Not all screws are manufactured in the same way, or are of the same quality. Ordinary wood screws have a thread that does not extend all the way from the point to the head, but rather stops short of the top, leaving a portion of the shank smooth. Another type of screw known as a tapping screw has threads that are continuous. The tapping screw also seems to have sharper threads, and they are much easier to drive.

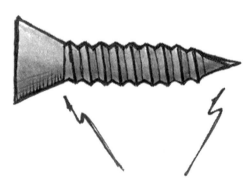

THREADS RUN THE ENTIRE LENGTH OF THE SCREW

TAPPING SCREW

Drywall screws are extremely popular. They were developed to hang wallboard in houses, which is also known as drywall. These screws are very long and thin, and have a distinctive appearance. They have what is called a bugle head, which looks and works much the same as a Phillips flat head. Drywall screws are most often black in color. They come in two gauges, #6 and #8. The lengths are somewhat odd, generally being ⅞″, 1¼″, and 1⅝″ for the shorter screws, and then jumping up into the 2″, 3″, and even 4″ ranges. Very recently, ¾″

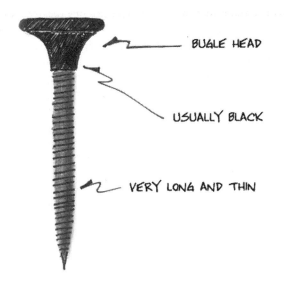

DRYWALL SCREW

- BUGLE HEAD
- USUALLY BLACK
- VERY LONG AND THIN

#8 drywall screws have become available, and are excellent for attaching theatrical hinges and other hardware.

Drywall screws are very hard and brittle, so the heads tend to break off if too much torque is used to drive them into the work. If a drywall screw is sticking through the back of a piece of scenery it can be easily snapped off with a hammer, or even your foot. This would not be even remotely possible with any ordinary type of screw, and serves as a demonstration of how hardness and malleability are inversely proportional, an issue that often comes up in the steel made to construct tools. Drywall screws need to be made of especially hard steel because of their length and their thin nature. Some drywalls have a fine thread and others are coarse. The coarse threads tend to hold better in wood.

Tech screws are also known as self-tapping screws. (If you spell tech with a K, it becomes Tek, a well-known brand name.) The tip is a small drill bit that can make

its own way into thin steel such as 16ga square tube, creating its own machine threads that then secure the screw in place. Tech screws are usually either 8, 10 or 12 gauge in diameter and are available in a variety of lengths. There are three types of heads, a large bugle head, a pan head, and a hex head. All of them are intended to be used in conjunction with a power driver, because tech screws cannot be driven by hand. The hex type is much easier to install, but it leaves a rather large and unsightly head above the surface of the wood. The flat-headed type is harder to spot once the scenery has been painted.

As mentioned earlier, the difference between screws and bolts lies in the type of thread that is used. Screw threads are pointy at the end that must start into the wood, and the threads flare outward so that they can gain more purchase on the surrounding material. Machine threads are exactly the same from beginning to end, so that they are in synch with the threads found on a matching nut. Tech screws have a drill bit on the end that creates the hole for it in the steel. The screw then taps its own treads in the metal. Normally, a bolt must have a hole drilled for it in advance, whereas a screw tends to make its own pathway. So tech screws are an interesting blend of the two.

Bolts are sized by their diameter and by their length in inches. The diameter is given first and the length second, as in "quarter-inch by three-inches." Metric bolts are not commonly used in scenery building in the states because scenery is not exported. Very small bolts less than $\frac{3}{16}''$ in diameter are sometimes referred to as machine screws and given a gauge number starting at #10 and going down.

Threads on a bolt are proportional to the size of the bolt itself, so that the threads of larger bolts are larger than the threads of smaller bolts. The number of threads is often listed with the size of the bolt, as in $\frac{1}{4}$ inch/20. The number 20 as used here refers to *threads-per-inch*, or *TPI*. Each diameter of bolt has a normal number of TPI, but sometimes manufacturers will deviate from the norm for

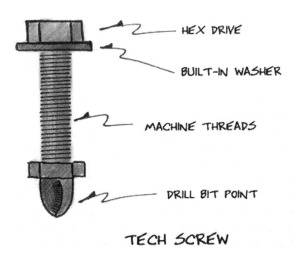

- HEX DRIVE
- BUILT-IN WASHER
- MACHINE THREADS
- DRILL BIT POINT

TECH SCREW

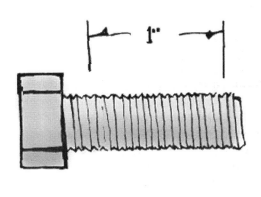

1"

16 TPI
(THREADS PER INCH)

a specific purpose, and you may find that even though your replacement bolt is of the same diameter, it still will not work properly. Quarter inch bolts have a standard 20 TPI, and three-eighths have a standard 16 TPI. Those sizes rarely have any other option. But very small machine screws like the #8 or #6 are often found with a variable number of threads.

Almost all screws and bolts are threaded right-handed, which means that to tighten them you should turn to the right, or clockwise. To remove, apply force to the left, or counterclockwise direction. Someone long ago came up with the phrase, "Righty tighty, lefty loosey."

The load capacity of heavy duty bolts is rated with marks on the bolt head. These marks relate to a numbering system for toughness. Rated hardware is guaranteed to hold a certain amount of weight. Grade 8 bolts are the strongest, but grade 5 is a more common hardware store variety. Many types of hardware have both rated and unrated versions.

Hex heads are a very popular drive for bolts, because they are intended to be used with a wrench. The amount of force used to tighten bolts is described as *torque*. A wrench applies much more leverage to a bolt than a screwdriver does. The higher torque of a wrench will get the bolt much tighter than a screwdriver can. Bolt head sizes naturally correspond to wrench sizes, in inches. The size of the head and the size of the shank of a bolt are two separate issues. The size of a bolt as it is listed at the hardware store refers to the size of the shank, not of the head. A ¼ inch bolt has a seven-sixteenths head.

The heads of *carriage bolts* are entirely different. They have a smooth, slightly rounded head with no gripping surface. The carriage bolt has a bit of square shank just below the head that is meant to be used in conjunction with a square hole in metal surface, or with a *torque washer* into wood.

A torque washer has a square hole in the center and teeth on the outside edge. The teeth dig into a wooden surface and prevent the carriage bolt from turning while the nut is tightened. If a carriage bolt is used in wood without a torque washer, and the threads of the bolt are

disrupted in some way, it may be impossible to remove the bolt without an angle grinder. Many people like the tight way the heads fit against the side of a platform.

Round heads are often found on *stove bolts*, the ¼" diameter bolts often used to hold scenery together. Stove bolts typically have threads all the way up to the head, while other types do not. The others may run out of threads before the bolt is completely snug. That is known as bottoming out.

Threaded rod can be purchased in lengths from 36" up. They come in all the popular diameters and can be useful when regular bolts are not long enough. Threaded rod does not have a head, but works quite well if you use nuts at both ends.

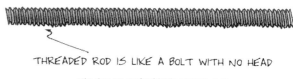

THREADED ROD IS LIKE A BOLT WITH NO HEAD

CUT ROD TO THE DESIRED LENGTH, AND
USE A NUT AT BOTH ENDS TO MAKE YOUR OWN HEAD

Nuts are most often hex shaped, but some older types are square. *Wing nuts* are just about the only other type, and they are very helpful because they can be made *finger tight* without the use of a tool.

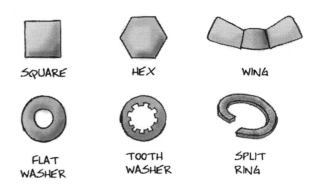

SQUARE   HEX   WING

FLAT   TOOTH   SPLIT
WASHER   WASHER   RING

BOLT HEADS, NUTS, & WASHERS

It is generally best to use *washers* with bolts because this spreads out the holding force of the bolt over a greater surface area for the pieces being bolted together. The larger footprint makes it much less likely that the bolt will pull itself through the hole and cause the joint to fail. Also, washers keep the action of tightening the nut from marring the surface of the work and make it easier to get the nut tight. You should always turn the nut, not the bolt, especially if the bolt is holding together steel pieces. This helps protect the threads on the bolt from becoming damaged. Regular washers are generally known as *flat washers*. *Split ring* washers and *tooth washers* may be used

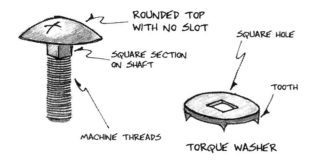

ROUNDED TOP
WITH NO SLOT

SQUARE HOLE

SQUARE SECTION
ON SHAFT

TOOTH

MACHINE THREADS

TORQUE WASHER

CARRIAGE BOLT

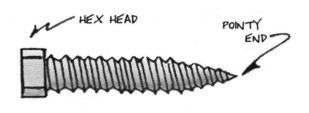

LAG BOLT

where vibration is a problem. These types of washers keep tension on the nut at all times and prevent it from working itself loose.

A *lag bolt* is a hybrid type of screw/bolt. They look like large screws that have a hex head on them. They are sized like a bolt, but go in like a screw. They are most often used to secure large items like lighting towers to the deck. Lag bolts often require a pilot hole for insertion.

CHOOSING THE CORRECT FASTENER

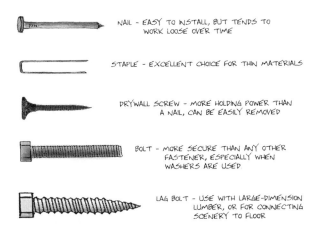

NAIL - EASY TO INSTALL, BUT TENDS TO WORK LOOSE OVER TIME

STAPLE - EXCELLENT CHOICE FOR THIN MATERIALS

DRYWALL SCREW - MORE HOLDING POWER THAN A NAIL, CAN BE EASILY REMOVED

BOLT - MORE SECURE THAN ANY OTHER FASTENER, ESPECIALLY WHEN WASHERS ARE USED

LAG BOLT - USE WITH LARGE-DIMENSION LUMBER, OR FOR CONNECTING SCENERY TO FLOOR

FASTENER COMPARISON CHART

In general, staples have more holding power than nails, screws have more holding power than staples, and bolts are more secure than screws. If two wooden pieces are glued together as well as nailed or stapled, the strength of the joint will be much stronger. A properly applied adhesive creates a much stronger bond than you might think, but the words *properly applied* should be considered very carefully. It is virtually impossible to disassemble wooden pieces that have been glued together, so don't use glue if you need to take something apart later on.

Screws work really well for joining wooden structures when disassembly is planned in the future, and drywall screws are very popular for that sort of thing. Bolting is generally the most secure way of fastening parts together. Anything that hangs overhead should be bolted for safety

reasons, and if there is any question at all about the weight of the piece, be sure to use rated bolts and other hardware. This is especially true when the load is pulling on the fastener along its length. A sideways force creates a shearing stress, which is generally less likely to pull two wooden structures apart, because that would require the total failure of the wood surrounding the joint. But if the force is one that pulls along the length of the fastener, it is much easier for a nail, staple, or screw to fail. In that case, a bolt with the appropriate sized washers has much more holding power.

HINGES

Hinges are crucially important to the rigging of stage scenery. Except for fasteners, they are used more than any other type of hardware. You are familiar with how hinges work when hanging a door, but in the theatre they are used in a much larger variety of applications. Hinges are often used on scenery as a fastening or connecting device and not because they can be made to swivel back and forth.

The shaft that runs through the *barrel* of the hinge and holds the two *leaves* together is known as the *pin*. Some hinges have tight pins that are permanently attached to the hinge. A loose pin hinge can be separated into two halves when its pin is removed. If one leaf of the hinge is connected to one piece of scenery, and the second leaf to another unit, you can disassemble the two units by simply removing the pin.

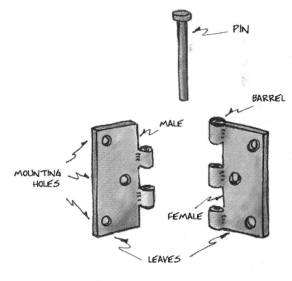

PARTS OF A HINGE

Butt hinges are used to hang doors. The name is derived from the fact that this type of hinge is intended to butt up against the edge of the door. In woodworking, boards that meet at their edges are said to be butting

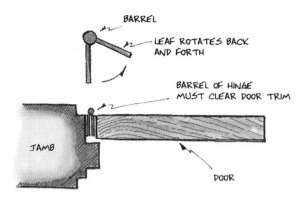

HOW A BUTT HINGE WORKS

against one another, and when connected in this way the result is called a butt joint. An inspection of any butt hinge will show that the two leaves or sides are much taller than they are wide. If you compare the shape of the hinge to the edge of the door where it is used, the specific shape of the butt hinge makes sense. Butt hinges are meant to be used in pairs, as one alone would not provide much stability when the door swings open. Heavy, or heavily used doors may have three or even four hinges on them. There is an online chapter about doors and hinges.

Butt hinges are usually sized by the height of the leaf. Three inch butts are fairly small, while 4 inch butts are quite large. The width of the leaves is proportional to the height. For theatrical use the 3 inch size is large enough for most applications. Some modern-day butts have rounded corners. These corners are intended to complement the use of a router and jig in creating the mortise that the hinge fits into. A straight corner hinge is generally more preferable when a jig is not used.

Strap hinges are shaped like two isosceles triangles joined at the base. This type of hinge is intended to be used on gates where they are meant to be bolted to the front. Butt hinges are shaped to fit the edge of a door, but strap hinges are shaped to take advantage of the large flat surface of the front of the gate. Strap hinges are best when a large, very heavy-duty hinge is required. Its shape makes it a natural candidate to be bolted to a bulky scenic unit. A close relative of the strap hinge is the *T hinge*, which is like a strap hinge on one side, and a butt hinge

on the other. The unique shape of this hinge can be useful in certain situations.

Another type of hinge may be referred to as a "saloon-door," or "kitchen-door" hinge, but is technically known as a *double action, spring loaded hinge*. Swinging doors are frequently required to facilitate stage movement. Directors love to have doors swing back and forth to reveal characters in a farce or other comedy. Mounting a swinging door hinge can be quite a challenge as it is somewhat more complicated than a butt or strap hinge. The common type of swinging hinge operates by using two spring loaded barrels that are located on either side of the door. Rather than having two leaves, as most hinges do, this type has three. The center one serves only to connect the two barrels. This leaf is not attached to either the door or the jamb.

DOOR SWINGS BOTH WAYS

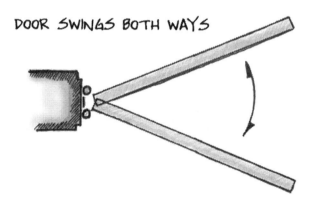

Around the top of each hinge barrel are a series of holes. A steel pin is used to turn the disk where the holes are located. (The manufacturer will most likely supply a special tool, but after you have lost it, a nail with the point ground off will do nicely.) Rotating the disk winds a spring that gives the hinge its ability to swing. A short pin is used to prevent the spring from unwinding. There are two barrels on each hinge, and all of the barrels on all of the hinges must be wound in order for the door to

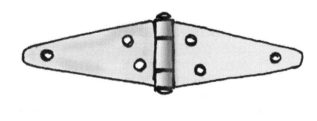

STRAP HINGE

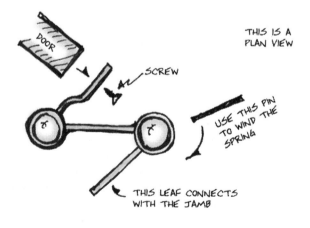

SWINGING DOOR HINGE

operate properly. It is possible to vary the speed of the closing of the door by adjusting the amount of tension on the springs.

This type of hinge comes in a variety of sizes, which mostly have to do with the thickness of the door slab. The hinge must be large enough to properly fit on the edge of the door. If the door is too thick for the capacity of the hinge, there will be no place for the barrels to fit. A close relative of the swinging door hinge is the *double action hinge* that swings in much the same way, but is not spring loaded. These may be used on folding screens, but are not sturdy enough to be used on heavy scenery.

There are a number of different types of cabinet hinges. Some of them greatly resemble butt hinges and are used in more or less the same way, but on a smaller scale. Some are meant to be face mounted like a strap hinge.

CONTINUOUS OR PIANO HINGE

The *backflap hinge* is a type of hinge made especially for theatrical use. It is generally not used in the traditional way—that is, to allow a piece to rotate. The backflap is more often used as a connector that holds scenery together. It allows stagehands to take scenic units apart, and then put them back together easily and quickly. Backflap hinges are indicative of the kind of methodology that gives scenery its knockdown, pull-apart, throw-on-a-truck, and then-reassemble-for-act-three-in-Peoria style. Early twentieth-century wooden scenery revolved around this portability factor. Traditional scenery is constructed so that it is lightweight and movable, whether the intent is to tour, or to allow for the production of a play with multiple scenes that must be reset. In commercial theatre, virtually all scenery is built elsewhere and must be trucked in to the theatre. The use of backflap hinges has traditionally been a critical link in this methodology. Hinging and bolting scenery together is covered in detail in the construction chapters.

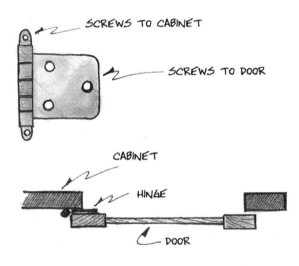

CABINET DOOR HINGES

The most popular type of cabinet hinge is the self-closing flush-mount. These are used for American-style doors that do not cover the entire front of the cabinet. On this type of cabinet the face frame and one half of the hinge are visible when the door is closed. This type of hinge attaches to the back of the door, and to the front of the face frame. The modern self-closing type does not actually close the door, but will hold it shut without using any type of catch or latch. Self-closing cabinet hinges are very cheap, plentiful, and easy to install without any special tools. An offset, or inset type, is available for doors whose backs are not on the same plane as the front of the face frame, but rather are inset ⅜″ into the opening.

The continuous or *piano hinge* is similar to the butt hinge, except that it has a very long leaf. Piano hinges run the length of a door of some type, like the lid of a piano. They provide a sturdier connection than a series of smaller hinges.

LOOSE-PIN BACKFLAP

You can examine the backflap hinge for clues on how to use it effectively. Notice that the leaf of the hinge is more or less square in nature. This would tend to indicate that it is not meant to be used on the edge of lumber as

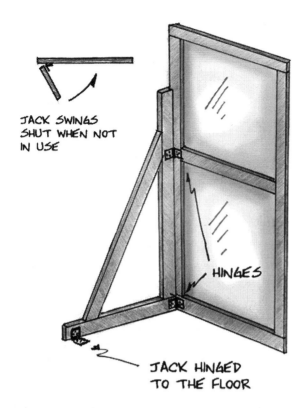

JACK SWINGS
SHUT WHEN NOT
IN USE

HINGES

JACK HINGED
TO THE FLOOR

BACKFLAP HINGES USED
ON AN L-JACK

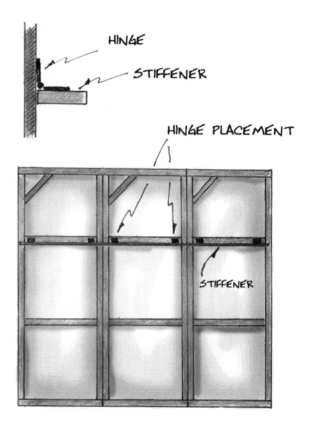

HINGE

STIFFENER

HINGE PLACEMENT

STIFFENER

BACKFLAP HINGES
ON A STIFFENER

a butt hinge is, but rather on the face of some framing member. Most backflaps are *loose-pin*, and the pin supplied is a bent shaft, giving it a small handle to grasp, so that it is easy to remove and replace the pin.

Loose-pin backflaps are often used to join groups of flats or other scenery. Attach the hinges to the backside of the framing so that removing the pins allows you to separate the flats from one another. This hinge may also be used to attach L-jacks to the back of a flat in order to keep it upright. When not in use, jacks can be folded over against the back of the flat, or if this is not possible for some reason, the pins can be pulled and the jack removed from the scenery. Sometimes several flats joined together will need to be stiffened so that they do not bend where they are hinged. A stiffener may be hinged to the back of the flats so that they remain rigid. Hinging the stiffener with loose-pin backflaps will make it possible to remove and reattach it easily. Even if scenery does not need to be moved during a show, being able to easily assemble/disassemble facilitates things like painting and moving the scenery around the shop.

Another use for this versatile hinge is to connect scenery to the floor. If it is not practical to use a stage weight to hold an L-jack to the deck, then a hinge may be used for the same purpose. You can also use this same

technique to secure the bottoms of stairs, newell posts, columns, and any other scenic element where a hinge will fit.

When using a backflap for some purpose where the pin will never need to be removed, it is best to use a tight pin hinge, or to replace the original pin with *pin wire*. Pin wire can be bent over at the ends to ensure that it does not fall out unintentionally. Although you can buy pin wire by the pound from a supplier, I have found it less expensive to buy the kind of wire that is used to hang suspended ceilings and to cut my own. This wire is quite stiff and useful for other projects as well.

You might try using the tight fitting original pin to put the scenery together, and then knock it out and replace it with a *bent nail*. This serves to give the joint just enough slack to fit together easily. Twenty-penny nails are a good fit for the 2″ backflap size.

If necessary, backflaps may be trimmed with a grinder to fit an odd shape. Sometimes you may need to bend them with a hammer and vise, or drill holes into them, and this can be done without too much effort.

Backflap hinges come in several different sizes, running from 1″ to 2″. There is some merit to having a variety of sizes, but the 2″ size is the most effective, so you may wish to stick with those. It is easy to recycle

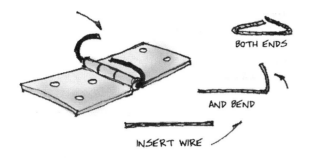

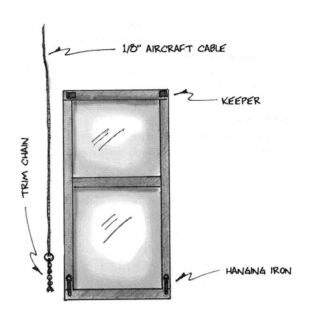

hinges, as there is little to go wrong unless they become bent in some way. The 2 inch variety is a heavier gauge and will last longer. It also has the advantage of being a good fit with the width of 1×3 lumber.

HANGING HARDWARE

Connecting scenery to a batten and flying it out overhead is one of the oldest methods of changing from one set to another. Soft goods like drops can be simply tied to a batten using their own tie lines, but built scenery is heavier and requires another approach. Specific pieces of hardware have been created for just this purpose.

PUT THE HANGING IRON AND TRIM CHAIN ON THE BOTTOM FOR EASIER ADJUSTMENTS

Notice that the hanging iron is placed at the bottom of the flat rather than the top. Suspended scenery rarely hangs exactly straight the first time, and generally needs to be adjusted after it is up in the air. It is much easier to make adjustments while you are standing on the floor rather than from the top of a lift or ladder.

Trim chains are used to adjust the length of a hanging rig. They typically consist of a welded ring, a 2 foot

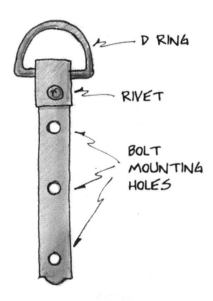

HANGING IRON

One of the oldest types of flying hardware is the *hanging iron*. It is basically a length of bar stock that has been doubled over to accommodate a *D-ring* at one end. The D-ring connects with a hanging cable. Holes along the length of the hanging iron are used to bolt it to a scenic unit. A hanging iron is actually made from steel, but it is quite common in theatre to call anything metallic an "iron." It is important to bolt the hardware on, so that it is very securely fastened.

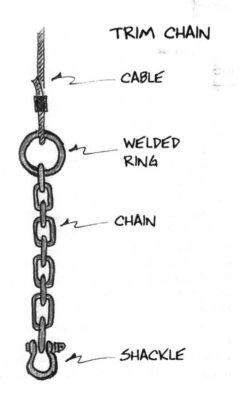

TRIM CHAIN

CABLE

WELDED RING

CHAIN

SHACKLE

length of ³⁄₁₆″ chain, and a shackle. The chain is used to adjust the length of the cable, and this in turn adjusts the trim of the scenery. It is a fairly easy thing to lift the low side of the piece and adjust a trim chain up or down a link or two. Since the chain passes through the D-ring, moving up a 1 inch link will raise the side only half an inch.

Chains are often also used at the top to attach the cable to the batten. They should be wrapped around the batten, and then use a shackle to connect the chain back to itself.

On occasion it is necessary to make smaller adjustments to a trim than are possible by using chain, which is often a problem when three or more cables are used rather than just two. A *turnbuckle* can shorten a hanging cable by a tiny amount. The turnbuckle is essentially a very long nut with an eyebolt sticking out of it at either end. One of the eyebolts has a left-handed thread, and when the center section is rotated the two eyebolts come closer together, or farther apart, depending upon the direction the center portion is turned. Turnbuckles are available in a large variety of sizes, from only a few inches to several feet in length. Turnbuckles can really help even out a complicated hanging job where many lift lines are needed.

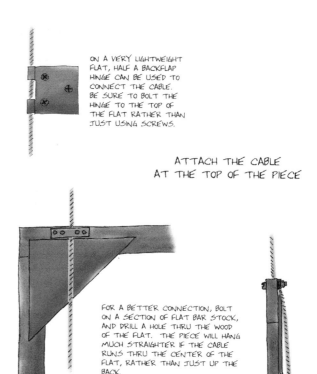

ON A VERY LIGHTWEIGHT FLAT, HALF A BACKFLAP HINGE CAN BE USED TO CONNECT THE CABLE. BE SURE TO BOLT THE HINGE TO THE TOP OF THE FLAT RATHER THAN JUST USING SCREWS.

ATTACH THE CABLE AT THE TOP OF THE PIECE

FOR A BETTER CONNECTION, BOLT ON A SECTION OF FLAT BAR STOCK, AND DRILL A HOLE THRU THE WOOD OF THE FLAT. THE PIECE WILL HANG MUCH STRAIGHTER IF THE CABLE RUNS THRU THE CENTER OF THE FLAT, RATHER THAN JUST UP THE BACK.

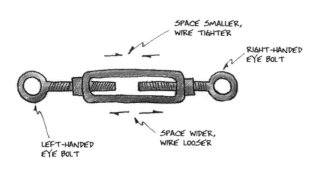

SPACE SMALLER, WIRE TIGHTER

RIGHT-HANDED EYE BOLT

SPACE WIDER, WIRE LOOSER

LEFT-HANDED EYE BOLT

TURNBUCKLE

There are several different ways to keep the cable firmly attached to the top of the flat. Half of a back-flap hinge works on a lightweight piece. A D-ring plate with no ring is a more heavy-duty alternative. One problem with either of those approaches is that the scenery tends to tip forward some, because all of the weight is hanging on the downstage side of the hanging cable. You can get around that problem by drilling a hole in the top of the scenery, and feeding the wire rope through it. If the framing of the scenery is beefy enough, the hole might be strong enough on its own, but it is generally prudent to install a steel plate on the back of the unit to keep the cable from pulling through the side of the hole. Be sure to use bolts rather than screws on any hanging hardware.

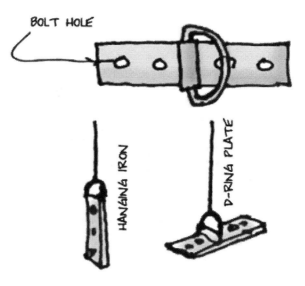

BOLT HOLE

HANGING IRON

D-RING PLATE

D-RING PLATE

A *D-ring plate* is used in a quite similar manner as the hanging iron. However this hanging hardware is shaped differently and may be used in places where a hanging iron might not fit. Most of the time, the hanging iron is used with the D-ring at the top and the iron vertical, while the D-ring plate is used lying flat, which makes bolting it securely even more important.

Aircraft cable is used to hang scenery because it has a very high load rating. Essentially, this is a twisted rope made from stainless steel strands. A large ⅜″ or ½″ variety is used in arena rigging. In a theatre, ¼″ aircraft cable is used in rigging counterweight arbors. Most scenery involves less weight, and the size of the cables used is correspondingly lighter. Most scenery is hung using ⅛″ cable, which is rated at about 1,000 pounds to its breaking strength. The actual amount varies from one manufacturer to the next and is stamped on the side of the reel that the cable comes on. The 1⁄16″ diameter cable is rated at about 400 pounds while the ¼″ goes up to 7,000 pounds. These are the breaking strengths, and it is prudent to maintain a safety factor of at least 4, so the safe load should be derated by that amount.

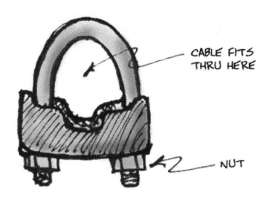

WIRE ROPE CLAMP

secure lift lines to a stage batten. It is the accepted practice to use two of these clamps when attaching cable to a thimble or a batten, as this better ensures that the connection will hold if one of them has been improperly installed or vibrates loose.

The bottom or *saddle* part of the clamp should be attached to the standing part side of the cable. This is often referred to as the "live" end.

SPOOL OF 1/8" AIRCRAFT CABLE

Quite frequently, the cables are painted black in the shop so that they don't show so much in the lights. It is also possible to purchase cable that has already been painted or powder coated by the manufacturer.

A *rope thimble* is used to protect the line from being bent over and kinked. It is very important to avoid a sharp bend when using wire rope. It is less forgiving than a line made from more pliable fibers like polypropylene or nylon. Kinking the cable will make it more difficult to use and will also greatly reduce its breaking strength. There are different sizes of thimbles for different diameter ropes and cables.

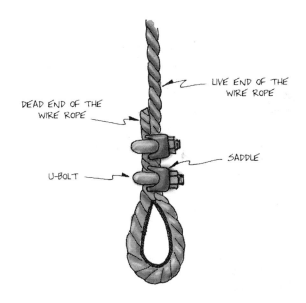

Swage fittings are used in the same manner as wire rope clamps, but the main difference is that the Crosby is removable, and the swage fitting is not. Once a swage fitting is secured to the cable, it is impossible to get it back off, unless you simply cut off the few inches of cable that are involved. Swage fittings are cheaper than wire rope clamps and they are much neater on the cable. They are also easier to put on but do require a special *crimping tool*. A different size crimper is needed for each size of cable. Some tools are made with several different apertures that will fit more than one diameter of wire rope. Special

WIRE ROPE   THIMBLE

Often called by its trade name *Crosby*, a *wire rope clamp* can be used to fasten the aircraft cable around the thimble. Wire rope clamps are quite commonly used to

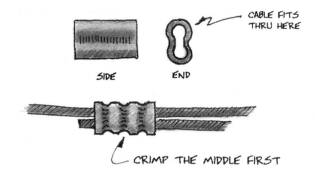

CABLE FITS
THRU HERE

SIDE   END

CRIMP THE MIDDLE FIRST

SWAGE FITTING

cutters must be used on the wire rope, so that the end is not overly deformed so much that it will not fit through the hole in the swage fitting. A common trade name for a swage is *Nicropress Sleeve*.

Screw eyes and *eye bolts* are very useful in rigging many different things backstage, but you avoid using them for hanging anything from a batten unless the weight of the item being hung is very, very low. It is generally unsafe to use this hardware to hang heavy items over the stage. A drop-forged rated eyebolt can be used through metal framing, but screw eyes should only be used for small prop items, and never to hang anything weighing more than a few ounces. When using an eyebolt in metal framing, be sure to use a flat washer to avoid having the nut pull through.

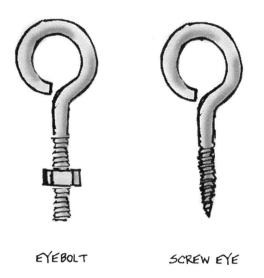

EYEBOLT   SCREW EYE

Eyebolts have a machine thread and are used with a nut, like a regular bolt. Screw eyes have a pointed, screw thread and are intended to be used in wood only, like a screw. Screw eyes come in a wide variety of sizes that are somewhat arbitrary. Eyebolts are described by the diameter of the rod they are bent from, such as ¼" or ½".

Take the direction of force of the cable pull into consideration when using a bent rod type of eyebolt. Cable pulling at an oblique angle is more likely to cause the eyebolt to fail. Rated hardware has a known load rating and is much safer to use in rigging.

Quick links resemble an oval chain link, but one side has a nut that may be used to create an opening for the passage of chain links, rope thimbles, and other hardware. When properly closed, the quick link is very secure and will not come open accidentally. Quick links are sized according to the diameter of the link material. It is problematic that the opening in the link is often not large enough to fit over what you would like to attach it to. Some quick links are rated for a specific load, but most are not, and thus are not appropriate for rigging purposes.

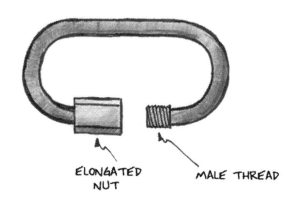

ELONGATED
NUT   MALE THREAD

QUICK LINK

Shackles are used in much the same way as quick links, but they are manufactured in much larger sizes, and for much heavier loads. The shackle has a bell and is designed to connect two lines to one in a Y configuration, but may also be used for a one-to-one connection. The removable bolt is called the *pin*, and it is accepted practice to use the shackle with the pin facing down since most of the time a bridle is hung in that way. Never rig two

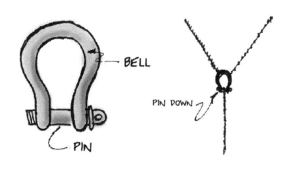

BELL

PIN DOWN

PIN

SHACKLE

cables to the bell of a shackle side to side, because it places stress on the pin. Shackles are almost always rated hardware and are the best choice for overhead rigging.

Snap hooks are used to quickly connect cables or chains. They have a somewhat oval shape, with one end of the oval being larger than the other one. They are very commonly used on lighting safety cables where the load rating is not such a concern. *Carabineers* are a type of climbing hardware that work in much the same way. Since they are used for climbing they almost always have a load rating, but they are somewhat clumsy to use for most rigging applications where steel cable is used.

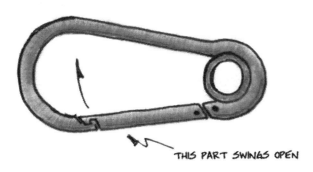

SNAP HOOK

An *S-hook* is a piece of heavy wire that has been bent into the shape of an S. A pair of pliers is used to close the ends around something you are hanging. This piece of hardware is not easily removed, except with a pair of bolt cutters. They should not be used for overhead hanging because the hook may open up and fail if too great a load is applied. Also, it is not uncommon to see someone forget to bend the ends of the hook closed, and if used in this way the hooks are almost certain to come loose at the worst possible moment. S-hooks are more appropriate to a variety of prop uses.

Some large-sized, shop-built S-hooks were being used for the national tour of *Grand Hotel* when disaster struck, as related by this story in the Denver Post on April 14, 1991.

PLAY HAS BRUSH WITH DISASTER

And the show went on. The old theatre adage was put to the test yesterday at the Auditorium Theatre. During the matinee finale of "Grand Hotel," with the entire cast on stage, a lighting and electrical harness weighing several hundred pounds fell from the rafters and crashed onto the stage. It missed the cast members, none of whom missed a beat; many members of the audience thought it was all part of the show. After the performance, a few cast members were overheard backstage saying that they had been frightened to death, but the evening performance was scheduled to go right on time.

The author witnessed the event from stage left, and found it an impressive lesson on the importance of safety in rigging. April 14 has always been a bad day for theatres.

Rota Locks are used to join two pipes together at a right angle. They come in two parts. One is a rod that has been bent into a double U shape and then welded together at the end. The other piece is a spacer that fits in between the two pipes that have been slipped into the U shapes. The spacer part has a bolt on it that may be turned to tighten the joint. Rota Locks are manufactured for all sizes of schedule 40 black steel pipe from 1″ to 2″ ID. The only real problem with the use of these clamps is that the pipe must be slipped into the clamp from the very end, and this is sometimes difficult to do.

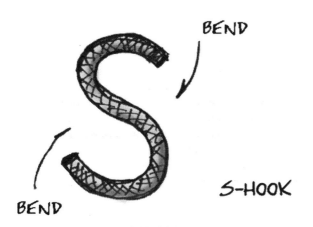

BEND

BEND

S-HOOK

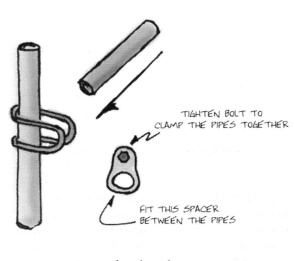

TIGHTEN BOLT TO CLAMP THE PIPES TOGETHER

FIT THIS SPACER BETWEEN THE PIPES

PIPE CLAMPS

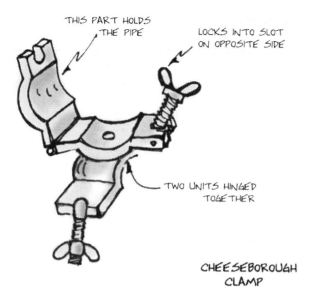

THIS PART HOLDS
THE PIPE

LOCKS INTO SLOT
ON OPPOSITE SIDE

TWO UNITS HINGED
TOGETHER

CHEESEBOROUGH
CLAMP

A similar piece of hardware, the *Cheeseborough clamp*, locks itself around the pipe by means of a bolt and wing nut and has the added advantage of working with the pipe at any angle, not just 90 degrees.

CLAMP USED TO CREATE A PIPE GRID

Casket or *coffin locks* are a great way to connect heavy pieces of scenery. Casket locks are most often used to lock two or more platforms together, and a discussion of that

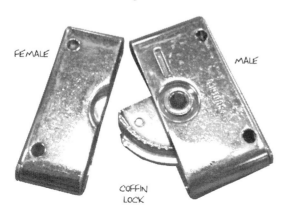

FEMALE

MALE

COFFIN
LOCK

process may be found in the chapter on decking. These locks can also be used in a wide variety of applications to join scenic units in much the same manner as loose pin hinges, although the method of attaching the lock is much different.

Casket locks consist of a male and a female side, with the male side having the moving parts. The two halves are connected to two different pieces of scenery, and then a ⁵⁄₁₆ hex key is used to lock them together. There is a cam-shaped hook inside the male half that rotates around and grabs two projections inside the female half. Since the hook in the male is a cam, it draws the female side toward it as it rotates.

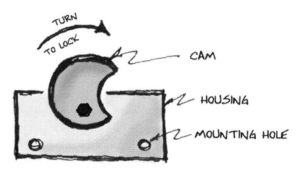

TURN
TO LOCK

CAM

HOUSING

MOUNTING HOLE

COFFIN LOCK

Screen door handles come in many sizes and weights. They are quite useful as a "gripping" point when attached to a unit of scenery. They are relatively inexpensive and reusable.

SCREEN DOOR HANDLE

A *cane bolt* is used to secure rolling scenery to the floor. It is very similar to a *barrel bolt* used on a door, with the exception that the cane bolt sinks into a hole drilled in the floor or deck. When the bolt is pulled upward and turned to the side, it will stay up and out of the way. When the handle is rotated to the center position, the bolt slides downward and into the hole in the floor, which holds the unit in place.

CANE BOLTS SECURE ROLLING UNITS TO THE STAGE FLOOR

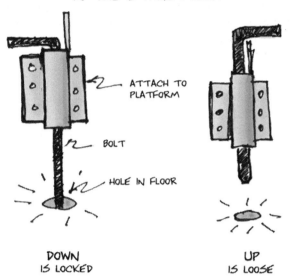

ATTACH TO PLATFORM

BOLT

HOLE IN FLOOR

DOWN
IS LOCKED

UP
IS LOOSE

There are several types of flat steel hardware that may be used to connect wooden framing members. *Corner braces* form a flat right angle and are especially useful on the bottom corners of stock 4×8 platforms to keep the 2×4s from pulling apart. *Angle irons* are similar in concept but are made by bending a straight piece of bar stock. Angle irons may often be used in the same connective manner as a backflap hinge, whenever the pieces need not be disassembled. Both come in a wide variety of sizes. You can easily bend an angle iron to an obtuse angle by laying it on a section of steel pipe and tapping it with a hammer.

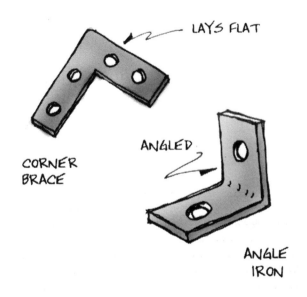

LAYS FLAT

CORNER
BRACE

ANGLED

ANGLE
IRON

Casters are wheels that have a steel mounting bracket, and are used to roll scenery on the stage. There are many different sizes, types, and styles to choose from, but only a few are really useful for moving scenery. Lots of casters are intended for use on furniture, and they are not nearly strong enough to move heavy scenery.

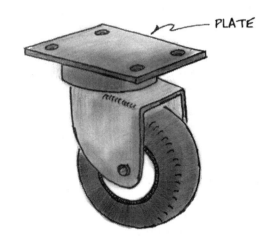

PLATE

SWIVEL CASTER

The best type of caster for theatre use has a plate on the top that can be bolted to the bottom of a piece of scenery. Casters that fit into a socket like furniture casters are not generally strong enough to fit theatrical needs. Casters are said to be of either the *swivel* type, or the *rigid* type. Swivel, or "smart" casters rotate and allow the scenery to be moved in different directions. Rigid, or "dumb" casters are fixed, and will run scenery back and

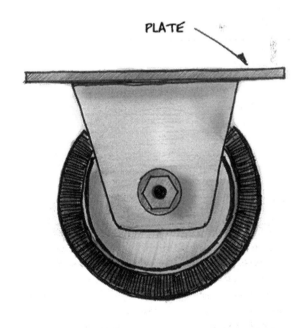

PLATE

RIGID CASTER

forth along the same pathway. Neither one is better than the other, because some situations call for swivel, and others demand rigid casters.

Casters are most often described by the size of the wheel and their load capacity. It is best to use casters that are rated significantly higher than the actual load. This makes for a much smoother ride. It is axiomatic that a larger diameter wheel will make it easier to move the wagon. Larger wheels are less prone to becoming stuck on or in irregularities in the stage floor. The other side of the coin is that large swivel casters require more clearance room to swivel and this makes it more difficult to stop and reverse direction.

One interesting type of caster is the *universal caster*, which has three small wheels on a revolving base. They are often seen on grand pianos, which are quite heavy. Using three small wheels allows the caster to fit into a lower space under a scenic unit. Universal casters also need less space around them for the offset to swivel.

UNIVERSAL TYPE CASTER

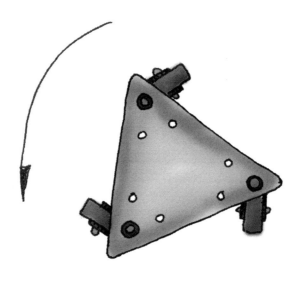

THIS TYPE IS USUALLY RATED FOR A HIGH LOAD
AND IS VERY LOW TO THE GROUND

Manufacturers use a variety of substances to construct the wheels used on casters. The best ones have a steel center hub and a tire made of neoprene or hard rubber. Plastic wheels or wheels that are made entirely of steel are not generally acceptable because of the amount of noise they create when the unit is being rolled. Plastic casters cannot carry very much weight. You can find more information about how to use casters for scenery in the appendix.

ADHESIVES

Aliphatic resin glue, which is often called *carpenter's glue*, is probably the most commonly used adhesive in building scenery. It has a yellow color that makes it easy to differentiate from white glue like Elmer's. Regular Elmer's is in the family of *polyvinyl glues*. Either one will do the same job, but yellow glue bonds more quickly and with greater strength than white glue. Carpenter's glue is the best choice for most woodworking, but not especially for adhering muslin to a flat. The white glue gives you a bit more time to work before it is too stiff to move the fabric around. White glue also dries clear, which can be an advantage in certain situations. As a rule of thumb, yellow glue bonds to two-thirds of its holding power in about 20 minutes, while white glue requires about an hour. To get the maximum hold from either takes 24 hours to cure.

Neither of these glues is a good gap filler, and as a result the parts being joined should be smooth, well fitting, and tightly held together in some way while the bond is formed. Jostling the joint while the glue is setting up will greatly reduce the holding power of the bond. When used on wood or some other porous material, the holding power of either of these two glues will generally exceed the strength of the material itself. Hence the wood will pull apart before the glue joint does. It is important to spread the glue evenly over the entire joint surface to achieve maximum holding power.

SMALL BLOBS OF GLUE DON'T HAVE VERY MUCH HOLDING POWER

SPREAD THE GLUE AROUND TO GET MORE CONTACT

USE A ZIG-ZAG PATTERN AND THEN SQUISH THE BOARDS TOGETHER FOR QUICK RESULTS

APPLYING WOOD GLUE

It is difficult to tell much difference in quality between the various brands of these two glues. Years ago yellow glue was somewhat more expensive than the white, but this is no longer true. You get a much better value if you buy these glues in gallon bottles. But the smaller applicator-type bottles are a must when actually using the glue. Of course you can also fill up other kinds of squeeze bottles and use those.

After about a year of storage, the yellow glue tends to form stringy clots in the jug that jam up the flow of

GALLON   PINT

WOODWORKING GLUE

the liquid. If that starts to happen, the glue is past the point where it is usable. A few years ago manufacturers developed a new type of yellow glue which is said to be waterproof. This may be a good choice of adhesive if the scenery is to be used outdoors, but it is not normally necessary for a show in the theatre.

Sobo is a brand of flexible white glue that can be used on materials that must bend after the adhesive has dried. It is often used on fabrics.

Most people are familiar with *hot melt glue* because it is used in a variety of craft situations. It is important to remember that this adhesive is indeed very hot when it comes out of the gun, so be careful not to burn yourself. The technical name for hot glue is thermoplastic adhesive, and it most often is sold in sticks.

Contact cement is an adhesive that works by first bonding to the two separate material surfaces, and then to itself. It is very commonly used to adhere laminates like Formica to a table or countertop. There are two basic types, the original that is quite flammable and really high

in *VOC* (*Volatile Organic Compounds*—not a good thing), and a newer type that is water-based. Clearly, the water-based type is a wise choice for use in the theatre, although it does not have all the holding power of the original.

The cement is rolled or brushed onto both of the two pieces to be joined. Use the cheapest possible short nap rollers and foam brushes for this purpose because the applicators will be ruined by the end of the project. It is important to let the adhesive dry for at least a half an hour or so, or until it is clear and dry to the touch. Oftentimes it will go on green or tan and dry clear. The contact cement will not bond properly unless it has dried prior to the two surfaces coming together. Exact times and conditions can be found on the label.

This type of glue bonds immediately on contact. Sometimes if only the least bit of touching has occurred the parts can be yanked quickly apart, but there are no guarantees. It is best to have a means of closely positioning the parts without having them touch each other. When laying countertops, rods are placed on the surface of the counter so that the laminate can be positioned. When all is ready, the rods are pulled out one at a time as the laminate is pressed against the wooden underlayment. It is important to press the two materials together firmly, perhaps using a roller or rubber mallet, but clamping is not required because the bonding occurs as soon as the pressure is applied. Laminate is generally cut a bit large and trimmed off later with a flush trim bit so exact positioning is not required.

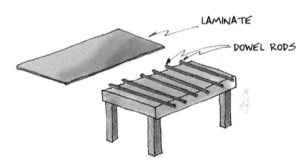

LAMINATE

DOWEL RODS

POSITION THE LAMINATE WITH THE RODS IN PLACE TO KEEP THE TWO SURFACES APART, THEN PULL THE RODS OUT ONE BY ONE

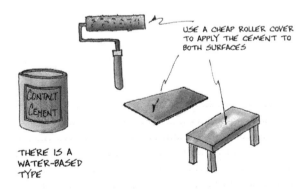

USE A CHEAP ROLLER COVER TO APPLY THE CEMENT TO BOTH SURFACES

THERE IS A WATER-BASED TYPE

AS SOON AS THE CEMENT IS NO LONGER WET YOU CAN JOIN THE TWO SURFACES TOGETHER, BUT REMEMBER THEY WILL BOND RIGHT AWAY

Contact cement is a good adhesive for building up blocks of polystyrene foam for carving. Unlike construction adhesives, it leaves no residue on the inside of the block that is difficult to carve through. The water-based cement will not "eat" the foam, and it makes a very good bond since it connects entire surfaces.

Barge cement is a flammable contact cement of the older type that is often useful for small prop jobs. It comes

Spray 77 is an industrial adhesive from 3M that has become available in retail outlets in recent years. It is an excellent glue to use in adhering either paper or a paper-thin material to a smooth flat surface. Shake well, line the nozzle up with the red dot, and spray an even coat over the entire surface of the paper. Use newspapers to prevent the over spray from ruining the tabletop or floor. Allow the glue 60 seconds or so get tacky on the paper before placement. That allows the paper to stretch out a bit and reduces the number of bubbles that may appear on large sheets. Wallpaper stretches in much the same way. You can make your own press with plywood and stage weights to push down on the paper for an hour or so, which will mostly eliminate the annoying bubbles. Small sections are not affected as much because the stretching of the paper is proportionally smaller. Spray 77 gets used quite often for mounting thin paper on heavier stock, but there are many, many, prop uses. It is great for foam rubber.

in a can with a brush applicator in the cap much like rubber cement. It is an excellent product for emergency repairs.

Construction adhesive is a very thick liquid glue, or mastic. It will stick foam to wood, steel, aluminum, acrylic sheet, or just about anything else when contact cement isn't practical. One of the advantages of this type of adhesive is that it is an excellent gap filler and can be used to connect parts that do not fit together well. Normally, this product comes in a caulking tube, but you can also find it in gallon cans. *Liquid Nails* is a brand of construction adhesive that has been around for many years. The original formula holds much better than any of the newer types. Construction adhesive also does a great job of connecting wood to metal tubing when mechanical fasteners aren't enough.

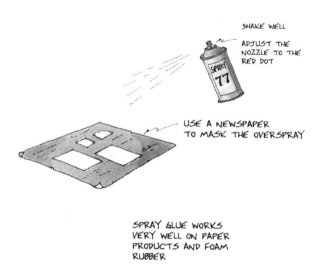

SHAKE WELL
ADJUST THE NOZZLE TO THE RED DOT

USE A NEWSPAPER TO MASK THE OVERSPRAY

SPRAY GLUE WORKS VERY WELL ON PAPER PRODUCTS AND FOAM RUBBER

The 3M company has several spray adhesives that are identified by a number and can be used in much the manner as the 77 is.

Zap is a brand of *cyanoacrylate* or super glue that is sold at woodworking stores. There are several different formulas for specific purposes, as well as a kicker that speeds up the bonding time. This product is not recommended for general woodworking, but it is handy to have around for the occasional odd problem. You can use it to glue small parts together when a strong bond is required. It is important to not use too much or the set-up time will take too long. It really does take just a drop. The kicker causes the glue to set up almost immediately. Be sure to follow the instructions exactly. Generic types of this glue are available just about anywhere, but you will most likely only find the kicker at a specialty woodworking store.

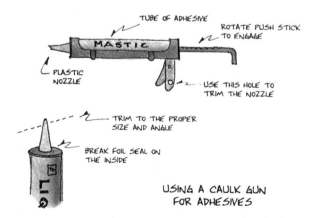

TUBE OF ADHESIVE
ROTATE PUSH STICK TO ENGAGE
MASTIC
PLASTIC NOZZLE
USE THIS HOLE TO TRIM THE NOZZLE

TRIM TO THE PROPER SIZE AND ANGLE
BREAK FOIL SEAL ON THE INSIDE

USING A CAULK GUN FOR ADHESIVES

TAPE

Gaffer's tape is a cloth tape with adhesive on the back that gets its name from movie electricians. It is available in many different colors, but black and white are generally the most useful. The standard size is a 2 inch wide, 60 yard roll. There are several different brands, and many stagehands have one they insist is the best. Some are thicker and stiffer than others and might be better suited to your particular situation. Some leave less sticky residue behind when you pull them off.

USE WHITE TAPE AND A MARKER TO MAKE TEMPORARY LABELS

GAFF TAPE RIPS EVENLY ALONG ITS LENGTH

GAFFER'S TAPE

The white can be used for putting labels on boxes and hampers, rail linesets, or dressing room doors. It can be ripped into strips to mark sightlines or to be used as spike marks. The black is useful when you need a tape that can disappear into the darkness of the backstage void. It is often used on electrical cables (hence the gaffer connection). The main advantage of gaff tape over ordinary duct tape is that the fabric nature of gaff tape makes it stronger and more malleable. One of the great things about this tape is that it can be ripped along its length into very narrow strips when odd sizes are required.

Glow tape is a plastic tape impregnated with a fluorescent powder that glows in the dark. The powder soaks up light energy and then releases it when darkness

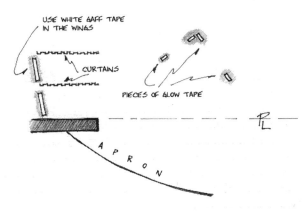

USE WHITE GAFF TAPE IN THE WINGS

CURTAINS

PIECES OF GLOW TAPE

APRON

GLOW TAPE CAN'T CHARGE UP IN THE WINGS WHERE THERE IS NO LIGHT. IF YOU USE TOO MUCH OUT ON THE STAGE, IT WILL BE DISTRACTING IN A BLACKOUT.

comes. It is often used for *spiking* the stage floor and for marking dangerous drop offs like stairs or the front of the stage. Spiking means to put marks on the stage floor that indicate the placement of scenery or props. The advantage is that, theoretically at least, the tape will glow in the darkness of a scene-change blackout. The pieces out on the stage floor that are exposed to direct stage lights glow very brightly in the darkness. On the other hand, the tape used in the wings where there is no light to charge up the chemical will hardly be visible at all. Strips of white gaffer's tape work better when the marks are in a place that is perpetually dark.

Vinyl electrician's tape is used to provide extra coverage for wiring insulation. It is stretchy and easy to bend around uneven joints. It is a good insulator. The most common color is black, but many other colors are available. Electrician's tape is often used to color code wires or even scenic units. It can be used when there are a great many spike marks on the stage floor, and there is a need to be able to differentiate between them. The most useful colors for electrical purposes are green for the ground, white for the neutral, and black, red, and blue for the hots. You can use the same tape to color code the different lengths of jumpers used for lighting purposes.

Some theatrical supply companies sell a narrow width variety gaff tape that comes in many different colors. It is meant for use as spike tape, and is really better than vinyl electrical tape for that purpose because it doesn't stretch so much. E-tape is designed to stretch to several times its own size so that it conforms to the odd shape of wires twisted together. That can be problematic when spiking the floor because the tape stretches when you pull it off the roll, and if you don't wait for it to shrink back up before sticking it down, it will tend to curl up off the floor later. The gaffer/spike tape won't do that.

Masking tape is a paper adhesive tape that was designed to be used as a temporary mask while painting cars. It works great when you are using a sprayer. The original type is a tan color, but a blue variety is currently marketed as *painter's tape*. Masking tape is cheap in comparison to other types of tape and is often used when some other type would really be better. Remember that masking tape is not designed to be left on any surface for more than 24 hours. After that length of time the paper and glue begin to dry out, and the tape will either let go entirely, or it will become so permanently stuck that it must be scraped off. It should not be used to mark the floor of a rehearsal space, or for any other semi permanent application.

Teflon tape is a non-sticky type of tape that may be used in the place of pipe dope to secure the threads of a pipe connection from leaking. It is wrapped around the male end two or three times in clockwise direction.

Floral tape is a paper tape that uses wax as an adhesive. As the name implies, it is often used in making floral arrangements, especially with silk flowers. It is

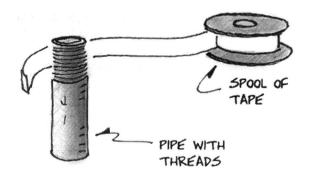

TEFLON TAPE ON PIPE THREADS

SANDING SUPPLIES

slightly stretchy and works well for wrapping the stems together. Its green or brown matte finish is more or less invisible when viewed from the audience.

Everyone is familiar with Scotch brand Magic Mending tape as it is used to hold papers together, but this type of tape is also useful on glass or mirrors. On paper, the slightly frosted appearance goes away when the tape is pressed down. On glass, the frosted look stays and can be used to create an etched or beveled look to the surface. If you need a tape that is perfectly clear, you might try clear plastic packaging tape used to seal boxes.

SANDPAPER

As the name implies, *sandpaper* is a sheet of paper or cloth that has a granular substance (but usually not really sand) stuck to one side. This abrasive side is used to wear away the surface of some other material, most often wood but also plastics and even metal. Sheets of sandpaper are a standard 9″×11″ size. Many power sanders use either one-half or one-quarter of a standard size sheet. Belt sanders use a round *belt* of sandpaper rotating between two drums. These belts are manufactured to fit a particular size of sander. Random orbit sanders use a round sanding pad with either an adhesive back or Velcro to attach the disk to the sander.

Most sheets of sandpaper are made in either an A or a C weight. The C weight is thicker and heavier than the A. The C weight is typically used for coarser grit sandpaper. The *grit number* is a measure of the size of the granules on the paper. Eighty grit is a coarse paper that may be used to roughly shape wood or plastic. It is very aggressive and will remove a large amount of wood in a short while. It leaves a somewhat rough surface, but one that most people would find suitable for painting with theatre techniques.

Many other grits are available. A grit of 150 is a reasonably fine number for sanding wood, while sanding coats of finish on furniture might require a grit in the 300 or 400 range. Most wooden scenery is smooth enough

for painting after a quick workout with 80 or 100 grit paper.

If an extraordinarily smooth surface is required, *steel wool* may be used. Steel wool is made from very fine steel shavings and is like an SOS pad without the soap. Steel wool comes in several grades from #2 to 0000. The #2 is fairly coarse while the 0000 is exceedingly fine. Steel wool is very handy for polishing metal surfaces like the top of the table saw.

FABRICS

Fabrics are very important in building scenery. Theatres have lots of curtains and drops, as well as fabric-covered flats and other scenery. Fabrics are often used as a means of creating painted scenery that is portable and lightweight.

Scenic *muslin* is the most common theatrical fabric. Muslin is a lightweight, all-cotton fabric that creates an excellent paint surface. It is often used for painted backdrops or for cycloramas. It is also used to cover the surface of soft covered flats, although when very high strength is required some shops may use canvas for this purpose. *Canvas* and muslin are both made from unbleached cotton threads, but the threads used for the canvas are larger in diameter, and as a result the fabric is heavier and coarser. It is important that theatrical canvas or muslin be manufactured from 100% cotton in order for the painting and sizing techniques of the theatre to be effective. Canvas tends to come in narrower widths, usually 72″ or less. The ounce weight of canvas refers to how much the fabric weighs per square yard, so naturally the heavier the weight the thicker and more durable the fabric will be.

Muslin is easily available in widths up to 120″, and much greater widths are possible, up to 35 feet in size.

The largest sizes are most often used for cycloramas, or for translucent drops where a seam would be unsightly. You should select the width of the fabric in the same way that you would choose the length of lumber being used for a specific project. The width chosen is a function of the width of flats being covered, or of drops being sewn together. The weight of the fabric may be light, medium, or heavy, but the heavy weight is recommended for most scenic uses. Canvas is often found in a variety of colors, but muslin is most often the natural off white. Sky cyc muslin is sometimes sold as a light blue color, as this enhances the ability to color the cyclorama a light blue sky hue.

Most theatrical fabrics are available as either flame proofed (FP) or non-flame proofed (NFP). Fabrics are very flammable, and if the fabric is not flame proofed from the manufacturer, it should be treated in the shop. Often-times flame proofing in the shop is more efficient, but some fire marshals won't allow it.

A number of theatrical specialty fabrics are available only from a theatrical supplier. One of these is *scrim*, which is a net-like material with rectangular openings. It is often used to create see-through curtains. White and black are the popular colors. Scrim is generally available

SHARKSTOOTH SCRIM

TINY TRIANGLES MAY RUN EITHER DIRECTION

BOBBINETTE

SCENERY NETTING

1-INCH SQUARES

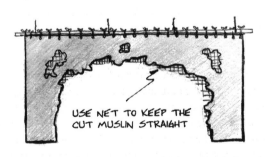

USE NET TO KEEP THE CUT MUSLIN STRAIGHT

NET-LIKE FABRICS

in widths around the 16 to 18 foot range, or in the 30 foot range. Thus you could construct a scrim that is either 18 feet tall by any width, or a scrim that is 30 feet tall by any width, or a scrim which is 30 feet wide by any height. It is not practical to sew two pieces of scrim together, as the seam would show when the translucent quality of the scrim is put to use. *Textilene* is a new material that looks very much like scrim, but is actually a non-woven plastic material. It is incredibly strong and resilient, but is not available in wide widths.

Scenery netting has square openings 1″ in either direction. This material may be used for cut drops, and is available in very large widths. Cut drops are made by painting on muslin first, then cutting out that design and gluing it onto the netting. This creates an open appearance to the outline.

Velour is a heavyweight, plush fabric used to make curtains. It is most often found as a 54″ wide fabric in a wide variety of colors. Velour has a nap like carpet does, which means that the pile will look different when it runs in different directions. Care must be taken to make sure that the nap on two adjoining panels is running the same way. You can do this by brushing the pile with your hand and seeing how the light reflects off the fabric. Black velour has incredible light and sound-absorbing qualities, and is an excellent choice for making a basic set of borders and legs. It is often used to cover masking flats, and other parts of scenery that the designer would like to disappear backstage. Like canvas, the thickness of velour is given in the number of ounces per square yard.

A less expensive alternative to velour is *duvetyn/commando* cloth. Sometimes, this fabric is called duvetyn when it is lighter in weight and commando cloth when it is heavier. Sometimes it depends on which part of the entertainment business you work in. Most people in theatre call it duvetyn. This fabric has no true nap like velour, but it does have a brushed, textural surface giving it a matte appearance. Like velour, duvetyn is most popular in black but comes in a variety of colors. The black is very handy for masking flats and can be stapled onto scenery to cover small gaps that were not foreseen in the design process. Duvetyn scraps can also be used to drape things backstage that you do not want the audience to see.

Burlap is a fabric made from jute. Jute is a rough fiber that has an oily resin in it. As a result it is quite flammable and must be heavily treated with a flame retardant. It has a rough texture much like the bags used to hold potatoes or coffee, which are made from the same material. Its natural color is, of course, that of jute, but burlap is also available in a wide range of colors. Colored burlap tends to be of a somewhat more regular weave than the natural. The texture of burlap makes it a favorite with designers, as is *erosion cloth*, a very loose type of jute netting.

Cheesecloth is a very lightweight, loosely woven fabric greatly resembling gauze. It is generally not used

CHEESECLOTH COMES FOLDED INTO FOUR LAYERS

100 YDS CHEESECLOTH

IN A BOX

TWO TYPES OF FLAME RETARDANT

ONE CAN BE ADDED TO PAINT, AND THE OTHER SPRAYED ON AS A FINAL COATING

as a fabric per se, but rather as a coating for other materials. This material is available from a theatrical supplier, but you may prefer the type sold in fabric stores where it is folded up in a box. The box type is easier to use for projects like coating foam-built scenery. The theatrical gauze or cheesecloth is much more difficult to apply.

Webbing is a narrow strip of heavy, stiff, material that is used to beef up the edges of a drop or curtain. It is typically used only on the top edge where the grommets are placed. It can sometimes be used in the construction of furniture, or to make straps of one sort or another. The original type of jute webbing is 3½″ wide and comes in a roll. There are two red (or sometimes blue) stripes down the length of the webbing, which are useful in lining up the placement of grommets. A newer type is made from polyester and is much more durable when used on a drop.

Grommets are brass rings used to reinforce the holes made in the top of a drop. They allow ties to be used in fastening the drop to a batten. Number 2 is the standard size for grommets used that way. Grommets must be installed with a grommeting hole cutter and setter. They are placed on 1 foot centers. More about webbing and grommets and how they are used can be found in the chapter on draperies and drops.

FLAMEPROOFING

It is important to *flame proof* scenery. Flame proofing means that a treated wooden or fabric material may char but will not support an open flame. "Fireproofing" is another thing entirely. It is generally not possible to accomplish that unless your scenery is built entirely from steel (or perhaps concrete and rocks for an outdoor drama). Many communities have a requirement that scenery should resist burning for a certain amount of time when heated with a match. The fire marshal in your community has the legal authority to make all decisions

as to how much flame protection is required, as well as other safety concerns like fire exits and such.

There are many different flame-retarding compounds on the market. Some are liquids that get sprayed on after the scenery is painted, and some are additives that you can put in the paint itself. Some are intended specifically for non-porous plastics. Follow the instructions that come with the compound. Retardants are available from most theatrical suppliers.

CORDAGE

Ropes and other lines used for tying are very important when working on stage. The most basic old-style type of rope is the hemp line, so called, but actually made from manila, a similar fiber that is derived from a relative of the banana tree. The rope itself is formed by twisting the fibers into several loose strands, known as yarns, and then twisting the yarns into a rope. This type of line has a definite right-hand twist, known as its lay. The lay becomes a factor when coiling a rope. Ropes of this type come in various diameters that are given in inches. The working strength of a rope is derived from its breaking strength, usually with a safety factor of 4. For example if the breaking strength of a certain line is 400 pounds then the safe working load limit would be 100 pounds. Knots, abrasions, and dirt will all greatly reduce the actual breaking strength, which is one reason the safety factor is used.

Many modern ropes are made from synthetic fibers such as nylon, polyester, or polypropylene. These ropes are generally more expensive than a hemp rope, but they are stronger and will last longer. Nylon is perhaps the fiber of choice, as it is fantastically strong and lightweight.

Sash cord is a very popular theatrical line. It was originally intended for use on the type of older window that used a counterweight hidden in the wall to balance out the weight of the sash. It is a woven rope, which means that there is an interior core of fibers that are surrounded by a woven casing. Since the fibers are not twisted together, the rope is less likely to become twisted up and tangled. Sash cord is excellent for tying knots, and for lashing together scenery back stage, but it is not especially strong. Modern-day sash cord has a cotton exterior with synthetic fibers on the inside, and is the line of choice for rigging a traveler track.

Tie line is used in many different situations backstage, and is technically known as #4 black trick line. It is about ⅛″ in diameter and seems very sturdy, but it is important to remember that according to the manufacturer, the safe working load is only 16 pounds. This kind of black tie line is most often available on a 3,000-foot reel and can be found either glazed or unglazed. The glazed version tends to last longer, but it is harder to tie. Ties for electrics should be about 30″ long in order to make two wraps around the pipe. Double wrapping makes it easier to keep the tie line tight when making a bow knot. Ties that are all the same length are easier to use.

Wire used to make suspended or drop ceilings is an excellent source of pin wire for loose pin backflap hinges. It is about the diameter of a thick wire clothes hanger, and comes in lengths 10 or 12 feet long. This wire can be used for all sorts of properties construction projects, because it is quite sturdy but can be easily bent with pliers.

Floral wire is a much thinner wire that can be used for much more than flower arrangements. It is a steel wire that has been painted green on the outside.

Cable ties are typically used to secure flexible cable or line to a rigid structure. They can be used in lots of different ways, especially when you would like to make a more permanent connection than tie line or tape would

allow. Cable ties are often made from nylon for strength, and have many ridges along their length. When the free end of the tie is pushed through a slotted head at the other end, the ridges catch on the head in a ratcheting fashion, so that the strip feeds in but cannot be pulled back out. This allows you to get the tie on very tight. But since the strip cannot be removed from the head, cable ties are essentially one use items, and wire cutters are generally required to get them off. They are at their best in a semi-permanent situation.

PAINT AND OTHER COATINGS

The artistic painting of scenery is outside the scope of this book, but it seems appropriate to have a *technical* discussion of paint and what it is made of. This short discussion of paint attributes will help you understand the types of coatings found in a scene shop. *Scenic Art for the Theatre* by Susan Crabtree is an excellent book covering the aesthetics and techniques of painting scenery.

Paint in general, no matter what type it is, is composed of three basic parts. The *pigment*, which gives the paint its color; the *vehicle*, which makes it a fluid; and the *binder* which causes it to stick to the surface you are painting.

PAINT

PAINT CONTAINS THREE ESSENTIAL ELEMENTS

PIGMENT — GIVES PAINT ITS COLOR, TRADITIONALLY MADE FROM GROUND UP MINERALS.

VEHICLE — MAKES PAINT A LIQUID. VIRTUALLY ALL THEATRE WORK DONE WITH WATER.

BINDER — THE GLUE THAT MAKES PAINT STICK. CAN BE ANYTHING FROM ELMER'S TO CLEAR POLYURETHANE.

For many centuries the pigment in paint was made from ground up minerals. Much of it still is. Raw sienna was literally made from soils found in Sienna, Italy. Renaissance painting masters employed apprentices who were charged with grinding up the pigments to a fine powder and then mixing them with linseed oil to make paint. They used the minerals as pigment, while linseed oil was both the vehicle and the binder. Up until fairly

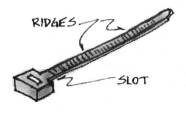

RIDGES ─

─ SLOT

RIDGES "RATCHET" THROUGH THE SLOT AND WILL NOT PULL BACK OUT

CABLE TIE

modern times, scenic artists used similar *dry pigments* to mix their paint with hide (animal) glue and water to make the paint used in theatre.

Some years ago, *casein* paints were developed that had their pigments already mixed together with binder into a liquid paste that could be purchased in gallon containers. This alleviated a lot of work in preparing the paints from scratch. Nowadays, most paint of this sort is made with a synthetic binder rather than the original casein milk-based type, but they work in very much the same way. There are a couple of dozen standard colors, and all others are mixed from those; much like an artist uses tubes of watercolor paints to mix the exact colors she needs for her painting.

SOME STORES SELL A CLEAR BASE THAT YOU CAN MIX WITH PIGMENTS TO MAKE YOUR OWN COLORS.

IDDINGS (NOW ROSCO) CASEIN-BASED PAINT HAS BEEN AROUND FOR MANY YEARS. IT HAS NO THICKENER LIKE LATEX PAINTS AND IS EASIER TO MAKE INTO WASHES AND GLAZES

On the other hand, ordinary house paint generally starts with a base made of *titanium oxide*, a whitish mineral that thickens the paint substantially. It also enhances the paint's ability to cover up whatever previous paint was applied to the wall. Water is the vehicle, and a latex or acrylic compound is used as the binder. Thick paint is less likely to drip off a brush and is easier for a homeowner to use, but the titanium oxide has the effect of "whiting out" the pigment color. Thus it is often difficult to get pure colors with latex paint. The thickness of latex paint is also problematic when painting a drop, because the flexible nature of the fabric demands a very thin, flexible coating that has more in common with a dye than with latex house paint. Synthetic casein paints come in gallon cans as a very thick paste, but can be reduced with water to make an extremely thin paint, which is excellent for fabrics like muslin. Latex paint cannot be thinned down in that way without losing a lot of its brilliance.

Another type of paint gaining appeal with scenic artists is made from *Universal Tinting Colors*. Paint stores use these colorants to add pigment to their products. There are a dozen or so standard colors, and a few other more exotic ones. Most paint manufacturers have several different *bases*, made up in advance, that have varying amounts of binder in them. Deeper colors have more pigment added, and thus need more binder in the base, and less titanium oxide. Binder and pigment are the expensive components in paint, so deeper colors are always more expensive. The tinting colors themselves do not contain the titanium oxide thickening agent, which is already in the base. It is important to remember that Universal Colorants are pigment only, and that a binder must be used with them in order to make the paint stick to the surface of anything you paint. Many different glue or glue-like products can be used for the binder, including

UNIVERSAL COLORANTS

THESE PIGMENTS ARE USED BY PAINT STORES TO COLOR THEIR PAINT. YOU CAN USE THEM IN THE SAME WAY, WITH WATER AND GLUE.

white glue, clear paint base, and water-based polyurethane. Mixing paint in this way allows the artist to create very specific colors from the tints, and to create a coating that is free of titanium oxide.

One scenic unit might be constructed of a combination of metal, wood, and plastic. Each of those materials reacts with paint in a different way. Treating them all with the same type of undercoat creates a smoother, more finished appearance. Several products can be used to create a solid base for faux finish painting on scenic units that were made from a mix of different materials. Products such as *Jaxsan 600*, *elastomeric*, and *Sculpt or Coat* work equally well to even out the appearance of the various parts of the scenery, and create a more homogenous texture. They are liberally applied to the scenery before painting.

DANGER!
WEAR A MASK!

THIS PLASTIC BOTTLE
CONTAINS SMALL
ALUMINUM PARTICLES
THAT CAN BE MIXED
WITH VEHICLE AND
BINDER TO MAKE A
SILVERY COATING

ELASTOMERIC COATING IS WIDELY
AVAILABLE AT HOME CENTERS

Water-based polyurethane is a much better choice for stage work than the original, which was made from some incredibly messy, high VOC chemicals. It can be tinted with pigment to form glazes, or can be used to protect a surface that has already been painted. Water-based polyurethane comes in gloss and satin varieties, but either one will impart a shiny depth to underlying paint. This substance is a favorite of faux finish painters.

Bronzing powders are ground up metallics like bronze, brass, copper, and aluminum. They are mixed together with glue and water to make a type of paint that creates a faux metallic surface. You should be very careful not to breathe in the unmixed, dry powder because it is bad for your lungs.

Drywall *joint compound* is used in construction to fill cracks in the wallboard used to cover interior walls. It is more or less the same thing that people mean when they use the word "spackle." It is often used to create smoother surfaces on wooden scenery as well. Joint compound is very easy to work with, and is not generally considered to be toxic, so there is no problem getting it on your hands. It is very easy to sand off with ordinary sandpaper. The one drawback to this material lies in its somewhat rigid nature, it tends to crack and fall off if the scenery is bent in some way. Scenic artists have several uses for a compound called "dope" which is made from joint compound and white glue.

Bondo can be used when joint compound is not strong enough. This material is intended for automotive body work, and is more or less indestructible. It can be sanded, sawn, and drilled into; much like plastic or wood. Bondo has two parts, the base material and a cream hardener. The two should be mixed with some precision, so that a proper set up time is achieved. This material must be used quickly, because Bondo hardens in a matter of minutes. It is an exothermic chemical reaction, so hot temperatures speed up the set up period. Joint compound must dry through evaporation, and a thick application can take several days, but a thick application of Bondo actually sets up faster than a thin one because the heat retained in the center causes a faster chemical reaction.

BUCKETS OF JOINT COMPOUND ARE USED TO FINISH DRYWALL IN A HOUSE. THEY ARE INEXPENSIVE, AND JOINT COMPOUND IS OFTEN USED TO FILL SMALL HOLES IN WOODEN SCENERY

Bondo will stick to just about everything, so some care must be taken when applying it. It is much harder to sand than joint compound, but can be molded with a Surform when it is not quite hardened.

Latex/acrylic caulk is more flexible than joint compound and has the added advantage of not needing to dry completely before painting begins. It is readily available in tubes that are used with a caulk gun to dispense the material into tight corners. Elastomeric and caulk are close cousins, but the caulk is much more viscous.

TERMS USED IN THIS CHAPTER

aircraft cable
angle iron
bent nail hinge pin
binder for paint
bolt: carriage, lag, stove, threaded
    rod
Bondo
bronzing powder
cable ties
cane bolt
carabineer
casein paint
caster, rigid, swivel
caulk
Cheeseborough clamp
coffin lock
corner brace
countersunk
crimping tool
D-ring
drive
dry pigment
elastomeric
eyebolt
fabric: bobbinette, burlap, canvas,
    cheesecloth, duvetyn, erosion
    cloth, muslin, scenery netting,
    scrim, Textilene, velour,
    webbing
fasteners
finger tight
flame-proofing

floral wire
glue: Barge, contact, hot melt,
    Liquid Nails, polyvinyl, Sobo,
    spray 77 yellow, white, Zap
grit # for sandpaper
grommet
hanging iron
head, flat, hex, pan, round
hinge: barrel, double action, leaf,
    pin, butt, loose pin, piano,
    strap, T
Jaxsan
joint compound
latex/acrylic caulk
machine screw
machine thread
nail gun
nail set
nail: box, brad, common, finish,
    spike
Nicropress sleeve
nut: hex, wing
paint base
pigment
pin wire
quick link
rope thimble
Rota Lock
saddle
sanding belt
sandpaper
sash cord

screen door handle
screw eye
screw: drywall, Phillips, tech
Sculpt or Coat
Shackle: bell, hub, pin
S-hook
snap hook
square drive
standard slot
staple: crown, leg
steel wool
swage fitting
tape: electrical, floral, gaffer,
    glow, masking, Teflon,
    spike
threads
threads per inch (TPI)
tie line
titanium oxide
torque
torque washer
trim chain
turnbuckle
Universal Caster
Universal Tinting Color
vehicle
volatile Organic Compound
    (VOC)
washer: flat, split ring, toothed
water-based polyurethane
wire rope/Crosby clamp

BUILDING SCENERY

CHAPTER 13

CONSTRUCTION DOCUMENTS

CONSTRUCTION DOCUMENT IS a catch-all term that means any sort of plan, drawing, photograph, parts list, model or other planning documentation that reveals information to the shop about how to build a particular show. Historically speaking the word "plans" meant sheets or plates of *drafting* drawn to scale. They were also known as a *set of plans* when put together in a group. But in today's world there's a lot more to it than that.

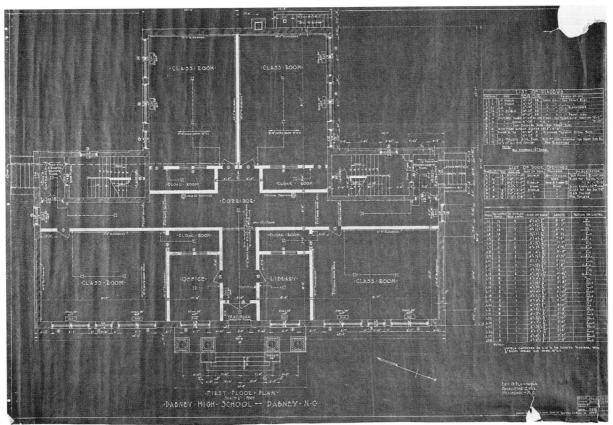

COURTESY OF NCSU LIBRARIES

OLD SCHOOL BLUEPRINTS HAD WHITE LINES ON A DARK BLUE PAPER

THIS ONE IS FOR A SCHOOL IN NORTH CAROLINA, AND IS TYPICAL OF A STYLE FROM THE MID-1900S THEY WERE ALMOST WORKS OF ART IN THEMSELVES.

For instance, construction documents could now include something you look at on a digital tablet. Or it could be something generated by a three-dimensional printer. Or perhaps a multi-page booklet of small drawings. In the past sheets of drafting were drawn out by hand on very large pieces of tracing paper, usually 36″×42″. The translucent sheets of tracing paper were used to make copies in the form of *blueprints,* so named because the paper was a dark blue color with white lines on it.

You would be hard pressed to find someone to make blueprints today, since virtually everyone now does drafting on a computer and then prints out drawings on a large format printer. As an alternative, modern drawings are often created on smaller, individual sheets that can be printed out on a desk printer. Lots of designers and tech directors are using smaller paper sizes for individual drawings. But ground plans (plan views of the setting as it will appear on the stage) and light plots are still generally printed in a large format. The reason is that construction plans are drawn to scale, meaning that a foot in real life is depicted as a proportionally equal, but smaller fraction in the drawing. A drawing of a door detail will easily fit on an 8½″ by 11 inch sheet of paper, but a drawing of the entire stage is much larger. A proscenium opening 50 feet wide would be 25 inches in ½″ = 1′-0″ scale, too large for the paper in most desk printers. And that doesn't include the surrounding architecture that defines where the set is located. With all of that, a drawing would be far too big for a sheet of paper much smaller than 36 by 42.

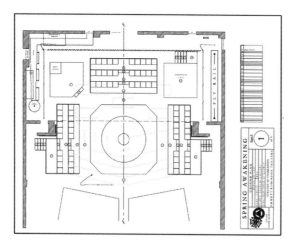

DRAWING COURTESY OF CHARLES CALVERT

PLAN VIEW OF THE ENTIRE STAGE

PLAN VIEWS ARE REALLY LARGE, SO THEY ARE USUALLY PRINTED ON A LARGE FORMAT PRINTER, EVEN IF MORE DETAILED DRAWINGS ARE MUCH SMALLER

Scale drawings of this sort are traditionally called drafting, and to call a drawing drafting assumes that it has been rendered in scale. But other sorts of drawings

that are less formal, and may also be considered a construction document. *Sketches* are free-hand drawings, usually of some small detail that was not clear on the drafting, or of a prop item, or of an idea of how to assemble something. One of the drawbacks of a sketch is its lack of accurate scaling, which may mean that the proportions are all wrong. As a result, the constructed piece may be much thinner or shorter than expected. One technique to avoid the unexpected is to scan the sketch into Photoshop or Vectorworks, and to use the computer program to measure the horizontal/vertical dimensions to see if they are proportionally accurate. If they are not, a Photoshop user can employ the transform command to show what the sketch would look like in the proper proportions.

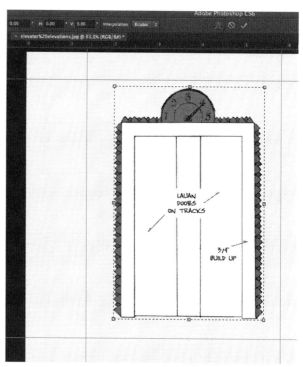

USE PHOTOSHOP AND THE TRANSFORM COMMAND TO CHANGE THE SCALE OF A SKETCH

SET GUIDELINES AT SPECIFIC POINTS BY USING THE RULERS. USE THE GRAB HANDLES TO CHANGE THE DRAWING'S SIZE.

TRADITIONAL DRAFTING

Architectural style drawings, like drafting, are generally done using several standard types of views that are immediately understood in the trade. A *view* literally means a way of looking at what you are drawing. A front view means looking at it from the front, a side view from the side, and so forth. A *plan view* means looking at the object, which here means the outline of the set on the stage, from up above in the "bird's eye" position. You may have seen drawings of a house in a magazine that depict where the living room is, where bedrooms are, all in relation to the garage or the laundry room. Those are plan views, which show the relationship of objects on the horizontal plane. They are often called *floor plans*. A plan view of the set in a theatre is also called a floor plan by some, and a *ground plan* by others. The term ground plan allows for the fact that not all scenery includes the use of an interior that has a floor. It might be something exterior or completely abstract.

Another type of architectural style drawing is an *elevation*. Elevations are drawings that show what something looks like in the vertical plane. In a plan view, something upright like a set of stairs looks just like a group of rectangles, but in an elevation view it takes a more familiar shape.

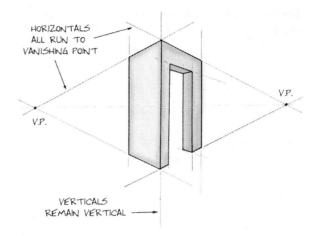

ESSENTIAL ELEMENTS OF PERSPECTIVE DRAWING

the vanishing point. Elevations make no attempt at demonstrating the relative sizes of near and far objects.

Construction elevations are generally drawn with a *CAD* program, but perspective drawings are often drawn by hand in an artistic manner. Elevations are much more mechanical but have the advantage of being proportionally accurate.

The last of the three most common types of architectural drawings is the *section view*. It can often be the most confusing to look at because it shows objects in a way that you don't generally see in real life. A section view looks as though you sliced through the middle of an object to see what is on the inside. One section view you probably already know is a sliced grapefruit.

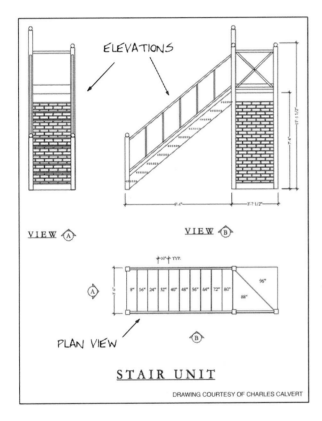

ELEVATIONS

VIEW Ⓐ   VIEW Ⓑ

PLAN VIEW

STAIR UNIT

DRAWING COURTESY OF CHARLES CALVERT

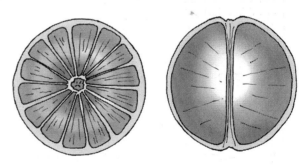

TWO SECTION VIEWS OF A GRAPEFRUIT

THE LEFT ONE IS WHAT YOU WOULD EXPECT, IT SHOWS MORE OF WHAT THE INSIDE OF THE FRUIT LOOKS LIKE.

STAGE SECTION VIEWS ARE THE SAME, THE STANDARD METHOD IS TO SHOW THE STAGE FROM DOWNSTAGE TO UPSTAGE, LOOKING TOWARD STAGE RIGHT.

A *perspective drawing* is usually a hand sketch that shows the relative sizes of identical objects that are closer as being larger while those farther away are smaller. They generally show the vertical surface of things like an elevation but there is a huge difference between the two types, perspective and elevation.

An elevation shows the exact size and shape of an object as though you were viewing it at a 90 degree angle from the front, so that a rectangle has no difference in size between the top and bottom, or the two sides. The lines of the top and bottom are parallel to one another and so are the sides. That is radically different from a perspective drawing where the vertical lines are indeed vertical, but all of the others are slanted toward

The left-hand section view is the one you expect, because that is how you would cut the grapefruit in order to eat it. The one on the right looks odd, because it was cut in the opposite direction, and would not be useful

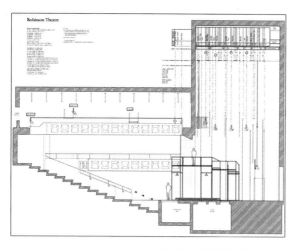

DRAWING COURTESY OF CHARLES CALVERT

SECTION VIEW OF A STAGE SET

THE PIPES HOLDING UP THE SCENERY ARE SHOWN
ON EDGE, SO THEY JUST LOOK LIKE ROUND DOTS.

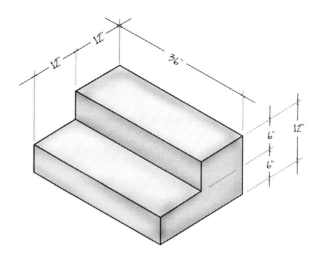

ISOMETRIC DRAWING

IT'S NOT A PERSPECTIVE DRAWING, BECAUSE LINES IN THE
FOREGROUND AREN'T LARGER THAN THOSE IN THE BACK.
ALL THE HORIZONTAL LINES ARE AT 30° ANGLE AND THE
VERTICALS ARE ALL VERTICAL.

because there would be no way to get out the meat of the fruit. Section views in a theatre are similar in that there is a standard way to do it.

As you can see, the drawing is done so that the theatre is cut in half down the *center line*, and we see the relative position of things like the height of the batten pipes, the tops of walls, the distance of those from the plaster line, and so forth. Section views are usually done so that designers can look at how well the sight lines of different units work together. Can the audience see the top of one unit over the other? Will lights from the third electric clear the top of a wall? Section views rarely influence the work of carpenters in the shop, but you should know what they are and be able to recognize them when you see them.

Another type of drawing is not a perspective drawing, but often looks like one. It is called an *isometric*

drawing. Iso means equal, and metric means measure. So an isometric drawing is made up of equal measurements.

Isometric drawings are easy to draw with a CAD program because all of the vertical lines are vertical, and the horizontal lines all have the same slant to them, most typically 30 degrees. In a perspective drawing, vertical lines farther away from the viewer are shorter, but that does not happen in an isometric drawing where all of the heights are accurate to scale. The same is true about the horizontal lines. An isometric drawing shows what

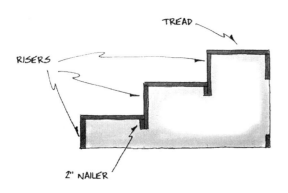

THIS SECTION VIEW <u>WOULD</u>
MATTER TO A SHOP CARPENTER
BECAUSE IT SHOWS HIDDEN PARTS
SHE WOULDN'T KNOW ABOUT OTHERWISE

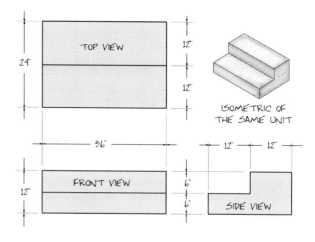

ORTHOGRAPHIC PROJECTION

THIS TYPE OF DRAWING SHOWS AN OBJECT FROM A
COMBINATION OF UP TO SIX SIDES; BUT THE TOP, FRONT,
AND RIGHT SIDE ARE THE MOST COMMON. THE VIEWS ARE
MORE EASILY DRAWN WHEN GROUPED IN THIS WAY.

something looks like from the corner which is almost always more revealing than just an elevation or plan view. In addition, this type of illustration allows the draftsperson to show the dimensions of all sides at once, rather than requiring two drawings showing different aspects.

In drafting, specific types of lines are used to give the viewer visual cues about how to understand the objects in the drawing. *Object lines* are dark and solid on the page. Their boldness is appropriate to what they are revealing, the outside perimeter of an object which defines its basic shape. Something solid like a wall often has small diagonal lines filling the inside. This is known as *cross hatching*. It is meant to fill an important object to make it stand out more.

Lines made of short dashes indicate an important corner or edge hidden behind the rest of the object. Lines made of long dashes are used when something hangs overhead, which isn't shown solidly because it would unnecessarily complicate the drawing. If a piece of scenery has an overhanging header, it will often be shown that way. The same lines are used to indicate the footprint of a unit that moves, and can be in different places at different times. Even longer dashes are used to indicate the *plaster line*, while alternating long and very long lines represent the *center line* or y axis of the stage floor. Usually the center line is also marked with the initials CL. Lines with arrowheads on them are used to indicate a *dimension*, or how far it is from one point to another.

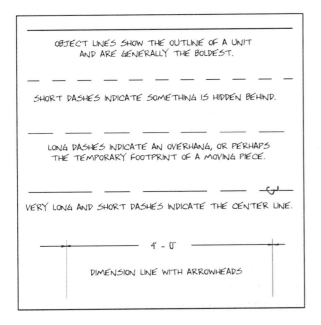

Most of the time architectural/mechanical drawings have dimensions on them that tell the carpenters how big they are. Knowing accurate sizes is crucial to making a cut list of the parts, and in fact you can't even begin without them. But sometimes there is a dimension

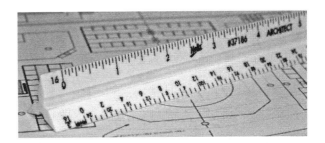

AN ARCHITECT'S SCALE RULE

THE MOST COMMON TYPE HAS THREE SIDES, LIKE THE ONE IN THE PICTURE. THE TOP PART ON THIS SIDE IS AN ORDINARY RULER THAT YOU ARE ALREADY FAMILIAR WITH.

missing, or perhaps the shop needs to know the size of something that the draftsperson didn't realize was necessary. Architectural drawings are always done to scale, so that all the parts are proportionally correct to one another. That allows you to use a *scale rule* to discover the length of distances that were not dimensioned when the drawing was done.

This type is known as an *architect's* scale rule, but there is another very similar type known as an *engineer's* scale rule which will not work at all for our purposes. The architect's rule gives dimensions in feet and inches, but the engineer's rule uses decimal equivalents, and is meant for measuring really large things like roads. You can use one of these when working in Europe because they are consistent with the metric system where every measurement scale is an order of magnitude bigger or smaller than the next one.

The notations on the rule seem really complex until you learn the secret of how they work, and then it's easy. Different scales are represented on different surfaces. There are three sections to the rule, which are often depicted by different colors to make them easy to spot. One of them is just a ruler of the sort you have used many times. It's usually black if there is a color code, and it is the only thing on the top of that side.

Across from the ruler on the black section are the numbers used for $3/16$ths and $3/32$ inch scales. They are at opposite ends of the ruler and cross over one another.

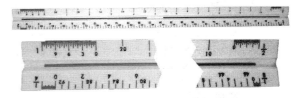

THIS SIDE OF THE RULE HAS FOUR SCALES, 1/8, 1/4, 1/2 AND 1 INCH.

THE 1/2 AND 1 INCH SCALES ARE NESTED TOGETHER. THE 1/2 INCH READS FROM RIGHT TO LEFT.

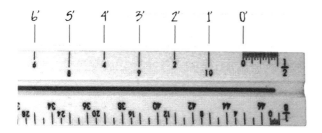

THE ½ INCH EQUALS ONE FOOT SCALE

THE FOOT NUMBERS READ FROM RIGHT TO LEFT.
THE ODD NUMBERED FEET ARE OMITTED BECAUSE
THE 1" SCALE NUMBERS SUPERSEDE THEM.

This works because the smaller scale is exactly half the size of the larger one. Both of those are really tiny and it is unlikely you will have a drawing done in either of those two scales. Most theatre work is done in either ½″ or ¼″ scales. If your rule is color-coded (and not all of them are) the ½ and ¼ inch scales are on the red side of the triangle. Eighth and ¼ are together on one side, ½ and 1 inch on the other. Remember that the different scales nest comfortably together because one is exactly half the size of the other.

Notice that the ½ inch scale measurements begin on the right side of the ruler and extend toward the left.

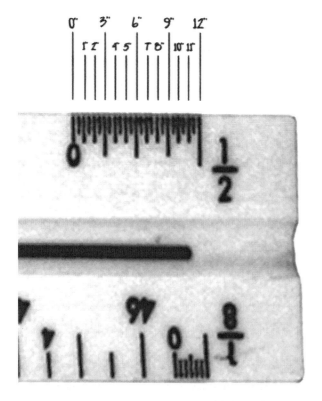

INCH MARKS ON THE HALF-INCH SCALE

That can be a bit confusing at first because we are so accustomed to reading from left to right. But that direction was reserved for the larger, 1 inch scale. All of the scales are done that way.

Look closely and you will see a number of lines very nearly together just to the right of the zero on the ½ inch scale. Those are inch markings and there are 24 of them because this particular scale is large enough to make it possible to view ½ inch at a time. Since there are 12 inches in a foot, that 12, plus the 12 half-inches makes 24 marks. Notice that the lines are not all the same length, which is done on purpose so that you can read them more easily. That is much the same as the lines on a tape measure, which have different lengths in proportion to their importance. In this case, the longer lines are at 3, 6, 9, and 12 inches. The other inch numbers are shorter, and the halves of an inch are shorter still. The numbering system for the inches goes left to right, which is the opposite of the way the feet are measured. There is a good reason for that. You can think of measuring a certain number of feet, plus a certain number of inches.

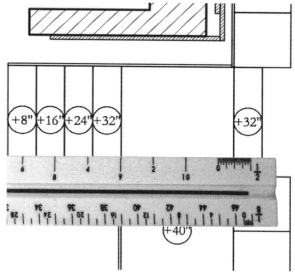

Here the distance is 3′-6″ as measured by the rule. The number of feet on the rule is actually 9, which is a number associated with the 1 inch scale at the other end of the rule. But since we are measuring with the ½ inch scale, we will interpret the number as the next one in the series between two and four. Look closely, the entire series is **20**, 1, **18**, 2, **16**, 3, **14**, 4, **12**, 5, **10**, 6, **8**, 7, **6**, 8, **4**, 9, **2**, 10, **0**. The numbers in bold are the ones that actually relate to the ½ inch scale, and not the 1 inch scale. You can see they have an order to them while all the numbers as a whole do not. This is similar to exams like the ACT or SAT that you took to get into college, and you should be able to apply the same sort of reasoning to deciphering this sequence. Notice that the non-bold numbers get larger from left to right, while the bold numbers read the opposite way from right to left.

In order to measure a distance with the ½ inch scale, place the rule on the paper so that the zero is just inside the distance you are measuring, and some amount of whole feet is on the other end of the distance. If what you are measuring is an even number of feet, you have finished measuring. If it is not, then add the number of inches to the right of the zero mark to the total number of feet, and that is the overall measurement.

You don't necessarily need a scale rule to get approximate measurements from a scale drawing. You can do the same thing with an ordinary tape measure and a little bit of arithmetic. The tape measure method has merit because if you are building something in a shop you already have the tape close at hand. The previous drawing was of an object drawn in ½ inch scale. (If you aren't sure about the scale of a drawing, there is very frequently a notation that indicates it in this way "Scale: ½" = 1'-0".") We already know that the object was 3'-6" wide. That means in ½ inch scale there would be three halves of an inch, and one half of a half. On a tape measure, that would equate to an inch and a half, plus one quarter of an inch.

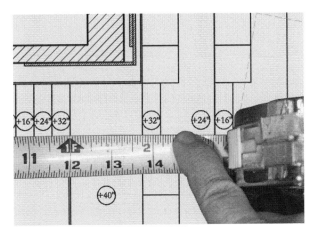

YOU CAN USE A TAPE MEASURE INSTEAD

1 AND 3/4 INCHES IS THE SAME
AS 3 FEET 6 INCHES IN 1/2 INCH SCALE

IF YOU "BURN A FOOT" YOU CAN AVOID DEALING WITH THE HOOK.

You can work the problem the opposite way by imagining you've used your tape to measure a distance that is four and one-eighths of an inch long. Each inch is 2 feet, while an eighth of an inch is half of a half of a foot, or 3 inches. The answer is 8'-3". Finding half of a distance is a very common practice when using imperial measurements since the entire system is based on dividing distances in half.

OTHER DOCUMENTS

Another category of construction documents is the paperwork used in guiding the process. A list of that might include:

- List of scenic elements
- Budget report
- Lineset schedule
- Prop list

ZOMBIETOWN

LIST OF SCENIC ELEMENTS

1 **Portal** With nose and Rotating eyes.

2 **Show Curtain** Painted on muslin with webbing and ties at top, pipe pocket at bottom.

3 **Tree Drop** Painted on muslin, cut out, and glued to netting. Netting needs to have webbing and ties at the top, and pipe pocket at the bottom.

4 **Drive in Movie Sign** Used for rear projection, on hanger, light up sign at the top.

5 **Raked Stage Decking** Needs to have a slot 4 feet from the top edge as a guide for the larger tombstone unit.

6 **Fence Posts** Larger at the top and/or uneven. Barbed wire larger than actual size.

7 **Windmill** Metal Constructed mostly from tubing of various sizes. Rolls on stage.

8 **Roll on House Unit** Ladder for actor access to top level. Top level not weight bearing. No glass in windows. Window needs to be boarded up as part of the action of the play.

9 **Large Tomb Unit** Actress dances on top of this. Zombie reaches in through swing-away insert. Actors roll it onstage from SL, must be guided by slot in stage deck.

10 **Gravestone** Slides in on push pallet from SR.

11 **Cemetery Bench** Slides in on push pallet from SL.

12 **Bench Car Seat** Slides in on push pallet from SR.

13 **Two Bucket Seats** Slide in on push pallet from SL.

14 **Projector Silencer** Used in the back of the house.

15 **Projector Stand** Use upstage in theatre, smaller projector, rear projects on drive in movie sign.

16 **Two Push Pallets** One for stage right and one for stage left. It might be easier to make four of them and not need to change the units that fit on them.

17 **Toyota Sign** Cut out letters mounted on tubing.

LIST OF SCENIC ELEMENTS

A list of the *scenic elements* can be helpful when doing a show that has many different parts to it, such as is often found in multi-scene musical. The shop can compare the list to the plans they have received to determine if all of the information is included. Also, this list is an overview of the scope of the work and can be used as a reference in that way.

The *budget report* is usually generated by the technical director (TD) or whoever is in charge of the shop. It details the cost of various things. The TD might well use the list of scenic elements to do that, making a notation of how much each item on the list costs. If the show is over budget, which frequently happens, having the list of elements and the budget report together can make it easier to decide which units are the most important and which might be more expendable.

Utah Shakespearian Festival

PRESENTS: "CAMELOT"		BRAD CARROLL, DIRECTOR		
PRELIMINARY ESTIMATES		R. ERIC STONE, SCENIC DESIGNER		
		ZAK STRIBLING, SCENERY SUPERVISOR		
UNIT: UNITS A & B		ROLLING PLATFORM UNITS W/ AIR CASTERS WITH PIVOT MOUNT SHIELD WALLS		

MATERIAL	SALE UNIT	COST	UNITS	COST
3/4" AC PLYWOOD	4 X 8 SHEET	$26.30	8	$210.40
1" SQUARE MT 1020 TUBE STEEL	LINEAR FOOT	$0.63	200	$126.00
1/4" MDF	4 X 8 SHEET	$11.00	11	$121.00
1/4" LAUAN	4 X 8 SHEET	$11.00	13	$143.00
1/4" MASONITE	4 X 8 SHEET	$14.99	2	$29.98
2x4x8 WHITE PINE	LINEAR FOOT	$0.45	200	$90.00
1x4x16 WHITE PINE	LINEAR FOOT	$0.50	0	$0.00
1.5" SQUARE MT 1020 TUBE STEEL	LINEAR FOOT	$0.85	80	$68.00
COFFIN LOCKS	EACH	$15.00	4	$60.00
AIR CASTERS AND WORKS	EACH	$75.00	8	$600.00
		$0.00	0	$0.00
SUB TOTAL				$1,448.38
CONTINGENCY 10%				$144.84
GRAND TOTALS				$1,593.22

BUILD PROCESS TIME ESTIMATE

PROCESS	CARPS	HOURS	ESTIMATED MAN HOURS
METAL CUTTING	1	2	2
WELDING	1	6	6
DECKING	2	1	2
PLATFORMING	2	6	12
STAIRS	2	4	8
PNEUMATICS	1	6	6
OTHER CASTERING	1	4	4
	0	0	0
	0	0	0
	0	0	0
CONTINGENCY 10%			4
TOTAL BUILD HOURS			44

REPORT COURTESY OF ZAK STRIBLING

Hanging Schedule for *Pajama Game*

Lineset	Usage	Distance from Plaster Line
1	Portal	1' – 0"
2	Show drop	1' – 6"
3	Star Drop	2' – 0"
4	Eagle Hall Banner	2' – 6"
5	Foliage cut drop	3' – 0"
6	Border	3' – 6"
7	Legs	4' – 0"
8	# 2 Electric	4' – 6"
9	Clear	5' – 0"
10	Factory Lights	5' – 6"
11	Hernando's Hideaway backing	6' – 0"
12	Black scrim	6' – 6"
13	Park drop	7' – 0"
14	Border (kick sheaves DS 12")	7' – 6"
15	Legs (kick sheaves DS 12")	8' – 0"
16	# 3 Electric	8' – 6"
17	Clear	9' – 0"
18	Clear	9' – 6"
19	Sign	10' – 0"
20	Border	10' – 0"
21	Legs	11' – 0"
22	Band overhead lights	11' – 6"
23	# 4 Electric	12' – 0"
24	Scrim	12' – 6"
25	Clear	13' – 0"
26	Border	13' – 6"
27	Legs & Cyc lights	14' – 0"
28	Sleep-Tite Band sign	15' – 0"
29	Clear	16' – 0"
30	Cyclorama	17' – 0"

HANGING SCHEDULE

A HANGING SCHEDULE LISTS THE NAME OF THE PIECE, THE PIPE NUMBER, AND THE DISTANCE FROM THE PLASTER LINE.

The *lineset schedule* is a way of determining at a glance what will be hung on each of the linesets in the theatre. This is generally easier to work with than a large plan view, which should have the same information but in a less user-friendly format. The lineset schedule should be worked out by all the interested parties, so that the electricians, carpenters, and designers are all satisfied. A set of drafted plans from a designer is not absolute. Alterations are frequently required because of budget or time problems. Negotiations may be required to find a way to fulfill the designer's vision but stay within budget constraints. The same is true of the hanging schedule in that more than just scenery will need to fit into the theatre.

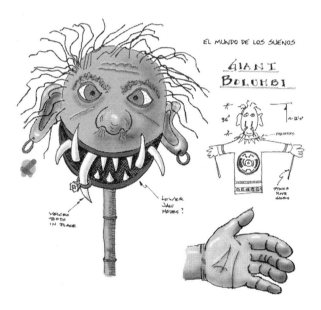

PROP SKETCH BY THE AUTHOR

The generation of a *prop list* usually takes a while, especially if the show is a new script, because the director and the actors don't yet know everything that will happen during the rehearsal phase. Some items on the list such as pocket watches, books, and teacups won't really matter to the shop because those are bought/found objects. But other things like unusual furniture or a magically lighted treasure chest may need to be constructed. Some theatres have a separate prop shop, and others do not. But if something cannot be purchased then it will have to be constructed by someone. It is good to have a list of the complicated props as early as possible so that they can be considered when making a schedule. Built props are often detailed with sketches rather than measured drawings like from a CAD program. Those sketches are the responsibility of the scenery designer.

CAD Drawings

Back in the day, all drafting was done by hand, using a T-square and triangles, but now computers reign completely. As mentioned earlier, drafting is different from free-hand drawing in that the images are done to scale, meaning that all parts of the drawing are proportional to one another, and that they are a specific amount smaller than the actual objects they represent. One of the most common scale sizes for theatrical drawings is ½″ equals 1′-0″. Half-inch scale works out to be ¹⁄₂₄th the actual size of an object. Proper scale is really important, because without it scenery might be drastically mis-proportioned.

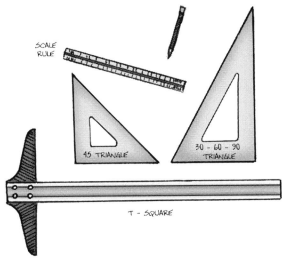

DRAFTING TOOLS OF YESTERYEAR

THIS IS WHAT YOU NEEDED TO DO WHAT IS NOW CALLED "HAND DRAFTING" TO DIFFERENTIATE IT FROM CAD. MANY DESIGNERS STILL USE THESE TOOLS FOR ELEVATIONS AND OTHER "DONE BY HAND" DRAWINGS.

One of the first *CAD* or *Computer Aided Drawing/ Drafting* programs was AutoCAD, which is very widely used today. *AutoCAD* originated in the early 1980s, when personal computers were in their infancy. You can intuit that by the way it works, with lots of DOS-looking typed in commands that predated the invention of the graphical user interface that brought us the mouse.

Vectorworks is a competing CAD program frequently used in the entertainment industry because there is an entertainment specific version called Spotlight. *Vectorworks Spotlight* has many tools for lighting designers, as well as the standard architectural drawing setup. VW was originally developed for Macs, but can now be run equally well on either Mac or PC. AutoCAD began as a PC program (actually pre-dating Windows) but there is now a Mac version. Vectorworks is quite popular with lighting designers, but many scenery designers and probably most TDs use AutoCAD instead. One of the advantages of AutoCAD for designers is the very useful 3-D software, while TDs appreciate the way it helps organize budgeting.

The name "Vectorworks" has an interesting connotation that speaks to the difference between any CAD program and a picture/drawing program like Photoshop or Paint. Whatever the type of computer or computer program, lines, shapes, and colors on the screen must somehow be documented and recorded. Photoshop does that using the *raster* method, which records the look of each individual pixel on the screen. As a result, you can manipulate the image one pixel at a time. That makes it possible for the brushes in Photoshop to move in any direction the mouse moves. You can also scan in images and manipulate their color pallets. But the tradeoff is that Photoshop files are huge, and would never have been possible using a 1980s computer and its very small memory. The amount of memory space needed for an AutoCAD file is much smaller by comparison, because *vector* programs work differently.

Instead of keeping track of each individual pixel, the program remembers line placement by creating a mathematical formula that says "this line starts here and stops there." You should think of the drawing as individual lines, rectangles, circles, polygons, and so forth; that come together to form a drawing. You might think of the drawing window (the space where the drawing is done) as an infinitely large Cartesian graph. A line is said to begin at two points such as (3,3) and end at another two points (11,9) and what you are drawing

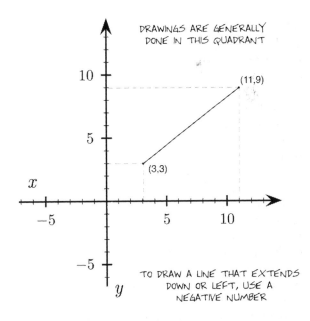

DRAWINGS ARE GENERALLY DONE IN THIS QUADRANT

TO DRAW A LINE THAT EXTENDS DOWN OR LEFT, USE A NEGATIVE NUMBER

DRAWING A LINE ON A GRAPH

THE LENGTH OF THIS LINE WOULD ACTUALLY BE THE SQUARE ROOT OF 8² PLUS 6², WHICH IS A REALLY CLUMSY NUMBER. MOST OF THE TIME YOU WOULD INSTEAD TAB OVER TO THE TEXT BOX REPRESENTING THE LENGTH OF THE LINE AND ENTER THE DESIRED DISTANCE. PRESS ENTER TO CREATE AN ARC THAT LENGTH. CHOOSE A PLACE ON THAT ARC WHERE THE LINE SHOULD STOP AND CLICK AGAIN TO ESTABLISH THE LINE. AUTOCAD DOES ALL OF THE POINT PLACEMENT FOR YOU.

on the screen is defined that way in the computer program. AutoCAD uses x and y coordinates for drawing in two dimensions like a plan view, and z coordinates to make three-dimensional drawings.

One of the best things about a vector program over a raster program like Photoshop is *scalability*. Scalability means that you can make an image larger or smaller without disfiguring it. If you enlarge a 72 dpi jpeg image to something like 500%, the pixels grow very large on the screen, and the image becomes a grainy collection of squarish dots. That does not happen with a vector program. The lines become thicker as you zoom in, but they don't break down into dots.

AutoCAD Basics

Both Nemetschek, which publishes Vectorworks, and Autodesk, which publishes AutoCAD, have student versions of their programs for no or extremely reduced cost. They are hoping of course that you will learn their particular program and continue to use it when you are a professional and can afford the much more expensive pro version. But anyone can download a trial version of the software just to see if they like it. Both programs have changed drastically in just the past few years, so it is good to have a later version, which you will get in either case. You can find really excellent video tutorials online.

The modern AutoCAD workspace has Windows-like menus with tabs similar to many other programs, and the button icons should look pretty familiar to you. The banner across the top of the workspace is called the *ribbon* and has many functional buttons. You can click on different tabs to bring up new menus that are arranged in much the same way as Microsoft Word. Another similarity is the big purple "A" in the upper left-hand corner which, rather than using a file menu, can be used for familiar functions like open, new, save, and print and is much like the Office Button in Word.

You can undock panels from the ribbon and move them around the workspace if you will use them frequently. At the bottom of the window is the *command line*, and under that another strip of buttons called the status bar. The command line is a way of entering commands to do almost anything that AutoCAD can do as a drawing program and was traditionally used to tell the computer how to draw lines. You can still do that, but you can also just click on icons from the ribbon. Newer users will probably prefer that method because it is much more familiar to them. But, even if you draw entirely using the mouse, the command line will still document what actions you have taken. Pressing the F2 key will bring up a list of all the commands you've entered since beginning your session.

When used as a two-dimensional drawing program, AutoCAD constructs all drawings from straight lines, arcs, rectangles, and other polygons. To make a line you select that tool from ribbon, or type in "line" in the command line followed by enter. Click the mouse on the drawing window where the line should begin and again where it should end. Press enter to stop drawing lines, or move the cursor to a third point and click again. The third click will create a second line from the end of the first line to the last click point. To close up the triangle, you can use "close" in the command line. Notice that the command line often prompts you to enter defining information. Rather than clicking randomly on the screen, you can enter exact sizes into the command line to create a scale drawing.

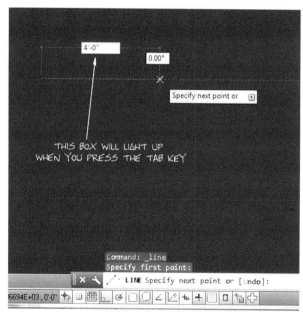

USE THE COMMAND LINE TO SPECIFY YOU WANT TO DRAW A LINE, AND THE TAB KEY TO ENTER EXACT DIMENSIONS. IT WILL GREATLY SPEED UP YOUR DRAWING TIME AND MAKE THEM MUCH MORE ACCURATE.

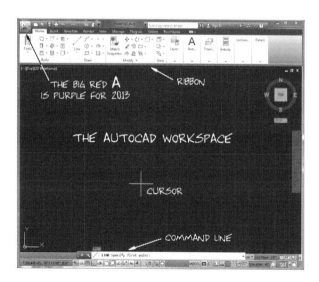

THE BIG RED A IS PURPLE FOR 2013

RIBBON

THE AUTOCAD WORKSPACE

CURSOR

COMMAND LINE

AutoCAD is set up so that the space bar is equivalent to the enter key, because it is used so frequently and it is easier to find the space bar than the enter key. That is one of very many aliases used in AutoCAD. The term *alias* is used to describe a keyboard short cut, which are often things like L for line and D for dimension which can be typed into the command line to initiate actions. Instead of typing the entire word, you can type in the shortcut letter and press enter. Experienced AutoCAD users will use them instead of clicking icons from the ribbon because it is faster for them. They use the mouse with their dominant hand, and use the other hand to type commands from the keyboard. If you have entered an incorrect value in the command line, you can press the escape key to back out of it. There are a couple of different levels to that, so it may be necessary to press escape more than once.

You can select previously drawn lines on the screen in a couple of different ways. One is to click on them with the mouse, which should be fairly self-explanatory. Notice though that when you move the cursor over an object that it lights up to let you know what you are about to select. This is important when there are many small items on the screen. Another method is to use either the *selection window* or the *crossing window*. They appear on the screen when you hold down the mouse button and move the cursor across the screen. The selection window appears when you move left to right and the crossing window when you move right to left. The selection window selects objects that it completely encompasses, while the crossing window selects anything that it touches.

Notice that when you select a line several boxes appear along its length. These are called *object snaps*. The snaps show up to let you know (among other things) where the ends of the line are. Lines frequently need to intersect exactly at their ends, and AutoCAD will automatically make that happen if you are within a certain distance when you click the mouse. One line "snaps" to another.

Polar tracking is a related concept that makes it easier to draw with accuracy. You can click that icon at the bottom of the window to begin restricting the movements of the cursor to make lines snap to vertical or horizontal placements. You can set your own preferences to include exact degree placements like 45°

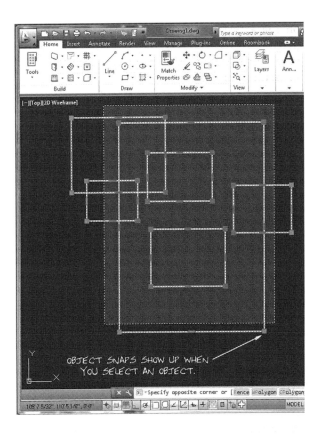

YOU CAN SELECT OJECTS BY CLICKING ON THEM ONE BY ONE, OR YOU CAN USE THE SELECTION OR CROSSING WINDOWS. THE SELECTION WINDOW GOES LEFT TO RIGHT, AND MUST ENCOMPASS THE ENTIRE ITEM. THE CROSSING WINDOW POPS UP WHEN YOU DRAG THE MARQUEE FROM RIGHT TO LEFT. IT WILL SELECT ANYTHING THE BOX TOUCHES.

OBJECT SNAPS APPEAR WHENEVER AN OBJECT IS SELECTED, AND CAN BE USED TO MANIPULATE IT AS WELL AS TO CONNECT SUBSEQUENT LINES.

from the horizontal. In this way, you can get very exact drawings without worrying too much about being so careful in manipulating the mouse.

Of course this is the briefest of overviews about a hugely complex program. It should though give you an understanding of the basic ideas behind using AutoCAD and perhaps let you know if it appeals to you. Similar tips for the Vectorworks program are found in the lighting chapter.

TERMS USED IN THIS CHAPTER

alias
architect's scale rule
AutoCAD
blueprints
budget report
CAD or Computer Aided
   Drawing/Drafting
center line
command line
construction document
cross hatching
crossing window
dimension

drafting
elevation
engineer's scale rule
floor plan
ground plan
isometric drawing
lineset schedule
object lines
object snaps
perspective drawing
plan view
plaster line
polar tracking

prop list
raster
ribbon
scalability
scale rule
scenic elements
section view
selection window
sketches
Vectorworks Spotlight
view

CHAPTER 14

FLATS

FLATS ARE THE most quintessential piece of theatrical scenery and have been around at least since the renaissance period when Serlio and Sabbatini were writing their now famous books. The basic rationale behind building flats is to provide a lightweight structure with a surface that represents a large flat area such as a wall. In earlier times, flats were essentially a large artist's canvas onto which all decoration such as windows, doors, wallpaper, and sometimes even furniture were painted. Early American stagehands would lash the flats together with ropes to form a room or box set. In the early twentieth century that was a method of constructing stage sets that were inexpensive and easily transported. At that time acting companies made a living "on the road" at theatres in small towns across the country. In this modern era, audiences expect to see a more realistic and three-dimensional setting and styles have changed. Even so, the old methods of flat building have a place in today's scenic studio where many structures are still built in similar ways.

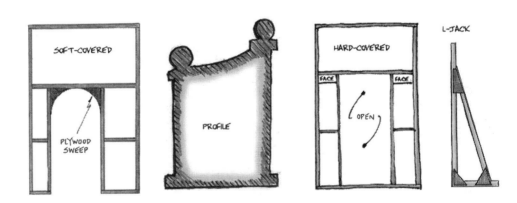

DIFFERENT TYPES OF "FLAT" STRUCTURES

MODERN THEATRE DESIGN HAS MOVED AWAY FROM ITS ROOTS IN MAKING BOX SETS FROM GROUPS OF FLATS LASHED TOGETHER. BUT EVEN SO, THE CRAFT OF CONSTRUCTING SCENERY STILL INCLUDES A HEAVY DOSE OF BUILDING LIGHTWEIGHT STRUCTURES - IN MUCH THE SAME WAY AS THE OLD-STYLE MUSLIN COVERED, PAINTED FLATS WERE MADE.

The skills you learn in building flats are easily transposed into building more complex units. Flat-like structures are used in making all sorts of things. The basic techniques of measuring, cutting, and joining are essential no matter what you are making. Cut lists of parts are used in all construction projects, whether you are building with wood, plastic, or metal. It is important to learn to visualize how units fit together, and how that interaction dictates the sizes of their individual parts. Flats are fairly simple structures, and are a great place to start that learning.

There are two main types of flats, the traditional type covered with a soft material such as muslin or canvas, and an alternate type that has a hard plywood covering. The two different

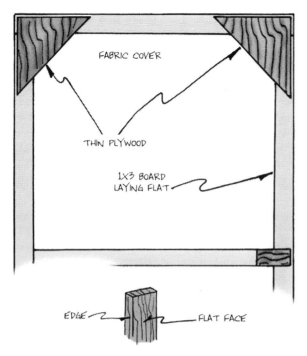

SOFT-COVERED FLAT DETAILS

THIS IS THE TRADITIONAL THEATRE TYPE. THE FRAMING IS DONE WITH THE FLAT FACE SIDE TO THE FRONT, SO THEY REALLY ARE VERY FLAT. THIS DRAWING SHOWS THE BACK SIDE OF THE FLAT, SO YOU CAN SEE PARTS THAT DON'T SHOW FROM THE FRONT.

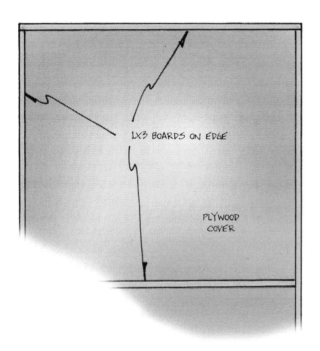

HARD-COVERED FLAT DETAILS

THIS TYPE IS VERY FREQUENTLY USED IN MOVIES AND TELEVISION, AND CAN BE CALLED A TV OR HOLLYWOOD FLAT.

approaches are called soft and hard-covered flats respectively. Hard-covered flats are often called TV or Hollywood flats because they are used in those industries. In either case, any kind of flat is constructed around a framework that delineates the outside profile and that provides enough internal support to maintain the structural integrity of the flat. This structure, usually unseen by the audience, is called the *framing*.

SOFT-COVERED FLATS

The most common *soft-covered flat* is a rectangular structure covered with fabric. The covering is often muslin, an all-cotton fabric that can be purchased in quite large sizes from theatrical suppliers. Sometimes duvetyn, velour, or some other type of specialty fabric may be used. Black duvetyn or velour can be used to make excellent *masking flats* that are set up backstage to improve sightlines. Masking flats are a very common use for soft-covered flats. Even so, heavyweight muslin is the standard type of covering for a painted flat.

The framing for a soft-covered flat is joined together in a traditional way, using framing parts with names derived from general woodworking practice.

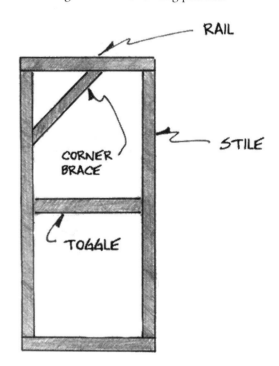

PARTS OF A FLAT FRAME

Any horizontal member is known as a rail. Any vertical member is a stile. Internal framing members that help to brace the rails or stiles are called toggles, whether they run vertically or horizontally. Quite often these are referred to with both names, such as in "toggle rail." A brace that runs diagonally across one corner of a flat is called a corner brace. This brace is used to reinforce the squareness of the flat and to keep it from deforming into a parallelogram.

The *corner brace* creates a triangular form at the corner of the flat. Triangles are a very strong structural form because there is no easy way to deform the shape. In order to do that you must change the size of a side, or bend it in some way, which requires a lot of force. The corner brace triangle is used to stiffen and reinforce the larger rectangle. If one corner of the rectangle is held rigid at 90 degrees, the other three corners must follow suit. You rarely need a corner brace on a flat unless it's very large, but these braces are frequently used on other structures.

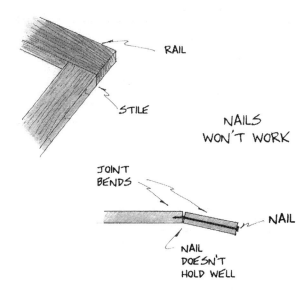

RAIL

STILE

NAILS WON'T WORK

JOINT BENDS

NAIL

NAIL DOESN'T HOLD WELL

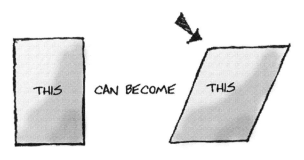

THIS   CAN BECOME   THIS

WHEN FORCE IS APPLIED AT AN ANGLE

The ¼″ thick plywood pieces are known as *corner blocks* and *keystones*. They form a *covered joint*. You can easily understand how corner blocks got their name, but keystone is a bit more obscure. The name comes from the shape of a stone block that forms the top of a Romanesque archway. These blocks were cut into the shape of a trapezoid and were used as a decorative and functional flourish.

ONE TRIANGLE WILL STRENGTHEN ALL THE CORNERS

90

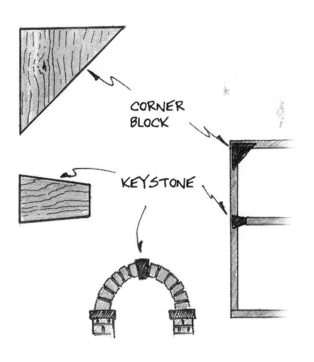

CORNER BLOCK

KEYSTONE

The rails, stiles, and toggles on this type of flat are joined together using thin pieces of plywood fastened to the back side of the boards. It is easy to see why when a flat is viewed from the side. Although they meet as a butt joint, the angle for nailing them together is awkward.

There is an obvious problem in nailing through the rail into the stile. There's a high probability that the wood will split because of the long distance the nail must travel through such a thin slat. It just looks wrong. This joint would be weak and prone to failure. A lot of carpentry work turns upon an intuitive grasp of things like that. You could overlap the boards and nail them together that way, but it would leave an uneven surface for the covering. Flats got their name from being flat structures.

Thin plywood blocks attached to the rear of the framing are an excellent way of connecting this joint.

Traditional keystones for flat building were made into this shape so that the wide portion of the keystone was attached to the stile, and the narrow portion (which is the same width as the toggle) attached to the toggle rail. That meant more surface area would be glued to the stile.

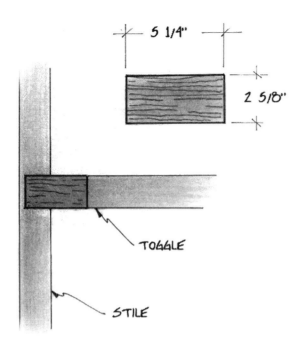

KEYSTONE PLACEMENT

extend all the way from side to side is such a hard-and-fast rule that the orientation of a flat can be determined just by observing the manner in which the framing pieces are overlapped. This is helpful when there is a mix of different flats and some of them are wider than they are tall.

A center support or *toggle* is used to maintain the inside shape of a flat. On larger flats the side stiles tend to curve inward when the flat's covering is attached and stretched. One or more toggles will prevent the stiles from bowing toward the center. The rule of thumb is to place a toggle every 4 feet or so.

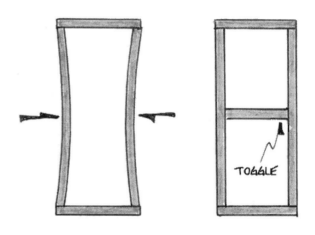

TOGGLES ARE USED TO PREVENT THE SIDES OF THE FLAT FROM BOWING INWARD

However, the trapezoid shape is difficult to cut because the sides are not parallel, and the angle of the saw must be changed repeatedly. Many shops forgo the traditional keystone shape and use a plain rectangle for the keystone.

On a flat, the top and bottom *rails* always extend to the very edge of the flat, covering the ends of the two stiles. This is done to protect the stiles when moving the flat. It keeps the wooden framing from splitting if the flat is dropped on its corner. Having the top and bottom rails

Other than corner blocks and keystones, all of the framing members of a flat are cut from one by material, traditionally white pine. In many shops, soft-covered flats are constructed from 1×3, and its milled size is ¾″ by 2⅝″.

The 1×3 has peculiar dimensions. As you may recall from the chapter on lumber, all nominally 1 inch thick boards are actually ¾″ thick after they have been through the milling process. So that dimension seems correct, but the width seems off. If you go to the lumber yard,

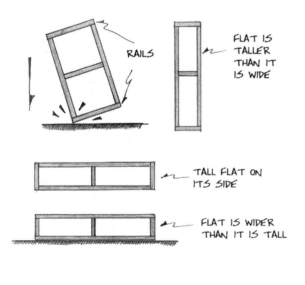

TOP AND BOTTOM RAILS RUN ALL THE WAY SIDE TO SIDE

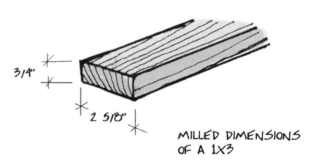

MILLED DIMENSIONS OF A 1X3

the nominal widths of one-by material are all even measurements like 4, 6, 8, 10, or 12. So a 1×4 is the smallest commercially available size. That turns out to be somewhat heavier than is actually required for most lightweight flats. The added weight of the wood actually makes the flat structure weaker. The heaviness of the flat makes it more likely that it will get twisted out of shape enough for the joints to come loose. A theatre 1×3 is made by ripping down a 12 inch wide board into four equal pieces that are 2⅝" wide. Four times 2⅝" is actually only 10 ½", but remember that the saw kerf takes away some of the material. Some carpenters use a 2½" size instead because the numbers are easier to work with.

The most common type of soft-covered flat is a tall rectangle. They are often used as wall sections or masking flats. But that is not the only type. You can also make door and window flats.

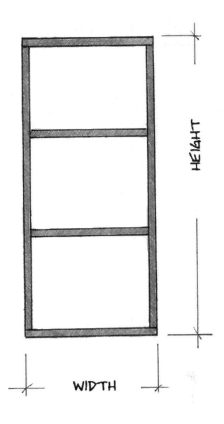

THUMBNAIL SKETCH

DOOR FLAT   WINDOW FLAT

You might often receive an elevation drawing showing only the external size of a flat, and perhaps the dimensions of a doorway as well. It may well be left to the carpenter to interpret what goes on inside. Or it might be that someone has done technical drawings of how the framing parts fit together. Some shops do a whole series of CAD drawings of the individual parts. If the latter is true, you can tell by the tech drawing how the rails and stiles overlap one another, but if not, you can make a thumbnail sketch to guide you in your work.

Carpenters often make small drawings to help them visualize construction issues. A sketch can be used to make up a cut list of the individual parts that you'll need and also serve as a construction guide during the assembly process.

No matter who does the technical drawings, certain guidelines must be met. Since this unit is 10 feet tall, two evenly spaced toggles have been sketched in. One toggle would have left two spaces 5 feet tall. Two toggles will leave three spaces, each about 3 feet 4 inches tall. Neither

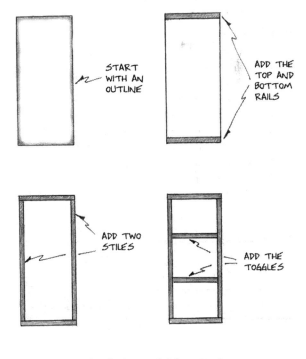

STEPS IN SKETCHING A FLAT

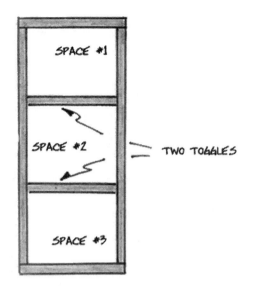

TWO TOGGLES MAKE THREE SPACES

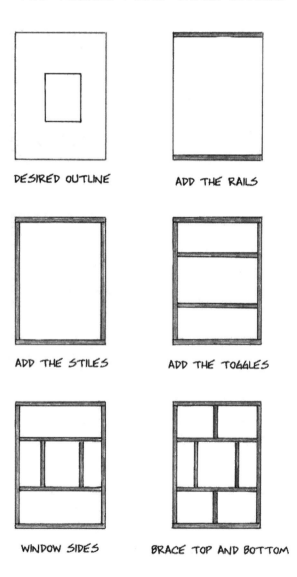

DESIRED OUTLINE   ADD THE RAILS

ADD THE STILES   ADD THE TOGGLES

WINDOW SIDES   BRACE TOP AND BOTTOM

one nor two works out to exactly 4 feet, but the best answer for the number of toggles in this example would be two.

As another example, imagine that you have been requested to build a window flat 6 feet wide and 10 feet tall. The window inside the flat should be 3 feet wide and 4 feet tall. The window is centered side to side in the space, and the bottom of it is 3 feet from the floor. It is easy to sketch out the flat using just this information. Begin with the outside profile, then continue with the inside profile of the window opening.

Keep in mind that your sketch should be of the *back* side of the framing, meaning that you are viewing it from the rear. If the flat is symmetrical from left to right there is no difference, but if not you must be sure to show the correct view. It will not be possible to install the keystones and corner blocks later on if the flat is laid out face up.

In the window flat example, there is a non-structural reason to place the toggles in a specific location. Rather than simply divide the available space into thirds, the two toggle rails are positioned so that they become the top and bottom of the window opening. Because the flat is more than 4 feet wide, two additional toggle stiles are used to brace between the toggle rails and the top and bottom rails.

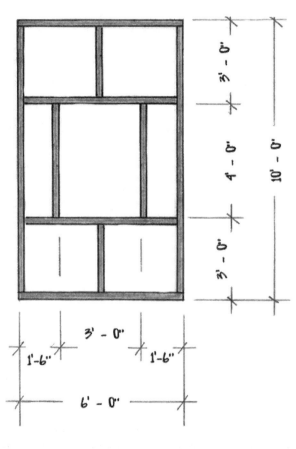

A DIMENSIONED SKETCH

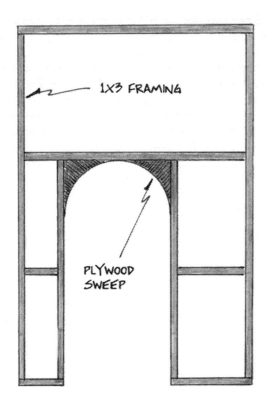

ARCHED DOORWAY

3/4" PLYWOOD

1X3 LUMBER

3/4" PLYWOOD IS THE SAME THICKNESS AS THE 1X3 SO IT WORKS WELL FOR A SWEEP

EXAMPLE OF A FLAT THAT IS NOT A RECTANGLE

1X3

START WITH THIS BASIC FRAMING

ADD PROFILE PARTS AS REQUIRED

A PROFILE FLAT

Door flats are framed in a similar fashion, excepting that the opening extends all the way to the floor, and the bottom rail is split into two parts. Toggle placement is used to delineate the top of the door opening. The door hole needs to be open at the bottom, or actors would trip going through.

All of the flats presented thus far have been rectilinear, but flats are not limited to that shape. One easy variation is to use a framing piece known as a *sweep*. Sweeps are used to create a curved profile, most commonly at the top of a window or doorway. Sweeps are cut from one-by or ¾″ plywood so that the thickness of the sweep matches the thickness of the one-by used to frame the flat. Sometimes the plywood is left whole when the sweep is very small, but more often the material behind the curve is trimmed away to reduce the weight of the unit. Use a large wooden compass or a set of trammel points to mark the curve. Connect the sweep to the main structure using keystones or specially cut shapes of ¼″ plywood as required.

There is no reason why flats must be composed of straight lines and 90 degree angles, other than that those are the easiest flats to build. The framing members can be cut at any angle and joined together with blocks and keystones cut to match.

Sometimes designs require flats that mirror an object with a completely irregular shape. To construct this type of flat, begin with an interior comprised of straight lines that fill most of the space. Then add to the profile with ¾″ plywood, much like when installing sweeps. The principle is the same; the shapes are simply more complex. The profile edges can be attached with ¼″ ply that has been cut to the specific size and shape of the profile.

CUT LISTS

A *cut list* is essential when building just about anything. You make a cut list the same way for any project, although the sizes of lumber and other materials change from job to job. Making a cut list involves using feet and inches, as well as fractional parts of inches shown on a tape measure. The divisions of the tape relate to repeatedly dividing 1 inch in half. One-quarter is equal to half of a half; one eighth is half of that, and so on. Before beginning an in-depth study of how to figure cut lists, here is a short review of adding and subtracting fractions.

FRACTIONS AND ENGLISH-STYLE MEASUREMENTS

Fractions are an indication of an amount that is divided by another amount. The symbol / actually means "divided by," so that the fraction ½ really indicates 1 divided by 2, that is to say, a whole that is split into two equal parts. The fraction ¼ represents a whole that has been divided into four equal parts. One-quarter could also be expressed as the decimal equivalent of 0.25, which is the number you will get when you divide 1 by 4 on your calculator. Many math problems are much easier to work when using decimal equivalents of fractions. That does not work well when making a cut list. Woodworking is always done using fractions. Many times fractions are actually easier to work with than decimal points, and with some practice you can do the math in your head rather than needing a calculator. At any rate, the answers you come up with must be measured with a tape that is marked in fractions, not decimal equivalents. You can buy a calculator that operates in feet, inches, and fractions rather than decimals. You may wish to try one but will probably find out that you don't really need it after a short

while because the problems are so easy once you get the hang of them.

The top number in a fraction is the *numerator*, and the bottom is the *denominator*. In order to add fractions together you must give them a common denominator. Before you can add ¼ and ½, you need to change the denominator 2 into a 4. You can do that by multiplying the fraction ½ by the fraction ²⁄₂. Two halves equal 1 and will not change the value of ½. Multiplying any number by 1 will not change its value. To multiply fractions you simply multiply the two numerators and then the two denominators.

$$\frac{1}{2} \quad \text{NUMERATOR}$$
$$\text{DENOMINATOR}$$

$$1/2 \times 2/2 = 2/4$$
$$1/4 + 2/4 = 3/4$$

Subtracting fractions is essentially the same process of finding a common denominator, and then subtracting the numerator. If you want to subtract ¼ from ½, then 4 will again be the common denominator, creating the equation 2/4 – 1/4 = 1/4.

Another example:

$$3/4 - 5/8 = ?$$
$$3/4 \times 2/2 = 6/8$$
$$6/8 - 5/8 = 1/8$$

$$1/2 = 1 \div 2 = 0.5$$

THE SLASH MARK
MEANS "DIVIDED BY"

WORKING WITH FEET AND INCHES

The *dimensions* used in a construction project have the added complexity of adding and subtracting whole feet and inches as well as just fractions. Although fractions are used to subdivide inches, you should never express foot measurements in fractional portions such as "two and one-half feet." Rather, you should say, "two feet six inches."

A shorthand method of expressing feet and inches uses an apostrophe ' for feet, and quotation marks " for inches. (Of course you don't call them that in measuring, they are just feet marks and inch marks.) Two feet 6 inches is written as 2'-6". Two feet, 6 and ½ inches is written 2'-6½". Always insert a dash between the feet and the inches, but not between the inches and the fraction.

If the measurement is an even 2 feet the notation should be 2'-0", with the zero inches included to make the reader certain that there are actually no inches included rather than that the writer has neglected to write the number of inches. On occasion, you will need to express a measurement that includes a fractional portion of 1 inch, but no whole inches, such as 2'-0½", and you are seeing the proper notation method written here.

Sometimes measurements are given in all inches rather than in feet and inches. A tape measure is equipped to deal with that because one side of the blade is in feet and inches and the other side is in all inches. Traditionally, if no part of what you are building is larger than 8 feet, then all dimensions are given in inches, but this rule is not always followed. Flats are generally bigger, and as a result flat cut lists are usually done in feet and inches. If you are building step units, or some other smallish scenery, it may be easier just to use all inches. There may be a specific reason to choose one method over the other,

but once you have, stick with it. Never mix all inch dimensions with feet-and-inches dimensions because it is very easy to get confused about the numbers. Twenty inches (20") and 2 feet (2'-0") tend to look very much alike, and they are very close in actual length. You cannot tell just from looking at the size on a scale drawing which one you have.

In my professional work I use all inches exclusively, no matter how big the pieces are. But that is just a personal preference. It avoids having to convert feet to inches, which is a cumbersome process. After a while you can easily remember the numbers of common lengths such as 96" for 8 feet and 144" for 12 feet.

Here are a few practice examples of adding and subtracting feet and inches:

Problem A is easy since it is possible to subtract the 4" from the 6½" cleanly and arrive at an answer of 2½". Three feet minus 2 feet leaves 1 foot, and therefore the answer to the first problem is 1'-2½".

The second problem B is a bit more of a challenge, because you need to convert the fractions first so that there is a common denominator. Multiplying ½" by ²⁄₂ gives you ²⁄₄". Two-fourths subtracted from three-fourths is one-fourth. The rest of the second problem is straightforward and the answer should be 1'-0¼". Note that a 0 is used to denote the absence of any whole inches.

Problem C involves shifting feet to inches in order to work the problem. 6'-0" is a whole number of feet, and doesn't allow you to subtract 2½". Before you can solve the problem, you'll need to convert one of the feet into inches. You can do that by borrowing 1 foot from the feet column and converting it to 12 inches. Since there are 12 inches in a foot, you have neither lost nor gained anything by re-expressing the amount as 5'-12". Go a step further and convert one of the inches into a fractional amount so that you have something to subtract the ½ inch from. Now the number is written as 5′-11½″. From here you can do the normal math and arrive at the answer 0′-9½″ for the third problem. Again, you can see that a 0 has been used to indicate that the number of feet is nil rather than simply missing.

The final problem D is one of addition rather than subtraction and is distinguished by the fact that the two inch amounts together are greater than 12. Proper form dictates reducing the number of inches by shifting 12 over to the foot column and adding 1 to that total. The answer to problem four is 9′-0¾″.

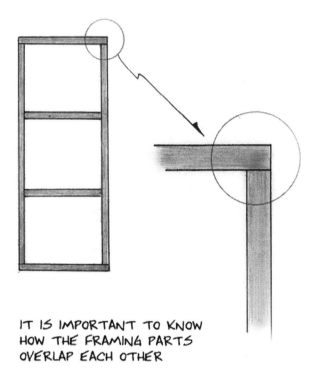

IT IS IMPORTANT TO KNOW HOW THE FRAMING PARTS OVERLAP EACH OTHER

It's important for any drawing to show exactly how the framing pieces intersect. Basically that means which pieces overlap which others. Dimensions are given to the outside of the structure. If covered butt joints are used to join the 1×3 lumber, only one of the pieces will extend all the way to the outside edge. Any other piece intersecting it will have its length shortened by the width of the 1×3. The math part of making a cut list is mostly about deciding which boards are the boards that get shortened, and then subtracting some amount from their length. This process is the same for all construction projects.

The next sketch shows that the top rail and the bottom rail run continuously from side to side, while the two stiles stop short of the top and bottom. Also, the center toggles do not run all the way to the outside, but are shortened by the width of the two stiles. This drawing has been dimensioned, and you can see the lines and numbers used to give the overall size of the flat.

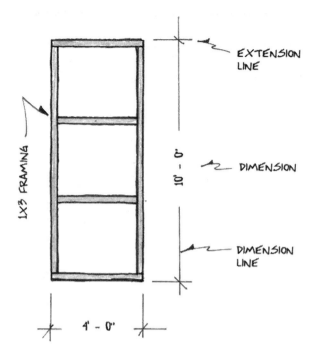

The flat in the drawing is 4′-0″ wide and 10′-0″ tall. There are two toggles. The framing will be cut from 1×3 #2 white pine. When forming a cut list, begin with the longest pieces first and work your way down to the shortest ones because that is the same order used to cut the pieces. It's good to cut the longest pieces first when you can be more selective about the stock of 1×3. Looking at the drawing, you can see that the two stiles are the longest pieces. The stiles are often the longest pieces if you are making wall flats for a box set. Most of the time flats are taller than they are wide.

The stiles are both the same size. It is normal to assume that the top and bottom of the flat are parallel with one another unless there is information to the contrary. You can see that the stiles don't reach either the top or bottom, and that their overall length should be decreased by twice the width of the framing material. In this case that is 1×3 lumber with an actual milled width of 2⅝″. The number to subtract from the overall height is twice 2⅝″, or 5¼″.

The exact size of the framing lumber in this example is not as important as realizing that calculations are made on the basis of whatever that size is. Sometimes 1×4 framing is used on flats, and of course in that case the milled size of the framing lumber would be 3½″. Or it could be that your 1×3s are 2½″ wide instead of 2⅝″. Whatever size you are using, you must subtract the width of the two pieces of lumber from the overall height in order to arrive at the proper length.

To get the length of the styles, subtract $2\frac{5}{8}'' + 2\frac{5}{8}''$ from the overall 10'-0" measurement. $2\frac{5}{8}'' + 2\frac{5}{8}'' = 5\frac{1}{4}''$. When that amount is subtracted from 10'-0" the answer is 9'-6¾". On the list you should make a notation of 2 @ 9'-6¾". This, of course, indicates that two pieces at this length are required to build the flat.

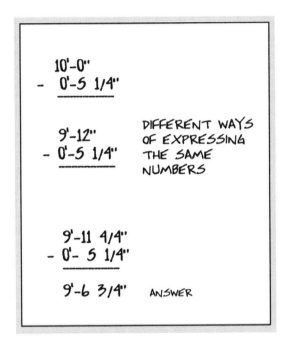

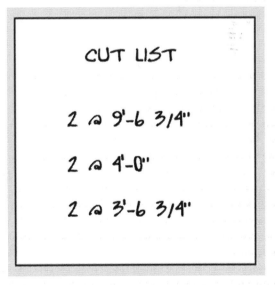

Years ago, it was necessary to explain that the @ symbol means "at," but thanks to the miracle of email, that explanation is no longer needed!

The next longest pieces are the top and bottom rails. You can see from the drawing that these two parts are continuous from side to side, and are dimensioned at 4'-0". Therefore the next item on our list is 2 @ 4'-0". No math is required because the dimensioned size on the drawing and length of the actual part are the same.

The final items for your cut list are the two center toggles. Again you can see that they don't run all the way from side to side, but rather dead end at the *inside* of the stiles. Again you need to add $2\frac{5}{8}''$ and $2\frac{5}{8}''$, and again the sum will be $5\frac{1}{4}''$. I have added these two numbers together many, many times over the years and somehow the answer is always the same. I'm sure that after you have worked a few of these problems, you will simply remember some of the most common math answers and will lose interest in a calculator. After subtracting $5\frac{1}{4}''$ from 4'-0", the answer is 2 @ 3'-6¾".

The answers to the practice problems (see p. 200) can be found at the end of the Helpful Hints section.

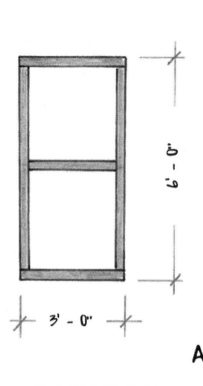

3' - 0"

6' - 0"

A

PRACTICE PROBLEM

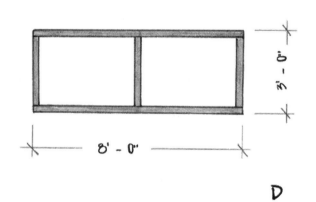

2' - 0"

9' - 0"

7' - 0"

3' - 0" 2' - 0"

6' - 0"

C

PRACTICE PROBLEM

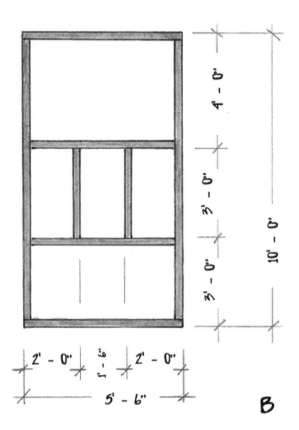

4' - 0"

3' - 0"

3' - 0"

10' - 0"

2' - 0" 1' - 6" 2' - 0"

5' - 6"

B

PRACTICE PROBLEM

3' - 0"

8' - 0"

D

PRACTICE PROBLEM

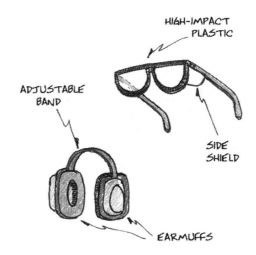
HELPFUL HINTS

- Remember to work in order from the longest to the shortest pieces.

- In order to keep track of what parts you have finished, make an x on the drawing over the appropriate part after you have listed it.

- If these problems have been difficult for you, make up some more and work them on your own. It is essential that you develop the skill of making cut lists in order to progress to the next level.

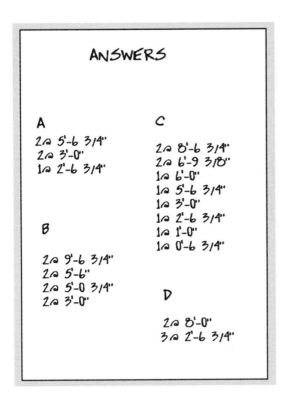

ANSWERS

A

2 @ 5'-6 3/4"
2 @ 3'-0"
1 @ 2'-6 3/4"

B

2 @ 9'-6 3/4"
2 @ 5'-6"
2 @ 5'-0 3/4"
2 @ 3'-0"

C

2 @ 8'-6 3/4"
2 @ 6'-9 3/8"
1 @ 6'-0"
1 @ 5'-6 3/4"
1 @ 3'-0"
1 @ 2'-6 3/4"
1 @ 1'-0"
1 @ 0'-6 3/4"

D

2 @ 8'-0"
3 @ 2'-6 3/4"

FLAT CONSTRUCTION

Now that you are armed with the ability to create a cut list from a drawing or sketch, it is time to bring together the skills learned in several different sections and try a construction project. Before using power tools in the shop it is important to review some safety issues.

Safety in a theatre shop should be stressed at all times. People of all different skill levels work there, and it is important to look out for one another. It is also important to wear safety glasses with any type of cutting tool, and hearing protectors with any tool that is loud enough to be annoying. Is it necessary to wear safety glasses and a hearing protector when using a hand screwdriver? Probably not, but if someone else is using an angle grinder right next to you, the answer would be a definite yes. The most important aspect of safety is common sense. If you think that something is dangerous, then it probably is, and you should take precautions.

Sometimes there are dangers that are not so obvious. That is why it is important to read and understand all the safety procedures outlined in the instructions that come with any tool. Although many tools are similar, individual examples have eccentricities that you may not know about unless you read the instruction book or receive specific instruction in the use of that tool from a qualified person. The most important safety consideration is to pay attention to what you are doing. Most accidents seem to occur when a worker has a lapse of concentration.

For this project, suppose that you have a drawing for a flat that is 3 feet wide and 12 feet tall. The cut list has been worked out to the side. If you are actually building this project, you may wish to use some other dimensions; just work up a drawing with sizes that meet your needs.

Rip down a 1×12 to get enough stock to build the flat. Of course, the 1×12 you start with will need to be at least 12 feet long, or the 1×3s will be too short to cut to the proper length.

Number 2 white pine has certain defects that prevented it from being sold as a higher grade of lumber, so the 1×3 laying on your shop floor has some imperfections in it. The process of sorting lumber according to quality is known as *culling*. The culls are the pieces deemed unusable for a particular purpose. But remember that a length of 1×3 that is totally unsuitable for a long stile might be just fine for a shorter rail, which is why it was important to list the parts of your flat in order from longest to shortest.

Some pieces are obviously too bowed or warped to use. (Cupping is not usually a problem with such narrow

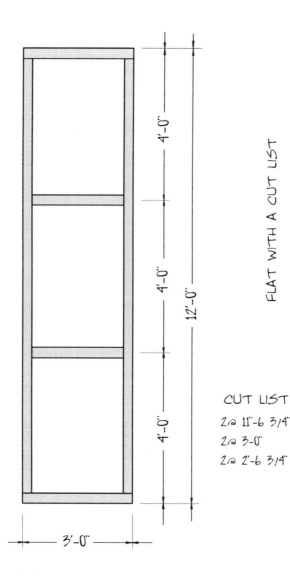

FLAT WITH A CUT LIST

CUT LIST
2 @ 11'-6 3/4"
2 @ 3'-0"
2 @ 2'-6 3/4"

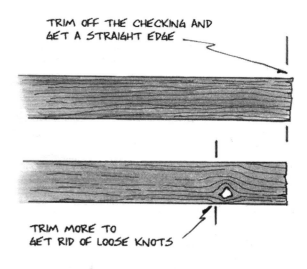

TRIM OFF THE CHECKING AND
GET A STRAIGHT EDGE

TRIM MORE TO
GET RID OF LOOSE KNOTS

TRIM THE END OF THE BOARD
BEFORE CUTTING A PIECE TO LENGTH

strips.) To get a good view of how distorted a certain board is, hold one end up to your eye and sight down to the end of it as though you were looking down a pool cue. This makes it easy to determine how much bow or warp there is over the length of the board. If the board has a gentle bow, it can be easily removed by correctly positioning the flat's toggles. If there is a sharp bend where a knot is located, that piece is probably not going to be usable with that kink still in it. Cull through all of the pieces, and set aside the ones that are best suited to cutting the long stiles.

Use the radial arm saw to cut the two stiles to their proper length. Remember to trim a small amount off the end of the 1×3 first so that you have a nice square starting point. Trimming will also remove the small drying out cracks, or checks, that often appear at the very end of a board. There should be plenty of length to do this even if you are using 12'-0" stock because the boards from the lumberyard are just a bit longer than that. Also, the stiles are shorter than 12'-0" because of the way they are interrupted by the top and bottom rails. On the cut list they are 11'-6¾".

Next cut the 3'-0" rails, and then the two toggles. Cut around large knots wherever it is possible. You can't always be too finicky, but do improve things when you can. Refer back to the chapter on woodworking and saws for more information on measuring and marking for the radial arm saw. If a RAS is not available, a power miter saw is the second best choice. You can set up a miter saw with benches on either side so that it works almost the same way as a radial arm saw.

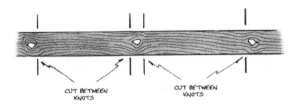

CUT SHORTER LENGTHS FROM LESS DESIRABLE MATERIAL

The corner blocks and keystones are next. The best material to use these days is ¼" B/C plywood. It's not a good idea to substitute lauan or Masonite for your corner block material. The lauan is far too spongy and will quite easily break under stress. Masonite is stiffer, but its lack of grain structure is a major fault. B/C yellow pine plywood is very strong, much stronger than either lauan or hardboard.

The size of corner blocks is somewhat flexible but should be somewhere in the neighborhood of 12 inches. Something slightly smaller than 1 foot, such as 11¾" is an excellent choice when you consider the 4×8 size of a sheet of plywood. You can rip four strips of 11¾" wide plywood on the table saw, and then cut those strips into squares with the radial arm saw. If you were to make the

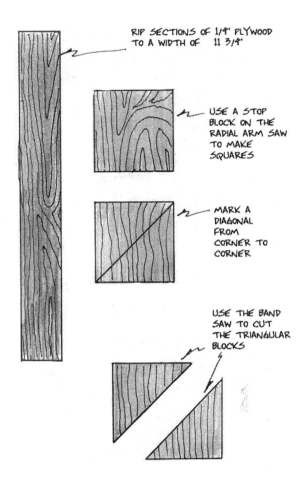

RIP SECTIONS OF 1/4" PLYWOOD TO A WIDTH OF 11 3/4"

USE A STOP BLOCK ON THE RADIAL ARM SAW TO MAKE SQUARES

MARK A DIAGONAL FROM CORNER TO CORNER

USE THE BAND SAW TO CUT THE TRIANGULAR BLOCKS

CUTTING CORNER BLOCKS

blocks exactly 12" square, you would only get three strips from a 4'-0" wide sheet because of the loss of material from the saw kerf. Use a stop block on the radial arm saw to ensure that all of the blocks are perfectly square. Use the band saw to slice the squares from corner to corner, creating the triangular shape required for a corner block.

Wood has much more strength along the length of its grain than it does across the grain. That is why plywood is manufactured with the grain of the various plies running in opposition to one another. As a result plywood is very strong in all directions. But when using ¼" plywood, that doesn't always work because thin plywood like it has only three plies. Obviously, there are two plies running one way and only one in the opposite direction. Therefore ¼" plywood has much more strength in one direction than it does in the other. When using it for a corner block you should make sure that the two grains visible on the top and bottom run *across* the crack resulting from the joining of the stile and rail. The tendency of the two 1×3s is to flex at the joint so you want the strength of the plywood to work against that. If the grain of the block runs in the same direction as the crack,

GREEN IDEAS TIP BOX

Trees are one of America's most abundant and renewable resources. Virtually all yellow pine trees used in making plywood are grown on plantations, farms where the trees are planted in rows like any other crop. They are just the right distance apart to grow straight and tall for maximum lumber production. When one crop is harvested, another is planted in its place. Most agricultural crops mature in a matter of months, but trees take decades. The cost of yellow pine plywood is more stable than for other varieties, because the industry that grows them has been planned and is predictable.

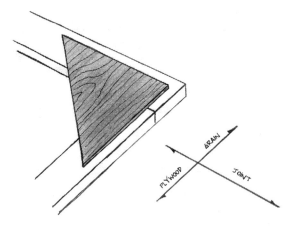

RUN THE PLYWOOD GRAIN
AT A 90 DEGREE ANGLE TO
THE DIRECTION OF THE JOINT

the joint will not be nearly as strong as when it runs across the crack.

The two blocks shown in the drawing cannot be cut from the same square unless one of them is flipped over after cutting. That would put the bad side up. It is more craftsman-like to show the good side of the plywood as the exposed side, the one you can see from the back. If you flip the triangle over, one of the sides will have to be the rough side.

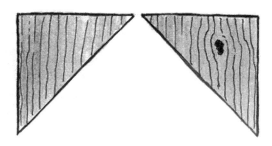

IT TAKES CUTTINGS FROM TWO
DIFFERENT SQUARES TO MAKE A
PAIR OF LEFT- AND RIGHT-HANDED
CORNER BLOCKS

You can avoid having the bad side show by making both left- and right-handed blocks when you cut them on the band saw. It's easy to do. Mark your diagonal cut lines in opposite directions for left- and right-hand blocks. When making a large number of corner blocks, it is more efficient to cut a number of them at one time by stacking the blocks together and cutting through all

TO MAKE LOTS OF CORNER BLOCKS
STACK THE BLANKS UP WITH THE
GRAIN ALTERNATING AND CUT THEM
ALL AT ONE TIME

the layers at once. It is possible to organize the left- and right-handed blocks by stacking the squares so that the grain on them is alternately vertical and horizontal. When a stack such as this is cut, there will automatically be an even number of left- and right-handed blocks.

There's one final step to take before the corner blocks are ready for use. It is common practice to chamfer the edges of the plywood blocks in order to keep them from splintering later on, and that is easily done on a stationary belt sander. A stationary belt sander is the same as a hand-held one, except that it is larger and you are meant to move the work in relation to the tool rather than the tool in relation to the work. If the stationary version is not available, you can do the same thing with a router table fitted with a chamfering bit.

This brings up an interesting point about whether you should bring the tool to the work or the work to the tool. In general that breaks down to which one is easier to manipulate. It's easier to bring the work to the tool when the part you are sanding is so lightweight that you would have to hold it in place anyway. Sanding or routing the corners should be a rapid process requiring no more than a few seconds for each block. Only the good side of the plywood needs to be chamfered, as the rough side will be pressed against the framing of the flat, and doing that side would just create an unsightly crack between the two pieces. Chamfering is one of those details that will give your work a finely crafted appearance.

Keystones are manufactured in a similar process, except of course that they are a rectangular shape rather than a triangle. Making the traditional trapezoidal shape

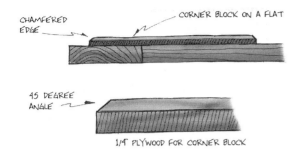

CHAMFERED EDGE

CORNER BLOCK ON A FLAT

45 DEGREE ANGLE

1/4" PLYWOOD FOR CORNER BLOCK

CHAMFERING THE EDGE REDUCES SNAGS AND SPLINTERING. IT GIVES YOUR WORK A MORE PROFESSIONAL APPEARANCE.

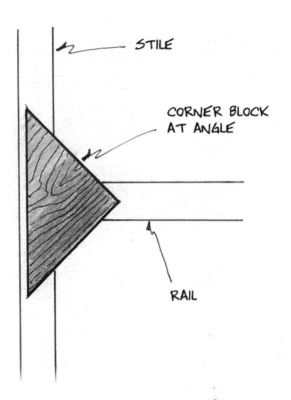

STILE

CORNER BLOCK AT ANGLE

RAIL

is usually too time-consuming for the amount of extra strength it allows. Some people call the rectangular version a strap. Rip down some of the ¼″ plywood into strips that are 2⅝″ wide. Cross cut these strips into pieces 5¼″ long, and then chamfer the edges of the good sides.

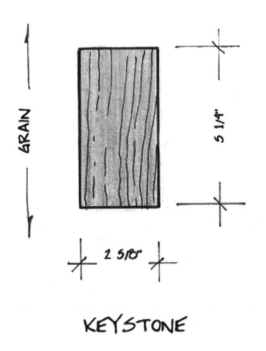

GRAIN

5 1/4"

2 5/8"

KEYSTONE

Remember to keep the grain of the plywood running the length of the keystone. That keeps the strength of the grain running across the joint as it did on the corner blocks. If for some reason you are building a structure that requires extra strength, use a corner block in place of a keystone.

A *template table* makes it much easier to assemble the parts of a flat. A template is a set of guidelines used to

SUBSTITUTE A CORNER BLOCK FOR A KEYSTONE WHEN MAXIMUM STRENGTH IS NEEDED

shape something else. Templates are used in such diverse pursuits as drafting and setting up word processing documents. In flat building (and other types of construction) they are used to square up the framing as it is put together. Many shops have constructed a large wooden table to use as a template, but a wooden floor works just as well. You can also use a number of platforms laid edge to edge for this purpose. It is imperative to be able to nail into the surface of the template in order to hold your parts in alignment while working on the flat. Blocks of wood along two adjacent sides form a guide. This guide is used to capture the framing and hold it in place. The resulting corner should be as square as possible because it will be used to square up your flats.

The first step in laying out the parts for assembly is to place the bottom rail against the bottom of the template. Any bow or *crown* in the board should point toward the inside of the flat so that the structure will not rock when it is in its upright position. (Crown is another word for bow.) There shouldn't be very much bow in such a short piece of 1×3. Next place one of the stiles along the side of the table where the positioning blocks are. Make sure that the crown of this piece is pointed toward the inside of the flat as well. Using 6d finishing nails, secure these two pieces to the table, taking care to straighten them out along the blocks as you go. Try not

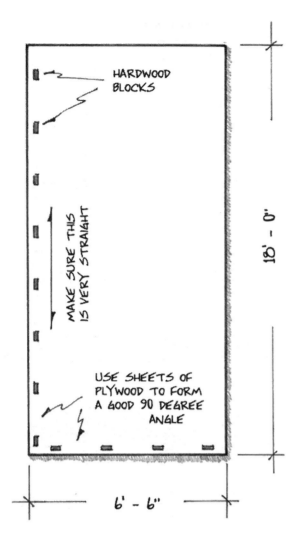

HARDWOOD
BLOCKS

18' - 0'

MAKE SURE THIS
IS VERY STRAIGHT

USE SHEETS OF
PLYWOOD TO FORM
A GOOD 90 DEGREE
ANGLE

6' - 6"

A TEMPLATE TABLE

NAIL

STILE

CROWN

CROWN

RAIL

SECURE THE STILE AND RAIL
BUT DON'T PUT NAILS WHERE
THE CORNER BLOCKS WILL GO

to put any nails in the places where the corner blocks and keystones will need to be connected. Do not drive the nails in all the way, but rather leave the heads up some so that it will be easier to remove them later on. Use the fewest nails possible to accomplish your purpose.

Set the remaining stile and rail in position, making sure to again point the stile's crown toward the interior of the flat. Adjust all corners so that they are flush with one another and nail down these last two pieces. When you are tacking down the second stile it is important to use nails only at the very ends of the piece. You might find that you can actually put the nails into the table, just next to the board but not actually into the board. That allows the stile to move as you remove the bow with the toggles. If the nails are too far from the end, the joints

will pivot around the nail when the stile is straightened. Very thin 6d finishing nails will make it less likely that the 1×3 will split when you nail so close to the end. Place the toggles in position and use them to press the second stile outward. If all of the pieces have been cut to the right sizes, the bow or crown should be removed and the flat should now be straight, square, and true.

If the amount of bow in the two stiles is relatively the same, it will have almost no effect on the finished product because the force of one side pushing in is an equal but opposite reaction to the force of the other side. If you are making flats for an entire show at one time, there will most likely be a number of same-length stile pieces to choose from, and you can pick matching pairs for the various flats. It is much easier to make many flats

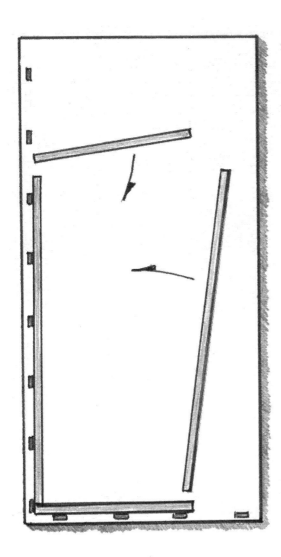

LINE UP THE CORNERS OF THE REMAINING RAIL AND STILE

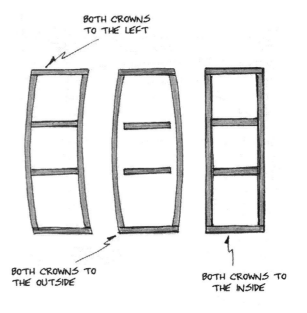

BOTH CROWNS TO THE LEFT

BOTH CROWNS TO THE OUTSIDE

BOTH CROWNS TO THE INSIDE

FOR BEST RESULTS, POINT ALL THE CROWNS OR BOW TO THE INSIDE OF THE FLAT

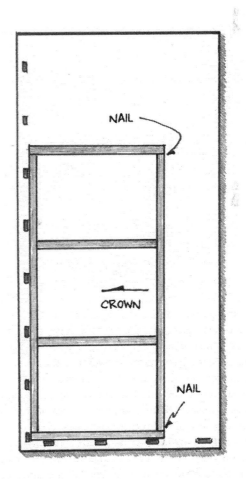

NAIL

CROWN

NAIL

TOGGLES SHOULD BE EVENLY SPACED

all at once than to cut and assemble them one at a time. In industry that is often referred to as *economy of scale*, meaning that if you spread the cost of preparing to build a product over many multiples, the cost per unit is reduced. That philosophy works for building all sorts of things.

The up/down position of the toggles has never been written down on any of the construction documents. Usually the exact location of internal bracing is not dimensioned, but is left to the discretion of the carpenter. It is a given that the toggles will be evenly spaced inside the opening. In this case, there are two toggles, but they create three spaces inside the flat. If you had three toggles there would be four spaces, and with four toggles five spaces, and so on.

The number of spaces is used to calculate the placement of the bracing rather than the number of toggles. Divide the total distance by the number of spaces to determine the size of each one. In this case you divide 12'-0" by three and arrive at 4'-0". Sometimes, the toggles are used to brace something that will be added to the flat later on, perhaps a chair rail, or some other piece of trim. In that case, dimensions may show the toggles are to be installed at a particular height from the bottom of the flat.

Imagine another case where the overall distance is 16'-0" and the number of toggles is five, resulting in six spaces. Dividing 6 into 16 gives 2⅔ feet, which is not an easy number to work with. Sometimes the numbers work better if you convert to all inches and try that way. Doing that for 16 feet gives 192 inches. The number 192 is easily divisible by 6. You can convert the resulting 32 inches back to 2'-8", or simply continue to work with the inches if that is easier. If you write it down anywhere, be sure to use 2'-8" because all of the other dimensions have been in feet and inches. If you write 32 instead, it may be misinterpreted as 3'-2". Those two dimensions are close enough together that a partner may not notice the difference until it is too late. This is one of the issues that may lead you to use all inches in all cases, despite the traditional use of feet and inches.

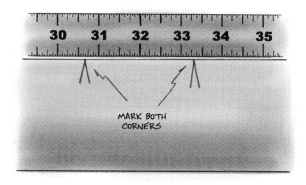

FOR A 1×3, MAKE A MARK 1 5/16" TO EITHER SIDE OF THE TARGET AMOUNT

The two toggles lay at 4'-0" and 8'-0" from the bottom. But that measurement is actually to the center of the toggles, and nothing on a 1×3 marks the center of the board. You could measure 1⁵⁄₁₆" to the center of the toggle and place a mark there, but the more accepted method is to locate the stiles at 4'-0" and 8'-0" but to make the marks 1⁵⁄₁₆" on either side of that point. That marks the two corners of the end of toggle itself and is a more accurate way than merely using the center of the toggle. 1⁵⁄₁₆" is half of 2⅝".

How did we get the fraction 1⁵⁄₁₆"? Of course half of 2 is 1, but an easy way to find half of any fraction is by doubling the denominator. In essence, you are multiply-

ing the fraction by 1/2. 1/2 times a/b = a/2b. 1/2 times 5/8 is 5/16.

When toggles are placed every 4'-0", you can hook the tape measure over the bottom of the flat and make a mark 1⁵⁄₁₆" to each side of each multiple of 4'-0". Mark both stiles since there are two ends to every toggle. Mark them all at once rather than moving the tape for each measurement because that allows placement error to creep in.

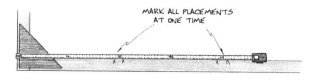

MARKING WHERE TOGGLES GO

After all of the framing for the entire flat has been tacked in place, you can attach the corner blocks and keystones. The traditional practice is to inset the blocks ¾" from the outer edge of the flat. This was done in order to allow another flat made from ¾" thick stock to fit evenly against it when making a 90 degree corner. This was done even if there was no immediate need for that to happen, since flats were often considered to be "stock" scenery, intended to be reused at a later date. But that is somewhat of an old-fashioned idea these days. Placing the blocks only a ¼ inch from the edge of the framing actually makes them much stronger. If you are making a duvetyn covered masking flat hinged together like a book, the ¼ inch distance is a much better choice.

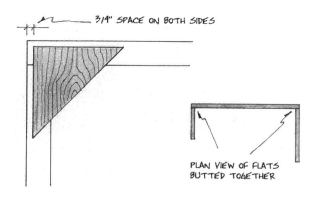

3/4' SPACE ON BOTH SIDES

PLAN VIEW OF FLATS BUTTED TOGETHER

CORNER BLOCKS TRADITIONALLY HAVE A 3/4' INSET TO ALLOW THEM TO FORM A CORNER WITH ANOTHER FLAT

You can easily mark the ¼" distance with a jig made from two short pieces of 1×3 offset from one another a quarter of an inch. Turn it the opposite direction for a ¾" space.

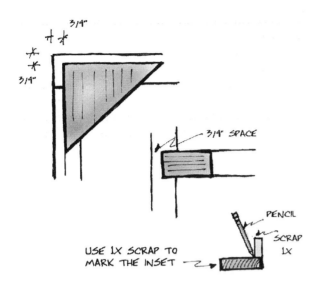

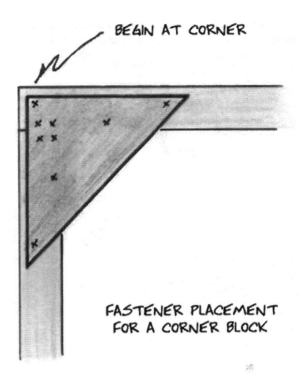

FASTENER PLACEMENT
FOR A CORNER BLOCK

Use a construction stapler with ¾" long staples in it to attach the ¼" plywood blocks to their proper positions. It's important to use staples rather than nails because the crowns of the staples won't shoot all the way through the thin blocks of plywood like finish nails are likely to do. Naturally, any sort of power tool is much faster than doing the job by hand.

possibly use. For the most part, fasteners really only hold the wooden pieces together while the glue sets up.

A traditional pattern is used to nail, staple, or screw the blocks in place. It is a good lesson in nailing technique, so you should use it for tradition's sake, even though using glue lessens the need for such exactitude. The pattern is as follows: one in each corner, two on either side of the joint, and one in the inside center on each leg. If you start with the staple that goes in the corner of the

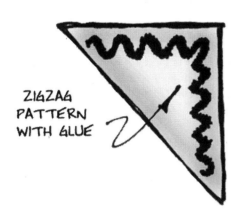

ZIGZAG
PATTERN
WITH GLUE

The strongest bond is formed by using a healthy application of aliphatic resin (yellow carpenter's) glue when attaching these blocks. Apply the glue using a kind of zigzag pattern. Put the block in place and then squish it back and forth a couple of times to spread the glue. You can pull one of the blocks back off every once in a while to confirm your gluing technique. The larger the surface area of the glue joint, the stronger the bond will be. Several small dots of glue on the back of the plywood block will just not do. You have only a couple of minutes to get things arranged after putting the glue on, because carpenter's glue will start to set after that time. So glue and staple the blocks one at a time rather than gluing them all at once before stapling. Remember that the glue will hold much better than any fastener you could

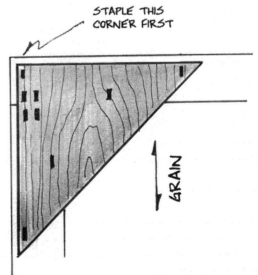

WHEN POSSIBLE,
MAKE STAPLE CROWNS FOLLOW
THE GRAIN DIRECTION

flat, it will make it much easier to line up the other two corners. From an engineering standpoint, it makes sense to secure the ends of the block and also the joint break. The center fasteners are added for good measure.

Keystones are fastened in the same way, but their rectangular shape creates a "double five" of dominoes appearance. Again, there is a staple in each corner, but this time four instead of three. If you are neat and tidy with the nail pattern, your work will have a more professional appearance.

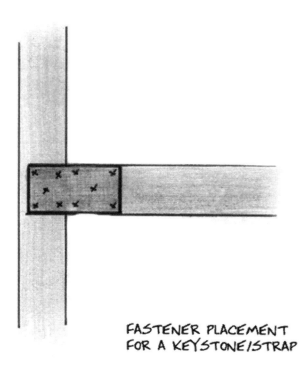

FASTENER PLACEMENT
FOR A KEYSTONE/STRAP

When all of the corner blocks and keystones have been put in place, it is a good idea to wait just a few minutes for the glue to set up somewhat before removing the nails that are holding it in place on the template table. After the flat has been separated from the table, check it over for defects and remove any puckers from the front that were caused by the 6d nails. This will prepare the flat for covering and sizing. When building a show, it is common to generate a large stack of flat frames before going on to the covering stage. Some flats are constructed for use as structural members and may never be covered at all.

COVERING THE FLATS

Old school painted flats are usually covered with heavy-weight muslin. This fabric is made from unbleached cotton fibers, and the type from a theatrical supply house comes in very wide widths for building scenery.

Some flats are covered with thin plywood rather than fabric. There may be a need to hang lots of artwork

on the walls. There may be trim pieces that cannot be accommodated in any other way. Traditionally, flats with a hard cover are made in the "Hollywood" style as described later on, but on occasion the traditional framing method is used. The main problem encountered in using a plywood cover on a traditional style flat is that when plywood is placed on the thin dimension of the 1×3, the framing tends to curl up, and it is difficult to get the flat to straighten out when it is assembled.

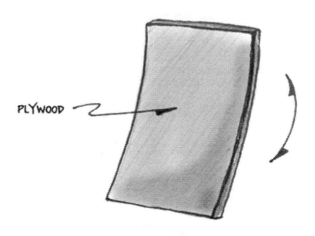

PLYWOOD

PUTTING PLYWOOD ON SOFT-COVERED
STYLE FRAMING CAN MAKE IT BOW

There are many different ways to affix muslin to a flat. The old-style method was to use tacks around the center of the flat, and animal glue (which is something akin to hot glue with a brush) to glue the muslin in place. Tacks are required due to the "instant stick" nature of this adhesive. The use of animal or hide glue has diminished in recent years both for political reasons (like where it comes from), and also because it is very messy to use. Hide glue must be heated in a special pot, and must be kept warm for hours on end. It is not the best thing you have ever smelled (because of where it comes from). Obviously, there is a risk of being burned by the glue. Today this sort of adhesive is mostly reserved for making expensive wooden musical instruments. For centuries luthiers have appreciated the tone that hide glue gives to stringed instruments. It is also used in antique furniture repair.

Some people stretch the muslin around the edges of the flat and staple it in the back as with an artist's canvas. This method does a good job of finishing off the raw edge of the flat. It is a good approach when the edges are likely to show to the audience, and is the way masking flats are covered with velour.

Another method is to glue the muslin onto the face of the framing using the technique shown here. Begin by laying the flat face up on top of some sawhorses. Pull enough muslin off of the roll or bale to cover the flat.

DOUBLE BOILER

FLAKE TYPE

HIDE OR ANIMAL GLUE IS BOUGHT BY THE POUND AND IS HEATED IN A GLUE POT

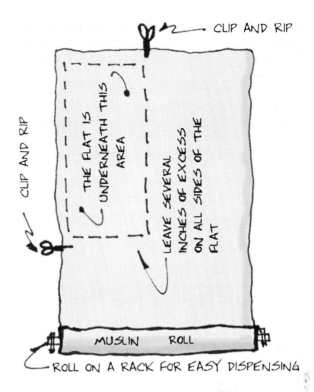

CLIP AND RIP

CLIP AND RIP

THE FLAT IS UNDERNEATH THIS AREA

LEAVE SEVERAL INCHES OF EXCESS ON ALL SIDES OF THE FLAT

MUSLIN ROLL

ROLL ON A RACK FOR EASY DISPENSING

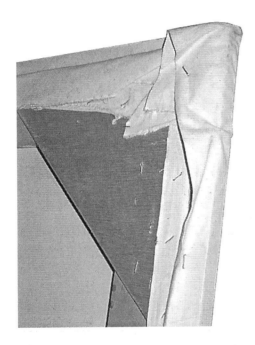

THIS FLAT IS USED BY A PAINTING CLASS, SO THE COVER IS JUST STAPLED ON

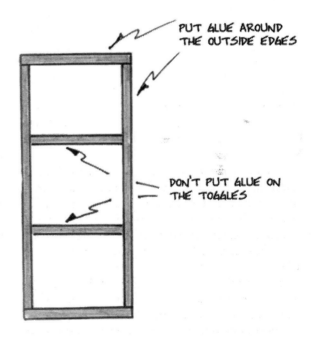

PUT GLUE AROUND THE OUTSIDE EDGES

DON'T PUT GLUE ON THE TOGGLES

Leave 3 or 4 inches of extra fabric around the outside edges, and rip the muslin to the desired size. Ripping is actually much better than using scissors for this purpose because the muslin will rip much straighter than you can possibly cut it. Scissors are helpful in making a small notch to start the rip. Pull off the excess strings and drape the muslin over the toggles on the inside of the flat.

Brush a generous helping of white glue onto the outer perimeter of the flat, spreading the glue over the entire surface of the 1×3. Do not put glue on any of the inside toggles or other framing. The muslin should be attached only on the outside, leaving the inside free. The only exception to this would be for a window flat, or some similar structure where the muslin is to be trimmed on the inside.

Pick up the muslin and place it gently on the surface of the flat and into the glue. This will take at least two people, and on a large flat, four. Walk around 90 degrees

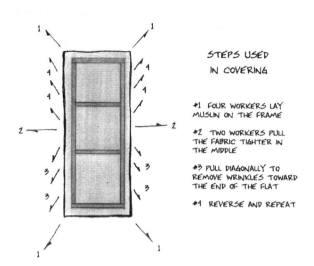

STEPS USED
IN COVERING

#1 FOUR WORKERS LAY
MUSLIN ON THE FRAME

#2 TWO WORKERS PULL
THE FABRIC TIGHTER IN
THE MIDDLE

#3 PULL DIAGONALLY TO
REMOVE WRINKLES TOWARD
THE END OF THE FLAT

#4 REVERSE AND REPEAT

MUSLIN LAYING ON TOP OF FRAMING

DRILL A 1/4" HOLE IN
THE CAP AND USE
THE ENTIRE
GALLON JUG AS A
GIANT SQUEEZE
BOTTLE

USE A 2"
POLY BRUSH, OR
SOME OTHER CHEAP
TYPE TO SPREAD
THE GLUE. DO NOT
USE EXPENSIVE
LINING BRUSH.

to the middle of the long sides of the flat and pull opposite one another to lightly stretch the muslin and press it very gently into the glue. Work together toward one end of the flat, straightening and pressing until that one end is finished, and then back to the middle, working toward the opposite end.

Try not smear the glue around too much when positioning the muslin, because if you wipe it all off, there will be nothing left to adhere the fabric to the wood. It is not necessary to stretch the muslin tightly. It is actually better to leave some sag in the material, but no more than an inch on a 4 foot-wide flat. You have used enough glue if you can feel a slight dampness through the fabric, but it is not good to have wet, sticky glue on the surface of the fabric. When it is dry, glue prevents scenic paint from soaking into the cotton fibers. Casein paint will have a noticeably lighter hue in the glue-coated areas.

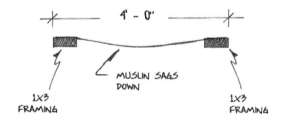

MUSLIN SHOULD SAG ABOUT 1" OVER 4 FEET

Once the cover is on, be sure to let the glue dry until the next day so that it cures completely. Otherwise it might pull away from the wooden framing when the fabric is sized. See the "Helpful Hints" section for additional advice.

You'll need to trim off the excess muslin from around the edges. It's easiest to do that with a utility knife, or perhaps just the blade from one. Hold the blade up against the side of the 1×3 and trim the muslin by running the blade along the edge of the flat. Try to make the muslin exactly flush with the framing. Use one long motion to slice the muslin so that the cut is as smooth as possible.

Sizing simply means to shrink the muslin fabric down to its proper size and tension by using a solution of very watery glue and/or paint. The normal ratio is in the neighborhood of 15 parts water to 1 part glue, but the exact amount is not all that crucial. A bit of paint in the mixture will make it easy to tell which part has been

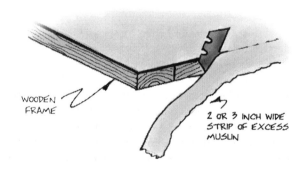

treated. You can actually see the cover shrinking and tightening right away. It may be necessary at some point to check the edges of the flat for small sections of loose muslin, and to re-glue these with a small bottle of Elmer's.

HELPFUL HINTS

Although it is likely that your first flat building experience will be in a class where you will make only one flat, it is more common to build a large number of flats all at one time. In our shop, we like to take the individual construction drawings and combine the cut lists into one master list that is used to do all the cutting. In this way, all of the longest pieces are cut first when the lumber selection is at its best.

Be sure to cut around knots when it is easy to do so. Often this will mean trimming only an inch or two from the 1×3, and it will result in a much better looking product. It will not be possible to exclude all knots from all parts. Cut away the ones that are easy to do.

Try to shoot the staples so that the indentation created by the setting of the crown runs *parallel* to the grain of the plywood. If the mark is *perpendicular* to the grain, tiny bits of the top ply tend to fly off and leave a messy appearance.

Do not rush the drying of the glue that holds the muslin in place on the flat frame.

Avoid muslin that has polyester thread in it, because this type will not size properly. It is the norm for a fabric store. They have a different use in mind than covering flats. Wide heavyweight muslin from a theatrical supplier is the best because they purchase goods with a knowledge of what it will be used for and are careful to select an appropriate type.

After flats have been sized or painted and have begun to dry, run your hand between the cover and any toggles that you can. This will ensure that the fabric does not stick to them by accident. If it does, the fabric will size in an odd way, which often results in puckering.

HARD-COVERED FLATS

Hard-covered flats are more popular these days. The name comes from the thin sheets of plywood that form the covering. Hard-covers are at their best when smaller flats are required, such as in a TV studio. The weight of the plywood becomes a major problem on larger flats. Most television scenery tends to be in the 9 to 10 foot tall range. The nice thing about the hard-covers is that it is possible to cut holes in them to run cables or fog hoses

or the like without destroying the structural integrity of the flat. Pictures can be hung just about anywhere without the need to install additional toggles as is necessary with a traditional muslin covered flat. These factors are especially helpful in television, where many decisions are not made until the very last moment and are difficult to predict. TV flats are often cut up to allow a new camera angle, or entire walls are moved around. The philosophy is that if the camera doesn't see it, it doesn't matter. In live theatre the audience is free to look wherever they wish, and you must pay a bit more attention to the overall appearance of the setting. Being as neat as possible backstage is important in live theatre because the stage manager cannot call out "cut" if something falls over backstage. The show must go on.

Hard-cover flats are definitely the more modern type, especially considering the high degree of realism required nowadays. Hard-cover flats are generally easier to build, more durable, and easier to connect together. But a stage carpenter should know how to build either type, as well as how to extend the techniques used to build them into the construction of other units.

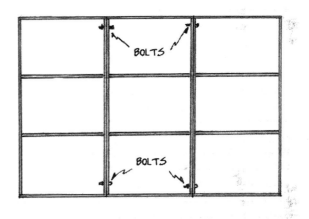

HARD-COVER FLATS CAN BE BOLTED TOGETHER THROUGH THE FRAMING ON THE BACKSIDE

TV flats are built with the framing on edge, so that the wall is quite thick by comparison to the standard type. They are more like the walls in a house. Flats are often bolted or screwed together edge to edge through the framing.

Since the entire face of the framing is covered with plywood, there is typically no need for corner blocks or keystones. Making a cut list is similar to the earlier process, but the sizes are different because of the way the framing is placed on edge. In the first example, the flat is smaller than 4 feet by 8 feet. You can build a hard-cover flat larger than 4×8, but special framing techniques must be used to connect the plywood covers.

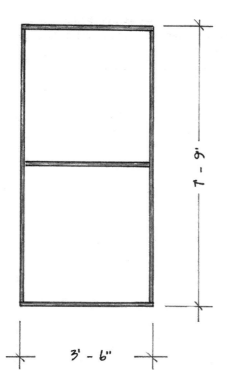

7' - 9'

3' - 6"

NOTE THE THINNER APPEARANCE
OF THE FRAMING WHEN IT IS
TURNED ON EDGE FOR A
HARD-COVER FLAT

The overall dimensions are $3'$-$6'' \times 7'$-$9''$. As you would expect, the stiles are the longest framing pieces, and should appear first on the cut list. Remember that the milled thickness of a one-by is actually $\frac{3}{4}''$. Just as with the muslin flat cut lists, you must subtract the thickness of the two rails from the overall height of the flat to determine the length of the two stiles.

MATH PROCESS

$3/4'' + 3/4'' = 1\ 1/2''$

$7' - 8\ 2/2''$
$- 0' - 1\ 1/2''$
$\overline{\quad 7' - 7\ 1/2''\quad}$

The length of the two rails is the overall width of the flat, $3'$-$6''$. The center toggle is found by again subtracting $1\frac{1}{2}''$ from the overall width. Hence our cut list is expressed as:

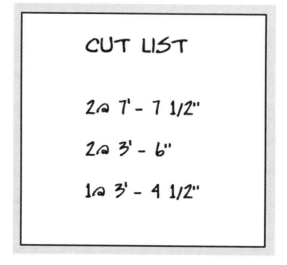

CUT LIST

2 @ 7' - 7 1/2"

2 @ 3' - 6"

1 @ 3' - 4 1/2"

A window flat can be designed in the same way that a soft-cover version is, with internal framing forming the window area. Here is an example of that process.

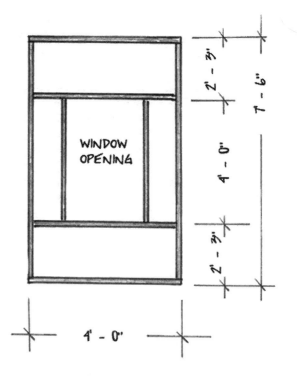

WINDOW
OPENING

2' - 3"

4' - 0"

7' - 9'

2' - 3"

4' - 0"

DIMENSIONS OF A HARD-COVER
WINDOW FLAT

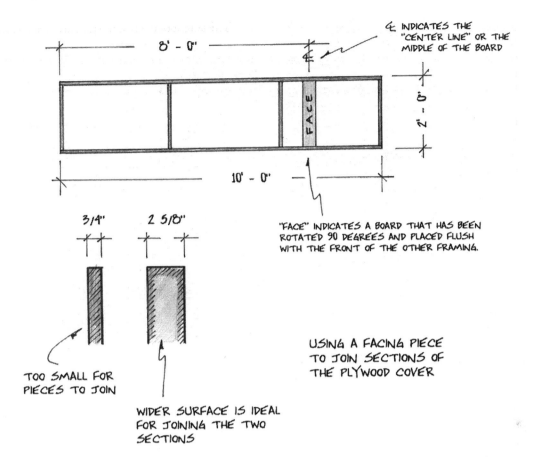

₵ INDICATES THE "CENTER LINE" OR THE MIDDLE OF THE BOARD

"FACE" INDICATES A BOARD THAT HAS BEEN ROTATED 90 DEGREES AND PLACED FLUSH WITH THE FRONT OF THE OTHER FRAMING.

TOO SMALL FOR PIECES TO JOIN

WIDER SURFACE IS IDEAL FOR JOINING THE TWO SECTIONS

USING A FACING PIECE TO JOIN SECTIONS OF THE PLYWOOD COVER

The examples so far have been flats smaller in size than 4 feet by 8 feet. Larger flats require more than one 4×8 sheet of plywood and need a way to join them together. You need some extra parts to make that happen.

The ¾″ width of a one-by is not wide enough to accommodate the joining process. Each plywood edge would have only ³⁄₈″ resting on the framing, and that is not really enough for a reliable connection. A good method of enlarging that surface area is to turn a framing member on its side so that the wider surface is flush with the front of the regular framing. This type of framing member is called a *facing piece*. The facing pieces do not add much to the structural stability of the flat, but they work well for attaching the cover. Here is an example of a flat that uses this technique. Notice that the facing piece is used in addition to the normal toggles.

The large surface area provided by the facing piece is excellent for gluing the plywood covering to the frame. You can see in the next drawing how the concept of facing pieces is used to frame a window flat that is larger than 4 by 8 feet.

Notice how the facing members are placed so that the plywood covering pieces will be easy to cut and easy to install. The plywood covers are all simple rectangles you can cut on a table saw. This method is much easier than trying to cut the lauan into a more complex shape, and also ensures that all edges of the covering are connected to the framing.

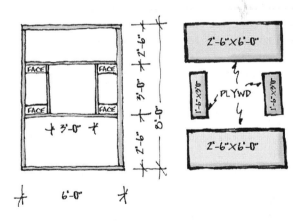

COVERING A HARD-COVERED FLAT

Sometimes a flat must have a solid covering wider than 4 feet. In that case, the facing pieces are arranged so that the plywood is applied horizontally. In reality, this would be a very heavy flat, and the excessive weight should be considered when deciding whether or not to use this method. Perhaps a series of smaller flats could be used instead. You can see a framing piece running up the middle of the flat that intersects the facing pieces. This internal stile must be notched to allow the facing pieces to cross.

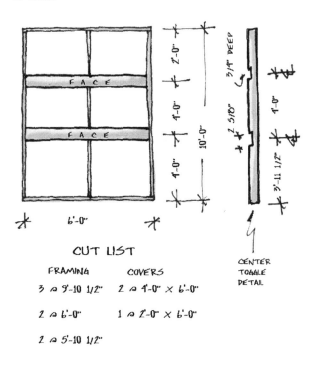

CUT LIST

FRAMING	COVERS
3 @ 9'-10 1/2"	2 @ 4'-0" × 6'-0"
2 @ 6'-0"	1 @ 2'-0" × 6'-0"
2 @ 5'-10 1/2"	

CENTER TOGGLE DETAIL

The final example is that of a door flat. The bottom rail passes all the way across the bottom of the flat, including the space left open for the doorway. This will leave a threshold that an actor must step over in passing through the door, but it greatly enhances the strength of the flat.

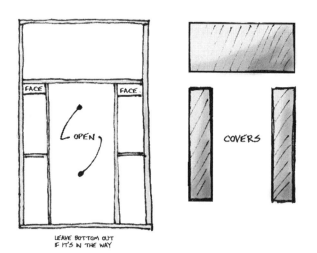

LEAVE BOTTOM OUT IF IT'S IN THE WAY

It is possible to build the unit without this framing member, but it is much stronger with the two sides connected. The action of the play may not allow it. Sometimes a flat piece of metal, or bar stock may be used in place of the lumber. If so, the *sill iron* should be made from ⅛" × 1" stock, and be made to run all the way from side to side, underneath the regular framing. Many years ago sill irons were a traditional part of soft-cover flats used in touring.

CONSTRUCTION

Joining the framing of a hard-covered flat is pretty straightforward, although it is necessary to bear in mind that the flat should be put together face up, rather than face down as with a muslin flat. It is not necessary to use the template method because the plywood covering will square up the flat. Be sure to use plenty of glue on the joints, although glue alone will not hold the framing together because of the small surface area involved. The glue does help, however.

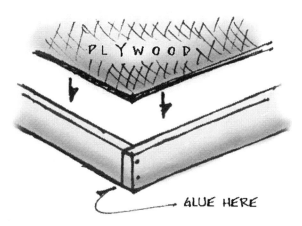

GLUE HERE

When measuring the placement of internal framing pieces, remember to use the measurement ¾" rather than 2⅝". A speed square is helpful for making sure that the toggles are square to the rest of the framing. After marking a location with two small Vs, use the square to mark a line through one of them and across the board. You can use this mark to line up the toggle when nailing.

Often there is a slight discrepancy in the widths of the various framing pieces caused by mistakes in the ripping process. Be sure to flush the tops of the boards with the top of the framing, because that is the front of the flat where the plywood will go.

Cut all of the plywood covering pieces for the front of the flat in advance of beginning the construction process, or you'll have a problem with the glue setting up prematurely. It is often best to cut the covering parts a bit large, say 1⁄16" or even ⅛". That will allow enough extra so that they can hang over the edge a small amount after

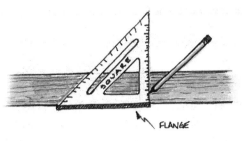

USE A PENCIL AND SQUARE
TO MARK TOGGLE PLACEMENT

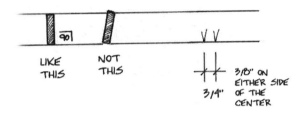

LIKE THIS   NOT THIS

90|

3/8" ON EITHER SIDE OF THE CENTER

3/4"

MARKING THE TOGGLE PLACEMENT

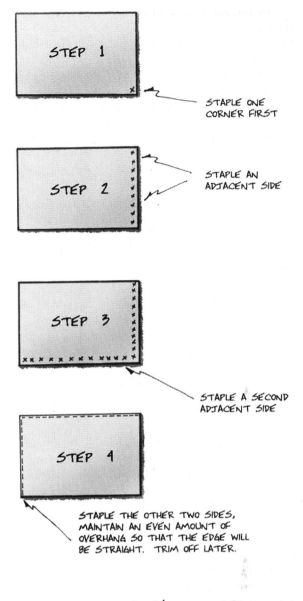

STEP 1 — STAPLE ONE CORNER FIRST

STEP 2 — STAPLE AN ADJACENT SIDE

STEP 3 — STAPLE A SECOND ADJACENT SIDE

STEP 4 — STAPLE THE OTHER TWO SIDES, MAINTAIN AN EVEN AMOUNT OF OVERHANG SO THAT THE EDGE WILL BE STRAIGHT. TRIM OFF LATER.

ATTACH THE PLYWOOD COVER

the cover is stapled on. You can trim this edge flush later. It is difficult to cut out all the framing parts, and the covering parts, and get them to all fit together closely without cheating a bit in this way. If the overall size of the flat were off by ⅛", it would most likely go unnoticed, but a crack that size in the covering would most certainly show.

Begin attaching the cover by putting glue on the tops of all framing parts that will be touched by the first section of plywood. Carefully lay the covering in place and adjust it so that one of the outside corners is aligned and flush. The other parts of the cover need not be exactly in place at this point, just close. Don't worry about them now. Staple the one corner, and then flush up and staple one of the adjacent sides starting from the corner where you began. Use a staple every 8 inches or so, aligning and stapling each point in turn. The most common mistake is to try and line up the whole thing at once. It is not really practical to do that, and it is completely unnecessary.

After the first side is done, return to the corner where you began and staple the adjacent side in the same manner as the first one. This process is used to square up the framing, and making one of the corners square should have the same effect on the rest. If the flat is 4×8 or smaller, it's an easy matter to finish up by stapling the remaining two sides. If you have oversized your plywood (sometimes even if you have not), there will be a small overhang on one or both of the two remaining sides. Do not pull the framing outward and flush the two surfaces in the middle unless it already fits that way at the corner. If you do, you will create a curve on that side of the flat.

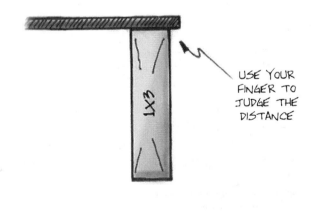

USE YOUR FINGER TO JUDGE THE DISTANCE

1x3

Try instead to leave the same amount of overhang along the entire length of the side. This is fairly easy to do if you feel the amount overhang at the corner with your finger and then use the same finger to judge the amount of overhang as you work your way around the flat. It's not really something you can measure with a tape.

If the flat you are constructing has multiple sections of plywood covering that must be joined with a facing board, use the point where the toggle, stile, and facing piece meet as the corner to start from. Don't leave extra material on the inside of the flat because there is no way to trim it off there.

Run a line of staples into the internal framing parts as well. Use a straight edge to mark the location of the framing by looking at nail holes on the side. Longer lines can easily be marked using a chalk line. A drywall square can also be helpful.

After the covering has been completed, you should trim and fill the flat. Use a router with a *laminate trimming bit* to shave off the excess covering material. This type of *flush trim bit* has a large roller bearing on the bottom that makes for a smooth passage along the side. Since the cutters are exactly the same diameter as the bearing that rides on the framing, the cover will be trimmed to exactly the same size as the framing. Before starting, be sure to check for any nails or staples that might be sticking out, as these will permanently damage the bit.

You can use joint compound to fill the joints and cracks that are a natural result of the construction process. If there will be a great deal of movement associated with the piece, it might be best to use auto body filler, but the joint compound is much easier to use and is incredibly cheap. A 5 gallon bucket costs only a few dollars and will last a very long time. Use the thicker variety, which has less shrinkage.

Lots of different types of scenery are made using the same techniques as described for the construction of hard-cover flats. You can extend these methods to many other projects.

It is very common to use plywood strips for the framing parts when the size of the unit is small, less than 8 feet in any direction. You can make the width of the plywood anything required by the plan, wider than would be possible with dimension lumber. Wider framing is used to make things like columns. If the unit needs extra strength, thicker plywood can be used for the covering. If you need to make a profile piece that has a decorative edge, try using ½" plywood for the cover, because this will hold up better if the profile is complicated. The profile edge can overhang the framing by several inches with no problem.

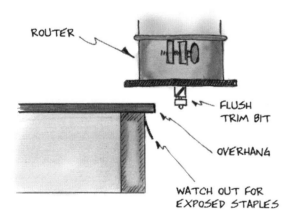

USE A ROUTER TO TRIM THE COVER

ROUTER

FLUSH TRIM BIT

OVERHANG

WATCH OUT FOR EXPOSED STAPLES

HELPFUL HINTS

- Be careful about where your fingers rest when a nail or staple is fired into the framing. It is fairly easy for the fastener to come out the side and into your finger, so don't leave your finger there. The flip side of this is that it is much easier to tell if parts are in line using your finger than by looking at them. Just be careful to move your finger before each shot.

- Remember that yellow glue begins to set in just a few minutes. Plan ahead and have all your parts ready in advance.

- Lightly sanding the corners of the flat with 100 grit sandpaper will reduce splintering and give the flat a more finished look. Do not round the corners over if the flats need to fit flush against one another, as this will only make the crack appear larger.

- Remember when applying joint compound that the idea is to fill the holes and not to create a build-up on the surface of the flat. Any amount extra that dries on the surface will have to be sanded off later, a time-consuming and thankless job.

- Staples must be used to attach the plywood covers, as finish nails will zip right through.

- The covering material of choice is often ¼" lauan or a current substitute. This material has a very tight grain structure, and this grain does not "telegraph" through a paint job. Just be aware that lauan is not terribly sturdy. ¼" domestic plywood is much stronger, but has a grain pattern that is very easy to spot even after it is painted. You can reduce that effect by sanding the surface after a base coat of paint is applied. Some shops glue muslin or even canvas on the outside of the plywood and framing to achieve a more paintable surface that is extremely durable.

TERMS USED IN THIS CHAPTER

corner block
corner brace
covered joint
crown
culling
cut list
denominator
economy of scale

facing piece
flush trim bit
framing
hard-covered flat
keystone
laminate trimming bit
masking flats
numerator

rail
sill iron
soft-covered flat
stile
strap
sweep
template table
toggle

CHAPTER 15

STAIRS

I T'S REALLY COMMON for stage sets to have different levels. Sometimes they are low and close to the stage floor, but often they are quite tall. A Shakespearean unit set often has a high level that serves as a balcony location. They all need stairs of some sort; performers can't get from one level to another without them. Most stage settings include steps in some way, whether it's just one step up to a low platform or as a long set of backstage escape stairs.

Three basic parts make up any set of stairs. The treads are what you step on when going up or down. Risers are the parts of the unit that "rise" from one tread to another, and the carriages are the side pieces used to "carry" the weight of the entire unit. Steps vary greatly depending upon the type of materials used, steepness, whether they are left open or boxed in, and differences of style. But they generally have those three elements.

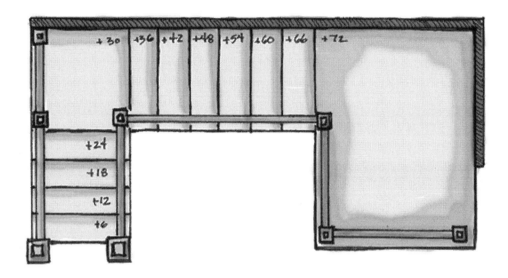

MANY DIFFERENT PARTS WORK TOGETHER
TO CREATE A SET OF STAIRS

STEP BASICS

You should understand a few general concepts about how the human body relates to moving through space. Everyone has tripped over a section of sidewalk that is randomly higher than the surrounding area. You've also sat in a chair that is lower than you thought it would be and had the sudden sensation of falling. This happens because your body gets accustomed to certain distances and rhythms and comes to expect them. The same principle makes it possible for you to text rapidly on a cell phone, or for a musician to play the piano without looking at the keys.

When you are walking up a flight of stairs your body gets into a rhythm based on the height of the risers and the depth of the treads. If one of the steps is suddenly different you are likely to trip at that point. For that reason, it's universally accepted that each step should be exactly the same, and carpenters take great pains to make that happen. If the design calls for an irregular look to the stairs, perhaps it would be better to make each one a different size so that no rhythm is established.

Most fire codes require at least an 11 inch tread and 7 inch rise for stairs in public buildings, but that doesn't apply to stage settings. They aren't open for the public to use. Even so, you might think of that as a place to begin deciding how steep a set of stairs should be. For a particular design that is likely an aesthetic concern that will be resolved before the plans get to the shop. Even so, it's good to realize what is involved. Quite often the design of backstage escape stairs is left to the discretion of the shop. *Escape stairs* are meant to be used out of view of the audience, and a utilitarian approach is generally taken to their design. The steepest you could imagine would be a set with 9 inch risers and 9 inch treads, which would be really steep and require a strong handrail and a good clip light for the actors to see where they are going.

It's probably not possible for actors to use a set of stairs like that on stage while acting and singing at the same time. It's just too much to think about. Nine inch by 9 inch is really steep even for a set of escape stairs, and if there is enough room backstage it would be much better to plan on something a bit less steep. The shallowness of the treads is more of a concern than the height of the risers because it doesn't leave enough room for your foot to land. The ball of your foot that you balance on would be out in space.

GOING UP THE STAIRS, THE BALL OF YOUR FOOT IS FIRMLY ON THE TREAD

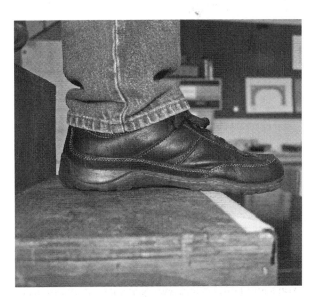

GOING DOWN IS LESS BALANCED, BECAUSE THE BALL OF YOUR FOOT TENDS TO HANG OVER

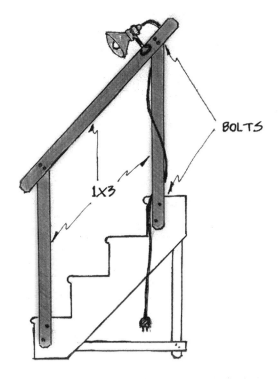

BOLTS

1X3

AN EASILY CHANGED HANDRAIL FOR ESCAPE STAIRS

Stair Terminology

Riser—The vertical connection of two levels or steps.

Tread—The part you step on.

Carriage—The side framing that keeps the treads and risers together.

Newel post—A large post that anchors the end of, or a bend in, a section of railing. The newel post at the bottom of a stairway is usually the most ornate.

Baluster or spindle—An upright piece used to support the handrail. Spindles are often rounded and turned on a lathe.

Landing—An area used for a change in a stairway's direction. This is most common when a number of different sections or flights of steps are used.

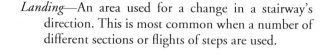

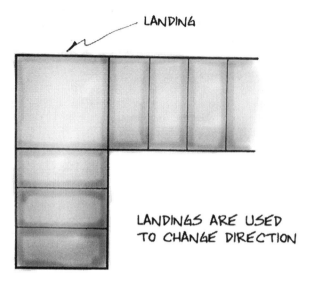

LANDINGS ARE USED TO CHANGE DIRECTION

Stage stairs are often easy to plan because stage platforms tend to be even amounts. If a platform is exactly 2 feet tall a rise of 6 or 8 inches (commonly used increments), would work well. Twenty-four inches can be divided evenly by either amount. A 9 inch rise wouldn't work because that height will not divide cleanly into 24 inches. Nine inch risers would fit neatly with a platform height of 36 inches. Divide the height of the platform by the individual riser height to get the number of rises you need. The number of rises is one more than the total number of treads, if the platform itself is used as the top step.

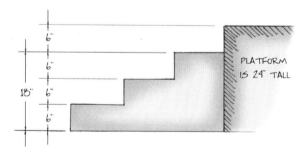

THREE STEPS ACTUALLY HAVE FOUR RISES

BECAUSE THE TOP OF THE PLATFORM IS ONE OF THEM. THAT ONLY WORKS WHEN THE STEP IS SMALL, AND RESTS ENTIRELY ON THE FLOOR WITH NO SUPPORT FROM THE PLATFORM.

The preceding problem was made quite a bit simpler because the numbers divided evenly. Unfortunately, this does not always happen, and quite often the process goes a bit more like this: imagine that the platform height is 8 feet 6 inches, which converts to 102″. Guessing that eleven rises might work, 11 into 102 works out to 9.3 inches per rise. A rise of 9.3″ is in excess of the 9″ maximum we have set for ourselves. If you substitute 12 for the number of rises and do the math, you will discover that for 12 risers each individual rise would be 8.5 inches. This is lucky because the decimal number 0.5″ is easy to convert to a fractional equivalent of ½″. If you need an easier climb, then 13 rises would give you an average of 7.8 inches each.

A decimal expression such as 7.8 may be converted to a woodworking fraction by using a ratio to determine the number of sixteenths that a base ten number equals. Use the equation z/10 = x/16. In this equation z represents the number of tenths and x is the number of sixteenths, a fraction that you can find on a tape measure. The conversion of 7.8 to a woodworking fraction goes like this:

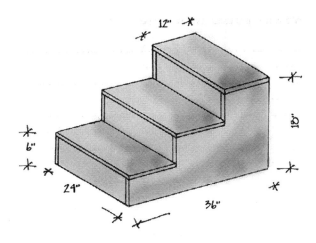

TO CONVERT BASE 10
DECIMALS TO SIXTEENTHS
USE THIS EQUATION FOR A RATIO:

$$Z/10 = X/16$$

EXAMPLE:

$$8/10 = X/16$$
$$X = (8 \cdot 16)/10$$
$$X = 128/10$$
$$X = 12.8$$

WHICH ROUNDS OFF TO ~ 13/16

The rounding off will leave a margin of error that is really too small to be of importance. As you can see, it is far easier to start out with a more user-friendly decking height, or to choose the 8½″ riser height. But that may not always be an option.

A Step Building Method

Here is a method of building steps that uses nothing other than ¾ inch plywood. It is presented first because it is an easy and straightforward way to build a small step unit based on very clear engineering principles. Using only one material streamlines the process, and it produces a neat and clean piece of work, which should be a major objective of any craftsman.

This step unit has a 6″ tall rise and a 12″ deep tread. There are three treads in total, and the width of the steps is 24″. Remember that the steps are constructed exclusively of ¾″ thick plywood. In order to construct this unit, you will need to develop a cut list of the parts. Most people find it easier to make the list of parts in order, from the most easily understood to the most difficult to figure out. The easy answers give clues to the difficult ones, which works well in many different situations. Remember that determining the overlapping members is critical to forming a cut list.

The drawing shows that the ¾″ plywood pieces used for the three treads stretch all the way from the left side to the right side of the unit. They also extend from the very front to the very back of the 12 inch dimension. There are no other structural members overlapping them that would make the tread pieces smaller than the listed dimensions, so you can determine that there are three treads @ 12″ x 24″. It makes sense that the treads rest on top of the other parts because they are weight bearing. If the treads were nailed on the inside of the other parts, only the nails would be supporting them. The shear (sideways stress) strength of a nailed joint like that is not very high.

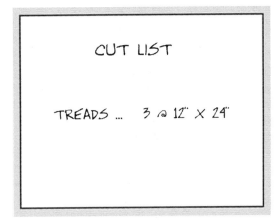

CUT LIST

TREADS ...   3 @ 12″ X 24″

The next part to consider is the bottom riser. Notice in the drawing that this riser piece fits inside, between the two carriages. The overall dimension of the width is 24″, so to get the width of just the riser piece add ¾″ + ¾″ and subtract that from the overall width of the unit.

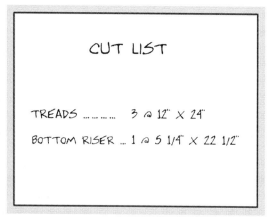

Similarly, you can see that the overall height of the tread from the floor is given as 6″, but that this measurement is to the top of the tread while the riser only reaches up to the bottom of it. The tread is ¾″ thick.

The remaining two risers require a bit of explanation because they have parts that join in a way that cannot be seen in the original drawing of just the outside of the unit. A section view through the center shows the hidden internal parts.

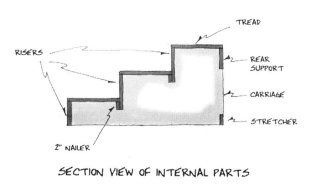

SECTION VIEW OF INTERNAL PARTS

You can see from the exterior drawing that the second and third risers have the same width as the first one did. The height of the next riser is not decreased by ¾″ as the first one was. It starts ¾″ *below* the *top* of the first tread, and winds up ¾″ *below* the *top* of the next one. So nothing is gained or lost. Even though ¾″ is lost by subtracting the thickness of the tread on top, it is regained by adding back the thickness of the tread on the bottom. The section view shows that these two risers extend below the underlying tread by a distance of 2 inches. This allows for a second piece of ¾″ ply to be scabbed onto the front of the riser

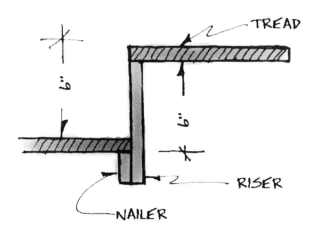

When the 2″ is added, the total height of the riser is 8″. These risers should be listed as 2 @ 8″ × 22 ½″. The 2″ piece of plywood is added in order to give the tread a framing member to rest upon. If this were not done, then the rear of the tread would be supported only by nails driven horizontally through the bottom of the riser next to it. Many steps are made in that way, but it proves to

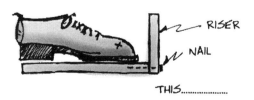

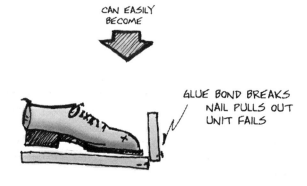

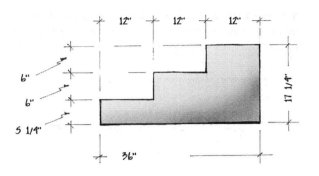

CUT LIST

TREADS .... 3 @ 12" X 24"

BOTTOM RISER ... 1 @ 5 1/4" X 22 1/2"

RISERS .... 2 @ 8" X 22 1/2"

NAILERS ... ... 2 @ 2" X 22 1/2"

be an inherently weak structure. The nails easily bend, and the glue bond breaks. The 2 inch nailer prevents that from happening.

There are a couple of rules that make it quite easy to figure a cut list. The first riser piece is always ¾" shorter than the overall height of the rise. All other risers, regardless of how many there are, will be 2" taller than the given riser height. The 2" wide nailers we have been discussing are of course only 22½" wide because they fit to the inside of the carriages. The horizontal member at the back of the step unit and which supports the top tread will also be 22½" wide, with the other dimension varying depending on the width of the step unit. Very wide steps require a beefier member, but a 3½" wide strip should prove sufficient for this small unit. The 3½" width was selected somewhat arbitrarily because it is the same as the milled width of a 1×4, but the exact size isn't all that important.

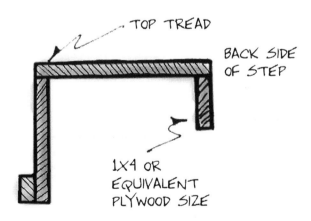

TOP TREAD

BACK SIDE OF STEP

1X4 OR EQUIVALENT PLYWOOD SIZE

The only remaining items for your cut list are the two carriages. These pieces are not rectangles like everything else so far, but rather are a more complex shape. Because of that you can't describe them merely by saying they are "so wide by so long." A good way to do it instead is to make a small sketch and dimension the parts.

The section of the carriage that corresponds to the bottom riser is dimensioned at 5¼" just as the riser was and for the same reason, because it fits under the tread rather than to the side of it. The next two rises are an even 6" each since they both lose and gain ¾" from their respective treads. The depth of the tread is given at 12 inches. Note that the overall height is 17¼", which is ¾" smaller than the height of the finished unit.

CONSTRUCTING THE STEPS

Use the table saw to rip the ¾" plywood into strips of the proper width and the radial arm saw to cut the strips to length. This project (and others) will be more aesthetically pleasing if the grain of the exterior veneer on the plywood runs the length of the pieces. B/C yellow pine plywood is probably the best choice of material, because it is readily available and will create a nice finished appearance. Use all of the measuring and marking skills you learned from the chapters on wooden joinery and flats. This method of construction depends upon a high degree of accuracy from the cutting process. Parts that are not the right size will not fit together well, so spend some time getting the cuts right.

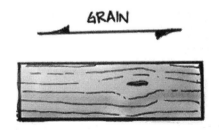

GRAIN

FOR BEST RESULTS, RUN GRAIN THE LENGTH OF YOUR PARTS

Since the carriages are not a simple rectangular shape, they require a bit more work to cut out. Mark lines using the sketch you made as a guide, transferring the measurements and connecting the marks with a straight edge. Use either a circular saw or a jigsaw or both to cut along the lines. Remember to make the kerf fall on the side of the line that will become scrap.

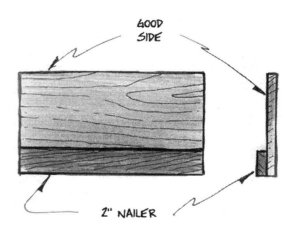

ATTACH THE 2" NAILER TO THE GOOD SIDE OF THE RISER

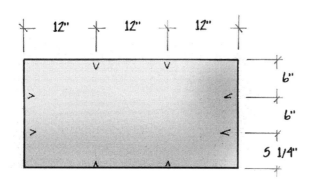

MAKE THE APPROPRIATE MARKS ON THE PLYWOOD

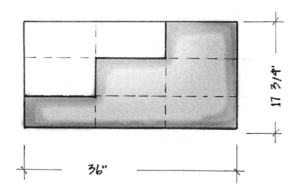

CONNECT THE DOTS WITH LINES, AND DRAW IN THE PROFILE OF THE CARRIAGE

It is easier to assemble this unit in a specific order. Connect the 2″ tall nailers to the 8″ tall risers first. Keep track of the good and bad sides of the plywood, because of course you want to put the good side facing outward. For the two riser parts, this means attaching the 2″ strips to the good side of the 8″ risers, taking care to align them with the bottom and the two sides.

A nail gun or a construction stapler will greatly speed up assembly. Use glue between the surfaces. Apply enough so that they are completely coated. You can learn to gauge this amount by putting the glue on in a zigzag pattern and then pulling the two pieces apart to see if that was enough to spread everywhere. Pressing the two pieces together and then squishing slightly from side to side will help to spread the glue. Yellow aliphatic resin (carpenter's) glue is the best. It has very fast bonding properties, so be aware that once this glue is applied you have only a couple of minutes before the glue begins to set. If you disturb the glue bond after it has begun to gel, but before the bond is completed, the strength of the connection will be reduced.

Nails or staples from a gun do not have a great deal of holding power, so the glue really is essential. It is good to make a habit of gluing together more or less every joint in every project, unless you know from the outset that they will need to be taken apart at some point in the future.

Finishing nailers of all brands typically *set* the nail an eighth of an inch or so into the surface of the plywood. The same is true of narrow crown staples. Be sure to bear this in mind when selecting the length of fastener to use. For a double layer of ¾″ thick plywood a 1½″ fastener is really too long. The set of the fastener by the nail gun would cause this length to protrude from the back of the underlying piece of plywood. That can lead to some nasty cuts on anyone handling the scenery. Use a slightly shorter 1¼″ nail or staple instead.

The second phase of assembling the steps is to connect the risers and the carriages together. Remember that the carriages have a good and a bad side, and of course the good side should face outward. It is easier to stand one of the center risers on end, put glue on it, and lay the carriage on top of the riser. If you nail the center riser first, you can balance the carriage while you go about the business of attaching the others. Standing the risers on end will also keep the glue from running off the edge as quickly. Be sure to flush what will become the top of the riser to the top of the carriage, and the face of the riser with the front of the carriage.

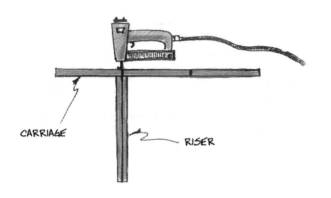

CARRIAGE

RISER

TURN THE RISER ON END TO
ATTACH THE CARRIAGE TO IT

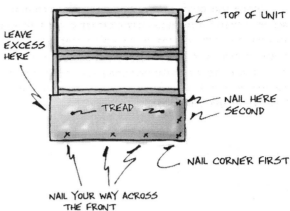

LEAVE EXCESS HERE

TOP OF UNIT

TREAD

NAIL HERE SECOND

NAIL CORNER FIRST

NAIL YOUR WAY ACROSS THE FRONT

START IN THE CORNER
FLUSH UP TWO ADJACENT SIDES
TO SQUARE THE STEP UNIT

Once you've completed the task of joining the three risers and the support that goes at the back of the top tread, flip the unit over and attach the second carriage. Use enough fasteners to hold the parts together well, but not so many that they split the plywood apart.

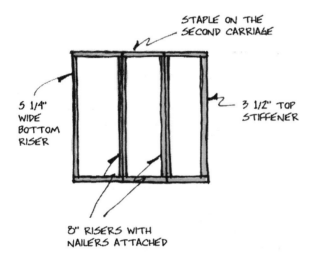

STAPLE ON THE SECOND CARRIAGE

5 1/4" WIDE BOTTOM RISER

3 1/2" TOP STIFFENER

8" RISERS WITH NAILERS ATTACHED

After attaching the second carriage, turn the step unit upright. The assembly of carriages and risers may not be especially square when you first look at them. That's because we've done nothing so far to square them up, but attaching the treads will do that. Each one has four 90 degree angled corners, and two sets of equal sides. This is the ideal shape to use in squaring up a structure and is a common practice in all types of construction.

Put glue on the surfaces that lie underneath the bottom tread, and set the tread into position. Adjust the tread until one of the front corners is perfectly aligned with the corner of the riser and carriage, and put one nail in this corner. Twist the entire step unit until the side of the tread is flush with the carriage, and secure the back

corner with a staple. You've connected the short side of the tread to the frame. Put in a row of nails/staples across the front of the tread, beginning at the first corner you attached and then working your way across to the other side. That will automatically square up the entire unit. It is the same process that was used to square hard-cover flats in an earlier chapter. Perform the same squaring up procedure on each tread to be sure the unit is as exact as possible.

A *stretcher* at the bottom of the step unit in the only remaining free corner will help to prevent the plywood from warping inward.

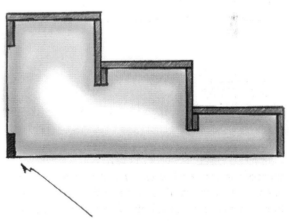

USE A STRETCHER ACROSS
HERE TO STRAIGHTEN OUT
THE CARRIAGES

The width of the nailer that holds up the back edge of the treads does not have to be 2″. That is simply a number I chose because it is easy to add with other numbers. If you are planning to construct a very wide unit of more than 60 inches or so, increase the size of this member to accommodate the longer span. You can build steps up to 96 inches in width using this method and a 3½″ wide nailer. The steps require no center carriage and are completely rigid, with no detectable deflection in the center. Methods that require the use of one or more center carriages are much more difficult to assemble.

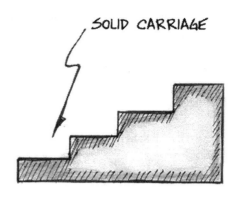

SOLID CARRIAGE

STRINGER

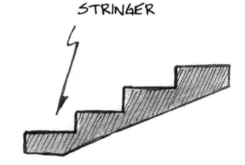

HELPFUL HINTS

- Don't try to align all the parts completely before you begin to nail. Line up only the section you are nailing at the time.

- You can use either nails or staples for this type of construction.

- All B/C plywood is ⅟₃₂″ thinner than the nominal size. There are two sides to the unit, so the stairs will be ⅟₁₆″ narrower than planned. You can cut the treads that much smaller to make them fit better, or increase the length of other parts.

- If the tread is slightly too small from front to back, leave a space in the back where it isn't so noticeable.

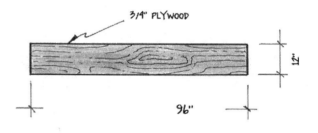

3/4″ PLYWOOD

12″

96″

IF YOUR STRINGER PIECE MUST BE LONGER THAN 8′-0′, YOU WILL NEED TO LAMINATE IT TOGETHER FROM 1/4″ THICK PLYWOOD

ALTERNATE BUILDING TECHNIQUES

Sometimes the design of a stair makes it necessary to use an alternate method of step building. This is often true for stairs with many steps, or when an open riser look is mandated. Some stairs are curved, or at an angle. Some must be made from metal.

Long or tall stairs are most commonly made using the *stringer* technique. Any step unit that rises more than 3 feet or so in height will be very heavy when constructed with a solid carriage. In this case the stringer style is much lighter and is a better way to go.

The drawing illustrates the difference between the two types, which appears quite significant. In reality, the stringer style is constructed in more or less the same manner as the previous demonstration, except for the diagonal nature of the carriage, and the method of marking the notches. Begin the process by ripping a strip of ¾″ plywood for the stringer. If an 8 foot long section of plywood will not be long enough, it is possible to *laminate* together thinner stock to make up the stringers. Be sure to offset the joints in the laminating process to produce a stronger member.

For most applications, a 12 inch wide strip of plywood is wide enough for the stringer. That is in keeping with the nominal width of a 2×12 that is often used as a stringer in home construction. If the stair has

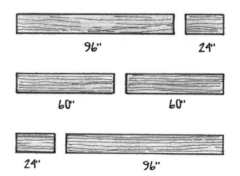

96″   24″

60′   60′

24′   96″

WHEN LAMINATING PARTS TOGETHER, OFFSET THE JOINTS AS MUCH AS POSSIBLE. PUT GLUE OVER THE ENTIRE SURFACE OF THE JOINT WITH A PAINTBRUSH OR ROLLER.

---

unusually high rises, deep treads, or a great many steps, it may be necessary to increase the width of the strip. It is important that the stringer be large enough to maintain its strength even after the notches have been cut into it. Any amount less than 12 inches will probably not be enough.

After the stock for your stringers has been ripped to the proper width, you can mark the location and angle of the notches for the steps. Use a *framing square* for this job. It is best to use a regular square that is 16 inches on one side and 24 inches on the other. Remember that with most framing squares, the markings on one side are in twelfths of an inch and in sixteenths of an inch on the other side. The twelfths are used to work on roof pitches and are of little use in scenery building, so you should use the side marked in sixteenths. If you are not sure which is which, count the number of small spaces between the inch marks.

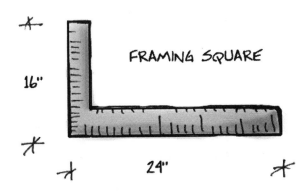

FRAMING SQUARE

16"

24"

A set of *stair gauges* can be very helpful when used with the framing square. Gauges are essentially small clamps that fasten to the edge of the square. They make it easy to find the same spot over and over, and function as a jig to increase the accuracy of your layout.

Assume that you wish to lay out a set of stairs with a rise of 6 inches and a tread depth of 10 inches. Lay a corner of the framing square across the plywood so that the 6 inch mark on the short side of the square is even with the near edge of the plywood. Rotate the framing square until the 10 inch mark on the long side of the square lines up with the same edge of the plywood strip. If you have a set of stair gauges, attach them to the square so that it is easy to return to the alignment you set up.

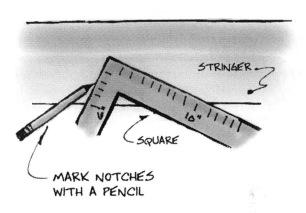

STRINGER

SQUARE

MARK NOTCHES WITH A PENCIL

Use a pencil to trace around the outside edge of the square and mark one tread depth and one rise. It is best to start at the bottom of the stringer when marking the layout. There is one really tricky part to the process. The bottom riser, as laid out on the stringer, must be shorter in height than the other risers by the thickness of the tread, which in our case is ¾″. Use the framing square to measure down from your tread line 5¼″.

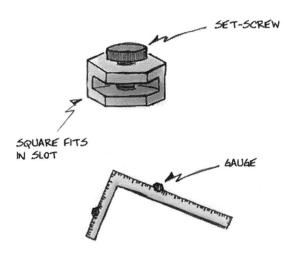

SET-SCREW

SQUARE FITS IN SLOT

GAUGE

STAIR GAUGES CLAMP ONTO THE SQUARE SO THAT YOU CAN EASILY RETURN TO THE SAME SETTING

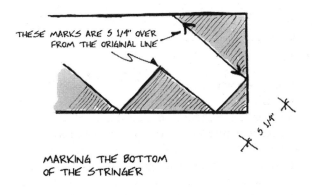

THESE MARKS ARE 5 1/4″ OVER FROM THE ORIGINAL LINE

5 1/4″

MARKING THE BOTTOM OF THE STRINGER

Use the square as a straightedge to draw a line parallel to the original tread line. You have established the very bottom of the stringer, the part that makes contact with the stage floor.

From this point it is a fairly simple matter of drawing in as many repetitions of the first riser/tread layout as are

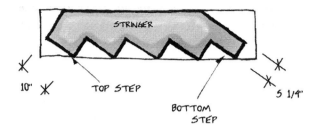

required to reach the desired height for the stringer. When the top tread line is marked, don't mark the corresponding riser line upward, but instead extend it downward from the tread line at a 90 degree angle to finish off the top of the stringer.

Construction of this type of step unit is basically the same as our first unit, save for the fact that that the carriage is shaped differently. The riser section sub assemblies are built first, and then attached to one of the stringers. Then the opposite stringer is connected, and finally the treads are used to square the unit. You will need help with these stringers because they are so much bigger and heavier than the carriages in the smaller unit discussed earlier.

The step unit with solid carriers was held up by the sides alone. But that won't work with a stair made with stringers as the carriages. There isn't anything to hold up the back side of the unit. A very common method is to make the height of the top stair the same as the top level of the platform it leads to. If the stairs are bolted to that platform, and hinged to the stage floor, the stairs become in effect a diagonal brace that helps to steady the platforms. But that isn't always possible, and instead you might put a system of legs on the stair to keep the unit erect. You will need two legs in the back and enough bracing to keep the whole thing together.

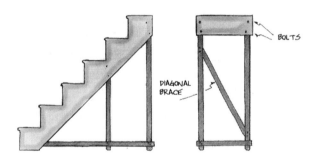

LEGS ON A STRINGER-TYPE STAIR

Notice the triangles formed by the bracing in the drawing of the freestanding stair on the last page. You can see one large triangle in the side view created by the horizontal rail, the upright member, and the stair itself. In the rear view you can see two triangles that share a hypotenuse. Triangles are a very strong structural form and are often seen in any kind of bracing.

Sometimes the design calls for stairs that have open risers, which is to say that the piece that physically makes up the riser itself is left off. These stairs have a more open appearance to them. In this case, the type of all-plywood construction we have been discussing will not work. A ¾ inch plywood tread is not nearly strong enough to support the weight of a person, even when the steps are very narrow, without being joined with a riser. Therefore a thicker and stronger tread material must be used. Most commonly, two-by lumber of some sort is used, probably a 2×12 or a 2×10, as any narrower dimension would be too small for the tread. This type of stair usually has carriages made from a 2×12 also, and they must be cut out with the stringer method if the overall height of the stair is more than 12 inches.

When 2×12s are used, the thickness of the treads will be 1½″ rather than ¾″. As a result, the bottom riser will need to be marked 1½″ smaller on the bottom of the stringer rather than ¾″ as noted in the earlier exercise. This type of stair unit may appear to be airier and lighter to the eye, but it is in reality much, much heavier. It lacks the "portability factor" required by most stage scenery. It will also tend to be less precise, and to warp out of shape more easily, so it is not such a good choice from an engineering standpoint.

It is possible to make this unit entirely from laminated plywood instead of lumber by using two layers ¾″ ply or three layers of ½″ ply to make up the stringers.

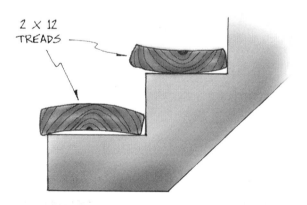

2 × 12 LUMBER TENDS TO CUP, AND MAY NOT LAY FLAT ON THE CARRIAGE. IT'S ALSO VERY HEAVY

The advantage of ½" material is to stagger the end to end joints so that longer stringers are possible, which isn't necessary if you don't need that length. You can use a double lamination of ¾" ply for the treads instead of dimension lumber, with the advantage being that the resulting material is more stable. If you glue the plywood together so that only the good side is out, its appearance is enhanced, and any natural bow in the plywood will tend to cancel itself out. Sometimes this method is said to use "engineered materials" because the plywood is created by a manufacturing process that removes some of the element of surprise that comes from using natural wood products.

In recent years stair units constructed from steel tubing have become very popular. *Square tube* is a popular choice for metal construction because it is much easier to fit together than other shapes. In general, a hollow tube has much of the strength of a solid structure the same dimensions but much less weight because the interior has been removed. Tube cutting and joining techniques are shown in the chapter on metal working where the properties of steel shapes are discussed. Steel square tube framing presents a very light, open quality to the audience. Although the steel itself is heavy, it can be joined in ways that use less material, and some structures are not as heavy as others when a light gauge material is used.

For steel square tube construction, make a pattern or jig in the shape of a carriage, as discussed earlier. Cut the square tube parts to fit the jig and weld them together. The metalworking chapter goes into detail about how to use wooden blocks to make a temporary jig that will hold the parts in position while they are being welded. After

the carriages have been constructed, use straight pieces of tubing to connect the two carriages and form the support for plywood treads.

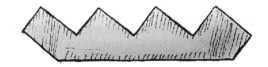

MAKE A PATTERN FROM SCRAP PLYWOOD AND USE IT TO BUILD A JIG FOR THE SQUARE TUBE STRUCTURE

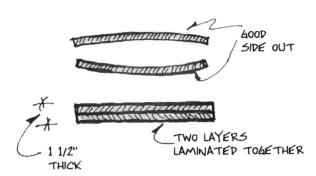

GOOD SIDE OUT

1 1/2" THICK

TWO LAYERS LAMINATED TOGETHER

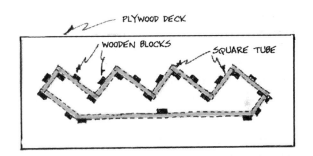

PLYWOOD DECK

WOODEN BLOCKS

SQUARE TUBE

An alternate method is to create rectangular metal frames for the treads, and join them together with runners on the sides of the step unit. Angle the bottom ends of the runners so that they mate with the floor at the proper angle.

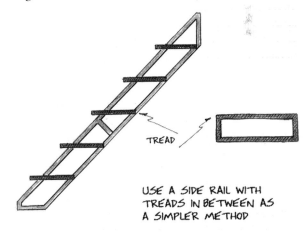

TREAD

USE A SIDE RAIL WITH TREADS IN BETWEEN AS A SIMPLER METHOD

TERMS USED IN THIS CHAPTER

baluster	landing	stair gauge
carriage	newel post	stretcher
escape stairs	riser	stringer
framing square	spindle	tread
laminate	square tube	

CHAPTER 16

DECKING

PLATFORMS ARE MORE heavily constructed than most other stage scenery because of the weight they must carry — not only the weight of the setting that is placed upon it, but the combined pounds of all the actors as well. Moving objects create what is known as a *live load*, which requires a sturdier structure than a *static load*. Actors who are dancing, or running, or jumping up and down create a live load that is really several times their combined weight, because their mass is multiplied by their acceleration to arrive at the force, or load acting on the platforms. A group of dancers running to one side of the stage and suddenly

COMMERCIALLY MANUFACTURED DECKING

THIS PLATFORMING SYSTEM WAS DESIGNED AS PORTABLE
STAGING FOR CONCERTS IN LARGE ARENAS. IT IS VERY
EASY TO SET UP, BUT IS NOT SUITABLE FOR THEATRE
WORK BECAUSE IT IS TOO HEAVY, AND ISN'T VERY ADAPTABLE.

stopping causes a great deal of sideways or *lateral stress* on a structure. Because people are standing on them and might fall, there is an additional safety concern added to designing and constructing platforms. That responsibility generally falls on the shop that builds them rather than the scenic designer.

Several companies manufacture *risers*, which are platforms that fold up for storage and are used by schools and convention centers to create a raised level for public assemblies. They are generally not used for theatre work because they aren't meant to be combined with other scenery, or the non-stock platforms built in a theatre shop. The words *platform* and *deck* are often used to mean the same thing. In a subtle way though, decking tends to indicate platforms that are part of a system.

In this chapter many of the techniques and processes mentioned earlier in the book are used in constructing platforms. Flip back to some of the earlier chapters for more information about tools, woodworking, and wood products like plywood and lumber.

STOCK DECKING

Most permanent theatre companies use stock decking units to decrease the cost of using platforms. The most common size for a stock platform is 4×8 because that's also the standard size of a sheet of plywood, and there is little waste in construction. A prudent designer considers the use of standard units in designing a show, so as to reduce the cost of construction. It is often cost effective to have some other stock sizes too, such as 2×8 and/or 4×4. These dimensions are a good fit with a 4×8, and in combination they create a large variety of decking shapes and sizes. Stock platforms are in constant use for years before they are no longer viable. It's best to take a global approach when considering stock decking, so that all the parts are interchangeable.

The projects discussed so far have mostly used one-by lumber or plywood for the framing. Platforms typically need something stronger and more rigid, so 2×4 lumber is often used. It will stand up to years of indifferent use. Sometimes 1×4 framing is enough for a throw-away that doesn't carry much of a load, especially if it sits on the floor. The best covering material is ¾″ plywood. It is thick enough to make a secure cover with minimal spring to it. A 4×8 platform built with a ¾″ plywood top requires a support framing member every 24″ in order to keep deflection and vibration to a minimum. Here is a sketch for the framing of a stock platform built with 2×4 lumber and a ¾″ thick plywood top.

You can see that the end rails are 4′-0″ long and run all the way from side to side, while the toggle rails fit to the inside of the stiles, and as a result are only 3′-9″ in length. Staggering the joints in this way locks the framing together securely. If all of the rails were 3′-9″, it would be remarkably easy to pull the stiles off of the sides of the

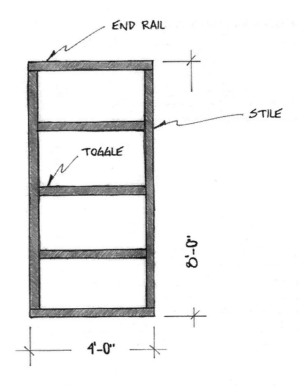

FRAMING FOR A
4X8 PLATFORM

CUT LIST
USING 2X4 LUMBER

2 @ 7′-9″
2 @ 4′-0″
3 @ 3′-9″

STILE IS TOO EASY TO PULL OFF.
OVERLAP END RAILS THE OPPOSITE WAY.

platform. You can connect the framing together with 16d box nails or 3″ drywall screws.

There are several methods of holding platforms together in groups after they are constructed. One is to c-clamp the framing members together. Another is to screw or bolt between the 2×4s. An altogether different method, which must be considered before constructing a platform, is to use coffin locks.

Coffin locks are cam-operated fasteners attached to the sides of decking and used to join the platforms together. Coffin locks allow you to lock platforms together quickly and easily, using a ⁵⁄₁₆″ *hex key*. During set up, the decking can be laid out top up in the position it will eventually

A COFFIN LOCK

THE WRENCH TURNS THE CAM FROM THE
MALE HALF, WHICH CONNECTS WITH
THE FEMALE HALF, LOCKING BOTH TOGETHER

If you center the locks exactly 1'-0" from each corner of a 4×8 platform, and alternate the male/female orientation, the locks in different decks will match up with one another. No matter how the platforms are turned the male/female locks will match up properly. When two sides or two ends meet, both of the locks on that side match. When the platforms meet from side to end only half of them do.

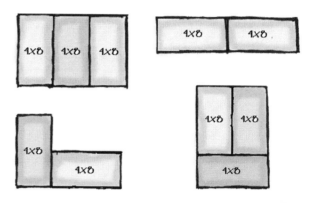

DIFFERENT WAYS OF JOINING 4X8 PLATFORMS

occupy. Bolting platforms together can be quite problematic when the height of the decking is too short for a person to crawl under. Bolting together a large number of heavy platforms upside down and then trying to flip them over can be quite a challenge, and it places a lot of stress on the decking. Coffin locks avoid all of that. The down side is the time and expense required to install them.

You can install the locks so that stock platforms fit together in many different ways. Most often, individual platforms are placed side by side, or end to end when they are used together. Sometimes you might want to place one platform across the ends of two others, or to create an L shape.

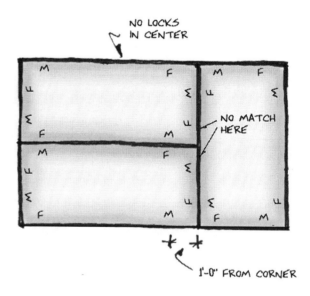

POSITIONING THE COFFIN LOCKS

PLYWOOD

DRILL KEY HOLE
FOR MALE HALF ONLY

You can avoid some tedious repetition in measuring and marking if you make a couple of jigs. This notch marking jig was made of plywood for strength.

Use the 1'-0" end for marking the rails, and the 0'-10½" end for the 7'-9" stiles.

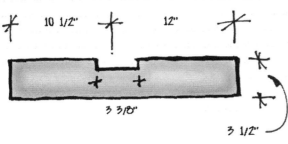

10 1/2"   12"

3 3/8"

3 1/2"

NOTCH MARKING JIG

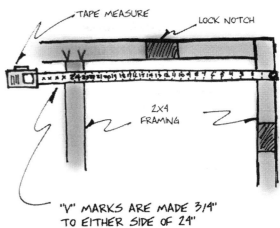

TAPE MEASURE   LOCK NOTCH

2×4
FRAMING

"V" MARKS ARE MADE 3/4"
TO EITHER SIDE OF 24"

2×4

CUT NOTCHES BEFORE
YOU ASSEMBLE THE
FRAMING

ASSEMBLE THE FRAME

Begin by connecting the perimeter box. It is important for all of the internal parts to be consistent so mark the toggles exactly. These are stock platforms, and having exactly interchangeable parts will pay dividends later on in ways that are not apparent now. Measure the placement for the toggles in the same way as you would for a flat. Using a standard tape measure, follow along the side until you reach 2'-0". Count backwards ¾", which is half of the thickness of the 2×4. Make a V mark. Count forward ¾" to 2'-0¾" and make another V mark. Move forward to the 4'-0" placement and repeat the procedure, and again at the 6'-0" toggle. Do this on both stiles, taking care to start the measurement from the *same end*. Marking the two corners is a much more accurate method of working, and once it becomes habit it takes no longer than marking just the center.

Lay the plywood decking in place and attach it. On a permanent unit like this it is best to glue the plywood down, as that is the most secure way to join the parts and will help to prevent squeaking later on. You can use yellow carpenter's glue, but if the 2×4 stock is a little rough, a construction adhesive like Liquid Nails may work better. Liquid Nails is thick and an excellent gap filler, while the aliphatic resin carpenter's glue is not. Following the common practice that you have seen before, begin by aligning one corner of the unit, while leaving the others merely close. Use 1⅝" drywall screws to secure the plywood tops. This may seem like overkill when used with the glue, but remember that these platforms will be around for a very long time. Work your way along the 4 foot side, squaring up and fastening as you go, one step at a time. Go back to the original corner and work your way along the 8 foot length in the same fashion. Since the framing of a platform is very rigid, you may need to use one or more pipe clamps to square the 2×4s to the plywood.

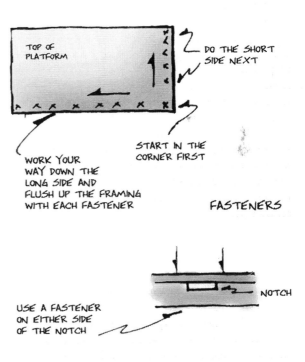

TOP OF
PLATFORM

DO THE SHORT
SIDE NEXT

START IN THE
CORNER FIRST

WORK YOUR
WAY DOWN THE
LONG SIDE AND
FLUSH UP THE FRAMING
WITH EACH FASTENER

FASTENERS

USE A FASTENER
ON EITHER SIDE
OF THE NOTCH

NOTCH

This procedure ensures that the finished platform will be square. Take one step at a time. Attempting to line up all parts of the platform at one time is a nightmarish procedure and a complete waste of time. It is far better to begin in one spot and let the procedure take its course.

You'll need to drill some holes in the plywood cover if you are using coffin locks. This is just the sort of task that jigs do well. Remember that in construction a *jig* is a shop-made device that helps to construct something else.

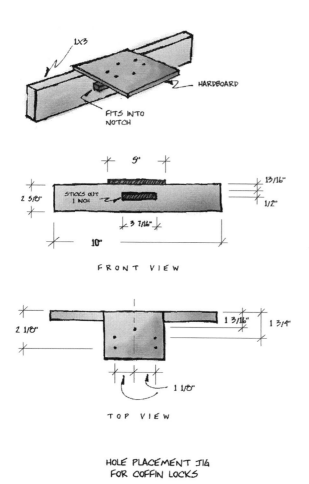

1x3

HARDBOARD

FITS INTO NOTCH

5"

13/16"

2 5/8"

STICKS OUT 1 INCH

3 7/16"

1/2"

10"

FRONT VIEW

2 1/8"

1 3/16"

1 3/4"

1 1/8"

TOP VIEW

HOLE PLACEMENT JIG FOR COFFIN LOCKS

The ½″ by ³⁄₁₆″ block is intended to fit inside the notches you cut into the framing earlier. The perforations on top are used to mark the exact placement of the holes to drill for inserting the ⁵⁄₁₆″ hex key, and for the two screws that hold the coffin lock in place.

LABEL UP

MALE HALF

There are different holes for male and female locks. If you place the male and females in standard locations that are the same on each platform, they will be interchangeable. That is a good thing for a stock unit.

Either large wood screws or flat-head bolts should be used to install the coffin locks. In either case, drill a *countersink* hole for the head to fit into. You don't want anything to stick up above the surface of the plywood.

Using casket locks greatly lengthens the service life of stock platforms, but installing them takes time. That may or may not be something that a particular theatre wants to do. But the coffin lock system really comes into its own when you are loading the show into the theatre; so they are invariably used on touring shows which are built once but set up many times. Tour shows often travel with their own deck, which might have special features for automation like winches. The decks are placed directly on the stage floor face up, and there is really no other way to connect them except for coffin locks.

Another procedure that will increase the life span of a stock platform is to use *corner irons* to hold together the outside perimeter of the framing. Use the flat type of iron on the bottom of the platform rather than bent ones that would fit on the inside of a corner. They won't interfere with the installation of legs later on. Legs may need to be attached to the inside corner of the framing. The iron will keep the end rail from pulling away from the stile, which it is prone to do.

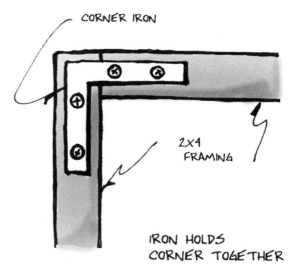

CORNER IRON

2X4 FRAMING

IRON HOLDS CORNER TOGETHER

ODDLY SHAPED DECKING

You can't platform every show with just rectangles. Quite often stock sizes are used for the majority, and then odd-shaped decks are built to fill in. The best method for constructing them is to cut out the plywood top first and then use this shape as a full-scale pattern in marking the 2×4 framing. You can simply cut the framing parts to fit

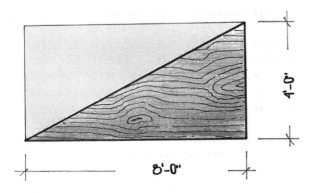

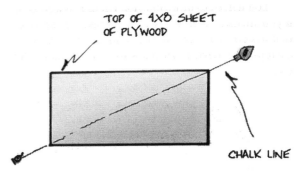

TOP OF 4X8 SHEET
OF PLYWOOD

CHALK LINE

MAKE A PLATFORM
FROM HALF A SHEET

the plywood lid. As an example, assume that you need to construct a triangular platform that is half of a 4×8 sheet of plywood. Drawing a line diagonally from corner to corner forms the shape.

The sketch provides all the information you need to construct this platform, even though you have not been given any information about the number of degrees in any of the angles other than the one factory corner. *Factory corner* refers to a plywood corner that was cut at the mill and is assumed to be a perfect 90 degree angle. Using the pattern method, it is not necessary to know these angles, which in any case are rarely given on the designer's plans.

To prepare the top for cutting, mark a straight line from corner to corner on a sheet of ¾″ ply. A chalk line is very handy for that. You might want to mark the back rather than the front, to reduce the amount of saw tearout on the good side. You can use a circular saw to make this cut. Try using a saw guide; it will make your cut exactly straight.

Most of the time you can free-hand with a circular saw, but on occasion it is nice to be able to work with more precision. In that case, you can use this shop-made *circular saw guide* to ensure a straight cut. Make exact cuts by lining up the edge of the guide with the line you would like to cut.

The jig is very simple to make from a couple of strips of plywood. After assembly, run the saw down the channel and trim off the edge of the guide so that it is exactly the width of the saw table. The kerf falls to the outside of the guide, so it is generally best to place the jig on top of the piece you want to keep.

The guide must be firmly secured to the work. You can do that by clamping it down or by using drywall screws. The clamps are sometimes problematic when the saw motor doesn't have enough clearance to move over the tops of the clamps but the screws leave holes, so you'll need to pick the most appropriate approach. Make sure the left side of the saw table stays securely against the thick part of the guide in order to make a straight cut.

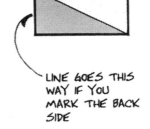

LINE GOES THIS WAY IF YOU MARK THE BACK SIDE

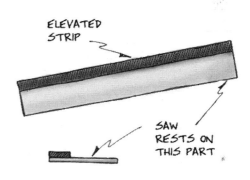

ELEVATED STRIP

SAW RESTS ON THIS PART

USE TWO STRIPS OF PLYWOOD
TO MAKE A CIRCULAR SAW GUIDE

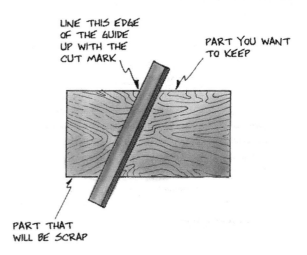

LINE THIS EDGE OF THE GUIDE UP WITH THE CUT MARK

PART YOU WANT TO KEEP

PART THAT WILL BE SCRAP

ADDING FRAMING TO THE PLATFORM

After you have cut out the top of the platform, lay it good side up across a pair of sawhorses so that the corners are unobstructed. Trim the end of a piece of 2×4 to make it square and line it up with the 4'-0" side of the triangle. Square up one end with the 90 degree angle corner, and use a pencil to scribe the length and angle of the plywood onto the 2×4 from underneath. Use a miter saw to cut the board to length. When you do, make a note of the number of degrees because you will need that same angle to cut other parts. For the moment, you need only to adjust the saw by eye so that it matches your marked line, and then cut the 2×4.

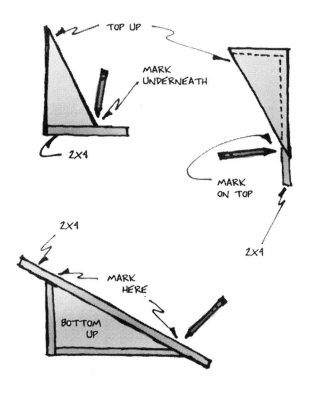

USE THE PLYWOOD
TO MARK THE FRAMING

When using this method, it is best to attach each framing member as you go along because it will simplify the marking process. Otherwise, the piece you just cut will tend to move while the next piece is being marked. For an irregular deck that will not go into stock at the end of the show, you probably won't want to glue the pieces in place. That makes it almost impossible to get anything back apart, and there may be some salvageable pieces you can use again later. It's enough to screw the top to the framing with 1⅝" drywall screws. After this first section has been attached, hold another length of 2×4

under the 8 foot long side and scribe the pointy angle from the plywood pattern. You will not be able to cut this angle on a miter saw because it is too steep. The saw will not swing around that far. The best way is to use a large band saw if you have one that will accommodate the piece. If not, use a circular saw instead. Cut halfway through on one side, and then turn the 2×4 over to do the same on the second side. The 7¼" blade found on most saws is too small to cut through the entire board at once.

After the piece has been cut, screw it into place and turn the entire platform upside down. Mark the last piece by laying a length of 2×4 stock in place and marking the two ends. One of the ends will match the same angle you cut before on the miter saw. The pointier angle will need the same process with the circular saw of cutting halfway through and flipping over.

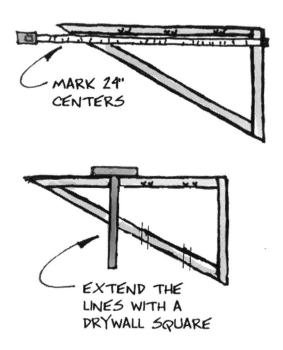

Each toggle will be a different length, but all of them will have one end that is a 90 degree angle, and another that is the same angle as was earlier cut on the miter saw. Before you can cut the toggles to length, you'll need to do some layout on the bottom of the platform to determine the toggle locations. Measure along the 8 foot side of the platform, marking both sides of where each 2×4 toggle should go. It isn't practical to measure on both sides, as the hypotenuse of the triangle is at an angle. You need a different way of marking that side. Use a drywall square to extend your existing marks to the angle side. You only need to mark the 2×4 framing, not the entire expanse of plywood. Set a length of stock in place flush with the straight side, and scribe the required length and angle from the opposite side. These three toggles can be cut on the miter saw.

Curved Platforms

When building a curved platform there is generally no way to bend 2×4 framing so that it exactly fits along the edge of the plywood top. If the design allows you to leave a small overhanging lip, you can use standard construction techniques with 2×4 framing. A ¾″ ply top is sturdy enough to have an overhang of 2 or 3 inches with no support. If the curve requires more than that, you may try doubling the thickness of the plywood along the edge.

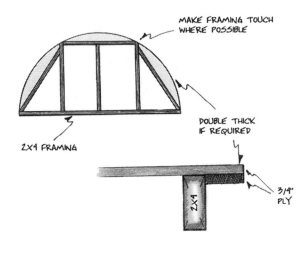

PLATFORM WITH A ROUND EDGE

To mark the curve, use a set of trammel points if it is part of a circle, or use the *grid method* if it is irregular. Gridding a piece means to lay out a 1 foot grid on the drawing in its particular scale, and actual 1 foot squares on the plywood you will cut out. This technique can be used to transfer lines of any sort from a small drawing to full size.

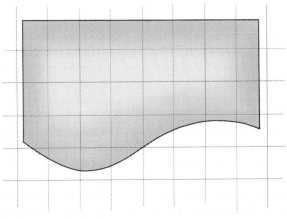

USE A GRID PATTERN FOR ODD SHAPES

MARK A 1 FOOT GRID IN SCALE ON THE DRAWING, AND AN ACTUAL 1 FOOT GRID ON THE PLYWOOD FOR THE TOP.

Trammel points are essentially small clamps attached to a strip of wood to form a very large beam compass. One of the clamps has a steel pin that serves as the pivot point, and the other clamp holds a pencil. You can use strips of white pine left over from ripping down 1×3s as the "beam" part of the compass. It is best to use a lightweight connection because it gives more control over the marking process. A substitute for the trammel points would be to use two small strips of wood that are held together with small spring clamps. Put a 4d nail through the end of one of the strips to use as the pivot point, and drill a pencil-size diameter hole through the end of the other. (Make it just a shade small.) Squeeze the pencil into place, and you are ready to go. The size can be adjusted by removing the clamps and sliding the strips of wood back and forth. Do not use a string with a pencil tied to the end of it, because the string will either stretch, break, or get caught on something. Sometimes, for a very large arc, you might consider driving a nail into the center point and using a steel measuring tape to strike an arc.

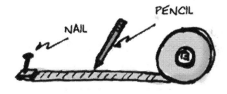

CIRCLE MARKING IMPLEMENTS

After the curve has been established, you can draw in some lines to represent placement of the framing members. It is best to do this in some logical way, but the actual placement is somewhat arbitrary, especially if the curve is irregular. The placement of the framing in the example is much like what you might expect from an angular platform, like those described earlier in this chapter.

Bending plywood is usually made from either lauan or birch that has been laminated together like regular plywood, except that there are two thick plies and one very thin ply. The barrel version has the grain of the thick plies running the 4 foot direction on the sheet. If you rip a 4″ wide strip from a sheet of that type, the resulting 8 foot long section of wood will be exceedingly bendable, and can easily be wrapped around the edge of a curved surface such as a platform.

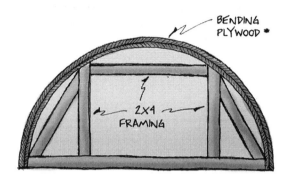

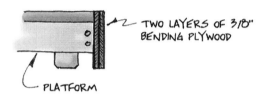

USE BENDING PLYWOOD AROUND THE OUTSIDE EDGE OF THE PLYWOOD TOP

* THIS WILL INCREASE THE SIZE OF THE PLATFORM

Make your framing touch the edge of the curve in as many places as possible in order to give the plywood more support. You can also add small braces that go between the platform top and the facing. Remember when you lay out the curve that anything you add to the outside will make it larger. Bending plywood is usually ~⅜″ thick.

LEGGING METHODS

There are many different ways to give height to the kind of platforms we have been discussing, but all of the methods fall into one of two general categories. The first is to put individual legs on each of the platforms, and the second is to build a structure that supports a number of platforms all at once. Choose the type that works best for the given situation.

Individual legs are generally the best solution when the platforms are either very low to the ground, and/or when the platform area is very small. On the other hand, a large expanse of decking several feet off the stage floor definitely calls for some kind of support structure. Back in the day, shops used fold-out legging structures to hold

up unframed plywood lids. They were called *parallel platforms* and were constructed like flats that were hinged together. The flat-like legging structures provided the tensile strength for the plywood tops. That method hasn't been popular for many years because the foldout units were hard to make and the style of stage design has changed.

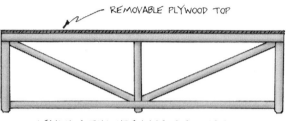

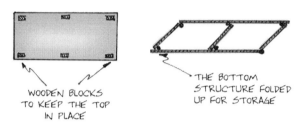

OLD-SCHOOL PARALLEL PLATFORM

SCENIC STUDIOS WOULD HAVE LOTS OF THESE IN STOCK, SO THAT THEY COULD RENT THEM TO VARIOUS SHOWS.

A major engineering problem associated with legging platforms is to provide enough *lateral* strength to keep the structure from twisting out of shape to the side, and/or from "corkscrewing." Care must be taken to keep the legging structure rigid. If all of the parts stay in position, the structure will be safe. If any of the parts bend or twist the structure will fail. Since that would most likely happen when people are on top of the platform, that is obviously something you should take great care to avoid.

The upright parts have a *compression* load that pushes straight down the length of the 2×4. We most often think of compression as a downward force compacting the leg. *Tensile strength* is the ability of a material to withstand a load that would cause it to bend and possibly break. We most often think of that in context to a framing member that snaps at a weak point along its length. When individual legs are used, the platform framing itself is responsible for providing the tensile strength. The 2×4 framing is okay as long as the legs are reasonably spaced so that the span isn't too great.

Stiffeners and *braces* are used to keep the upright parts in position. Lateral forces from things like actor movement tend to disturb the equilibrium of the system and work against the bracing, which must be designed to counteract those forces.

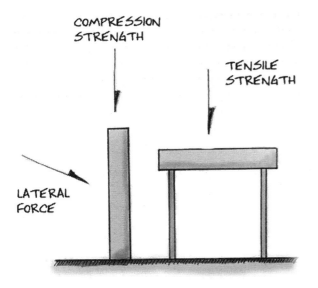

COMPRESSION
STRENGTH

TENSILE
STRENGTH

LATERAL
FORCE

Determine the length of the leg from the height of the platform less the amount of the thickness of the material covering that platform. If the lid of a platform is ¾" ply and the height of the decking overall should be 12", then the length of the leg stock should be 11¼". If you will be covering the top surface with Masonite and sound deadening, be sure to account for that as well. Plan on using six legs on a 4×8 stock platform so that the span between legs doesn't exceed the tensile strength of its framing.

Perhaps the most popular way of legging in small theatre companies today is to bolt 2×4 legs into the corners of the platforms. A 2×4 on end has a great deal of compression strength and is more than up to the task, as long as it stays upright.

LEG PLACEMENT
ON A 4X8 PLATFORM

Cut all of the legs at one time using the radial arm saw and a stop block. Use the miter saw to put a small bevel, or chamfer, on the outside edges of the leg. This increases the chance that the leg will sit flat on a slightly uneven surface, and besides, it is a very handsome look.

Another way to leg a platform is to use a *V-leg* instead of a 2×4. They are called this because of the shape of their cross section. Some people call that shape a *hog-trough*. It is essentially two pieces of 1×4 that have been glued and stapled together. You can rip down strips of ¾" plywood as an alternative. Plywood tends to split less when the legs are screwed to the platform framing. V-legs have two sides forming a corner, and that shape has more ability to withstand twisting. Also, since two boards are joined at a right angle, the leg is strengthened against bowing out of shape. One single 1×4 would be very dangerous in that regard. It is important to glue the two halves of the leg together so that they remain firmly attached to one another.

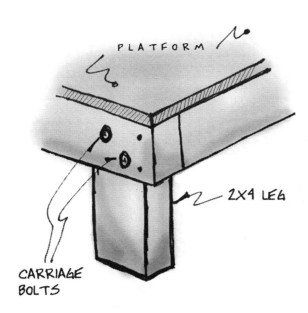

PLATFORM

2X4 LEG

CARRIAGE
BOLTS

Platform legs are generally much longer than they are wide, and the narrowness of the surface attached to the platform framing gives them a tendency to twist and pull away from it. Bolting on 2×4s is a good way to avoid pulling away, but bolting is generally harmful to the platform, especially when a large number of holes have been drilled right in the corner. To lessen that effect you should attempt to drill through existing holes in the platform, and then through the 2×4 leg.

Attach the V-legs to the platform from the inside with 1⅝" drywall screws. Put one screw on the skinny side, and two on the wide side. Bear in mind that the farther apart the fasteners are, the more secure the leg will be. Six legs on a 4×8 platform will leave no unsupported span of more than 4 feet. That's compatible with the strength of a platform constructed with 2×4 lumber and a ¾" plywood top.

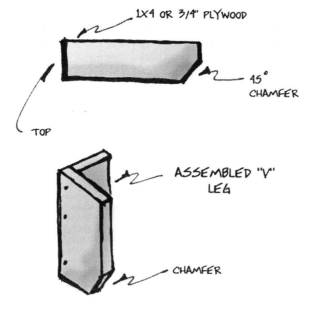

1X4 OR 3/4" PLYWOOD

45° CHAMFER

TOP

ASSEMBLED "V" LEG

CHAMFER

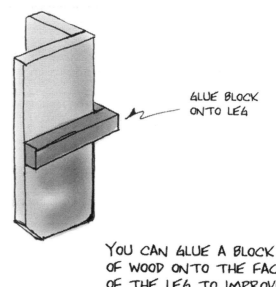

GLUE BLOCK ONTO LEG

YOU CAN GLUE A BLOCK OF WOOD ONTO THE FACE OF THE LEG TO IMPROVE ITS LOAD-CARRYING CAPACITY

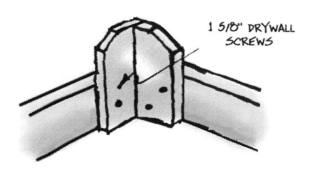

1 5/8" DRYWALL SCREWS

PLYWOOD TOP UPSIDE DOWN

As a rule of thumb, you can consider that a platform with V-legs or 2×4 legs needs no lateral support if it is no more than 16″ or so in height. The width of the leg is large enough, and the distance of the platform from the floor low enough that the structure has little danger of breaking loose under normal conditions. Less than a foot of each leg is exposed below the bottom of the framing. It is imperative though, that the platforms and legs be properly constructed and assembled.

For taller legs some sort of bracing is required to keep them upright under stress. This applies to legs made in either the 2×4 or V-leg style. Sometimes it is enough to simply band the bottom of the legs with a strip of ¾″ thick material that will keep the legs from being twisted outward. If the height warrants it, diagonal bracing should be used. Note how the bracing runs in different directions for added strength. Bracing in this way makes the unit look suspiciously like an old-school parallel platform.

HELPFUL HINTS

- If you bolt on 2×4 legs and need to add facing to the platform later on you might consider using carriage bolts so that the heads don't stick out so far.

- When using V-legs it is important to use 1⅝″ screws and to make sure that they are tightly installed. There should be no gap of any kind between the leg and the framing.

- Make sure to use the proper number of legs in your system. Six legs per 4×8 platform is slightly redundant and will provide extra protection.

- You can add a safety feature by gluing blocks on the outside of V-legs so that the load from the platform frame is transferred to the leg by more than just the screws holding the leg to the frame.

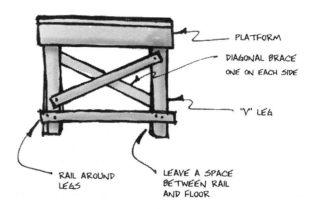

PLATFORM

DIAGONAL BRACE ONE ON EACH SIDE

"V" LEG

RAIL AROUND LEGS

LEAVE A SPACE BETWEEN RAIL AND FLOOR

Putting individual legs on a large number of platforms can become quite difficult, because of the unnecessary duplication of the upright members and also the problem of how cumbersome the units can become. It is quite easy for one or more of the decking units to become unlevel, especially if they are tall. The more of them there are, the less likely they will all fit together properly. Individual legs are fine when the decking area is very small and/or low to the stage floor, but larger decks require a different approach.

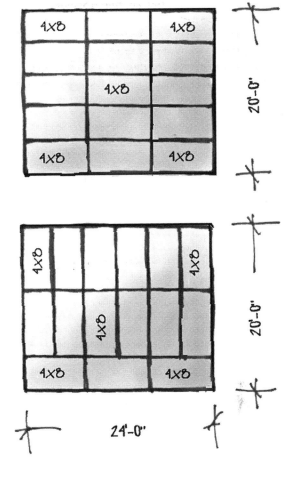

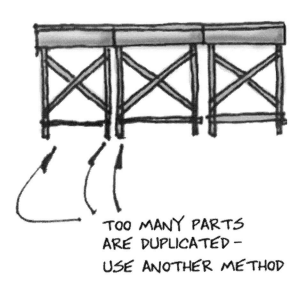

TOO MANY PARTS
ARE DUPLICATED –
USE ANOTHER METHOD

CARRIERS

Carriers get their name from the way they carry the weight of the decking. They are intended to hold several platforms at once, and the effectiveness of this method increases with the number of platforms involved. It does not work particularly well with just one or two. Carriers are essentially short *stud walls*, like those in a house but made from different materials. Stud wall is such a good description that it is a very popular name for the same thing.

The size and shape of the decking area is of great importance in designing the carrier or stud wall system. For the example shown, the deck under construction is 20 feet by 24 feet in size and 18″ tall. Here are two possible ways to get this size using standard 4×8 platforms.

It's important to support the deck so that there is no span greater than 4'-0″. You can accomplish that by running the carriers on 4 foot centers. If the carriers are made from 2×4 stock, the 3½″ wide lumber is spacious enough to support the 2×4 framing of two platforms at once. It is crucial that the platform framing rest firmly on the carrier and not to the side. The platforms should be securely fastened together.

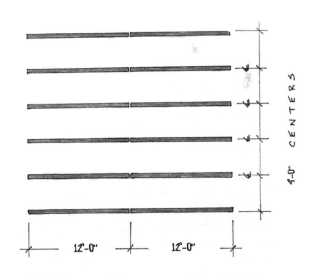

PLAN VIEW OF CARRIER LAYOUT

You need to determine the overall height of the carriers. For individual legs, you subtracted only the thickness of the platform covering material, but for this type of support it is necessary to account for the thickness of the entire platform, framing and all, because all of the platform will be resting on top of the carrier. In this demonstration the thickness of the platform is 4¼". Hence the overall height of the carrier would be 13 ¾". The cut list contains quite a few pieces, but many of them are identical parts that can be cut out all at once using a stop block. Remember to rank the cut list from the longest pieces to the shortest because that's the order you should cut them. It will be easy to find material suitable for the short sections even after the long ones are finished.

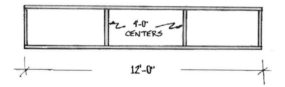

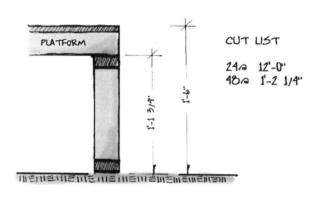

CUT LIST

24@ 12'-0'
48@ 1'-2 1/4'

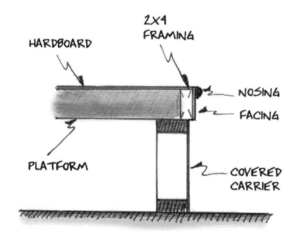

MAKE SURE THAT THE PLATFORM
FRAMING STAYS ON THE CARRIER

One really advantageous aspect of using the stud wall method is that resting the framing of the platform on the carrier increases the stability of the platform. The load on top of the platform is assumed by the entire structure and the full width of the cord of the framing members rather than just the portion connected by bolts or screws.

If they are tall, the carriers need some kind of lateral bracing. Without it, they tend to rack out of shape into a parallelogram, and the entire deck might fall. The importance of keeping the upright members vertical is paramount. The 2x4 uprights have enough compression strength to hold up a huge load, but compression assumes only a downward force. If the uprights are allowed to tilt, failure is imminent. You can avoid this by bracing the uprights diagonally.

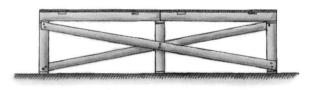

USE TRIANGLE FORMING RACK BRACES
AS REQUIRED

Most theatres cover the decking with a layer of hardboard, which creates a much smoother and more uniform surface than the plywood tops of the platforms themselves. That's especially true of stock platforms that may have been in service for a number of years. If you do that, the hardboard will tend to lock the individual decks together, lessening the need for coffin locks or bolts that connect the platform units.

SOUND DEADENING

Hard shoes pounding against the ¾" plywood top of a platform can make a most distracting and drum-like noise. The clomping and thudding of feet in a blackout removes much of the magic of the moment. Here is a method of deadening sound with insulation and hardboard that works quite well and has the added bonus of also improving the appearance of the deck.

You can use any of several different types of thin insulating material. Homosote works well, or perhaps extruded foam insulation. Either of these loosely compacted materials is intended to insulate a house from cold, but it will insulate sound vibrations just as well.

Place the insulation so that the edges don't fall in line with the joints of the 4x8 platforms. This will prevent the *telegraphing* of uneven joints upward toward the finished surface.

The insulation material itself is far too delicate to be the finished floor. You can lay sheets of hardboard to create a durable surface. The finished product will appear

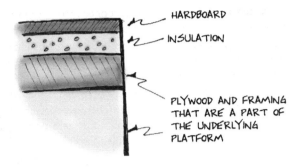

HARDBOARD

INSULATION

PLYWOOD AND FRAMING THAT ARE A PART OF THE UNDERLYING PLATFORM

much flatter and more solid than just using the tops of the platforms themselves. In fact, you can use a layer of just hardboard with no foam at all if sound deadening is not an issue. In either case, be sure to stagger the hardboard away from the underlying joints.

Make small *countersink* holes in the surface of the hardboard about every foot around the outside perimeter of the sheet. Use drywall screws to fasten the hardboard to the deck. Add a few fasteners to the interior of the sheet to keep it from bulging upward. You should leave a small gap about the thickness of a dime all around the sheet to account for expansion if the weather turns humid.

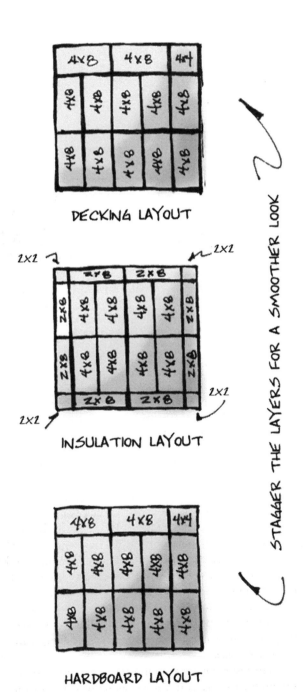

DECKING LAYOUT

INSULATION LAYOUT

HARDBOARD LAYOUT

STAGGER THE LAYERS FOR A SMOOTHER LOOK

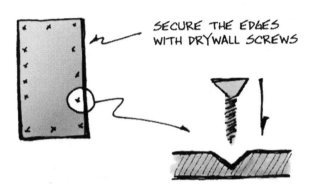

SECURE THE EDGES WITH DRYWALL SCREWS

MAKE COUNTERSINKS SO THAT SCREW HEADS DO NOT STICK UP PAST THE SURFACE

The surface of hardboard is very slick. You should plan on painting new sheets before any scheduled rehearsals.

🌹 GREEN IDEAS TIP BOX

Re-Use the Masonite

If you are careful at the strike, you can re-use the hardboard panels a number of times. It's actually easier to use the hardboard the second time because the countersink holes are already there, which is the time-consuming part of installing them. You can save even more by planning ahead to use stock parts. The audience won't really notice the difference between a deck that is 40 feet wide and one a few inches larger or smaller.

Stressed-Skin Panels

Sometimes a special type of platform is required, for which the standard construction methods simply won't work. Sometimes a platform must cover an unusually large span, and/or must have a clean and streamlined appearance. Sometimes the bottom of the platform will be seen. These are all factors that might lead you to select the stressed-skin construction method. *Stressed-skin panels* have both a top and a bottom cover, so the bottom looks just as good as the top. The way they are constructed makes them much more rigid, and more supportive than the traditional construction method, even though they may be thinner than a platform made with 2×4s. Stressed-skin panels can be used in a variety of ways, not just platforms. Hollow-core doors are a good example of the engineering principles involved.

The secret to stressed-skin manufacture lies in the way the bottom cover or "skin" keeps the platform from bending. These platforms have exceptional tensile strength. In general, for any framing member to bend, two things must occur. The top of the member must compress, and the bottom must stretch. Bending of this sort will eventually cause the lumber to break when the force applied is enough to stretch the material past the breaking strength of the fibers that hold it together.

The bottom skin in a stressed-skin platform prevents the bottom of the structure from stretching too far because it spreads the stress of the load over the entire platform rather than letting it concentrate on one framing member. All of the materials used in a stressed-skin structure are intended to work in concert, and they must be securely joined together, or the structure will fail. All of the joints in a wooden platform must be properly glued together in order for the system to work. This concept cannot be over-emphasized.

You can build this type of platform using ½″ plywood for the tops and ¼″ ply for the bottoms. It is possible to use ½″ ply rather than the normal ¾″ for the top surface because the framing members of the platform are much closer together and that will reduce the amount of flex created by footfalls.

Space the framing members no more than 12″ apart, on center. This will provide sufficient support for the ½″ plywood top. Notice that all the framing runs continuously from one end to the other. The platform in the illustration is intended to be supported at the ends only. Longer spans need a thicker *cord*, the distance from top to bottom of the framing.

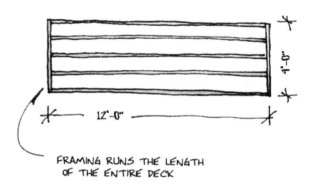

FRAMING RUNS THE LENGTH OF THE ENTIRE DECK

WIDTH OF THE FRAMING MEMBER DEPENDS ON THE LENGTH OF THE SPAN, WEIGHT, AND TYPE OF LOAD.

After the framing has been glued and fastened together, the top of the platform can be attached. The plywood should be used to square up the framing in the usual way, by starting at one corner and working the two adjacent sides. If there is a problem keeping the internal framing in place during this process, cut a number of spacers to keep the framing from wandering.

Use enough yellow aliphatic resin glue to ensure that the plywood completely adheres to all of the lumber framing over the entire surface of the framing. It is very important to glue every inch of every joint on a stressed-skin platform. Staple the top plywood to all of the framing, not just the perimeter, so that it will be held together firmly while the glue sets up.

If the size of the top requires more than one sheet of plywood, the two adjoining sheets should be scabbed together securely. This is very important, and the structure will fail if it is not done properly. Glue and nail a 4″ wide slat of ½″ plywood to the underside of one of the plywood sheets, half on and half off. The protruding

LINES CLOSE TOGETHER COMPRESSION

LINES FARTHER APART STRETCHING

THIS DRAWING MIMICS THE EFFECTS OF BENDING. NOTICE HOW THE LINES ON THE CURVE ARE FARTHER APART ON THE BOTTOM AND CLOSER TOGETHER ON THE TOP. THE BOTTOM STRETCHES, WHILE THE TOP COMPRESSES.

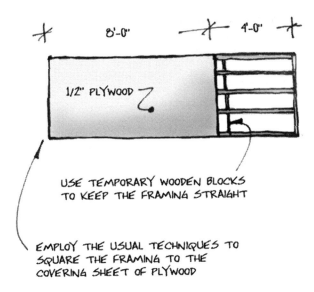

USE TEMPORARY WOODEN BLOCKS
TO KEEP THE FRAMING STRAIGHT

EMPLOY THE USUAL TECHNIQUES TO
SQUARE THE FRAMING TO THE
COVERING SHEET OF PLYWOOD

failures occur very quickly, with no warning. Make sure that the plywood joint on the bottom falls in a different place than the top did.

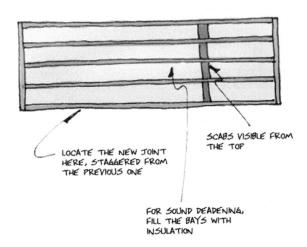

LOCATE THE NEW JOINT HERE, STAGGERED FROM THE PREVIOUS ONE

SCABS VISIBLE FROM THE TOP

FOR SOUND DEADENING, FILL THE BAYS WITH INSULATION

BOTTOM OF THE UNIT

half will be used to connect the second sheet. Do not cut notches in the framing to let in the connecting slat, but rather use several small pieces. Notches may well remove too much of the framing for it to support properly in that weakened condition. Extend the connecting slat so that it covers as much space as possible between framing members. Again, it is very important that all wooden surfaces that touch each other have a proper glue bond. Nails alone will not hold.

After the glue has cured overnight, use a flush trim router to clean up the edges. Stressed-skin platforms must use some kind of carrier-type structure to elevate them, because there is no place to attach any sort of individual leg. If steel frame legging is used, the decking can usually be held in place by virtue of its own weight when wooden blocks are attached to the underside of the platform to keep it from sliding. This is very similar to the way old-style parallel platforms were used.

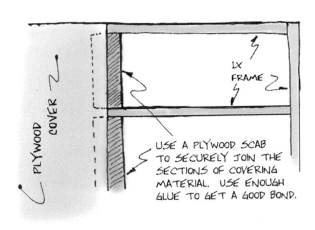

PLYWOOD COVER

1X FRAME

USE A PLYWOOD SCAB TO SECURELY JOIN THE SECTIONS OF COVERING MATERIAL. USE ENOUGH GLUE TO GET A GOOD BOND.

BLOCKS GLUED TO THE BOTTOM OF THE PLATFORM

The ¼″ bottom ply should be attached in the same manner as the top was, including the use of the connecting scabs. Proper installation of the joining scabs is even more important on the bottom skin, which is subjected to stresses that want to pull it apart. The bottom plywood is what gives this technique its name, because the ¼″ plywood is the "skin" that is "stressed." If the bottom skin comes loose from the structure, or two connected pieces come apart from one another, a catastrophic failure of the structure will occur. Catastrophic

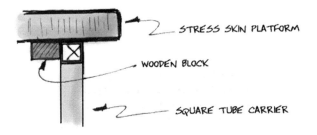

STRESS SKIN PLATFORM

WOODEN BLOCK

SQUARE TUBE CARRIER

TERMS USED IN THIS CHAPTER

$5/16''$ hex key
carrier
circular saw guide
coffin lock
compression load
cord
corner iron
countersink
decking

factory corner
grid method
hog-trough
jig
lateral stress
live load
platform
riser
static load

stiffener
stressed-skin platform
stud wall
telegraphing
tensile strength
trammel points
V-leg

CHAPTER 17

METAL WORKING

I N RECENT YEARS metal framing has become increasingly popular as a medium for scenic construction. The use of welded steel or aluminum tubing allows scenery to be constructed from materials that are smaller in cross section, more securely joined, and in some cases lighter than traditional wood framing. This method has the added advantage of being very quick to assemble using easily constructed jigs. Furthermore, there is actually more salvageable material left from steel framing than from the wooden type. Metal framing from tubing is the only logical approach to constructing some scenic units with open structures and odd angles.

WELDING PICTURES ARE VERY DRAMATIC. SPARKS FLY IN ALL DIRECTIONS!

MATERIALS

The phrase "metal framing" could mean either aluminum or steel. There are advantages and disadvantages to either product. Aluminum is much lighter than steel, but steel is considerably stronger than aluminum, which has a tendency to crack and shatter. Steel square tubing is much less expensive than its extruded aluminum counterpart. Aluminum is more difficult to weld than steel is, and requires special inert gas techniques that are more difficult to produce. Aluminum framing is very popular with companies who build scenery for tours of rock and roll shows because of its light weight, but they have almost unlimited financial resources. Steel framing is much more popular with schools and theatre companies.

TUNGSTEN INERT GAS WELDER, OR TIG

UNLIKE A MIG WELDER, THE TIG DOESN'T USE
A SPOOL OF WIRE. YOU MUST HOLD A WELDING ROD
IN YOUR HAND INSTEAD, MUCH LIKE AN OLD-STYLE
OXYACETYLENE WELDING RIG. THE TUNGSTEN TIP
HEATS THE METAL AND THE ROD BECOMES THE FILLER.
THE FOOT-PEDAL IN THE FOREGROUND IS USED TO START
THE WELDING PROCESS, AND CAN BE USED TO "EASE INTO"
HEATING UP THE TIP WHICH IS VERY IMPORTANT WHEN
WELDING ALUMINUM STOCK.

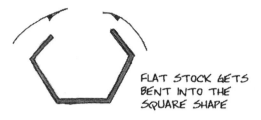

FLAT STOCK GETS
BENT INTO THE
SQUARE SHAPE

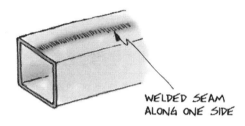

WELDED SEAM
ALONG ONE SIDE

Square tube gets its name from the shape of the cross section, which is, of course, square. It is quite often the most useful shape, although tubing is also manufactured in round or rectangular cross sections. Steel tube is bent into shape from flat bars of metal, and as a result one side of it has a seam where the edges of the bar have been welded together. This seam generally appears as a slightly darker, sometimes bluish stripe.

Aluminum is extruded through a die in order to get whatever particular shape is required and has no such seam. Cutting and grinding steel framing requires the use of special metalworking equipment, whereas the much softer aluminum can usually be cut and shaped with ordinary woodworking tools. Welding aluminum requires a TIG welder, whereas steel may be worked with an ordinary arc welder, or even *oxyacetylene*.

This chapter is written with steel tubing in mind because it is more widely used, but there isn't that much difference in the types of structures you can build with either one.

OXYACETYLENE RIG

Building the structural parts of a set from steel square tube can actually be less expensive than using wooden parts. The difference in price is due to the way steel joints are welded together. The resulting connections are much stronger than any kind of wooden joinery, and you can easily make angular shapes that are much more difficult with wooden scenery. Less bracing is required, so fewer running feet of material are needed for steel structures than for traditional wooden methods.

 GREEN IDEAS TIP BOX

When wooden scenery is struck, most non-stock parts wind up in the trash, but with steel framing, no part is too small to be recycled. Even small scraps left over from cutting parts to length during construction can be collected and recycled.

Steel tubing is available in many sizes and cross sections. A reasonably well-stocked supplier should have square tube in a variety of sizes from half-inch to 4 inch. *Rectangular* tubing is available in sizes like 1×2 inches, 1×3 inches, 2×3 inches, and so forth. Other useful shapes are *angle iron*, which has two sides and is shaped like an L, *channel*, which is U shaped, *flat bar*, which is one flat piece and *round bar*, which is a solid round shape. *Round tubing* is hollow on the inside, which makes it different from round bar. Round tubing and steel pipe are not the same thing. *Black steel pipe* used in plumbing is generally much thicker than the tubing meant for welding structures. Even so, black steel pipe is frequently used in constructing scenery.

Pipe is sized by its *inside diameter* or ID. The wall thickness varies in proportion to the diameter according to the *Nominal Pipe Size*, or NPS, but is generally between ⅛" and ³⁄₁₆", so 1 inch pipe is actually almost an inch and ⁵⁄₁₆ on the outside. Other types of structural steel such as square or round tubing are sized by their *outside diameter* or OD. Of course it is much easier to make up a cut list if you are given the exterior dimensions of the materials.

The two most common wall thicknesses of black steel pipe are known as Schedule 40 and Schedule 80. *Schedule 40* is the most available, while Schedule 80 is much thicker and heavier. Pipes are meant to hold pressurized water on the inside, while tubing is not.

On the other hand, the wall thickness of tubing is described with a *gauge system*. The smaller the gauge number, the thicker the tubing wall. As in the case of wire gauges, this is the exact opposite of what would seem logical. As a point of reference, 10ga tubing is approximately ⅛" thick, while 16ga tubing is about ¹⁄₁₆" thick. (16ga,

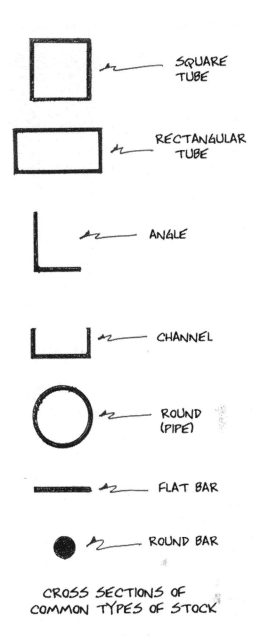

CROSS SECTIONS OF COMMON TYPES OF STOCK

¹⁄₁₆" is easy to remember.) The same gauge numbers are used to describe the wall thickness of all steel pieces, no matter what their size or shape. From a structural standpoint, the outside dimension of the tubing has the most impact on the rigidity of something you make from it, rather than the thickness of the wall. For lightweight structures it is generally best to use the thinnest wall available. 20-gauge tubing is an excellent lightweight material, but it can be somewhat difficult to find because it is not very popular for general construction. The 16-gauge is much more common. Unless you are building something that must withstand extreme forces (perhaps you should consult a professional engineer), it is best to steer clear of really thick tubing like 10ga. It is just too heavy for most theatrical use. You can spot thick wall tubing by looking at the corners. Thicker wall tubing has

SHARPER CORNER
ON THIN 16 GA STEEL

CORNER OF THICKER
10 GA STEEL IS
MORE ROUNDED

THICKER STEEL HAS
MORE ROUNDED CORNERS

more rounded corners. This makes sense when you think about how square tubing is made by bending a flat piece of steel into a square shape and welding the sides together. The thicker material is harder to bend.

Most square tubing comes in 24 foot lengths, which is an excellent thing if you need long pieces. It is not so good when looking for a place to store the material. Many construction projects that include plywood parts are centered around 8 or 12 foot lengths, so the 24 foot size is appealing in that regard, since those numbers divide into 24 evenly. Some smaller size tubing comes in 20 foot lengths, while black steel pipe is a standard 21 foot length.

The 1½″ size square tube is very popular for several reasons. First of all, 1½″ is the same thickness as any wooden two-by. It is often handy to work with materials that are the same thickness, because the parts line up better. Second, it is difficult to obtain thinner gauges in larger tubing that is really intended for heavy construction purposes, and in theatre we are always concerned about the weight of portable scenery. Last of all, and perhaps the most important, the cross-section of 1½″ square tube is large enough to have a fair amount of rigidity all on its own, without being doubled, or made into a truss. For most projects, you can estimate that it has approximately the same strength and rigidity as a 2×4. Some small units are better constructed from 1″ or even ¾″ stock when that rigidity is not required. *Structural Design for the Stage*, by Holden and Sammler, is an excellent resource for anyone interested in studying the structural properties of specific materials.

Structural steel tubing of the sort used to construct scenery is composed of mild steel, a name given to steel with a low carbon content that has excellent malleability and a Rockwell C scale hardness number in the 20s. It is easily drilled with ordinary tools.

WELDING EQUIPMENT

Two very common types of welders are used to join steel. One is the generic arc welder and the other is the Metal Inert Gas type, which is abbreviated as *MIG*. A MIG welder is by far the easiest kind of welder to use for welding mild steel and is far and away the most popular choice. A MIG welder is somewhat more expensive to

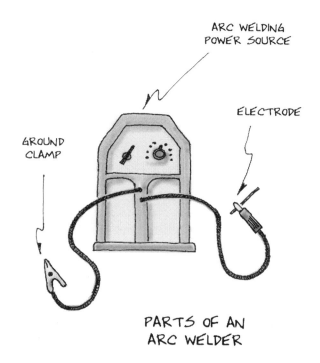

ARC WELDING
POWER SOURCE

ELECTRODE

GROUND
CLAMP

PARTS OF AN
ARC WELDER

purchase than a standard arc welder because its mechanism is much more complicated.

An *arc welder* is essentially a very large rectifier unit that changes AC power into DC power. Electronically, some machines are constant current while others are constant voltage. Two long cables are attached to the output of the machine. The *ground* has a clamp on the end that gets connected to the steel you are welding. The other cable has a smaller clamp to hold an *electrode*, which is a consumable wire stick coated with *flux*. The flux is a catalyst that aids in the welding process by producing CO_2 gas when heated by the welding process. The inflammable gas prevents the steel from oxidizing at high temperatures. When the electrode is brought into close contact with the steel, a circuit is completed between the (usually) positive output of the welder, the electrode, the steel being welded, the ground clamp, and the negative terminal of the welder.

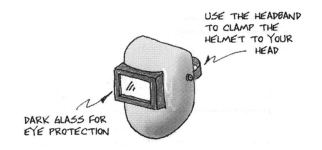

PROTECTIVE HELMET
FOR MIG OR ARC WELDING

ARC WELDING MELTS THE STEEL ELECTRICALLY

Since the electrode is only tangentially in contact with the steel, the electricity must jump across that small gap in order to complete the circuit. When that happens, a small spark or *arc* is created. The arc is very hot and melts the steel. The electrode gets hot also, so the tip of it melts as well. Protected from burning by the flux, molten steel from the electrode mixes with the molten steel on the edges of the joint being welded. Three pieces of steel are melted and joined, the two pieces being connected, and the electrode from the welder itself. When the molten steel cools and hardens, all three should be joined at the molecular level, so that theoretically they are all one homogenous crystalline structure. (In reality, the heating and cooling make a slight difference in the composition of the welded area.)

There are several fairly problematic consequences of arc welding. Of course the light produced is extremely bright and will cause serious injury to your eyes if you look at it from a close distance. (The distance from the arc while you are welding is very close.) Special equipment must be worn to protect your eyes while welding, and the glass is so dark that you cannot see anything through it when it is in place. The electrode will complete the circuit the instant it is in close proximity to the steel. (Close enough for the voltage pressure to force electrons across the gap.) So it is difficult to coordinate your

movements to get the electrode in position, get the helmet in place, and then strike the arc.

The helmet is strapped securely to your head. The traditional type is hinged on the side so that a quick neck motion will cause it to fall down into place. Newer types have a lens that senses the light from the welding process and electronically darkens in an instant. That type is much easier to use because the jerky head motion is not required, which often spoils your careful pre-placement of the electrode. In addition, sensitivity controls on most models allow you to set how dark the lens gets, and how fast/when it happens.

The electrode is consumed by the welding process and must be frequently changed. The flux, the very hot steel, and oxygen from the air combine to form *slag* on the surface of the steel while you are welding. The slag is messy and can get in the way of future welding. It must be removed by hand after the welding process is completed.

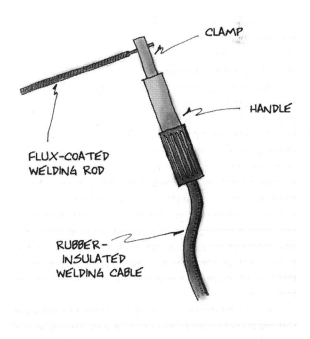

The *MIG welder* addresses many of the difficulties of using an electric arc when welding. A MIG welder also uses a large rectifier to change AC power into DC power. It also has two cables that carry electric current and complete a circuit. One of them has a grounding clamp, but the other has a *nozzle* in place of the electrode found on a regular arc welder. The nozzle emits an *inert gas* that surrounds the joint while welding is taking place. The inert gas, most often an *argon/CO_2 mix*, protects the molten steel from oxygen in the air. There is no flux on the wire, and as a result no slag is formed on the weld. (Some wire welders do not use the inert gas method, and *do* in fact have flux-coated wire. They are not technically considered to be MIG welders.)

SPOOL OF WIRE IN A MIG WELDER

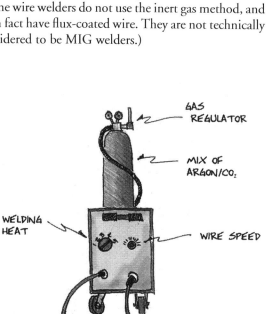

GAS REGULATOR

MIX OF ARGON/CO_2

WELDING HEAT

WIRE SPEED

GROUNDING CLAMP

TRIGGER

WIRE STICKING OUT OF NOZZLE

BASIC PARTS OF A MIG WELDER

A MIG welder is sometimes called a *wire welder* because it uses a spool of wire in place of the electrode that is found on a standard arc welder. The wire is fed through the nozzle from a spool that contains enough of the wire to last for a very long time in even a very busy shop, so it does not need changing very often. This means that you do not have to stop welding to insert a new rod. The arc on a MIG welder is not struck until you pull a trigger on the nozzle. This makes coordinating the welding process much easier. You can rest the wire in the nozzle on the joint to be welded, cover your eyes with

the hood, and then pull the trigger to start the welding process. With a modern helmet the process is even more seamless.

Remember that welding requires you to melt both of the parts forming the joint, and to allow the resulting metals to flow together so that they become indistinguishable from one another. A good weld should have a *"puddled"* appearance, because the steel is highly viscous when in the liquid state.

NOTE THE EVEN PUDDLING ALONG THE LENGTH OF THE WELD

You should be able to see that both parts melted and that the resulting joint line shows evidence of it. If the weld looks like many globs of steel stuck on the surface, the metal did not really flow together. There has been no *penetration* of the heat into the underlying metal.

If the metal you are welding is really thick, it may be necessary to prepare the joint by grinding so that the heat from the arc can melt the steel all the way through its thickness. If you are welding 16ga tubing, that will not be necessary because the wall is so thin.

Make the weld itself by slowly moving the electrode or wire back and forth across the joint line. Make sure

LOTS OF BLOBS AND SKIPS

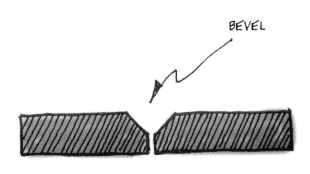

BEVEL

GRIND DOWN THE CORNERS OF
THICK STEEL PIECES FOR
BETTER WELDING PENETRATION

welding thicker materials. ~.035 is a good size for 16ga tubing.

The MIG welder has a *heat control knob* with numbers like 1 through 5 that can be used to regulate the voltage pressure of electrons through the welder, and hence the temperature of the arc. (Some machines control current instead.) The higher the voltage, the more heat concentrated on the weld. Use a higher setting for thick materials and a lower setting for thin materials. If the steel surrounding the weld tends to melt and fall through the tubing, the temperature is too hot. Coordinate the temperature with the wire speed for a good weld.

HEAT SELECTION KNOB

that heat from the arc is applied to both surfaces. If you move too quickly, there will not be enough heat to properly melt the two parts. If you move too slowly, there will be too much heat and the steel will completely melt and drop out, creating a hole. Some people describe the movement across the joint as a zigzag pattern, and others as making small circles with the nozzle. On a MIG welder, pulling the nozzle back from the joint will reduce the amount of heat present at the weld. Moving closer will make the weld hotter. If you pull back too far, the gas will not be able to completely encase the welding area, and also the wire may melt before it gets close enough to the steel to complete the circuit. This can cause a popping sound while you are welding. It will also happen if the wire speed is too high. Different diameters of wire are available, and of course the heavier gauges are meant for

Another variable is the speed of the wire coming out of the nozzle. Generally speaking, the *wire speed* should be higher if you are welding at a higher temperature, but this is somewhat variable, so you will need to experiment to discover the best setting. If the wire pushes the electrode away from the weld, the wire speed is much too fast. If the end of the wire melts into a ball before getting to the weld, the speed is too slow. Again, you need to adjust the wire speed and temperature in tandem, so that a good balance is struck. It is different for thicker/thinner materials, but after a while you will have an intuitive understand of the appropriate settings for the type of welding you most frequently do.

WIRE SPEED KNOB

The newest type of welder has a different scheme, in that you must select the thickness of the material and wire gauge. The welder automatically sets the voltage and wire speed parameters.

One other variable is the pressure of the *gas flow*. This is set by a regulator on the tank of gas, and generally doesn't need to be adjusted after setting up the tank when you first get the welder. A glass vial has a small bead inside it that should float about half way up when the argon/CO_2 mix is running through the welder. It sits on the bottom of the vial when the welder is idle.

Reading this chapter will not qualify you as an expert at using either an arc or MIG welder. It takes more time than that, and you need to have personal instruction. The few preceding paragraphs were meant as an overview of the process to prepare you for that. The rest of this chapter is concerned with how to cut and assemble parts for welded steel scenery. That is actually the most difficult and time-consuming part of the job.

This book describes some special methods developed over the years to enhance accuracy and speed up production. The processes are intended to be used with a MIG welder, which is an excellent investment for any shop. Some people describe a MIG welding set-up as "the hot glue gun of metalworking" because of how easy it is to use. If you have experience in other forms of welding, it should be possible for you to do fairly good work with only a few minutes' practice.

SOME SAFETY CONCERNS

The light produced by any type of welding will cause extensive retina damage if you stare at it, especially if you are very close at hand, i.e., when you are the person welding. But the light can be problematic from a distance as well, so it is good to use protective screens if others are in close proximity. The lenses found in sunglasses, or even cutting torch goggles, are not enough protection from the bright light.

The welds are very hot for some time after you make them, and will cause a severe burn if you touch the steel shortly after welding it. You can get a nasty sunburn on exposed skin if you weld for a long period and don't cover up your arms and neck. Use all the protective gear required for your particular equipment. This includes at the very least: safety glasses, a helmet, special gloves and clothes, and screens to mask other workers from your welding. Be sure to read, understand, and follow all of the safety instructions that come with your welder.

Cutting And Fitting The Parts

The most difficult part of metal construction is cutting the pieces and making them stay put while you are welding them. Of course, any cutting job necessitates the development of a cut list. Here is an example of a cut list for a simple project:

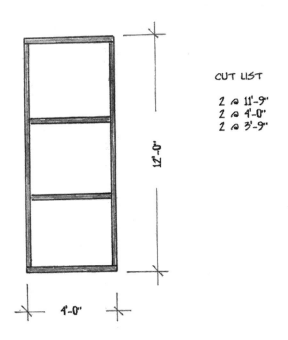

CUT LIST

2 @ 11'-9"
2 @ 4'-0"
2 @ 3'-9"

12'-0"

4'-0"

MAKE FROM 1 1/2"
STEEL SQUARE TUBE

The process of making a cut list for this welding project is exactly the same as the process of making a cut list for a flat, or a step unit, or a platform. Overall dimensions are given on the drawing, and your task is to determine which framing members overlap the other members. This drawing indicates that the top and bottom rails overlap the upright members in the same way they would on a hard-cover flat. The directions say to construct the unit from 1½" 16ga square tube. As a result, the length of the upright stiles will be 3 inches shorter than the overall dimension, while the rails run the full width of the nominal size. The gauge of the metal is not a factor in the cut list, because the dimensions of metal tubing are to the outside, and not the inside as is true with pipe.

Now that you have a cut list, you must shape the steel. Aluminum can be cut with woodworking equipment, but steel requires special techniques.

The most practical tool for cutting small sections of steel in a small shop is the *chop saw*, sometimes known as a cut-off saw. This is really sort of a misnomer, as a chop saw is really a type of grinder and not a saw at all. Rather than using the teeth of a blade to cut, this tool

grinds the metal away with an abrasive blade. The blades must be changed frequently, as the abrasive material is also worn away during the cutting process. Small chop saws are relatively inexpensive, around $300, and are a very expedient way to cut steel.

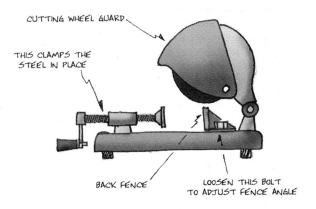

CUTTING WHEEL GUARD

THIS CLAMPS THE
STEEL IN PLACE

BACK FENCE

LOOSEN THIS BOLT
TO ADJUST FENCE ANGLE

PARTS OF A CHOP SAW

They function in much the same way as a miter saw, with a hinge in the back that lets the user press the grinding blade down onto the work. This allows gravity to work for you when cutting. There should be a metal plate or fence on the table of the saw that allows the user to cut angles. This is done by loosening a pair of bolts and rotating the plate to the desired angle. There are marks on the plate to indicate angles, but they are often not very accurate. Perhaps the manufacturer of your particular chop saw will have improved on the design, but if not, you might try using a speed square to set the saw to either 90 or 45 degrees. For other angles, use the miter saw to cut a 3 or 4 inch wide board to the desired angle, and then use this pattern to set the angle on the chop saw. Adjust the fence so that the angle of the pattern board matches the blade, and tighten the fence into place.

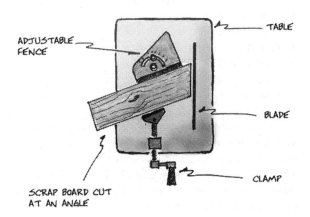

ADJUSTABLE
FENCE

TABLE

BLADE

CLAMP

SCRAP BOARD CUT
AT AN ANGLE

CUT A BOARD ON THE MITER SAW
AND USE IT TO SET THE ANGLE

The saw should have a clamp in the front so that the steel can be securely held in the saw while cutting. Be sure to follow all the safety rules listed on the tool. A chop saw sprays out a shower of sparks while it cuts the steel, and you should take care to protect yourself and others. Be especially mindful of the fire danger from the sparks. If you've never used a chop saw before, you will most likely be surprised by the abundance of sparks that the tool creates. They can get into sawdust and smolder for a very long time before a fire is noticed.

BE CAREFUL!

THE CHOP SAW MAKES
LOTS O' SPARKS

A *metal cutting band saw* is another common steel cutting tool. This type of band saw is very different from the kind used in woodworking, but the blades are similar in either case. The metal cutting band saw blade greatly resembles one used in a hack saw, with small teeth that weave back and forth to create the necessary set for cutting. A metal cutting band saw warps the blade outward so that it can cut through material that would otherwise be too large for the throat of the tool. There are both portable and stationary versions of this tool. Either one is much quieter than a chop saw, and does not produce sparks, but they are much, much slower at cutting through the material.

If you have the room, and will be cutting a lot of steel, it might be worth your while to set up a radial-arm-saw-type bench for your saw. The steel pieces are quite long and supporting them with a bench is very convenient. If you place a fence all down the length of the table, you can easily attach stop blocks for making multiple cuts. Create a holder for a chop saw by installing wooden blocks to hold the feet in place. A stationary metal cutting band saw has feet on it that you can attach to the floor.

If no wall space is available, you can work with a chop saw on a concrete floor instead. Make up a number of wooden blocks that are the same height as the top of the saw table. They can be used to hold the tubing up off the floor and level with the saw. This creates a flexible method of supporting the tubing while cutting, because you can move the blocks around as required.

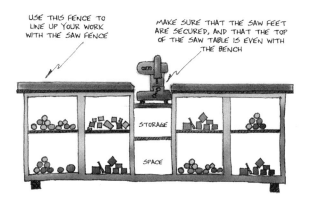

USE THIS FENCE TO LINE UP YOUR WORK WITH THE SAW FENCE

MAKE SURE THAT THE SAW FEET ARE SECURED, AND THAT THE TOP OF THE SAW TABLE IS EVEN WITH THE BENCH

THIS BENCH FOR A CHOP SAW IS SIMILAR TO ONE FOR A RADIAL ARM SAW

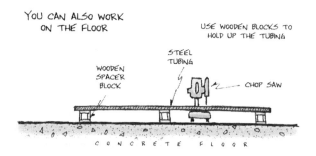

YOU CAN ALSO WORK ON THE FLOOR

USE WOODEN BLOCKS TO HOLD UP THE TUBING

WOODEN SPACER BLOCK

STEEL TUBING

CHOP SAW

CONCRETE FLOOR

Each piece must be marked and cut in turn, in much the same manner as working on a radial arm saw. Don't try to rush the cut; let either type of saw work at its own pace. The speed used to cut any material is called the *feed rate*. If the motor begins to slow down and bind excessively, you are moving too fast. It is also possible to move too slowly, causing the work to heat up unnecessarily from excess friction. A metal cutting band saw usually has a knob that will set how fast it moves through the material when cutting.

THE CONTROLS ON THIS METAL CUTTING BANDSAW AREN'T LIKE OTHER TOOLS YOU MAY HAVE USED. THE KNOB WITH THE NUMBERS CONTROLS A HYDRAULIC VALVE THAT GOVERNS THE PRESSURE USED TO FORCE THE SAW BLADE INTO THE WORK. THE LEVER OPENS AND CLOSES THE VALVE, THUS STARTING AND STOPPING THE MOVEMENT OF THE SAW. AFTER YOU OPEN THE VALVE THE SAW MOVES ON ITS OWN.

One of the advantages of the slower band saw is that the burrs it leaves are much smaller, perhaps insignificant. A *burr* is a thin ridge of steel that is left by the cutting process. Burrs from a chop saw are much larger and probably need to be removed before attempting to fit the pieces together. It is pretty easy to do this with a few strokes of a large, rough *file*, or by using an *angle grinder*. The grinder is of course much faster. The ends of some of the pieces will be exposed in the finished product, and

may need to have an interior burr removed as well. A file will fit inside easily. It is not necessary to spend a great deal of time in treating the ends of pieces that will be welded together. However, it is sometimes difficult to jig up the parts if there is a large burr on the end of the tubing. If the defect is small it will most likely melt away during the welding process. Most burrs on the inside will not show.

Steel tubing is often coated with a layer of oil. The steel mill does this to keep the product from rusting while it is at the supplier. It is generally a nasty, grimy sort of oil and for years I have suspected that it is one

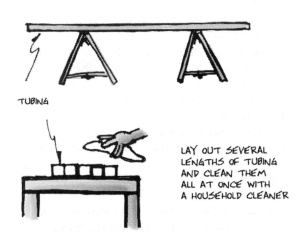

TUBING

LAY OUT SEVERAL LENGTHS OF TUBING AND CLEAN THEM ALL AT ONCE WITH A HOUSEHOLD CLEANER way of recycling used motor oil. Sometimes there's a little, and sometimes there's a lot. It is best to take care of the oil problem shortly after the stock arrives by wiping it down with a spray cleaner like 409 or Simple Green and rags or paper towels. It's a dirty job, but someone has to do it! It is important to get at least the major portion of the oil off the tubing, so that it is not there when you are welding. It seems problematic that the suspect oil will otherwise be vaporized into an inhalable gas by the welding process. Besides, it is very messy.

ASSEMBLY

Unless you are making something really small like a cane bolt holder that doesn't need one, you may find that creating the *welding jig* takes more time than any other part of the fabrication process. It is really important to hold the tubing steady while you are welding, because heat from the arc causes the steel to expand and warp out of shape, a process generally referred to as *heat distortion*. Heat distortion can move the parts you are welding a significant amount, and cause your project to be very un-square. There are many different ways of creating a welding jig. The easiest is to make marks on the floor and hold the steel members in place with stage weights. This method is best when the parts are very large, and the number of units is very small.

Tape out a sizable right-angle pattern on the concrete floor of the shop, and use it in much the same way as a template table is used to square up flats. Lay down several sheets of plywood and use them to mark the right

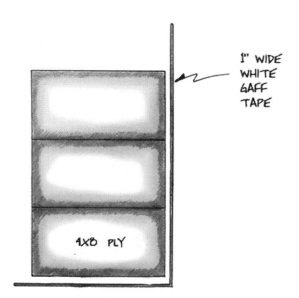

1" WIDE WHITE GAFF TAPE

4X8 PLY

USE SHEETS OF PLYWOOD AND WHITE TAPE TO MARK OUT A REALLY LARGE RIGHT ANGLE

angle. The plywood will ensure that the angle is proportionally large enough to enhance accuracy in the layout.

Start with the bottom rail, and then add a stile. Stage counterweights may be used to hold the ends of the square tube in place. They are quite heavy and, of course, will not burn. If your theatre uses old-style lead weights it would probably not be a good idea to use them for this purpose, as they might easily melt and/or become toxic.

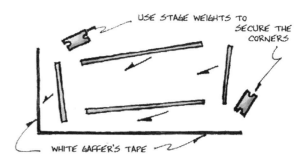

USE STAGE WEIGHTS TO SECURE THE CORNERS

WHITE GAFFER'S TAPE

SQUARING THE FRAME

Concrete floors are often uneven. Make a supply of small wooden wedges to use in leveling the joints. You can make these from short sections of 1×12 which are cut diagonally on the band saw. That will keep the grain going the length of the wedge. It is important to use wedges or some other type of *shim* to arrange the faces of the square tube so that they are on the same plane with one another before welding.

If you will be tech screwing some other material to the square tube, avoid having the welded seam side up when laying out the unit. Because the heating and cooling of the welding process tempers the metal, the seam is oftentimes much harder steel than the regular mild steel of the rest of the tube, and it will be more difficult to get the tech screws to start there.

Using stage weights to pin down the corners of a unit lying on a concrete floor is a good way to stabilize the parts of a large frame, but if the parts are smaller and more complex another method is called for. It is at its best when you need to reproduce a number of the same units. A welding shop uses a template table with a sheet of steel on its top. Individual parts are tack welded to its surface to hold them in place while welding the joints, and that is a good method, but if your shop is mostly a woodworking facility you probably don't have space for that kind of table. Instead, use the same wooden-topped template table used to build flats or a group of 4×8 platforms. Use small wooden blocks to hold the parts in place. Cut a number of them from half-inch plywood, somewhere in the neighborhood of 1 inch by 2 inches. The exact size doesn't matter as much as that they all be the same.

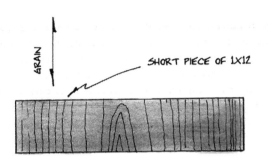

GRAIN

SHORT PIECE OF 1X12

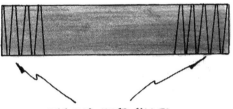

USE THE MITER SAW TO
CUT A FEW WEDGES FROM
EACH END OF A LONG PIECE

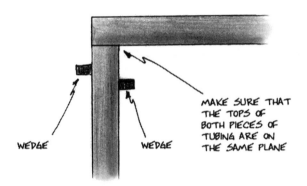

WEDGE   WEDGE

MAKE SURE THAT
THE TOPS OF
BOTH PIECES OF
TUBING ARE ON
THE SAME PLANE

USE WEDGES TO LEVEL OUT
THE DIFFERENT PIECES OF
SQUARE TUBE

USE 1/2" PLYWOOD TO CUT A LARGE NUMBER OF
UNIFORM BLOCKS, ALL ABOUT 1" BY 2".
IF THESE BLOCKS ARE ALL THE SAME
IT WILL BE EASIER TO MAKE UP A WELDING JIG.

Plywood is best because it won't split apart the way dimension lumber can. Half-inch is a good thickness because it doesn't interfere with welding the sides of the steel as much as a thicker block would. They are very easy to attach to the table using a nail gun. If you use nails or staples about 1″ long, it will be easy to remove the blocks when you are finished.

The first step in laying out the jig is to establish a right angle of wooden blocks on the table, which you can do with the same trick as before, using a sheet of plywood. Lay down the first couple of parts that go in that corner, and hold them in place with more blocks, especially toward the ends. Add more sections of pre-cut tubing and lock them in place with more blocks. Use only as many as necessary, but enough to positively hold the steel tubing in place. After you've welded this first unit together and removed it, you can fit more pre-cut sections into the jig and weld another almost instantly. It takes a bit of time to put the jig together, but once you have it, you can make a large number of identical units in a very short time.

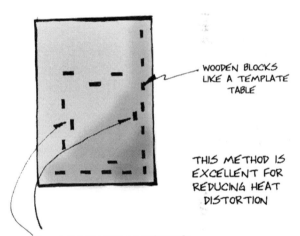

WOODEN BLOCKS
LIKE A TEMPLATE
TABLE

THIS METHOD IS
EXCELLENT FOR
REDUCING HEAT
DISTORTION

ADD MORE BLOCKS AS REQUIRED
TO LOCK THE TUBING INTO PLACE.
THE SAME SETUP CAN BE USED
FOR MANY COPIES OF THE SAME
PIECE.

A wooden surface is important so that you can nail down the blocks, you can't do this on concrete. Be careful when welding though, because the steel gets very hot, about 2600 degrees, and wood ignites at around 500. It's a good idea to keep a spray bottle of water around to douse small flames that pop up from the plywood. Of course you should always make sure that the area is clear of sawdust and other flammable materials. The wood often gets slightly charred, but rarely are there actual flames.

The process of creating jigs from wooden blocks will arise several more times, when special situations are discussed. Making up a welding jig is an important part of the metal frame construction concept.

If you examine the butt joint between two pieces of square tubing, you will see that there are four seams between the two pieces. The most obvious are the face seams, which occur between the end of one piece and the side of another. They result in a *face weld*. The inside corner between the two can be joined with a *fillet weld*. Opposite to the fillet is a seam that shows the thin edge of the end of the tubing. It is generally not practical or advisable to weld that seam.

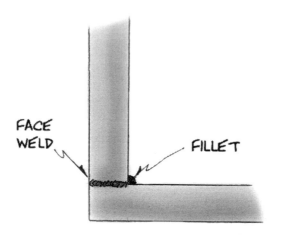

All welds leave at least a small bump out on the surface of the seam, so that another piece of steel will not lay perfectly flat against it. In order to smooth out the bump, you must grind off the part of the welded seam that is sticking out from the face of the tubing. An *angle grinder* is used to do that. The grinder blade is actually a gritty material very similar to what you would find on a chop saw used to cut the metal to length.

As you grind away metal, the blade is also consumed, eventually becoming too small to be useful. The blades come in different thicknesses, and the thinnest ones are called *cut off blades* because they are really meant to cut through steel rather than to flatten welds. Very similar disks are made for cutting masonry materials, but are not the same thing.

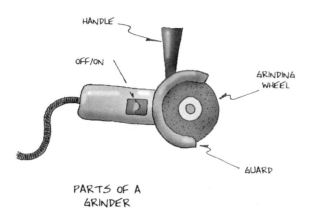

PARTS OF A GRINDER

Much like a belt sander, the way you hold a grinder has a lot to do with how aggressively it removes unwanted material. If you hold it at a steep angle to the work, it will remove the metal very rapidly, but also tends to create an uneven surface. Holding it at a flatter angle will create a smoother surface.

GRINDING AT A STEEP ANGLE TENDS TO DIG INTO THE WORK

GRINDING AT A SHALLOW ANGLE CREATES A FLATTER SURFACE

You do not need to grind all of the welds, but rather only the ones that create a problem in fitting other parts together. It is only necessary to make the area flat, or nearly so. Most novices tend to go too far and create a depression at the site of the weld, which requires more work than necessary and also tends to weaken the joint. Grinding is a noisy, smelly, and somewhat unpleasant chore, and it is best to keep it to a minimum whenever possible. Remember to consider where the sparks are going. Always wear eye and hearing protection when using any type of grinder.

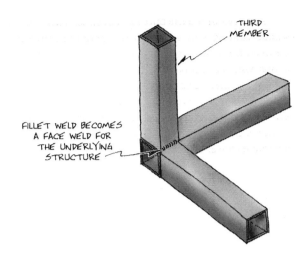

THIRD MEMBER

FILLET WELD BECOMES A FACE WELD FOR THE UNDERLYING STRUCTURE

ADDING A THIRD PIECE OF STEEL ON THE "Z" AXIS CREATES SOME INTERESTING DIFFERENCES

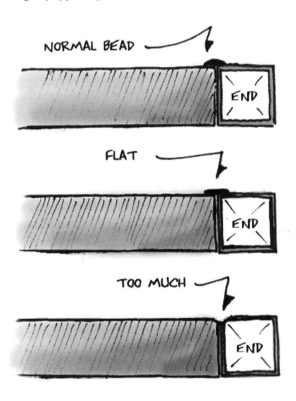

NORMAL BEAD

END

FLAT

END

TOO MUCH

END

DON'T GRIND OFF SO MUCH AS TO WEAKEN THE WELD!

Fillet welds don't need to be ground down because they don't fit up against anything. Because of that, many people tend to connect units with fillets rather than face welds, which means that no grinding is necessary. That technique works really well when a third member will be welded at a right angle to the first two, as would happen when making a box-like structure. The process of welding the third member actually makes the face weld for you.

But welding the fillets alone does not connect the steel parts as securely as the face welds do. If you are concerned about the structural integrity of what you are building, it is best to weld all the seams together. If your welding skills are good, you won't really need to grind that many of them, especially not those that don't show and don't affect the assembly of the parts.

If you are making a large number of multiples, weld all the frames on one side first, and then stack them with the un-welded side up. That makes it easy to weld all of the reverse sides at one time. You can attach the ground to the bottom frame, and it will not need to be moved until the entire stack of frames has been completed. Electrical contact will be preserved through the entire group.

A PRACTICAL EXAMPLE

The following concept of how to arrange steel square tube supports for decking is based on using three standard 4×8 platforms that are joined together with coffin locks, bolts, or clamps. The finished deck will be 2 feet tall. When designing decking systems involving square tubing, it is best to think of the platforms as a group, rather than as separate pieces. The system is put together from five main subassemblies that bolted together to form an overall structure. This is very much like building stud walls out of 2×4s, but using metal instead.

The decking frames require an upright member about every 4 feet when using 1½″ 16ga steel square tube, similar again to wooden 2×4 construction. That spacing is enough to hold the weight of the decking and a reasonable amount of live load as well (live load indicating movement, as with people). *It is critical to keep the upright members vertical.* The compression strength of a 1½″ section of steel square tube is tremendous, but if the support structure is allowed to warp out of shape, disaster is imminent. Generally speaking, the greater the surface area of a decking unit the more stable the structure will be. No matter what type of legging system you use, ten 4×8 platforms linked together will have much, much more stability than one alone.

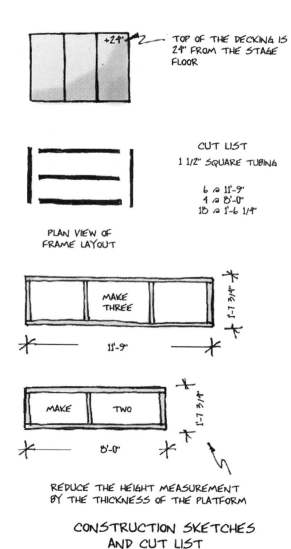

TOP OF THE DECKING IS 24" FROM THE STAGE FLOOR

CUT LIST
1 1/2" SQUARE TUBING

6 @ 11'-9"
4 @ 8'-0"
18 @ 1'-6 1/4"

PLAN VIEW OF FRAME LAYOUT

MAKE THREE

11'-9"

1'-7 3/4"

MAKE   TWO

8'-0"

1'-7 3/4"

REDUCE THE HEIGHT MEASUREMENT BY THE THICKNESS OF THE PLATFORM

CONSTRUCTION SKETCHES AND CUT LIST

frame. That amounts to approximately 9 feet of square tube material out of 115 feet total, which is less than 10% extra.

Notice that the interior toggles are placed on approximate 4'-0" centers, meaning that the centers of the uprights are 4 feet apart. On the 8'-0" frames it is essential to locate the uprights at precisely the center in order to facilitate the connection of the middle frame.

Connect the metal frames together using ¼" bolts and wing nuts. Bolting is a very secure method of joining them. ¼" bolts are heavy duty enough considering that the connecting bolts have almost no load on them; they are just used to keep the parts from separating. Washers are a good idea, especially if you oversize the holes at ⅜". Over sizing the holes makes it much easier to get the bolts through the frames. That's important if you consider that each bolt must pass through four walls, two on each piece of square tubing. A ¼" hole is barely large enough for a bolt to fit through one hole. A larger ⅜" opening allows for easy alignment and bolting of what can be awkwardly large frames.

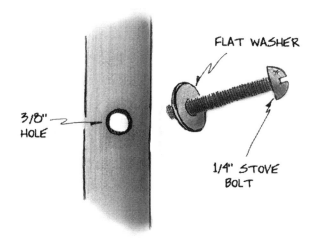

FLAT WASHER

3/8" HOLE

1/4" STOVE BOLT

Rather than legging three separate 4×8 platforms, one system is used for all of them. The 11'-9" frames stretch all the way from one side of the deck to the other, and therefore tie the three platforms together for more stability. Notice that all of these sections are designed to fit inside the shorter, 8'-0" frames. This is done in order to reduce the number of different-sized units to be constructed, and feeds into the wooden block jig philosophy of construction. Although five frames need to be built, there are only two different jig set ups.

The word *frame* is used to indicate a flat, welded together section. One of the advantages of using flat sections is that they stack and store in a small amount of space. Another is that the overall unit can be dismantled easily, and just as easily reassembled using bolts. The tradeoff is that some parts are duplicated. When it is assembled, this carrier system duplicates a few of the uprights used to hold up the weight of the load. That is especially true in the corners where two frames come together. In this example, six extra uprights must be cut, one for each corner and two at the ends of the center

ACCOMMODATING ODD SHAPES

Stud wall carriers made of steel that support stock platforms work great when you are making a large decking system. But you may need a much smaller and oddly shaped unit. You can use square tubing to make very open platforms with tops that don't need to be framed with 2×4s first. In this example the unit can be broken down into frames that are connected together to make the total unit.

In this case the steel framing members must meet at angles, but cutting miters on all of the frames is too difficult a process, and even if you did manage it, the angles on the horizontal parts would not fit the sides of the uprights well. It isn't possible to change the geometry

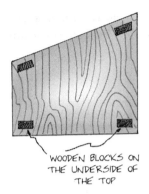

IF YOU PULL THESE PINS THE FRAME WILL FOLD UP

WOODEN BLOCKS ON THE UNDERSIDE OF THE TOP

METAL FRAMES HELD TOGETHER WITH BUTT HINGES

OPEN SPACE

STEEL FRAMING

STEEL FRAMING STOPS SHORT OF THE CORNER

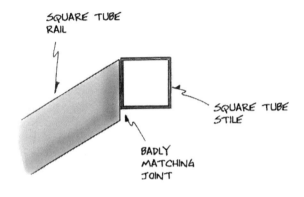

SQUARE TUBE RAIL

SQUARE TUBE STILE

BADLY MATCHING JOINT

IF YOU CUT THE END OF THE RAIL AT AN ANGLE, IT WILL NOT MATCH WELL WITH THE UPRIGHT

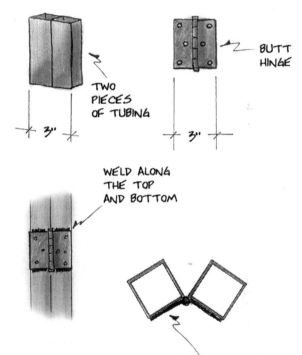

TWO PIECES OF TUBING

3"

BUTT HINGE

3"

WELD ALONG THE TOP AND BOTTOM

HINGE ALLOWS THE TWO UPRIGHTS TO BE JOINED AT AN ANGLE, AND CAN ALSO FOLD UP IF REQUIRED

of the square tube into a triangular shape, as you might with a wooden part.

It is better to hinge the frames so that they touch *corner to corner*. This means that the frames will need to be shorter than the overall dimensions of the platform faces. Hinges will allow you to break down the unit into smaller parts, but if that isn't necessary you could just weld the corners together.

A method of computing a cut list must be developed. Cut out the plywood top first. Use a piece of 1½″ tubing to mark a line along the edge of the decking to simulate the placement of the square tube framing. Measure from corner to corner where the lines cross to get the width of the legging frames.

Hinges will connect the uprights at odd angles. You can attach the hinges with tech screws, or you can simply weld them in place. Welding is more secure, but you won't be able to use the hinges again later. It would be disastrous if the screws were to come out of the hinge because that might cause the platform to collapse. 3″ butt hinges fit rather well on 1½″ square tubing. Most hinges are brass plated, which will not affect the process, but solid

brass hinges won't work when welding. You can use a magnet to test what type you have.

Weld the hinges on after the frames have been constructed and trial fitted on top of the pattern. Setting up on the pattern ensures that the angles are properly adjusted. Vise grip clamps are an excellent way to hold hinges in place while they are being welded. If the hinges are located to the inside of the unit, they will not be in the way of any covering that might be attached to the frame. Loose pins made from bent 30 or 40-penny nails will make it easy to connect the hinges together.

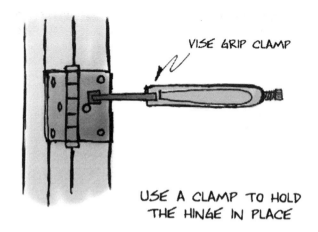

USE A CLAMP TO HOLD
THE HINGE IN PLACE

IMPACT DRIVER FOR LAG BOLTS

Sometimes the decking system is so large, heavy, and solid that there is no need to attach it to the floor. This is especially true of wide and low decks that have no tendency to tip over. When the footprint of the platform is small, and the height is substantial, it is best to lag bolt the bottoms of the frames to the floor. A ⅜″ × 4″ lag bolt is a good size. Drill ½″ holes in the steel frames while they are still in the shop.

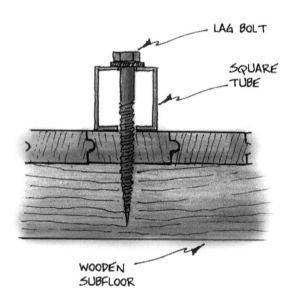

MAKE SURE THAT THE BOLTS
GO FAR ENOUGH INTO THE FLOOR

A ¼″ pilot hole into the wooden floor will make it easier to screw in the bolt. This method may be used to secure spot towers, lighting towers, and other such metal frames. Use lag bolts of a proper size, and be sure that the flooring is solid enough to hold the threads of the lag bolts.

The kind of steel framing discussed so far can be dismantled and stacked against the wall when not in use.

It is very easy to move about (except for the weight) and can be fitted into a truck without using up too much space. The flat nature of all of the pieces makes them easy to assemble with the types of jigs already discussed. Sometimes though, it is preferable to put the frames together into cubes. This method will avoid the doubling of vertical support elements in the corner of an assembled frame and hence will require less material. It also creates an airier, more open look if the framing is to be visible to the audience. This approach is at its best when the size of the decking piece involved is small and won't need to be disassembled.

Begin by constructing two side frames in the normal manner. These frames will be connected directly by

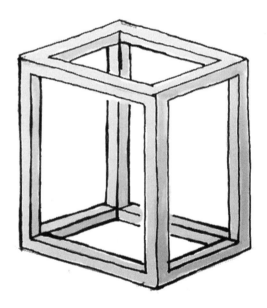

MAKING ONE SOLID PIECE
HAS A NEATER APPEARANCE,
BUT IT IS MUCH MORE
DIFFICULT TO CONSTRUCT

horizontals rather than by using additional frames. You don't need a 2×4 framed platform to finish off the top. Tech screw ¾″ plywood to the top instead.

It is best to *tack weld* this sort of work and get all of the parts in position before completing the welding. Double check for squareness, because heat distortion is a problem and might warp the entire structure out of alignment. When a piece of tubing is welded on one side, it tends to draw up toward that side as it cools. Tacking the parts together first, and making sure that they are firmly braced during welding, will avoid the negative consequences of that effect.

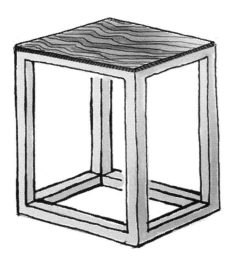

YOU CAN MAKE THE TOP WITH JUST A LAYER OF 3/4″ PLYWOOD. IT DOESN'T NEED TO BE FRAMED WITH 2X4S, BECAUSE THE UNIT NEVER COMES APART.

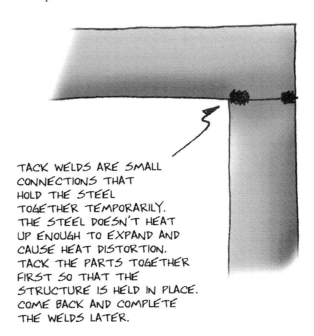

TACK WELDS ARE SMALL CONNECTIONS THAT HOLD THE STEEL TOGETHER TEMPORARILY. THE STEEL DOESN'T HEAT UP ENOUGH TO EXPAND AND CAUSE HEAT DISTORTION. TACK THE PARTS TOGETHER FIRST SO THAT THE STRUCTURE IS HELD IN PLACE. COME BACK AND COMPLETE THE WELDS LATER.

The concept is simple, but the execution is somewhat more complicated. The problem lies in arranging all the parts so that they are square to one another in a three-dimensional rather than two-dimensional setting. Arranging two dimensions on the jig is easy, but working in three dimensions requires some new techniques.

Use an unattached frame to hold the upright section in place and vertical. As shown in the diagram, the frames are easy to clamp to one another, and if all has gone well they should be a perfect right angle.

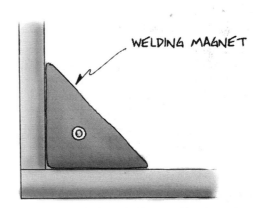

WELDING MAGNET

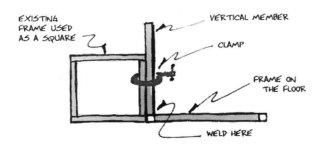

EXISTING FRAME USED AS A SQUARE
VERTICAL MEMBER
CLAMP
FRAME ON THE FLOOR
WELD HERE

TACK WELD EVERYTHING FIRST. THIS ALLOWS FOR SOME ADJUSTING AND REDUCES THE EFFECTS OF HEAT DISTORTION.

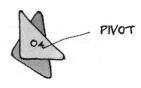

MAGNETS ON ALL THREE SIDES

PIVOT

SPIN TO ADJUST TO DIFFERENT ANGLES

Welding supply shops carry *magnetic squares* that work in the same way as the larger squaring up frames. They are much easier to put on, but their small size can be a drawback. Use whichever method seems the best at the time.

HEIGHT ADJUSTMENTS

Not all stage floors are exactly level. Sometimes bumps are left over from old paint, tape, or uneven boards. Consider adding small wooden or plastic feet to the bottoms of the carriers at regular intervals.

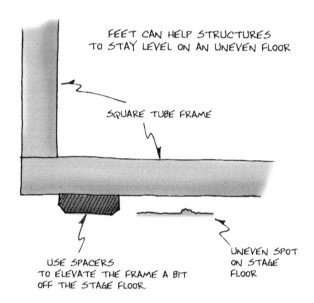

FEET CAN HELP STRUCTURES
TO STAY LEVEL ON AN UNEVEN FLOOR

SQUARE TUBE FRAME

UNEVEN SPOT
ON STAGE
FLOOR

USE SPACERS
TO ELEVATE THE FRAME A BIT
OFF THE STAGE FLOOR.

Sometimes you may need to ensure that a structure can be exactly leveled out over a slightly uneven surface and the best way to do that is to use *leveling feet*. There are several different kinds, but be sure to use heavy-duty ones with at least a ⅜″ bolt on them.

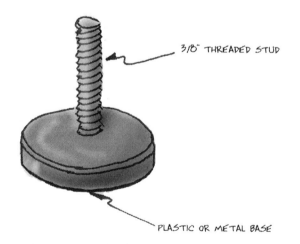

3/8" THREADED STUD

PLASTIC OR METAL BASE

LEVELING HARDWARE WITH THREADED STUD

There are several ways of tapping threads for the bolt, and the simplest is to drill an appropriate size hole, and then ream out threads with a tap.

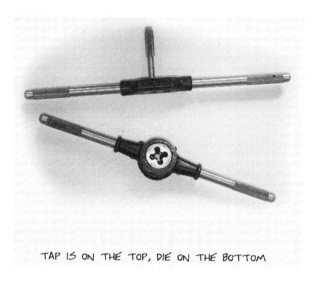

TAP IS ON THE TOP, DIE ON THE BOTTOM

Taps and *dies* are designed to thread all sorts of things. Dies are used to put male threads on a shaft, while taps are used to install female threads inside a hole. The problem with tapping this tubing is that the 16 gauge metal isn't thick enough to produce more than one thread, and the leveler will soon work itself loose. Try welding on a thicker metal plate for more grip.

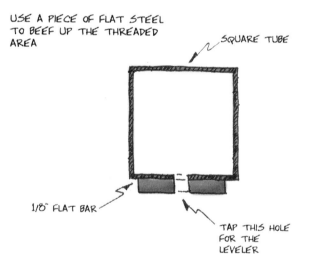

USE A PIECE OF FLAT STEEL
TO BEEF UP THE THREADED
AREA

SQUARE TUBE

1/8" FLAT BAR

TAP THIS HOLE
FOR THE
LEVELER

Another approach is to weld a nut to the bottom of the frame. This variation isn't as craftsman-like, but it gets the job done.

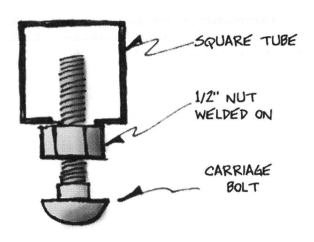

SQUARE TUBE

1/2" NUT WELDED ON

CARRIAGE BOLT

CUTTING STEEP ANGLES

A chop saw won't cut an angle steeper than 45 degrees. You may occasionally find the need to do so, especially if constructing a metal L-jack brace.

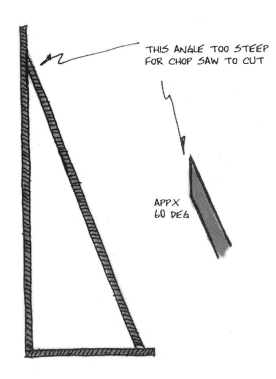

THIS ANGLE TOO STEEP FOR CHOP SAW TO CUT

APPX 60 DEG

FIND ANOTHER WAY TO CUT ACUTE ANGLES

The stile and rail end in right angle cuts, but the rack brace is different. The bottom angle where it intersects the rail is less than 45 degrees, but the top angle is more like 75 degrees. The exact amount isn't so important because you can mark the angle directly on the steel with a straightedge. But you can't cut it on a chop saw. Use a grinder with a cut off wheel to do the actual cutting.

The *cut off wheel* is essentially a very thin grinding wheel meant to cut through the steel rather than to smooth it out. Its thinness produces less of a kerf, and allows the wheel to move through the metal more easily. Hold it at a right angle to the work when you are cutting. After a bit of experience you will notice that there is a tendency for the wheel to get caught in the steel while you are cutting, and that sometimes it may shatter

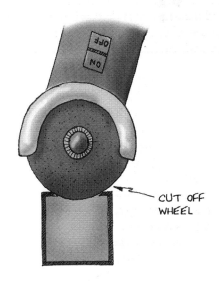

CUT OFF WHEEL

DON'T GO TOO DEEP WITH THE CUTTING WHEEL, OR IT WILL BIND IN THE STEEL because it is so thin. You can avoid this problem to some extent by marking the steel all the way round, and not penetrating the tubing by more than a small amount. This method of cutting requires some practice. Be sure to wear protective gear.

CASTERS ON STEEL FRAMING

Casters can be attached to steel framing in several ways. The first is to use a *stemmed caster* that has a bolt sticking out the top. Stemmed casters are different from the normal type that has a metal plate with mounting holes. You can drill a hole through the steel itself, insert the stem of the caster through it, and then use a locking nut or a regular nut with a lock washer to hold it in place. This method is very easy, but the stemmed casters are less available than the plated kind. They are only available in the swivel type.

Another method of attaching casters is to weld on a mounting plate that matches the mounting plate on the caster itself. Drill holes in the shop-built plate that match the ones in the caster.

Either of these two methods results in a very solid attachment. You can also weld the caster plate to the metal tubing, but then the caster can't be easily removed.

BENDING METAL TUBING

A *tube bending machine* consists of three wheels, two of them stationary, and a third drive wheel that can be moved toward them in small increments. The drive wheel is put into motion with a crank. It is used to force the tubing through the machine.

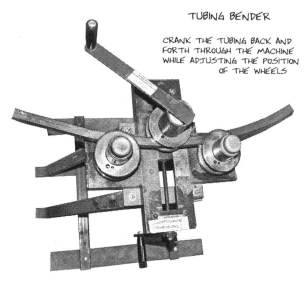

TUBING BENDER

CRANK THE TUBING BACK AND FORTH THROUGH THE MACHINE WHILE ADJUSTING THE POSITION OF THE WHEELS

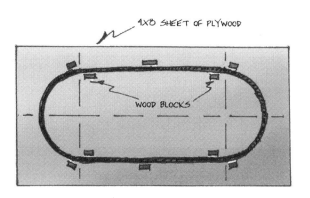

4X8 SHEET OF PLYWOOD

WOOD BLOCKS

DRAW OUT A FULL-SCALE PATTERN ON A SHEET OF PLYWOOD AND CURVE THE PIECES TO MATCH IT. LATER ON YOU CAN USE THE SAME PATTERN AS A JIG TO HOLD THE PARTS TOGETHER

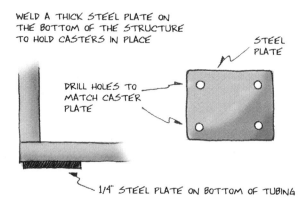

WELD A THICK STEEL PLATE ON THE BOTTOM OF THE STRUCTURE TO HOLD CASTERS IN PLACE

STEEL PLATE

DRILL HOLES TO MATCH CASTER PLATE

1/4" STEEL PLATE ON BOTTOM OF TUBING

The drive wheel is cranked toward the two stationary wheels in very small amounts via a screw thread. Turning the bolt forces the wheels toward each other. Each time that happens the tubing is forced to curve just a bit more in order to fit between the wheels when you crank it through. It is best to do this slowly, and to make many passes back and forth rather than to hurry, because that places too much strain on both the equipment and the tubing.

A full-scale pattern can be used to judge when the curve is correct. You should keep track of how many turns you've made on the bolt that brings the wheels together so that multiple copies can be made using the same formula. If you need several arcs all with the same radius, try making a longer piece of the curve and then cutting it into sections.

outdoor set-ups, where the terrain is apt to be extremely variable. They are created by using two differently sized pieces of square tubing that nest inside one another. They can be adjusted by extending or collapsing the interior section in proportion to the exterior one. Holes along the side make it possible to insert a pin to lock the members into position. An outer leg of 1½" tubing is approximately 1⅜" on the inside, so that a 1¼" tubing leg can easily slide in and out.

Since the legs are meant to be used as a group, it is important to standardize construction so that all pieces are identical and interchangeable. The parts are easily cut to the same length, but the holes must also be identical. To do this, a jig is required.

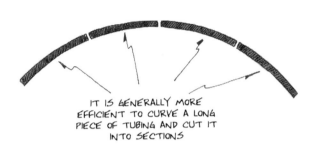

IT IS GENERALLY MORE EFFICIENT TO CURVE A LONG PIECE OF TUBING AND CUT IT INTO SECTIONS

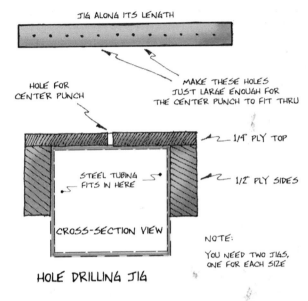

JIG ALONG ITS LENGTH

MAKE THESE HOLES JUST LARGE ENOUGH FOR THE CENTER PUNCH TO FIT THRU

HOLE FOR CENTER PUNCH

1/4" PLY TOP

STEEL TUBING FITS IN HERE

1/2" PLY SIDES

CROSS-SECTION VIEW

NOTE: YOU NEED TWO JIGS, ONE FOR EACH SIZE

HOLE DRILLING JIG

EXTENSION LEGS

Extension legs are used to adjust the height of decking or some other unit, when the amount of difference between one leg and another is very great. They are excellent for

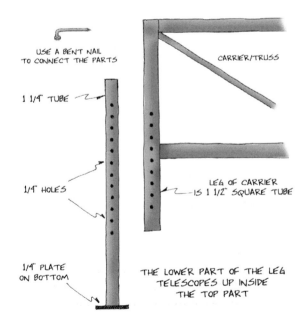

USE A BENT NAIL TO CONNECT THE PARTS

CARRIER/TRUSS

1 1/4" TUBE

1/4" HOLES

LEG OF CARRIER IS 1 1/2" SQUARE TUBE

1/4" PLATE ON BOTTOM

THE LOWER PART OF THE LEG TELESCOPES UP INSIDE THE TOP PART

A JIG LIKE THIS MAKES CUTTING ON THE DRILL PRESS MUCH EASIER

The holes are placed on 1 inch centers, which is close enough to allow for small adjustments, but not so close as to require excessive drilling to create them. Notice that one of the jigs is meant to fit snuggly on the 1½″ and the other on the 1¼″ tubing. The holes in the jig are just large enough for a *center punch* to fit through. A center punch is used to make a small dent in metal so that a drill bit naturally goes to the center of it. Punch both sides of the leg rather than drilling all the way through it, this will increase precision and all burrs will be to the inside of the tubing.

Make a square plate from ~³⁄₁₆″ steel and weld it to the bottom of the smaller extension leg. That will prevent it from sinking into the dirt. When setting up the decking, a collection of ½ and ¾ inch plywood blocks can be used as shims to spread the load even more, and adjust the height of individual legs to plus or minus ¼ inch.

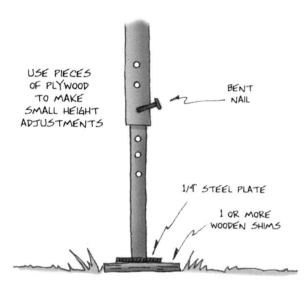

USE PIECES OF PLYWOOD TO MAKE SMALL HEIGHT ADJUSTMENTS

BENT NAIL

1/4″ STEEL PLATE

1 OR MORE WOODEN SHIMS

How Trusses Work

A *truss* is a structural member that is specially designed to be both strong and lightweight at the same time. It is strong because it is made up of many small triangles, and it is lightweight because the interior is composed mostly of open space. Thin steel or wooden members are used to create the triangles. The connection points are called *nodes*.

Triangles are very strong geometric shapes because it isn't possible to deform them without bending one of the members, or destroying a node that connects them. This is not true of any other polygon, all of which can be distorted by altering the connection angle of a node.

Trusses are very *rigid structures*, and are not intended to bend. If a truss deflects over a certain amount, catastrophic failure is imminent. Bending is a sign that

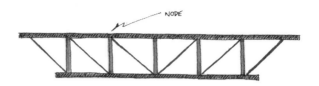

NODE

THIS TYPE OF TRUSS MADE OF WELDED STEEL IS COMMONLY USED TO SUPPORT ROOFS

THE DIAGONALS MAKE TWO TRIANGLES OUT OF ONE SQUARE

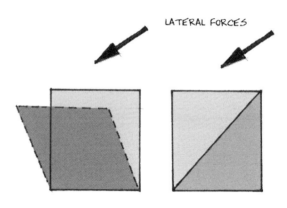

LATERAL FORCES

A SQUARE CAN BE DEFORMED INTO A PARALLELOGRAM WHEN LATERAL FORCES ACT ON IT. THE SIDES OF THE SQUARE ROTATE AROUND THE NODES. THAT ISN'T POSSIBLE FOR A TRIANGLE UNLESS ONE OF THE SIDES IS BENT.

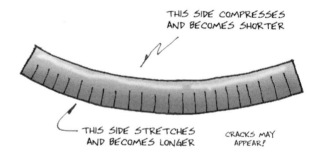

THIS SIDE COMPRESSES AND BECOMES SHORTER

THIS SIDE STRETCHES AND BECOMES LONGER

CRACKS MAY APPEAR!

HOW MATERIALS BEND

THINNER MEMBERS BEND MORE UNDER THE SAME AMOUNT OF FORCE

either the nodes or the connecting members have been loaded past capacity. That is generally not reversible. On the other hand, a single piece of steel tubing can flex to a curved shape and then return somewhat to its original linear shape.

The closer the top and bottom are to one another, the easier it is for a member to bend, because the top and bottom don't need to compress and stretch as much. Thinner members bend more easily than thicker ones, which is a fairly intuitive concept. The top to bottom measurement is known as the chord, and trusses have very large ones.

A truss creates a rigid structure that is lightweight, yet able to support large loads by separating the top and bottom beams. Greater separation means that the top and bottom must stretch/compress more than they are able to do. The most common type of truss is created by top and bottom beams connected with verticals, where diagonals are used to stiffen the structure by dividing it into triangles.

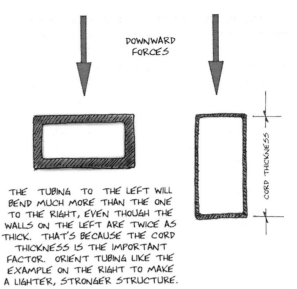

DOWNWARD FORCES

CORD THICKNESS

THE TUBING TO THE LEFT WILL BEND MUCH MORE THAN THE ONE TO THE RIGHT, EVEN THOUGH THE WALLS ON THE LEFT ARE TWICE AS THICK. THAT'S BECAUSE THE CORD THICKNESS IS THE IMPORTANT FACTOR. ORIENT TUBING LIKE THE EXAMPLE ON THE RIGHT TO MAKE A LIGHTER, STRONGER STRUCTURE.

TERMS USED IN THIS CHAPTER

angle grinder	flat bar	oxyacetylene
angle iron	flux	puddled weld seam
arc welder	frame	rectangular tubing
argon/CO_2 mix	gas flow regulator	round tubing
black steel pipe	gauge system for steel tubing	Schedule 40 black steel pipe
burr	ground for welder	shim
center punch	heat control knob	slag
channel steel	heat distortion	square tube
chop saw	inert gas	stemmed caster
cut off blade (metalworking)	Inside Diameter (ID)	tack weld
cut off wheel	leveling feet	tap
die	magnetic square	truss
electrode	metal cutting band saw	tube bending machine
extension leg	Metal Inert Gas (MIG)	weld penetration
face weld	node on a truss	welding jig
feed rate	nominal pipe size	wire speed knob
file	nozzle	wire welder
fillet weld	outside diameter (OD)	

STAGE LIGHTING

ELECTRICAL THEORY

*T*HOMAS EDISON AND *Nikola Tesla* were engineers who led the way in developing electrical power at the end of the nineteenth and beginning of the twentieth centuries. Actually though, Edison was more of an inventor who was primarily interested in practical devices. Tesla studied electrical engineering at a prestigious Austrian school where he learned the mathematics of electrical theory. Eventually the decidedly quirky Tesla immigrated to the US and worked at Edison's think tank in Menlo Park, New Jersey. The men soon had a falling out, probably because Tesla's mathematical background helped him understand the

THOMAS EDISON AND HIS ORIGINAL "DYNAMO"

importance of alternating current in efficient power transmission. Edison was convinced that DC power was better, and when Tesla joined forces with George Westinghouse, the newspapers called it the "War of the Currents." Although Edison was a brilliant inventor, he was wrong about the AC/DC controversy and lost the war.

ATOMIC THEORY, DEFINITIONS OF TERMS, AND UNITS OF MEASUREMENT

In 1911, a theory of atomic structure was developed that described an atom as having a central positive nucleus surrounded by orbiting negative *electrons*.

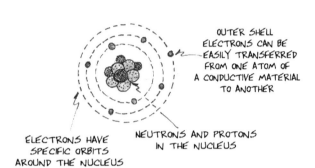

OUTER SHELL ELECTRONS CAN BE EASILY TRANSFERRED FROM ONE ATOM OF A CONDUCTIVE MATERIAL TO ANOTHER

ELECTRONS HAVE SPECIFIC ORBITS AROUND THE NUCLEUS

NEUTRONS AND PROTONS IN THE NUCLEUS

LIGHTNING

ATOMS MOVING PAST EACH OTHER IN CLOUDS FORM A NEGATIVE CHARGE WHICH JUMPS TO THE POSITIVELY CHARGED EARTH. LIGHTNING HAS A HUGE VOLTAGE PRESSURE, MUCH LARGER THAN ANYTHING MAN-MADE. IT NEEDS A LARGE AMOUNT OF PRESSURE TO JUMP SO FAR ACROSS AN OPEN GAP WITH NO CONDUCTOR.

BATTERY

CHEMICALS IN A BATTERY REACT WITH ONE ANOTHER CAUSING ELECTRONS TO GATHER AT THE NEGATIVE TERMINAL -, BY DRAWING THEM FROM THE POSITIVE TERMINAL, +. WHEN THE TWO TERMINALS ARE CONNECTED BY A CONDUCTIVE MATERIAL, THE ELECTRONS MIGRATE FROM - TO +.

INDUCTION

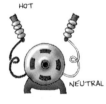

A COIL OF WIRE SPUN IN THE PRESENCE OF A MAGNETIC FIELD CREATES A VOLTAGE PRESSURE, BUT RATHER THAN FLOWING IN ONE DIRECTION LIKE LIGHTNING OR A BATTERY, THE ELECTRONS EBB AND FLOW ON A SCHEDULE DETERMINED BY THE SPEED OF THE GENERATOR.

A further development of this idea gave the electrons specific orbits around the nucleus in "shells," and can be used to explain how certain elements combine with one another to make compounds. Although more complex atomic theories have been developed since then, Rutherford's original concept is an excellent model for electrical theory discussions, and can be used to explain how electrons work in producing electricity.

Electricity is formed when electrons are pushed from one atom to another. This can happen in a number of different ways; statically like lightning; chemically like a battery; or by a generator using the process of induction.

Lightning strikes the earth when large numbers of electrons gather on the bottom of rain clouds and are attracted to atoms in the earth which are missing electrons and are thus positively charged. As the number of electrons increases, so too does the pressure they are under. When the pressure becomes great enough, the electrons make a giant spark as they dramatically jump through the air. The farther the distance, the greater the pressure required to jump across the open gap. Lightning

strikes are measured in billions of volts, which is much higher than earthbound electrical circuits. When electricity is used for practical purposes, electrons move through a discrete substance called a *conductor*. That material conducts, or moves electrons from one place to another.

All metals conduct electricity, some better than others, and they are often used to form conductors. Although copper is the metal of choice for most electrical wiring in a building, high-voltage power lines are generally made from aluminum because it costs less and isn't as heavy. Brass and steel are also commonly used for electrical devices, but not for wiring because they are too rigid and inflexible.

Some elements and/or compounds are extremely poor conductors. They are called *insulators*, and are critical to the practical use of electricity. If every element conducted electrons there would be no way to contain or control electricity. Rubber, plastic, glass, ceramic, and air are frequently used insulators.

The name given to the force that makes electrons move is EMF or *Electro Motive Force*. The amount of the force applied is measured in *volts*.

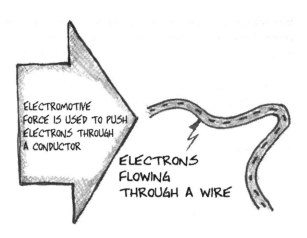

ELECTROMOTIVE FORCE
(EMF)
IS MEASURED IN VOLTS

E   is the symbol used for mathematical computations using volts. (from EMF)

v   is the symbol used to express an amount of voltage.

Example: E = 12v.

Where does the force to move electrons come from? The static electricity formed by a thunder and lightning storm is a very visible example, but lightning is not useful in a practical sense, indeed it is something to be avoided. The *battery* is a much more stable and controllable source of electromotive force. The type shown in the illustration is often called a *wet cell* storage battery and is the kind used in a car. (At least a car that runs on fossil fuels!) Two dissimilar metals are suspended in an electrolytic solution like sulphuric acid. Technically speaking, a battery is

CERAMIC INSULATORS ARE USED FOR
HIGH-VOLTAGE LINES. THE HIGHER THE VOLTAGE,
THE LARGER THE INSULATOR.

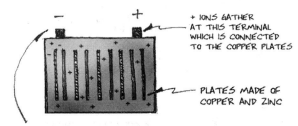

"WET CELL" BATTERIES ARE OFTEN FOUND
IN CARS OR BOATS (OR STAGE LIFTS)

actually a number of *cells* linked together to form one, larger power source. Each plate in a storage battery is a cell. A number of cells make up a battery, or group of them.

When placed in series with one another, a group of cells produces a higher voltage, because the separate voltages are added together to get a total. The D cell batteries pictured here work in the same manner as the wet cell battery, but the electrolytic solution has been made into a highly viscous gel so that it stays put even when the battery is turned upside down.

BATTERY CELLS IN SERIES

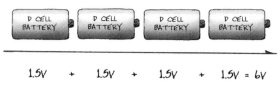

4 D CELL BATTERIES IN SERIES
ADD UP TO 6 VOLTS OF TOTAL PRESSURE

A chemical reaction occurs between the two metals in the battery, using the fluid they are suspended in as a catalyst. The fluid provides ions that move electrons between the metallic plates. In the case of a wet cell car battery, lead and copper are frequently used, but other types of batteries use other metals. Rechargeable tool batteries may use nickel and cadmium suspended in a gel. Acids create a high number of ions and are often used as the catalyst, so take care in working with them. Wet cells are often used as a power source for stage lifts, and if you turn that sort of battery upside down, there is almost sure to be at least some leakage.

Batteries produce a type of current known as *DC* or *direct current*. They create an electromotive force that pushes electrons away from the negative terminal, which

is a gathering point for all of the negatively charged ions. In a DC circuit, the electrons flow in only one direction, from the negative terminal to the positive one.

This graph shows the voltage pressure, E, from a 12 volt car battery over a period of 5 minutes. The x axis represents time, and the y axis the pressure of the voltage as supplied by the battery. The origin, or intersection of the two axes, is the zero starting time. The graph is a straight and horizontal line, because the pressure of the voltage does not change during the 5 minute interval. Battery graphs do go down over time as the battery wears out, but this wouldn't happen in so short a time as 5 minutes.

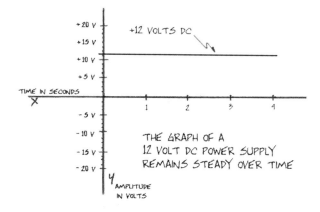

Quadrants II and III are not generally used in electronics graphs, because they fall before time begins at the origin. Quadrant I is used to indicate a positive voltage pressure, and Quadrant IV a negative voltage pressure. DC currents are generally depicted as positive, because the voltage pressure is pushing the electrons forward.

The electrons in direct current flow in only one direction, but *alternating current* or AC is different. AC is produced by a generator, using the principle of induction, and that process will be covered in detail later on. Alternating is a good word to describe this type of current, because it alternates between flowing forward, a positive voltage pressure, and backward, a negative voltage pressure. The graph of an AC voltage looks like this:

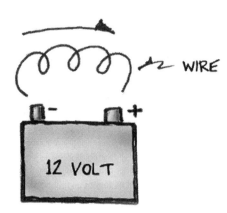

ELECTRONS FLOW FROM
NEGATIVE TO POSITIVE

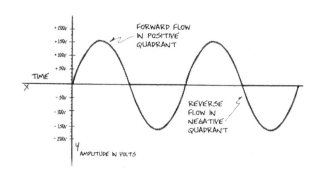

AC CURRENT OVER TWO TIME INTERVALS

The electrons flow forward during the first time interval, and backward during the second time interval. The forward flow is positive, and the backward flow is negative. AC is often said to be pushing and pulling the electrons. The curious shape of this curve is known as a *sine wave*, and is a function of how the electrons are induced to flow in the generator.

The flow of electrons or *current*, as described here is often compared to water. A river has a certain amount of water flowing in it, a very large but finite number of H_2O molecules. The amount or number of water molecules represents the current, while the pressure of the moving water represents the voltage. Current is measured in *amperes*, or *amps*.

I   is the symbol used for mathematical computations using amps.

A   is the symbol used to express an amount of current in amps.

Example: I = 20A.

Technically, 1 ampere is defined as 6×10^{18} electrons moving past a given point in one second. That's not very useful information in and of itself, but does demonstrate how a measurement in amperes denotes an actual amount or number of electrons. The mathematical relationship between volts and amps is very important.

IMPORTANT

Remember that amps refer to an amount or number of electrons flowing, whereas volts are used to measure the pressure of that flow.

AMPERES = AN AMOUNT OF CURRENT

VOLTS = THE PRESSURE USED TO PUSH THEM

Electrical *circuits* are created when current flows through wires and other devices that form a completed pathway. *Schematic* drawings are used to show the electrical connections between various electronic components. Lines represent conductors. Other components are represented by graphic symbols.

In this circuit, closing the switch causes the bulbs to glow. The brightness of the bulb is a function of the voltage pressure applied to the filament. Increasing the pressure of the voltage makes a bulb brighter. Notice that these bulbs are not connected one after the other, in series, like the cells of a battery. Instead, they are connected

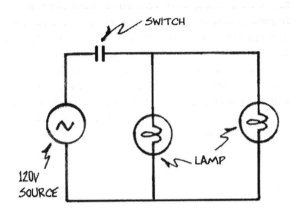

SCHEMATIC FOR A CIRCUIT WITH A SWITCH AND TWO LIGHTBULBS

across two parallel lines. It is an example of a *parallel circuit*. In a parallel circuit, each resistance (in our case light bulb) has its own path back to the power source.

Resistance is defined as the opposition to current flow. Resistance comes from a number of sources; devices like light bulbs or clocks, but also the wires used to connect them. Even good conductors resist the flow of electrons to some degree, and a longer conductor creates more resistance than a shorter one. At the opposite end of the spectrum, insulators conduct electrons so poorly that they are generally regarded as not conducting at all, so in a practical sense they have infinite resistance.

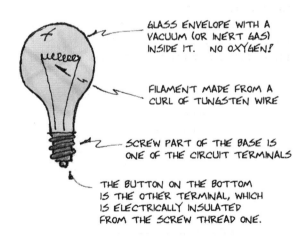

GLASS ENVELOPE WITH A VACUUM (OR INERT GAS) INSIDE IT.   NO OXYGEN!

FILAMENT MADE FROM A CURL OF TUNGSTEN WIRE

SCREW PART OF THE BASE IS ONE OF THE CIRCUIT TERMINALS

THE BUTTON ON THE BOTTOM IS THE OTHER TERMINAL, WHICH IS ELECTRICALLY INSULATED FROM THE SCREW THREAD ONE.

PARTS OF A LIGHTBULB

The tiny tungsten *filament* in the light bulb resists the flow of electricity, and in the process of doing that, changes some of the electrical energy into heat energy.

If the voltage pressure is high enough and the wire gets hot enough, it will incandesce, or glow. The nichrome wire inside a toaster-oven turns a bright red when heated to its maximum value in the same way. Nichrome wire is specially designed to resist oxidizing in the atmosphere, but a light bulb is different. An inert gas in the glass envelope keeps the tungsten filament from burning up through oxidation. The curl in the filament creates a longer filament, and produces more light in a smaller bulb.

The amount of resistance to electron flow in the wire filament is measured in *ohms* using the uppercase omega, Ω, as a symbol.

R is the symbol used for mathematical computations using resistance.

Ω is the symbol used to express an amount of resistance.

Example: R = 150 Ω.

SYMBOLS TO REMEMBER

E = EMF . . . measured in . . . Volts (v)

I = Current . . . measured in . . . Amps (A)

R = Resistance . . . measured in . . . Ohms (Ω)

One additional unit of measurement is watts, which is used to quantify an amount of *power*. Power describes how much work is being done. Light bulbs do work when they produce light. Toasters do work when they get hot, as well as when they make toast. Other power measurements are things like horsepower, decibels, and BTUs.

P is the symbol used for mathematical computations using power.

W is the symbol used to express an amount of power in watts.

Example: P = 100W.

OHM'S LAWS AND THEIR EFFECT ON CIRCUITS

Georg Ohm was a German physicist and electrical experimenter back in the 1800s. He discovered a series of formulas that define the mathematical relationship between amperage, voltage, resistance, and watts. His work and primary research led to an understanding of the basic laws of how electricity behaves, and the formulas that connect these four units of measurement are named in his honor, as well as the unit of measurement for resistance itself, the ohm (Ω).

The first of Ohm's laws states this mathematical formula:

Voltage is equal to resistance
multiplied by the current flow, or
E = IR

As with any algebraic formula, it is possible to rearrange the terms in order to solve the equation for a specific unit of measurement. Two algebraic equivalents of the formula would be:

I = E/R

R = E/I

A very handy *magic triangle* is available that makes it easy to remember the different permutations of this formula.

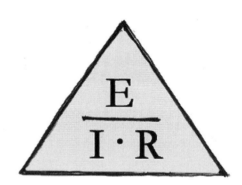

Cover the value to be determined with your finger, and the relationship of the other two is revealed in their proper algebraic form. Example: you need to know the amount of current flowing in a circuit with 100Ω of resistance and 120 volts of pressure. Cover I, the symbol for current, and the remaining two symbols, E and R, appear in their correct relationship E/R. The answer would be 120/100 or 1.2 amps. Whenever you solve any equation using Ohm's law, be sure to write the unit of measurement after your answer so that your answer is defined by that unit of measurement. Otherwise it is just a meaningless number.

A second formula includes the measurement for power. Ohm's power formula states that:

Power is equal to the current flow
multiplied by the voltage pressure, or
P = IE

Another magic triangle is available for this formula, which for obvious reasons is often called the "pie" formula. Stage electricians generally find the pie formula to be the most useful one, because it helps determine how many lights can be powered from a known amount of current.

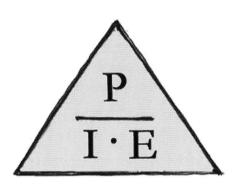

RESISTANCE IN SERIES

One of Ohm's laws states that when resistances are arranged in *series* one after the other, the total amount of resistance in the circuit is equal to the sum of the various resistances. Furthermore, that the voltage applied to the circuit is shared between the different resistances in proportion to their size. Current remains constant, since the same number of electrons flow through every point along the path. This concept has some very important implications so far as dimmers are concerned, especially the early kinds.

A practical example: ACL (*Air Craft Landing*) lights are sometimes used for special effects lighting on stage because they put out a tightly focused shaft of light. These lamps were designed to help airplanes land at night, and are mounted on the aircraft like a headlight. Planes use a voltage of 28v, rather than the earthbound 120v. If ACLs were simply plugged into a standard wall voltage of 120v, the filaments would burn out immediately because the voltage pressure would be far too much for them to handle. A special power supply could be constructed, but there is an easier way to solve the over-voltage problem and get the lamps to work from a regular wall outlet.

Ohm's law can be used to demonstrate a way to divide up the regular line voltage by using a series circuit created by placing four of the lamps in a row. However it should be noted that if one of the lamps burns out, all

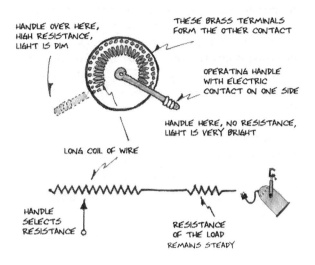

BECAUSE THE RESISTANCE OF THE DIMMER AND LIGHT ARE IN SERIES WITH ONE ANOTHER, ADDING RESISTANCE AT THE DIMMER DECREASES VOLTAGE AT THE LIGHT.

of them will go dark because the conductive pathway will be disconnected, or open. A circuit that has been disconnected in this way is called an *open circuit* and is an indicator that the circuit is not working. The total voltage, 120v, is shared equally between the lamps so that each one receives 1/4 of the total, or ~30v. The voltage pressure does not have to be exact, and this amount will work okay.

Another example of resistance in series is one that can occur at any time in a scene shop. If you use several power cords plugged together to reach a motorized power tool, you might find that the motor has trouble running properly. It might make a buzzing noise and not start at

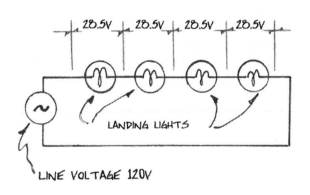

28.5V × 4 = 114V
WHICH IS ACTUALLY CLOSE ENOUGH

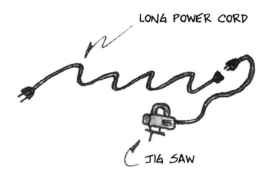

LONG POWER CORD

JIG SAW

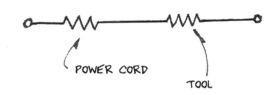

POWER CORD

TOOL

**POWER CORD AND TOOL
AS VOLTAGE DIVIDER**

all. That is because the resistance of the electric motor on the tool is in series with the resistance present in the power cord itself, and a *voltage divider* has been created. That means that the voltage has been divided between two parts of a circuit, in our case between the long power cords, and the power tool.

All wires have a certain resistance to the flow of electrons. A thick diameter conductor has less resistance, per foot, than a thin one. Also, a shorter cable has less resistance than a longer one of the same diameter because there are fewer feet of it creating resistance. A long power cord, especially a small gauge one, could provide quite a bit of resistance to current flow. The resistance in the cord will split the voltage between the tool and itself. AC electric motors are designed to operate at the full line voltage, and using them with a lower voltage will eventually burn out the windings. You can avoid trouble with the tool motor by using a larger gauge cable that is as short as possible. You should never operate an AC motor with a stage dimmer because dimmers work by lowering voltages, which would of course be destructive.

RULES FOR SERIES CIRCUITS

Add together the individual resistances to find the total resistance for the circuit.

The current flow is the same in every part of the circuit.

The voltages across each of the resistances add up to the total voltage for the circuit.

THE JABLOKOV CANDLE

The first public lighting systems were begun in the 1860s, before the invention of a practical incandescent lamp. These outdoor street lights were often of the *Jablokov* type, an arc lamp made by placing two carbon rods next to each other, with an insulator between them. Contact was made at the tips of the rods, and an electrical arc began. Electrical arcing is extremely bright and produces a very strong light, as any welder can tell you. The insulation between the rods burned down at the same rate as the rods themselves, and the lamp would stay lit as long as the rods lasted.

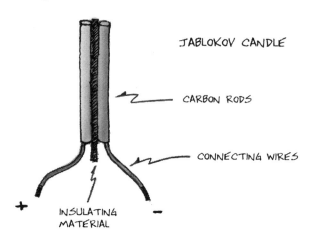

JABLOKOV CANDLE

CARBON RODS

CONNECTING WIRES

INSULATING
MATERIAL

THE INSULATING MATERIAL SEPARATED THE TWO CARBON RODS, BUT AN ARC JUMPED ACROSS THE ENDS, CREATING A LIGHT SOURCE. THIS CONCEPT WAS AN EARLY VERSION OF WHAT BECAME CARBON ARC FOLLOWSPOTS. THE INSULATOR BURNED UP WITH THE RODS, WHICH NEEDED FREQUENT REPLACEMENT.

At the time, the complexities of Ohm's Laws were not universally understood. Arc lamps generally require a DC current. DC currents are difficult to regulate when long wires are used because the voltage pressure can't be controlled by a transformer, like with AC current. Jablokov candles farther away from the power source tended to get a lower voltage because of a voltage divider set up with the resistance in the lamp itself in series with the wiring. As a result, some of them burned faster than others, or did not want to start at all. The late 1800s saw a "war of the currents" to decide whether DC or AC would be the standardized choice. AC won out, but not without a struggle.

PARALLEL CIRCUITS

We've been looking at series circuits, where devices are connected together one after another along a conductor, but these are actually quite rare. Parallel circuits are the norm in stage lighting systems, as they are elsewhere.

They allow a number of different devices to be connected to the circuit, all of them using different amounts of power/watts, but all at the same voltage pressure. In addition, loads can be removed from the system without causing it to go open circuit. Most electrical devices in the US, Mexico, and Canada are constructed to operate on 120v, the standard line voltage from a wall receptacle. Here are several schematics showing the same parallel circuit, but with the wires placed differently.

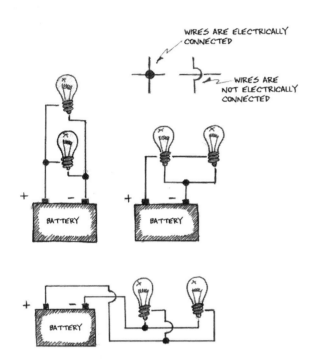

VARIATIONS ON PARALLEL CIRCUITS

In this example, each lamp has its own discrete path to the voltage source, and if one of the pathways is opened, the others will still operate. In a parallel circuit, the voltage pressure in each part of the circuit remains constant, but the current varies in proportion to how many loads are fed by the conductor that feeds that part of the circuit. This is the opposite of the way a series circuit operates.

RULES FOR PARALLEL CIRCUITS

The reciprocals of all the individual resistances added together are equal to the reciprocal of the total resistance.

The voltage is the same everywhere.

The current draws in the individual branches of the circuit add up to the total current draw.

Although the wiring running between the lights is arranged differently, all of the lamps in the drawing have the same electrical connection to the same voltage. No matter how convoluted the wiring in a lighting system may appear to be, all of the circuits involved are still in parallel, and all of the outlets have the same 120v service.

Ohm's rules for parallel circuits are most often used to determine what the total *current draw* will be for an entire network. Remember that the measurement for current is taken in amperes, which is an indication of how many electrons (an amount of them) are moving through the wires. Theatre lighting systems are protected by either fuses or circuit breakers which will disconnect the flow of electricity if too much demand for current is placed on that system. The purpose is to protect the component parts from damage from overloading.

If too many electrons pass through the wiring inside the wall of a house, or through a jumper feeding a stage light, the copper wire will overheat just like the tungsten filament inside a light bulb. The filament is housed inside a glass bulb, and the entire lamp is constructed to cope with such overheating. Wiring is *not* intended to withstand that sort of extreme use, and a fire will result if too great a load is placed on it.

The amount of current draw can be determined by the mathematical relationship between the total power consumed by a circuit in ratio to its voltage pressure. The greater the wattage of lamps in a circuit, the greater the current flow will be.

The pie formula is used to determine current draw when the voltage pressure and wattage are known.

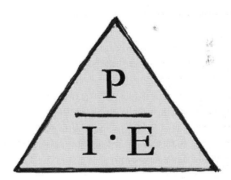

Suppose that the schematic at the top of p. 286 is given, and that the problem is to find the total current draw.

We are seeking the value of the current flow I, and covering that symbol on the magic triangle gives the formula:

I = P/E

First the total power consumed by the circuit must be determined. Add the power used by the various lamps to get the total power for the circuit.

$$P_{TOTAL} = P_1 + P_2 + P_3 \ldots$$

$$P_{TOTAL} = 500 \text{ W} + 1000 \text{ W}$$

$$P_{TOTAL} = 1500 \text{ W}$$

Solving:

$$I = P/E$$

$$I = 1500 \text{ W}/120 \text{ v}$$

$$I = 12.5 \text{ A}$$

PARALLEL CIRCUIT WITH TWO LAMPS

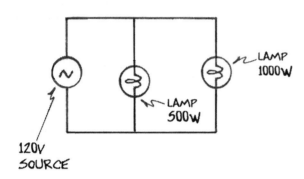

If we were checking to see if these two lamps would be safe for the 20A circuit breaker in a D20 dimmer, the answer would be yes.

Remember that there are two basic types of electric current, *direct* (DC) and *alternating* (AC). These two types are defined by the way each one causes electrons to

DIMMER RATINGS

The most common rating or "size" of modern stage dimmers is 20 amps. Stage lamp ratings are generally given in watts, just like household variety. The permissible wattage on a 20A circuit can be determined via Ohm's law to be:

P = 20 Amps × 120 volts

or 2400 Watts

It is often easiest to remember the 2400W rating, and just add up the wattages of the individual lamps to see if they are more or less than that amount. If your dimmers have a lower or higher current rating, use the same formula to determine the total wattage permissible on them. You can determine the amperage of a breaker by looking on its switch.

500 WATT LIGHTS

500 WATTS   500 WATTS   500 WATTS

ADD THE WATTAGES TOGETHER TO GET A TOTAL AMOUNT

```
     500
   + 500
   + 500
```
TOTAL 1500   WHICH IS LESS THAN 2400.

1000 WATT LIGHTS

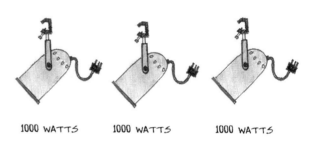

1000 WATTS   1000 WATTS   1000 WATTS

```
    1000
   +1000
   +1000
```
TOTAL 3000   WHICH IS GREATER THAN 2400.

move through a conductor. In direct current (DC) electrons move in one direction only, from a source of surplus electrons known as the negative terminal (–), toward a collection point known as the positive terminal (+). A *terminal* is an ending point for a circuit. You can find the plus and minus signs on any battery next to its terminals.

Incandescent lamps will work equally well with either AC or DC. But batteries are not very useful for lighting work, because the power requirements of the lights are too high. Direct current is not often used for lighting purposes except for very special arc-type lamps that require DC to operate. These are found mostly on followspots or large movie lights, most notably xenon or HMI lamps.

THE TERMINALS OF MOST BATTERIES ARE MARKED WITH PLUS AND MINUS SIGNS THAT STAND FOR POSITIVE AND NEGATIVE

9 VOLT BATTERIES ARE COMMONLY USED IN VOLT- OHM METERS AND IN HOME SMOKE DETECTORS

Any type of ordinary filament bulb will operate with either direct or alternating current with no problem, but electric motors are wired for one or the other. The speed of DC motors can be adjusted by varying the voltage supplied to them; much like varying the voltage will cause a light to vary in brightness. Reversing the polarity of the current will make the motor run backward. DC motors are used for equipment like gobo rotators because their speed and direction are so easily controlled. Alternating current motors will burn out if you try reducing their voltage. AC motor speed can be controlled by altering the frequency of the sine wave, but that is a much different process. Rotators must be connected to a special DC power supply in order to work. They typically use a stepper motor, which can be stopped at specific points in its rotation.

AC Current from Power Generation

Alternating current was long ago adopted as the standard method of producing electrical current. It is easier to transmit long distances and requires smaller and less expensive wires. It is the type of current supplied to most homes and businesses. AC differs from DC in that its electrons move through the conducting wire in two opposite directions following a regularly scheduled pattern. There is a constant ebb and flow from the source of power, with electrons first being forced down the wire and then being pulled back toward the source. The speed at which this change of direction occurs is given in cycles or *Hertz* (Hz). Sixty cycles per second is standard in most of the western hemisphere. A 50 Hz ~230volt system is used in European countries, Australia, and New Zealand.

POWER GRIDS

It is more efficient to connect groups of power stations together in a grid, or network that can operate together to provide power. When one of the generating stations is offline, another can take its place. When demand is extraordinarily high, extra stations can be started to meet the challenge. It wouldn't be generally possible to connect power stations that use a different number of cycles per second. As a result, North America, Central America, and parts of South America all use the same 120volt 60 Hz power generating standard. In the European market, which is also interconnected, the 230volt 50 Hz standard is used. Most modern electronics can operate on either standard by adjusting a switch. The connector plugs are vastly different. The US system uses the Edison plug, but others use the Schuko.

GOBO ROTATOR

THE WIRES ON THE MOTOR ARE MARKED PLUS AND MINUS, WHICH IS AN INDICATOR OF A DC CIRCUIT

IF THE VOLTAGE PRESSURE INCREASES THE MOTOR WILL RUN FASTER. IF THE POLARITY IS REVERSED THE MOTOR WILL RUN BACKWARD.

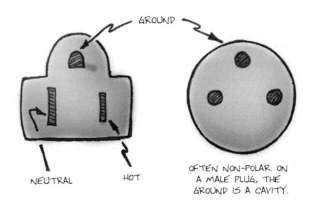

GROUND

NEUTRAL   HOT

OFTEN NON-POLAR. ON A MALE PLUG, THE GROUND IS A CAVITY.

USA EDISON AND EUROPEAN SCHUKO PLUGS

THE GROUND PIN OF THE SCHUKO IS ACTUALLY ON THE WALL. THE PLUG HAS A HOLE IN IT THAT THE GROUND FITS INTO. NOT ALL COUNTRIES USE THE SAME EXACT TYPE.

AC current is produced in a generator by the interaction of coils of wire and a strong magnetic field. The reaction of the electrons contained in a wire to the effects of an outside magnetic force is called *induction*. When a coil of wire moves through a magnetic field, the magnet forces a current to flow through the wire. The magnetic field thus "induces" a current to flow in the wire, but only so long as either the wire or the magnetic field is in motion. The relationship between magnetism and EMF is crucial to the operation of many common electrical devices. In fact, the entire system of power circuits everywhere in the world is dependent on the principles of the magnetic induction of current flow.

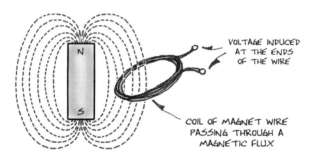

VOLTAGE INDUCED AT THE ENDS OF THE WIRE

COIL OF MAGNET WIRE PASSING THROUGH A MAGNETIC FLUX

The force of the current, or voltage, induced in the wire by the magnetic force is largely dependent on these factors:

1   The strength of the magnetic force.
2   The proximity of the wire and the magnetic force.
3   The angle of movement through the lines of magnetic force.

The first two factors regarding the strength of an induced voltage are fairly intuitive. It makes sense that the effect would be more pronounced with a stronger

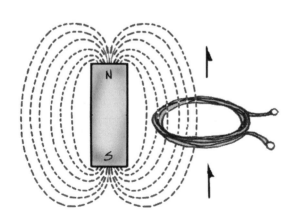

MOVING **ALONG** THE LINES OF FORCE INDUCES **LITTLE**, IF ANY, CURRENT

magnet, and also by being closer to it. We all know that stronger magnets cling together with more force, and that a magnet must be touching the refrigerator in order to stick to it. But the angularity factor is less obvious. As it turns out, more voltage is induced when the wire is passing *across* the lines of magnetic force rather than when the wire is passing *along* the lines of magnetic force.

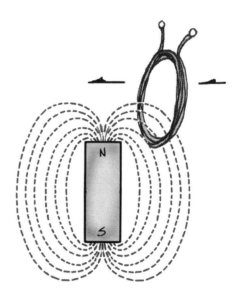

MOVING **THROUGH** THE LINES OF FORCE INDUCES MUCH **MORE** CURRENT

This important factor explains the unique way alternating current is produced in a generator, where an extremely useful fluctuation in the current is created. If either the wire or the magnetic field is spun in a circular fashion, then the direction of travel through the magnetic field changes from across to along as it completes the circle. As a result, the pressure of the voltage induced will rise and fall in a predictable manner.

AC is formed in a generator by using magnetic force and electrical induction to create a voltage in a coil of wire. Generators can be powered by wind, falling water, or steam from coal/gas/nuclear reactor, or any other mechanical means that will rotate the coils of wire.

As the generator rotor spins, its coil of wire passes through different parts of the magnetic field, and the voltage pressure pushing the electrons changes constantly as a result of its angular motion through the field.

Once the coil has rotated 180 degrees, the voltage is pulled in the opposite direction because the wire has, in effect, flipped over. The polarity of the magnetic force is then the mirror image of what it was in the beginning. The net effect is to push electrons through the wire during the positive portion of the rotation, and to pull electrons in the opposite direction during the second half of the rotation.

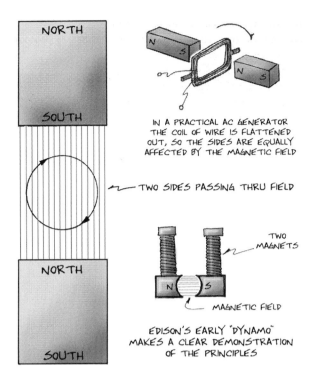

IN A PRACTICAL AC GENERATOR THE COIL OF WIRE IS FLATTENED OUT, SO THE SIDES ARE EQUALLY AFFECTED BY THE MAGNETIC FIELD

TWO SIDES PASSING THRU FIELD

TWO MAGNETS

MAGNETIC FIELD

EDISON'S EARLY "DYNAMO" MAKES A CLEAR DEMONSTRATION OF THE PRINCIPLES

AS THE COIL OF WIRE MAKES A CIRCULAR PATH THRU THE MAGNETIC FIELD, THE ANGLE OF ITS INTERSECTION WITH THE LINES OF MAGNETIC FORCE IS CONSTANTLY CHANGING. THAT ANGLE, AT ANY ONE MOMENT, DETERMINES THE FORCE OF THE EMF/VOLTAGE.

ANGLE DETERMINES STRENGTH OF EMF

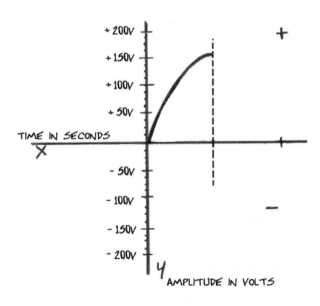

THE POSITIVE PRESSURE OF THE VOLTAGE INCREASES DURING THE FIRST 1/4 TURN OF THE COIL OF WIRE IN THE MAGNETIC FIELD.

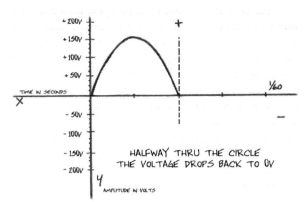

HALFWAY THRU THE CIRCLE THE VOLTAGE DROPS BACK TO 0V

A graph is typically used to display the manner in which alternating current produces a voltage. The x axis represents time in seconds, while the y axis represents the strength of the EMF, given in volts. The graph on p. 290 shows one complete, 360 degree circle through the magnetic field. The shape of this graph is a special type of curve known as a *sine wave*.

A sine curve is a specific shape. You may have noticed that it appears to slope upward most rapidly near the x axis, and that its rate of change slows dramatically near the top of the curve. The slope of the line is a function of the *angle* of the rotation through the lines of magnetic force. It is the ratio of the *angle of the intersection*. So it makes sense that it is described as a value related to ratios of angles used in triangles, the sine.

Notice that the peak voltage of the graph is around 151 volts, in either the positive or negative quadrants, which is 31 volts higher or lower than the nominal voltage. Even so, the voltage represented on most of the graph is less than 120 volts. Since the voltage pressure is constantly changing over time, a special method is used to describe that pressure. AC voltages are expressed as an *RMS* average. RMS stands for *Root Mean Square*, which is a mathematical method of determining the mean distance of points on the graph of a sine curve from the x axis. For standard line voltage that mean is 120VAC. The sine wave graph is important to stage electricians because it is the only way to graphically demonstrate how modern stage dimmers work. You will see it again in the discussion of dimmers. This type of graph is also used to show how 220v single phase or three phase power works.

Rather than having a positive and a negative terminal like a direct current battery, AC is said to have a *hot* and a *neutral*. The "hot" is the wire used to push and pull electrons through the circuit. The word hot is indicative of the fact that this conductor is energized. The neutral wire provides a resting place for electrons to go to when they are not being used. The neutral must be in place for the circuit to be closed and to operate. When wiring electrical devices, it is important to make sure that the

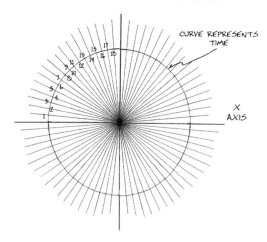

CURVE REPRESENTS TIME

X AXIS

THE CIRCUMFERENCE OF THE CIRCLE REPRESENTS ONE CYCLE OF ALTERNATING CURRENT, AND THE RAYS DIVIDE THE TIME INTO SECTIONS. EACH SECTION REPRESENTS ONE TIME DIVISION ON THE GRAPH BELOW. MEASURE FROM THE X AXIS UP TO THE INTERSECTION OF ONE OF THE RAYS AND THE CIRCLE. PLOTTING EACH ONE OF THE INTERSECTIONS ON THE GRAPH WILL PRODUCE A SINE CURVE, BECAUSE THE RATIO OF THIS PROCESS IS THE SAME AS WHEN A WIRE TRAVELS IN A CIRCLE THROUGH A MAGNETIC FIELD.

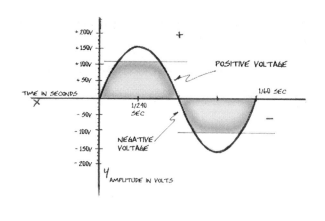

ONE CYCLE OF ALTERNATING CURRENT

THE USEFUL VOLTAGE APPLIED TO THE LOAD IS THE AVERAGE VOLTAGE. THE RMS AVERAGE VOLTAGE IS INDICATED BY THE SHADED-IN AREA. THE ACTUAL PEAK VOLTAGE IS MUCH HIGHER.

ELECTRONS TRAVEL IN ONE DIRECTION WHEN THE CURVE IS IN THE POSITIVE QUADRANT, BUT REVERSE AND FLOW THE OPPOSITE DIRECTION WHEN IT IS IN THE NEGATIVE ONE.

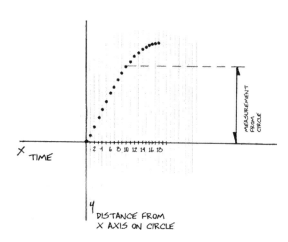

X TIME

DISTANCE FROM X AXIS ON CIRCLE

CONNECTING THE DOTS WILL FORM A SINE CURVE

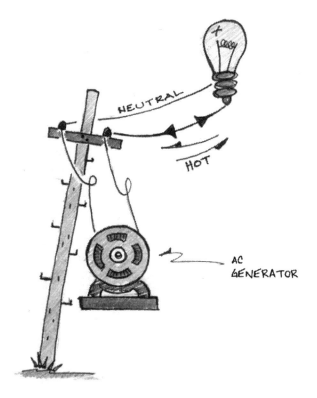

NEUTRAL

HOT

AC GENERATOR

ALTERNATING CURRENT

AC HAS A HOT AND A NEUTRAL RATHER THAN A PLUS AND MINUS LIKE IN DIRECT CURRENT

hot and neutral wires are attached to the proper terminals, or they may not be safe.

The hot wire is connected to the generator on the side where electrons are being pushed because of the inductive force. The neutral wire is used to complete the electrical circuit, but in many ways mimics the action of a capacitor.

In electronics, *capacitors* are used to store electrons. Electrons can be "bunched up" inside a capacitor in proportion to the voltage pressure in a circuit, and released later on when the pressure drops. The neutral conductor acts in a similar manner, allowing electrons a place to rest temporarily. When the voltage pressure of the sine wave increases, as it does in the positive quadrant of the sine wave, electrons are fed into the neutral. When the voltage pressure drops below zero, electrons begin to move out of the neutral and back into the hot conductor. That happens because the pressure of the collected electrons in the neutral is higher than the pressure of electrons in the hot conductor.

Touching a hot conductor will allow at least some electrons to flow into your body, a hand perhaps. It may be that the resistances of the various pathways are such that you will receive only a tingling sensation. However,

if you are "grounded out" by a puddle of water or some other method of conduction, you might receive a severe shock as the current passes through you to get to the ions in the puddle of water/earth.

Normally, a ground wire is used to make AC current safer by providing an alternate path or circuit for electrons to take that has less resistance than the pathway through a person's body. Since the body acts as a resistor in series with a short circuit, and the ground wire has only the very small resistance of the wire itself, it will naturally draw off most of the current. If no ground wire is present, the full amount of the current will pass through your body, which can be deadly. The ground wire is usually connected to the metal housing of something like a stage lighting fixture. Grounding does not guarantee safety; it merely makes things safer than they would be otherwise. Many electrical devices are said to be *double insulated*, meaning that there is no metal structure on the outside for the user to touch and be shocked by. They do not require ground wires and generally don't have them.

TRANSFORMERS, AC TRANSMISSION, AND THE POWER LOSS FORMULA

Power on overhead lines runs at a very high voltage because that is the most efficient method of transmission. High voltage electricity loses less power to resistance over long distance wires. Power loss in a circuit is determined by the formula $P_{LOSS} = P^2R/E^2$. Since the value of E is squared in the denominator, the higher the voltage is, the smaller the total power loss will be for a given amount of current and resistance. The current running through transmission lines is actually quite tiny. The current can be small because a large voltage and a small current will still create a reasonable amount of power, as demonstrated by the P = IE formula. High voltage power lines are very dangerous, and you should avoid them.

Transformers

A transformer can be used to transform, reduce, or step down the high voltage to a more user-friendly 120 volts. *Transformers* are aptly named, because their function is to "trans-form" or change the voltage in a circuit. A basic transformer consists of two coils of enamel-coated magnet wire that are wrapped around an armature made of laminated steel plates. The coil of wire that is in series with the incoming voltage is known as the *primary*. The coil of wire that is in series with the outgoing, altered voltage is known as the *secondary*. Both of these coils of wire are wrapped around the same iron core. The iron core is used to focus the magnetic force created by the primary. It is important to realize that the electrical currents in the primary and secondary coils are electrically insulated from one another. Although magnet wire looks as though it has no insulation on its exterior, it in fact does. The

OHM'S LAW AND GROUNDING

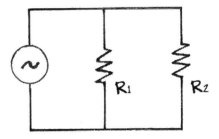

R₁ = HUMAN BODY = 1000 OHMS
R₂ = GROUND WIRE = 1 OHM
E = 120 VAC

I = E/R

HUMAN BODY

I = 120/1000 = .12 AMPERES

GROUND WIRE CIRCUIT

I = 120/1 = 120 AMPERES

IF A 20 AMP CIRCUIT BREAKER IS IN PLACE, THE 120 AMPS DOWN THE GROUND WIRE SHOULD TRIP THE CIRCUIT BREAKER IMMEDIATELY

MATHEMATICS OF
POWER TRANSMISSION

POWER STATION
BUILT NEAR
COAL DEPOSITS

THE CITY IS
20 MILES AWAY
~ 100,000 FEET

THE CITY NEEDS 120 KILOWATTS
OF ELECTRICAL POWER

THIS ALUMINUM WIRE HAS
A RESISTANCE OF
10Ω/1000 FEET

$R_{TOTAL} = 100 \times 10\Omega = 1K\Omega$

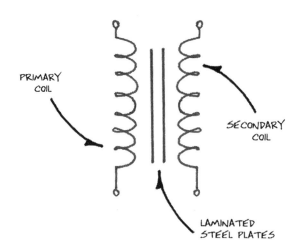

PRIMARY
COIL

SECONDARY
COIL

LAMINATED
STEEL PLATES

SCHEMATIC SYMBOL
OF A TRANSFORMER

USING THE POWER LOSS FORMULA

$$P_{LOSS} = \frac{P^2 \times R}{E^2}$$

P = 120KW
R = 1KΩ
E = 120KV #1
OR
12KV #2

EXAMPLE ONE

$$P_{LOSS} = \frac{(120KW)^2 \times 1K\Omega}{(120 KV)^2}$$

$$P_{LOSS} = \frac{120^2 \times 1}{120^2} = \frac{14400}{14400} \quad = 1KW \text{ OF LOSS}$$

EXAMPLE TWO

$$P_{LOSS} = \frac{(120KW)^2 \times 1K\Omega}{(12 KV)^2}$$

$$P_{LOSS} = \frac{120^2 \times 1}{12^2} = \frac{14400}{144} \quad = 100KW \text{ OF LOSS}$$

insulation is a clear varnish type that keeps the copper wire a reddish gold color.

In order to understand how a transformer works, you must study it in conjunction with the AC current that feeds it. The rise and fall of an alternating current in relation to its sine wave is central to the workings of a transformer. As the incoming current, in series with the primary coil, gains voltage strength in the first part of its cycle, a building magnetic field is formed around the iron core of the transformer. As the alternating current cycle continues, the magnetic field reaches its peak, and then

collapses to zero as the voltage reaches the x axis on our graph. It then re-forms with its magnetic poles *in the opposite direction* as the AC cycle reverses its current flow. That process is repeated over and over, 60 times per second. This creates a constantly moving magnetic field, but it is due to electrical forces, not the physical forces found in a rotating generator.

In a transformer, the graph of the voltage in the secondary is the exact opposite of the primary. If the function of the transformer is to lower the voltage of the circuit, a graph of both the primary and secondary voltages might look like the following figure.

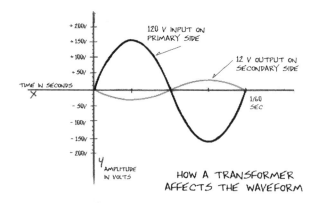

120 V INPUT ON PRIMARY SIDE

12 V OUTPUT ON SECONDARY SIDE

TIME IN SECONDS

1/60 SEC

AMPLITUDE IN VOLTS

HOW A TRANSFORMER
AFFECTS THE WAVEFORM

Transformers do not work with DC current; in fact they are used to block it from some audio circuits. Even though DC develops a magnetic field in the primary coil as its voltage builds, once it has established that field it becomes static, and remains in a steady state. Since the field is static and not moving, it will not continue to induce a current in the secondary coil.

Different types of transformers are used for specific jobs, sometimes to create a lower voltage, and sometimes to create a higher one. Fluorescent lighting requires a very high voltage, so those fixtures or lamps have a special step-up transformer in them. Center-tapped transformers are a special type used to create two voltages of equal but opposite polarity. They are used to create the ubiquitous 120/240 volt service, found in homes and elsewhere. The secondary winding of the transformer has a tap in the middle, which means that there are three wires coming from that side.

The center one is the ground, or neutral potential. The other two have the same voltage, but the graphs of the sine curves are opposite to one another. The voltage potential from one of the hots to the neutral is 120 volts. From one of the hots to the other hot is 240 volts, average peak to average peak. So this type of transformer can supply either 120 volts of pressure, or 240 volts of pressure, depending on how the wires are connected.

THIS TRANSFORMER IN A RESIDENTIAL AREA STEPS DOWN VOLTAGE TO SEVERAL HOUSES.

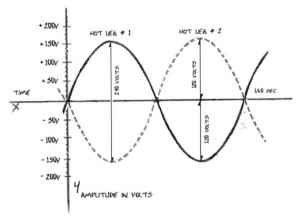

THE CENTER-TAPPED TRANSFORMER CREATES VOLTAGES THAT ARE EQUAL TO EACH OTHER, BUT OPPOSITE. THE RMS VOLTAGE FROM EITHER ONE TO THE X AXIS IS 120 VAC, BUT FROM THE TOP OF ONE TO THE BOTTOM OF THE OTHER IS 240 VAC. IN THIS DRAWING, THE X AXIS REPRESENTS THE POSITION OF THE NEUTRAL.

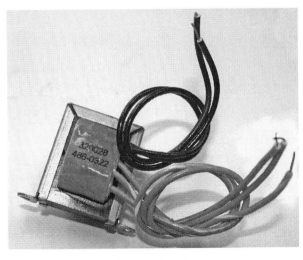

LOW-CURRENT, CENTER-TAPPED STEP DOWN TRANSFORMER

THE TWO DARK WIRES ARE THE LEADS TO THE PRIMARY. THE STRIPED WIRE IS THE NEUTRAL CENTER TAP. THE OTHER TWO LIGHT WIRES ARE THE HOTS FROM THE SECONDARY COIL. THE SAME SYSTEM IS USED FOR HIGH-CURRENT POWER TRANSFORMER.

In Edison's day, using DC current, it was necessary to have a power generating station every few blocks because the resistance of the distribution wires themselves, in series with the intended load in a home or business, would seriously degrade the voltage available to the end user. Even though Edison's power company used extremely large conductors for their DC grid, the distances they could effectively span were quite short by modern standards. Today, power transmission lines can be hundreds of miles long because they use AC power in conjunction with transformers rather than DC.

COPPER WIRE RESISTANCE TABLE

AWG	Feet/Ω	Ω/100ft	Ampacity*
10	490.2 ft	.204Ω	30A
12	308.7 ft	.324Ω	20A
14	193.8 ft	.516Ω	15A
16	122.3 ft	.818Ω	10A
18	76.8 ft	1.30Ω	5A
20	48.1 ft	2.08Ω	3A
22	30.3 ft	3.30Ω	2A
24	19.1 ft	5.24Ω	1A

A LARGER AWG NUMBER MEANS A SMALLER WIRE, JUST THE OPPOSITE OF WHAT YOU MIGHT THINK. LARGER WIRES CARRY MORE CURRENT, AND HAVE LESS RESISTANCE TO CURRENT FLOW. MOST BUILDINGS HAVE AWG #12 AS A STANDARD SIZE FOR LIGHTING CIRCUITS, BUT SOME WIRES ARE MUCH LARGER.

TERMS USED IN THIS CHAPTER

ACL
alternating current
ampere
battery cell
capacitor
circuit
conductor
current
current draw
direct current (DC)
double insulated
Edison, Thomas
electromotive force

electron
filament
Hertz
hot
induction
insulator
Jablokov candle
magic triangle
neutral
ohms
open circuit
parallel circuit
power

primary coil
resistance
schematic
secondary coil
series circuit
sine waves
terminal
Tesla, Nikola
transformer
voltage
voltage divider
wet cell

CHAPTER 19

POWER
DISTRIBUTION

POWER CIRCUITS ARE USED to supply AC current to devices throughout a theatre. Often the words *line voltage* or *main* are used to describe the supply of 120VAC power. This chapter is concerned with the methods used to distribute line voltage from an external source into a theatre, and within the theatre itself.

Some of the information in this chapter would apply to electrical work in any field, but the entertainment business uses some very specialized equipment that differs substantially from what may be used in other industries. A lot of theatre practice is meant to be temporary, given the changeable nature of the business. Power distribution systems may be set up for one show, and changed for another. Portable cables are used to bring power and data to equipment, rather than using traditional hard-wired methods. Because entertainment depends on rapidly changing from one show to another, special devices are used to quickly connect parts of the system together, and just as quickly strike them at the end of the show.

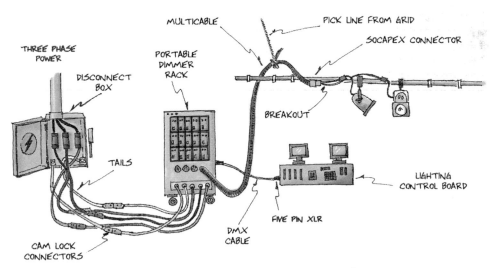

PARTS OF A PORTABLE SYSTEM

A TOURING RIG MAKES A GOOD EXAMPLE, BECAUSE IT IS EASIER TO SEE HOW THE PARTS FIT TOGETHER WHEN THEY AREN'T BURIED INSIDE A WALL

120/240 Volt Split Phase Power

Most homes, and some theatre installations, use a *240v service*. The three conductors that make up the system consist of a bare aluminum neutral and two insulated hot legs. The twisted pair of black insulated wires is usually twined around the neutral.

A pole transformer steps down a higher voltage (frequently 12kv) to 120VAC using a center tapped secondary to create two separate hots. The sine curves of the two hot legs are inversely proportional to one another, and as a result, voltage measurements show a 120 volt potential between either of the two hot legs and the neutral, but 240 volts between the two hots. This is just like the description in the previous chapter. Sometimes this arrangement is known as a *split* or *opposite phase hookup*.

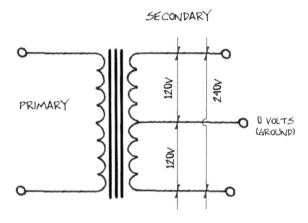

SECONDARY

PRIMARY

120V 240V

120V

0 VOLTS (GROUND)

A TRANSFORMER FOR 240 VOLT SERVICE STEPS DOWN VOLTAGE LIKE THIS.

THERE ARE TWO 120 VOLT LEGS AND ONE NEUTRAL. A CENTER-TAPPED TRANSFORMER CREATES A +120 VOLT LEG, AND A -120 VOLT LEG BECAUSE THE TWO SINE CURVES ARE EXACTLY OPPOSITE OF ONE ANOTHER. MEASURING THE VOLTAGE ACROSS EITHER HOT LEG AND THE NEUTRAL GIVES 120 VOLTS. MEASURING THE VOLTAGE ACROSS THE TWO HOTS GIVES 240 VOLTS.

You may have noticed by now that several different numbers have been used to describe line voltage. Some devices are marked 110 volts, others 115 volts, and just now I used the numbers 120/240 volts. The actual amount of voltage pressure in a system varies for many reasons, demand on the system, amount of resistance between the measuring point and the transformer, and even the temperature or corrosion on the outlet. Any number between 110 and 120 is entirely possible,

and any voltage pressure in that range will work just fine for most electrical devices. The actual standard is somewhere in the middle at 117/234 volts, but you rarely see those numbers.

In a 120/240 split phase system one neutral is used for both hots. It might seem as though the neutral would be carrying twice the current load as either of the two hot wires, and thus should be physically larger in size than either of them in order to carry the load. But, because the two voltages are opposite one another, the electrons in the current from one are gone when the other arrives.

A theatre system using 240v service must split up the current between the dimmers so that half of them are connected to the first hot leg, and the remainder are connected to the second one. The neutral completes the circuit for both of them. No dimmers should be connected to both of the hots, as this would supply too much pressure and would burn them out in short order. Most temporary hook-ups are done from a disconnect box of the type shown. Notice that there are two fuses, one for each of the two hot legs, but none for the neutral. It is not necessary to circuit protect the neutral with a fuse or circuit breaker. A hook-up of this type would be a very small installation; most theatres use something larger, such as a three phase supply.

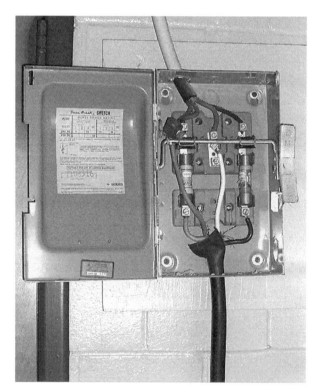

A DISCONNECT BOX FOR 220/240 POWER

THE FUSES CONNECT THE TWO HOTS, THE NEUTRAL IS IN THE CENTER, AND THE GROUND RUNS UP TOP

THREE PHASE POWER

In a power station generator, the circular movement of a coil of wire inside a magnetic field produces an alternating current that fluctuates from positive to negative in a regular pattern called the sine wave. That was discussed in the previous chapter. A power station generator is a very large device, and operates more efficiently if more than one current is produced at the same time. *Three phase power* (3φ) is the most common type of polyphase circuit. The phi symbol φ is used to denote phase. Remember that a standard 120v sine wave looks like this:

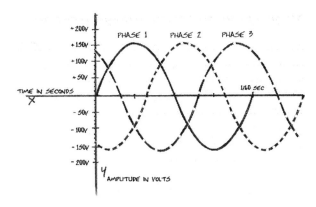

VOLTAGE FLUCTUATION IN THREE PHASE POWER

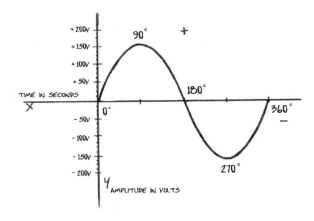

STANDARD 120 VOLT SINE WAVE GRAPH

THE DEGREE MARKINGS REPRESENT THE POSITION OF THE WIRE COIL IN THE GENERATOR.

As the coil of wire in the generator makes its 360 degree circular journey through the generator's magnetic field, the voltage induced rises to a peak after the first 90 degrees, drops back to zero after 180 degrees, reaches a peak reverse flow at 270 degrees, and then returns to zero at the 360 degree mark. What would happen if there were more than one single coil of wire in the generator? If three *electrically separated* coils are used instead of one, three separate and distinct currents are formed. If the coils of wire are equally spaced inside the generator, then the sine waves of the three currents will be identical in shape but happen at different times or in different *phases*. The generator produces three times the electrical power, but uses the same amount of mechanical energy to do it. The resulting three phase current is represented graphically like the following diagram (top next column).

It is important to realize that the three phases are actually present on three different conductors that are electrically insulated from one another, and that this graph only represents how the phases relate to one another. The actual wires don't touch.

After the three phase power is generated, it must be distributed on different conductors, in order to maintain the separate phase arrangement. On a pole, the conductors might be arranged like this:

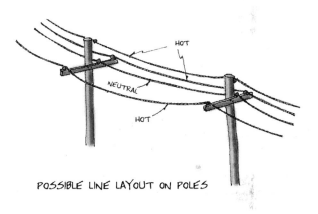

POSSIBLE LINE LAYOUT ON POLES

Notice that there are three hot legs, but only one neutral. Because the current of the phases is running at different times and each places a demand on the neutral in a different way, it is not necessary to have separate neutral conductors for each of the hot legs. Larger lighting systems are virtually universal in their use three phase power rather than 240 split phase.

There are two configurations of three phase power, *wye*, and *delta*. The delta configuration is used primarily in factories and is not often seen in theatres, where the wye configuration is standard. Wye gets its name from the "Y" shape formed by the three secondary coils that form the output of the transformer. These coils are contained within a transformer that is part of the building structure, probably in a vault in an inaccessible place. A stage electrician would never access them directly, but it is helpful to understand how they supply power to the dimming system.

THREE PHASE POWER, Y CONNECTION

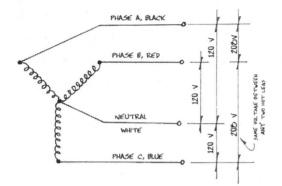

THIS TRANSFORMER IS SET UP IN THE "Y" CONFIGURATION. NOTICE THAT ONE END OF EACH OF THE SECONDARY COILS IS JOINED TOGETHER. EACH OF THE FREE ENDS BECOMES ONE OF THE HOT CONDUCTORS OR "LEGS." THE VOLTAGE POTENTIAL OF ANY HOT LEG AND THE NEUTRAL IS 120 VAC. THE VOLTAGE POTENTIAL BETWEEN ANY TWO OF THE HOT LEGS IS 208 VAC BECAUSE OF THE WAY THE TWO SINE WAVES MERGE TOGETHER. SOME EQUIPMENT IS INTENDED TO OPERATE ON 208 VOLTAGE, BUT MOST OF THE TIME SEPARATE CONNECTIONS ARE MADE TO EACH HOT LEG TO MAKE THREE SEPARATE 120 VOLT SERVICES.

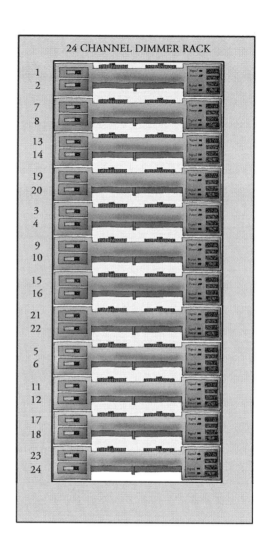

For a wye connection, the pressure between any two of the hot legs is 208 volts, and the voltage between any one of the three hot legs and the neutral is 120 volts. Remember that with 240 power, half of the dimmers are connected to one of the 120 volt legs, and the other half are connected to the other hot leg. In 3φ power, one third of the dimmers are connected to each of the three hot legs. In the rack, dimmers are arranged so that one third are connected to the *phase A* hot leg, one third to *phase B*, and one third to *phase C*. As a result, each dimmer has an input of 120 volts, but from different sources. All phases use the same neutral connection, which works out okay because the different phases are using the neutral at different times. If the loading on each phase A, B, and C is the same, the neutral will not have a voltage potential on it with respect to ground, but if the phases have unequal loads a dangerous imbalance may exist. In that situation it is possible for the neutral to produce an electrical shock.

You may notice that the dimmers in an ETC Sensor rack seem to have a very odd numbering system, and that the numbers skip around something like this (see figure on right).

THE NUMBERING SYSTEM SEEMS PECULIAR

There is a reason for the number skipping. When dimmers are inserted into a rack, connectors on the back meet up with a *bus bar*, which is the end of the phase connection. The bus bar is one solid piece, and one third of the dimmers in the rack must mate with each of the bus bars. The dimmers are in groups of two, so the numbers 1, 2, 7, 8, 13, 14, 19, 20 fall together in order on the phase A bus bar; 3, 4, 9, 10, 15, 16, 20, 21 on the phase B; and 5, 6, 11, 12, 17, 18, 23, 24 on the phase C. *(Note: Sensor racks often have more dimmers in them, but this number makes it easier to demonstrate.)*

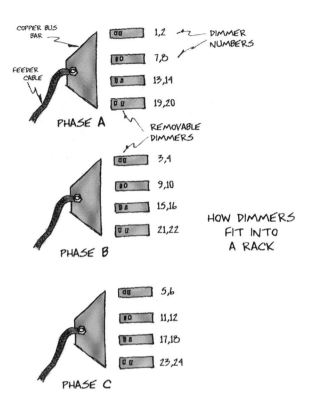

COPPER BUS BAR

FEEDER CABLE

PHASE A

1,2 — DIMMER NUMBERS

7,8

13,14

19,20 — REMOVABLE DIMMERS

PHASE B

3,4

9,10

15,16

21,22

HOW DIMMERS FIT INTO A RACK

PHASE C

5,6

11,12

17,18

23,24

THE ODD NUMBERING SYSTEM IS INTENDED TO KEEP ALL PHASES AT THE SAME LOAD LEVEL

of fuses in the panel. 240 volt service has two fuses inside, one for each of the two hot legs. Three phase power has three fuses. Voltages in either case should be 120 volts from any hot to the neutral. If the panel contains 240 split phase the potential from one hot to another should be 240 volts, and for three phase 208 volts.

USE SOME CAUTION

Be very careful when you open a disconnect box of this type, because you can easily get a shock from the components inside. They are not nearly as well shielded as consumer equipment, especially older model boxes. Don't try hooking up to one without proper supervision by a qualified electrician. A finger in the wrong place could result in serious injury or death!

The system design engineers would like to spread the load of all the dimmers evenly between the three phases of the power supply so that the load on the neutral is balanced between them. If the dimmer numbers of all circuits on the first lighting position are 1 through 24, and all of the lights hung on it are on at the same time, the load should be evenly shared between the three phases. Although it is impossible to predict in advance how a lighting designer may choose to divide up which lights are on at any particular moment, lighting systems engineers feel that this is their best attempt at doing so.

CABLES AND CONNECTORS

In a large, permanent, theatre installation the *feeder cable* to the dimmer racks is most likely in a conduit that runs directly into the dimmer racks, and does not need to be changed from show to show. Portable equipment on the other hand must be supplied with power by means of a *disconnect box*. This set-up is by its very nature temporary, and is the type used by touring shows that travel with their own dimming equipment. The disconnect panel could be either a smaller 240 single phase type, or it could be three phase as in a professional theatre. The type of disconnect you have can be determined by the number

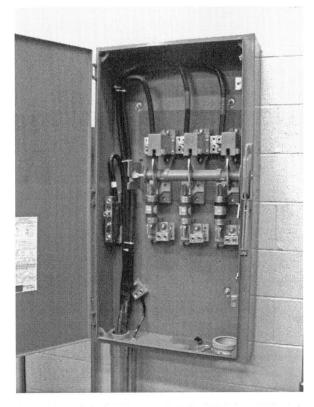

DISCONNECT FOR 3 PHASE POWER

NOTE: THREE HOT LEGS WITH FUSES. WHITE TAPE ON NEUTRAL BUSS AT LEFT. GROUND CONNECTION AT THE BOTTOM.

Typically, a disconnect box has a handle on the right-hand side that must be pulled down before the box will open. The handle disengages the power to the connections inside making them safer to handle. Large *cartridge fuses* denote the current carrying capacity of the system. There should be a fuse for each hot leg, but none for the neutral. The total amperage available from the panel is the total of the amounts stamped on the fuses. If 200 amp fuses are in use, the total available current would be 600 amps, which is enough for 30, 20 amp dimmers working at full capacity. At the bottom of the box, directly under each of the fuses, is a set of *terminal lugs*. When a disconnect is used for a permanent installation, the dimmers are hard wired to the box, which then may be used more or less as a giant off–on switch for repair purposes.

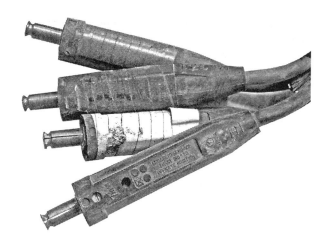

CAM LOCKS ARE USED FOR SINGLE CONDUCTOR CABLES

IF THE PICTURE WERE IN COLOR YOU COULD SEE HOW THE TAPE IS USED FOR COLOR CODING.

THIS TYPE OF CARTRIDGE FUSE IS FREQUENTLY USED IN A LARGE CAPACITY DISCONNECT PANEL

On a touring set up, the disconnect box is used to supply power to portable dimmer racks. Very special wiring is used for this purpose, most often *#0000 (four ought)* entertainment cable with a heavy *SO* rubber sheathing on the outside that provides insulation. Each conductor is run separately, and each has its own connector for just the one wire. *Cam lock* connectors are used to connect various sections of the wire. Cam locks come in male and female versions just like other connectors, with the female being the source of current, and the male pointing toward the power. Obviously, if the male connector with its exposed brass fitting were energized, the risk of electrical shock would be huge. Sometimes the neutral wire is run backward, since the theoretical chance of electrical shock is small, and reversing the connectors makes it impossible to accidentally miss-connect the neutral and one of the hots.

Tails are used to make the connection with the disconnect box. These are short sections of cable that have a female connector on one end, and bare wire on the other. The bare wire is wrenched down to one of the lugs in the disconnect box. It feeds out through an appropriate opening and is given a *strain relief*, which might be a

conduit clamp, or simply tying all the conductors up with line, so that pulling on the extensions will not place a mechanical strain on the terminal lug. It is common practice when working with #0000 feeder cable that one should make the ground connection first, then the neutral, and then the three hots. If there is some mis-adventure, this procedure will ensure that the ground is in place before any current can reach the equipment. It is important not to energize the system via the disconnect handle until all of the system connections have been made. Even female cam locks are really dangerous if left exposed.

TWO PIN AND GROUND MALE PIN CONNECTOR

The most common theatrical connector for regular 20 amp power circuits is the *pin connector*, but a second type, the *twist lock*, is also popular. The pin connector has been around for many decades and is extremely durable. The ¼ inch diameter brass pins are almost impossible to break off. As a safety feature, the ground pin in the center is slightly longer than the other pins, so that the ground connection makes up first when you put them together. The neutral is located closest to the ground, and the hot is on the far side. Early versions were not grounded, and had no center pin.

20 AMP JUMPER WITH PIN CONNECTORS, COLOR CODING TAPE, AND TIE LINE FOR STORAGE PURPOSES.

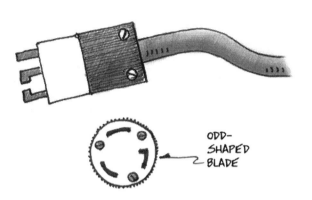

ODD-SHAPED BLADE

TWO PIN AND GROUND TWIST LOCK MALE

Twist locks have the obvious advantage of a positive method of making sure that the connection stays together. A stagehand twists them together slightly causing the two halves to lock. On the other hand, pin connectors can come apart when someone accidentally pulls on the cable unless they are tied or taped together. But twist lock connectors are not as sturdy as the pin connector, the blades tend to bend easily, and it is sometimes difficult to line them up with the proper holes without looking closely. There are many brands and types of twist locks, for different ampacities. Pin connectors come only in 20 amp (the most common) and 60 amp (very rare) versions.

When a lighting fixture in a theatre is hung too far away from a circuit box for its own pigtail to reach the receptacle, a *jumper* is used to bridge the gap. They are like extension cords for lighting. Most theatres have readymade jumpers in specific lengths on hand at all times. If a theatre has lots of circuits in all the right places, it may not need many jumpers. If the circuits are in inconvenient places, it may need many jumpers.

Socapex makes a multi-connector with 19 pins for *multi-cables* that have that many conductors. They are often used when a large number of wires must be run, perhaps in a touring rig. A six circuit multi-cable is

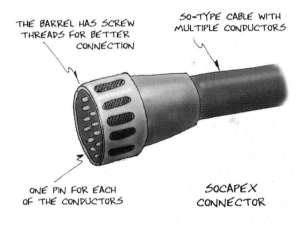

THE BARREL HAS SCREW THREADS FOR BETTER CONNECTION

SO-TYPE CABLE WITH MULTIPLE CONDUCTORS

ONE PIN FOR EACH OF THE CONDUCTORS

SOCAPEX CONNECTOR

much easier to manipulate than six separate runs of 12/3 SO jumpers. A 19 pin Socapex connector can be used to make up a multi that services six lighting circuits, each having a separate hot/neutral/ground, with one pin left spare.

The wire itself has many different conductors color-coded within it. A *breakout* is used at the end of the cable, to separate it into individual circuits. Frequently, the dimmer system has female Socapex connections on the back so that no breakout is required at that end.

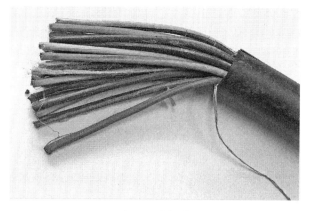

MULTI-CABLE

THE VARIOUS CONDUCTORS EACH HAVE THEIR
OWN COLOR-CODED INSULATOR. THE EXTERIOR
IS A HEAVY-DUTY SO TYPE RUBBER.

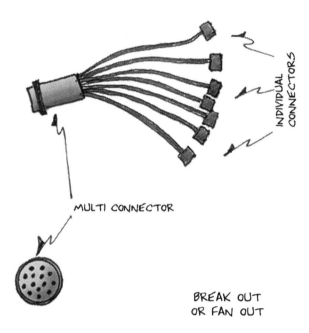

INDIVIDUAL CONNECTORS

MULTI CONNECTOR

BREAK OUT
OR FAN OUT

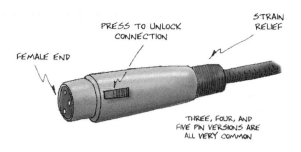

FEMALE END

PRESS TO UNLOCK
CONNECTION

STRAIN
RELIEF

THREE, FOUR, AND
FIVE PIN VERSIONS ARE
ALL VERY COMMON

THREE PIN XLR CONNECTOR

DON'T BE FOOLED!
THIS PICTURE IS GREATLY ENLARGED.
AN ACTUAL CAT 5 IS VERY SMALL.
CATEGORY 5 IS REALLY A WIRING
TERM, BUT THIS TYPE OF CONNECTOR
IS GENERALLY USED, SO THE NAME
USUALLY APPLIES TO EITHER OR BOTH.

CATEGORY FIVE
OR "CAT 5" CABLES
ARE OFTEN USED FOR
ETHERNET CONNECTIONS

Modern lighting systems also use *XLR connectors* for control functions between the board and dimmer racks, moving fixture lights, and other peripheral equipment that requires a digital signal to operate. These cables are not expected to carry large amounts of current, and as a result they are physically much smaller. Three pin XLRs of the sort very commonly used for microphones, are also used for moving fixture lights.

Four pin XLRs are often used for color scrollers. Two of the pins transmit data, and the other two carry the DC voltage used to run the motors. The five pin version of the XLR is meant for DMX transmission from the light board. DMX 512A is the computer program protocol used in the entertainment industry. In reality the DMX signal only uses two of the pins plus a shield/ground, but those cables have extra shielding built in. It is sometimes very frustrating to have three different, but very similar connector types, but they are actually used for different purposes, so the variety in pin numbers helps to keep the wrong cable from being plugged in where it shouldn't go. *Category 5 computer cables* are also used, if the system has an *Ethernet* hub. None of these cables is used to distribute line voltage, but they are all used to control equipment that is used with line voltage.

ELECTRICAL WIRES

The size of a wire used to conduct electricity is determined by its *AWG* (*American Wire Gauge*) number. For the most part, the larger the gauge number, the smaller the wire is. So #20 gauge wires are actually much smaller than #10 wires, just the opposite of what might seem intuitive. The largest wire used in the entertainment industry is #0000 (four ought) feeder cable, which is larger in diameter than #00. The strands of copper wire in #0000 cables are all together about as big in diameter as a roll of pennies, so you can imagine how heavy they are.

Wire can be made *solid*, or *stranded*. Stranded electrical cable is much easier to bend, so it only makes sense that portable cables such as those used in theatres should be of the stranded variety. Solid copper wire is used in permanent installations where the wire never needs to be moved about. Solid wire mistakenly used in a situation requiring mobility will soon develop metal fatigue and become dangerous.

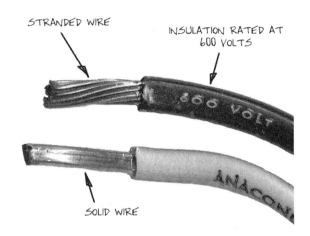

SOLID AND STRANDED WIRE TYPES

STRANDED WIRE IS MUCH MORE FLEXIBLE THAN THE SOLID TYPE, AND IS WHAT YOU SHOULD USE FOR A PORTABLE CABLE LIKE A 20 AMP JUMPER

Larger gauge wires with more copper in them are able to carry more current than small ones, but the voltage capability depends on the insulation surrounding the conductor. Rubber insulation is preferred for theatre cabling, and the code for that is type *SO* or *SJ*. SJ insulation is somewhat lighter and thinner than SO. It is rated at 300 volts, while the SO is rated at 600 volts. Notice that the copper wire is rated in amps, while the insulation is rated in volts. Remember that insulation is designed to contain the voltage pressure, and to keep the wire from shorting out. The copper wire is designed to carry the actual electrons.

The exact ampacity of any conductor is affected by a large number of factors like the metal alloy used, the size and number of the strands, the frequency of the sine wave, temperature, and all sorts of other peculiar details. The list above is the one actually used by electricians. Most portable lighting cables are made from #12 wire, because it can handle a 20 amp load, which is the most common dimmer rating. This cable may be referred to as "12/3 SO" which indicates that it is 12 gauge, 3 conductor (hot/neutral/ground) with type SO rubber insulation on the outside. On occasion you might see 12/2 with ground, which would be the same thing.

APPROXIMATE AMPACITIES OF GAUGES

#0000	225 amps
#00	175 amps
#4	80 amps
#8	46 amps
#12	20 amps
#16	13 amps
#20	7.5 amps
#30	0.5 amps

Type SO has been the standard for many years, but recently SJ has become very popular as well. SJ is much lighter in weight, and thus more easily carried, but its smaller diameter can be problematic when making a connection to the strain relief of a pin connector designed for the larger diameter SO.

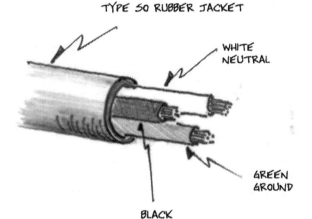

12/3 SO CABLE FOR JUMPERS

The various conductors inside a jumper are each sheathed in insulation of their own to keep them separated from one another. Although the outside insulation is black, a standard *color coding* is used to tell the individual conductors apart. This color code is not just for theatres, but is used in all different types of electrical work.

TROUBLESHOOTING

Troubleshooting is the name given to a methodology for fault finding. In electrical work, troubleshooting most often occurs when something either doesn't work at all, or doesn't work properly. It requires the use of logic to deduct and infer from a given set of facts what could be the cause of a certain fault. Efficient troubleshooting requires an understanding of Ohm's law, series and parallel circuits, induction, and so forth. In short, all of the things you have been reading about so far.

Fault finding requires a logical process of investigation. To save time it is generally best to check the components most likely to have failed first. Checking to see that the fixture is properly plugged in and that it has a lamp in it is very easily accomplished, so it intuitively makes sense to try that first. An amazing number of electrical faults are just that simple.

FAULT-FINDING PROCESS

FAULT FINDING CONSISTS OF A LOGICAL AND LINEAR STREAM OF CHECKING ALL THE COMPONENTS IN A SYSTEM TO DISCOVER WHICH ONES ARE NOT WORKING PROPERLY. BEGIN WITH THE USUAL SUSPECTS.

LIGHT IN QUESTION NOT WORKING AT ALL:

IS IT PLUGGED IN?
IS THE POWER ON TO THAT CIRCUIT?
IS THE LAMP GOOD?

AFTER ANSWERING THOSE QUESTIONS, GO ON TO THINGS LIKE BAD CABLES OR CONNECTORS.

LIGHT WORKS, BUT ONLY SOMETIMES OR FLICKERS ON AND OFF:

THIS IS ALMOST ALWAYS A BAD CONNECTION OF SOME TYPE, MOST LIKELY A PROBLEM WITH A CONNECTOR. OPEN UP THE PLUG AND CHECK THE WAY THE WIRES LOOK. QUITE OFTEN THERE MAY BE BURN MARKS FROM ARCING.

SOMETIMES A BAD LAMP SOCKET WILL CAUSE A LIGHT TO GO OFF AFTER BEING ON FOR A WHILE, BECAUSE THE HEAT CAUSES EXPANSION.

Imagine that a group of lights have been hung side by side on the first electric. You bring up all the lights with the lightboard to see if they all work. One does not, but why? The first thing you might try is to unplug a light next to the defective one, and plug it into the circuit of the light that didn't work. If the second light works, then logic dictates that the problem must be in the non-working light itself and not in the power coming from the outlet. If the second lamp does not light, you should intuit that there is no power at the outlet, or at least that you should check to see that there is.

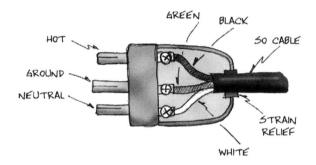

THE APPROPRIATE
MECHANICS INSIDE A 20 AMP
PIN CONNECTOR

MAKE SURE THAT ALL THE TERMINALS
ARE TIGHTLY SCREWED DOWN
AND THAT THE STRAIN RELIEF HAS A
GOOD GRIP ON THE SO INSULATION

When a theatre light is moved from one place to another it is necessary to unplug it first. It is human nature to tug on the cord at least a little bit when doing that. The wires inside a pin connector or twist-lock often come loose, so it makes sense to look there for the source of trouble. Burned out lamps and connectors with wires loose are the most common causes of a fixture not lighting up, if there is actually power to the outlet.

Sometimes, the problem inside a fixture cannot be easily detected with the naked eye. You can use a VOM, or volt-ohm-meter to check all of the components in an entire fixture all at one time, without taking anything apart. The fixture must be *de-energized*, which is to say not connected to a source of power.

Set your meter to read Ωs. Connect the lead from one probe (it doesn't matter which) to the hot pin on the connector, and then touch the other probe to the neutral. If the connector is old, and has a lot of corrosion on it, you may need to press the sharp point of the probe into the metal just a bit to get a proper reading. If you get a reading of some low number of ohms, which is to say <20Ω then the fixture should be able to light up normally. If you get a reading of infinitely large resistance, then the circuit is open, and most likely a wire is loose or the lamp is blown.

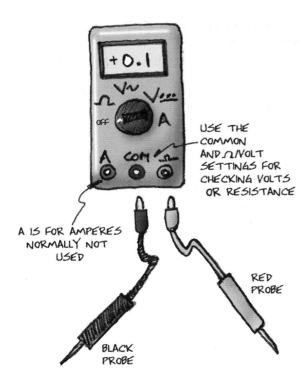

USE THE COMMON AND Ω/VOLT SETTINGS FOR CHECKING VOLTS OR RESISTANCE

A IS FOR AMPERES NORMALLY NOT USED

RED PROBE

BLACK PROBE

TO CHECK RESISTANCE, SUCH AS WHEN TESTING FOR CONTINUITY THROUGH A FIXTURE OR CABLE, SET THE DIAL ON THE METER TO OHMS - Ω. WHEN CHECKING THE VOLTAGE AVAILABLE IN A CIRCUIT SET THE DIAL TO ~V. THAT SETTING IS CORRECT FOR ALTERNATING CURRENT. NOTICE HOW THE TILDE IS SIMILAR TO A SINE WAVE. SOME METERS AUTOMATICALLY SET THEMSELVES TO THE CORRECT RANGE, BUT OTHERS MAY REQUIRE YOU TO MAKE A SELECTION.

If you get a very low reading of less than 1 ohm, then there is a short circuit in the fixture. You can tell that because the meter is reading only the resistance of the connector, and not the resistance through the wire and the lamp filament. Lastly, measure the resistance from the ground pin to the metal housing of the fixture itself. A low ohmic reading indicates that the ground wire is working properly, and that it is connected to the metal exterior of the light. An infinitely high reading indicates that the ground wire has become disconnected somewhere.

It is possible for the copper wire inside to break if it is bent back and forth enough times. Stranded wire is meant to take more of that abuse than a solid wire (which should not be used for portable conductors) but even so it will break after a while. This most often happens right where it bends the most, near the connector or the fixture housing. A fixture that comes on when you jiggle the wire often has a broken conductor.

Your meter can also be used to check the power outlet itself. Set your VOM on AC Voltage, which on most meters is marked with a ~ representing the sine wave. You may need to set the range of values. Some meters are "auto-ranging" meaning that they will automatically determine the range appropriate to what you are measuring. If not, set the range on the meter in accordance with what value you logically expect to find. AC power circuits for stage lighting are always 120VAC plus or minus a few volts when the dimmer is at full. The ranges on most meters are set an order of magnitude apart—2, 20, 200, and 2k. The 200 volt range is the lowest one larger than 120 volts.

If the power is working properly, you should get a reading of 120 volts between the hot and the neutral conductors. You should also get a reading of 120 volts between the hot and the ground. You should get a reading of 0 volts between the ground and the neutral. It may seem dangerous to connect the meter to 120v service, and you may be worried that it will *short* out, but it will not as long as you don't accidentally touch anything else with the metal part of the probe. The meter has a very large internal resistance when checking voltage, so the actual current flow inside it is very, very small.

SHORTING OUT VERSUS A BAD CONNECTION

Short circuits and *loose connections* are two radically different things. If a fixture "shorts" the hot wire has come loose inside it, and has come into contact with either the neutral or the ground. The entire exterior of a theatre fixture with a metal housing is connected to the ground wire. If the hot should come loose from the socket on the inside of it and it should brush up against the housing, a short circuit will occur when a maximum amount of current rushes through the wires all at once. Oftentimes sparks can be seen as the voltage arcs at the point of contact. When that happens, the circuit breaker will trip because the very low resistance of the newly created and "shortened" circuit allows too much current to flow all at once. Shorts are common occurrences in connectors where the hot, neutral, and ground wires are very close to one another. The problematic area often has a scorched, blackened look, and is easily recognized.

Loose connections are actually more common than shorts, and most shorts start out as loose connections. When a wire is loose in a connector, an open circuit is formed. Since the circuit is no longer complete, no current can flow, and the light will not come on. The loose wire can be either a hot or a neutral, as both are necessary in order for the circuit to be closed. In either case the circuit breaker will not have tripped, even though the light remains dark.

A break in the ground wire often goes unnoticed because lamps work just as well without one. It is a good idea to check fixtures with a meter from time to time to ensure that the grounds are functioning.

In stage work, jumpers are often used to bridge the gap between a circuit box and the light. Since a jumper has a connector on each end, and connectors are frequent failure points, you should consider them in your troubleshooting process. You can use a meter to check them without taking apart the connectors. Set your meter on ohms and check for continuity between the hots, neutrals, and grounds on each end. You should get a very low reading, because the only resistance is that of the copper wire.

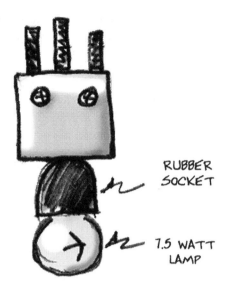

RUBBER SOCKET

7.5 WATT LAMP

A SHOP-BUILT LIGHT LIKE THIS IS SMALL ENOUGH TO CARRY WITH YOU

CIRCUIT TESTER

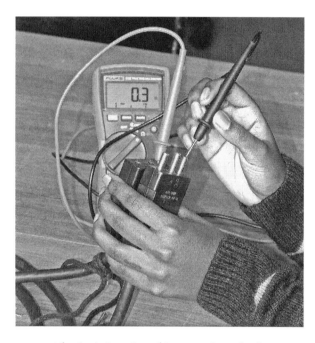

CHECKING A JUMPER WITH A METER

YOU CAN USE A VOLT-OHM METER TO TEST A JUMPER TO SEE IF IT IS WORKING PROPERLY. SET THE METER ON OHMS, AND CHECK THE RESISTANCE THROUGH THE HOT, NEUTRAL, AND GROUND CONNECTIONS. THIS JUMPER IS OK BECAUSE THE RESISTANCE (0.3OHMS) IS SO LOW.

The process of checking outlets with a meter is somewhat time consuming. You can make the job go much faster by investing in a tool that automatically checks an energized circuit. A simple shop-built checker can be made from a male pin connector, a standard rubber screw base socket, and a 7.5 watt bulb. This unit is small enough to go in your back pocket, but will only tell you if a circuit is live.

The *GamChek* is a tool made by Great American that can not only tell if the circuit is live, but also if the ground is okay, and if the hot and neutral are properly wired. Your shop-built tester can't tell you about those things. Similar devices are sold for household use, but of course they aren't meant for use with a pin connector.

Theatre lights have another layer of complexity our troubleshooting example didn't cover, in that they are fed by a dimmer system, which is controlled by a dimmer rack and/or computer. The light may not come on even if all of the electrical connections we've looked into so far are in perfect working condition. If you check the circuit output with either of the two devices above and the circuit is not energized, you should turn your attention to the dimmer itself, and/or functions of the light board that may need to be corrected. But that is really a control issue, and not an electrical one. Detailed information about the operation of modern dimming equipment is located in another chapter, but here are a few of the most common problems:

• Assuming a dimmer per circuit system, is there in fact a dimmer in the slot?
• On many dimming systems, if the dimmer is receiving a DMX signal from the board telling it to turn itself on, an LED will light up on the dimmer. If the LED is not lit, no signal is being received.
• If no lights are on anywhere in the system there may be a global problem with the wiring transmitting the DMX signal and you might need to troubleshoot it, but it is highly unlikely that a cabling issue would affect just one dimmer. You should check to make sure that the proper channel is up on the board, and that the blackout function is not engaged.

- Check to make sure that the dimmer has been properly patched with the channel you are using. If the patch is still set at 1 to 1, then the dimmers should match the channels.
- Very rarely, a problem may develop with a panel-mount connector on a drop box or in a floor pocket.

In general, mechanical issues develop at points of stress, and stress occurs wherever people use the equipment the most.

TERMS USED IN THIS CHAPTER

#0000 four ought cable	feeder cable	Socapex connector
240 volt service	GamChek	solid wire
AWG wire gauges	jumper	split phase hookup
breakout	line voltage	strain relief
bus bar	loose connection	stranded wire
cam lock	mains power supply	tails
cartridge fuse	multi-cables	terminal lug
category 5 cable	opposite phase hookup	three phase power
color code	phase A, B, C	troubleshooting
de-energized	pin connector	twist lock connector
Delta connection	short circuit	wye connection
disconnect box	SJ insulation	XLR connector
Ethernet	SO insulation	

CHAPTER 20

LIGHTING CONTROL

MODERN LIGHTING CONTROL methods are governed by complex computer systems that make it possible to operate hundreds of dimmers at one time. They also make it possible to use digitally controlled lights, color media, and LED fixtures developed over the past several decades. Although each manufacturer has its own particular method of handling technical issues, the core technology that makes all of them work is basically the same. As a result, if you learn how to program one board the others are easier to master. Each manufacturer publishes an operator's manual that provides information about their equipment. The manual is the best source of information about any specific type of system. Virtually every company makes these manuals available for download online, which is an excellent way to get information about new products. The most popular manufacturers, ETC and Strand, have some really great online "how-to" videos which you should sample.

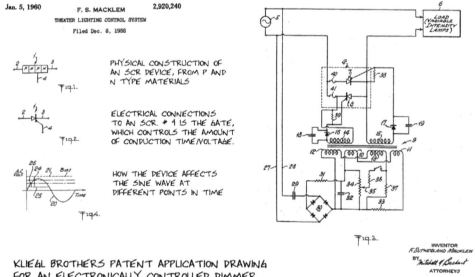

KLIEGL BROTHERS PATENT APPLICATION DRAWING
FOR AN ELECTRONICALLY CONTROLLED DIMMER

HISTORICAL PERSPECTIVE

In today's modern world it is hard to imagine a time before electric lights, but historically speaking they are a relatively new concept. Gas made from coal was used to light theatres through most of the nineteenth century, and even into the twentieth. The system of controlling the flow of the gas, and hence the brightness of the stage; and the distribution of light across it was quite complex. Gas lights were manipulated by plumbing valves, which could make the flames higher or lower, creating artistic effects. That artistic philosophy is similar today, however we control brightness by varying the voltage to incandescent lights. But when electric lights were first invented, the only means of adjusting them was to switch them on and off in large groups. Of course theatre artists would like to have more subtle control over the look of the stage than simply on/off, so electrical dimmers were invented in order to fade lights in and out, and to provide lowered settings for scenes that required them.

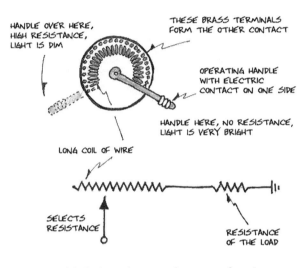

RESISTANCE DIMMER CONCEPTS

WHEN THE RESISTANCE OF THE DIMMER ITSELF IS LARGE, IT TAKES THE LION SHARE OF THE VOLTAGE, AS PER OHM'S LAW THAT STATES RESISTANCES IN SERIES SHARE THE TOTAL VOLTAGE IN PROPORTION TO THEIR RELATIVE VALUES.

Early dimmers worked on the principle of resistance, and created a voltage divider in series with the light bulbs such that as the dimmer increased its resistance, it got a larger share of the available voltage. When voltage was reduced to the lamps, the light from them faded down. The dimmer's resistance was variable, so lights could fade up and down smoothly. The dimmer's share of the power was converted to heat energy. Resistance dimmers of this sort work equally well with either AC or DC current. Most Broadway theatres used DC rather than AC until much later than the rest of the country because of Edison's influence in New York. Ironically, resistance dimmers remained popular there until the 1970s because theatre owners were reluctant to pay for upgrading their old DC power service to AC. But the rest of the country was almost exclusively AC powered decades earlier.

One of the major issues with resistance dimmers lay in the method that their levels were adjusted during a performance. It took a number of electricians to run this type of system, bearing in mind that one person could pull at most three or four levers at one time. Resistance systems tended to concentrate more lights into one dimmer, which was bad for flexibility of control. It was also difficult to get consistent results on a complex cue. The *auto-transformer* was another type of dimmer, popular in the 1950s and 1960s. It worked by using a transformer with a large number of taps on the coil of wire making up the secondary. In essence, the auto-transformer was a type of variable transformer. But it too required a number of operators for each show, and was physically very much like a resistance dimming system.

Modern electronic dimmers gained widespread acceptance in the late 1960s. Electronic dimmers have the distinct advantage that a control system, such as a modern computer board, can be used to operate all of the dimmers at one time. Prior to the invention of electronic dimmers, running lights for a show required numerous electricians all struggling with switches and dimmer handles to produce smooth crossfades.

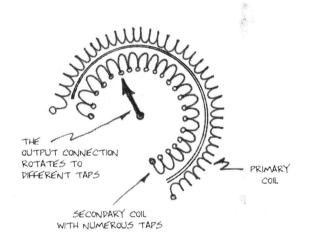

AN AUTO-TRANSFORMER TYPE DIMMER

THEY LOOKED AND OPERATED VERY MUCH LIKE A RESISTANCE DIMMER, BUT BEING TRANSFORMERS THEY DIDN'T USE THE FULL CURRENT AND WERE THUS MORE COST EFFICIENT FOR YOUR ELECTRIC BILL.

Thyristors are a family of semiconductor switching devices that can be used to turn AC electric circuits on and off in relation to a specific point in their sine wave cycle. One of the earliest versions of this device used in theatre lighting was the *Silicon Controlled Rectifier* or *SCR*, which is still quite common in many power control circuits. More modern dimmers may use different components such as the *IGBT* or *insulated gate bipolar transistor*, but the general principle of how they alter the voltage in an AC circuit remains essentially the same.

Modern electronic dimmers vary the voltage pressure to a lamp by switching the current on and off at specific moments in the sine curve. In the case of an SCR, a control voltage applied to the input gate of the rectifier

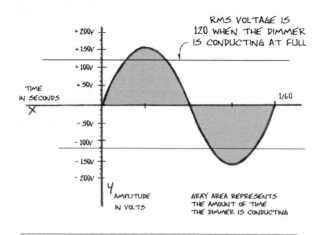

RMS VOLTAGE IS 120 WHEN THE DIMMER IS CONDUCTING AT FULL

TIME IN SECONDS

AMPLITUDE IN VOLTS

GRAY AREA REPRESENTS THE AMOUNT OF TIME THE DIMMER IS CONDUCTING

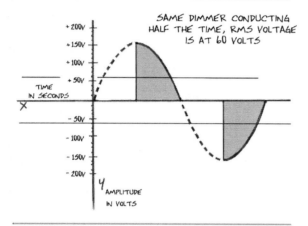

SAME DIMMER CONDUCTING HALF THE TIME, RMS VOLTAGE IS AT 60 VOLTS

TIME IN SECONDS

AMPLITUDE IN VOLTS

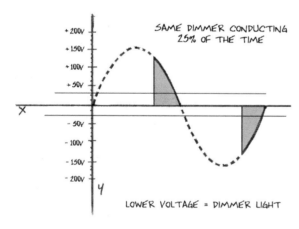

SAME DIMMER CONDUCTING 25% OF THE TIME

LOWER VOLTAGE = DIMMER LIGHT

tells it when to conduct. When the line voltage of the circuit drops to zero as it crosses the x axis of the sine wave graph, the SCR shuts off and stops conducting. It must be told by the control circuit to begin conducting again, and remains off until that signal is received. As a result, the control circuit can vary the precise moment that conduction resumes.

Remember that the effective voltage of a sine wave is expressed by its root mean square, or RMS. The graph shows how much time the wave spends conducting, and

what affect this has on the RMS voltage. If the control circuit tells the SCR to begin conducting late in its cycle, a smaller average voltage is produced. If conduction begins sooner, a larger voltage is produced. SCRs conduct in one direction only, somewhat like a diode, so in order to make use of the entire sine wave, two inversely mounted SCRs are generally used.

The newest development in dimmers is the *Sine Wave* type from ETC. Sine Wave dimmers work by lowering the amplitude of the sine curve itself, and thus lowering the RMS apparent voltage. One advantage of the new type lies in its lessening of an effect known as *60 cycle hum*. The filament in most lamps has a curled shape, which mimics the coils of wire used to create a magnetic field through induction. When a current passes through the filament, a magnetic field is established, and when the electrons reverse flow the magnetic field also reverses. The change in polarity of the magnetic field causes the filament wire to move slightly. When an AC current has a period of 60 cycles per second, the filament moves back and forth at that frequency, which is well within the range of human hearing. Sometimes that movement produces a sound pressure level large enough

DIMMER CLOSE UP

A STRAND CD 80 RACK AND DIMMMER

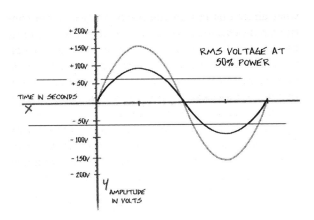

RMS VOLTAGE AT 50% POWER

TIME IN SECONDS

AMPLITUDE IN VOLTS

SINE WAVE DIMMERS WORK DIFFERENTLY, IN THAT THEY ALTER THE AMPLITUDE OF THE WAVEFORM, RATHER THAN CHOPPING IT UP. THE RESULT IS THE SAME, A LOWER VOLTAGE TO THE LIGHT

to make it audible, especially when the filament is large, as they are in high wattage lamps. When many lamps are used together in a theatre the noise can be quite loud. When a standard dimmer alters the sine wave to dim lights, the wave form becomes a very rough shape, which increases the hum, especially at reduced voltages when the curve is at its roughest. Sine Wave dimmers don't do that, because they don't "chop up" the wave form like a traditional thyristor dimmer does. Altering the amplitude reduces the hum effect at lower settings.

Standard SCR or IGBT dimmers use a large copper-wire *choke* to lessen the 60 cycle hum by smoothing out the waveform. The chokes are the large toroidal-shaped inductors in the middle of a dimmer, which occupy most of the space on the inside. In an ETC Sensor dimmer there is one choke for each of the two dimmers in the unit, which is generally true of Strand dimmers and others as well. Inductors tend to round over the jagged edges of a waveform, thus reducing 60 cycle hum. Changing the

ETC SENSOR DIMMER

THERE ARE TWO SENSOR DIMMERS IN EACH MODULE, AND THUS TWO CIRCUIT BREAKERS BOTTOM LEFT AND TWO INDUCTION COILS, OR CHOKES, WHICH ARE IN THE CENTER. A CHOKE IS USED TO SMOOTH OUT THE SINE WAVEFORM.

MOST OF THE ELECTRONICS ARE HELD IN THE "POWER CUBE" TO THE REAR LEFT OF THE MODULE. TYPICALLY, ANY FAILURE OF THE DIMMER CAN BE REPAIRED BY CHANGING OUT THE POWER CUBE

shape of the waveform doesn't always change the voltage pressure, at least as long as the area between the curve and the x axis remains the same.

CONTROL EQUIPMENT

The earliest control boards that could take advantage of electronic dimmers came about in the late 1950s, before computers were commonly available. They worked on the principle of presetting groups of dimmer values, which were used by designers to set up a *look* on stage. A look is a specific set of light values created by dimmers that produces an overall artistic effect on stage. The controller can vary the value of each light individually. Quite frequently, designers work by setting up a specific look for a scene, and then varying it to support the action of the play as time passes. If the action of the play returns to the same location several times, the same look, or a variation of it, may be reused each time the action returns.

This method of working developed from the use of *presets*, which could be made up in advance of the cue being revealed on stage. A group of *sliders* was pre-set ahead of time. Each slider controlled one dimmer, which in turn affected a small number of lights. One of the earliest examples of this was the *two-scene preset board*, which was very popular in the 1960s, and is still popular in some small venues. The board was constructed with two sets of sliders, also known as *potentiometers*. The two

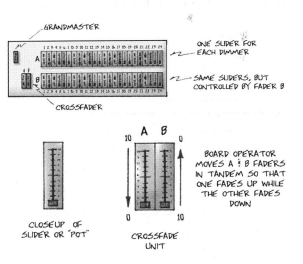

GRANDMASTER

ONE SLIDER FOR EACH DIMMER

SAME SLIDERS, BUT CONTROLLED BY FADER B

CROSSFADER

CLOSEUP OF SLIDER OR "POT"

CROSSFADE UNIT

BOARD OPERATOR MOVES A & B FADERS IN TANDEM SO THAT ONE FADES UP WHILE THE OTHER FADES DOWN

TWO-SCENE PRESET BOARD

THE SYNTAX OF A SYSTEM MEANS THE BASIC GRAMMAR OF HOW IT WORKS. EVEN THE MOST MODERN THEATRE CONTROL CONSOLES OWE MUCH OF THEIR METHOD OF WORKING TO THESE EARLY BOARDS. THAT INCLUDES IDEAS LIKE:

* DESIGNING LIGHTS AROUND THE "LOOKS" CONCEPT

* LINEAR PROGRESSION FROM ONE LOOK TO ANOTHER VIA A "CUE LIST"

* CROSSFADING FROM ONE LOOK TO ANOTHER

sets were often called *banks*, and were labeled X/Y or A/B. Each bank had one potentiometer for every dimmer in the system, perhaps 1 through 64. Larger numbers were problematic because of the time needed to reset all the sliders between cues by hand. The sliders in a bank were set to specific levels to arrive at a look on stage. The operator would write the numbers down on paper to record them. In performance a second bank of values could be set up in advance while the first was still in use on the stage.

Crossfaders were used to make a smooth transition from one preset to the next. A pair of inversely proportional sliders made up the crossfade unit. One read 10 (full) when positioned all the way up, and the other 10 when positioned all the way down. The operator moved both sliders in tandem, causing one scene to fade up while the other faded down. The output control voltage from the board to the dimmers was literally 10VDC, and lowering that voltage would in turn lower the voltage output to a stage light.

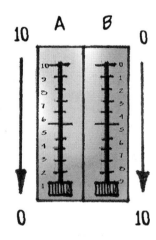

PROPORTIONAL CROSSFADERS

PROPORTIONAL CROSSFADERS WERE VERY IMPORTANT TO FLOW SMOOTHLY FROM ONE LOOK TO THE NEXT. WHEN PUSHED TOWARD THE TOP, THE ONE ON THE LEFT FADED ITS LOOK UP WHILE THE ONE ON THE RIGHT FADED ITS LOOK DOWN. YOU COULD LEAD WITH ONE OF THEM TO CREATE DIFFERENT UP OR DOWN FADE TIMES. THE SAME IDEA FOLLOWS THROUGH TO LIGHTING COMPUTERS OF TODAY, BUT OF COURSE THE BOARD DOES THE MOVING FOR YOU DIGITALLY.

A refinement of this system led to the creation of a *preset panel* that had many different banks of sliders for various scenes. That allowed more time for a second operator to manipulate the banks of sliders and set up a number of cues in advance. Thus the cuing could be more complex that what was possible with just one person doing everything. The final link in that technology was the introduction of the card-reading board.

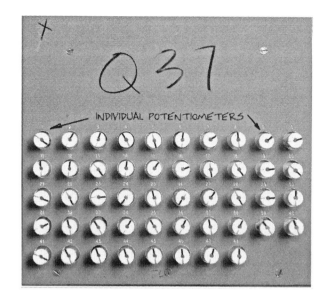

CUE CARD FROM A CARD READING BOARD CIRCA 1968

APPARENTLY THIS WAS CUE NUMBER 37.! THIS TECHNOLOGY WAS VERY SHORT LIVED, BUT INTERESTING AS IT SHOWS THE SHIFT TO USING A MACHINE MEMORY VERSUS AN OPERATOR MEMORY. THE BOARD USED A SEPARATE CARD FOR EACH CUE, THEY WERE INSERTED INTO A SLOT SO THAT THE BOARD COULD READ THE DATA BEFORE CROSSFADING TO THAT CUE

A *card-reading board* used presets stored on a printed circuit board (similar to a card that fits into the frame of a computer tower) to store intensity data for a given cue. In order to work as intended the user needed to have one card for each cue in the show, which could mean a huge and expensive number of them. But this system allowed the machine to store all of the data in a mechanical way so that the operator didn't have to do any programming (by adjusting potentiometers) during the show. Instead, all of the cards were set during a tech rehearsal by manipulating the small dials, each of which in turn controlled a dimmer. You can see how many mechanical parts might be subject to failure! This technology didn't last very long, but it is interesting to consider how it was a direct ancestor of the modern computer and how it works in controlling dimmers for a show. Instead of storing data mechanically, computers do it in digital format. But the concept of recording information for a series of cues and then playing them back is essentially the same.

Computer boards such as the *Kliegl Performer* were a huge change in the lighting design and technology fields, but it is easy to see how they were directly related to earlier types. A careful study of the Performer's keyboard shows its close affiliation with earlier preset board types. Most notably, there is an A/B fader that has A full at the top, and B full at the bottom. This was so that the operator

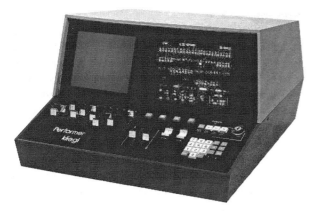

VERY "RETRO" LOOKING NOW, THIS KLIEGL PERFORMER
BOARD WAS STATE OF THE ART IN 1980.
THE MONITOR SCREEN WAS BUILT INTO THE HOUSING.
THE KEYPAD FUNCTIONS HAD CLOSE TIES TO THE
TWO-SCENE PRESET BOARDS THAT PREDATED IT.

could manually fade from one cue to another as was done on a preset board. As an alternative, the operator could use the X\Y fader, which would make the cue happen at the press of the button. This illustrates an important difference between a computer board and *any* earlier type, the ability for the machine itself to complete a cue over a period of time with no help from the operator. The fast/slow buttons were used to speed up a lengthy cue to save time while reviewing cues.

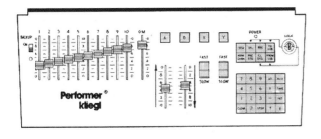

THE KLIEGL BROTHERS PERFORMER KEYPAD
WITH A CROSSFADE UNIT VERY SIMILAR
TO WHAT WAS ON PRESET BOARDS OF THE PERIOD

An interesting feature of this board was the inclusion of a backup plan at the left-hand side of the keyboard. The on/off switch can be seen at the far left. *DIP switches* were used to assign one or more channels to each of the sliders. This same type of switch is still used today to address some types of digital equipment. By carefully assigning channels into useful groups, and then manipulating them manually, the operator could run a show even if the computer crashed. That was sort of like using submasters, but in disaster recovery mode rather than programming mode.

Modern control systems don't generally have a backup mode, perhaps because they are more reliable, but more likely because people have become much more trusting of computer systems in general, and lighting systems in particular.

Early computer boards stored information digitally, but they still used a 0–10v analog DC signal to operate the dimmers. It would not be possible to use most of today's accessory equipment with an analog signal, so today digital signals are used instead. In the 1980s, various manufacturers agreed to adopt a common system of digital rules that would work with all stage equipment.

DMX 512

The modern *protocol*, or system of rules governing the way that the computer and dimmers communicate with one another is known as *DMX 512A*. DMX 512 stands for "Digital Multiplexing with 512 channels" the method used by lighting equipment manufacturers to send information from a lighting controller to a lighting device. *Multiplexing* is a generic computer term that means to send several different signals over the same line at the same time by varying a factor such as time, space or frequency. The DMX 512 protocol was first agreed upon in the 1980s as the standard computer "language" for the entertainment industry. It has been revised on occasion, and the newest version is known as DMX 512-A by ANSI, the American National Standards Institute. Before DMX became the accepted method, each manufacturer developed their own proprietary code, used only by their company, and as a result a lighting console from one company would not work with dimmers from another one. The adoption of DMX 512 as a standard by all manufacturers meant that incompatibility would no longer be an issue. It is hard to say how long this arrangement will last, because that technology is very dated by this point. It is possible to buy some types of budget dimmers today that don't use the DMX signal, and that will only work with a controller supplied by the same manufacturer.

Computers communicate with one another via a series of high and low voltages that may also be described as the numbers 1/0 or true/false. Electronically, these high and low pulses have the graphed appearance of a *square wave*, which is significantly different from the sine wave generated by an alternating current source. In the DMX standard, the ideal high voltage is +5v and the ideal low voltage is –5v. If the wiring involved in connecting the system is very long, has defects in it, or is not the right type, problems with the signal can occur. Resistance may form a voltage divider and cause a drop in voltage on the line, or if the data cable runs too close to an inductive source like a coiled stack of feeder cable the shape of the square wave could be distorted enough to be unrecognized by the recipient. The DMX 512-A standard

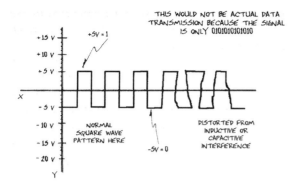

THIS WOULD NOT BE ACTUAL DATA
TRANSMISSION BECAUSE THE SIGNAL
IS ONLY 0101010101010

+15 V
+5V = 1
+10 V
+5 V

X

-5 V
-10 V   NORMAL   DISTORTED FROM
          SQUARE WAVE   INDUCTIVE OR
-15 V   PATTERN HERE   CAPACITIVE
                          INTERFERENCE
-20 V   -5V = 0

Y

DIGITAL INFORMATION IS SENT VIA SQUARE WAVE

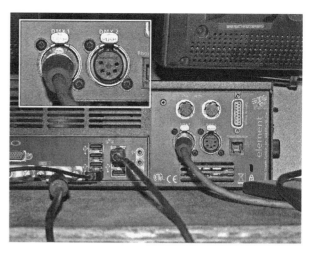

THIS ELEMENT CONSOLE HAS TWO
UNIVERSES OF DMX

requires that devices be able to receive information when the difference in high/low voltages is as small as 200mv, or one-fifth of a volt, so in most practical work there shouldn't often be a problem with the voltage drop.

The "512" part of the name comes from the number of separate lines of information that are transmitted by a light board, and corresponds to the number of *channels* available. Each channel has *256 possible values*. Computer code numbers are generally some value of 2^n, because they use only two characters (1 and 0) to communicate. 256 is 2^8, and 512 is 2^9.

The light board repeatedly sends out a string of information which tells a dimmer how much voltage to emit, or a moving fixture light what position to take. Each string of information is made up of a long series of high/low pulses that represents each of the 256 values for each of the 512 channels, plus a special start code at the beginning, and a stop code at the end. The start and stop codes are used to synchronize transmission by the light board and its reception by a device. Most electricians won't need to know the intricacies of the code itself, but knowing that there is one makes it easier to understand how the system as a whole operates.

When the DMX 512 standard was set up in the 1980s it was seen only as a way to control dimmers, and not all of the digital equipment in use today. It seemed unlikely at the time that any installation would have more than 512 dimmers, which even now would be a very large number of them. But today the DMX signal is used for much more than just dimmers. As time passed and the issue of digital control of accessory equipment was revealed, it became obvious that 512 channels would no longer be enough, especially when using moving lights. They may require dozens of channels for each fixture, so the numbers added up rapidly. The DMX standard was set at 512 channels and it was not possible to add more to it without making all previous equipment obsolete. Instead, manufacturers opted to use more than one group of DMX in a single light board.

One group of DMX signals became known as a *universe*, because it was its own complete world, not connected to any other. It is common for a lighting console to contain two or three universes, and at least one automated board has six universes for working with moving fixture lights. A recently manufactured light board may have multiple *5 pin XLR* outputs, one for each universe. They will be numbered 1-512, 513-1024, and so forth.

Another very interesting and important development used in digital control equipment from the very beginning was the use of *channels* in setting up data recording. *Dimmers* are real, physical devices that control the intensity of lighting fixtures. A channel on the other hand is a pathway for information to flow down, and is similar in concept to a television channel. A TV station is brick and mortar, but its channel number is more ethereal. The numbers are assigned by the FCC so that the public can differentiate between channels. To the receiver, channel 22 has one program on it, and channel 37 has another. Information is broadcast, or a cable provider flows into the television and a program appears on the screen. In the same way, information from the lighting computer flows down a control cable to one or more dimmers, and they in turn cause one or more lights to change brightness.

Channels only exist in the digital realm and are really just a means of assigning information to different devices. A channel does not necessarily have to be connected to a dimmer. Accessories like color scrollers, gobo rotators, and even fog machines can have assigned channel numbers.

Channels and dimmers today can be connected with one another by what was once known as *soft-patching*, and now simply *patching*. Although a modern *dimmer-per-circuit* system has a dimmer for every outlet, old-style systems generally had a smaller number of dimmers and a larger number of circuits or outlets. This was a holdover

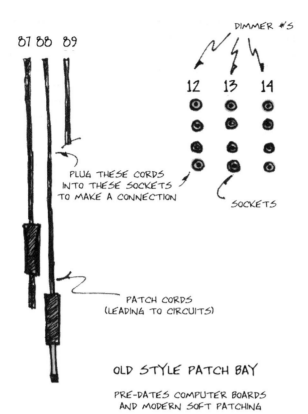

87 88 89

DIMMER #'S

12 13 14

PLUG THESE CORDS
INTO THESE SOCKETS
TO MAKE A CONNECTION

SOCKETS

PATCH CORDS
(LEADING TO CIRCUITS)

OLD STYLE PATCH BAY

PRE-DATES COMPUTER BOARDS
AND MODERN SOFT PATCHING

of dimmers. In a dimmer-per-circuit system the dimmer and circuit numbers are the same. Circuit 22 is always connected to dimmer 22.

The older approach made sense in a time when dimmers were controlled by hand, and operating too many would be physically difficult. In the present day, all of the dimmers in a system are manipulated by one electrician, literally at the press of a button, so a large number of dimmers has become an asset rather than a liability.

HOOKUP SHEET

Channel	Dimmer	Use	Type	Color	Location
1	2	Down Left Platform	36 deg	Rx 08	3FOH1
2	22	Down Left Platform	36 deg	Rx 60	3FOH12
3	4	Center Platform	36 deg	Rx 08	3FOH2
4	24	Center Platform	36 deg	Rx 60	3FOH13
5	8	Down Right Platform	36 deg	Rx 08	3FOH3
6	26	Down Right Platform	36 deg	Rx 60	3FOH14
7	56	Upstage Platform	36 deg	Rx 08	1FOH7
8	63	Upstage Platform	36 deg	Rx 60	1FOH13
9	5	Front Color Wash	1kFres	SCRLR	3FOH6
10	15	Front Color Wash	1kFres	SCRLR	3FOH12
11	23	Front Color Wash	1kFres	SCRLR	3FOH20
12	98	Back Special	26 deg	NC	2ELEC3
13	97	Scrim Pattern Left	50 deg	Rx 55	1ELEC2
14	107	Scrim Pattern Right	50 deg	Rx 55	1ELEC4
15	96	Down Pattern Wash	50 deg	Rx 16	1ELEC1
16	99	Down Pattern Wash	50 deg	Rx 16	1ELEC3
17	93	Down Pattern Wash	50 deg	Rx 16	1ELEC5
18	102	Down Pattern Wash	50 deg	Rx 16	1ELEC6
19	111	Down Pattern Wash	50 deg	Rx 16	1ELEC7
20	167	Center Side Special Low	26 deg	NC	3ELEC1
21	168	Center Side Special High	26 deg	NC	3ELEC2
22	169	Window Pattern	19 deg	Rx 34	3ELEC3
23	21	Spare	36 deg	NC	3FOH4
24	172	Spare	26 deg	NC	3ELEC4

from resistance dimmer days when there was a limit to how many dimmers the stagehands could manually operate at one time. A patch panel was used to hard patch one or more circuits to a dimmer with plugs and sockets. If the lights in circuits 12, 20, and 58 were designed to always be on at the same value and at the same time, they could all be patched into the same dimmer for convenience and to save on using up a limited number

```
Screen 1                                          _ □ ×
                        Patch
                        02:57 PM              Dim 58

Chan  Dimmer/Proportion/Profile

 1      12    20    58

 2      2

 3      3

 4      4

 5      5

 6      6

         Select dimmer numbers, then press ENTER to assign to a channel,
     or press AT to assign a proportion, or press PROFILE to assign a profile
   S1       S2       S3       S4       S5       S6       S7       S8
  Dimmer                      Previous Next              More     Fixture
  Double     A        B        Page     Page    Unpatch  Softkeys  Patch
```

YOU CAN USE THE PATCH SCREEN TO ASSIGN DIMMERS TO
CHANNELS ON AN ETC BOARD. HERE DIMMERS 12, 20, ?
58 HAVE BEEN PATCHED INTO CHANNEL 1, AND ALL THREE
WILL BE ACTIVATED WHEN USING THAT CHANNEL. IN
REALITY THOUGH, THERE IS LITTLE REASON TO PATCH
MULTIPLE DIMMERS INTO ONE CHANNEL ON A COMPUTER
LIGHTING SYSTEM. THE PROGRAM CAN HANDLE AN
UNLIMITED NUMBER OF CHANNELS IN ONE CUE.

A HOOKUP SHEET IS USED TO DESCRIBE HOW
CHANNELS AND DIMMERS ARE CONNECTED
TOGETHER OR "HOOKED UP." CHANNELS ARE
LISTED IN CONSECUTIVE ORDER, BECAUSE
THEY ARE USED TO PROGRAM THE BOARD.
DIMMER NUMBERS ARE RANDOM, AN
INDICATION OF HOW THEY ARE SCATTERED
ABOUT THE THEATRE. THE HOOKUP ALSO
GIVES DETAILS ABOUT HOW AN INSTRUMENT
IS USED, TYPE OF FIXTURE, COLOR, AND ITS
LOCATION IN THE THEATRE. 3FOH4 = THIRD
FRONT OF HOUSE POSITION, FOURTH LIGHT
FROM STAGE LEFT.

A patch panel was a real, physical entity, but soft-patching occurs only in the computer's memory. After the appropriate menu is selected, dimmers or other accessories are matched with channel numbers. This can be a distinct advantage for a designer or technician, because consecutive channel numbers can be chosen for lights that will commonly be used together, regardless of what circuit/dimmer they may be plugged into. This makes the numbers much easier to remember, and to enter on the keypad. Each target device, like a dimmer, rotator, or strobe unit, has a discrete number location known as its *address*. Dimmers are usually the lowest number addresses, so for a 192 dimmer system they would be addresses 1 through 192. Addressing devices is covered in more detail later on.

Entering the patch is guided by use of the *hookup* sheet, a spreadsheet-like document that lists all of the channels in use, and the dimmers/addresses that are connected to them. Most of the time the dimmer numbers aren't known until after the lights are hung and plugged in. Electricians write down the dimmer numbers during the hang, and a designer makes up the hookup to reflect the order she desires.

PROGRAMMING THE BOARD

Theatre light boards are meant to run a single list of cues from the beginning of a show to its end. It is assumed that the show will be very tightly scripted, and be exactly the same each night. This is different from other types of entertainment like concerts which may be different from night to night, or from more mundane gatherings such as a business meeting that may have no rehearsal and no set cues. A lightboard is often used in either of the two alternative cases, even though they are very different from a play. Another difference in how a board is used lies in the types of fixtures it is meant to control. Light boards, or *desks* as the new nomenclature describes them, were originally developed to program cues for static fixtures,

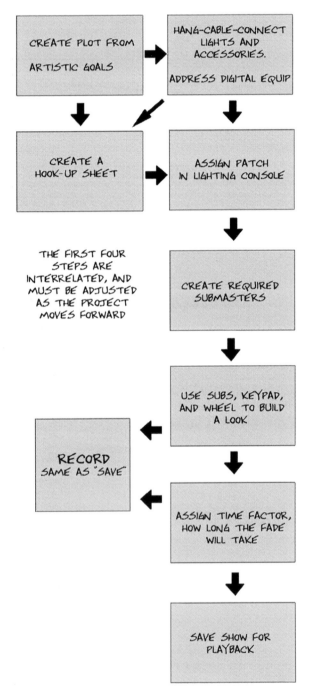

FLOW CHART FOR PROGRAMMING LIGHTING CUES

CREATE PLOT FROM ARTISTIC GOALS

HANG-CABLE-CONNECT LIGHTS AND ACCESSORIES. ADDRESS DIGITAL EQUIP

CREATE A HOOK-UP SHEET

ASSIGN PATCH IN LIGHTING CONSOLE

THE FIRST FOUR STEPS ARE INTERRELATED, AND MUST BE ADJUSTED AS THE PROJECT MOVES FORWARD

CREATE REQUIRED SUBMASTERS

USE SUBS, KEYPAD, AND WHEEL TO BUILD A LOOK

RECORD SAME AS "SAVE"

ASSIGN TIME FACTOR, HOW LONG THE FADE WILL TAKE

SAVE SHOW FOR PLAYBACK

MOVE-FADE AND TRACKING PHILOSOPHIES

THE TWO DIFFERENT WAYS THAT LIGHTING CONSOLES WORK

MOVE-FADE, ALSO KNOWN AS PRESET

THIS IS THE TRADITIONAL WAY FOR A LIGHT BOARD TO OPERATE, AND WAS THE MOST COMMON UNTIL RECENTLY. THE PROGRAMMER SETS LIGHTS AT VARYING INTENSITIES. THOSE LEVELS BECOME CUES. EACH CUE RECORDS THE LEVEL OF EVERY CHANNEL, EVEN ONES THAT DON'T CHANGE.

TRACKING

THIS PHILOSOPHY IS CURRENTLY GAINING IN POPULARITY. ON A TRACKING BOARD, THE ONLY INSTRUCTIONS SENT OUT ARE FOR CHANNELS THAT CHANGE VALUE, SO WHAT THE BOARD IS DOING IS "TRACKING" THOSE CHANGES. IT'S POSSIBLE THAT LIGHTING COMPANIES PREFER THIS METHOD BECAUSE IT IS EASIER FOR THE ENGINEERS WHO WRITE THE SOFTWARE CODE TO USE THIS METHOD IN DEALING WITH MOVING LIGHTS.

meaning regular theatre lights which are not "movers." One company describes that difference as being between *move-fade*, which is the traditional model; and *tracking* which has become much more popular as moving lights switch from concert to theatre use.

The difference is essentially this: move-fade programming assumes that each recorded cue is a standalone item and that you move between them with a fade that gracefully segues from one to the other. That is very much how an old preset board worked. On the other hand, a tracking system keeps the values of individual channels the same from one cue to the next until told to change or stop. Tracking channels is a more efficient way of programming moving lights and has become the popular modern method. With some boards it is possible to select either mode, which is sometimes known as the difference between tracking and cue-only. You might consider that tracking is most helpful when originally setting cues, while cue-only is more user friendly for editing them.

Many manufacturers offer PC-based versions of the software that is used in their desks, and some programs can be configured to actually run a show. With others, the computer versions are meant to be offline editors, so that the operator can change programming while away from the theatre. Light boards can be visualized as hardware interfaces that allow you to access the features of the program more easily. It is certainly possible though to program lighting cues with the mouse and keyboard found on a personal computer, but the console makes it more ergodynamically convenient.

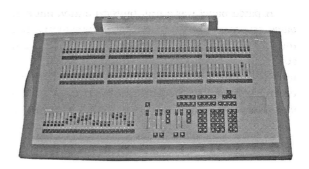

EXPRESS CONSOLE

THE EXPRESS CONSOLE HAS A SLIDER FOR EACH CHANNEL, NOT UNLIKE AN OLDER TWO-SCENE PRESET BOARD

channel when you begin working with it. The *wheel* can be used to adjust levels in a fluid way. The Expression family of control boards has a moveable wheel to the right of the keypad that allows the user to ramp selected channels up or down by rotating it. Express has a track pad that works in a similar fashion.

Channel selection through the numeric keypad is made easier by the function keys found just to the right of it. The *and* key allows several numbers to be added together and manipulated all at the same time, for example 4 *and* 5 *and* 7 *and* 8, which can then all be set at the same level. The – or *thru* key, allows for a sequential series of numbers, for example 4 *thru* 8, to all be selected at once. The *at* key is used to preface entering a level command, such as channels 4 thru 8 *at* 40%. This same arrangement can be found on just about any type of computer light board from the Kliegl Performer onward.

Submasters are frequently used to speed up the cuing process. They are a way of storing chunks of information that you can use in building a cue. You might view them as a sort of workaround for not being able to cut and paste information like most computer programs. The workflow

PARTS OF THE EXPRESSION CONSOLE

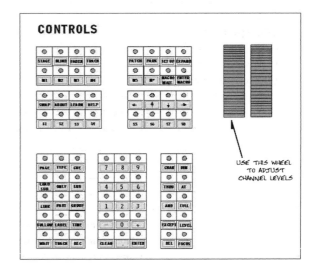

SUBMASTERS   FADERS   KEYPAD   WHEEL

The ETC Express–Expression family of light boards are a good example of a move-fade desk. Looks are created by *capturing* channels using the numeric keypad and the function keys just to the right of it. Channels can be manipulated singly or in groups to light the stage by entering their channel number(s) and assigning a value between 00 and full. Although the DMX signal has 256 steps, the board divides them into percentages, 0% to 100%. The display only has a two digit capability, so 100% shows up as FL rather than 100. Quite often, you may not know the exact level you would like to set for a of how these boards operate predates that sort of thinking. Submasters function by grouping together sets of channel numbers and values so that they all work as one unit. If you would like to use the same look a number of times, record it as a submaster so that you can bring it back as needed. Sometimes systems of light are put into a sub so that they can be brought up as a group on the way to creating a look. For example, red cyc lights in one sub, green and blue in others. The subs aren't just on/off, you can set any value between 0 and 100% using the slider. This sort of arrangement is a common feature in lighting boards made by many different manufacturers. Channels recorded in a submaster are not cues, but you can use them to make a cue.

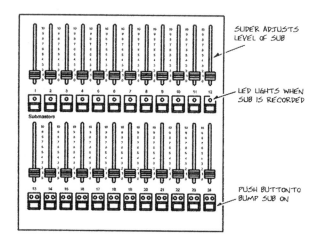

SUBMASTER SECTION OF AN ETC EXPRESSION

A LIGHT BOARD DOESN'T HAVE THE SAME MEMORY FUNCTIONS COMMONLY FOUND ON A PC OR A MAC. THERE IS NO MOUSE, AND IT DOES NOT ALLOW FOR NAVIGATION BETWEEN FILES. SUBMASTERS ARE A GOOD WAY TO STORE FILES SO THAT THEY CAN BE RECALLED LATER.

THE LED LIGHTS UP WHEN A SERIES OF CHANNELS HAS BEEN RECORDED INTO THE SUBMASTER. THE BUTTON 'BUMPS' THE SUB ON FULL. THE SLIDER CAN BE USED TO ADJUST THE LEVEL OF THAT PARTICULAR SUB

Using submasters brings up an interesting topic, that of *Highest Takes Precedence*, or HTP. This occurs when there are two or more ways to bring up a channel at the same time. There must be some sort of hierarchy about which control takes precedence over another. It could be that the values are added together, but that wouldn't work well as it would give totally unpredictable results. It could be that of *Latest Takes Precedence*, in which case the second set of instructions overrides the first one. That mode is actually a choice on the Strand Light Palette. But HTP is the rule most of the time. So if you are bringing up a submaster slider and one or more of the channels are already up via the numeric keypad or a cue, you won't see any effect until the submaster value is larger than the cue or keypad value.

The next step in programming a show on a lighting console is to record each look or other type of change as a *cue number*. Generally speaking, the cues are numbered sequentially, one after the other so that they will be in order for playback. A problem arises when adding cues later on. Additional cues are frequently added during dress rehearsals, so *inserting* cues is necessary and can be done by using the dot "." key. That creates a cue sequence such as 24, 24.1, 24.2, 25, 26.

Each cue number must have a period of *time* associated with it, even if that time is zero. There are actually two timing sequences in a crossfade, the *fade down* time of the previous cue and the *fade up* time of the following cue. Depending on how the board is configured, the computer may ask for them separately, but remembers the fade down time when asking about the fade up time. If a straight cross fade is required (as it usually is) from an Expression board, entering a time in seconds and pressing the enter button twice will make the up and down times the same. An Ion board is different, hitting the enter key will set both times the same unless you've entered them differently to start with such as [time, 3s, time 5s, enter]. You can set an overall default time in the computer's memory such as 3 or 5 seconds so that each cue is automatically given that fade time when it is recorded. You can change that value later on.

Running a show from the *fader controls* is a matter of selecting the required cue from the numeric keypad, and (on command from the stage manager) pushing the *GO button*. There are often multiple go buttons, which

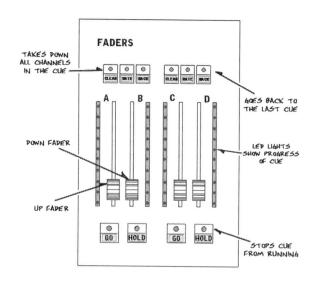

FADER SECTION OF AN ETC BOARD*

THERE ARE ACTUALLY ONLY TWO FADERS, A/B AND C/D. THE SLIDERS MUST BE IN THE UP POSITION FOR THE GO BUTTON TO WORK. IF THE SLIDER IS DOWN, THE CUE WILL RUN BUT THE CHANNELS WILL STAY AT ZERO UNTIL YOU PUSH THE SLIDER UP

*EXPRESSION SPECIFICALLY, OTHERS ARE SIMILAR

means that it is possible to run two completely separate cues at the same time. If a background cue is needed, perhaps a cyc change which happens over several minutes, that cue can run in one fader while the general show cues are run in the other. Or an effects cue can be run in the background on one of the faders. If you are merely running a sequence of cues that happen one after another, you should avoid using more than one fader, because doing so will cause cues to remain up even when the next one should have taken its place. Any channels that are higher in the first cue won't be affected by the second cue, and frequently the stage doesn't get dark in a blackout. This is an instance of how highest takes precedence works.

All of the cues line up in a list on the monitor screen. Pushing the GO button will automatically segue to the next cue on the list, without having to request that cue number. Be sure to remove unwanted cues from the list, or they may be brought up by mistake.

Both the ETC and Strand lighting companies use the word *softkey* to describe keys that are changeable and whose exact function for the moment is visible on the monitor screen. The regular "hard keys" that allow you to access the *softkey* items are usually labeled S1, S2, and so forth. You can look to the monitor to see what pressing S1 or S2 might do. That is sort of like function keys on a PC, but the outcomes are variable. The companies do this so that the number of buttons on the board doesn't get too large and cumbersome. One of the softkeys is generally a "more softkeys" access, which leads to another series of options. Softkey functions are not necessarily the same for all modes of operation.

There are several different modes of operating the board that have to do with what you see as you program it. In general, the commands *live* or *stage* mean that your actions will be transmitted to the stage lights in real time, and that you can see the effect as you do it. *Blind* allows

the operator to make programming changes that are not seen on the stage, perhaps to other cues while a rehearsal is continuing. Some boards use the term *preview* to mean the same thing.

One of the greatest difficulties of using a board in the Expression family is saving the cues. Unless attached to a separate server, Expression and Express can only save to an internal memory or to a 3.5″ floppy disk. Newer equipment has an interface that allows you to save to a jump drive. They also allow you to save as, so that you can keep multiple copies of your work on different drives.

TRACKING BOARDS

Tracking boards have some different features. The most common ones for theatre are the Strand Light Palette and the ETC Ion/Eos family. Each of them has a number of available variations. Other desks are intended for concerts and they aren't as commonly used in theatres. Desks from Whole Hog, Avolites, Martin, and others have incredible effects engines that make it much easier to do a flashy job of programming moving lights. Theatre shows are less likely to be doing that, and theatre designers are generally more accustomed to the older move-fade type. Concert lighting directors are much more likely to prefer a desk

STRAND LIGHT PALLETTE

that is dedicated to moving lights.

The Light Palette and Ion are amazingly similar in the way they work. They are both tracking boards that work well with moving fixtures, but have their roots in the tightly scripted theatre world. You will recall that tightly scripted refers to the idea that the show has gone through a tech period where the lighting cues have been carefully crafted and are expected to stay exactly the same from night to night.

Both of the boards have a command line that is very much like what you would find in AutoCAD, and which

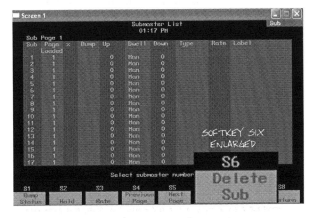

SOFTKEYS ON AN ETC BOARD

SOFTKEYS ARE A MEANS OF PROVIDING MORE FUNCTIONS WITHOUT ADDING A LOT MORE BUTTONS TO THE CONSOLE. THIS PARTICULAR ONE BROUGHT UP A LIST OF SUBMASTERS.

ETC ION BOARD

THIS ONE HAS A COUPLE OF WINGS ADDED,
WITH SLIDERS THAT MANAGE SUBMASTERS
AND INDIVIDUAL CHANNEL SLIDERS

ETC CHANNEL TILES

INTENSITY MEANS HOW BRIGHT THE LIGHT IS. THE
LETTERS F, C, AND B REFER TO FOCUS, COLOR, AND BEAM.
THOSE ARE OFTEN EDITABLE ATTRIBUTES FOR MOVING LIGHTS.

works in much the same way. Information is typed in via the numeric keypad and appears on the command line. Pressing enter causes the command to be taken, which is somewhat different from Expression, where pressing full brings up the light automatically, but is exactly like AutoCAD where commands need *enter* to make them happen.

Either of the two consoles saves data by recording it to a hard drive, and or to a flash drive. The external drive is handy to ensure that your programming data can survive a total crash of the board itself. The boards can save multiple versions of the show you are working on, as well as others. The memory is large enough to save a virtually unlimited number of shows and cues.

Both consoles have the capability to configure the attributes of specific moving lights when you select your type from a menu. After selection, the board is able to automatically display the functions of many different types and brands of intelligent lighting fixtures.

Encoders are used to manipulate the values of the attributes. Use hard and/or softkeys to select the attribute

you would like to adjust, and the encoder wheels can be used to change values. On the Light Palette, a track ball is used for pan and tilt, and a color picker such as found on Photoshop can be used to click on a specific color with the mouse. Either board will mix LED or dichroic filters to the shade of standard gel filters made by all the major companies, so you can match whatever else is already going on with the conventional fixtures.

The monitor displays use individual tiles for channel information, rather than just a number on a screen. This is to organize the information in an easily understood way. In keeping with the philosophy that channels can be more than just dimmers, the tile can also show information about focus, color, and beam. These are known as *non-intensity parameters*.

WORKING WITH DIGITAL EQUIPMENT

In the early 1980s digital lighting technology was brand new, and moving fixture lights were the exclusive domain of the *Vari-Light* Corporation. This company didn't sell their fixtures, but rather rented them to rock and roll tours and kept their technology a closely guarded secret. The High End Systems *Intellabeam* came on the market as an alternative. Intellabeams used the same digital approach, but the mechanical systems were very different. Although this particular fixture has been discontinued, High End still sells a much smaller but similar product, the *Trackspot*.

In a *moving fixture* light, a motorized *yoke* allows the optical section to pan and tilt so that the light beam shines in different directions. This is very much like a

SOFTKEYS AND ENCODERS ON AN ION BOARD

NOTE THAT THE KEY ON THE FAR RIGHT
IS THE "MORE SOFTKEYS" BUTTON

mechanized version of a traditional light. There are two basic versions, wash and spot. The differences are just about what you would expect. But a Trackspot is a *moving mirror* light. As its name implies, a mirror in front of the light beam is used to reflect it in different directions, and the body of the fixture itself does not move. Moving mirror lights respond much more quickly than moving fixture lights, and there is less pressure to keep the light physically small since only the mirror moves.

Moving lights have *attributes*, which is a name used to describe the different controllable properties of the lights. Moving fixtures may have several dozen attributes and require the same number of channels to control them. If a light has 20 different attributes, it requires 20 channels of the DMX signal. Each channel controls one specific attribute, which in turn controls what the light looks like on stage. Setting a value for the channel may affect the appearance of the light beam by changing color, shape, intensity, beam angle, pan or tilt. Setting cues for moving lights requires that levels be entered for the different channels/attributes so that the desired look is achieved. That is much easier to do on a modern tracking

HIGH END SYSTEMS

CYBERLIGHT

STUDIO SPOT

ENTIRE HEAD MOVES
ON A ROTATING YOKE

CYBERLIGHT ATTRIBUTES

CHANNEL	ASSIGNMENT
1	Pan Coarse
2	Pan Fine
3	Tilt Coarse
4	Tilt Fine
5	Color Wheel
6	Cyan (red)
7	Magenta (green)
8	Yellow (blue)
9	Static Litho (pattern)
10	Rotating Litho
11	Rotate
12	Zoom
13	Focus
14	Iris
15	Effects Wheel
16	Frost
17	Shutter
18	Dimmer
19	Motor Speed
20	Control

console because when you select the proper fixture from a list, it automatically sets up all the channels for you. In addition the program will configure the softkeys so that they open windows that contain sliders, wheels, and color pickers that allow you to manipulate that particular fixture.

The digital age has made other sorts of equipment easier to control as well. *Color scrollers* are motorized strings of gel color on a scroll, which can be rotated across the front of a lighting instrument so that the position of the string determines the color of the filter in the light. So a wash of top lights can be many different colors instead of just one. But there is a disadvantage, because the transition from one color to the next isn't very smooth unless they are right together on the gel string. Often times, scrollers must be reset during a blackout of some sort. Newer sorts use dichroic filter technology to crossfade more easily from one color to the next.

Dichroic filters are used in architectural applications as well as entertainment because they are extra-durable; much more so than a standard polyester gel. To make one, very thin metallic coatings are deposited on glass. They refract white light rays very slightly in much the same way as a prism does. Several are used in tandem to mix colors in an RGB manner. Each color has its own channel so that they can be proportionally mixed. Some moving lights use a color wheel instead, which in actual use is much like a scroller. The wheel has to rotate to the desired color, and that will show if the light is on at the time.

Gobo rotators are tiny motorized units that spin the gobo in its slot. In early versions, they were controlled entirely by an analog 0–10 volt DC signal, the same type used on analog electronic dimmers. Nowadays, a digital signal is sent to a control unit, and the motors are powered from there. The same method is used to control hazers and fog machines. A standard theatre type console can be used to program all digital devices used in a show, within the limitation of how many channels are available.

Each accessory device (moving light, color scroller, strobe light, etc.) has an *address*, which is the controller's target when sending out information. This address is changeable, and can be reset by the user. When loading in the show, electricians set the address of each device at a specific number between 001 and 512, depending on what the hookup requires. A multi-channel device set at a certain address may automatically take up whatever following channel numbers are required to assign a different channel for each attribute. Thus, a 16 channel moving light addressed at channel 301 will also use all the following channels up through 316. This illustrates how quickly 512 channels can be taken up in lighting a show.

The dimmers in a system generally use the lowest numbers in universe one, and are semi-permanently addressed as devices 001 through 096, 192, 288, or

GOBO ROTATOR AND POWER SUPPLY UNIT

THE SUPPLY UNIT INTERPRETS THE DMX SIGNAL AND SENDS THE APPROPRIATE DC + OR - VOLTAGE TO THE ROTATOR.

SCROLLER

THIS UNIT IS TYPICAL OF MECHANICAL COLOR CHANGERS. THE OPENING IS CLEAR IN THE PICTURE, WHICH IS USUALLY ONE OF THE CHOICES MADE IN GEL STRING COLORS.

however many dimmers are in use. As a result, any accessory device must have an address higher than that. If moving light addresses were in the zone used by the dimmers, changing dimmer values would inadvertently affect the fixture and vice versa. When no more addresses are available in the first universe, a second can be used. The address numbering system starts over again in the second universe. The next address after universe 1, #512 is universe 2, #001. A single universe cannot recognize a number higher than 512.

Restarting the address number after 512 works perfectly well for individual universes that do not interact with one another, but the control board must communicate with every universe, and a different numbering system must be used so that each address in each universe has a unique channel number for cuing purposes. Channels for the first universe in ETC equipment are numbers 001 through 512, the second are 513 through 1024, the third 1025 through 1536, and so forth. Strand does that differently with a numbering system that uses a decimal point. The first universe is 1.xxx, the second is 2.xxx and so forth, which is a bit easier to visualize. The universe numbers are used by the console only, and not by the device. All address numbers have three digits, and are 512 or lower.

To configure a light or other device to the board, you need to run a cable from a DMX port to the first fixture in the line. Most DMX-operated devices have both input and output connectors for the DMX signal so that up to 32 of them can be run from one board output by *daisy chaining* them together. The output cable runs from the console to the input of the first device. From that point a *jumper* runs the signal from the output of the first device to the input of the second device. This continues until all of the fixtures are hooked up. A DMX-controlled device will only react when its particular section of the data stream (its address) tells it to do so. Information for other devices passes through it without difficulty. The end device in the chain should have a *terminator* on it to end the signal. A terminator is an XLR connector with special electronic components that eliminate signal corruption.

ETC equipment and others use an Ethernet system and *nodes* to distribute the DMX signal rather than the outputs on the back of the console. The *Node Configuration Editor* is used to assign the node output to a particular universe of addresses. The node converts the Ethernet signal to a DMX signal.

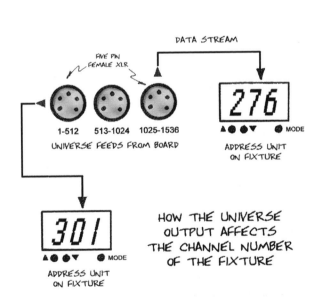

HOW THE UNIVERSE OUTPUT AFFECTS THE CHANNEL NUMBER OF THE FIXTURE

THE CHANNEL NUMBER OF THE FIXTURE AT LEFT WILL BE #301 ON THE BOARD, BECAUSE IT IS IN THE FIRST UNIVERSE. BECAUSE THE FIXTURE ON THE RIGHT IS IN THE THIRD UNIVERSE, ITS CHANNEL NUMBER WILL BE 1025 + 276, OR #1301.

THIS NODE HAS AN ETHERNET INPUT PORT ON THE SIDE, AND FIVE PIN XLR OUTPUTS FOR DMX ON THE FRONT

TERMS USED IN THIS CHAPTER

60 cycle hum
address
attribute
auto-transformers
bank on a preset board
captured channel
card-reading board
channel
choke
color scroller
crossfader
Cyberlight
daisy chain
desk
dip switches
DMX 512
Electronic Theatre Controls (ETC)

fader controls
five pin XLR
gobo rotator
highest takes precedence (HTP)
hook up
IGBT (insulated gate bipolar
    transistor)
Intellabeam
Kliegl Performer
latest takes precedence (LTP)
look
move-fade
moving mirror fixture
moving yoke fixture
multiplexing
node
non-intensity parameters

patch
potentiometer
preset
preset panel
SCR
SineWave dimmer
slider
softkeys
square wave
submaster
terminator
thyristor
tracking
two scene preset board
universe
Vari-Light

CHAPTER 21

PHOTOMETRICS

T ECHNICALLY, *PHOTOMETRICS* MEANS "those things pertaining to the measuring of light." In common usage though, photometrics is used to describe how lighting instruments, or fixtures, are defined as to their sizes, light output, and uses. In his groundbreaking 1936 work, *A Method for Lighting the Stage*, Stanley McCandless coined the phrase lighting *instrument*, which he used in referring to lights used for the stage. Perhaps he was attempting to use a scientific name to enhance the image of something that, up to that point, was not given much thought. Lights today are still very often called instruments, but the term *fixture* is also popular as it fits in well with the terminology used in commercial lighting practice. In most situations, the words instrument, fixture, and light are used interchangeably.

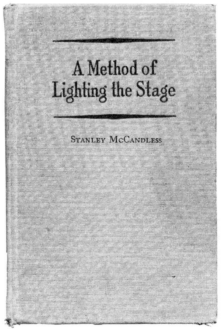

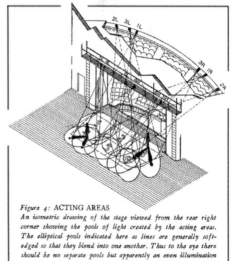

Figure 4: ACTING AREAS
An isometric drawing of the stage viewed from the rear right corner showing the pools of light created by the acting areas. The elliptical pools indicated here as lines are generally soft-edged so that they blend into one another. Thus to the eye there should be no separate pools but apparently an even illumination over the whole acting area. However, the two shadows of the actor are always present and the lights should be so focused that the actor can move in any portion of the numbered areas and be sure that his face and the balance of his body will be lighted. Note that 1L, *3R, 4L and 6R instruments are mounted so that their outside rays are parallel with the side extremities of the whole acting area.*

THIS BOOK BY STANLEY McCANDLESS WAS THE BEGINNING
OF THE ACADEMIC STUDY OF ENTERTAINMENT LIGHTING

LIGHTING FIXTURE COMPONENTS

The earliest electrified theatre-specific fixtures were basically just light bulbs with a shiny surface behind them to reflect more of the light in one direction. Not long after, lenses were added to help focus the light beam down to a more specific shaft of light rather than a simple wash going in all directions. Lenses completed the triad of mechanical parts that make up the core of photometrics as used in a modern lighting instrument. These are: the light source or *lamp*, the *reflector*, and the *lens*. Most modern fixtures contain all three of these elements, though some of them place two or more within the lamp itself.

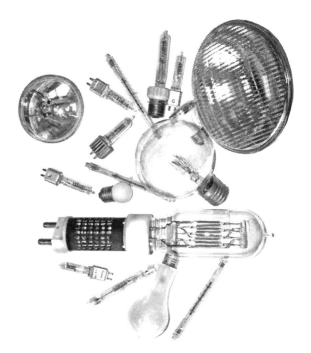

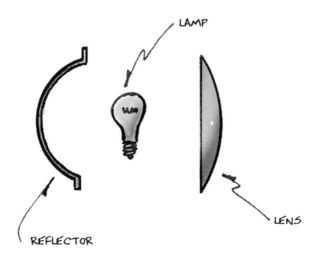

THREE BASIC COMPONENTS
OF A LIGHTING INSTRUMENT

In any sort of electrical lighting fixture, the lamp is used to create light, the reflector helps to gather the part of that light that emanates in the wrong direction, and the lens helps to either focus or diffuse the beam into a useful shape. It seems appropriate to start this discussion with the lamp since that is where light begins.

LAMPS

Most lamps generate light by resisting the flow of electricity through the *filament* of the bulb. The tiny wire filament becomes so hot that it incandesces, which means that it has so much heat energy that some of it is dissipated in the form of light energy. To keep the filament from oxidizing, or burning up in the atmosphere, the first light bulbs used a glass enclosure to create a vacuum around the wire filament. Modern versions have an inert gas like argon inside of them which creates pressure to keep the filament from off-gassing and make it last longer.

A longer filament generally produces more light energy, so the wire is often curled inside the glass bulb so that it can be made longer without using up too much space. Making a bulb smaller in relation to its output is very important for theatre lights because they are much brighter than ordinary commercial fixtures. A large lamp requires a large fixture, which is problematic when trying to hang a number of instruments in a small space. One of the problems facing engineers a half century ago was that the high wattage lamps used in theatre lights got too hot for the glass bulbs of the period, and they tended to melt from overheating. To accommodate the heat produced, the glass envelope surrounding a 1000 watt lamp had to be several inches in diameter, which was just too big for a practical fixture.

About that time *quartz glass* was developed to create a lamp that could be tiny in size, but put out a very large amount of light. That type of glass is used extensively today for modern stage and studio lamps. Quartz glass (which is made from a finely ground powder of that mineral) can absorb a tremendous amount of heat without being destroyed. It is important not to touch a quartz lamp with your bare hand when installing one in an instrument because dirt and oil on your fingers will adhere to the glass. The oil turns black when heated, and that part of the glass will get hotter than the rest. It will melt in short order as a result. It's important to unplug fixtures before changing lamps. If the power to the light has not been switched off, the instantaneous heating of the lamp will seriously burn your hand.

The arrangement of the filament in the lamp is very important to its ability to work well in concert with the reflector and the lens. In a theoretical sense, the source

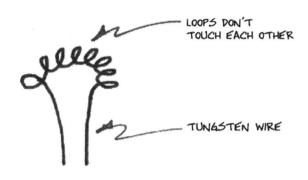

LOOPS DON'T TOUCH EACH OTHER

TUNGSTEN WIRE

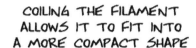

COILING THE FILAMENT ALLOWS IT TO FIT INTO A MORE COMPACT SHAPE

ANSI CODE AND WATTAGE MARKED ON BASE

TWO PIN LAMP

EACH END HAS A SINGLE CONTACT

DOUBLE-ENDED OR RECESSED SINGLE CONTACT

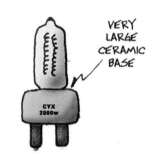

VERY LARGE CERAMIC BASE

HIGH-WATTAGE MOGUL BIPOST

METAL HEAT SINK HELPS PREVENT DAMAGE TO SOCKET

HPL FAMILY

COMMON LAMP TYPES

of the light should be from one single point for the reflector to work at its highest efficiency. Of course this is not entirely possible given the coiled nature of a practical filament, but even so manufacturers strive to design the filament so that it is extremely compact, and comes as close as possible to the theoretical model. The desire for a compact light source has made arc lamps more attractive, because theirs is extremely small. Even so, they are generally not used in static fixtures because of the dimming issue. Instead of dimming, arc lamps sputter and go out when their voltage supply is reduced.

The *base* is the part of the lamp used to make connection with the *socket*, which is part of the fixture itself. Everyone is acquainted with the screw base because this is the type most commonly used in everyday life. Other common types include the *two pin*, the *RSC or double ended*, and the *mogul bipost*. The *HPL* is a two pin lamp that is fitted with an aluminum heat sink to dissipate the extreme amount of heat that is generated by this quartz lamp inside a small fixture. Earlier versions of similar lamps were prone to failure in the base and socket because of the heat factor. Even though the glass part of the lamp coped well with high temperatures, the metallic base did not.

The letters "HPL" are an example of listing lamps by their *ANSI* code. The American National Standards Institute creates standards for many different industries in the United States. They ensure that devices are compatible with one another, and that, for example, any standard screw base light bulb will fit into any standard screw base socket. They provide a three letter ANSI code for every new lamp manufactured. The code is stamped on the shipping container, and should also be visible on the base of the lamp itself. Lamps of the same basic type, but different wattages, have different codes.

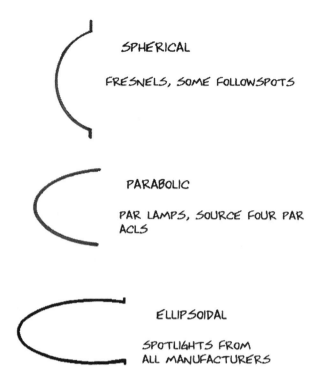

SPHERICAL

FRESNELS, SOME FOLLOWSPOTS

PARABOLIC

PAR LAMPS, SOURCE FOUR PAR ACLS

ELLIPSOIDAL

SPOTLIGHTS FROM ALL MANUFACTURERS

TYPES OF REFLECTORS

REFLECTORS

A reflector is used to "reflect back" the light rays that are going toward the rear of the fixture. More than that, it is designed to do this in a way that is optically efficient with the rest of the instrument, creating a specific type of light beam. The most commonly used shapes for a reflector are *parabolic*, *ellipsoidal*, and *spherical*. The type of reflector used defines how the light rays travel after they leave the fixture.

The study of how light interacts with the natural world is known as optics. *Geometrical optics* is the study of the *reflection* and *refraction* of light when it interacts with lenses and mirrors. Although light is often described as either waves, or as particles called photons, for the purposes of a study of geometrical optics it is helpful to visualize light in terms of *rays*. A light ray is assumed to travel in a straight line unless acted upon by a device like a lens or reflector.

Reflectors are in fact mirrors that have a curved shape, and the properties of that curve affect the manner in which the light rays are reflected. On a flat planer reflector, light rays bounce off the surface so that the *angle of incidence* is equal to the angle of *reflection*. The angle of incidence is the angle at which the light ray strikes the mirror's surface.

If the mirror is held at an angle and the light source remains in the same place, the angles of incidence/reflection will still be equal, but the size of the angle will be altered, and the light will be reflected to a different place.

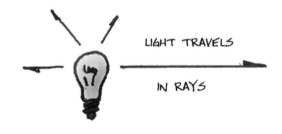

LIGHT TRAVELS

IN RAYS

GEOMETRICAL OPTICS

LIGHT RAYS MOVE OUTWARD IN A STRAIGHT LINE UNTIL ACTED ON BY A REFLECTOR OR REFRACTOR

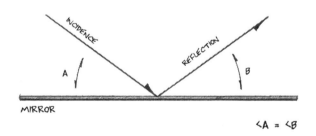

LIGHT RAY IS REFLECTED AT THE SAME ANGLE IT STRIKES THE MIRROR

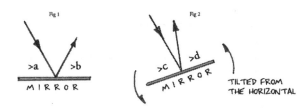

In Fig 1, angle A and angle B are equal to one another, because the angle of incidence is equal to the angle of reflection. The same statement is true for angles C and D in Fig 2.

The angle of the light ray striking the first mirror is the same angle (to the horizontal) as the second one, yet the final direction of the two reflected rays is different, because the second mirror has been tilted from the horizontal.

The axiom of *angle of incidence equals the angle of reflection* also holds true for curved surfaces, but the curve affects what the angle will be for each particular point on the curve. Sometimes it is helpful to think of a curve as a series of infinitely small flat surfaces connected together. Viewed in that context, a curved mirror becomes a series of reflectors each with its own angle of incidence/reflection.

A curved surface can be visualized as a series of flat surfaces arranged together.

It is important to remember that reflectors are three-dimensional forms, but it is generally easier to visualize them using two-dimensional shapes. Hence, a spherical 3-D form becomes a 2-D arc when depicted on a flat piece of paper like the one you are looking at right now.

Many early fixtures used a spherical reflector derived from lights originally designed for lighthouses. On paper they are approximated with an arc of a circle. It is the nature of a mirror curved with this shape that rays from a source in the center will be reflected back toward the center. This method is not perfect however, and in the process light rays on the extreme edges of the reflector are deflected in a more random pattern. Light that falls outside the desired pattern is said to be *ambient*. Imperfections in the reflection of light from a spherical reflector create a good deal of ambient light mixed in with the intended light beam.

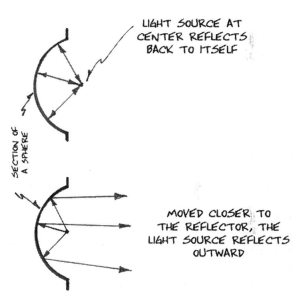

SPHERICAL REFLECTOR

The *parabola* is a very interesting shape that occurs in nature in many different ways. When a string is draped between two points and allowed to hang downward in a curve, the shape it forms is a parabola. The arc of a baseball through the air is also a parabola. Parabolas are a frequent object of mathematical study because they occur in the natural world, yet have a scientifically predictable shape. When a parabola is used as a reflector, a light source at its natural focal point is reflected outward with all rays pointing in one direction. That aspect has obvious advantages when constructing a light fixture to project organized beams of light. In this theoretical construct, the light source is viewed as a single point. In a practical lighting instrument, the filament is not a single point, but rather a coil of tungsten

ANGLE OF INCIDENCE IS EQUAL TO
THE ANGLE OF REFLECTION

PARABOLIC REFLECTOR

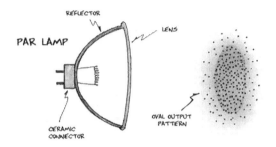

PAR LAMP

REFLECTOR

LENS

CERAMIC
CONNECTOR

OVAL OUTPUT
PATTERN

THE ACTUAL OUTPUT OF A PARABOLIC
REFLECTOR IS GENERALLY AN OVAL SHAPE,
PARTLY DUE TO THE SHAPE OF THE FILAMENT,
AND PARTLY BECAUSE THEY WERE DEVELOPED
TO BE CAR HEADLIGHTS.

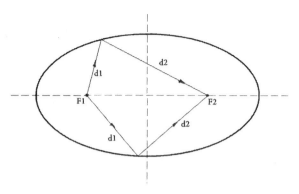

MATHEMATICAL PROPERTIES OF AN ELLIPSE

D1 + D2 SHOULD HAVE THE SAME VALUE NO MATTER
WHICH DIRECTION THE RAYS EMANATE FROM ONE OF
THE FOCAL POINTS. A RAY FROM ONE FOCAL POINT
WILL ALWAYS REFLECT TO THE SECOND FOCAL POINT

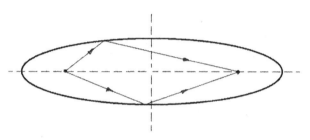

AN ELLIPSE MAINTAINS ITS
MATHEMATICAL PROPERTIES
EVEN WHEN ELONGATED

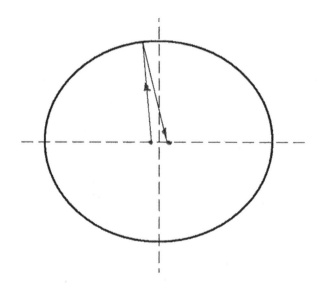

MOVING THE FOCI TOGETHER
WILL EVENTUALLY PRODUCE A CIRCLE

wire with dimensional qualities. If the filament is arranged laterally across the reflector, the light from an instrument of this type will have a beam that is somewhat oval in shape.

A third type of commonly used reflector draws its shape from the *ellipse*. In plane geometry, an ellipse is formed by using two *focal points*, F_1 and F_2. The curved surface of the ellipse is defined by adding (distance) $d_1 + d_2$, where any two values of d_1 and d_2 should equal any other two values for d_1 and d_2. This sum should be the same for any point on the curve.

A string can be used to demonstrate this. Fix the ends of the string to the two focal points and stretch it taut in any direction. Use a pencil to draw a line all the way around. The resulting curve will be an ellipse. *Varying the distance between the focal points produces ellipses of different proportions.* If the focal points are moved close to one another, an approximate circle will be formed. If the focal points are so far apart that the string is almost tight between them, a long thin curve will be formed.

The string method of forming an ellipse makes it easier to visualize how light rays are affected by an elliptical reflector because the curved surface is such that a ray emanating from one focal point will be reflected toward the second one, in the same way that the string was running. The string approximates the angles of incidence and the angles of reflection. In a theoretical construct, all of the light from a lamp in the position of F_1 that hits the reflector will be bounced off and converge again on F_2. Of course in a practical lighting instrument, the reflector cannot be an enclosed unit because there would be no way for the light to get out and reach the stage. Only part of the ellipse is used, and because of that, some light from the lamp will not be properly reflected and will become ambient light. Even so, the elliptical reflector is very efficient when compared to other types.

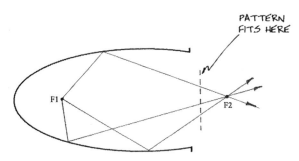

LIGHT RAYS CONVERGE AND DIVERGE, SO ANY TEMPLATE INSERTED BETWEEN THE TWO FOCAL POINTS WILL BE PROJECTED UPSIDE DOWN AND BACKWARD

One interesting aspect of a fixture with an elliptical reflector is that the light rays actually cross over each other as they pass through the second focal point. If this type of fixture is used to project an image by using a metal *pattern* placed between the two focal points, the image will be upside down and reversed. The area where patterns are placed is called the *gate*. Projecting patterns is a very useful quality of an ellipsoidal instrument.

The exact shape of the ellipse is important in determining the width of the beam of light projected by an ellipsoidal. A narrower ellipse will produce a narrower beam, and a fuller ellipse a wider beam. Different beam angles are important to lighting designers so that they can efficiently shape the light that will be projected onto the stage. Early fixtures used differently shaped reflectors, but the manufacturing process was very expensive, so the modern trend is to construct one type of reflector and create different beam angle spreads with lenses instead. If the reflector is made of glass with a dichroic coating, it is possible to construct it so that invisible infrared light rays pass through to the back of the instrument, which keeps the gate and lenses cooler.

LENSES

Glass lenses were first invented at the end of the thirteenth century, and use the principle of *refraction* to change the angle at which light rays travel. In the case of a magnifying glass, light rays are gathered by the lens as they pass toward the human eye. In the case of a lighting instrument, light rays are affected as they pass out of the fixture, but the optical principles involved are the same.

Dutch mathematician Willebrord Snell determined that light rays passing through a denser medium were slowed, and that this process bent, or refracted the rays so that they moved in a different direction. Most everyone is familiar with the "broken straw" example, where a straw in a transparent glass appears to bend where it enters the water. The straw is not really bent or broken, but rather only appears to be, because light passing through the water and glass is slowed, and according to Snell that refracts the light into a new direction.

You might actually observe several different effects on the straw, because not only is light bent by the water, it is also affected by the transparent glass container. The density of the material makes a difference in how much refraction takes place. A denser material creates more refraction than a less dense material, so the glass has more of an effect than the water. The angle at which a light ray intersects with the refractive medium is also important. A light ray that strikes the refractor at a steeper angle is bent more than one striking at a shallower angle. If the intersection is at a 90 degree angle, there is no refraction.

A STRAW IN WATER APPEARS TO BE "BROKEN" WHEN THE LIGHT IS REFRACTED

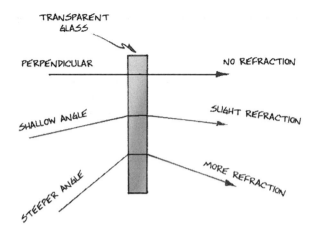

TRANSPARENT GLASS

PERPENDICULAR   NO REFRACTION

SHALLOW ANGLE   SLIGHT REFRACTION

STEEPER ANGLE   MORE REFRACTION

AMOUNT OF REFRACTION IS AFFECTED BY:

DENSITY OF MATERIAL
ANGLE OF INCIDENCE
THICKNESS OF MATERIAL

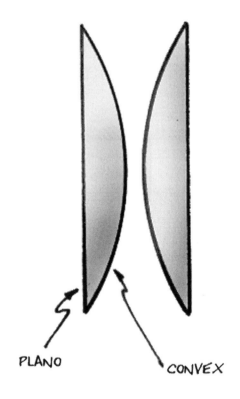

PLANO   CONVEX

TWO THINNER LENSES
CAN HAVE THE SAME
EFFECT AS ONE
THICKER LENS

Useful lenses for the theatre are generally of a type known as *Plano-convex*, meaning that they are flat on one side, and curved on the other. The curvature of the lens affects the amount of bending that occurs, and by carefully calibrating the curve it is possible to focus light rays from an instrument into a cohesive unit. The thickness of the lens is directly proportional to the amount of bending the lens will create, because a thicker lens has a more pronounced curve. In the typical ellipsoidal instrument, two Plano-convex lenses are used as a pair to reduce the thickness that would be required if only one were used.

Augustin Fresnel was a nineteenth-century French scientist working with the properties of light who developed a specific type of lens often used in lighthouses, and also in theatrical lights. One of the problems of the day was that the very thick lenses used in lighthouse lights tended to crack. This was because impurities made the glass less than 100% clear, so part of the light passing through them was converted to heat energy. This would cause the lens to heat up when the light was turned on, and the heat caused the glass to expand. When turned off, the glass would contract, and this movement often meant that the somewhat brittle glass would crack, ruining the lens. Fresnel solved this problem by creating a stepped lens that maintained its convex shape on the curved side, but did so in steps, so that the resulting lens was much thinner.

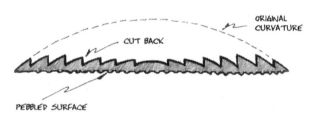

ORIGINAL CURVATURE

CUT BACK

PEBBLED SURFACE

FRESNEL LENS

Although this works perfectly well in theory, the formation of the glass is not completely exact, and a certain amount of ambient light is created. Fresnel lenses are used theatrically in the *Fresnel* lighting instrument, which creates a soft pool of light where precision is not required, unlike an ellipsoidal instrument. Fresnel lenses often have a slightly pebbled surface on the flat, plano side in order to diffuse the pool of light they create. This helps to hide light and dark spots resulting from the imprecision of the stepped lens.

Diffusion is the main objective of some lenses, especially those used on fixtures with a parabolic reflector such as PAR lamps, or the ETC Source Four Par. In either of those two types, the lens serves to spread the beam

WIDE

MEDIUM

NARROW
(PEBBLED SURFACE)

VERY NARROW
(CLEAR)

SOURCE FOUR PAR LENSES

PICK THE PROPER BEAM ANGLE

THIS GRAPHIC SHOWS THE RESULT OF 36 AND 70 DEGREE
FIXTURES AT THE SAME DISTANCE. IF YOUR GOAL WAS TO
LIGHT UP THE GUITAR PLAYER, THE 70 IS MUCH TOO SPREAD
OUT. YOU CAN SHUTTER IT IN, BUT THEN YOU'VE LOST A
GREAT DEAL OF LUMINOSITY.

outward a specific amount. The lenses have a similar appearance, and can be identified by the texture of the surface.

Modern ellipsoidals use lenses to create different *beam angles*. A beam angle is the divergence of the light as it leaves the fixture, measured in degrees. If each light has the same output in lumens or candlepower, the brightness of a light on a reflective surface should be determined by what percentage of the output of the entire fixture falls on that reflective surface. If the reflective surface is far away from the fixture, a narrower, tighter beam of light will preserve more of its luminosity than a wider one would. Thus the apparent light from the narrow angle fixture will be brighter.

THE FRESNEL

The *Fresnel* is perhaps the oldest kind of still existing lighting instrument and has been around longer than any type still in common use. Because Monsieur Fresnel was French, his name has a pronunciation that is odd for most English-speaking persons. The word is pronounced fruh-nell, rather than frez-nell.

FRESNEL LIGHT

Fresnels use a spherically shaped reflector to bounce light vaguely back in the direction of the lens. Both the lamp and the reflector are fastened to a sled that can be moved back and forth, toward or away from the lens. The closer the sled is to the lens, the more spread out the beam pattern will be. This position is referred to as *flood*. When the sled is moved away from the lens, the beam output is sharpened into a position known as *spot*. There are an infinite number of stops between the two extremes.

Regardless of the number of degrees of beam spread, the light output of a Fresnel is always somewhat diffuse, with a bright or hot spot in the center, and a gradual lessening of intensity toward the edge of the beam. A common accessory used in limiting the beam spread of a Fresnel is a set of *barn doors*. This is a set of hinged metal flaps on a mounting plate that can be fitted into the gel frame at the front of the light. They are especially popular in a television studio. By adjusting the angle of the flaps it is possible to mask the leakage of unwanted ambient light that tends to angle obliquely outward from the imperfect Fresnel lens. A *top hat* is a rounded masking device based on the same principle.

BARN DOORS   TOP HAT

It is interesting to note that ETC does not currently offer a true Fresnel lighting instrument in its family of theatre lights. PAR lamps in general and the Source Four Par in particular have lessened the popularity of Fresnels in theatres.

THE ELLIPSOIDAL SPOTLIGHT

Sometimes ellipsoidals are called *Lekos*, because they were developed by two people named Lee and Cook at Century Lighting in New York, and that company uses Leko as a trade name. Strand Lighting bought that company and sells ellipsoidals using the name Leko Light, but the name is often used in a more generic way, as are the names of a popular brand of facial tissue and/or cotton swabs. Ellipsoidals are the workhorse units of the theatre and are the most commonly used fixtures in stage lighting. An ellipsoidal can be used in more subtle ways than other kinds of lights because it can be more

finely controlled. They are used extensively in theatre because theatre lighting is a more subtle art form than TV or concert lighting. TV lighting tends to center around high wattage Fresnels, and concerts (where the PAR once was king) now use moving fixture lights almost exclusively. The qualities of high intensity, a coherent beam, and adjustable focus, account for the most useful feature of an ellipsoidal: its ability to shape the light beam.

The optics of an ellipsoidal reflector were covered earlier, where you learned that the light beam can be shaped when it is in the space between the two focal points created by the elliptical reflector. The area of an ellipsoidal where shaping of the beam occurs is known as the *gate*. The shaping operation occurs before the light rays have merged and crossed over themselves at the second focal point. Consequently, any image projected by a Leko will be reversed when the beam reaches the stage.

Several different approaches to masking the beam may be taken. The most common is to use *shutters*, four thin pieces of metal that slide in and out of the gate and are a permanent part of the instrument. Shutters can make the beam of light into a semicircle, or a square, or, by angling the shutters, a triangle. Shutters are quite useful in shaping the light to fit a specific object such as a window or a door. Most modern instruments have a rotating barrel so that the entire shutter assembly can be turned a few degrees to a more advantageous angle. Lights are hung at all different attitudes, and without this feature it is sometimes difficult to angle a shutter enough to get the desired shape.

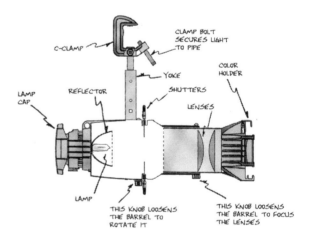

PARTS OF A SOURCE FOUR ELLIPSOIDAL

The left shutter affects the right side of the beam, the bottom the top of the beam, and so forth. It is not possible to precisely shape the output with barn doors, top hats, or any other equipment fitted into the gel frame holder, those devices only work on Fresnels, or possibly a wide angle PAR lamp.

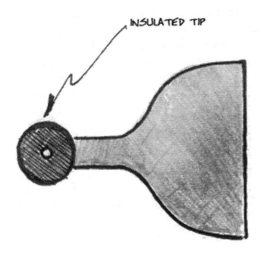

INSULATED TIP

SHUTTER

There are several ways to describe the size and use of ellipsoidals. An early method was to use the distance between the focal points in a fixture. The farther apart the two focal points were, the narrower the angle would be. Focal lengths for traditional lights varied from 6 inches to 22 inches. Many of these lights are still in use. The beam spread of a 6×6 is much wider than that of a 6×22, and as a result, the pool of light emitted by the 6×6 (at the same distance) will cover more area on the stage than the 22 will.

An *iris* can be used to reduce the size of the light beam to a small, round spot. Irises are most often used in followspots, but they are also made in a size that will fit into a standard gobo slot so that it is possible to use a standard ellipsoidal as a followspot, perhaps from a spot tower.

A VINTAGE ALTMAN FIXTURE

THE TYPE OF LIGHT, 6×9
IS CLEARLY MARKED ON THE YOKE

THIS TYPE OF LABELING DOESN'T
WORK ON ETC SOURCE FOURS
BECAUSE THE LENS TUBES CAN
BE SWAPPED, AND THE LABEL
WOULD BE WRONG AFTER THAT

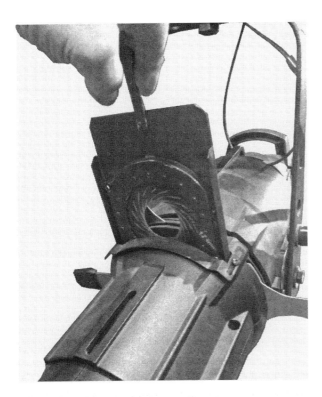

DROP-IN IRIS UNIT

THE SLIDE-OPEN GOBO SLOT ON THIS SOURCE FOUR FIXTURE
ALLOWS YOU TO INSERT A DROP-IN IRIS. THAT MAKES IT
MUCH MORE EFFICIENT AS A FOLLOWSPOT.

The newer system uses degree angles to describe the *beam angle* spread. This system came about partly because of a change in manufacturing philosophy. Companies began to design their fixtures so that they all use the same housing and reflector making manufacturing them less expensive. Instead of reflectors, different lens arrangements are used to produce different beam angle spreads. These range from a very narrow angle of 5 degrees to an extremely wide angle of 90 degrees. It is possible to purchase extra lenses so that one body can produce different angles by switching *lens tubes*. The most commonly used degree angles are 36° and 26°, which correspond to 6×9s and 6×12s in the older numbering system.

Source Four fixtures are made with 90 degree and 70 degree spreads, but several manufacturers produce fixtures with these angles:

50°
36°
26°
10°
5°

COLOR CODING TAPE

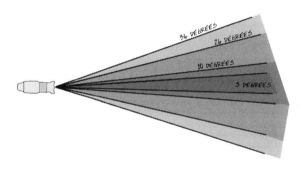

RELATIVE BEAM SPREADS

EVEN THOUGH THE FACTORY STICKER HAS FALLEN OFF, THIS LENS TUBE IS STILL RECOGNIZABLE AS A 36° BECAUSE OF THE COLORED TAPE ON THE BARREL

Most of the lenses are interchangeable from one fixture body to the next. The 5 and 10 degree lenses are much larger than the others, which all have the same general appearance. A *Beam Angle Chart* is included in the appendices. It shows the approximate size of various beams at different distances.

When fixtures were separated according to their reflector size, there was little need to transfer the lens tube from one fixture to another - they were all the same. It was common practice to *color code* the light as to its focal length, and the marking was often placed on the yoke of the instrument, frequently writing it on the metal surface with a paint marker.

Today, when ellipsoidals use the same standard body but different lenses another approach is needed. The specification of the light cannot be marked on the yoke, but rather must be on the lens tube itself. Companies place stickers on the tube at the factory, stating 19, 26,

36 degrees, and so forth; but these stickers often fall off, and are difficult to read from a distance. It is much easier to tell the lights apart if the lens tube is color coded in such a way that the code can be read from the ground when the fixture is hanging in the air.

THE PAR LIGHT

Traditional *PAR cans* are essentially round car headlights that have been manufactured to operate at 120 volts, rather than at the standard automobile voltage of 12v. The fixtures themselves are very simple, lightweight, and inexpensive because all of the optics are built into the lamp itself. As a consequence, PAR lamps tend to be somewhat more expensive than other types, but the fixtures themselves are cheap. The parabolic reflector creates a naturally tight beam of light, and the on board glass lens is used to diffuse it.

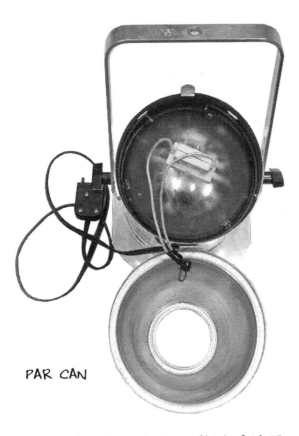

PAR CAN

NOTICE THE CERAMIC ON BACK OF LAMP

THE CERAMIC CONNECTS POWER
TO THE LAMP, AND CAN BE USED TO ROTATE
THE OVAL "HOT DOG" WHEN
FOCUSING THE LIGHT

SOURCE FOUR PAR

NOTICE THAT THE LENS ROTATES
TO ALTER THE DIRECTION OF THE "HOT DOG"

PAR cans were the standard rock-and-roll light for many years because they are so lightweight and durable, and because rock shows did not require a great deal of precision in focusing. The beam that comes from a "can" is similar to that generated by a Fresnel, except that it is oval in shape and the instrument does not allow for changing from spot to flood. Instead, a variety of lamps must be used. They range in angle from wide to medium to narrow to very narrow.

It is possible to rotate the lamp within its housing in order to change the orientation of the oval beam shape from vertical through horizontal, in accordance with how the light can best cover its intended area. PARs come in two main sizes, the 64 and the 56, with a few much smaller sizes. PAR 64s are far and away the most common. Birdies are tiny PAR 16 lights which can be mounted on scenery to provide light in odd spaces. The peculiar sizes refer to the diameter of the lamp given in one-eighths of an inch. (PAR 64 = 8″ while PAR 16 = 2″.)

The *Source Four PAR* is physically very different from a PAR can, but emits a very similar light. It has a traditional reflector and lamp, and only the lens is changed to alter the beam angle of the light. A ring known as the *bottle* is rotated to change the direction of the oval, like a regular PAR except only the lens rotates. These fixtures are more expensive than a standard PAR can, but they have the advantage of using the much cheaper HPL lamp used in many other lights.

CYCLORAMA LIGHTS

Cyc lights, also known as *border lights*, or *strip lights* are used to produce a wide swath of light on stage. As the name implies, these fixtures are manufactured in strips, where a number of lamps are ganged together in a parallel circuit. Mini Strips have a large number of very small lamps. They are 12 volt lamps connected in series of 10, and if one filament blows, all the lights go out. The fixture itself is very small and will fit into places that others will not.

//	//	X	//	X	//	//	X
RED	GREEN	BLUE	RED	GREEN	BLUE	RED	GREE

COLORS IN CYCLORAMA LIGHTS

CYC LIGHTS OFTEN HAVE EITHER THREE OR FOUR DIFFERENT COLORS TO THEIR CIRCUITS. THEY ARE USED TO PROVIDE AN EVEN COLOR WASH ON THE CYC. RED, GREEN, AND BLUE ARE THE PRIMARIES OF LIGHT, AND THUS SHOULD BE MIXABLE TO ANY COLOR.

THE FAR CYC IS TYPICAL OF MOST MODERN "STRIP" LIGHTS. IT DOES NOT HAVE A GROUPING OF CIRCUITS, BUT RATHER EACH CELL HAS ITS OWN PIGTAIL.

The Mini Strip is not the typical type, which tends instead to be a group of two or three cells in a row. Plugging several strip light units together end to end, it is possible to create a swath of light across the entire stage, and/or as they are most commonly used, across a sky *cyclorama*. Strip lights are evenly spaced to provide a wash of color. Usually there are three different circuits for different colors. By using different colors in each circuit, colors on the cyc can be mixed together. If red, green, and blue are used (the primary colors for lighting) a theoretically infinite color range may be achieved. A common practice for cyc lighting is to use a set of strip lights on a batten above, and a set of lights on the floor. A scenic ground row is often used to mask the bottom strips. Confusingly, the bottom strips themselves are also referred to as a *ground row*, and this term can be used to describe either the lights or the scenery.

Strip light circuits are easy to overload because of the large number of individual lamps that are used. Care should be taken to determine the individual lamp wattage and multiply it by the total number of lamps in use.

Compare this wattage rating with the dimmer capacity, or use the P=IE formula to convert to amps. It is possible to buy dimmers of a higher wattage rating, but cables become an issue when the 20 amp rating for standard jumpers is exceeded.

LED Cyc Lights

LED lights are considered by many to be the technology of the future. They use less power to produce light than incandescent lamps and give off much less heat. One problematic aspect of LEDs though, is that like moving lights they don't work with existing dimmer installations. That isn't too much of a concern because a modern computer board is intended to control them without using dimmers. The intensity control circuits are in the fixtures themselves and you only need to run line voltage power to them. Very often a dimmer can be set to 100% in the control panel and that circuit can then be a constant source of power for an LED or moving light fixture. When that happens, you have created what is often called a *non-dim*.

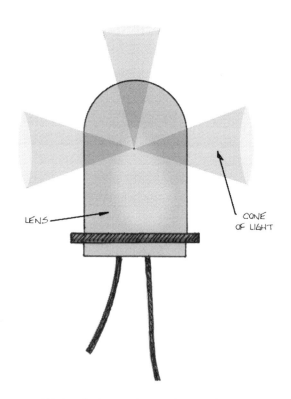

LIGHT EMITTING DIODE OR LED

LEDS PRODUCE LIGHT WHICH EMANATES IN SPECIFIC DIRECTIONS CALLED "CONES." THE ACTUAL MECHANICS ARE MUCH MORE COMPLEX THAN SHOWN HERE, BUT THE ILLUSTRATION DEMONSTRATES THAT LIGHT DOESN'T TRAVEL OUTWARD EQUALLY IN ALL DIRECTIONS LIKE THE FILAMENT OF AN INCANDESCENT LAMP. THAT'S PROBLEMATIC WHEN DEALING WITH OPTICAL DEVICES LIKE REFLECTORS AND LENSES.

LED stands for light emitting diode. LEDs produce light when a current passes through their semiconductor material, usually some variety of gallium alloy. The light is emitted in a process known as electroluminescence. Current passes in one direction only, from the cathode to the anode, but not in reverse. This is the same way that all diodes operate not just LEDs, and is similar to the physical characteristics of transistors which also use a junction between P and N type materials. The basic material is made in larger wafers that are split apart into smaller pieces. A diode "chip" is mounted in a plastic housing with wiring leads attached. The chip itself is very small, often about 1 millimeter, but the case can be much larger, especially for a brighter variety. The lights are very efficient and long lasting.

The light is emitted through what is known as an escape cone, and there may be several on one LED. Many of the chips have a multifaceted surface with multiple escape cones. It is difficult to construct a light fixture that can accommodate the way LEDs emit light through the escape cones when using traditional optics such as what you might find in a standard ellipsoidal spot light. You will recall that an ideal light source for such optics is a single point, as small as possible. The technology required to make that happen with LEDs is still in its infancy. As a result, LEDs are much better suited to wash-type lights that have a pattern like a PAR or Fresnel.

LEDs are perfect for cyc lighting because it is possible to mix their red, green, and blue hues together to make a variety of colors, and also because cyc lighting typically involves creating washes of light on the fabric. As an aesthetic aside, you might notice that the colors created by LED fixtures lean toward what could be called "neon" or "electric" in nature and might not be appealing to all designers for all types of shows.

CHROMA-Q COLOR FORCE LED LIGHT

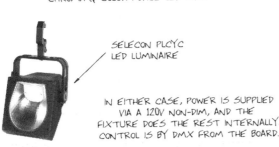

SELECON PLCYC
LED LUMINAIRE

IN EITHER CASE, POWER IS SUPPLIED
VIA A 120V NON-DIM, AND THE
FIXTURE DOES THE REST INTERNALLY.
CONTROL IS BY DMX FROM THE BOARD.

LED CYC LIGHTS

TWO DIFFERENT APPROACHES. THE CHROMA-Q FIXTURE
SHAPED LIKE A TRADITIONAL STRIP LIGHT, AND THE SELECON
MORE LIKE A FAR CYC, OR PERHAPS AN OLD-SCHOOL SCOOP.

FIXTURE STORAGE RACKS

Lights must be stored when they are not in use. Of course storage can be handled in a multitude of different ways, but one of the most popular is to use lamp racks. The advantage of using rack storage is that the lights can be rolled around to a specific location where they are being hung. It is a good idea to mark the racks so that all the electricians know which fixtures go where. Color coding is very popular.

THIS LAMP RACK IS ON WHEELS
SO THAT IT CAN BE EASILY ROLLED
INTO POSITION

COLOR MEDIA

Sheets of plastic are routinely used to create colored light for the stage. They can be called by several different names—*gel*, *filters*, *color media*, or simply "color." Modern intelligent lighting often uses *dichroic* filters to change the color of light. Dichroic filters use the principle of prismatic action to change light color, where white light is split and divided into specific colors through refraction. Dichroic filters are very different from a standard plastic gel, which is much more commonly used. The *SeaChanger* is a color changing device that fits in the middle of a standard fixture, and uses dichroic filters to alter the color of the light's output. A different type of device, the color scroller, can be used to automatically shift from one standard gel color to another. Scrollers use the standard plastic media, but it is cut into specific sizes and the different colors are connected together to form a *gel string*, which is then shifted back and forth in front of the light in order to change the fixture's color output.

Gels got that name because they were originally (until the mid-1970s) manufactured from the same sort of gelatin material used to create Jell-O, the popular dessert item. Gelatin is an organic animal substance used in many different products. It was used to create the original stage lighting gels because it is easy to insert dye into the material. A method of dying clear plastic sheets was not invented until later. Gelatin-based gels would dissolve in water, and that was the basis of a joke where a new stagehand would be asked to "wash the dirty ones."

Most modern color media is created from a mix of polyester and/or polycarbonate plastics. Some manufacturers are able to insert the dye in the base material, while others apply it to the surface. The theory is that when color is an integral part of the plastic, it is less likely to bleach out over time and exposure to bright light. The original gelatin gels tended to lose their color saturation rather rapidly, and needed frequent replacement. Modern gels last much longer, and typically only need replacement in a long-running venue.

Gel color comes in either a roll form, which is more popular in television and film, or in 20 inch by 24 inch sheets. Film electricians, or gaffers, tend to use rolls of color so that they can cut a large piece and attach it with clothespins to the barn doors of a lighting fixture. The nature of film is that a "set-up" for a certain shot will last for only a few minutes before moving on to the next one, so the use of theatre-style frames is not time efficient. If one were to use the film method in a theatre where shows last from weeks to months to years, pinned on gels would tend to work themselves loose and are not practical. The 20x24 sheets are more suited to cropping on a paper cutter that can be used to trim them to the appropriate sizes.

The most common sizes are:

19°–90° ellipsoidals:	6¼" × 6¼"
Source 4 Par:	7¼" × 7¼"
Older ellipsoidals:	7¼" × 7¼"
6" Fresnel:	7¼" × 7¼"
8" Fresnel:	10" × 10"
PAR 64:	10" × 10"

Quite frequently, these sizes are marked out on a paper cutter, so that it is easy to tell at a glance where to cut.

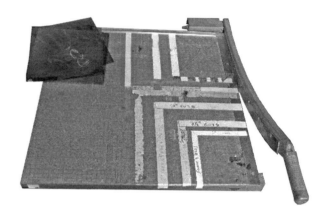

USE TAPE TO MARK OFF
COMMONLY NEEDED GEL SIZES

Gels are often called "filters" because of the nature of how they work in changing the color of light. Light from a theatre instrument at full intensity is white, subject to certain limitations imposed by the Kelvin scale of color temperature. White light is a combination of all different wavelengths of visible light, from just past infrared to just short of ultraviolet. A red-painted surface appears as red because the paint only reflects the wavelengths of light which the human eye perceives as the color red. All other wavelengths are absorbed by

RED LIGHT

WHITE LIGHT

THE RED PAINT OF THE SPORTS CAR
REFLECTS ONLY THE RED WAVELENGTHS
OF THE WHITE LIGHT

the object and converted to heat energy. This is why dark objects, which reflect very little light, become much hotter when exposed to direct sunlight on a sunny afternoon than white objects do.

White paint theoretically reflects all wavelengths of light and absorbs none of them. If a red gel is used to illuminate a white object, the object will appear as red. Not because the gel is making the object that color, but because the red gel has filtered out the other wavelengths of light, so they are not present to be reflected. Filters subtract undesirable wavelengths as light leaves the instrument, and so not all wavelengths are present in the beam of light emitted from the fixture. The gel removes or "filters" the unwanted wavelengths from the mix before the light from an instrument has a chance to reach the stage.

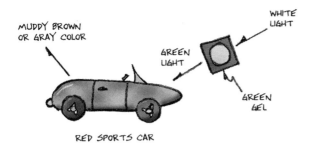

RED SPORTS CAR

THE GREEN GEL FILTERS OUT MOST OF THE RED WAVELENGTHS OF LIGHT, SO THERE ARE NONE TO REFLECT OFF THE SURFACE OF THE CAR.

BECAUSE THE FILTER MECHANISM IS IMPERFECT, THE GEL IS NOT COMPLETELY SATURATED, AND THE PAINT IS NOT PURE RED, SOME REFLECTION TAKES PLACE ANYWAY.

An interesting paradox develops. If a fixture is filtered with a primary green gel so that its output is restricted to green wavelengths only, and the light from it strikes a red object which reflects *only* red wavelengths, there should be no reflection at all, and the red object should be invisible. What a boon that would be for magicians everywhere. In reality, this does not happen because the filter is not perfectly constructed and transmits some light other than that which is intended. The red paint is not perfect either, but rather a mixture of colors where red predominates. Thus the object will not be invisible, but rather a muddy shade of grayish brown. There is a long standing prohibition against using any sort of green gel in a light that may hit an actor's face, because green is the opposite, or *complementary color* of a healthy, sanguine face and would make the actor look sick. The musical *Wicked* is a good example of how rules are meant to be broken.

The primary colors of light are red, green, and blue, which is different from pigments where the primaries are red, yellow, and blue. The debate about why the

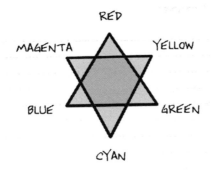

COMPLEMENTARY COLORS IN LIGHT

THIS CHART SEEMS VERY ODD TO A PAINTER, WHO IS ACCUSTOMED TO PIGMENT PRIMARIES OF YELLOW, RED, AND BLUE, AND SECONDARIES OF ORANGE, VIOLET, AND GREEN. COLOR THEORY USED IN LIGHTING IS CLOSER TO A TRUE, MATHEMATICAL UNDERSTANDING OF THE SUBJECT, WHICH WORKS WELL WITH ELECTRONIC EQUIPMENT. CYAN IS A LIGHT BLUE COLOR, SLIGHTLY TINGED WITH GREEN.

difference exists has not been settled, but RGB is used as a standard for all fields where color is produced by lighting. The mixing of red, green, and blue should produce a white light. The mixing of any two of them will produce a secondary color, just as with pigments. Sometimes there is a need to produce white light from a mixture of two different colors. White is desired so that the true color of the scenery/costumes can show through, but the use of two different colors to achieve the white light means that interesting shadows are cast that help in making the stage picture seem more three-dimensional. If two lights are used, one having a primary color, and the other the opposite secondary color, then a white light will result on any surface receiving an equal amount of each color.

The *CIE color chart* is used to reference how colors react with one another. Pick a color on the chart and draw a line from it through the middle of the white area to a color on the other side. The color at the end of the line will be the complementary, or opposite of the first one. Using those two colors together should produce a white light. The artistic goal of producing a white light on the stage in this fashion has become less popular than it once was, but knowing the method re-enforces your knowledge of how subtractive mixing works.

The effect of gels is governed by factors other than just the chroma, or hue of the color. *Saturation* refers to the amount of color present. Saturated gels have a darker appearance, and they have more dye in the plastic, so that more of the white light is stopped. Most color media is not designed to stop all of the white light going through them, but rather boost the amount of the chosen color

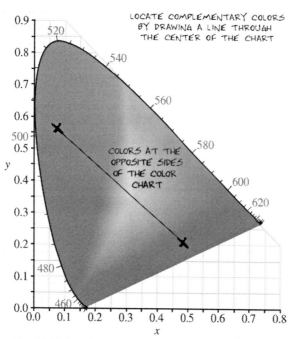

LOCATE COMPLEMENTARY COLORS
BY DRAWING A LINE THROUGH
THE CENTER OF THE CHART

COLORS AT THE
OPPOSITE SIDES
OF THE COLOR
CHART

OF COURSE SINCE THIS IS IN BLACK AND WHITE YOU CAN'T
SEE THE COLORS! BUT IF YOU LOOK IT UP ONLINE YOU'LL
SEE THAT THE OUTSIDE EDGE HAS THE MOST SATURATED COLOR
AND THE MIDDLE IS WHITE.

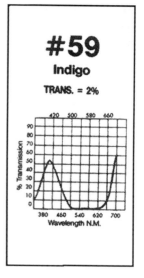

TWO DIFFERENT GRAPHS
OF COLOR TRANSMISSION
IN ROSCOLUX COLORS

wavelength by reducing all the others. A very dark color such as Rx59, Indigo, is highly saturated with dye and transmits only 2% of the available light. The very next color in the Roscolux swatch book is No Color Blue, Rx60. It is not very saturated, and transmits 62% of the available light. As a result, the Rx60 also transmits a large amount of ~white light wavelengths along with the blue ones.

The "big three" lighting gel manufacturers are *ROSCO*, The Great American Market or *GAM*, and the European company *Lee Filters*. ROSCO has a series of colors for the European market that all begin with the letter E, but are not commonly used in the States. Sheets of gel from any company have a tag on them with the color number. Pieces of gel cut for individual lights are usually marked with a grease pencil so that they are identifiable from each other.

The letters Rx, G, and L are used to denote the company, and the number of the gel follows. For example: Rx60, L202, and G820 are all very close to the same shade of light blue, which is a very commonly used color, and it is difficult to tell them apart. So marking is mandatory. But each company has colors that are more specific to their line, and most designers have favorite colors that they like to use. At one time, ROSCO had a second line of gels known as *Roscolene*, which are no longer popular because they tend to fade more over time. RL and Rx were used to differentiate between the two.

Gel manufacturers regularly hand out samples of their products in the form of filter *swatch books*, which contain small pieces of the color media in a flip out deck such as paint manufacturers offer. Each color is backed by a piece of paper that gives the name and number of the color, its transmission percentage, and a graph showing its transmittance curve. The graph shows the relationship between the wavelength of the light in nanometers, and the percentage of transmittance. In reality,

MARKING THE COLOR WITH A GREASE PENCIL

YOU CAN GET ONE FROM A SUPPLY HOUSE,
THEY ARE OFTEN FREE WITH A GEL ORDER.

a theatre practitioner has little reason to be concerned about the precise wavelengths of light being used, but in an academic way the graph is a good indicator of how tightly compacted and narrow the filter is when transmitting light.

There are some non-color related reasons to use gels. *Neutral density* is a type of filter that reduces the amount of light transmitted without changing its apparent color. It is used to reduce the light output of one fixture in relation to another. The graphs of neutral density colors are not a peak like most others, but rather tend to flow across the spectrum in a wavy line. *Frost* and *diffusion* gels are used to scatter light from a fixture that may be too close to spread out normally in accordance with the mechanics of the fixture. Some diffuse the light in all directions, while others work in a more linear fashion. The primary colors of red, green, and blue often have frost versions, so that they will scatter and blend together better on a cyclorama. Another type of filter has color, but is not used for artistic reason. *Color correction* filters are used to change the Kelvin temperature of an incandescent lamp to 56k for film or television purposes.

PATTERNS, GOBOS, TEMPLATES AND OTHER PROJECTION MATERIALS

There are a number of different ways to project an image onto the stage using a pattern or slide fitted into the gate area of an ellipsoidal instrument. The most common is to use metal *templates*, also known as *patterns* or *gobos*. There are several hundred stock types to choose from, or for a fee supply companies will create a custom metal template from your user-supplied artwork. It is also possible to have color images transferred to glass plates, but this technology is newer and more expensive. ROSCO offers plastic slides under the name Image Pro.

One of the problematic aspects of all patterns is that they are fitted inside an instrument where temperatures can reach several hundred degrees Fahrenheit. ROSCO's Image Pro circumvents that issue by cooling the plastic medium with a fan, but even so the images fade after a short while. Color glass break-ups are available, as well as deformed glass that adds no color, but rather creates a texturally interesting, swirling sort of light on the stage.

The standard type of pattern is created by etching an image onto a thin sheet of stainless steel. Stainless is preferred because it holds its shape better under high heat. If a pattern is removed from a light while it is on, the metal can often be seen to glow from the heat. Some patterns are made from other alloys when the pattern is too intricate for the normal method.

Patterns are manufactured in several different sizes, for use in different sorts of lights. Size A is intended to fit most modern ellipsoidal fixtures, and has the largest image area. The larger image area is generally more efficient. This size pattern fits the standard-size holder used for Source Four and Altman ellipsoidals. Strand Lekos use size B.

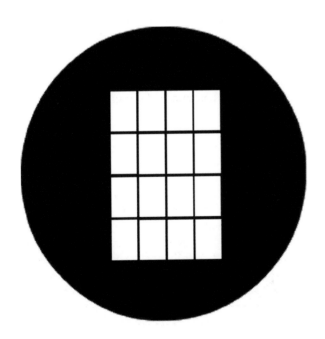

STANDARD GOBOS ARE ETCHED INTO STAINLESS STEEL SHEETS THAT CAN WITHSTAND THE INTENSE HEAT INSIDE A LIGHTING INSTRUMENT

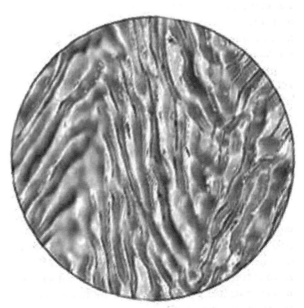

THIS DEFORMED GLASS GOBO FROM ROSCO CREATES SWIRLING PATTERNS OF LIGHT WHEN USED IN A ROTATOR

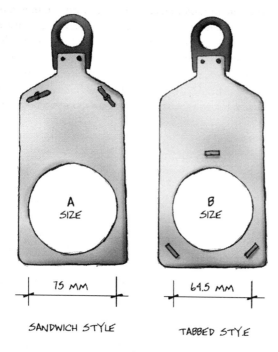

SANDWICH STYLE   TABBED STYLE

TWO DIFFERENT TYPES OF GOBO HOLDERS.

THE ONE ON THE LEFT OPENS UP AND IS
DESIGNED FOR RECTANGULAR PATTERNS,
WHILE THE ONE ON THE RIGHT IS DESIGNED
FOR ROUND PATTERNS.

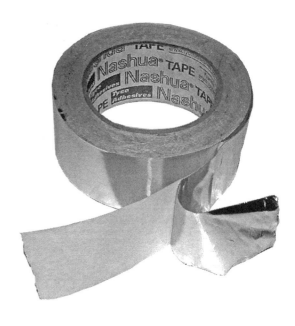

THIS TYPE OF DUCT TAPE IS MADE FROM
ALUMINUM FOIL, AND HAS A STICKY SIDE
THAT IS REVEALED WHEN YOU PULL THE
TAPE AWAY FROM ITS PAPER BACKING.
THE FOIL DOESN'T BURN UP IN THE LIGHT,
BUT SOMETIMES THE GLUE LETS GO.

Gobo rotators typically use size B, and their patterns must have a round shape to fit in the holder. Although the round B size is intended for a rotator, it will also work in a regular fixture, but a special holder with a smaller opening is generally necessary. That's because the outside diameter of the pattern is almost the same size as the image area of an A size pattern holder, and they tend to fall out of it. It is generally not possible to tape a gobo in the holder because the tape will burn at the high temperature found inside the ellipsoidal, but aluminum duct tape works okay in a pinch. This type of tape is made from aluminum foil and an adhesive backing and is not the usual kind of plastic duct tape. It won't burn but the adhesive will leave a mess that is difficult to remove.

Size M is used in Source Four Juniors, and is much smaller than the other types. The holder for M gobos is very different looking from the normal kind. Moving lights use patterns also, but each manufacturer tends to use a different size.

Gobos are often used in groups to provide a textural wash across the stage. In that context, they tend to be repeating irregular shapes that have no definite orientation. Others are used to project a specific image such as a logo or the outline of a building. Remember that patterns fit into the gate of an ellipsoidal, in a place where the light rays from the lamp and reflector have yet

STANDARD SIZE A
FOR REGULAR
SOURCE FOUR LIGHTS

FRAME FOR A SIZE
M PATTERN
FITS A SOURCE FOUR
JUNIOR

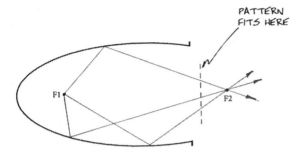

LIGHT RAYS IN AN ELLIPSOIDAL INSTRUMENT
CONVERGE AT FOCAL POINT TWO

to converge and cross over themselves. So the image of the pattern will be projected upside down and backward of the way you have placed in the fixture. When the pattern has a discernible top and bottom, be careful to insert it into the holder in the proper orientation. Left and right can be altered at the fixture by turning the holder over, but since the holder has a handle on it, right side up can only be accomplished when loading the pattern.

Gobo rotators are used to spin a pattern, so that the resulting projection is animated. One end of the rotator unit fits inside the light, while the motor is on the outside. Rotators require some sort of external controller, which is connected to the unit via a cable. Speed and direction can be manipulated. Some rotators spin two different patterns at the same time, and can achieve more complicated effects.

Most gobos are made by etching a pattern onto a metal sheet. In doing so, the area occupied by the image is eaten away, and left open. If the design is intricate, a system of islands and bridges is used to create a stencil-like form. Islands are the cut away part, while bridges hold interior parts of the design in place. If a custom-designed pattern is required, the artwork must have sufficient bridges to create a stable design when the metal has been etched away. Another approach is to use many small dots through the metal to create a *mesh* appearance. This method works especially well for amorphous shapes like clouds on a cyclorama. Throwing the fixture slightly out of focus will create a more realistic image.

THIS ROTATOR HAS A FOUR PIN XLR PLUG
THAT PROVIDES BOTH DATA AND POWER TO
THE UNIT

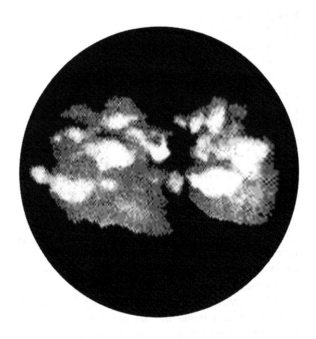

MESH GOBOS ARE FORMED BY MANY
SMALL PINHOLES, SO BRIDGES ARE
NOT NEEDED. THIS RESULTS IN
A MUCH MORE DETAILED IMAGE.

ROSCO invented the Image Pro so that slides can be projected by a standard ellipsoidal fixture. An image is printed onto a special plastic sheet with an inkjet computer printer. The plastic is mounted in a holder. The holder is fitted into the Image Pro unit, which is in turn inserted into the gobo slot on the fixture. The unit itself has a fan built into it, which serves to cool the slide. These images are quite bright, but have a stated life span of only 15 hours when the light is full power. After that the ink forming the image tends to bleach out.

THE IMAGEPRO UNIT PROVIDES A COOLING BREEZE TO KEEP THE SLIDES FROM MELTING IN THE INTENSE HEAT OF THE LIGHTING INSTRUMENT

TERMS USED IN THIS CHAPTER

ambient light	gate	plano-convex
angle of incidence	gel string	plugging strip
ANSI	geometrical optics	quartz glass
barn doors	gobo	reflector
base	gobo rotator	refraction
beam angle	ground row	ROSCO
bottle on a Source Four Par	hotdog	Roscolene
CIE color chart	HPL	RSC or double ended
color correction gel	iris	saturation
color filters or media	lamp	shutter
complementary color	Lee Filters	socket
cyc light	Leko	Source Four PAR
dichroic filter	lens	spherical reflector
diffusion gel	lens tube	spot
ellipsoidal instrument	mesh gobo	strip light
filament	mogul bipost	swatch book
fixture	neutral density gel	template
flood	PAR can	top hat
focal point	parabolic reflector	two pin
Fresnel	pattern	two pin lamp base
GAM	photometrics	

CHAPTER 22

HANGING AND FOCUSING

ANGING THE LIGHTS is done to specifications laid down by a designer, who should provide a *light plot*. Most of the time this is a scale representation of the theatre and its lighting positions, showing the lighting equipment types in their proper locations. Occasionally, plots are more like a schematic drawing, and are not to scale. Computer-Aided-Design (CAD) plots are often used. *CAD* programs came into their own early on in lighting design because they are really good at keeping track of all the numbers used for dimmers, channels, circuits, gel colors, and the like. It is also much easier to add and delete lights on the computer and then print out a new plot than it is to do any sort of hand drafting. However, it should be noted that there were many very artistically satisfying lighting designs created in advance of CAD technology. The computer makes the paperwork a lot easier to put together, but doesn't make anything more artistic. The art part must come from an actual human being.

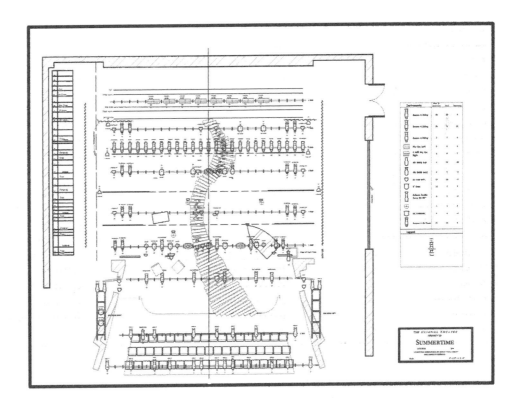

The aesthetic quality of individual light plots tends to vary greatly, but there is a general consensus about the information that should be on the plot. The plot is a plan view that shows all of the lighting positions in the theatre, in relation to one another. Different types of lighting instruments are shown on the plan as icons that graphically represent the various instruments. It should include a *legend*, which is a guide to the meanings of various symbols for different types of lights. Part of this is the *key*, an instrument symbol that details the numbering system for gel color, channel numbers, dimmer numbers, and instrument numbers. This is the same sort of legend used on a road map to indicate symbols used for types of roads, hospitals, airports, etc. Front-of-house positions should be labeled, as well as the battens being used as electrics. Electrics should have an indication of their *trim height*.

Some plots have marks on the battens at 18 inch centers. This is the most common spacing for instruments on a pipe, unless the lights will be focused directly to the side, where 24 inch centers are more realistic. Maintaining an even spacing ensures adequate room to properly focus the lights. Using corresponding marks on the battens can make a light hang go really fast, because the electricians can simply count over from center to find the proper place for a fixture.

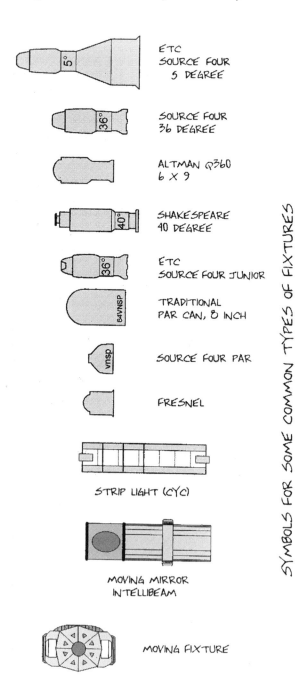

SYMBOLS FOR SOME COMMON TYPES OF FIXTURES

ETC SOURCE FOUR 5 DEGREE

SOURCE FOUR 36 DEGREE

ALTMAN Q360 6 X 9

SHAKESPEARE 40 DEGREE

ETC SOURCE FOUR JUNIOR

TRADITIONAL PAR CAN, 8 INCH

SOURCE FOUR PAR

FRESNEL

STRIP LIGHT (CYC)

MOVING MIRROR INTELLIBEAM

MOVING FIXTURE

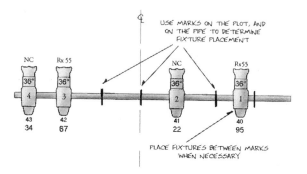

USE REGISTRATION MARKS TO AVOID MEASURING

If no marks are shown, you will need to *scale off* the placement of lights using a scale rule. Half-inch scale is standard for theatrical drawings of all types, but ¼″ is also quite common. Generally speaking, placement is close enough if you can get the measurements correct to within a few inches. An ordinary tape measure works well if the plot is in ½″ scale. For that scale, ½ inch on the drawing is equal to 1 foot on the pipe. Experienced designers tend to use a standard spacing, rather than making each space a different size. This speeds up the hang and leaves more time for focusing.

VECTORWORKS

Vectorworks is used by many people in the entertainment industry because of an entertainment-specific version called Spotlight. *Vectorworks Spotlight* has many tools for lighting designers, as well as the standard architectural drawing setup. Although this book is mostly concerned with the implementation of designs, you might like to know something about how Vectorworks operates. VW was originally developed for Macs, but can now be used on either Mac or PC. Lighting design requires a lot of detail in record keeping, and computers are great at that.

The Vectorworks Spotlight program is very complex, and this section is only the briefest outline of how to visualize its properties. There are some very fine online resources that can help you with the details of this program. You should think of this as a sampler, just to help you get started. Students can download a copy of the program online, for free.

THE WORKSPACE

When you open VW, go to FILE/Workspace preferences and choose Spotlight. That will set up the workspace so that all of the theatre specific tools are available. If you choose any other workspace the spotlight tools won't be on your monitor. An unnamed file will open with the program, and if you are starting something from scratch, you can use that file to begin your work. Or, you can open some other file that was already established.

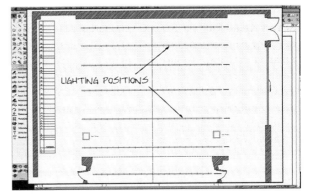

TEMPLATE FOR LIGHTING DESIGNS

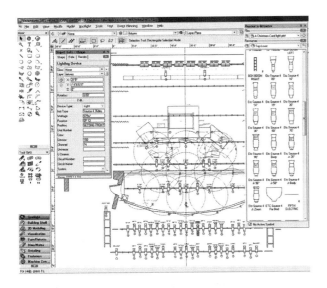

VECTORWORKS SPOTLIGHT WORKSPACE

THE OBJECT INFO BOX, RESOURCE BROWSER, AND SPOTLIGHT TOOL SET ARE SHOWN OPEN. THEY ARE THE MOST IMPORTANT FOR A LIGHT PLOT.

Theatres that are road houses, meaning that they are for rent to touring companies, usually have a *tech package* that details how the theatre is laid out, what lighting and sound equipment they have and so forth. Frequently they may have a CAD drawing of the theatre space that shows where lighting positions are located. Most schools and resident theatres have the same thing, and in that case it is best to open the standard drawing and use that as a template.

A template will allow you to get right down to making up a plot, without having to draw the theatre first. Vectorworks can import an AutoCAD .dwg file and convert it to a .mcd file, the standard extension for Vectorworks files. You can also import a CAD version of the scenery designer's ground plan and merge that with the theatre template. Import is a command located under the file menu. Then copy the parts of the ground plan

you need to use in your light plot, and paste it into your drawing. Import and export are often used in computer programs when files need to be transcoded to another file extension.

Vectorworks uses *layers* to help organize complicated drawings. It is often helpful to separate drawings according to things like: the theatre itself, Act I scenery, Act II scenery, light fixtures, lighting positions, or whatever separations make sense for your particular situation. It is especially good to separate the fixtures to their own layer, because this makes it much easier to select them on the page without accidentally grabbing other objects as well. There are a number of layer options that allow you to protect parts of the drawing while working with others. The layer you are working on is the *active layer*. You can change layers using the Layers dialog box at the top of the workspace.

Layer options/*gray others* will keep the active layer black but make all other layers a gray color. That makes it easier to spot what is in the active layer. With that

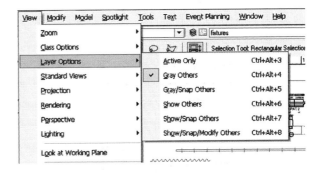

THE LAYER OPTIONS MENU DETERMINES HOW THE INACTIVE LAYERS WILL REACT.

"ACTIVE ONLY" SHOWS ONLY THE LAYER YOU ARE ON, NONE OF THE OTHERS ARE VISIBLE. "SHOW/SNAP OTHERS" MEANS YOU WILL BE ABLE TO ALIGN YOUR WORK WITH OTHER LAYERS. "SHOW/SNAP/MODIFY OTHERS" IN EFFECT TURNS OFF THE LAYERS FEATURE SO THAT ALL OBJECTS ON ALL LAYERS ARE EDITABLE.

setting you can select objects in the active layer and move them around the page without accidentally moving anything from another layer.

You can select various pallets by using the *window* menu on the top ribbon. A really important one for lighting work is the *resource browser*, a window that allows you to import already constructed objects from a catalog. You can navigate through different layers of the browser to find lighting fixtures, and the specific brands you will be using. Like all browsers, it has the ability to retain favorites.

Another important pallet is the *object info box* which is very similar to what one would expect after right-clicking and choosing "properties" on a PC. It is very helpful in assigning information like color and dimmer numbers to lighting instruments. You can move the object info box and resource browser pallets around the workspace in a fairly predictable way. You will also need the basic tools pallet, which contains the instrument insertion tool.

The *spotlight* menu on the ribbon has commands related to placing theatre-specific items on a plot. It can also be used for generating paperwork like a hookup sheet or an equipment inventory list.

There are many other palettes and menus for other purposes. The tops of the palettes have small pushpins on them that allow you to pin them to the blue bar across the top of the screen. Clicking on the pin changes its orientation from up and down to sideways. When the pin is sideways, the palette will collapse upward out of the way when it is not in use.

Use the Resource Browser to select lighting fixtures you would like to place on the plot. Navigate through the browser to find the appropriate company products, and the specific fixture, and click to select it. Click next on the *fixture insertion tool* from the Spotlight palette (or double click on the appropriate fixture icon). Click the place on the drawing where the fixture goes and a ghost image of the icon for your light will show up there. You have the option of rotating it before clicking again. If you want to place more of the same type of fixture, click the drawing in other places to do that, you do not need to go through the selection process again.

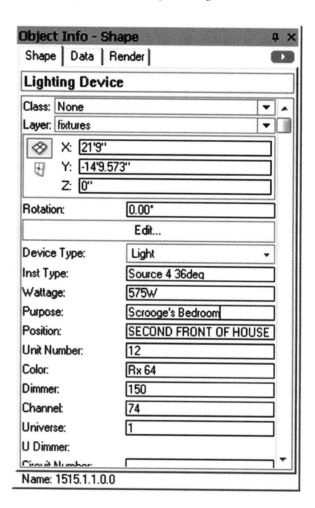

USE THE RESOURCE BROWSER TO SELECT OBJECTS YOU CAN THEN PLACE ON THE LIGHT PLOT

DOUBLE CLICK ON ANY ONE OF THEM TO SELECT, AND IF IT'S A FIXTURE, THE "INSERT FIXTURE" TOOL WILL ALSO BE SELECTED. CLICK THE MOUSE ON THE PLOT TO PLACE AN INSTRUMENT.

THE OBJECT INFO BOX

USE IT TO DEFINE PURPOSE, COLOR, DIMMER, AND CHANNEL AND OTHER PARAMETERS THAT SHOW UP ON THE LEGEND.

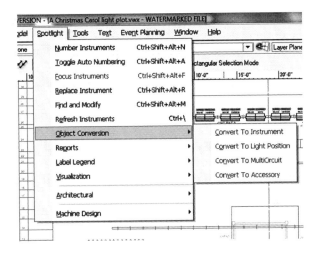

VECTORWORKS SPOTLIGHT MENU

YOU ONLY GET THIS MENU WHEN YOU ARE USING THE
SPOTLIGHT VERSION OF THE PROGRAM. IT ALLOWS YOU TO
CONVERT AN OBJECT ON THE DRAWING TO A LIGHTING
POSITION SUCH AS AN ELECTRIC. THIS DRAWING IS
WATERMARKED, MEANING IT WAS MADE AVAILABLE FREE TO
TEACHERS AND STUDENTS, A REALLY GREAT DEAL!

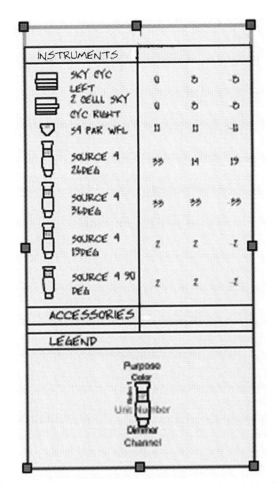

KEY TO INSTRUMENTATION

USE THIS TOOL TO DEFINE THE ICONS USED ON THE PLOT.
THE LEGEND AT THE BOTTOM TELLS THE ELECTRICIANS
WHERE THE COLOR, CHANNEL, AND DIMMER NUMBERS ARE.

Use the Object Info Box, to include information about the light. Type in all necessary information about color, purpose, and templates in the dialog boxes. The placement and unit numbers will be automatically added by the program.

Use SPOTLIGHT/utilities/*key to instrumentation* to place an inset on the drawing that informs electricians as to the meanings of the various icons from the resource browser.

Use SPOTLIGHT/generate paper work to create a hook up for your light plot. *Generate paperwork* opens a dialog box with lots of different possibilities. You can configure the Excel-like spreadsheet to display the information in many different ways. The process works much better on newer versions of the program. The program *Lightwright* has been around for many years and is an excellent resource for managing paperwork. Newer versions of Lightwright and Vectorworks are more compatible with one another and can be used in unison on either a Mac or a PC.

PREPARE FOR THE HANG

In an IATSE union theatre, the job of managing a light hang falls to the house electrician. In other venues, the title master electrician or ME is often used. If you become one of those you will probably already realize that hanging lights can be done very quickly if you organize the event before starting. Research the plot and other paper work to find out which gel colors you need, as well as how many and which sizes. Cut the gels and load them into the proper frames. Resident and university theatres often have a filing cabinet filled with previously used gels stored in folders. They are usually sorted according to the color number each is assigned by the manufacturer. The colors have names too, but most everyone uses the numbers to specify.

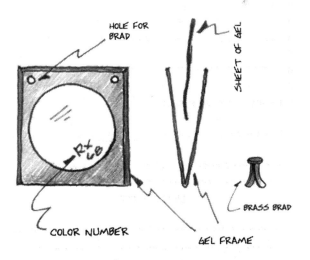

GEL FRAME HOLDER

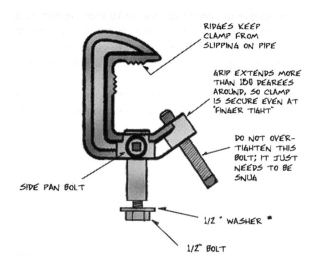

RIDGES KEEP CLAMP FROM SLIPPING ON PIPE

GRIP EXTENDS MORE THAN 180 DEGREES AROUND, SO CLAMP IS SECURE EVEN AT "FINGER TIGHT"

DO NOT OVER-TIGHTEN THIS BOLT; IT JUST NEEDS TO BE SNUG

SIDE PAN BOLT

1/2" WASHER *

1/2" BOLT

* IF A LOCK WASHER IS USED INSTEAD OF A FLAT WASHER IT IS OFTEN POSSIBLE TO FOCUS WITHOUT USING THE SIDE PAN BOLT.

STANDARD IRON C-CLAMP

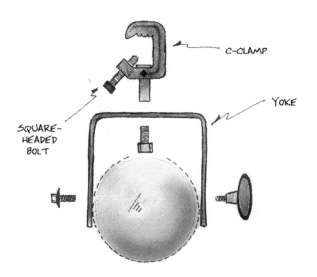

C-CLAMP

YOKE

SQUARE-HEADED BOLT

FOCUSING HARDWARE

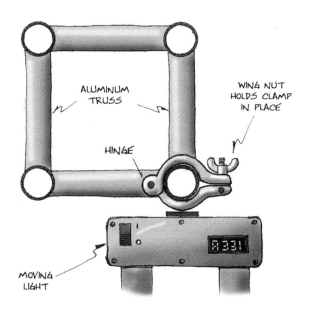

ALUMINUM TRUSS

WING NUT HOLDS CLAMP IN PLACE

HINGE

MOVING LIGHT

HALF-BURGER

SAFE TO USE ON ALUMINUM TRUSS

It is helpful to mark the color numbers with a grease pencil. If the marks are placed nearer the center than the edge of the gel they can be easily read in the dark. Some purists will disagree, but the output of light and the quality of the color will not be noticeably affected, and readable labeling will make finding the proper color during focusing in semi-darkness much easier.

Holes are provided in the corners of the gel frames so that brass *office brads* can be used to secure the gel. Some people use tape instead, but over a period of time the intense heat generated by the light will cause the tape either to fall off, or to become permanently bonded to the frame, depending on the type of tape used. The manufacturers clearly intend for brads to be used to secure the gel.

Virtually all theatres use some form of *c-clamp* to attach lights to a pipe such as a boom or an electric. This c-clamp is a specialized type that is able to grasp a round pipe easily. At the bottom of the c-clamp is a ½″ bolt that connects the clamp to the *yoke*. It also allows the light to move from side to side, or *pan*. Most of the time the yoke is a piece of flat steel that is bent into a U shape. It curves around the sides of the body of the light and is attached on either side with bolts or handles. They allow the light to move up and down, or *tilt*.

When hanging lights on aluminum box truss, a small section of PVC pipe can be used to prevent damage to the soft aluminum pipe making up the truss. Some lights are intended for use on a truss bar and have special hardware for that purpose, especially in the concert world. The *half-burger* is an interesting offshoot of the Cheeseborough clamp used to connect pipes together. (The original type is often called a "cheeseburger.")

The half-burger is often used in hanging moving fixture lights. This type of clamp requires no wrench, because the large wing nut can be tightened with just your fingers.

If a light is secured to a tower, ladder, box boom, or some other position made of square tubing, the yoke is usually bolted straight to that frame with no clamp. Half-inch bolts are an excellent fit. A washer placed between the yoke and the metal tubing of the tower makes it much

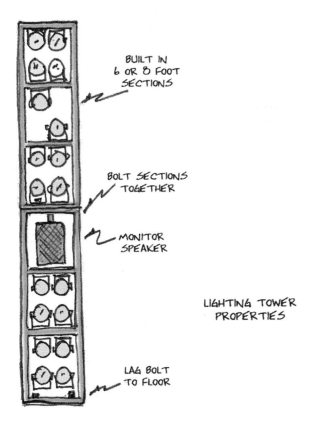

BUILT IN
6 OR 8 FOOT
SECTIONS

BOLT SECTIONS
TOGETHER

MONITOR
SPEAKER

LIGHTING TOWER
PROPERTIES

LAG BOLT
TO FLOOR

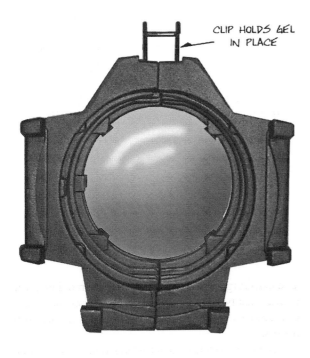

CLIP HOLDS GEL
IN PLACE

THE CLIP SHOULD BE ON THE TOP
IF THE LIGHT IS RIGHT SIDE UP

easier to pan the light back and forth when focusing. If one of the washers is the split ring type there will be much less chance for the bolt to work itself loose, and it is often possible to pan the light a small distance without using a wrench to loosen/tighten.

On the front of a light is a slot where *gel frames* go. On the back is a power cord, or *pigtail*, that is used to plug the light into a circuit. Although many lights have a retaining clip that will prevent the gel frame from falling out of the fixture, it is still best to hang the light right-side up. Gobos won't stay in the slot when the light is hung upside down.

LIGHTING POSITIONS

In a theatre, lights are hung in specific areas, some over the stage itself and some out in the auditorium. Hanging positions in the audience seating area are called *Front of House* positions or FOH. They may have other names like cove or beam or balcony rail in some theatres. Unless they have those specific names, it is common practice to number the FOH positions starting from the *plaster line*, an imaginary line across the front of the stage just behind the proscenium. The closest position to the plaster line is the first front of house or 1FOH, the second is the 2FOH, and so forth. FOH positions are extremely variable from theatre to theatre.

Theatres frequently have a lighting position on either side of the proscenium in an area where nineteenth-century theatres had their box seats. For this reason, they are known as *box boom* positions. A *boom* is any vertical pipe used as a hanging position. The stage left boom is called box boom left (BBL), and the stage right is the box boom right (BBR). The exact configuration of box boom positions tend to vary widely from one theatre to another, but most have some sort of hanging position in that area.

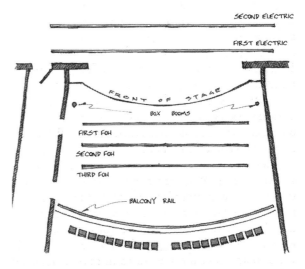

SECOND ELECTRIC

FIRST ELECTRIC

FRONT OF STAGE

BOX BOOMS

FIRST FOH

SECOND FOH

THIRD FOH

BALCONY RAIL

PLAN VIEW OF LIGHTING POSITIONS

An onstage pipe used for hanging lights is called an *electric*. These are normally regular system pipes used for hanging curtains and scenery. Some theatres have dedicated electrics, meaning that certain pipes have been chosen to always be the electrics, and as a consequence they have a plugging strip that connects the lights with dimmers. Electrics are numbered from the plaster line just like FOH positions, but since they are on the upstage side of the line the most downstage pipe is the first electric and the numbers increase toward the upstage wall. The first electric is a very popular place to hang lights, and is almost always used in any show. It is often made a dedicated electric and has a plugging strip even if no other pipe does.

Other positions frequently found on stage are *torm booms*, vertical pipes attached to the back of the proscenium opening, free-standing booms sometimes called *trees*, lighting *towers*, and *ladders*. Booms often have heavy steel bases to help them stay upright, while towers are enclosures of steel tubing that totally encase the lights.

Ladders are metal structures that hang down off the end of an electric, and increase the number of fixtures that can be used there for side lighting. Another backstage placement method is the *floor mount*, which can be scattered wherever the design specifies. *Set mount* fixtures are attached directly to scenery when that is the best method of placing them in a desired position.

HANGING AN ELECTRIC

If both the plan and the batten are marked with 18″ centers it is an easy matter to count the number of marks and determine the exact placement of an instrument. If not you will need to measure the placement of each light as scaled off the drawing. In any case, you should always begin from the *centerline* of the pipe and work toward the two sides because it is very likely that the designer may not have known the exact length of the pipe when the drawing was done. The center of the batten is a well-defined location, and the hang will be more accurate that way. Think of the centerline as the y axis on a graph.

When measuring distances on the plot, it is best to do all of them at one time. Take all the measurements from the center of the pipe to the fixture and not from one fixture to the next. This will lessen the chance of inaccuracy compiling itself. After getting the measurements from the plot, use a piece of chalk to mark them on the pipe all at one time. Measuring and marking is a job for only one or two hands, but once the chalk marks are in place a larger crew can jump in to hang the lights *finger-tight* on the pipe. Finger tight means to snug the bolt without using a wrench, and makes it easy to change the placement if necessary. After all the lights are

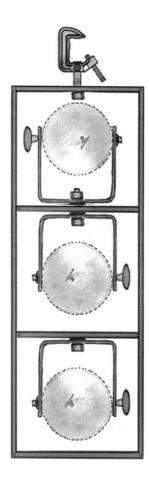

LIGHT LADDER

MEANT TO BE HUNG
UNDER A BATTEN

ALWAYS MEASURE FROM THE CENTER OF THE PIPE

JUST MAKE IT SNUG, DON'T OVERTIGHTEN

Recording circuit/dimmer numbers is essential so that a patching hook-up sheet can be generated later on. Most theatres today are dimmer per circuit, meaning that each circuit runs straight to one dimmer and they both have the same number. Writing down the circuit number is the same as recording the dimmer number.

Some theatres use drop boxes instead of plugging strips. A *drop box* typically consists of a long piece of *multicable* (a large cable with many conductors) that ends with a box containing a number of panel-mounted female connectors.

The multicable extends downward from the grid, allowing the drop box to be moved around the stage. When lowering a drop box it is important to lower the

hung, double-check placement with the plot, and make any changes before it becomes more difficult to do so. C-clamps are constructed so that they will not come off unless the bolt is very, very loose. Finger tightening will prevent the lights from falling during the short time that you are hanging and double-checking.

Tighten the bolts with a 6 or 8 inch C-wrench only enough so that they do not vibrate loose. Over tightening with a wrench that is too large will damage both the clamp and the batten. Having one person go along and tighten all of the bolts in order, at one time, is an efficient way of ensuring that none of them are left loose accidentally. If you are not sure, it is always best to go through and double check. Finger-tight bolts will vibrate loose over a long period of time.

Rotate the lights so that they are pointed up or down stage in the direction shown on the plot. Most lights have a "this side up" orientation that becomes obvious when you look at the gobo slot. Check to see that all the handles and bolts used in focusing are snug, but not overly tight. This will speed up the focus time later on. Make sure that all shutters are pulled out on all of the ellipsoidals. Shutters are often completely closed when the fixture is in storage, so that they don't get bent. When left in that position, they won't allow any light to escape and the instrument will become overheated, possibly ruining the shutters.

Safety cables should be attached so that they go through the light and around the batten. This will keep the light from falling should someone have forgotten to tighten the C-clamp.

If your theatre is equipped with *plugging strips* that are permanently attached to dedicated electric battens, the process of cabling is very easy. Simply plug the lights into the nearest circuit and record the number on the plot.

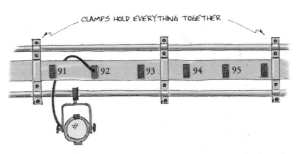

CLAMPS HOLD EVERYTHING TOGETHER

91 92 93 94 95

4

PLUGGING STRIP ON A DOUBLE BATTEN

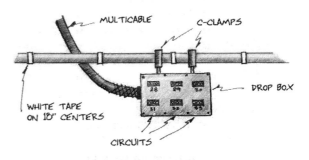

MULTICABLE   C-CLAMPS

WHITE TAPE
ON 18" CENTERS

DROP BOX

CIRCUITS

DROP BOX ON A BATTEN

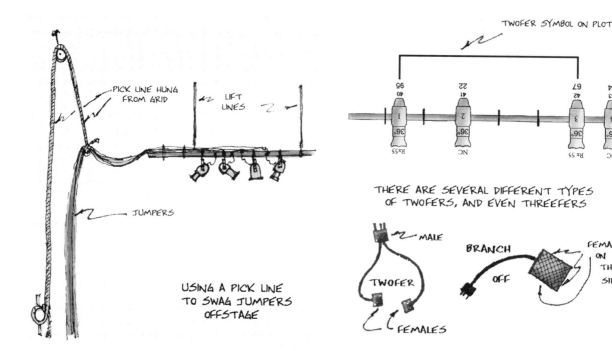

USING A PICK LINE TO SWAG JUMPERS OFFSTAGE

TWOFER SYMBOL ON PLOT

THERE ARE SEVERAL DIFFERENT TYPES OF TWOFERS, AND EVEN THREEFERS

MALE

TWOFER

FEMALES

BRANCH OFF

FEMALES ON THREE SIDES

cable directly over the batten, so that the cable does not foul any of the surrounding pipes. Sometimes drop boxes are hung off to the side of the rigging system and are maneuvered with a *pick line*. As another alternative, individual jumpers can be run off the end of the pipe and from there to a circuit box.

When cables hang down off the end of a pipe it is important to leave enough *swag* in them so that the batten can be flown in and out. It is much easier to do repair work from the ground than off a ladder or *Genie* lift. Since the hanging process occurs when the electric is all the way down, there will automatically be enough cable for it to reach this point if you create the swag while the pipe is in.

You can determine the number of circuits needed, and hence the number of drop boxes, by counting the number of lights on the batten as described by the light plot. Sometimes the designer will know in advance that two or more lights will be ganged together into one dimmer and will show that on the plot. If so, you won't need to provide an entirely different circuit for each fixture. The designer indicates ganged-together lights by drawing a line on the plot from one light to another, which is the normal way of indicating two-fering (two for one). A special *twofer* cable having one male plug connected with two female plugs is used for this purpose.

Although it is the designer's responsibility to have determined in advance the proper power requirements dictated by connecting lamps together in this fashion, it is a good practice to double-check how much power will be required by the total number of lamps. That's especially true when a number of lights are linked together by two-fering, three-fering, or perhaps four-fering. Use

the P = IE formula, by adding the wattages together, and dividing by the voltage to get a result. 2400 watts of lighting power translates to a 20 amp circuit, the most common rating. The 575W HPL lamp was designed to make it just possible to have four lamps on one 20A circuit. If your lights have the alternate 750-watt lamp, the four-fering won't work and the designer might not know it.

Extension cords used to connect the pigtail of a lighting instrument with a drop box circuit are referred to as *jumpers*, because they "jump" power from one location to another. Jumpers consist of a single circuit with a male plug at one end and a female at the other. 20A jumpers made with 12 gauge wire are the most common, because they work well with the 20A dimmer capacity. Be careful though, some jumpers use 14 gauge wire instead, and are only rated at 15A. The wire gauge should be printed on the outside of the rubber insulation.

Jumpers of varying lengths are needed to cover the distance from the fixture pigtails to circuit boxes. It is helpful to color code the different jumper lengths with vinyl electrical tape so that you can easily tell them apart. You can tell at a glance which jumper is the proper length for the job. Fasten cables to the batten with tie line. It might seem more expedient to tape everything together, or to simply wrap the cable around the pipe several times. But those two methods are quite difficult to remove, and the entertainment business is all about quickly changing from one show to another.

To connect a light to a drop box circuit, begin by tying the female end near the c-clamp of the light. Tie it close enough so that there is enough slack in the pigtail for the instrument to pivot easily during focusing. Run the jumper along the floor and plug it into a circuit/dimmer. Record this number next to the light as it appears on the plot. Repeat this procedure until all of the lights have been plugged.

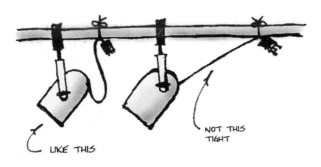

LIKE THIS

NOT THIS TIGHT

LEAVE SOME SLACK FOR FOCUSING

It is best to save tying up the cables until the last thing. Fewer ties are needed that way. But before you do that, take a moment to test the system. Run each dimmer to full one at a time to see if the lights come on as they should. It is important to test your hang while it is still on the ground and relatively easy to troubleshoot, and it is much easier to trade out or repair any faulty equipment before the cable has been tied to the batten. Make sure all of the shutters are pulled out and that safety cables are in place.

If the show has not been patched yet, use the light board to set the patch at 1-1. That means dimmer 1 is patched to channel 1, 2 to 2, and so forth. You can bring up the appropriate channel numbers by reading the circuit/dimmer numbers off the drop box or plugging strip and punching them into the computer.

A remote focus unit or RFU is often used to control the dimmers during the light hanging and focusing. The buttons on the panel typically match those on the regular console, and can be used to bring the channels up and down. An RFU is more convenient than running back and forth from the stage to the tech table. Recently smart phone apps have become available, which you can download and use to turn your phone into your own personal RFU.

YOU CAN RUN MOST BOARD FUNCTIONS WITH THIS REMOTE. A WIRELESS VERSION IS ALSO AVAILABLE.

RFU OR REMOTE FOCUS UNIT

Once troubleshooting is over, and all the lamps are working, you can bundle up all of the wiring at once. Start at the end farthest from the drop box and use tie line to secure the cable. Put on a tie every 4 feet or so, and pick up the additional jumpers as you go along, tying them all at the same time using a bow knot. Thirty inches is a good length for tie lines because it will usually allow the line to be double wrapped around the cable. Two turns around the pipe makes it easier to get a tight bundle. Most stagehands use *#4 black tie line*, because those ties can be recycled several times. When you reach the drop box, squish the excess cable against the batten and tie it on as tightly as possible. A bit of tidiness now will pay off when you focus, and will also help keep other flown pieces from snagging on the electric. Try to keep the rubber insulation of the jumpers away from the instrument housings, which get very hot during the show. The pigtail wires are usually okay, as they are manufactured from a heat resistant material.

USE TIE LINE TO SECURE CABLES
TO THE ELECTRIC

DON'T USE TAPE, OR WRAP THE CABLES AROUND THE PIPE.
IT'S TOO HARD TO STRIKE WHEN THE SHOW IS OVER.
BE AS NEAT AS YOU POSSIBLY CAN.

When the electric is ready to be flown out to its trim, use a small piece of *gaffer's tape* to secure the end of a steel tape measure to the pipe before it goes up. Use it to tell when the batten has reached the proper trim height. Reel off the tape so that you can hold the exact length on the floor with your foot. When the slack is out of the tape you are at trim. Once the trim is set the tape measure can be yanked down. (Don't use too much gaff tape!)

Front-of-house positions are so varied that it is impractical to discuss in detail how they may be hung or circuited, but the basic principles just covered should still apply. Most of the time the FOH positions have much easier access to circuit plugs because they are always in

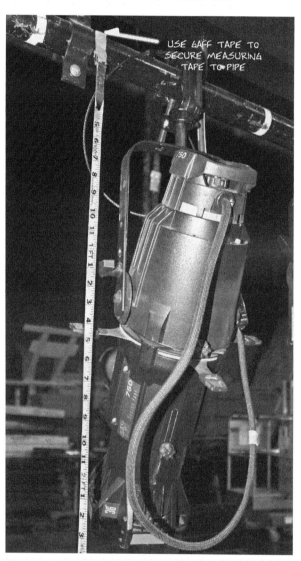

USE GAFF TAPE TO
SECURE MEASURING
TAPE TO PIPE

USE A TAPE MEASURE TO SET THE
TRIM OF THE PIPE OVER THE STAGE

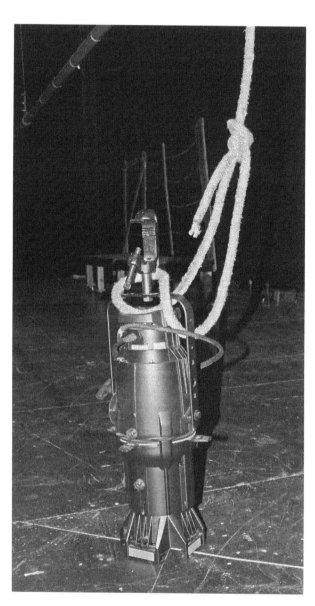

USE A BOWLINE THROUGH THE YOKE
FOR HOISTING A LIGHTING FIXTURE

THAT WAY YOU WON'T NEED TO TIE
AND RE-TIE THE KNOT

the same place and the circuits are hard-wired. Getting the lights to the position is often the hardest part. If you need a number of lights up high, try raising them with a large diameter, soft hand line, perhaps the same type that is used by carpenters as a bull line. Tie a 2 foot bowline in the end of the rope. Slide that under the yoke and around the c-clamp. It won't come off as long as there is tension on the line. That way you won't need to retie the knot each time a new light is lifted.

TECHNIQUES USED IN FOCUSING THE LIGHTS

Focusing lights is like dancing a tango. You need to observe what your partner is doing, and be ready to respond. The lighting designer leads, and if the electrician follows well the job can be done very quickly. On tour where the designer is not available, focusing is usually done with the stage manager instead.

Use a 6 or 8 inch C-wrench to focus lights. Some people use a safety line on the wrench, to prevent it from falling. The lights get hot in a hurry, so you might consider a pair of gloves, but a bulky pair will definitely get in your way. If you are quick, the lights will not heat up fast enough to make the gloves necessary, and experienced electricians usually avoid them, or use a fingerless type.

It is best to have one person on the board or *RFU* to bring up the proper channels, two moving the lift,

FOCUSING FROM A GENIE, WITH TWO HANDS AT THE BASE.

and one who actually focuses. Either a lift or a ladder is required to focus lights that are up in the air, which means almost all of those on an electric. You might consider two electricians to focus the front of house so that one can move to a new position while the other is actually focusing.

It is common for a designer to begin with a fixture at one end of an electric and work her way down to the other end one after another, rather than to hop around from place to place. This prevents having to reposition the lift frequently, which wastes a lot of time. Most experienced designers accommodate that process in order to save time, even though it makes their work more difficult.

Often, the designer asks for a channel number to be brought up, goes to the light's focus point and just stands there waiting. The general idea is to focus the center, or hot spot, of the light on the chest or back of the designer, and then lock off the bolts that hold the light in place. Most designers stand with their back to you and watch where their shadow falls within the light. If a relationship of mutual respect is developed, the designer may simply trust that the electrician has the hot spot in the proper location without looking too much.

The designer gives directions on moving the light. Up and down movement is called *tilting*. Side-to-side motion is known as *pan*. The designer might say something like pan left, and tilt up a bit, or she may just point: up, down, left, right, especially if there is a lot of noise. A clinched fist means "Stop, you've got it." If you are exceptionally in tune with your focusing partner, you will most likely be able to hit them just right without so much talking, and they will just say "Lock it" when you've got it right. *Locking* means to tighten the bolts that hold the light in place. It's important to do that so that the light doesn't move when you shutter it. You often need to make *shutter cuts* when focusing an ellipsoidal.

You'll probably need to sharpen or loosen the focus of the light first by moving the barrel back and forth, just like focusing a projector. A knob on the barrel can be loosened, which allows it and the lenses to move back and forth to adjust the sharpness. It is important to get the barrel set first before going on to the shutters, because adjusting the lens tube changes the size of the light beam, and thus the placement of the shutter cuts.

Push in on the top shutter to mask the bottom of the light beam. Push in on the left shutter to change the right side. Very often, the shutters are hard to move and you'll find that it is easier if you jiggle the handle back and forth a bit to get it started. Shutters don't just travel straight in and straight out. It is quite possible to tilt them to a severe angle, but not always as far as the designer would like. You can rotate the barrel on some fixtures, but don't immediately start doing that for every light, because it will take too much time. Try angling the shutters first and rotate the barrel as a last resort.

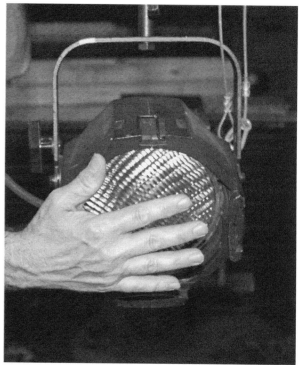

FLAG THE LIGHT TO
SEE ITS EFFECT

THIS KNOB LOOSENS THE BARREL
SO THAT YOU CAN SLIDE IT BACK AND FORTH

If the designer is uncertain which light is casting which shadow, she may ask you to *flag* the light. This means to pass your hand or foot or some other convenient body part in front of the light. This will cause the beam to flash on and off, making it easy to spot its effect on the stage.

Patterns/gobos require a special technique. Running the barrel for a sharp focus can make a huge difference in the appearance of the pattern effect. On occasion, a *donut* is used to sharpen the focus even more. A donut of this sort is a black metal sheet that fits into the gel holder slot. It has a hole in the center, and cuts down on ambient light. A donut often has a dramatic effect on contrast.

If you are focusing a PAR, it might be necessary to change the direction of the lens or lamp in order to adjust the direction of the oval, or *hot dog*. The ceramic socket in the back of the light can be used for this purpose. There is a limit to how far it will turn in one direction, so it may be necessary to try both ways. Source Four PAR fixtures use a ring around the outside to "spin the bottle" of the reflector.

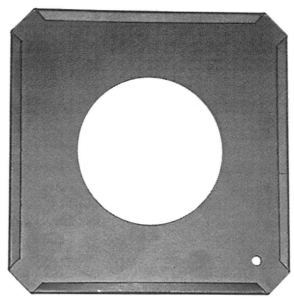

USE A DONUT LIKE THIS IN THE
GEL FRAME HOLDER OF AN ELLIPSOIDAL
TO SHARPEN THE OUTLINE OF A PATTERN.

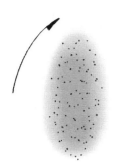

ROTATE THE CERAMIC IN AN OLD-SCHOOL PAR, OR SPIN THE BOTTLE ON A SOURCE FOUR PAR. EITHER WAY THE EFFECT IS TO CHANGE THE ORIENTATION OF THE OVAL PATTERN.

HOW TO CHANGE THE OVAL PATTERN OF A PAR

If you are focusing a Fresnel, you may need to change from *spot* to *flood*. Some fixtures have a crank on the back or side, but most have a knob on the bottom. Loosen it and move it in the right direction. Flood forward, spot back.

If you are on the lift doing the actual focusing, there are several things you can do to speed up the process. If you position yourself properly, you can most likely reach several lights before moving. But don't lean too far out of the basket just to save time. When you are ready to move, tell the guys moving the lift on the deck. If you loudly announce, "Moving stage left," they will know exactly what to do. If you mumble, "OK," or "Go," or make some other nebulous statement they may not. Remember that moving *onstage* means toward the center, and moving *offstage* means toward the wing of the side you are closest to.

If there is ever a hold-up of some sort, be sure to announce what it is and that you are working on the problem so that people on the ground have some idea of what is happening. As a result they will be less frustrated and impatient.

Bumpers are used on electrics whenever a working piece on the next batten might get fouled in an instrument or knock one out of focus. A bumper is a section of flat iron bar that has been bent into a circle about 18 or 20 inches in diameter. A c-clamp is used to fasten the bumper to an electric at a convenient location along the pipe. Often three or four are needed for each electric.

A *side arm* is used to attach lighting equipment that will not fit on the pipe in the normal way. It is really just a long extension of the yoke and c-clamp. The yoke of the fixture bolts to a sliding T, so that the length can be adjusted.

Side arms have been adapted for many other purposes. One of these is to prevent a batten from rolling. Lights are usually hung with the yoke pointing straight down, but sometimes there is a reason to *yoke them out* to the side, or even to hang them standing up on the top of the pipe. Sometimes this is to get a better

LIFT AND LADDER SAFETY

Be sure to employ any and all of the safety devices that come with the lift you are using. Follow the instructions given in the instruction booklet. If you do this there is very little chance of the lift being knocked over. The same cannot be said if you choose to ignore the safety rules. Never set up a lift or a ladder on a raked stage for any reason. It's a good practice for two stagehands to move the lift, and to stand by while work is being done. Use a safety harness when it is required.

OUTRIGGERS HELP TO STABILIZE THE LIFT - BE SURE TO USE THEM

BUMPER

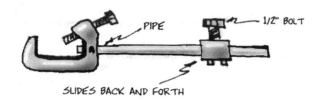

PIPE
1/2" BOLT
SLIDES BACK AND FORTH

SIDE ARM

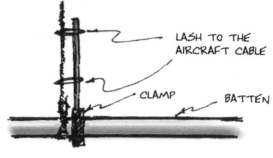

LASH TO THE
AIRCRAFT CABLE
CLAMP
BATTEN

USE A SIDE ARM TO KEEP A BATTEN FIXED

LIGHT "YOKED" OUT TO THE SIDE

NOTICE THAT A SIDE ARM WAS USED
TO KEEP THE PIPE FROM ROLLING

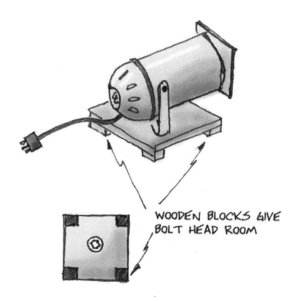

WOODEN BLOCKS GIVE
BOLT HEAD ROOM

MAKE A SMALL BASE
FOR "ROVER" LIGHTS

angle with the light, and sometimes it is just a matter of getting more units into less space.

Hanging lights to the side makes the pipe want to roll, and if that happens it will change the focus of the lights. To keep the pipe from rolling, fasten a side arm to the batten near one of the lift lines and tie the pipe to the aircraft cable.

A shop-built base is excellent for *floor mount* lights. A square section of ¾" plywood can be used to form the base, and the yoke of the light is bolted to the center of the wood. Feet on the bottom of the wood will keep the assembly from rocking on the bolt. These floor mounts can be easily moved about, or screwed to the deck to prevent being knocked out of focus.

TERMS USED IN THIS CHAPTER

#4 black tie line
ambient light
barn doors
boom
border light
bottle on a Source Four PAR
box boom
bumper
CAD
c-clamp
center line
Crescent wrench
donut
drop box
electric batten
ellipsoidal instrument
finger tight
flag
flood
floor mount

FOH, front-of-house
gaffer's tape
gel frame
Genie
half-burger
jumper
key to instrumentation
ladder
legend
lens tube
light plot
lock it off
office brad
offstage
onstage
pan
PAR can
pattern
pick line
pigtail

plugging strip
RFU
safety cable
set mount
shutter cut
shutter
side arm
Source Four PAR
spot
tech package
template
tilt
torm boom
towers
trees
trim height
twofer
yoke

SECTION FIVE

AUDIO AND VIDEO

CHAPTER 23

AUDIO THEORY

FROM THE BOOK

THE SECRETS OF SCENE PAINTING
AND STAGE EFFECTS

BY

VAN DYKE BROWNE

BACK IN THE DAY, MOST SOUND EFFECTS HAD TO BE LIVE

THESE TWO METHODS HAVE BEEN IN USE AT LEAST SINCE
WILLIAM SHAKESPEARE'S GLOBE THEATRE

THERE ARE THREE elemental ways to use sound in a play; live sounds—including those made by actors, playback of previously recorded elements, and sound reinforcement through amplification. Historically, sound effects were made using live devices in the manner of an old radio program or a modern day foley artist. Later on records were used for playback, and then audiotape, and now digital recordings to create effects. Sound reinforcement requires a host of electronics to amplify a singer's voice, and that equipment requires a lot of study to understand. But it is more than just equipment; the physical arrangement of an auditorium is itself an object of study. The way audible sound waves are affected when they bounce around a room is known as *acoustics*, the study of waves in (among other things) air.

METHODS OF PRODUCING SOUND

Some sounds are aesthetically better when performed as *live sounds*. Gun shots (unless there are lots of them), telephone rings, and doorbells are all good examples of when live sounds are more appropriate. It is difficult to get a realistically loud and sharp gunshot report through a sound system, or to sync it up with an actor pulling a trigger. The sound from a telephone is very directional, so having it emanate from the phone itself is more realistic. If a land line itself rings, it will stop when the actor picks it up. Other sounds like door chimes are so easily set up that it only makes sense for them to be done live. Sometimes the timing of a cue is better when an actor does it, such as a doorbell, rather than when a stage manager calls the cue to a board operator and it rings only after a short delay.

Playback is used when sounds are recorded and stored on a machine, and then played back during the performance. Playback includes things like pre-show music and *underscoring*, music that is played under a scene like in a movie. Rain, thunder, cars driving by, and crickets are all good examples of sound effects that may be played back. Playback was once done with analog devices like records or tape recordings, but is now exclusively digital.

Sound reinforcement is used when the voices of actors are not strong enough to provide sufficient volume. It is obviously impossible for actors in a rock musical like *Spring Awakening* to make themselves heard over the band without help, but reinforcement is also useful in a straight play when the timbre of an actor's voice needs to be softer than that used when "projecting" to the rear of the theatre. Microphones can also be used to amp up the musical instruments in an accompanying orchestra. Sound reinforcement requires a complex system of microphones, mixer, signal processing, amplification, and speakers. There is a separate chapter on that process.

SOUND AS WAVES

Sound is created when pressure waves move through the air. The waves are created by vibrating objects that in turn vibrate the air around them. The speed at which that happens determines the frequency. Frequency is the number of times per second the vibration happens. The vibrating air can be imagined as waves that travel outward from the source, in much the same way that waves radiate outward from a stone thrown in water. Water doesn't compress, so the waves cause it to rise up from the surface—which makes it easy to see them. Because air is compressible, sound waves take the form of alternating areas of compression and rarefaction, high and low pressure, and their movement is invisible.

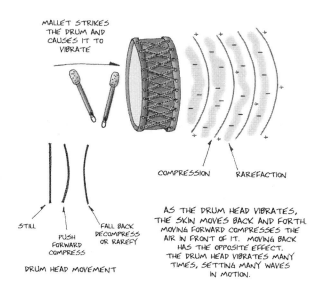

Sounds can be displayed using a graph, in which the x axis represents time, and the y axis represents the amplitude or loudness of the sound. The frequency is indicated by how often the wave crosses over the x axis from the positive to the negative zone and back. The positive quadrant represents an area of compression and the negative quadrant an area of rarefaction. The height or amplitude of the line above the x axis is representative of the volume of the sound. If a pure tone were to make 27 oscillations per second, there would be 27 peaks on the graph. That is the frequency of the lowest A on a standard piano keyboard.

In a sound editing program, the graph of a sound is a time/loudness representation instead. Virtually all real-world sounds are a composite of many different tones, all at their own phases and amplitudes with many harmonics, and a realistic graph of that would be so complex as to be meaningless to the viewer. In fact, it would merge into a solid area that is bounded only by the extreme amplitude of all the tones mixed together.

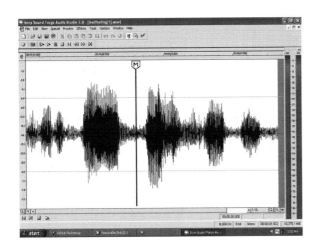

THIS GRAPH SHOWS THE
RELATIVE LOUDNESS OF THE SOUNDS

Sound editing programs offer a generalized representation of how loud a sound is.

In a theoretical model, the waves move through air in all directions, in the form of a sphere. As the waves travel farther from the source, their power is reduced according to the law of squares, which is derived from finding the surface area of a sphere. In a practical situation, sound doesn't usually radiate outward equally in all directions. Instead, a structure such as a proscenium opening works like a megaphone to focus the sound waves in a particular direction, which causes them to seem much louder by comparison. Speaker cabinets do much the

same thing with amplified sound, and are often focused toward a specific part of the audience.

Sound waves are created when a vibrating source compresses and rarefies the air around it, and the same thing happens in reverse when those atmospheric waves strike a solid object—the waves cause it to vibrate too. Some materials are more affected by sound waves than others are. A thin, semi-rigid material vibrates more readily than a thicker one. The plastic "skin" on the head of a drum is an excellent vibrator, being thin and expansive. In the human ear, the ear drum is a flat layer of skin that reacts in the same way. Small bones in the ear transfer the vibrations to nerves that interpret them as sounds.

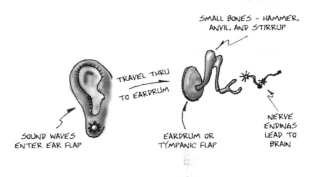

THE HUMAN EAR IS A TYPE OF TRANSDUCER
BECAUSE IT CHANGES SOUND WAVE ENERGY INTO
SMALL ELECTRICAL IMPULSES THAT ARE INTERPRETED
AS SOUND BY THE NERVE ENDINGS

SOUND FREQUENCIES

The frequency of a sound is relative to its pitch and is measured in *Hertz* (Hz) as you might expect from studying other wave fields. Frequency means exactly what it seems to, how frequently the oscillations occur. High-pitched sounds have a higher frequency, while low-pitched sounds have a lower frequency. The human ear can detect only a limited range of sound, although audio frequencies higher than that are possible. Dogs have much more acute senses than humans and can hear higher and lower frequencies, as can many other animals. Hearing ability changes over time. As a person ages, the "skin" on the ear drum tends to thicken and is not as good a sound receiver as it once was. Higher frequencies are more heavily impacted than lower ones. Thus older people have less acute hearing, especially in the higher frequency ranges. The eardrum is a very sensitive instrument and should be protected. Sounds that are too loud, and especially high pitched ones, will damage the drum permanently.

Audible sound occurs approximately between 20 Hz and 20,000 Hz, but the amounts are not exact because

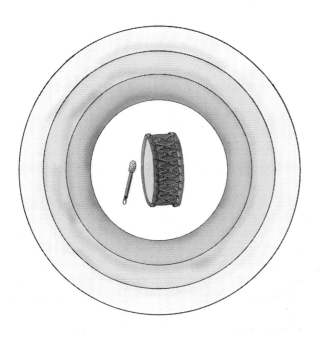

THE ENERGY OF THE DRUMBEAT FADES
AS IT TRAVELS OUTWARD IN ALL DIRECTIONS

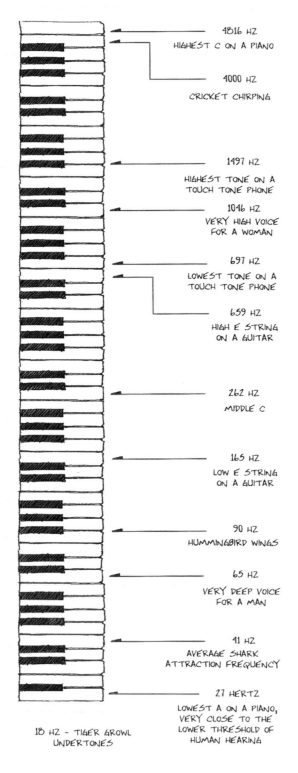

HUMAN HEARING TOPS OUT AROUND 20,000 HERTZ. THE EAR CANNOT PROCESS VIBRATIONS FASTER THAN THAT.

25 KHZ + ... BAT SONAR CLICKS

4816 HZ
HIGHEST C ON A PIANO

4000 HZ
CRICKET CHIRPING

1497 HZ
HIGHEST TONE ON A TOUCH TONE PHONE

1046 HZ
VERY HIGH VOICE FOR A WOMAN

697 HZ
LOWEST TONE ON A TOUCH TONE PHONE

659 HZ
HIGH E STRING ON A GUITAR

262 HZ
MIDDLE C

165 HZ
LOW E STRING ON A GUITAR

90 HZ
HUMMINGBIRD WINGS

65 HZ
VERY DEEP VOICE FOR A MAN

41 HZ
AVERAGE SHARK ATTRACTION FREQUENCY

27 HERTZ
LOWEST A ON A PIANO, VERY CLOSE TO THE LOWER THRESHOLD OF HUMAN HEARING

18 HZ - TIGER GROWL UNDERTONES

HUMAN HEARING BOTTOMS OUT AROUND 20 HERTZ. BELOW THAT LEVEL VIBRATIONS ARE PERCEIVED AS MOVEMENT RATHER THAN SOUND.

some people hear better than others. As a frame of reference, middle C on a piano is 262 Hz, and the highest C is 4186 Hz. Any note an octave above another is twice the frequency of the beginning one, in a logarithmic scale. Middle A is 440 Hz, and is considered a standard from which other pitches are measured. The concept of an octave is important when considering an equalizer, which is a system of filters that allows the user to boost some frequencies and reduce others.

Another way of looking at the pitch of a sound is to describe its wavelength, which is the distance from one peak to another when plotted on a time graph. The numbers for frequency and wavelength are inversely proportional to one another such that a low frequency sound has a long wavelength and a high frequency sound has short wavelength.

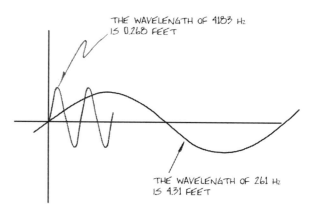

THE WAVELENGTH OF 4183 Hz IS 0.268 FEET

THE WAVELENGTH OF 261 Hz IS 4.31 FEET

WAVELENGTH AND FREQUENCY ARE INVERSELY PROPORTIONAL

The size and shape of an enclosed space such as a theatre can have a large impact on how sound behaves within it. Sound waves bounce off the walls in a room with hard surfaces and are reflected back into the space in a similar way to how light waves react to a mirror. A room that creates a lot of reflected sound is said to be *live*. You can gain an intuitive sense of how live a theatre auditorium is by standing on the apron and clapping your hands. The reverberation in a live room is apparent. Very often soft materials like curtains are used to keep a theatre from being overly live, because excessive echoes can interfere with intelligible speech. The shape and size of a space can also produce an undesirable side effect when sound is reinforced electronically. A few specific wavelengths that match the geometry of the room will tend to bounce around more than others. Their corresponding frequencies will *feedback* into the amplification system disproportionally, creating a loop that becomes over amplified. This is often corrected by using an equalizer to attenuate the feedback frequencies.

How Loudness Is Measured

The standard unit of measurement for sound is the *decibel*. In the SI system of prefixes for units of measurement, the prefix deci means one tenth. Thus a decibel or *dB* is one tenth of a bel, a power measurement for sound that is named for telephone inventor Alexander Bell. The scale is logarithmic, so that 2 bels is twice as loud as 1, and 5 is twice as loud as four. This causes the sounds to become louder very rapidly, so the smaller decibel unit of measurement is used to give the scale more sensitivity. A chart is often used to demonstrate the relative values of dB numbers, so that a frame of reference can be established.

A *VU meter* is closely related to decibels, but is generally used to reference the force of an audio signal in sound equipment rather than sound waves in the air. VU stands for Volume Units. The output of a device is considered to be optimum when the needle is at 0. A volume in the plus range means that the equipment has reached a point where some distortion will occur. The higher the output into the plus range, the higher that amount of distortion will be. Modern sound equipment often has an LED readout instead of an analog meter, in which a series of green LEDs represent VU measurements up to 0, and red LEDs represent the passage into positive numbers. Sound editing programs have virtual LED bars that reference the same thing. The term *clipping* is used to indicate when a meter has reached the end of the scale.

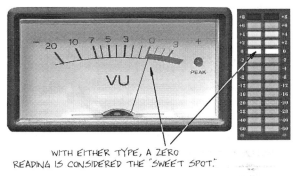

WITH EITHER TYPE, A ZERO READING IS CONSIDERED THE "SWEET SPOT."

TWO TYPES OF VU METERS

DECIBEL REFERENCE CHART

180 dB — KRAKATOA EXPLODING IS CONSIDERED TO BE THE LOUDEST SOUND EVER

100 dB — JACKHAMMER AT CLOSE RANGE. REALLY LOUD, BE SURE TO WEAR HEARING PROTECTION. ABOUT THE SAME AS ROCK CONCERT VOLUME.

80 dB — ANNOYINGLY LOUD VACUUM CLEANER

63 dB — THE VOLUME OF A TV AT "NORMAL" LISTENING LEVEL

10 dB — LEAVES BLOWING IN TREES IS CONSIDERED TO BE A REALLY FAINT SOUND, BUT CLEARLY AUDIBLE FOR SOMEONE WHO DOES NOT USE A JACKHAMMER

0 dB — THE BUZZ OF A MOSQUITO YOU CAN JUST BARELY MAKE OUT EVERY ONCE IN A WHILE

TINNITUS

Tinnitus is a condition whereby a person's ears tend to have a persistent ringing sensation. Short-term tinnitus is a common result of exposure to loud sounds, especially high pitched sounds. The problem is proportional to the duration of exposure, and a long exposure is more problematic than a short one. A loud arena concert may reach a noise level of 100dB or more, and if the show is two hours long, an (at least) short-term ringing in the ears is almost sure to occur. (Remember that 100dB is twice as loud as 90dB.) Tinnitus is symptomatic of hearing loss, and by the time you notice that your ears are ringing, it is already too late to do anything about it. In recent years musical artists have come to rely upon wireless *in the ear* monitors rather than using monitor speakers pointed directly at them. The older style needed to be very loud in order to overcome the ambient sounds of the concert, but the in-ear type can be much softer. This protects the ears of the performers, but doesn't help the audience.

ANALOG VS DIGITAL SIGNALS

It is important to make a distinction between an analog signal and a digital one. Microphones are analog devices, and the electrical signal they produce is proportional to the sound waves in the air, and can be graphed like any other wave. Digital signals are a long string of plus and minus voltages that make up a simulation of an analog signal. Analog equipment cannot process a digital signal and digital equipment cannot process an analog signal, unless some sort of conversion is made between the two types. Technically, all digital signals are in the form of a square wave, just like the DMX signal discussed in the chapter on lighting control. Quite often converters are used to change back and forth from analog to digital. A computer's sound card does that when it changes the digital signal from an MP3 file into an analog signal that comes out your speakers. Speakers are inherently analog, as are all devices that deal with audible sound.

In order to become a digital signal, sounds must be sampled. *Sampling* is a process that tests the signal at certain intervals to see what its properties are. The *sample rate* is the time interval involved. A higher sample rate is generally better, because this will ensure that the "samples" of sound are taken often enough to create an accurate digital picture. This is especially true at higher frequencies. The sample rate must be several times the analog rate in order to be effective. Early programs weren't able to sample very rapidly, but the modern type use a fairly standard 44.1 kHz rate. That allows the computer to sample a 20 kHz audio signal twice for every alternation of the analog signal. Of course a 20 kHz sound is a very high-pitched squeak, which is inaudible to some people. Pleasing tones are for the most part a much slower frequency, and thus more accurately sampled.

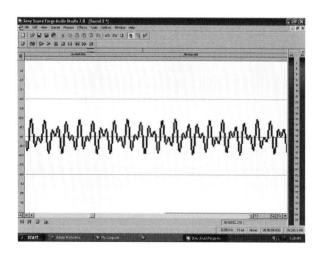

DIGITAL SAMPLE OF THE LOWEST TONE PRODUCED BY A TOUCH TONE PHONE, 697 Hz. THE TONE WAS SAMPLED AT A VERY LOW RATE OF 8000 Hz, SO THE SQUARE WAVE APPROXIMATION IS CLEARLY EVIDENT.

SOUND QUALITIES

Sound is often considered to have certain qualities, or controllable properties. The apparent quality of a sound can be changed by altering or controlling the properties.

The most obvious of these is *pitch*, which is how high or low a sound is. That is a function of its frequency, in that high frequency sounds have a higher pitch than low frequency sounds. As discussed earlier, the frequency is described by how many hertz, or oscillations occur per second. Singers are said to be "on pitch" when they have hit the correct musical note.

Another easily understood quality is that of *loudness*, which is quite literally how loud a sound is. In the past couple of decades a situation has developed known as the *loudness war*, in which recorded music has been made louder and louder by digitally controlling its dynamic range through limiting and compressing the sound. In that process soft sounds are made louder, while loud sounds are kept just within the range of being not so loud as to be distorted. That was not really possible with analog equipment.

A third quality is that of *timbre*, pronounced tamburr. Timbre is a bit more subtle, but just as important as frequency and loudness. It is often used to describe how rich or full a sound seems to be. When pure tones are created at a certain frequency by a musical instrument, harmonic sounds are also created at related frequencies. That happens with other resonators as well, like the human voice. The number and variety of these resonant frequencies is related to how full, rich, or warm a sound is. All of those terms are used to describe the aspect of timbre.

Another aspect of timbre comes from the impression that sound is coming from a variety of sources. This is often caused by *reverberation*, which is another word for echo. We have all been guilty of singing in the shower, but why is that so popular? A shower stall is composed of all hard surfaces so that the sound of your voice bounces around the space for some time before it *decays*, or becomes too soft to hear. That results in many small echoes, or reverberation, which makes the sound of your voice (at least to you) fuller and more pleasing.

SOUND QUALITIES

- Pitch

- Loudness

- Timbre

- Direction

- Distance

Two more controllable properties of sound are *direction* and *distance*. Our ears and brains are trained from birth as direction finders so that we can tell where a noise is coming from. This can be quite important in theatre sound because an audience can tell right off if the PA speakers are not focused with their sound coming from the stage. Sometimes you might want a sound like thunder to come from the rear, as if it were off in the distance somewhere. If a radio is playing on the stage, planting a speaker nearby (for the actual sounds) will make the moment seem more realistic. Sounds in the distance are softer, but they are also fuzzier and more indistinct.

TERMS USED IN THIS CHAPTER

acoustics	in the ear monitor	sound types: live/playback/
clipping	live sounds	reinforcement
dB/decibel	reverberation	tinnitus
direction/distance	sample rate	underscoring
feedback	sound qualities: loudness/pitch/	VU meter
Hertz	timbre	

CHAPTER 24

SOUND REINFORCEMENT

SOUND REINFORCEMENT IS used to amplify the sound you hear from a stage whenever it isn't loud enough all on its own. Usually that means the singers and orchestra for a musical, but increasingly it is used for a straight play as well. The process is somewhat complex since the acoustical sounds of the various actors and orchestral instruments must be transformed into electrical impulses, transmitted to a central location, mixed, processed, amplified, and transmitted to a set of speakers that in turn transform the electronic signal back into acoustical sound. That's only possible because of a system of electronic devices that work together in concert to make it all happen. When sound impulses are converted to electrical impulses and travel through the system, the route they take is known as the *signal path*. Each part of the system along the signal path has a specific job to do in creating an amplified version of the show that is true to the artistic goals of the performers.

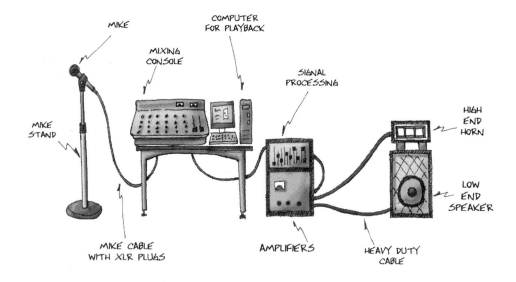

HOW EQUIPMENT IS CONNECTED

MICROPHONE DESIGN

The first duty of the system, picking up aural sounds and converting them to electrical impulses, is the job of the *microphone*. Any device that changes energy from one form to another is called a *transducer*, and microphones do that when they change the energy of sound waves traveling through the air into analog electrical impulses. A number of different types of microphones are used in specific situations that relate to how sound is produced by actors, or perhaps by musicians in the orchestra pit.

A *dynamic microphone* uses a coil of wire suspended in a magnetic field to make the transformation. As mentioned in the chapters on electrical theory, a coil of wire moving in a magnetic field produces a voltage. Sounds enter the microphone and vibrate a diaphragm that in turn vibrates a coil of wire. The electrical pulses formed are proportional to the vibrations picked up out of the air. This arrangement requires significant energy to move the coil of wire, because it is somewhat heavy. Dynamic microphones operate best in the middle frequency ranges where the human voice lies, and are often used for vocal purposes. It's much better if the singer is really close to the mic.

Condenser microphones work on a different principle, that of the capacitor. As mentioned in the chapter on electricity, capacitors have two metal plates separated by an insulating material and can be used to hold an electrical charge. The closeness of the two plates has an effect on the size of the charge. In a condenser microphone (condenser is an older word for capacitor—they mean the same thing) one of the metal plates is free to move in relation to the sound waves that enter the mic. The other is fixed, and as the distance between them varies an electrical signal is created. The very small voltage is proportional to the sound waves, but is generally too small to reach the mixing console without some sort of amplification. The *preamp*, as it is called, in a condenser microphone amplifies the signal so that it is stronger, but requires a supply of energy in order to do that.

That power supply is known as *phantom power*, usually 48DC. Phantom power is supplied via the mixing console. Most boards offer the option of turning it on or off, so it must be turned on when a condenser mic is in use. Most dynamic microphones are not affected by the phantom power supply.

Other types include carbon microphones, which aren't often used for high fidelity reproduction, and ribbon microphones which are, but are often considered to be a bit too delicate for theatre use. Ribbon microphones are much more likely to be found in broadcast or recording studios.

Mics Used on Stage

The Shure model SM58 is easily the most recognized type of microphone, and has been around for years. They are available in the standard corded version, but also as a wireless type that transmits a signal to a receiver so that the performer can move about anywhere on stage. The SM58 is a dynamic mic, and is designed to pick up sounds close to it, such as when the performer is holding it in their hand, or is positioned behind a mic stand. There are lots of similar microphones by Shure and

ALTHOUGH THE PICTURE IS OF A SHURE MICROPHONE, THERE ARE MANY OTHER MANUFACTURERS WITH SIMILAR PRODUCTS

TAKE A COUPLE OF WRAPS AROUND THE STAND TO HOLD CORD IN PLACE

CLUTCH USED TO SECURE EXTENSION

THIS STYLE OF SOLID METAL BASE IS THE MOST POPULAR, BUT THERE ARE SOME LIGHTER ONES

other manufacturers, and they work about the same. But the 58 is pretty iconic in its appearance. The large metal enclosure is actually a windscreen that protects the interior cartridge that contains the electronics. The cartridge is tiny by comparison to the protective screen.

These types of microphones are meant to be used by one, or perhaps two people at a time because of the way they pick up sound waves. A mic that picks up sounds from all directions is said to be *omnidirectional*. But this type of personal microphone is of the *cardioid* type, which means that its directionality pattern is heart-shaped. It picks up sounds mostly from the front and/or slightly to the sides. This is helpful when a stage monitor speaker is used, because these microphones will not easily feedback sounds that come from their rear.

An actor with a hand-held microphone makes a very presentational statement, which might be okay for some theatrical productions when the characters are meant to be in the act of performing, but most of the time a less distracting approach is used. One method is to place a type of microphone on the front of the stage that can pick up sounds from a larger area than would be possible with a personal mic like the SM58. *PCC (phase-coherent-cardioid)* microphones are sometimes used across the front of the stage to capture generalized sound from many different actors. They are often meant to pick up the voices of a chorus of singers, when it would be difficult to mike each individual member of the group.

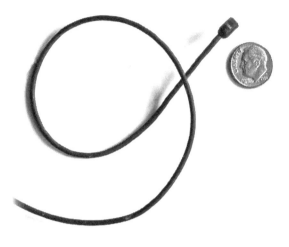

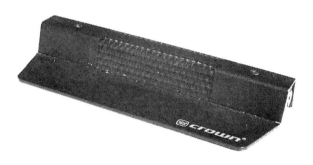

PCC MICROPHONES LIE FLAT ON THE STAGE FLOOR AND TEND TO PICK UP MORE GENERALIZED SOUNDS THAN OTHER TYPES.

Group mikes like the PCC are useful for capturing the overall ambient sound from the stage, but used alone at high gain they tend to amplify unwanted sounds like footsteps and fabric rustling. In most modern theatre productions, wireless microphone systems are used to boost the voices of individual actors. They use a type of microphone known as a *lavaliere*, which is tiny by comparison to the others, and may be hidden on the body of the performer. This type is used by newscasters as well, but broadcast lavs are quite large and worn like a tie pin. They are immediately noticeable when watching a news program where no attempt is made to hide them. The theatrical type is much smaller and is most often worn behind the ear, or perhaps on the forehead after passing under a wig. The mike is connected to a transmitter via a small wire. The transmitters are tiny also, and if worn in a pouch connected directly to the actor's body, the performer can change costumes without disturbing the mike.

The wireless microphone receivers are generally of the *diversity* type, meaning that they have two antennas installed at different angles, so that if one is unable to pick up the signal the other one takes over. The receivers are usually rack mounted so that many of them can be fitted

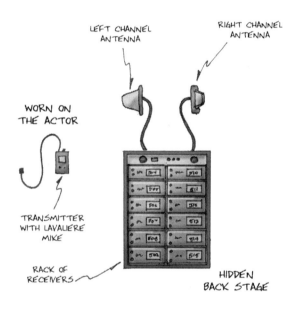

WIRELESS BODY MIKE SYSTEMS CONSIST OF LAVALIERE MIKE TRANSMITTERS AND DIVERSITY RECEIVERS. MOST OF THEM UTILIZE THE SAME BROADCAST FREQUENCIES AS UHF TELEVISION STATIONS – 470 MHZ THROUGH 698 MHZ. JUST RECENTLY THE 698 – 806 MEGAHERTZ BAND WAS ALSO AVAILABLE, BUT THE FCC AUCTIONED OFF THOSE FREQUENCIES AFTER THE SHIFT TO DIGITAL MEANT THEY WERE NO LONGER REQUIRED FOR THAT ORIGINAL PURPOSE. MOST SYSTEMS ALLOW THE USER TO SELECT APPROPRIATE, UNUSED FREQUENCIES IN THEIR AREA.

POWER SUPPLY UNIT ON TOP
WITH LIGHTS THAT SHINE DOWN

THE RAILS HAVE
PRE-DRILLED AND TAPPED
HOLES AT STANDARD
DIMENSIONS

HANDLE

19" WIDE SPACE

CASTERS

AUDIO RACK

A 19" RACK IS VERY STANDARD, AND PROFESSIONAL
SOUND EQUIPMENT IS GENERALLY MANUFACTURED TO
FIT THAT SIZE. "TWO RACK SPACES" MEANS THAT A UNIT
WILL TAKE UP THAT MANY SECTIONS OF THE RACK.
AN AMP OR MICROPHONE RECEIVER UNIT HAS A FACEPLATE
WITH HOLES ON THE SIDES THAT MATCH THE ONES
THAT ARE IN THE RACK.

WIRELESS MICROPHONE FREQUENCIES
AS OF JANUARY 1, 2014

THERE ARE SEVERAL "SLOTS" OF FREQUENCIES THAT
MANUFACTURERS TEND TO FAVOR.

482.000 MHz TO 507.000 MHz
THAT'S TV CHANNELS 16 TO 20

541.500 MHz TO 566.375 MHz
THAT'S TV CHANNELS 25 TO 30

655.50 MHz TO 680.375 MHz
THAT'S TV CHANNELS 44 TO 49

YOU CAN BUY A TRANSMITTER RECEIVER COMBO THAT
CAN BE SET TO AN EXACT FREQENCY IN THE RANGE.
USE THE CHART TO SELECT A RANGE OF FREQUENCIES
THAT IS APPROPRIATE FOR YOUR LOCATION, SO IF YOU HAVE
LOCAL STATIONS ON CHANNELS 25 AND 29, YOU SHOULD
AVOID THE MIDDLE GROUP OF FREQUENCIES.

into a small space. That is especially important when each actor is wired up individually and 20 or more are in use at one time. Frequently a pair of outboard antennas is used to gather the output of all the transmitters at once, when a large number of individual antennas would be impractical.

The housings of most pieces of sound equipment like receivers and amplifiers are designed to be 19 inches wide, which works well with audio equipment racks which are the same width. Very often the specifications of a piece of equipment will tell how many spaces it takes up on the *rails*, which are used to attach the system components. Mounting holes are at 1.25 inch intervals. An amplifier that works this way is said to be *rack mountable*. Microphone receivers are often constructed so that two of them sit side by side in the rack.

In 2010, the *FCC* or *Federal Communications Commission* ruled that wireless microphones used by broadcast, concert, theatre, and church groups would no longer be allowed to transmit on the 700 megahertz band, because those frequencies would be needed for other purposes. 700MHz was in the UHF television spectrum, as are the remaining frequencies still used today. Each microphone transmitter needs its own discrete

frequency to operate. Those frequencies must be chosen from a list that excludes UHF television transmissions from stations within a 50 mile radius. If a station is outside that radius you may use their frequency, if it is clear enough. Modern systems are said to be *frequency agile*, which means that you can set the frequency for a transmitter/receiver to one that is (within certain limits) suitable for your area. Being able to change frequencies is important because not all of the legal ones work as well as others. How well they actually do work can change from day to day.

CABLES AND CONNECTORS

Three pin *XLR connectors* are universally used to connect microphones to sound equipment. Most sound mixing consoles have an input strip along the back, and each mic compatible module has an XLR input. Most mic cables have a metallic shield around them just under the insulation, so that the wires inside are protected from interference from other electrical sources. Wires from

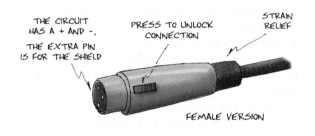

THE CIRCUIT
HAS A + AND -.

THE EXTRA PIN
IS FOR THE SHIELD

PRESS TO UNLOCK
CONNECTION

STRAIN
RELIEF

FEMALE VERSION

XLR MICROPHONE CABLE

lighting equipment, like a 20 amp jumper or feeder cable, create an inductive field around them that can interfere with the very small voltages present in a microphone cable. You should avoid running mic cables and lighting cables in the same space, especially if the lighting cable has been neatly coiled, because a coil of wire creates a much larger inductive field than straight wires.

A playback device like a CD player often uses *RCA connectors* as outputs. They are used on many televisions and DVD players as well, and will seem quite familiar. Most mixing consoles don't have RCA connectors on the back, so you will need an RCA to ¼″, or RCA to XLR adaptor to connect a CD player to a sound board.

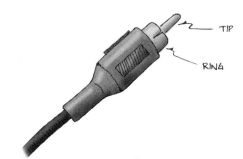

RCA CONNECTORS
ARE OFTEN USED TO PATCH DIFFERENT SORTS
OF CONSUMER ELECTRONICS. AUDIO OUTPUTS ARE
USUALLY RED AND WHITE, AND VIDEO YELLOW.

Many modern devices use a ⅛″ jack. It is really similar to the older and larger ¼″ version that has been around for decades. There are two types, one for mono and one for stereo. It is important to use the right one, which is usually but not always, the stereo type. A stereo jack has either three or four discrete regions separated by insulators rather than the two you will find on a mono plug. This connector is immediately recognizable as what you use for a pair of ear buds.

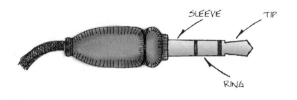

AN EIGHTH-INCH STEREO PLUG

VERY SIMILAR TO THE LARGER QUARTER INCH SIZE, THIS
TYPE OF CONNECTOR IS VERY FREQUENTLY USED TO
PATCH AN IPOD OR COMPUTER TO A SOUNDBOARD.
THE TIP AND RING CONNECTIONS ARE THE TWO POSITIVE
OUTPUTS, ONE FOR EACH CHANNEL, AND THE SLEEVE IS
THE GROUND CONNECTION FOR BOTH OF THEM. AN IPOD JACK
HAS TWO SEPARATE SLEEVE CONNECTIONS, BUT IS STILL
COMPATIBLE WITH THE STANDARD TYPE.

In most systems, the wireless microphone receivers are placed just off stage so that a backstage electrician can access them easily if something has gone wrong. This means that all of the signals from those microphones must travel from that location to the mix location in the back of the auditorium. An *audio snake* is used for efficiency. The snake is a multicable that can carry many different signals at once, each on different pairs of wires. Usually there is a breakout of XLR connectors at each end so that the snake can be connected to both the wireless rack and to the mixing console. A newer trend is to use a converter that translates the microphone signals to one that can be sent via Ethernet cables, which are physically easier to manage.

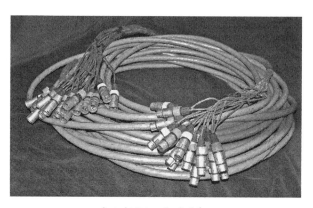

AN AUDIO SNAKE

THIS PARTICULAR SNAKE IS FOR A 16 CHANNEL
MIXING CONSOLE. ONE END HAS MALE XLR CONNECTORS
AND THE OTHER HAS FEMALES.
THE ENDS 'BREAK OUT' TO INDIVIDUAL COLOR-CODED CHANNELS.

MIXING CONSOLE

A sound *mixing console* takes all of the inputs from different microphones, as well as playback devices, and blends them together into a unified output that is heard by the audience. The inputs require mixing because the signals come in at different volumes and need adjusting to create a workable sound. What one performer is singing might be more important and given a boost. Other singers might have louder voices that need to be dampened. The mixer allows you to make very selective choices about how to balance out the different sounds in a show. Operating a mixing console is not a purely mechanical exercise, like running a light board. Mixing sound requires a great deal of focus to listen to the sound of the show and tweak the individual channels to get an artistically satisfying result. Other than playback cues, a sound mix stagehand runs the show on her own; the stage manager doesn't call cues for her.

Mixers generally have many more inputs than outputs. A *mono* output means that all speakers have the same sound, whereas *stereo* indicates that there are two slightly different versions coming from different sides of the stage. Stereo imparts a sense of directionality to the sound, so that some specific effects seem to be coming from one side of the stage or the other. You might choose to pan a sound effect such as a car driving by from one side to the other to enhance the idea that the car is actually moving somewhere. Much more complex multichannel systems are available, but stereo is a fairly standard type of arrangement. Many boards have more than two outputs which may have different uses as monitors, audience assisted listening, or perhaps alternate speakers backstage or in the lobby. A monitor signal specifically for the artists is often called a *foldback* output. The signal path is folded back to the stage or orchestra pit so that the performers can hear it via a monitor speaker. You can select specific channels for that purpose rather than sending the entire mix that the audience hears. That's important, because routing the singer's voices to a stage monitor can be problematic when wireless lavaliere mics are used. Feedback would be sure to happen.

Another use for an alternate output might be for delay purposes. The speed of sound is approximately 1000 feet per second, which sounds fast but is really quite slow compared to light. Light is much faster, so that lighting is visible long before the thunder arrives. In a really large venue, especially an outdoor one, it may be

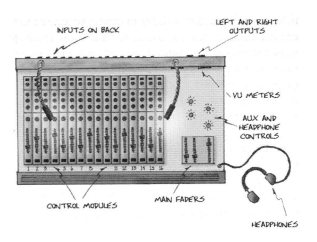

LAYOUT OF A COMMONLY USED MIXING CONSOLE

DESPITE THE SEEMINGLY HUGE NUMBER OF KNOBS AND BUTTONS, THE CONTROL MODULES ARE MOSTLY ALL THE SAME, SO MIXING A SHOW IS NOT AS DAUNTING A PROCESS AS YOU MIGHT THINK.

necessary to set up a second speaker array some distance back from the stage so that the back seats get enough volume to hear well. If both sets of speakers emit the exact same sound at the exact same time, there will be a noticeable phase mismatch between the two sounds. At a distance of 100 feet that would be a very obvious tenth of a second. To prevent that, a *delay* is used, such as will cause the signal to the auxiliary speakers to be delayed by the same amount of time that it takes sound to get from the stage PA to the middle of the house speakers.

There are two major variations in mixing consoles, analog and digital. As you might well imagine the analog type is the old standard, while digital is the newer variety. They both do the same job, mixing together multiple inputs into at least a stereo output. But the way they do that is very different. In an analog board the signal is analog from start to finish, from the microphone to the speaker. A digital board samples the analog signal from a microphone and converts it to a digital signal, which is then converted back (usually) in the output stage so that it can be fed into an amplifier. All this sampling and converting adds a layer of complexity to the process, but it is worthwhile. One advantage is that the board can use computer programs to alter the various signals with complex algorithms that sweeten it in subtle ways. The mixer can apply all of the same effects that a sound editing program can, equalizer, chorus, reverb, as well as adding compression to make soft sounds louder, and limiting to avoid distorting louder sounds.

Possibly the biggest advantage of digital boards is that they can remember settings for certain scenes. Cues are recorded in a manner similar to what you would expect from a lighting console. The operator adjusts the faders on the board so that the mix is appropriate for a specific scene. Those settings can be recorded in the board's memory. When that preset is recalled, the faders move

A WEDGE MONITOR LIKE THIS ONE IS MEANT TO BE USED FOR SINGERS IN A BAND, WHERE A CARDIOID MICROPHONE IS POINTED AWAY FROM THE SOUND COMING OUT OF THE SPEAKER. IT WOULDN'T WORK AT ALL FOR A SHOW WHERE THE ACTORS ARE ALL WEARING WIRELESS LAVALIERE MICROPHONES BECAUSE FEEDBACK WOULD HAPPEN INSTANTLY.

"FLYING FADERS" ON A DIGITAL CONSOLE

THE COMPUTER MEMORY STORES PRESETS,
SO WHEN YOU RECALL A CERTAIN CUE THE SLIDERS
MOVE INTO POSITION AUTOMATICALLY. THE SOUND
ENGINEER CAN THEN MOVE THEM MANUALLY TO
TWEAK THE DESIRED MIX.

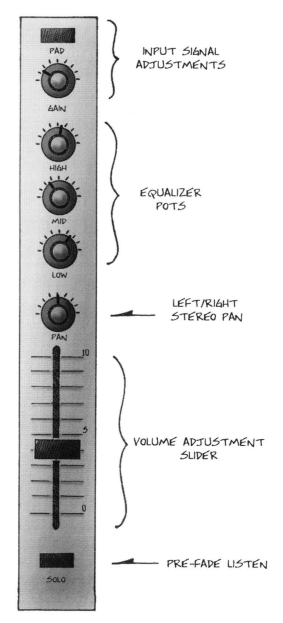

INPUT MODULE

into position, on their own. This type of console is known as a *flying fader* board. Moving the faders into position is important because the show changes from night to night, and continuous changes must be made to the mix. That wouldn't be possible if the faders didn't move to the positions their volumes require. The operator can adjust them once that happens.

Whether digital or analog, any type of mixer has a number of input channels. Each input to the mixer board has its own discrete and individual module. The numbers of *input modules* tend to come in multiples of 16, so that 16, 32, and 48 channel boards are common, but that is not a universal truth and other combinations exist. Input modules are somewhat different from model to model, but some features are standard. Each of the input modules on a board is identical in most respects, so that although the mixer may have hundreds of knobs and sliders, many of those controls have identical functions, and the set-up is not as complex as it may first appear.

At the top of each module on an analog board are the *pad* button, and the *gain* knob that are meant to be used together in preparing the module to receive a signal that is more powerful or less powerful. Microphones emit a very low power *mic level* signal, while playback devices such as a CD player or a computer headphone jack emit a much stronger signal. The latter are often referred to as *line level* inputs. The pad button is used to switch between the two, and the gain knob is used to make finer adjustments to the input power. A digital board might have the same set up, but more likely will have a feature that does the same thing automatically. It is important to adjust the input gain so that the signal is strong enough to be useful, but not so strong as to be out of line with others.

The word *gain* is generally used to indicate an amount of amplification. It is important to make the distinction that the overall amplification of the signal is

adjusted by moving the module slider at the bottom. The gain knob at the top of the module is really meant only to adjust the input signal. Use the input gain knob to create a level where the module slider works effectively in the middle of its travel. If the gain is too high, the input sound will be instantly loud the moment you move its slider upward. If the gain is too low, the sound will be faint even when the slider is all the way up. Sometimes the word *headroom* is used to describe leaving some space between a level that would be normal and one that is too high, so that the faders can be manipulated easily without clipping.

Most input modules have at least three *equalizer* knobs, but many have more than that. They are used to

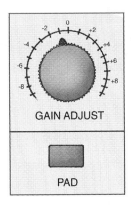

GAIN ADJUST

PAD

GIVE YOURSELF SOME HEADROOM

USE THE GAIN KNOB AND PAD IN TANDEM TO ADJUST
THE INPUT GAIN SO THAT THE OUTPUT SLIDERS
WORK WELL IN THE CENTER OF THEIR TRAVEL.

A DIGITAL BOARD WILL PROBABLY DO THIS FOR YOU
AUTOMATICALLY

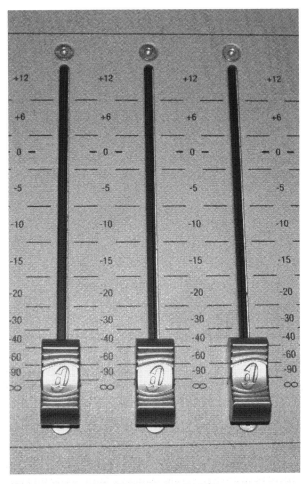

FADERS ON A MIXER

THE NUMBERS REPRESENT VALUES LIKE YOU MIGHT
EXPECT FROM A VU METER, WHERE 0 IS THE SWEET SPOT.
IN REALITY THOUGH, MIXING AUDIO IS AN ARTISTIC
PURSUIT AND IS DONE MORE OR LESS BY EAR.

EQ the sound coming into that one single input. *High end*, or high frequency tones can be enhanced or reduced. The same is true of *low end* sounds. The human voice tends to be in the lower mid range of audible frequencies. Adjusting the EQ can create a richer than normal sound. It has been said that modern Americans are "addicted to bass" and require more of it than would actually be found in nature.

The *solo* or *PFL* (pre-fade listen) button allows the operator to preview the contents of a channel before bringing it up with the slider. Press the button to hear that channel over your headphones, or to check its strength with the VU meter. These actions do not affect the sound being heard by the audience.

The *slider* or *fader* below the knobs is used to adjust the volume of the microphone patched into that particular input module. Each channel is controlled separately so that the sound reaching the audience is a balanced mix of all the available sounds. Sliders to the far right of the console are used to adjust the overall master left and right stereo volume. Sliders/faders are used in place of knobs because they are so much easier to manipulate.

SIGNAL PROCESSING

Several different devices can be used to process the signal, which means to alter it in some way to make it work better for the listening audience. The most common are equalizing, limiting, and compressing. The equalizer section of the input channel is used to sweeten the sound but a *third octave equalizer* is generally used post mix and is intended to reduce the effects of feedback. Feedback occurs when a specific frequency of sound feeds itself back into the microphone from a speaker. A *feedback loop* occurs when the tone reproduces itself louder and louder until it becomes a squeal that drowns out everything else. Often, feedback can be reduced by positioning the microphones away from the speakers.

Another cause of feedback has to do with the length of sound waves, and how they interact with a specific room. Each theatre is different in size and shape, so the exact frequency involved is different for each room, but some wavelengths are just the right size to bounce back stronger than others—like an echo. A third-octave EQ has filters similar to those found on the input module, but there are many more of them, three per octave of frequency variation. As you will recall a musical note one octave higher than another has twice the frequency. So the octave between 200Hz and 400Hz would have third octave stops at ~250 and 315Hz. You might find that one of the room's natural feedback frequencies is right around 315Hz, and thus reducing the slider for that specific frequency will cut feedback at that frequency. The EQ could be either an analog device with physical sliders or a digital one with virtual sliders.

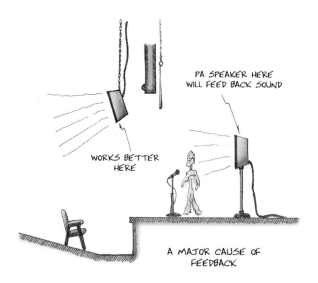

PA SPEAKER HERE
WILL FEED BACK SOUND

WORKS BETTER
HERE

A MAJOR CAUSE OF
FEEDBACK

PLACE THE SPEAKERS WHERE THEY DON'T
SEND SOUND DIRECTLY TO THE MICROPHONES

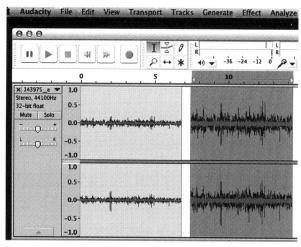

UNCOMPRESSED   COMPRESSED

THIS EQ RANGES FROM 20 Hz TO 20 kHz,
THE LIMITS OF HUMAN HEARING

THERE ARE TWO INDEPENDENT CHANNELS

Really experienced sound engineers might be able to tell what frequency is feeding back just by listening to it, and make the correct adjustments. More likely though, the problematic frequencies can be discovered through a process known as "pinking the room" in which *pink noise*, random sound on all frequencies at once, is injected into the PA system. A *spectrum analyzer* is then used to determine which frequencies are loudest (if not for idiosyncrasies of the room they should all be equal) and these are the ones that should be adjusted down on the EQ.

It is also possible to use a device that automatically detects and stops feedback, sometimes known as a "destroyer." Many professional audio engineers avoid them because they may have unintended effects on the general use of the signal, and perhaps cause more problems than they solve.

A *limiter* is used to prevent a signal from becoming so strong as to create distortion or perhaps clip. *Clipping* means that the amplification of the signal has maxed out, and has no more flexibility or headroom. That can create a murky sound in an analog signal, but is even worse in a digital signal because it causes problems with sampling. A limiter can be considered a "line in the sand" in that it stops the signal from going any further.

A *compressor* is often used in conjunction with a limiter. The compressor makes adjustments in the signal's *dynamic range* which is the difference between the loudest and softest sounds. In life, 10dB is the softest audible value and 100dB is considered the loudest safe volume. Those decibel endpoints, and all of the levels in-between, are the range of values that can change and be changed. A compressor is used to boost the value of soft sounds in proportion to louder sounds. That means really soft sounds are made much louder, while really loud ones don't change at all. Values in-between change in proportion to those extremes. The same process is used for a music CD, where the difference between the loudest sounds and the softest ones is generally less than 10dB. The process of compressing can make the system's output much more intelligible.

AMPLIFICATION

Sounds are amplified after leaving the mixer. Amplifiers are designed to have a low *noise to signal ratio*. Noise is the unintentional buzzing that comes from (among other things) the 60Hz AC line voltage. Each amp has a DC power supply inside it that is used to run the electrical components, and great care is taken by manufacturers to shield the system from inductive magnetic fields. You should avoid connecting them to a power source that also feeds dimmers because the switching nature of a modern dimmer causes multiple small voltage spikes in the system, which can create noise in the amplifier. A wide range of different amplifier power outputs is available, but most are in the range of several hundred watts. The power of an amplifier is rated in watts rather than volts or amps, which makes sense because watts is a unit used to measure power while volts and amps are not.

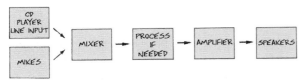

THE AUDIO SIGNAL FOLLOWS THIS BASIC PATH

It is important for amplifiers to be connected to the signal path after it emerges from the mixer/processors and not before. Amplifiers by their very nature greatly increase the strength of the signal, and if they were used in advance of the mixing console, they would seriously overload its circuits. Most amps can be used either mono or stereo, depending on how they are configured via a selection switch on the back. If one amp is used to power both the left and right speakers in a system, stereo should be selected and the left and right inputs patched in accordingly. But it is also very common to use multiple amps, one for each speaker or each group of speakers. In that case, configure the amp to mono so that maximum power reaches the speakers.

Sometimes amplifier/speaker assignments are made on the basis of high end and low end designations. *Low end* means the lower bass frequencies and higher ones are the treble *high end*. If an active crossover is placed ahead of the amplification section in the signal path, separate amps are used for the high and low ends. Other times the speaker themselves have a passive crossover system.

LOUDSPEAKERS

The amplified signal travels down wires to the *loudspeakers*, which are used to transform the analog electrical signal back into sound waves consisting of compacted and rarefied air that can be heard by the human ear. If all has gone well, the sounds are not unnecessarily distorted, other than as intended by the signal processing equipment.

Some older speakers are connected using a *¼" jack*, which appears to be one single conductor, but actually has a ring and a tip component. This sort of cable has two conductors in it, one being connected to the ring and one to the tip of the *jack*. This type of connector is also used for things like a guitar cable, so be careful because the current output of a guitar is much less than that of a speaker. Speaker cables are much more heavy duty.

Other speakers, especially more modern ones, use a *Speakon* connector, which has the advantage of making a more secure connection to the speaker cabinet. Small tabs on the sides must be manipulated to pull it loose. This type of connector is for speakers only, so there is no confusion with other types of cables.

The terminology surrounding a public address system can be confusing when it comes to the speakers. You may often hear someone call the speaker section the "PA," or that designation might mean the entire system

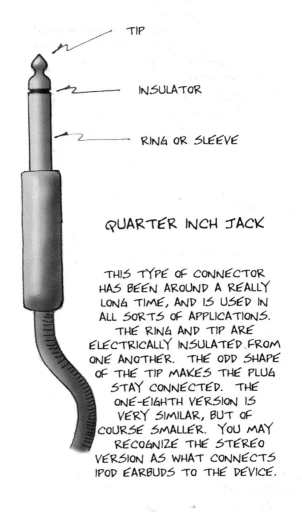

TIP

INSULATOR

RING OR SLEEVE

QUARTER INCH JACK

THIS TYPE OF CONNECTOR HAS BEEN AROUND A REALLY LONG TIME, AND IS USED IN ALL SORTS OF APPLICATIONS. THE RING AND TIP ARE ELECTRICALLY INSULATED FROM ONE ANOTHER. THE ODD SHAPE OF THE TIP MAKES THE PLUG STAY CONNECTED. THE ONE-EIGHTH VERSION IS VERY SIMILAR, BUT OF COURSE SMALLER. YOU MAY RECOGNIZE THE STEREO VERSION AS WHAT CONNECTS IPOD EARBUDS TO THE DEVICE.

SPEAKON CONNECTORS ONLY FIT ON AMPS AND SPEAKERS, SO THEY AREN'T EASILY CONFUSED WITH SOMETHING LIKE A 1/4" GUITAR CABLE

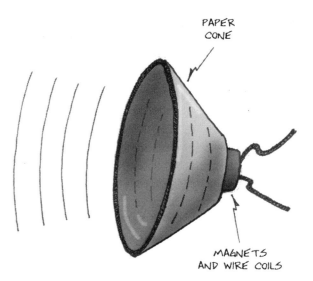

PAPER CONE

MAGNETS AND WIRE COILS

THE CONE OF A SPEAKER IS MADE OF PAPER AND IS QUITE FRAGILE. THE THIN, DELICATE NATURE OF THE CONE MAKES IT MAGNIFY THE VIBRATIONS OF THE MAGNETS AND WIRE FOUND IN THE BACK OF THE PAPER CONE. LOUDER SOUNDS MOVE THE CONE MORE THAN SOFT ONES. IF THE CONE MOVES TOO FAR OR TOO FAST IT WILL BE DAMAGED.

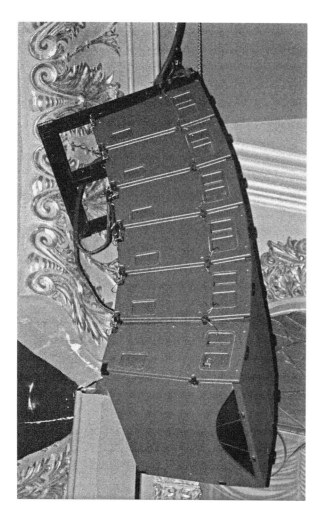

LINE ARRAY OF SPEAKERS

THESE PARTICULAR CABINETS WERE HUNG FROM THE CEILING OF THE THEATRE USING ONE TON CHAIN MOTORS.

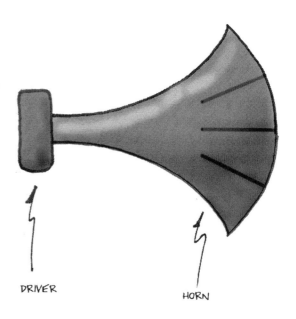

DRIVER

HORN

HORN AND DRIVER

THE DRIVER HAS THE MAGNET AND WIRE THAT MAKES THE ACTUAL SOUND, BUT THE HORN PART IS ESSENTIAL AS A RESONATOR

from microphones to speakers. Modern systems tend to use more efficient multi-purpose speakers housed in what is known as a *line array* that is very frequently flown over the stage and focused very carefully to give the best dispersion of sound over the entire theatre.

Other times the speakers are divided by different types for high and low end sounds. Most speakers are enclosed in a cabinet, and the way they are designed is critical to the way the speaker works. Cabinets are often very robust structures with interior baffles and chambers that resonate with the vibrations of the sounds the speakers produce. As a result, they are often much heavier than you would expect.

Cone speakers have a paper cone in them that is moved back and forth by a system of magnets and coils of wire. The process is not unlike that used by a microphone to convert, or transduce, aural sound into electrical impulses. In this case, the magnetic impulses move a much heavier paper cone much larger distances, which is why the amplifier was necessary. The back and forth motion of the cone pushes the air in front of it forward to compress it, and when it moves backward an opposite area of rarefaction is created. Thus an audible sound wave is created. This process is quite visible in larger speakers. The larger cone moves back and forth a proportionally large distance.

Lower pitched sounds have a longer wavelength, and are best reproduced by a larger cone. *Woofers* and *subs* are sometimes used to reproduce low end tones. Higher frequencies are often handled by *horn* and *driver* loudspeakers. A system of magnets and wires similar to that found in a cone speaker is used to vibrate a thin metal diaphragm instead of a paper cone. The plastic horn is used as a resonator. The horn is aptly named, having a small throat and a much larger outer opening. The horn greatly increases the volume of sound from the diaphragm.

TERMS USED IN THIS CHAPTER

¼" jack	gain	phantom power
audio snake	headroom	pink noise
cardioid mic pattern	high end	preamp
clipping	horn and drive speaker	rack mountable, rails
compressor	input modules	RCA connectors
condenser microphones	lavaliere	signal path
cone speakers	limiter	slider
delay	line array speakers	solo or PFL (pre-fade listen)
diversity receiver	line level inputs	button
dynamic microphone	low end	Speakon connector
dynamic range	mic level input	spectrum analyzer
equalizer	microphone	stereo
FCC/Federal Communications	mixing console	subs
Commission	mono	third octave equalizer
feedback loop	noise to signal ratio	transducer
flying fader	omnidirectional	woofer
foldback	pad button	XLR connectors
frequency agile	PCC (phase-coherent-cardioid)	

CHAPTER 25

DIGITAL
AUDIO FILES

NOT SO LONG AGO, recorded sound in a theatre meant playing music from a reel-to-reel tape recorder, which was still popular as late as the 1990s. Starting the tape machine created a loud clunking noise, so it was best for the sound man to be in a booth somewhere. Playback was accomplished by turning the tape transport lever to the right for

TAPE REELS

BUILT-IN EDITING BLOCK FOR SPLICING

TWENTY YEARS AGO, THIS WOULD HAVE BEEN A DREAM MACHINE FOR THEATRE SOUND REPRODUCTION, BUT TIMES HAVE CHANGED!

play or fast-forward and to the left for rewind. Modern transport controls have the same icons as back then, although they are of course now computer generated and completely silent. Back then, light-colored splicing tape helped you locate your cue in the right spot on the tape. Editing magnetic tape was done by rotating the reels back and forth by hand to move the tape over the "head" which read the magnetic code. That made an eerie, slow motion sound from the speakers. When you found just the right spot, a Sharpie was used to mark the tape, which was then cut with a razor blade and spliced back together to create an edit. Lots of things have changed since then, to say the least! Editing and playback now are of course done with a computer.

Numerous sound editing programs are available today, some are free downloads and some are not. With a wide array of possibilities comes a wide range of differences in the sort of features they have. Some of them just work with mp3s, some are primarily used for music recording, and some lean toward video production. Even with those differences there are similarities at the basic editing level. The greatest similarity is the way sound editing programs use a *timeline* as an editing tool. Timelines are also popular with video editing software, and the reason is that both audio and video files play over a period of time, so a static snapshot won't work. A video is usually made up of both pictures and audio, so the editor can follow the narrative with the visual cues. Sounds have narratives too, which makes them part of the storytelling process. But you can't see those sounds on a computer monitor. You can however make a graph of how loud or soft the sounds are. A timeline is used to represent that, and allows you to visualize what is happening at different moments. "Seeing" the sound is a great improvement over moving tape back and forth to find a particular moment in a cue.

A computer equipped with sound editing software has become known as a *Digital Audio Workstation*, or *DAW*. You can download some of them for free, or perhaps like *Garage Band* one came pre-installed on your new computer. The most popular professional editing programs of the moment are *Pro Tools*, *Adobe Audition*, and *Sound Forge Pro*. Sometimes you can download a trial version for a brief review period, which is a great way to see if you like it or not. These programs are packed with all sorts of cool features that a professional sound engineer needs to have.

As an alternative, *Audacity* is a free, open source program that can work cross-platform on either PC or Mac. It doesn't have all the features of the big three, but does a really good job of editing together sound effects cues for a play. You can download sounds from the internet, record them yourself, or rip them from effects CDs. I've picked Audacity as my sample demonstration program because it's free for you to download, works cross-platform, and is a very intuitive workspace. There is a good online support community. If you use a different program now, or step up to a more professional one in the future, many of the basic concepts of cutting, pasting, mixing, and volume adjustment are very much the same across the board.

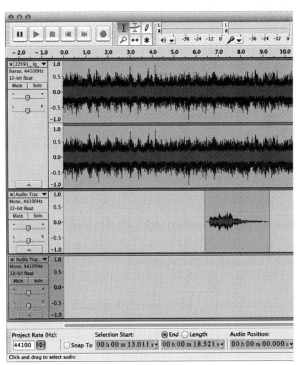

AUDACITY WORKSPACE

AUDACITY IS A CROSS-PLATFORM PROGRAM, MEANING THAT YOU CAN USE IT ON EITHER MAC OR PC. YOU CAN DOWNLOAD IT FROM THE INTERNET FOR FREE.

PRO TOOLS WORKSPACE

PRO TOOLS IS CAPABLE OF DOING JUST ABOUT ANYTHING YOU CAN DREAM UP WHEN IT COMES TO EDITING AUDIO, ESPECIALLY MUSIC.

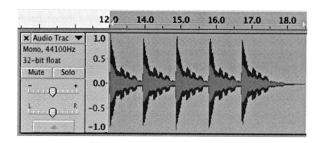

AUDACITY TIMELINE WAVEFORM

AUDACITY DISPLAYS A LOT OF INFORMATION IN THIS WINDOW.

AT THE LEFT: MONO TRACK AND 44.1K SAMPLE RATE.

AT THE TOP: THE SOUND STARTS AT 12 SECONDS INTO THE TRACK, AND ENDS 6.5 SECONDS LATER.

LOOK AT THE WAVEFORM TO TELL WHEN CERTAIN EVENTS HAPPEN. IN THIS CASE, YOU CAN EASILY SEE WHERE A NEW CLANG OF THE BELL STARTS.

THE LEFT RIGHT STEREO IS VERY INTERESTING, WITH IT YOU CAN DESIGNATE WHETHER A MONO TRACK WILL BE LEFT, RIGHT OR CENTER IN A FINAL STEREO MIX.

USE THE MUTE BUTTON TO SILENCE SOME OF THE TRACKS WHEN YOU ARE MIXING VARIOUS LAYERS TOGETHER.

RIPPING DATA FROM A CD

Audacity does not extract data directly from a CD, perhaps because of the intellectual property issues that brings up. It's probably something the open source creators would like to avoid. Lots of theatres have a library of sound effects on CDs. If you have effects CDs, the legal hurdle has already been passed because the makers expect you to use the sounds in a show in accordance with their user agreement. Otherwise they would be of very little value. If you are using a PC, the Audacity website has suggestions for third party programs that will extract the data from a CD and convert it to a WAV or AIFF file, which you can then import into the Audacity workspace. If you are a Mac user, opening the CD file on your computer will automatically convert the files to the AIFF extension which is native to Apple products. This is the clumsiest part of the process. Either way, you might consider gathering all of the sounds you need at one time, and keeping them in a folder you can easily find.

All of the programs use a graphical, visual approach to displaying the sound file, so that you can look at it to see what the sound is doing at various points in its progress. You can't hear a sound all at once with your ears, but you can visualize an entire cue all at once graphically. Sounds occur over time and are fluid in nature, so the visual approach is a good way to look at them in a static form.

The graph shows how the volume of the sound rises and falls over time, which allows the user to look and see where a landmark event takes place. This particular Audacity graph has five distinct parts, each of them separated by silence. It is a bell clanging at a railroad crossing, and was ripped from a CD of *sound effects*. Later on I'll demonstrate how to use this and other sounds to build an effect using tools found in the program. You can also download sound effects, or *SFX*, from the Internet. Several pay sites are aimed at the television and movie industry. These commercial sites have incredible selections, but are rather pricey. Other sites offer free downloads, but some of them have very limited selections and poor quality. A few are *sharing sites*, that allow you to upload sounds you've recorded, and download sounds from others; they tend to be the best. You might try one called Freesound.org.

The quality of downloaded sounds can be quite variable. Things that might affect quality include bit depth and sample rate. *Bit depth* refers to the amount of data used to record the sound. It is sort of like the resolution of a photograph where higher resolution is a more faithful representation of the subject. But of course that also increases the file size, which is somewhat problematic when it comes to storing and editing. The default Audacity setting is *32 bit float*, which seems to work quite well. That's also the natural bit depth of most computers. 64 bit has recently become available for Pro Tools, but won't work on a lot of machines and is probably much more than you really need for most sound effects. A commercially recorded music CD has a bit rate of 16, which is considered standard for that media and produces high fidelity. But that is somewhat misleading, because a higher bit rate is much more useful when editing the sounds than when listening to them.

Another fidelity component is the *sample rate*, which was mentioned earlier in the audio theory chapter. A human (or a dog for that matter) cannot hear a digital signal. All sounds must begin as analog waves, because that is the way the natural world works. The process of converting an analog sound wave to a digital file requires a conversion program to test, or sample, the shape of the wave to see what it looks like. Of course the sound wave is changing amplitude and frequency over time as waves do. So the sampling must occur at regular intervals to determine what those changes are. If the interval between samples is too large the true nature of the wave will be missed.

The current standard for sample rate is 44,100Hz, and that is the default rate for the Audacity program. But you may find that sounds downloaded from the internet have a different sample rate, usually slower, especially if

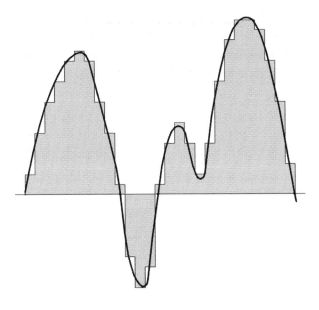

DIGITAL SAMPLING OF AN ANALOG WAVEFORM

THE MODERN STANDARD IS 44,100 TIMES PER SECOND, WHICH
IS FAST ENOUGH TO RECORD THE WAVE EFFECTIVELY. IF
THE SAMPLE RATE IS TOO LOW, THE ANALOG WAVEFORM
WON'T BE TESTED ENOUGH TIMES TO REFLECT ITS TRUE
SHAPE AND THE SOUNDS WILL BE DISTORTED.

they were recorded some years ago. Audacity will play the file as though it were 44.1kHz, but if you look at the sample rate on the left of the timeline window; you can see the actual rate. Slow sample rates are generally not as good.

When you open a source file from a CD it's a good idea to save it to your computer with a name that can help you to identify it later. You'll notice that files taken from a CD have names like sound 1 or track 2 rather than the name of the sound as it might appear on a media player. That's because extracting, ripping, or transcoding from a CD often removes the metadata that was attached to the file. So the name of the sound (which wasn't part of the actual audio file) doesn't copy. That won't happen if you open a downloaded file, or one you've already named. The problem is that the generic title doesn't tell much about what the sound actually is. If you give it a descriptive name you will automatically recognize it later.

File extensions are the (usually) three-letter .xxx that you see at the ends of computer files. That is a type of metadata that tells the computer which program to use when opening the file. *Metadata* is ancillary information about a media file that is not the actual sound or picture itself. When you *save as*, and choose a different file type than currently exists, the program will *transcode* the file to the type that works with that extension. Often the process is called importing or exporting. Transcoding does more than just change the extension letters; it rewrites the file entirely to the new code, something you

might visualize as being like translating a book from French to German. Video files are notorious for taking a very long time to transcode. Audio files are much faster because they are so much smaller, but still take a few seconds. The three main audio types, WAV, CDA, and AIFF are almost identical, so transcoding from one to another takes very little time. Moving from Audacity's .aup file type to a WAV or AIFF takes a bit longer. Transcoding from a program's native, proprietary, working language is important, and must be done so that the file can be accessed by others who aren't using that specific program. A .aup file can only be opened by Audacity.

Some file formats use *data compression*, which is a way for them to take up less space on your computer, or other media player. The mp3 is a very well-known type, which is widely used to compress files so that more of them will fit onto the memory chip of your audio listening device. That type of compression is said to be *lossy*, which means that some data is lost during compression. It is really better to use a non-lossy file type such as the *Windows Audio File, WAV*. Or the *Audio Interchange File Format* abbreviated *AIFF*. WAV files are native to Windows, and AIFF is native to Apple OS, but either one will work just fine cross platform. There isn't much need to save space on a drive when building sound cues for a show, and either of the two uncompressed file types is much better for editing than an mp3. Some versions of Figure 53's playback program QLab caution against using mp3 files and specifically suggest using the WAV format instead. You might want to check to see if the media server or playback program you use has any special requirements.

When you start up the Audacity program you'll see a workspace with a menu bar across the top that includes very familiar titles like file, edit, and view. Choosing

---

AUDIO FILE FORMATS

- WAV or Windows audio file
  Often used for music playback, non "lossy".

- AIFF or audio interchange file format
  Native to the Apple operating system, and very similar to the WAV format.

- MP3 or MPEG III
  A compressed type of file used for playback devices like an MP3 player, although they sound just fine for playback, editing compressed files is problematic. The MP4 is very similar to the MP3, but has restrictions placed on copying and transferring.

File/new will open another copy of the workspace; File/open will allow you to open one of the files from your sounds folder. File/import will *add* another sound file to the project you are currently working on so that you have more than one sound open at a time. If you are building an effect, use the *import* command to add all of the files you need to use into one project.

When you open a non .aup sound file, Audacity asks if you would like to use a copy of the sound or use it directly. It's almost always better to use a copy, so that you don't lose the original sound, even though it takes a few seconds to transcode the original file. Most media editing programs create their own file type for the period you are working with the media, and then convert to an easily used WAV or AIFF when you are finished. Making a copy is a type of *non-destructive editing*, in that the original sound is kept intact. It allows you to return to a set point later if you change your mind about actions you take during the editing process.

Suppose you would like to build a stereo cue in which a crossing bell rings twice, a train passes by on the tracks from left to right while the bell continues to ring, after which the bell rings twice more and stops. The first step in building that cue would be to find the two different sounds you need. The bell clangs many times, but each clang sounds the same, so it is really just one sound with lots of copies. Import each of the two different files so that their timelines appear on the screen. Notice how the use of volume-based graphics in the timeline makes it easy to identify when the bell clangs, and where the silence between sounds is located. I've also added a train whistle to the cue to add more of a *soundscape* or background of environmental sounds.

Let's begin by creating a bell sound that continues for 30 clangs, more than you will likely need. You can

trim off any excess later. Audacity allows you to copy and paste in the same way many other programs do, but it doesn't support doing that with a right click. So use the drop down edit menu, or the shortcut keys C and V to speed things up. Use the cursor to select data by clicking and dragging. If you want the entire file you can just double click to select the whole thing. Those are normal computer program actions that you probably already know, which is one of the things that make Audacity fairly intuitive.

You need to have approximately the same amount of time between each of the bell clangs. If you are good at guessing distances you can probably just click in the spot you think is right, and most of the time that works fine. But on occasion you need to be more exact, and that is when *labels* come into play. You can set labels on the timeline at important points you would like to find again. You do that by adding a *label track* from the TRACKS menu.

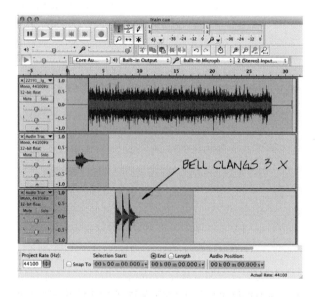

IT'S OBVIOUS WHEN THE BELL SOUNDS

Place the cursor where you want the label to appear, and chose *add label at selection* from the menu. You can assign a name by typing in the name you'd like.

Use labels to show the same spot on different bell clang sounds, where the sound has decayed the same amount. The selection properties of the cursor will snap to the label points, making it easy to grab just the right amount of sound.

Copy and paste bell clangs. Repeat the procedure several times until about 30 clangs are lined up in the window. (After you've pasted a couple, reselect a group of them and paste that selection to speed up the process.) I pasted at the head of the sound rather the end, because that last clang decays over a period of time, and I didn't

ADD A LABEL TRACK TO MARK POINTS ON
THE TIMELINE

THEN YOU CAN ADD NAMES TO THE LABELS WITH
INSTRUCTIONS AS TO WHY THEY ARE THERE.

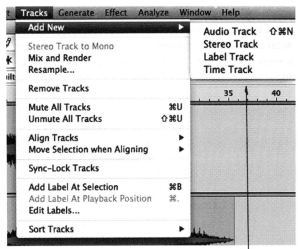

"ADD NEW" GIVES YOU THESE OPTIONS

"AUDIO TRACK" IS GENERALLY THE MOST USEFUL, BECAUSE
IT ADDS ONE MONO TRACK.

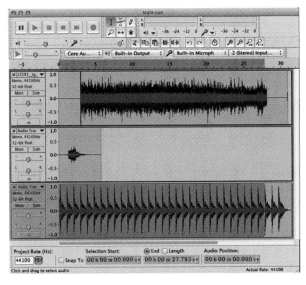

COPY AND PASTE BELL CLANGS

MAKE ENOUGH OF THEM TO COVER THE ENDS OF THE
TRAIN SOUND AT THE TOP. I ADDED THESE TO THE HEAD
OF THE TRACK BECAUSE THE LAST CLANG SUSTAINS A BIT
AT THE END, AND IT SOUNDS BETTER IF YOU LEAVE THAT
LONG DECAY OF THE SOUND.

want to lose that feature. Lots of sounds "ring out" at the end, and if you cut that portion off the sound will seem to jerk to an end unnaturally.

At a certain point the data in the timeline will exceed its viewable width. You can change the visible portion of the timeline using the magnifier icon to zoom in or out, or to fit the entire project. If everything has gone correctly, you should have 30 or so bell sounds that are perfectly spaced. If you used the "eyeball" method to measure you might wind up with too much time between

sounds. You can select a portion of the silence between clangs and delete it to remove a few seconds. If on the other hand there isn't enough time between sounds you can add more by putting the cursor where you need it and choose silence from the GENERATE menu. Pick an amount of time from the dialog box.

Your other file is the sound of the train passing by. Both it and the clang file are recorded in *mono*, meaning there is only one track. The design calls for the sound to *pan* from left to right showing that the train crossed in that direction, so we will eventually need a *stereo* version of the sound to do that. Audacity will create a stereo WAV file when you export your sound. For now we can continue to work with mono tracks in building the effect.

It's a good idea to trim off any silence at the beginning and end of the train file so that you have a clean edge to work with, and you can do that by selecting what you want and using the *trim command* from the edit tool bar. Open a new mono, audio track from the tracks menu and copy/paste the train sound into the new track. That creates two separate tracks with the same sound in each. The EFFECTS menu contains two processes called fade-in and fade-out. Use them to make the tracks fade in and out so that the sound builds as the train approaches and falls at it goes away. The design called for the sound to begin stage left and pan toward stage right. You can use the panel at the right of the screen to set left or right stereo channel for the sound on a specific track. Mix the left sound to the left speaker and the right to the right. I staggered the timing of the two tracks so that the left is heard first and the right last.

The *time shift tool* is a double-headed arrow, ↔ in the Audacity tools toolbar. Use it to move the train sounds back and forth until they are correctly aligned with

LAYERING SOUNDS DURING PLAYBACK

The process of building this sound cue brings up an interesting decision making issue. Should you mix the sounds together when building the cue, or should you leave the bell and train as separate sounds that they can be mixed by the playback computer? If you mix the sounds together now they will automatically play back as a stereo file with left right components once the Audacity file has been transcoded to a WAV. When played back during the show the operator has only one cue to play and the sound will pan between left and right. But what if you would like the bell clangs to come from a different speaker? If you are using a playback application like QLab or SFX, you can program the computer to play the bell sounds first. The train pan sound can be cued to automatically follow exactly two bell clangs later and come from the theatre's left/right stereo speakers. If you make all the decisions early on in the editing phase, you won't be able to easily change them at a tech rehearsal without a re-edit. But setting all the parameters in the theatre takes a lot more time during rehearsal. This section is about editing digital files with Audacity, so I've taken that approach.

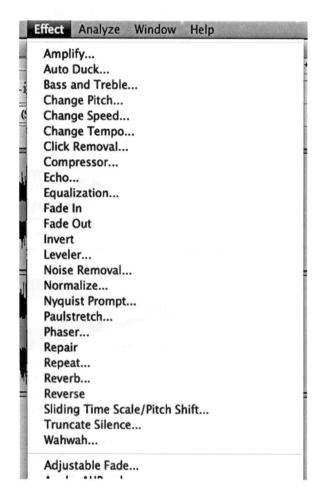

SOME OF THE BUILT IN EFFECTS
THERE ARE MANY MORE PLUG-INS ONLINE

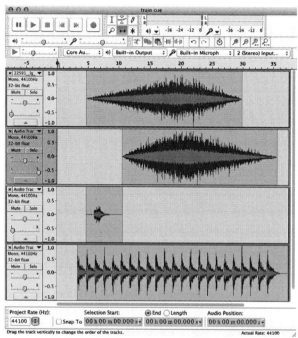

FINISHED EFFECT READY FOR EXPORT
AS A WAV OR AIFF FILE

WHEN YOU EXPORT THE FILE IT WILL AUTOMATICALLY BE
CONVERTED TO STEREO.

A NUMBER OF THINGS HAVE BEEN DONE:

THE TRAIN SOUND HAS BEEN PASTED IN TWO MONO TRACKS, AND HAS BEEN MADE TO FADE IN AND OUT. THE TOP TRACK IS SET TO PLAY ON THE LEFT SIDE, AND THE SECOND ONE ON THE RIGHT SIDE SO THAT IT PANS ACROSS. A TRAIN WHISTLE IS ON THE THIRD TRACK, ALSO SET TO COME FROM THE LEFT. THE BELL CLANGS COME FROM BOTH SIDES.

THE TIME SHIFT TOOL HAS BEEN USED TO ARRANGE THE VARIOUS TRACKS SO THAT THEY HAPPEN AT THE PROPER TIMES.

the bell clanging track, remembering that there should be two bell clangs before the train sound begins. You can remove any extra clangs by selecting and deleting.

A multitude of processes can be used to change the character of the sounds in your effects. Fade in and out were two options from the EFFECTS menu. As you can see there are many more of them, and you can use them to adjust volume (amplify), EQ, add compression, and time stretch among others. In addition Audio Units or AUs are added from time to time as plug-ins. Because Audacity is an open source program that is supported by volunteers, you will often see the name of the programmer who invented the plug-in at the top of an effect's dialog box.

The process of building the train cue has given some insight into how to use the cursor to select parts of a sound, how to cut and paste them, how to add different types of tracks, and how to mix sounds together.

You might want to record sounds of your own directly into Audacity. To do that you need to connect a microphone to the computer, possibly through an existing port (usually the pink mini phone plug on your computer's sound card) or by using an audio interface that connects to your computer via USB. An audio interface or external soundcard will provide lots of choices for connecting multiple microphones. You must set some very specific parameters to record on your particular equipment, so consult the online manual to see what is best for you. To do the actual recording, open a new file and press the red record button. Within reason, it doesn't really matter all that much if you have silence at the beginning or ending, because you can remove that with the regular editing tools. Editing the sound you capture is the same as editing any other sound.

AUDIO PLAYBACK

After you've built your sound cues, a playback program is used to play them over the sound system during the performance, where they become an important element of the show. *Playback* indicates that sounds have been recorded earlier and are played back during the performance rather than being produced live. Many different types of equipment have been used over the years, beginning with a record player, and progressing to audio tape, mini-disks, CDs, and now to sounds stored as digital files on a computer. It is difficult to imagine what the next thing will be, but it seems like playing digital files of one sort or another is here to stay.

Mini-disks were a type of read/write digital media that was used for a few years before CD burners were inexpensive enough to be purchased by the general public. Before that only record companies had them. With either minis or CDs there were two different ways of playing back on a disk player. One was to make a separate disk for each cue, so that the operator pressed

play to make the cue run. Problematically, the CD player might or might not begin playing immediately. Another method was to record the cues as separate tracks, and to use a specially made DJ type player that could toggle from one track to another. That was more likely to make the cue start with no delay. Some players had a track name feature, so that you could insert the actual name of your cue rather than just a number. Either of these two methods points out a feature of theatre sound playback that is very important. It doesn't matter at a party if your dance music starts instantly, but in a show with set cues and split second timing it is crucial for cuing to be tight.

Nowadays, there are several different possibilities of how to play back digital files, other than using a CD player, and no matter which you use it will work much better. It's possible to run sounds from something like Windows Media Player or ITunes by attaching the headphone output to the mixing console. Press play and the cue will begin immediately, as long as you've cropped out any silence from the cue file. But the problem with that is one of reliability and organization.

Media Player isn't set up to properly organize the files so that they form a tight *cue list*. Entertainment-specific audio programs such as *QLab* and *SXF* have important features that make them better for playing back digital files. A playback program will allow you to fade sounds in and out, automatically follow one another, and to run multiple sounds at the same time. The files can be organized into a cue list that automatically updates to the next cue in line once the previous cue has been run. That's amazingly similar to the way a lighting console program works. You can configure the outputs so that media (video as well as audio) goes to the correct target device such as a mixing console, amplifier, or video projector. Either QLab or SFX has enough program outputs for most theatre work.

More complex systems are available. A heavy-duty media server will run numerous audio and video feeds at the same time. Media servers are computer systems designed with complex output devices. They are purpose built to handle all of them at once. Some systems are meant specifically for nightclub DJs, who weave together audio, video, and lighting. That environment is much more free-form than theatre is. In that case the DJ is the performer, but in theatre the use of media is meant to enhance a performance rather than be it.

Many media control programs and devices can be configured to run other devices like a light board, or to configure with computers that control on-stage automation. That capability is generically called *show control*, meaning that it can control an entire show. Show control is very popular when the show in question has lots of time up front to program computers when in tech and previews, and when it has the potential to reduce the number of operators required. In a commercial venue fewer operators means a lower overall operating cost for a show that might run for years. Non-commercial venues may find that the reduction in workforce for a short run isn't all that beneficial.

Theatre shows are tightly scripted, which means that the same things happen in the same order for every performance. To aid that workflow a good playback program must provide these features:

1. Keep the cues in an ordered list, from the first one to the last one.
2. Allow the operator to play them back in a dependable fashion, using some type of "GO" command.
3. Allow the sound designer to designate which speakers the sound cues will output to, and hence where the sounds will come from.
4. Allow the designer to set volume levels for the individual cues.
5. Provide a means of fading cues in and out.
6. Make it possible to link cues together.
7. Allow you to apply non-destructive effects and edits to your sound files.

There has been an ongoing debate about which is better, QLab or SFX, for several years. In reality they are very similar. At a certain point it can boil down to: Are you a Mac person or a PC person? QLab is a Mac program that uses the OSX architecture, and only works on a Macintosh computer. SFX is a PC program that will also work on a Mac—if Boot Camp has been installed as a PC interface. (Boot Camp is a way of running Windows on a Mac.) One other thing to consider is that just about any newer Mac can play QLab right out of the box, if you limit yourself to the single stereo and single video outputs from the back of the computer. To make use of more complex outputs you'll need an auxiliary sound card. SFX needs a more complicated sound card/audio interface from the get-go.

You can download a limited functionality version of QLab for free to see if you like it. Interestingly, at present they will also rent their software to you by the day at a very low cost.

The biggest advantage of using a computer program rather than individual CDs for playing back sound effects during a show is the *cue list*. It can be arranged so that the sound you need first is cue 1, the next one is cue 2, the next 3, and so forth. The program automatically loads the next cue as soon as the first one begins to run, so that the operator can play all the cues in order by giving a series of GO commands. This eliminates the difficulty of loading disks into a machine and booting them up. Unless you set the default differently, a long playing cue will continue to run, even after the succeeding cue has been called up. This allows two cues to run simultaneously and avoids the need for multiple cue lists.

If you only need a left and right stereo output, QLab can use the sound card that comes with the Mac

WHAT IS A SOUND CARD?

The term "card"—when used in context with a computer—means additional electronics that can be inserted into the tower of a desktop computer. For a sound card, that generally means a printed circuit board that plugs into the computer's electronics in the back of the tower. It gives you additional audio handling capacity. But in the modern vernacular a broader *sound card* definition means any additional piece of hardware that adds to the computer's audio handling capability. PCs often have a sound card that is physically a part of the mother board (the core electronics) that is fine for everyday use but is less sophisticated than what is required for SFX. Most computers of any sort have limited input/output connectors built in, usually just a pink microphone in, a light blue line level in, and a lime green line level out. As a result you may need to add an auxiliary sound card. That card can be one you install inside the computer, but more likely an external unit that you connect via USB. External cards have multiple inputs and outputs for more flexibility. *ASIO* or *Audio Stream Input Output* is a driver used to bypass your computer's regular sound hardware, allowing the audio data stream to go directly to the added sound card.

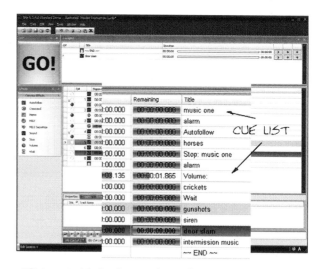

SFX WORKSPACE—NOTE THE GIANT GO BUTTON

ONE OF THE BEST THINGS ABOUT EITHER QLAB OR SFX IS THE WAY THEY ALLOW YOU TO SAVE CUES IN SEQUENTIAL ORDER FOR BETTER PLAYBACK.

SIGNAL PATH FROM COMPUTER

YOU MAY BE ABLE TO FEED A SIGNAL STRAIGHT FROM THE COMPUTER TO THE MIXER BY USING THE HEADPHONE JACK, BUT YOU WILL ONLY HAVE TWO OUTPUTS

PLAYBACK PROGRAM

↓

COMPUTER SOUND CARD

↓

DIGITAL/ANALOG INTERFACE

IF NEEDED

MIXING CONSOLE

AMPLIFIERS AND SPEAKERS

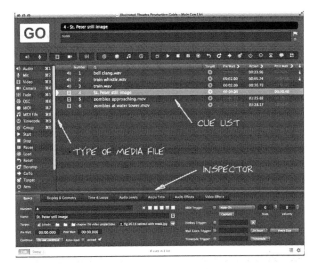

QLAB WORKSPACE

USE THE LIST AT THE LEFT TO INSERT A CUE FOR THE TYPE OF MEDIA FILE YOU WANT TO PLACE. YOU CAN EASILY MOVE THE CUES AROUND THE CUE LIST AND RE-NUMBER THEM. THE INSPECTOR AT THE BOTTOM ALLOWS YOU TO CHECK THE PARAMETERS OF THE SELECTED CUE.

computer, and doesn't require any specialized hardware. You can use the feed from the computer's headphone jack, but an additional sound card interface must be used if more outputs are required. The interface connects to a USB port, and receives the digital signals from the computer. It translates them into an analog signal that can be fed into a mixing console, or perhaps directly to your system amplifiers.

Both QLab and SFX have quite similar workspaces that allow you to drag and drop your sound files. This works best if you save all the cues in one folder when you are building them. It is important that all of your cues be in sequential order when running the show, so try to do that as you bring each one in, but if you need to make changes you can select a cue and drag to a new position between two others. Don't worry too much about that, you can renumber/name things later if you need to. If the same cue is used several times, create a new cue for each instance by dragging in the same file a number of times. Although the operator could back up in the cue list to repeat a sound, there will be fewer mistakes if everything works from repeatedly pressing go. Also, you might want to set different volume or fade parameters. Click the large GO button on the screen to start a cue, or you can configure either program to use the space bar as a substitute GO button.

The sound cues are not stored directly in the program's show file, but rather the playback program uses a link to them when the go command is given. As a result, it is important to leave a copy of the file on the computer itself, and not just on a removable travel drive. That is important to remember if you've built your cues on another machine and are using a flash memory drive to transfer them to the sound playback computer. If you accidentally remove an original sound file from the playback computer, a red X will appear next to the affected cue indicating that the link has been broken. After the cue list has been established in the playback program, you can click on the sounds one at a time to bring up a dialog box allowing you to set certain parameters such as sound level and patch designations.

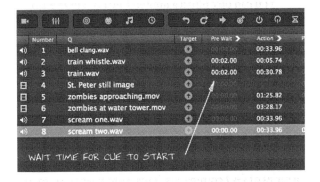

NON-DESTRUCTIVE CUES

INSTEAD OF MIXING THE SOUNDS TOGETHER AS ONE CUE, YOU MIGHT TAKE THIS APPROACH: SET UP EACH OF THE SOUNDS AS A DIFFERENT CUE AND LINK THEM ALL TOGETHER. THIS ALLOWS YOU MORE FLEXIBILITY TO ADJUST INDIVIDUAL TIMING AND VOLUME PARAMETERS. IN THIS EXAMPLE CUES 2 AND 3 AUTOMATICALLY FOLLOW THE PREVIOUS CUE, BUT A WAIT TIME HAS BEEN INSERTED SO THAT THE SOUNDS BEGIN AT STAGGERED TIMES.

In the earlier part of this chapter you learned how to mix sounds together to build a more complex cue, which is often a good way to create them. But consider this problem: What if the relative volumes of the train and bell were wrong? What if the train were too loud or the bell too soft? With the two sounds pre-mixed there is very little you can do about that at the tech rehearsal. An alternate method would be to have different cues that play at the same time. That way you can adjust the volume of the two parts individually.

Either SFX or QLab can configure the volume of cues to fade up, even if the original cue file wasn't built that way. They do this by creating a fade up edit that is applied to the cue. That doesn't change the original file, it just tells the program to fade the sound up over a set period of time. Since nothing destructive has happened to the file, you can change the fade up time, or get rid of it entirely without having to rework your original cue. QLab has a window at the bottom of the screen called the *Inspector*, which contains controls for fade ins, volume setting, and outputs. SFX has the same set up, but they call it the properties area.

Although you can use Audacity to edit the end of a cue so that it fades out, it is more likely with an underscoring sound that you will want to fade out on cue. That happens when you don't know how long the cue should last, and it changes a bit each night. Both SFX and QLab have a panel to the left of the screen that contains effects you can drag to the cue list. Selecting a fade effect creates a cue in the list that doesn't itself have any sound data. A fade cue only exists to fade out the previous cue. You can adjust the length and character of the fade using the properties or Inspector windows. When the original cue is running, the fade cue will be highlighted as the next cue. When go is pressed, the fade will happen.

Both programs have a method of *looping* a cue, so that it starts over as soon as it finishes. You might want that option with something environmental like rain or crickets, sounds that are fairly amorphous and play in the background. A looped cue is a good example of a cue you might want to end with a fade out cue, as was just described.

Another process is to link cues together so that one follows after another. If you do that, pressing go once causes a cascade of cues to run. As a refinement to that, you can set a wait time so that there is a set amount of distance between the starts of the two cues. Consider the train cue again. If the design calls for the train pan sound to start two clangs after the bell, give the linked cue that much wait time.

If you would like more information about the QLab program, you might consider *QLab 3: Show Control*, by Jeromy Hopgood.

After your show has been established on the computer, there are a couple of things you should do to make sure it works well for the run of the show. Either program will allow you to lock your show, so that no changes can be made until it is unlocked. That will prevent the operator from accidently clicking on the

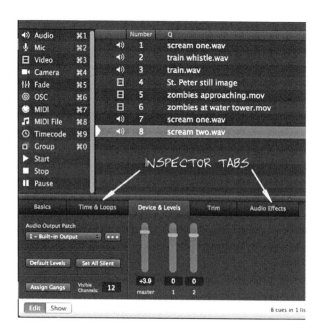

THE QLAB INSPECTOR

ONE OF THE TABS IN THE INSPECTOR ALLOWS YOU TO SET THE VOLUME OF THE SOUND YOU ARE LISTENING TO.

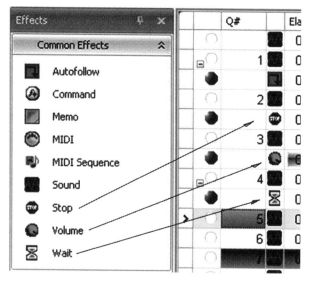

SFX EFFECTS PANEL

DRAG AN EFFECT OVER INTO THE CUE LIST JUST AFTER THE CUE WHERE YOU NEED IT. AN ICON WILL APPEAR BETWEEN SOUNDS IN THE CUE LIST. A WINDOW OPENS ALLOWING YOU TO SET PARAMETERS APPROPRIATE TO THE EFFECT THAT WAS APPLIED.

wrong thing and deleting some of your programming. You should also consider changing the computer's preferences to prevent it from doing any automatic updates or virus scans that might occur during the show. As with any type of computer used for live performance, make certain to disable Wi-Fi, networking, and Bluetooth as these can create interference and cause problems with playback. You can also set the monitor to remain on so that it doesn't accidentally time out when you have a long space between cues. The same is true about "sleep" events that may cause the hard drive to shut down to save power.

TERMS USED IN THIS CHAPTER

Adobe Audition	Label track/Audacity	sound card
Audio Interchange File Format (AIFF)	looping	sound effects (SFX)
	metadata	Sound Forge
Audio Stream Input Output (ASIO)	non-destructive editing	soundscape
bit depth/32 bit float	pan	stereo
cue list	playback	SFX playback program
data compression	Pro Tools	Timeline
decay of a sound	QLab	Time shift tool/Audacity
Digital Audio Workstation (DAW)	sample rate	transcode
	sharing website	trim command/Audacity
Inspector/QLab	show control	Windows Audio File (WAV)

CHAPTER 26

VIDEO PROJECTION FOR THE STAGE

*U*NITED SCENIC ARTISTS, the union for theatrical designers, recently added the position of *Projection Designer* to its existing design categories of scenery, lights, sound, and costumes. Projections have become an important part of the theatrical experience. Most musicals on Broadway today have a projected image component. But they aren't the only place projections are used. Many museums have video displays that discuss historical events as a component of their exhibits. Concert video walls have become standard in arenas everywhere because they give the audience a much more intimate view of the performer than would normally be possible from hundreds of feet away. Sports venues also use video walls to give fans the option of watching replays of exciting moments. Probably the least well-known, but most frequent use of video is at corporate events like sales meetings. As technology progresses it's very likely that projected video will become even more important to entertainment production.

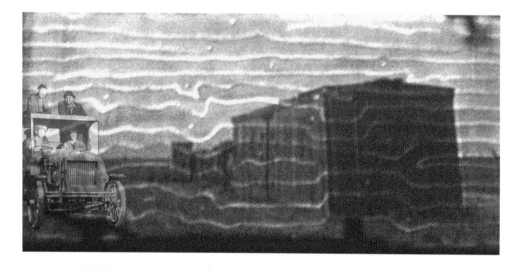

IN THIS PRODUCTION OF GRAPES OF WRATH, A PAINTED SCRIM, LIVE ACTORS, AND A FRONT-PROJECTED MOVIE OF A RAILROAD TRAIN WERE USED TO CONVEY A SENSE OF WONDER AS THE JOAD FAMILY TRAVELED ACROSS THE WESTERN UNITED STATES.

PROJECTION METHODS

There are three basic ways to deliver an image to the stage; front projection, rear projection, and video wall.

Although it could be several flat screens side by side, the term *video wall* generally means an assembly of LED screen units that are *tiled* together to form a much larger screen. Tiling means to assemble an image from smaller parts. In a video wall of the sort commonly used for large concerts, small LED screens are connected together to form a seamless image with very thin or virtually nonexistent spaces between them. The LED semiconductors are often seated inside a black mesh to provide extra contrast between the lighted LEDs and the background. A computer program is used to decipher the digital screen configuration and apportion the overall image between the separate, tiled units of the screen. This type of arrangement is also used for outdoor signs or billboards that can shift from one advertisement to another. The display is extremely *luminescent*, as it must be to work in a brightly lit environment.

The individual LED red, green, and blue clusters are small, but much larger than the individual pixels of a television or computer monitor. As a result the appearance of the image close up is very *pixilated*. But remember that these screens are meant to be viewed from quite a distance, perhaps hundreds of feet, and from that far away the pixels tend to blur together into a smoother image. This type of video display works really well in a concert environment because the image is so bright it can easily overpower the other stage lighting reflecting off atmospheric haze. The content of the video background is often a mix of a live feed of the artist blended with music-video background material.

Video projectors are much more commonly used for theatrical productions than a video wall. That may in large part be due to the very high cost of the walls, but there are aesthetic concerns as well because LED screen images are anything but subtle. A high-end projector may cost tens of thousands of dollars, but a video wall the size of a theatre cyc can run into the millions. LED screens are by their very nature only useful for images at the rear of the performance space.

Rear projection of video requires a screen material that allows light from the projector to pass through it and appear to a viewer on the other side, and as a result must be *translucent*. Translucent materials allow light to pass through, but are not completely clear or *transparent*. If the rear projection material were entirely transparent the light would pass through and create no image. An *opaque* screen blocks all the light and would be completely dark. It is a delicate balance, because if the screen material allows too much or too little light to pass through the luminosity of the image will be adversely affected. A rear

LED PANEL WITH A BLACK MASK

LED PANELS FOR THE CONCERT ENVIRONMENT OFTEN USE TRI-COLOR LEDS EMBEDDED IN A BLACK MASK TO HEIGHTEN THEIR CONTRAST. THIS ILLUSTRATION SHOWS A 96×96 PIXEL PANEL, WITH A TOTAL IMAGE SIZE OF 9216 PIXELS. THOSE ARE THE SAME SPECS AS THE ELATION EPV6 PANEL, WHICH IS ABOUT 22" SQUARE. AT THE VENUE, THE INDIVIDUAL PANELS ARE CONNECTED TOGETHER TO MAKE ONE LARGE SCREEN.

BARCO 11K LUMEN PROJECTOR

THIS PROJECTOR IS USED FROM THE BACK OF THE THEATRE AT THE UNIVERSITY OF KENTUCKY

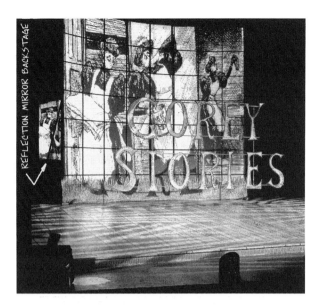

REAR PROJECTION WITH A MIRROR

IN THIS SHOW, A MIRROR WAS USED BACKSTAGE TO REFLECT THE IMAGES, MAKING THEM LARGER THAN THEY WOULD HAVE BEEN OTHERWISE. THAT'S USUSALLY DONE WHEN THERE ISN'T ENOUGH DISTANCE FOR THE IMAGE TO SPREAD OUT ON ITS OWN.

THE GRID PATTERN WAS PART OF THE DESIGN.

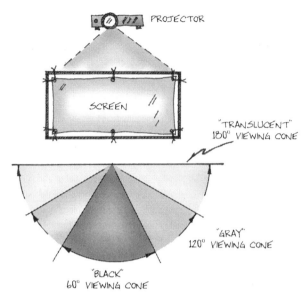

THREE TYPES OF REAR PROJECTION MATERIAL

IF THE AUDIENCE SEATING IS WIDER THAN 60 DEGREES, THE VIEWERS ON THE EXTREME SIDES WON'T SEE WELL WHEN USING BLACK SCREEN MATERIAL.

projection screen must capture a certain amount of the light, diffuse it, and make it visible on the other side where the screen glows with the image. The material does not necessarily need to be specifically designed for this purpose, but purpose-built screens are much better at the task. Any material used for rear projection must be made in a seamless fashion or the joints will show to the viewer. As an alternative, you can mask the seams by giving the screen a tiled appearance, so that the tiling covers the seams, making them invisible.

Commercial rear projection screen material comes in three basic types, standard translucent, gray, and black. The standard type has the most luminosity when used with a projector but the black is much darker on stage when no image is being projected. The screen material is manufactured in relatively narrow widths and must be joined together in order to make a large screen. The material is a type of plastic, and the process of connecting the strips is called *plastic welding*. The resulting seam is nearly invisible. That process takes special equipment and is not a do-it-yourself project. The darker colors have a narrower viewing angle that must be taken into account. This means that the brightness of the image drops off if the viewer is at an angle to the screen.

It is problematic that light from the lens of a rear projector can be seen by the audience, usually visible as a bright spot on the screen. This problem can be reduced or eliminated if you position the projector at a slight angle so that it is not directly in the line of sight of the audience.

The major challenge of rear projection is to get the projector far enough away from the screen so that the image has an acceptable size. The light from the projector emanates as a pyramid shape (similar to the cone from a standard ellipsoidal, but rectangular) and thus the resulting image becomes larger as the pyramid spreads out farther from the projector. Manufacturers create different lenses with different focal lengths, just as lighting equipment manufacturers do, but the wide angle lenses are much more difficult to make and as a result are much more expensive. Even if cost is no problem, there is a limit to how wide angle the lens can be, and if the idea is to rear project an image near the upstage limits of the stage house, it is very likely that there will simply not be enough room.

Mirrors can be used to increase the distance by bouncing the image off one or more of them on its way to the screen. But there are limits to this process as well because at a certain point the size of the mirror required to bounce the image is so large that it is problematic in a backstage environment. But even so this technique works well if the increase you need is small. Another solution to the problem is to use a smaller screen, but from a design standpoint a smaller screen is generally not as dynamic as a larger one.

A third option for projecting is to mount the projector in the auditorium so that it creates its image from the front. In this configuration the projection has much more space to spread out before it hits the projection surface, and can be a much larger image. In a

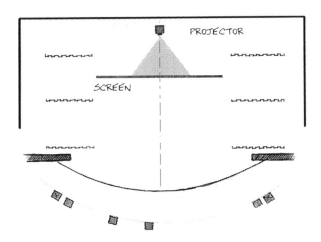

REAR PROJECTION TO AN UPSTAGE SCREEN
CAN BE PROBLEMATIC

EVEN IF THE LENS IS AT FULL ZOOM, THE IMAGE MIGHT NOT
FILL THE ENTIRE SCREEN. WIDE ANGLE LENSES ARE THE
MOST EXPENSIVE, AND MIGHT STILL NOT BE ENOUGH.

PROJECTORS IN A BROADWAY THEATRE

THE TWO PROJECTORS YOU SEE HERE ARE HUNG FROM
THE BALCONY RAIL POSITION. TWO ARE USED IN TANDEM,
SO THAT IF ONE GOES DOWN THE IMAGE WILL STILL BE
SEEN, ALTHOUGH DIMMER, ON THE STAGE.

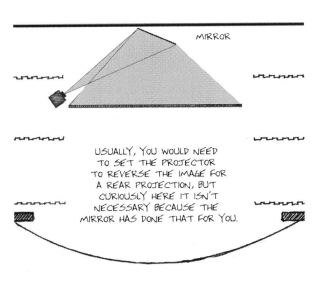

USUALLY, YOU WOULD NEED
TO SET THE PROJECTOR
TO REVERSE THE IMAGE FOR
A REAR PROJECTION, BUT
CURIOUSLY HERE IT ISN'T
NECESSARY BECAUSE THE
MIRROR HAS DONE THAT FOR YOU.

BOUNCE THE IMAGE OFF A MIRROR TO
INCREASE ITS SIZE OVER DISTANCE

THE PROBLEM IS OF COURSE THAT THE MIRROR MUST
BE REALLY HUGE, IN THIS CASE OVER 8 FEET WIDE.

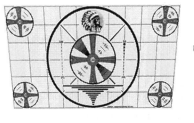

PROJECTOR LOWER
THAN SCREEN
CENTER

KEYSTONE AT TOP

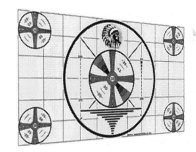

PROJECTOR TO
ONE SIDE

KEYSTONE TO ONE SIDE

Broadway theatre the projectors are often mounted on the balcony rail near the center.

That position gives them a straight shot at the stage and reduces the issue of keystoning. *Keystone* occurs when the projector is not completely square to the center of the screen. If the projector is slightly high and the bottom of the screen is farther away than the top, the image will appear slightly larger at the bottom. The same thing can happen from one side or the other. Most projectors have a means of correcting this as a part of the set up of the machine, or the computer used as a playback device may be able to do the same.

Projectors are not usually designed just for a theatrical environment. Most of them are used in more formal ways in lecture halls, movie theatres, convention centers, and so forth. A projector used that way can be formatted to exactly match the screen used in that space alone, with the arrangement lasting for the life of the projector. But in theatre shows the demands of an artistic statement may require much more complex arrangements. Rather than having an actual projection screen, most designers opt for a surface that is part of the set itself, and has a life outside of the light from the projector. If the surface has a relatively light value and is somewhat reflective, the image from the projector will show up quite well. This approach avoids making the statement: "Okay, we will show you a movie now." Rather than that the video component becomes a more subtle addition to the performance.

One issue that arises from the use of front projections is that of the actor who becomes a part of the screen surface. The projection appears on the body and face of the performer as well as on the background scenery. That is sometimes called "wearing the projection." Some designers desire this, as it becomes a textural light in the style of a gobo pattern wash. If not acceptable, light from traditional theatre fixtures and/or a followspot may be used to overpower the texture of the image on the performer. The spots are in effect used as a "projection eraser." Another issue arises from the shadow cast by the actor on the image behind him, and there isn't a lot that can be done about that. It's worth noting though that the same thing happens when using a traditional followspot.

One of the most common uses of video is to produce *supertitles*. Supertitles are used to add captions so that the audience knows what a character is saying even if they don't speak that language. They are frequently used in opera for audiences that don't speak Italian, but *Thoroughly Modern Millie* is a good example of how titles are called for in plays as well. In that musical they are used as an interpreter when the Chinese men speak, and are an integral part of the humor of the show. Instead of being at the bottom like movie subtitles, supertitles are usually projected somewhere near the top of the pro-scenium opening or some other neutral zone near the stage. The same technique can be used to add captions that tell a date or time that the action is taking place which is called for in many different plays.

DEFINITION OF VIDEO

What is meant by video? The word can be used in a couple of different ways. One way of looking at it might mean a YouTube presentation that you watch online. Or as a verb it could mean to use a camcorder. Modern nomenclature would have us use the words this way:

Video—The output feed to a projector.

Movie—Images that show movement like those you might get with a camcorder.

Motion Graphic—A still image that, through a series of computer-generated mutations, shows movement on the screen.

Still Image—An image that does not show motion.

PROJECTOR SPECIFICATIONS

A projection system is made up of several different components that work together in creating images on the stage. The projector itself is a vital part of that system, and has various properties. Several key factors to consider are brightness, ANSI contrast resolution, aspect ratio, and throw distance. Each of those will be discussed in this section.

There are two basic types of image production technologies, LCD and DLP. Each of these methods uses white light from an arc lamp source that is altered when it passes through one or more chips containing regions that represent the pixels in an image. The chips alter the white light passing through them, and the filtered light is then projected toward the stage via the projector's lens.

LCD stands for *Liquid Crystal Display*. In this technology a screen made of liquid crystal material is used to alter light shining through it. The crystal material is arranged so that the screen is divided into tiny individual squares, one for each pixel on the display. A control device manipulates each individual pixel to create an image. LCD technology is used in many different applications such as flat screen televisions, computer monitors, watches, and alarm clocks. In each of those devices, the glass screen of the device is the viewing plane. In a projector, the backlight passes through the LCD screen, through a lens, and onto the stage, which becomes the viewing plane. One issue arises when the pixels on the screen are large enough to be seen, and appear as tiny square spaces. It is similar to looking at something through a window screen.

DLP stands for *Digital Light Processing*. In a three chip system, three different chips made of very small prisms are used to filter the light from a white (usually) arc lamp by refracting it into differing colors. A control device positions the prisms (one for each pixel) so that they emit a desired color. This technology allows for many more colors than the human eye can differentiate. DLP is the preferred technology for very high-end projectors such as are used in a movie theatre as a replacement for a traditional film projector. The process of switching over is now underway because the cost of handling film reels is difficult and expensive. The digital transmission of a movie is very easily accomplished, and over time the new technology pays for itself.

Both LCD and DLP technologies depend on a light that passes through their processing mechanics, and consequently they use a lamp in a similar way to a film projector. The light from the lamp passes through the filtering medium, be it film or crystal display or tiny prisms and an image is projected. These lamps eventually burn out and must be replaced. They are often xenon or metal halide arc lamps and can be quite expensive. They should last for several thousand hours but will become noticeably dimmer near the end of their lives. The lamp should have a stated rating for the length of its service life, and many projectors have a timer that records the number of hours of use so that you can keep track of approximately how much time is left. Thus the lamp can be replaced before it actually goes out.

The brightness of a projector is measured in lumens. The *lumen* is the metric used for measuring luminous flux, or the amount of light that you see. The preferred method of comparing projectors is by the term *ANSI lumens*, which assures that the method used to determine the number of lumens is standard and can be judged fairly between types. The brightness of projectors has risen sharply over the years, which has made it possible to use them as a cinema projector, which must be extremely bright, perhaps as much as 20 thousand lumens (20k). The range useful for theatre work is less and might be in the 2k to 10k range. It is difficult to assess an exact number because the way projections are used is so variable. If the size of the projection area is small, the brightness required is less because the energy of the lamp is concentrated in a smaller space. The amount of light from stage lighting fixtures is also a factor because it takes more power to overcome ambient light that spills onto the projection. A dark, brooding production of Hamlet might need much less luminosity than a cheerier production of a musical.

Some shows use two projectors in tandem to protect against failure. Each projector sends out the same images over the same space, each duplicating the other. If one goes offline temporarily the other will carry on in a limited way. If that is the case, when working as planned the brightness of each projector can be half of the required amount. Something to consider though is the noise from fans used to cool the projector's mechanism. A larger, brighter projector needs a more powerful fan, which tends to be louder. In a quiet theatre the fan noise can be a problem, so getting the largest possible projector is not always the right thing to do. It is possible to build a sound-dampening box to house the projector, but the cooling fans are there for a reason, and care should be taken not to seriously restrict the airflow around the projector.

The *contrast ratio* is the difference between the highest and lowest values of illumination in an image, which would be the difference between a white pixel and a black pixel. High contrast is important to creating a strong image, perhaps even more important than the actual brightness of the projector. You might find that black pixels from the projector are so bright that they show up during a dark scene or transition. Some projectors have a dowser-like feature that blacks out the light when the screen must be completely dark. Another method can be to mount a layer of neutral density color filter a few inches in front of the lens. That will lower the brightness of the total image, but will make blackouts on stage more acceptable.

4×3 ASPECT RATIO

4 units wide by 3 units tall or any multiple

QVGA (quarter video graphics array)
= 320 pixels wide by 240 pixels tall

XGA (extended graphics array)
= 1024 pixels wide by 768 pixels tall

16×9 ASPECT RATIO

16 units wide by 9 units tall or any multiple

HD = 1360 pixels wide by 768 pixels tall

Full HD = 1920 pixels wide by 1080 pixels tall

The *resolution* of a projector means the number of pixels it has. These numbers are generally stated by the number horizontally versus the number vertically, as in 1024×768, which is also known as XGA. There are many different possibilities, but two main *aspect ratios* are 4:3 and 16:9. The *4:3 ratio* means that if there are four units wide there will be three units high, the units could be feet or inches or meters or multiples of pixels. That is the traditional shape of an older movie screen or a CRT television set. Notice that $4 \times 256 = 1024$ and $3 \times 256 = 768$, which correlates to the XGA standard. Another aspect ratio is *16:9*, which is also known as *widescreen*. Notice that in this example $16 \times 120 = 1920$ and $9 \times 120 = 1080$, which correlates to the nomenclature as *Full HD* (High Definition). Most projectors should handle either of these aspect ratios via an onboard menu, but it is good to consider them when considering a projection space on the stage. The number of pixels in an image defines its resolution. In general the higher the resolution the better the image, but there are limits to this. Higher resolution also means a larger file size, perhaps much larger. A larger file size translates to more time for a computer to generate the image. Full HD would be 1920×1080 or 2,073,600 pixels multiplied by ~30 frames per second, which is a really huge number. Taking into account that the audience is sitting quite a distance away from the projection, you may not need such clarity.

The *throw distance* of a projector is determined by the lens and is calculated by figuring the distance of the lens from the screen in context with the angle of the light coming from it. Again a ratio of one value to another is used, and this time describes the angle of the beam that comes from the projector. You can determine the size of an image at a specific distance by plugging in numbers. If the ratio of a certain lens is 2:1, and the distance from the screen is 50 feet, the image width will be 25 feet. The image grows 1 foot for every 2 feet of distance. You can find online calculators for most projector angles. Frequently the throw distance in a theatre is not all that changeable if the projector must be located on the balcony rail, or in a booth, or some other fixed location. So the only variable would be to use a different lens that is appropriate for the venue. Most projectors have a zoom feature that can, to a degree, change the size of the image.

BIGGER IS NOT ALWAYS BETTER

As mentioned earlier, the resolution of a video is defined by its resolution, and is often identified by an acronym like XGA or VGA. This relates to how many pixels wide, and how many tall the resolution is. Although a playback program may be able to handle a large resolution, your computer's graphics card may not. To solve that problem you could use a better graphics card, step up to a media server with greater capabilities, or you could consider using a smaller resolution for the video content. Bear in mind that the audience is viewing the picture from a distance, and the resolution tends to blur. The makers of Isadora suggest that when playing multiple videos at once you should think about using *QVGA*, or *Quarter Video Graphics Array*. QVGA has half as many pixels in its height and width, but only one-fourth the amount of data as regular VGA. One consequence of too large a file size is that your video program may not play each frame, or picture in the video. It may skip some in order to keep up. Sometimes you may notice areas of pixilation on the screen, or the image may stutter.

THE NUMBERS ADD UP

XGA	1024×768 or 786,432 pixels
VGA	640×480 or 307,200 pixels
QVGA	320×240 or 76,800 pixels

CREATING AND CONTROLLING IMAGES

This chapter is titled "Video Projections for the Stage," and gives the impression that live action moving pictures are the standard, but most of the time a projection is a still image instead. Or perhaps a still image that has been animated in some way. Projectors are capable of projecting either live motion images or stills; it really just depends on the digital file type you supply. When supertitles are used on stage, the words are typically not

a continuous movie, but rather a series of still images that progress as the action continues and more words are required. Each change is a separate cue, which makes it much easier to sync up to performers. Subtitles are done the same way, one sentence at a time.

The moments when an actual movie is used can be quite stunning. Projecting rain, or police lights, or lightning can create a large emotional response from an audience. The images projected onto the stage are sometimes called *program* or perhaps *content*, and are computer files that have been stored on a playback device that is used to tell the projector what to project. Content is a design responsibility rather than a technical one. That might be a set designer, or a lighting designer, or using the USA Broadway model, a projection designer engaged solely for that purpose.

Still images can be created using *Adobe Photoshop*, *Illustrator*, or any other program for editing image files. There are many different types of image files, which have extensions like .bmp, .jpg, .psd, .gif, or .png. The extensions are a way for the computer to know what program to use to open the file. A computer will not be able to open a file without its associated program, so if you save

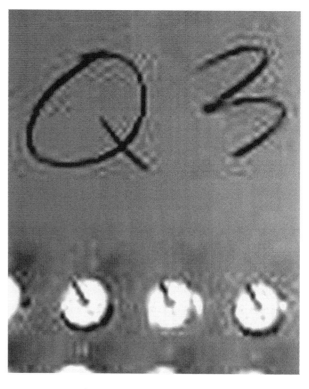

NOTE WAVY LINES AROUND THE DARKER "Q"

A COMPUTER PROGRAM COMPRESSES AN IMAGE BY LOSING SOME INFORMATION TO SAVE SPACE, AND THEN GUESSING WHAT IT WAS WHEN THE IMAGE IS RE-OPENED. THAT CAN LEAD TO SOME PRETTY DISTRACTING DISTORTION.

IF A FILE EXTENSION LIKE GIF, TIFF, OR PNG IS DESCRIBED AS "LOSSY," THAT MEANS IT LOSES DATA TO COMPRESSION.

---

an image as a Photoshop document or psd, it can only be opened by a computer that has that program on it, or if the playback program is capable of opening it on its own. Virtually any computer will open a jpg (Journalists Photographic Experts Group) file, which was originally intended for printing out pictures for a newspaper or magazine. Png (Portable Network Graphic) files are a newer type used to create digital images for the web. Both of those file types are actually methods of compressing files so that they are smaller. Compressing a jpg image means that some of the data is lost. When saving from Photoshop you are given a choice of what quality jpg is desired from low to high quality, and generally speaking higher quality is a better choice in that case. Compressing digital images is a very complex procedure in which the program tries to guess what will happen next to the pixels in the image. It is better not to require too much guessing.

Frequently you may wish to project an image onto a part of the stage that is smaller than the image size that comes from the projector. Most of the playback managers mentioned later can scale and place the image for you, but you can also mask a projected image in the way it is created, getting rid of parts you don't want or need.

The process is fairly straightforward; you can use Photoshop to select what you want to see, copy it, and paste it onto a black background. Photoshop has several default video background sizes you can choose from the NEW window. The transform tool can be used to resize the image and move it to a particular part of the stage. This process isn't particularly exact though, because it is difficult to say where the image will fall when it is actually projected on the stage. A program like Isadora or Watchout can do a much better job with that. You could equate this process with the one used to edit audio files with Audacity, or editing them with QLab. The latter method makes it easier to change the character of your media after you are in the theatre.

Photoshop is a great way to edit still images, but you need something else for moving pictures. You can edit live action movie video on a number of different programs. *Final Cut Pro* is a Mac-based program that is used by professionals to edit movies. *Adobe Premier* is a similar, competing program. *iMovie* and *Windows Movie Maker* are consumer-oriented programs. All of them are similar to audio editing programs in that the workspace contains a timeline that displays how the content changes

SAINT PETER RESIZED, WITH A BLACK MASK

ORIGINAL IMAGE OF SAINT PETER

over time. It is possible to cut and paste sections of video so that the movie is edited together as required. *Adobe After Effects* is an associated program, which among other things uses filters to alter the appearance of images. It can also animate still images to create motion graphics. Most image editing programs of any sort create their own proprietary file types/extensions for the period you are editing with them, which must be *transcoded* before the files can be used for a projector. Transcoding means to change file types, and it may take a while because each individual frame must be transcoded one at a time. If the resolution is set at a very high level the time required for transcoding is greatly extended. Acceptable file types may vary depending on which playback program is used, but *QuickTime* and *AVI* are fairly universal.

Adobe After Effects is a program you can use to add motion graphics to your video or stills. Photoshop users will recognize familiar Adobe concepts like layers, masks, adjustment layers, and so forth. After Effects is aptly named, as it is meant to add effects to your video after it has been edited together by another program. The timeline is divided into layers, which can be individually edited by dividing them into *key frames*, which are then used as time edit points for fading, moving, and so forth. You can use this program to alter the appearance of the video by changing colors and textures.

PLAYBACK

Playback means to play back something that has been recorded, either audio or video. The playback system is used to provide the projector with the still and motion images that make up the content. A comparison can be made to the systems used to control stage lighting, in that that projector is like a light fixture, the designer's looks and cues the image content, and the lighting console the playback device. There can be several components to this system, a computer program that stores data, a computer that transmits the data, and perhaps a media server that routes the data stream to the appropriate projectors.

A *media server* is a computer used to route data to various outputs like audio amplifiers and projectors. You need one if you will be using multiple projectors with different content, but probably not if you have only one data stream coming from the computer. The Watchout program requires a separate computer for each video display, each of which could be described as a server. Or you may consider that the one computer in use is the media server.

However the hardware is arranged, you need a computer program to playback the digital images to a projector. The program you select dictates how the system is connected. Something like a DVD player is very hard to control when you consider the timing of a cue beginning at one precise moment, or the need to fade in and out. It is possible to use a program like PowerPoint,

but that doesn't have the features of others that are specifically intended for playback in a live situation.

You might consider that three basic approaches are used to play visual media; *cue list based, module based,* and *timeline based.* The simplest type arranges video into a cue list similar to the way an audio playback program like QLab does. In that model the cues are listed in a sequential order so that the "timeline" is vertical up and down the list. Pressing go segues to the next cue. It is possible to link cues together so beginning one cue may cause a number of others to follow in sequence. The program can fade images in and out in a non-destructive manner by applying commands that control the output of the program rather than the content of the media.

Another method of running video cues is to use a modular system like *Isadora*. In that program movies are represented on the screen by modules that can be linked together, and that have dialogue boxes to define their editable behavior.

The third method is timeline based, like the *Watchout* program. In that example media events are placed on a timeline that determines when the cues will happen. This type can easily be linked to show control, because the cues happen at very specific moments in a constantly running timeline. You can adjust the timing and content by dragging the media into and along the timeline.

QLab, as you will recall, is also frequently used for audio playback. It is aimed at a show where the same thing happens at every performance. Some types of entertainment are not like that and instead change from night to night. For them a more flexible arrangement is needed that accommodates changes made "on the fly." Plays and musicals are exactly the same as possible each time, so having a lineup of cues that are played back in sequence is very desirable.

WITH QLAB, YOU CAN EASILY BUNDLE ALL OF YOUR AUDIO AND VIDEO CUES TOGETHER.

QLab is convenient in that audio and video cues are run by one operator. There is a sequential cue list, and pressing the go button plays the selected cue, in much the same way as a lighting console segues from cue to cue. Pressing go again will play the next cue and so forth. This syntax is very comfortable for theatre workers who are accustomed to that sort of control for lighting, which has been around for many years. If you need the same effect for several cues, it is best to add it to the sequence for each one of them so that the operator can simply press the go button each time. It's also possible to set up the cuing so that one cue auto-follows another when the timing is close together. Video cues cancel each other on the same output, so moving to the next image generally stops the original one. You can set the program to fade from image to image rather than having it bump from one to another. If no following image is required, you can fade to a black screen as a means of fading the image.

The *Isadora* program is very popular with VJs and multi-media crowd events. It is radically different from

QLab, which is a cue-based program. As you've seen, a cue in those programs is set up with specific media, which are controlled by setting fade times and follows. Isadora is based on controlling modules that are inserted into *scenes*, which then become your playback cues. Isadora calls the modules *actors*, because they create actions. You name the scenes yourself. You can give them cue numbers like 1, 2, 3; or you can label them with more descriptive titles like "pulsating dots" or "lighting flashes." A theatre show with a stage manager calling cues might do better with numbers that are played in sequence. A club VJ would probably prefer to label them with descriptors that make it easier to jump back and forth. The scenes don't have to be played back in a specific order, but that is an option you can choose.

The *toolbox window* at the left side of the workspace contains different sets of tools. You can navigate between them to find the modules you'd like to use, and adding the modules to the workspace by clicking to select and clicking again to place, which is a little different than what you might expect. The large open area is the *scene editor*, where the actors are manipulated. The ribbon across the bottom contains a list of different scenes.

Before editing any video you must import it to the *media window* at the top right. If you select a large number of files, Isadora will import only the ones it is able to use, leaving the rest. The media window automatically sorts them into different file types. The *stage window* at the bottom right is used to view the projector output, even if the projector isn't connected at the moment. That allows you to program video output without necessarily being in the performance space.

The actor modules control different aspects of the video. You place them onto the scene editor workspace from their positions in the left-hand tool box. Each actor has dialogue boxes that allow you to set the parameters that particular actor controls. The actors are connected by leads or wires that you draw between them that, for instance, might link a *movie player* actor to a *projector actor*.

The movie player is used to specify the video or still images you want to use, which can be added from the media window. Isadora doesn't drag things like that, you must type the movie's number into a dialogue box instead. You can only have one movie per movie player actor, but you can have multiple actors in the scene at one time. So that allows you to play more than one movie at the same time, but output them to the same projector. Use the *projector* actor to output the movie to the stage window. Use dialogue boxes to set parameters like how large the image will be and its location on the screen. That's one of the most interesting aspects of the Isadora program, the fluid way that it moves images around the screen, which is possibly why it is named Isadora, other than its roots in dance performance. When used in conjunction with the *mouse actor*, you can use the

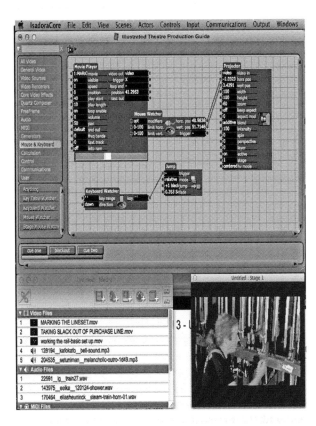

ISADORA WORKSPACE

THIS PROGRAM CALLS THE CUES "SCENES" WHICH YOU CAN NUMBER AND LINK TOGETHER SO THAT IT IS EASY TO RUN A SHOW. ONE OF ISADORA'S KEY FEATURES IS THAT YOU CAN EASILY CHANGE THE SIZE AND POSITION OF IMAGES ON THE STAGE, IN ORDER TO MAKE YOUR PROJECTION FALL ON A SELECTED TARGET. TOOLBOXES ARE AT THE RIGHT, AND ALLOW YOU TO PLACE "ACTOR" MODULES ON THE WORK AREA, OR SCENE EDITOR. DIALOG BOXES ALLOW YOU TO MANIPULATE PARAMETERS LIKE IMAGE SIZE AND POSITION.

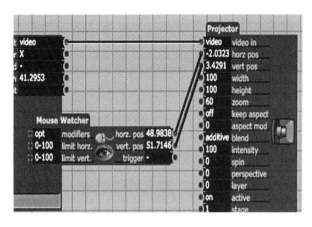

MOUSE WATCHER ACTOR
CONNECTED TO THE PROJECTOR ACTOR

NOTE THE WIRES BETWEEN THEM.

YOU CAN CLICK ON AN OUTPUT AND DRAG IT OVER TO AN
INPUT TO CONNECT THE ACTORS TO EACH OTHER. HERE
THE MOUSE WATCHER IS USED TO CHANGE THE VERTICAL
AND HORIZONTAL POSITION OF THE IMAGE ON THE STAGE.
THERE ARE LOTS OF DIALOG BOXES TO CHANGE PARAMETERS.

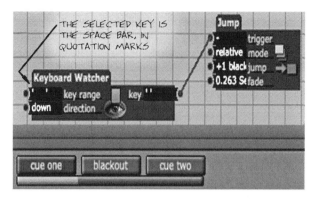

THE KEYBOARD WATCHER AND THE JUMP
ACTOR WORK TOGETHER TO ADVANCE CUES

YOU CAN SELECT THE ACTION KEY BY ENTERING IT IN
THE DIALOG BOX, IN THIS CASE THE SPACE BAR. THE JUMP
ACTOR USES THAT KEY AS A TRIGGER. IN A DIALOG BOX, +1
WAS CHOSEN AS THE ACTION, SO THE PROGRAM JUMPS
AHEAD ONE SCENE WHEN THE SPACE BAR IS PRESSED.
IN THIS CASE A FADE TIME WAS SELECTED, WHICH MAKES
THE JUMP FADE SMOOTHLY FROM ONE CUE TO ANOTHER.
A BLACK CUE WAS INSERTED BETWEEN CUES SO THAT THE
IMAGE WILL FADE OUT BETWEEN IMAGES.

computer's mouse to drag the image around the screen at will.

Each scene becomes in essence a cue, although they aren't called that. Scenes can be numbered and placed along the bottom of the window. You can copy and paste the same scene in multiple places to make the program more like a cue-based system. You can insert scenes between other scenes when necessary. To form the scenes into an automatically advancing cue list, use the *keyboard watcher* and *jump* actors from the tool box. You need to add these to each scene to create sequential cues, except possibly the last one if it doesn't need to jump anywhere.

The keyboard watcher allows you to define the function of keys on the keyboard. If you define the space bar as the trigger and connect it to the jump actor, you can use it to jump forward a cue each time the space bar is hit. You can set the jump actor to move forward or backward any number of cues, which means you can jump backward to form a loop.

Watchout is a program meant specifically for PC and is available as a free download. But in order to use the program to output video to a projector a series of *USB keys* is required. A system consists of the playback computer, a networking device, and a separate PC for each projector or other display device. Each of them must have a USB key attached in order to operate. The series of PC computers is used rather than a media server.

The Watchout workspace has a stage view area to the top left that allows you to see the effects as you edit them, and a media window on the right that holds the different media files you want to use in building your video affect cues. Remember that "video" just means electronically

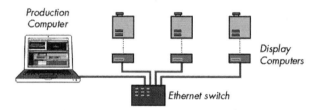

WATCHOUT NETWORKING DIAGRAM

FROM THEIR INSTRUCTION MANUAL. THE SYSTEM CONSISTS
OF A CENTRAL COMPUTER TO RUN THE PROGRAM, AND
ANOTHER COMPUTER FOR EACH OF THE DISPLAYS, WHICH
COULD BE A PROJECTOR, LED VIDEO WALL, OR FLAT SCREEN.
YOU NEED A SEPARATE KEY, OR DONGLE, FOR EACH OF
THE COMPUTERS TO ACTUALLY RUN THE VIDEO, BUT YOU
DON'T NEED THEM JUST TO WORK WITH THE PROGRAM.

reproduced images, and can mean movies, motion graphics, or still images. The bottom of the workspace contains the timeline, which is divided into different layers. Layer 1 is on the bottom. Much like Photoshop, the layers on the bottom are at the back of what you see on the screen, so that an item in layer 3 may cover part or all of an item in layer 2. You can drag the media content from layer to layer to adjust which image is in front.

The timeline is at the heart of what is so different about the philosophy of how Watchout works. It is used to organize the timing of how your media files interact with one another. In addition, the layering aspect allows you to develop very complex compositions. Together these two aspects allow Watchout to serve as an image animator.

WATCHOUT WORKSPACE

THE "STAGE" WINDOW AT THE TOP CONTAINS THE OUTPUT
IMAGE OF WHAT YOU WILL BE PROJECTING. THE TIMELINE IS
UNDERNEATH THAT, AND THE MEDIA WINDOW IS TO THE
RIGHT. YOU CAN DRAG STILLS OR MOVIES TO THE TIMELINE.

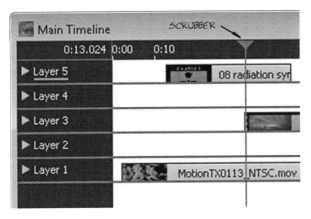

WATCHOUT TIMELINE

USE THE SCRUBBER TO MOVE BACK AND FORTH THROUGH
TIME, AND SEE WHAT IMAGE APPEARS WHEN. LAYERS ON
TOP TAKE PRECEDENCE, UNLESS YOU ALTER THAT
WITH A TWEEN POINT TO MAKE THEM TRANSLUCENT,
SMALLER, OR FADE IN AND OUT.

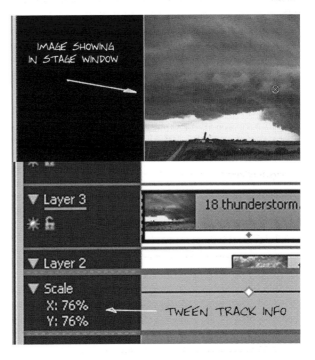

ENLARGED VIEW OF TWEEN TRACK

IN THIS INSTANCE, THE TWEEN TRACK IS BEING USED TO
MANIPULATE THE SCALE OF THE THUNDERSTORM MOVIE.
SLIDE THE DIAMOND-SHAPED CONTROLLER BACK AND FORTH
TO CHANGE THE SCALE.

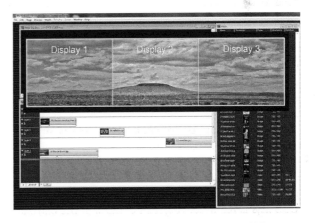

WATCHOUT MULTI-DISPLAY FEATURE

WITH MULTIPLE DISPLAYS OR PROJECTORS, YOU CAN TILE
TOGETHER ONE IMAGE FROM A NUMBER OF SOURCES.
THE PROGRAM CAN BE SET TO EDGE BLEND THE DIFFERENT
PROJECTORS INTO ONE SMOOTH IMAGE.

To insert media into your programming, drag a file from the media window onto a layer in the timeline. You can change the layer position by simply dragging the file from one layer to another. More than one file can be on a layer, but they shouldn't overlap one another, the program isn't equipped to do that. Time notations on the top of the timeline represent the location, in time, of the media you have placed there. Click on the middle of an item to drag it forward or backward in time. Click on either end of the selection to shorten or lengthen it. That's very similar to Final Cut Pro.

Watchout uses *tween tracks* to control editable properties such as fade in/out, rotation, scale, color, and motion path. A tween track can be applied to a layer by selecting it and choosing the type of effect you want from the tween menu. The track will appear on the screen with a line on it that has grab handles or "tween points." Use the tween points to adjust features of the effect. Manipulating the tween points will seem fairly intuitive. Watchout uses this method to add fades and to adjust scale, color, and other editable properties.

The motion path effect is especially intriguing. It allows you to animate an image so that it moves from one place to another on the screen. The path is set by a series of tween points that can be manipulated as a straight line or as a curve. The speed of the movement can be controlled differently at various points along the path. When a curved trajectory is used, the image in motion can be made to point its way along the path.

Watchout is intended to be used with multiple projectors, although that is not a requirement. The software is able to blend images from different projectors onto one screen by overlapping the edges a specific amount, and then fading the image intensity in those areas. That makes the image appear to be from one source rather than multiple sources, and allows for the use of a very wide screen. That's somewhat different from two projectors used to create the same, completely overlapping image on a Broadway stage. That technique is used when the second projector is a hedge against equipment failure.

TERMS USED IN THIS CHAPTER

Adobe After Effects	Liquid Crystal Display (LCD)	resolution
Adobe Illustrator	lumen	supertitles
Adobe Photoshop	luminescent	throw distance
Adobe Premier	media server	tiled
ANSI lumens	opaque	transcoded
aspect ratio	pixilated	translucent
AVI	plastic welding	transparent
content	playback	video wall
contrast ratio	program	Watchout
DLP/Digital Light Processing	Projection Designer	widescreen
Final Cut Pro	QLab	Windows Movie Maker
Full HD/1920×1080	QuickTime	
iMovie	QVGA (Quarter Video Graphics Array)	
Isadora		
keystone	rear projection	

APPENDIX

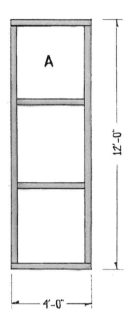

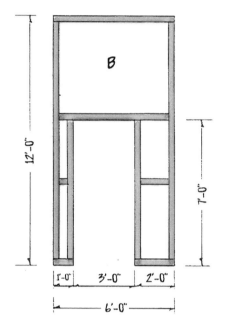

NOTE:

CONSTRUCT FROM 1X3 #2 WHITE PINE
MILLED DIMENSIONS = 3/4" X 2 5/8"

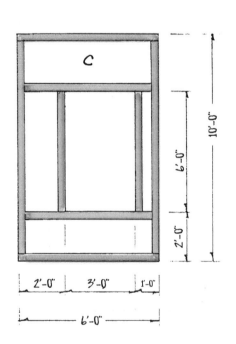

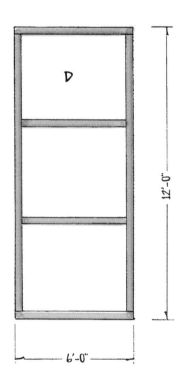

PRACTICE CUT LISTS FOR HARD-COVER FLATS

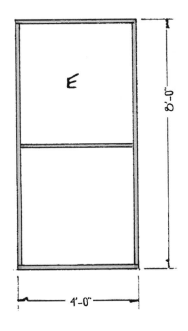

E

8'-0"

4'-0"

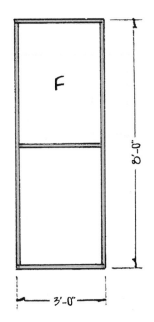

F

8'-0"

3'-0"

NOTE:

CONSTRUCT FROM 1X3 #2 WHITE PINE
MILLED DIMENSIONS = 3/4" X 2 5/8"

DON'T FORGET TO LIST
THE PLYWOOD COVER PARTS

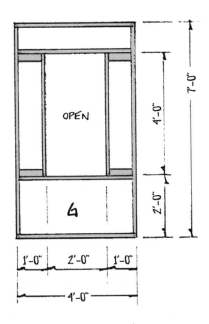

OPEN

G

7'-0"

4'-0"

2'-0"

1'-0" 2'-0" 1'-0"

4'-0"

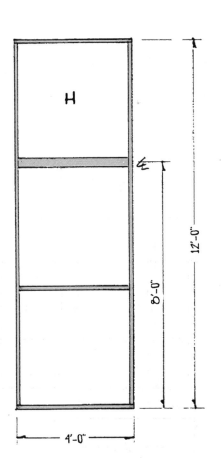

H

12'-0"

8'-0"

4'-0"

OHM'S LAW PRACTICE PROBLEMS

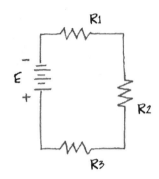

E = 100 VOLTS
R1 = 100 Ω
R2 = 200 Ω
R3 = 300 Ω

WOULD THIS CIRCUIT FOLLOW THE RULES FOR
PARALLEL CIRCUITS OR FOR SERIES CIRCUITS?

THE TOTAL RESISTANCE IN THIS CIRCUIT
WOULD BE _____

THE CURRENT DRAW WOULD BE _____

THE VOLTAGE ACROSS R₁ WOULD BE _____

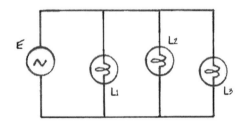

E = 120 VOLTS
LAMP 1 IS RATED AT 575W
LAMP 2 IS RATED AT 575W
LAMP 3 IS RATED AT 575W

WOULD THIS CIRCUIT FOLLOW THE RULES FOR
PARALLEL CIRCUITS OR FOR SERIES CIRCUITS?

WHAT IS THE TOTAL POWER DRAW? _____

WHAT IS THE VOLTAGE ACROSS L₁? _____

WHAT IS THE TOTAL CURRENT DRAW? _____

WOULD THIS AMOUNT OF CURRENT TRIP A
20 AMP BREAKER?

OHM'S LAW PRACTICE PROBLEMS

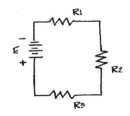

CIRCUIT A   CIRCUIT B

WHICH CIRCUIT IS PARALLEL,
AND WHICH IS SERIES?

WHAT IS THE CORRECT ARRANGEMENT
OF THE TERMS TO SOLVE FOR:

E = _____   I = _____   R = _____

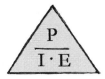

WHAT IS THE CORRECT ARRANGEMENT
OF THE TERMS TO SOLVE FOR:

P = _____   I = _____   E = _____

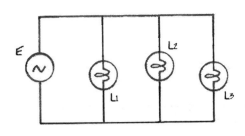

E = 120 VOLTS
LAMP 1 IS RATED AT 300W
LAMP 2 IS RATED AT 500W
LAMP 3 IS RATED AT 1KW

WOULD THIS CIRCUIT FOLLOW THE RULES FOR
PARALLEL CIRCUITS OR FOR SERIES CIRCUITS?

WHAT IS THE TOTAL POWER DRAW? _____

WHAT IS THE VOLTAGE ACROSS L1? _____

WHAT IS THE TOTAL CURRENT DRAW? _____

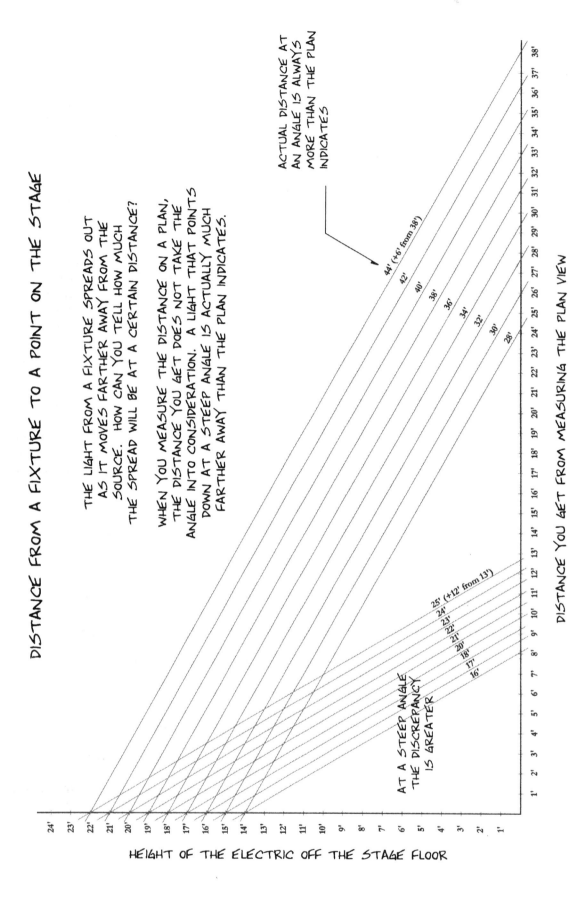

DISTANCE FROM A FIXTURE TO A POINT ON THE STAGE

THE LIGHT FROM A FIXTURE SPREADS OUT AS IT MOVES FARTHER AWAY FROM THE SOURCE. HOW CAN YOU TELL HOW MUCH THE SPREAD WILL BE AT A CERTAIN DISTANCE?

WHEN YOU MEASURE THE DISTANCE ON A PLAN, THE DISTANCE YOU GET DOES NOT TAKE THE ANGLE INTO CONSIDERATION. A LIGHT THAT POINTS DOWN AT A STEEP ANGLE IS ACTUALLY MUCH FARTHER AWAY THAN THE PLAN INDICATES.

ACTUAL DISTANCE AT AN ANGLE IS ALWAYS MORE THAN THE PLAN INDICATES

44' (+6' from 38')
42'
40'
38'
36'
34'
32'
30'
28'

25' (+12' from 13')
24'
23'
22'
21'
20'
18'
17'
16'

AT A STEEP ANGLE THE DISCREPANCY IS GREATER

HEIGHT OF THE ELECTRIC OFF THE STAGE FLOOR

DISTANCE YOU GET FROM MEASURING THE PLAN VIEW

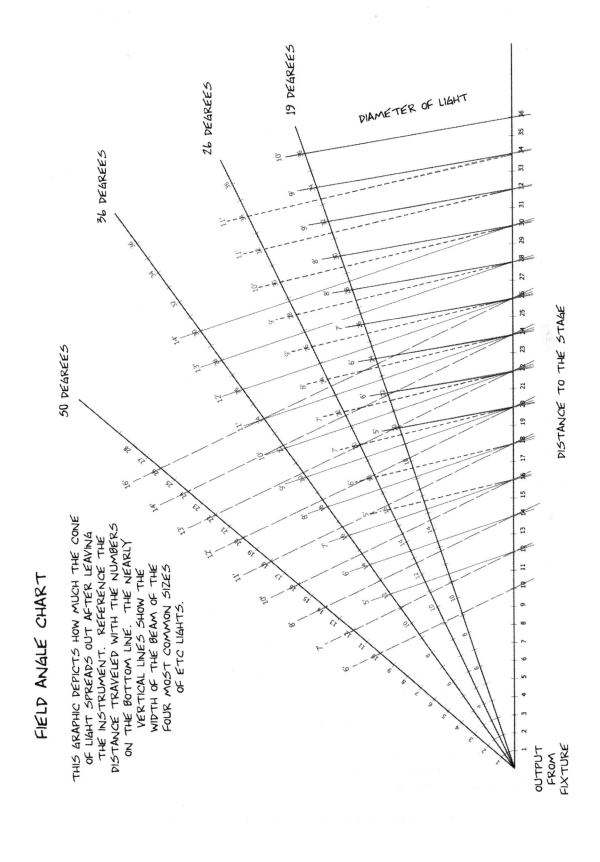

FIELD ANGLE CHART

THIS GRAPHIC DEPICTS HOW MUCH THE CONE OF LIGHT SPREADS OUT AFTER LEAVING THE INSTRUMENT. REFERENCE THE DISTANCE TRAVELED WITH THE NUMBERS ON THE BOTTOM LINE. THE NEARLY VERTICAL LINES SHOW THE WIDTH OF THE BEAM OF THE FOUR MOST COMMON SIZES OF ETC LIGHTS.

50 DEGREES

36 DEGREES

26 DEGREES

19 DEGREES

DIAMETER OF LIGHT

DISTANCE TO THE STAGE

OUTPUT FROM FIXTURE

ANGULAR DISTANCE CHART

HEIGHT OF PIPE	DISTANCE IN FEET ON THE PLAN VIEW															
	4	6	8	10	12	14	16	18	20	22	24	26	28	30	32	34
30	30	31	31	32	32	33	34	35	36	37	38	40	41	42	44	45
28	28	29	29	30	30	31	32	33	34	36	37	38	40	41	43	44
26	26	27	27	28	29	30	31	32	33	34	35	37	38	40	41	43
24	24	25	25	26	27	28	29	30	31	33	34	35	37	38	40	42
22	22	23	23	24	25	26	27	28	30	31	33	34	36	37	39	40
20	20	21	22	22	23	24	26	27	28	30	31	33	34	36	38	39
18	18	19	20	21	22	23	24	25	27	28	30	32	33	35	37	38
16	16	17	18	19	20	21	23	24	26	27	29	31	32	34	36	38
14	15	15	16	17	18	20	21	23	24	26	28	30	31	33	35	37
12	13	13	14	16	17	18	20	22	23	25	27	29	30	32	34	36

USE THIS CHART TO FIND THE ACTUAL DISTANCE FROM THE FIXTURE
TO A POINT ON THE STAGE.

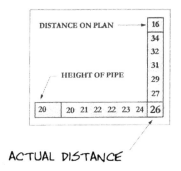

ACTUAL DISTANCE

MEASURE THE DISTANCE ON A PLAN VIEW.
CHECK TO SEE THE HEIGHT OF THE PIPE FROM THE STAGE FLOOR, OR
THE TOP OF THE DECKING IN THE SHOW. CROSS-REFERENCE THE
TWO NUMBERS TO GET THE ANGULAR DISTANCE.

INDEX

Page numbers followed by the letter 'f' refer to pages that contain illustrations, either figures or photographs.

#0000 (four ought) cables 300, 301, 302
#4 black tie lines 61–62, 171, 357, 358f

¼" jacks 383, 383f
⅛" jacks 378, 378f
1×4 lumber 54, 54f
⁵⁄₁₆" hex keys 233
32 bit float 388
60 cycle hum 11, 310–311
120/240 volt split phase system 296, 296f, 299

A

A2 cabinet-grade plywood 141
AC (alternating current) see alternating current (AC)
ACL (Air Craft Landing) lights 283, 283f
acoustics 368
acrylic/latex caulk 174
acrylic sheets 143
acting edition-type scripts 20
Actor's Equity Association 4, 17, 18; equity contracts 17f
Actor's Studio 34
addresses (lighting control) 316, 322–323
adhesives see cements; construction adhesive (Liquid Nails); glue
adjustable/Crescent wrenches 10, 97, 97f, 355, 359
Adobe After Effects 406
Adobe Audition 387
Adobe Illustrator 404
Adobe Photoshop: comparison with Light Palette 320; comparison with Vectorworks 185–186; comparison with Watchout 408; sketch scaling 178, 178f; video image editing 404–405
Adobe Premier 405
AEA see Actor's Equity Association
African Americans, chitlin' circuit 4
AIFF (Audio Interchange File Format) 389, 390
air compressors (pneumatic tools) 102f, 109
aircraft cables: cable cutting pliers 99–100; cable grids 36; counterweight rigging systems 72, 72f, 159; hanging hardware 77, 159; spool of 159f

Air Craft Landing (ACL) lights 283, 283f
aliases (keyboard short cuts) 187
aliphatic resin glue (carpenter's glue): characteristics 164; flat construction 209, 209f; step construction 226; stock decking construction 235; stressed-skin panels 246
alternating current (AC): Broadway theatres 309; definition 280–281, 280f; hot/neutral wires 289–291, 290f, 296, 297, 298; parallel circuits 286–287; from power generation 287–291, 287f–291f; resistance in series 284; sine waves 281, 287, 289, 289f, 290–291, 290f; transformers 292; see also power distribution
Altman fixture 335f
aluminum metal framing 249–250
ambient light 329, 331, 332, 334, 360
American National Standards Institute (ANSI) 313, 327, 402; ANSI lumens 403
American Panel Association 142, 327
American SAE (Society of Automotive Engineers) vs metric 98
American Wire Gauge (AWG) 302
amperes (amps): definition 281; electrical wires 303; Ohm's laws 282–283, 282f–283f
amphitheatres: Greek amphitheatres 25–27, 25f, 26f, 27f; Roman amphitheatres 26f, 27–28, 27f, 28f
amplifiers 382–383, 383f
amps see amperes (amps)
analog signals, vs digital signals 372, 372f
angle grinders (metal framing) 259, 262–283, 262f
angle irons 163, 163f, 251, 251f
angle of incidence (optics) 328–329, 328f–329f
angles, cutting 124–126, 124f–126f
animal/hide glue 172, 210, 211f
ANSI (American National Standards Institute) 313, 327, 402; ANSI lumens 403
apex (bridles) 88–89, 88f, 89f
apprentice stagehands 7
apron stages 39
arbor heavy 77

arbors: circular saw blades 113–114, 114f; counterweight rigging system 72–76, 72f, 81f

arches 27–28, 27f

architect's scale rules 181, 181f

arc lamps 284, 327; LCD and DLP technologies (Liquid Crystal Display) 402–403

arc welders 252–253, 252f, 253f

arena rigging: bridles 87–88, 88f (baskets 89, 89f; practical example 88–90, 88f, 89f); chain hoists/motors 82–83, 82f (1 ton motors 83, 84, 87; 2 ton motors 83, 84, 87; chain bags 83, 83f, 85–86; chain running 83, 83f, 86; CM Lodestart 82, 83f; connectors 84, 84f; pickles (motor controllers) 84, 84f; running 83, 83f; running the chain out 83–84); deck chains 88, 88f; shackle hubs/bells/pins 87–88, 87f–88f, 89, 89f, 90; slings and bowlines 86, 86f, 89f, 90; slings and chokes 85, 85f; steel cables 86, 86f, 87 (steel cable eye 87f); trusses (box trusses 84, 84f; delta trusses 84); wells (large beams) 86–87, 87f, 88; see also rigging; theatre rigging

arena theatres/theatres in the round 31–32, 31f, 34

argon/CO_2 mix (MIG welding) 254, 256

artisans 3–4

artistic directors 4

ARTSEARCH 7

asbestos, fire curtains 42

ASIO (Audio Stream Input Output) 394

aspect ratios (video projectors) 403, 403f

assistant directors 18

assistant stage managers 10, 18, 20, 21, 22, 23

atomic theory: amps and volts 281; batteries 278, 278f, 279–280, 279f–280f; circuits 281, 281f; conductors 279, 279f; currents 280–281, 280f; electrons 278–279, 278f; EMF and volts 279, 279f; insulators 279, 279f; light bulbs 281–282, 281f; lightning 278–279, 278f; power and watts 282; resistance and ohms 281–282; summary of symbols 282

attributes: Cyberlight 321f; moving lights 321

Audacity (sound editing software): bit float 388; fading out 396; label tracks 390, 391, 391f, 392f; layering sounds 392; open source program 387; practical example 390–393, 390f–392f; ripping data from CDs 388; sample rates 388–389; timeline waveform 388f; time shift tool 391, 393; transcoding 389; trim command 391; workspace 387f, 389–390

audio file formats 389; see also digital audio files

Audio Interchange File Format (AIFF) 389, 390

audio racks 377, 377f

audio signals: basic path 383f; from computer 395f

audio snakes 378, 378f

Audio Stream Input Output (ASIO) 394

audio theory: analog vs digital signals 372, 372f; loudness measurement 371, 371f; sound frequencies 369–370, 370f; sound production methods 368; sound qualities 372–373; sound waves 368–369, 368f–369f; see also digital audio files; sound; sound reinforcement

auditions: audition forms 18; stage management 18

auditoriums, proscenium theatres 38–39

Austrian curtains 48–49, 49f

AutoCAD: basics 186–187, 186f–187f; command line 186, 186f; compared with tracking boards 319–320; crossing window 187; object snaps 187, 187f; polar tracking 187; ribbon 186, 186f; selection window 187; vs Vectorworks Spotlight 185–186; see also CAD (Computer Aided Drawing/Drafting)

automation 41

auto-transformers 309, 309f

auxiliary tables (table saws) 119, 119f

AVI 406

Avolites boards 319

AWG (American Wire Gauge) 302

awnings (Roamn theatres) 28, 28f

B

backdrops see curtains and backdrops

backflap hinges 155–157, 155f, 156f, 157f

bad connections vs short circuits 305–306

balconies 39

balcony rails 39, 353, 401, 404

ball peen hammers 101, 101f

ballyhoos (followspots) 16, 16f

balusters (or spindles) 222, 222f

band saws: band saw wheels 129f; blade guides 130–131, 131f; blades 129–130, 130f; cutting circles 131–132, 132f; cutting notches 132, 132f; cutting sharp curves 133, 133f; decking construction 238; flat construction 203, 204; metal cutting 258–259, 258f, 259f, 260; safety 131, 133; "soft side" cuts 131, 131f; tires 130, 130f

banks (preset boards) 312

bar (pipe) clamps 101, 101f

Barco 11K lumen projector 399f

barge cement 165–166

barn doors (lighting) 334, 334f, 340

barrel bolts 162

barrel hinges 153, 153f

bases: lamp parts 327, 327f; paints 172–173, 172f; routers 107f, 108

baskets (bridles) 89, 89f

batten-heavy 71

battens: counterweight rigging system 73–74, 73f–74f; cyclorama (cyc) pipes 47, 47f; drop boxes 355f; hemp rigging system 69–70, 69f, 70f; marrying battens/pipes together 76–77, 77f; plugging strips 39–40, 40f, 355, 355f; side arms 362, 362f batteries: atomic theory 278, 278f, 279–280, 279f–280f; D-cell batteries 280, 280f; direct current (DC) 286; green tips 103; hand-held tools 103–104; Li-ion batteries 103; Ni-Cad batteries 103; wet cell batteries 279–280, 279f

battery-powered drills/screw guns 103–104, 103f; *see also* drills

BBL (box boom left)/BBR (box boom right) *see* box boom positions

beam angles 333, 333f, 336, 336f, 416f–418f

beam lighting positions, proscenium theatres 38

belaying pins 71, 71f

Bell, Alexander 371

bells (shackles) 87–88, 87f, 90, 160–161, 160f

belt packs 11, 11f

belt sanders 106, 106f, 168

bench saws *see* radial arm saws

bent nail hinge pins 146f, 147, 156

binders (paint) 171–172, 171f

bit depth (sound recording) 388; 32 bit float 388

bite-lights 6, 6f

bits: drills/screwdrivers 104f, 105, 105f; routers 107–108, 107f–108f

black box theatres/flexible seating 32, 32f

blackout curtains 46–47, 50, 55–56

black steel pipes 161, 251, 252; *see also* steel pipes

blades: band saw blade guides 130–131, 131f; band saws 129–130, 130f; blade set 114, 114f, 116; circular saws 108, 108f, 113–115, 115f; cut-off blades 262; heat expansion 114f; jigsaws 106–107, 106f, 107f; power miter saws 123–124; ripping blades 114; table saws 116, 116f; tang style blades 106, 106f, 107f; tape measures 94, 94f

blade set 114, 114f, 116

bleacher seats 32

bleed-through 48

blocking rehearsals 18–19, 20, 21, 22f

blocks: head blocks 70–71, 70f; loft blocks 70, 70f

blueprints 177f, 178

board feet 138–139

bobbinette 169f

body mike systems 376, 376f

bolt cutters 99, 99f

bolts: barrel bolts 162; cane bolts 162–163, 163f; eyebolts 49f, 51, 160, 160f; head shapes 149–150, 150f, 152–153, 152f, 153f; hex heads 150, 152, 152f, 153; lag bolts 153, 153f, 266, 266f; load capacity 152; machine threads 149; nuts 149; vs screws 149, 149f; sizes 151; stove bolts 152; threaded rods 152, 152f; threads-per-inch (TPI) 151–152, 151f; tightening method 152; torque washers and carriage bolts 152, 152f; washers 152–153, 152f

Bondo 173–174

boomerangs (followspots) 13, 13f, 14–15, 15f, 16f

booms 353; free-standing (trees) 354; torm booms 354

booths, proscenium theatres 39

border lights 337–338, 338f

borders (curtains) 45f, 46, 55–56

bottles (Source Four Par lamps) 337f, 360, 361f

bottom pipes 53, 53f, 57

bowing: flat construction 192–193, 192f; lumber defects 139, 139f

bow knots 62–63, 62f, 63f

bowlines: arena rigging 86, 86f, 89f, 90; left-handed 65f; tying method 64–65, 64f

box boom positions 39, 39f, 353, 353f

box-end wrenches 98, 98f

box nails 146

box seats 39

box sets 30, 30f

box trusses 84, 84f, 352

braces (legging methods) 240

brads 146, 352; office brads 352

braided/woven (ropes) 60f, 61

breaking strength: cables (counterweight rigging system) 72; ropes 61

breakout/fanout cables 301, 302f

bricks (counterweights) 75–76, 75f

bridles: baskets 89, 89f; downlegs 88, 88f; eyes (thimbles) 87, 87f; practical example 88–90, 88f, 89f

Broadway theatres: balcony rails 39; commercial theatres 4; DC vs AC current 309; dressing rooms and rail 38; fly towers 41; plugging strips 39–40; projection designers 404; prop departments 12; proscenium theatres 37; stagehands 5–6; touring shows and proscenium theatres 30; trap rooms 41; *Trip to Bountiful* 48; video projections 398; video rear projections 401, 401f; without lighting circuits 39–40

"broken straw" example 331, 331f

bronzing powders 173, 173f

Browne, Van Dyke, *The Secrets of Scene Painting and Stage Effects* 367f

budget reports 184f

building materials *see* wood and building materials

bull lines 76, 76f, 77, 78

bump (chain motors/hoists) 84

bumpers (electrics) 361, 361f

burlap/jute 169

burrs (metal framing) 259

bus bars (dimmer racks) 298

business agents (IATSE) 6

butt hinges 153–154, 154f

butt joints 112, 112f

C

cabinet (self-closing) hinges 155, 155F

cable coiling 10, 10f

cable cutters (Felco) 99–100, 99f
cable grids 36, 36f
cable picks (pick lines) 40, 40f, 356, 356f
cables: #0000 (four ought) cables 300, 301, 302;
    breaking strength 72; breakout/fanout cables 301,
    302f; category 5 ("cat 5") computer cables 302,
    302f; feeder cables 299; and microphones
    377–378, 377f–378f; multi-cables 301, 302f, 355;
    and power distribution 299–302, 299f–302f; safety
    cables 355, 357; steel cables 86, 86f, 87, 87f;
    twofer/threefer cables 356, 356f; *see also* aircraft
    cables; electrical wires; solid wire; tie lines
cable ties 171, 171f
CAD (Computer Aided Drawing/Drafting):
    AutoCAD (basics 186–187, 186f–187f; command
    line 186, 186f; compared with tracking boards
    319–320; crossing window 187; object snaps 187,
    187f; polar tracking 187; ribbon 186, 186f;
    selection window 187; vs Vectorworks Spotlight
    185–186); elevations drawings 179; isometric
    drawings 180; lighting positions 349; light
    plots 347
calculations: amps 281; base 10 to sixteenths 223f;
    feet and inches 197, 197f; fractions in
    woodworking 196, 196f; framing cut lists 199,
    199f; framing practice 200–201, 200f–201f;
    ohms/resistance/power 282; stair riser height
    222–223, 222f–223f; volts 279
call boards (auditions) 18
"call for line" 18, 20–21
call lights 11
"call the show" 22
cambium (sapwood) 135–136, 135f, 136f, 137, 140
cam locks 300, 300f
cane bolts 162–163, 163f
canvas 168–169
capacitors 290, 375
captured channels (light boards) 317
carabineers 161
carbide steel blades 115, 115f
carbon dioxide (welding) 253; *see also* argon/CO$_2$ mix
    (MIG welding)
carbon microphones 375
cardioid microphones 375; PCC (phase-coherent-
    cardioid) microphones 376, 376f
card-reading boards 312, 312f
carpenters: carpentry department 5; head carpenters 6;
    "joiners" 113; shop carpenters 7–8, 8f; *Stage
    Carpenter, The* (Monroe H. Rosenfeld) viii; stage
    carpenters 8–9, 8f, 10, 45; student stage carpenters
    111f; tools of the trade 8f; *see also* wood and
    building materials; woodworking; woodworking
    tools
carpenter's glue (aliphatic glue) *see* aliphatic resin glue
    (carpenter's glue)
carriage 220, 222; *see also* stairs

carriage bolts 152, 152f
carriers: decking 243–244, 243f–244f; master carriers
    50, 50f; traveler tracks 49, 49f
cartridge fuses 300, 300f
casein paints 172, 172f, 212
casket/coffin locks 162, 162f, 233–234, 234f, 236,
    236f
casters: plated casters 270, 270f; rigid (dumb) casters
    163–164, 163f; stemmed casters 270, 270f; swivel
    (smart) casters 163–164, 163f; universal casters
    164, 164f
cast lists 18
category 5 ("cat 5") computer cables 302, 302f
catwalks 35, 36
caulk 129, 166; latex/acrylic caulk 174
caulk guns 166f, 174
c-clamps: characteristics 101, 101f; decking
    construction 233; hanging lights 352, 352f, 357,
    359, 361
CDA file format 389
CDs: bit depth 388; CD file names 389; playback
    393; ripping data from 388
cements: barge cement 165–166; contact cement 165,
    165f; *see also* construction adhesive (Liquid Nails);
    glue
center lines: drafting documents 180, 181; hanging
    curtains 52, 52f; hanging electrics 354, 354f;
    proscenium theatres 39
center punches 272
center-tapped transformers 293, 293f
CFLs (compact fluorescent lamps): and dimmers 328;
    ghost lights 44; in loft areas 41; work lights 22
chain bags 83, 83f, 85–86
chain motors/hoists: arena rigging 82–83, 82f (1 ton
    motors 83, 84, 87; 2 ton motors 83, 84, 87; chain
    bags 83, 83f, 85–86; chain running 83, 83f, 86;
    CM Lodestart 82, 83f; connectors 84, 84f; inverted
    chain motors 82; pickles (motor controllers) 84,
    84f; running 83, 83f, 86; running the chain out
    83–84); theatre rigging 69
chalk lines 96, 96f
chamfer bits (routers) 108, 204
chamfering: flat construction 204–205, 205f; V-legs
    242f
channels: DMX 512A protocol 314, 315–316, 321,
    322–323; intercom systems 11, 11f; lighting
    317–318, 320; traveler tracks 49
channel steel 251, 251f
character shoes 20
charcoal lines 96
chariot and pole system 30, 30f
checking (lumber defect) 121, 121f
Cheeseborough clamps (cheeseburgers) 162, 162f,
    352
cheesecloth 169–170, 170f
Chicago, IATSE Local Two 6

chitlin' circuit 4

chokes 63, 63f, 85, 85f, 311

chop/cut-off saws 257–258, 257f, 258f, 269

chorus (Greek theatre) 26–27

chuck/chuck keys 104, 104f

CIE color chart 341–342, 342f

circles: circle marking implements 239, 239f; cutting 131–132, 131f

circuits: circuit testers 306, 306f; concept 281, 281f; Ohm's laws 282–283, 282f–283f; open circuits 283; parallel circuits 281, 284–287, 285f–287f; series circuits 283–284, 283f–284f; terminals 286, 287f; see also power distribution

circular saws: arbors 113–114, 114f; blade sizing 108, 108f, 113–115; carbide blades 115, 115f; circular saw guides 237, 237f; cross cutting blades 114; heat and expansion 114, 114f; kerf 115, 115f, 116; ripping blades 114; set 114, 114f, 116; tearout 114, 114f; theatre use 108–109

clamps: bar (pipe) clamps 101, 101f; c-clamps see c-clamps; Cheeseborough clamps (cheeseburgers) 162, 162f, 352; grounding clamps (welders) 253, 254; half-burger clamps 352, 352f; hanging clamps 49–50, 49f, 50f; opera clamps 54, 54f; pipe/bar clamps 101, 101f; radial arm saw clamping mechanism 120, 120f; Rota Locks (pipe clamps) 101, 101f, 161, 161f, 235; spring clamps 102, 102f; Vise Grip clamps 102, 102f, 122, 265, 266f; wire rope (Crosby) clamps 72, 159, 159f; wooden clamps 101, 101f

cleats 71

clews (hemp rigging system) 71, 71f

clipping: signal processing 382; VU (Volume Units) meters 371

clove hitches 64, 64f, 73f

CM Lodestart chain motors/hoists 82, 83f

CO$_2$ (welding) 253; see also argon/CO$_2$ mix (MIG welding)

coatings see paints/coatings

coffin/casket locks 162, 162f, 233–234, 234f, 236, 236f

coiling techniques 10, 10f

college theatre students 7, 7f, 111f; see also university shows/theatres

collets (routers) 107–108, 108f

color changers see boomerangs (followspots)

color coding: electrical wires 303–304; jumpers 357; lamp storage racks 339; lens tubes 336, 336f

color correction gels 343

color filters/media 340–343, 340f–342f; see also gels

color frames (followspots) 14–15, 15f; see also no color (followspot boomerangs)

color media see color filters/media

colors, complementary 341, 341f

color scrollers 302, 322, 322f, 340

color temperature scale, and gels 340, 343

color transmission, Roscolux 342, 342f

Colosseum 28, 28f

Columbus McKinnon 82, 83; CM Lodestart chain motors/hoists 82, 83f

commando cloth/duvetyn 46, 169, 190, 208

commercial theatres 4, 5, 6, 21, 24

common nails 146, 146f

community theatres 4

compact fluorescent lamps (CFLs) see CFLs (compact fluorescent lamps)

companies of actors 4

company managers 6

compasses 96, 96f

complementary angles 124–126, 125f

complementary colors 341, 341f

compression load 240, 241f

compressors (signal processing) 382, 382f

computer programs: Adobe After Effects 406; Adobe Audition 387; Adobe Illustrator 404; Adobe Photoshop see Adobe Photoshop; Adobe Premier 405; Audacity see Audacity (sound editing software); CAD see CAD (Computer Aided Drawing/Drafting); Digital Audio Workstation (DAW) 387; Digital Light Processing (DLP) 402–403; Final Cut Pro 405; Isadora 404, 405, 406, 407–408, 407f–408f; playback (audio) 393–397, 394f–396f; playback (video) 406–410, 406f–409f; Pro Tools 387, 387f, 388; QLab see QLab; raster computer programs 185, 186; scalability 186; SFX 392, 393, 394–396, 394f, 396f; show control software 393–394; sound editing 387–388, 387f–388f (see also Audacity (sound editing software)); Sound Forge Pro 387; Vectorworks 178; Vectorworks Spotlight see Vectorworks Spotlight; Watchout 405, 406, 408–410, 408f–409f; Windows Media Player 393; Windows Movie Maker 405

condenser microphones 375

conductors 279, 279f

cone speakers 384–385, 384f

conferences, theatre conferences 7

connectors: loudspeakers 383, 383f; and microphones 377–378, 377f–378f; multi connectors 301, 302f; pin connectors 300f, 301f, 304, 304f; power distribution 299–302, 299f–302f; RCA connectors 378, 378f; Socapex connectors 301, 301f; see also jacks

construction adhesive (Liquid Nails) 166, 166f, 235; see also cements; glue

construction documents: CAD see CAD (Computer Aided Drawing/Drafting); definitions (blueprints 177f, 178; drafting 177, 178; sketches 178, 178f); other documents (budget reports 183, 184f; hanging schedules 184, 184f; lineset schedules 184; prop lists 184; scenic elements lists 183, 183f); traditional drafting (cross hatching 181; dimension lines 181; elevations 179, 179f; floor/ground plans 179; isometric drawings 180–181, 180f; object lines 181; perspective drawings 179, 179f; plan views 178–179, 178f; scale rules 181–183, 181f–183f; section views 179–180, 180f; tape measure method 183, 183f; types of lines 181, 181f; views 178)

construction-grade lumber 138

construction staples/staplers 148, 209, 226

contact cement 165, 165f

contact sheets 20, 20f

content (video projections) 404

contrast ratios (video projectors) 403

converters 372, 378; and microphones 377–378, 377f–378f

coping (crown molding) 129

copper wires: breakage 305; resistance table 294f; types of 302–303

cord (framing) 246

cordage 170–171, 171f; *see also* ropes

corner blocks: flat construction 203–204, 203f–204f, 208–209, 208f–209f; hard-covered flats 213; soft-covered flats 191, 191f; *see also* keystones

corner braces 163, 163f; soft-covered flats 190–191, 190f, 191f

corner irons 236, 236f

costume fitting 20

countersunk holes 150, 236, 245, 245f

counterweight rigging system: advanced techniques (bull lines 76, 76f; hanging hardware 76–77, 77f; lineset safety 77–78, 77f; marrying battens/pipes together 76–77, 77f; pipe weights 76); aircraft cables 72, 72f, 159; all components 81f; arbors 72–76, 72f, 80f; batten-arbor relationship 73–74, 73f–74f; breaking strength 72; bull lines 76, 76f, 77, 78; clove hitch 73f; double purchase system 74, 74f; hanging hardware 77f; marrying battens/pipes together 76–77, 77f; rail 73f; spreader plates 75, 75f; tension pulleys 73; trim chains 72, 73f; T-tracks 73, 74, 74f, 75f; weight loading/unloading 76, 77–78; weights (bricks) 75–76, 75f; wire rope clamps 72; *see also* arena rigging; hemp rigging system; rigging; theatre rigging

counterweights: counterweight rigging system 75–76, 75f; metal framing assembly 260

covered joints 113, 113f, 191

Crabtree, Susan, *Scenic Art for the Theatre* 46, 171

Crescent/adjustable wrenches 10, 97, 97f, 355, 359

crimping tools 159

Crosby clamps/wire rope 72, 159, 159f

cross cuts 112, 112f, 120

cross cutting blades 114

crossfaders 312, 312f

cross hatching 181

crossing window (AutoCAD) 187

crossovers: amplifiers 383; proscenium theatres 38

crown molding 126–129, 126f, 127f, 128f

crowns: flat construction 205, 207f; staples 148, 148f

crow's foot (V mark) 121–122, 121f

cues: cue flow chart (lighting control) 316f; cue lights 8, 9, 23, 79f, 79–80; cue lists (playback software) 393, 394, 394f, 395–396, 395f, 406; cue numbers (lighting control) 318–319; cue sheets 79–80, 79f; go cues 22; non-destructive cues 395f, 396; pulls (flymen's cues) 79–80; QLab audio and video cues 406–407, 406f; "slide over" cue 15; standby/warn cues 22

cue-to-cue rehearsals 21–23

culls/culling 201–202

cupping lumber defects 139, 139f

current: AC (alternating current) 280–281, 280f, 284, 286–287; AC from power generation 287–291, 287f–291f; current draw 285; direct current (DC) 280, 280f, 284, 286–287, 292–293, 309; *see also* power distribution

curtains and backdrops: basic curtain types (blackouts 46–47, 50; borders 45f, 46; drops 45–46, 46f; leg and order sets 45f, 46; legs 45f, 46; tab curtains 51–52, 51f, 52f); construction techniques (curtains 56–57; grommets 57, 58–59, 58f, 59f; muslin drops 45, 47, 56–59, 57f–59f; pipe pockets 57, 57f; webbing 57–58, 57f, 58f); hanging (bottom pipes 53, 53f; drops 52–53, 53f; drops (too large) 53–54, 54f; legs 52, 52f); knot tying, bow knots 62, 63; masking 46–47; rigging (hemp system) 69–71, 69f, 70f, 71f; sightlines 46, 46f; specialty curtains (Austrian curtains 48–49, 49f; cyclorama (cyc) curtains 47, 47f; grand drape/main 48, 48f; oleo curtains 49, 49f; scrims 47–48, 47f; show drops 48, 48f); spring clamps use 102, 102f; storing (folding 55–56, 55f; folding a leg 56f; hampers 55–56, 55f, 56f; west-coasting a scrim 56f); *see also* fabrics; fire curtains; traveler tracks

curved claw hammers 100, 100f

curved platforms: bending plywood 239–240, 240f; circle marking implements 239, 239f; grid method 239, 239f

cut lists: carriers (decking) 244, 244f; flat with 202f; fractions and English-style measurements 196, 196f, 208; hard-covered flats 213–214, 214f, 216f; hard-covered flats (practice cut lists) 413f; metal framing 257, 257f; softcover flats (practice cut lists) 412f; step building 223, 223f, 224f, 225, 225f; working with feet and inches 197–199, 197f–199f, 208 (practice problem 200–201)

cut nails 146, 146f

cut-off/chop saws 257–258, 257f, 258f, 269

cut-off wheels 269–270, 269f

cut-off blades 262

cut types: angles 124–126, 124f–126f; circles 131–132, 131f; cross cuts 112, 112f, 120; dado cuts 113, 113f; double miter cuts 120, 124, 129;

half lap joints 112, 112f; miter cuts 112, 112f, 120; nibble cuts 132; notch cuts *see* notch cuts; rip cuts 112, 112f; sharp cuts 133, 133f; slots 132, 132f; "soft side" cuts 131, 131f; steep angles 269–270, 269f

c-wrenches *see* Crescent/adjustable wrenches

cyanoacrylate/super (Zap) glue) 166

Cyberlight 321, 321f

cyclorama ("cyc") curtains/pipes 47, 47f, 65, 65f, 345; sky cyc 47, 48, 169, 338

cyclorama ("cyc") lights 337–338, 338f, 343; *see also* LEDs

D

dado cuts 113, 113f

daisy chaining (lighting) 323

Dallas Theater Center 35f

data compression 389

DAW (Digital Audio Workstation) 387

dB (decibels) 371, 371f

DC (direct current) 280, 280f, 284, 286–287, 292–293, 309

D-cell batteries 280, 280f

Deadblow hammers 101

dead-end pulleys 50–51

dead hang: arena rigging 86, 88; curtains 51, 64; hemp rigging system 70, 70f

dead limbs (trees) 136, 136f

dead-man switches 84

decay (of a sound) 372, 390

decibels (dB) 371, 371f

deck carpenters *see* stage carpenters

deck chains 88, 88f

deckhands 8f, 9, 10, 23; *see also* stage carpenters

decking: basics 232–233; carriers 243–244, 243f–244f; commercially manufactured 232f, 233; curved platforms (bending plywood 239–240, 240f; circle marking implements 239, 239f; grid method 239, 239f); hardboard layer 244; legging methods 240–243, 240f–243f; oddly shaped decking 236–237, 237f (adding framing 238, 238f); sound deadening 244–245, 245f; stock decking 233–235, 233f (coffin locks 233–234, 234f, 236, 236f; corner irons 236, 236f; frame assembling 235–236, 235f–236f; key hole 234f; notch markings 234, 235f; stiles 233, 235, 236); stressed-skin panels 246–247, 246f–247f

decks (stage floor) 69

de-energized fixtures 304

delay (mixing consoles) 379

delta connections 297

delta trusses 84

denominator (fractions) 196, 197, 208

de-rated ropes 61, 61f

designers 3, 4, 6, 18–19, 21; *see also* lighting designers

desks (lighting control) 316–317; *see also* Electronic Theatre Controls (ETC)

diagonal pliers/dikes 99, 99f, 100

diameter, inside/outside 251

dichroic filters 320, 322, 331, 349

dies, metal frame leveling 268, 268f

diffusion 332–333

diffusion gels 343

digital audio files: audio file formats 389; bit depths 388; CD file names 389; data compression 389; before digital age 386–387; playback 393–397, 394f–396f; practical example (Audacity software) 390–393, 390f–392f; sample rates 388–389, 389f; sound editing programs 387–388, 387f–388f; sound effects 388; transcoding 389

Digital Audio Workstation (DAW) 387

Digital Light Processing (DLP) 402–403

Digital Multiplexing 512A (DMX 512A) protocol 302, 313–316, 314f, 321, 322–323, 323f

digital signals, vs analog signals 372, 372f

dikes/diagonal pliers 99, 99f, 100

dimension lines 181

dimension lumber 120, 137, 142, 218, 231, 261

dimmers: and 240 volt service 296; addresses 322–323; and amplifiers 382; auto-transformers 309, 309f; card-reading boards 312, 312f; CFLs (compact fluorescent lamps) 328; crossfaders 312, 312f; disconnect boxes 300; DMX 512A protocol 313–316, 314f; electric dimmers 309–310; ETC Sensor dimmers 311, 311f; IGBT (insulated gate bipolar transistor) dimmers 309, 311; Kliegl Performers 312–313, 313f, 317; look 311; patching 314–316, 315f; per circuit 355; presets/preset panels 311–312, 311f; ratings 286; resistance dimmers 283f, 284, 309, 309f; RFU (remote focus unit) 357, 357f, 359; Silicon Controlled Rectifiers (SCRs) 309–310, 309f, 311; Sine Wave dimmers 310–311, 311f; Strand dimmers 311; and three phase power 298–299, 298f, 299f; thyristor dimmers 309; troubleshooting 306–307; two-scene preset boards 311–312, 311f; wattage 286, 311, 338; *see also* connectors; lighting control

diodes *see* LEDs

dip switches 313

direct current (DC) 280, 280f, 284, 286–287, 292–293, 309

direction (sound) 373

directors 17, 18–19, 21; *see also* rehearsals

disconnect boxes 296, 296f, 299–300, 299f

distance (sound) 373

diversity receivers 376–377, 376f

DLP (Digital Light Processing) 402–403

DMX 512A protocol 302, 313–316, 314f, 321, 322–323, 323f

donuts 360, 360f

door flats 193, 193f, 195, 195f, 216, 216f

doors: loading doors 38; pass doors/"passages" 38; smoke doors 44, 44f; stage doors 23f, 24; *see also* barn doors (lighting); door flats

"dope" (compound and glue) 173

double action hinges 155; *see also* swinging/saloon door hinges

double-ended/recessed single contact (RSC) lamp bases 327, 327f

double-headed (duplex) nails 147, 147f

double insulation 291

double miter cuts 120, 124, 129

double muff headsets 11

double-overs (knots) 62, 63f

double purchase rigging system 74, 74f

dovetail 113, 113f

downlegs (bridles) 88, 88f

downstage 29

dowsers (followspots) 13–14, 13f, 14f, 15

drafting: definition 177, 178; hand drafting tools 185, 185f; traditional drafting (cross hatching 181; dimension lines 181; elevations 179, 179f; floor/ground plans 179; isometric drawings 180–181, 180f; object lines 181; perspective drawings 179, 179f; plan views 178–179, 178f; scale rules 181–183, 181f–183f; section views 179–180, 180f; tape measure method 183, 183f; types of lines 181, 181f; views 178)

drapes: terminology 45; *see also* curtains and backdrops; grand drapes (main drapes)

drawings *see* CAD (Computer Aided Drawing/Drafting); drafting; schematic drawings (electrical circuits); sketches

dress circles 39

dressers 6f

dress rehearsals 23

drill presses 104, 104f

drills: basics 102; battery-powered drills/screw guns 103–104, 103f; chuck/chuck keys 104, 104f; drill direction 105; driver bits 104f, 105, 105f; hammer drills 104, 104f; hole saws 105, 105f; safety precautions 102; twist drills 105, 105f; variable speed reversible drills 104

D-ring plates 158, 158f

D-rings (hanging irons) 157, 157f, 158

driver bits 104f, 105, 105f

drives: Phillips drives 104f, 105, 150, 150f; Robertson (square) drives 105; screwdrivers 98; screws 150, 150f; slotted drives 150, 150f; socket wrenches 98, 98f; square drives 150, 150f; standard slot drives 150, 150f

drop boxes 40, 40f, 355–356, 355f

drops: construction techniques 56–59, 57f, 58f, 59f; definition 45–46, 46f; hanging 52–53, 53–54, 53f; hanging "too large" drops 53–54, 54f; shortening (rolling) 53, 54, 54f; show drops 48, 48f;

storing/folding 55–56, 55f, 56f; *see also* curtains and backdrops

dryness, grading lumber 137

dry pigments 172

dry tech rehearsals 21–23

drywall screws 150–151, 151f

drywall squares: definition and usage 96, 96f; extending lines 238, 238f; flat construction 218

duct tape 167, 344, 344f

dumb (rigid) casters 163–164, 163f

duplex (double-headed) nails 147, 147f

duvetyn/commando cloth 46, 169, 190, 208

dynamic microphones 375

dynamic range (signal processing) 382

E

echoes 370, 372, 381

economy of scale 207

Edison, Thomas 277–278, 277f, 293, 309

Edison plugs 287, 287f

editing: non-destructive editing 390, 395f, 396, 406; *see also* sound editing programs

elastomeric coating 172–173, 173f, 174

electrical current *see* current; electrical theory; power distribution

electrical hand tools: drills (basics 102; battery-powered drills/screw guns 103–104, 103f; chuck/chuck keys 104, 104f; drill direction 105; driver bits 104f, 105, 105f; hammer drills 104, 104f; hole saws 105, 105f; safety precautions 102; twist drills 105, 105f; variable speed reversible drills 104); routers 107–108, 107f, 108f, 218, 218f; sanders (belt sanders 106, 106f, 168; random orbit sanders 106, 106f); saws (circular saws *see* circular saws; hole saws 105, 105f; jigsaws 106–107, 106f, 107f; reciprocating (Sawzall) saws 108f, 109); *see also* hand tools; pneumatic hand tools; woodworking tools

electrical tape (vinyl) 19, 167, 357

electrical theory: atomic theory (amps and volts 281; batteries 278, 278f, 279–280, 279f–280f; circuits 281, 281f; conductors 279, 279f; currents 280–281, 280f; electrons 278–279, 278f; EMF and volts 279, 279f; insulators 279, 279f; light bulbs 281, 281f; lightning 278–279, 278f; power and watts 282; resistance and ohms 281–282; summary of symbols 282); Edison and Tesla 277–278; Jablokov candles 284, 284f; Ohm's laws (circuits 282–283, 282f–283f; parallel circuits 284–287, 285f–287f; series circuits 283–284, 283f–284f); power generation and alternating current 287–291, 287f–291f; *see also* transformers

electrical troubleshooting 304–305, 304f–305f, 306–307

electrical wires 302–304, 303f–304f

electricians 5, 9–11, 10f, 11f; master electricians 351; *see also* spot operators

electrics (electric lighting positions): definition 354; first electrics 40, 69; hanging 354–359, 354f–358f; proscenium theatres 39–40

electrodes (welders) 253

Electro Motive Force (EMF): definition 279, 279f; magnetism-EMF relationship 288–289, 289f; strength 289, 289f; symbol 282

Electronic Theatre Controls (ETC): channels and addresses 320f, 323, 323f; Ethernet system 323; Express-Expression light boards 317, 319, 320 (console and controls 317f; fade down/up 318, 318f; softkeys 319f; submaster and fader sections 318f); "how to" videos 308; Ion tracking boards 318, 319–320, 320f; Sensor dimmers 311, 311f; Sine Wave dimmers 310–311, 311f; Source Four Par lamps 332–333, 334, 336, 337, 343, 360 (lamp and "hot dog" 337f; lenses 333f; oval pattern changing 361f)

electrons 278–279, 278f

elevations (drafting) 179, 179f

Elizabethan times, thrust theatres 31, 34

ellipsoidal reflectors 328, 328f, 330–331, 330f–331f

ellipsoidal spotlights (Lekos) 334–336, 334f–336f, 355, 359

Elmer's glue 164, 213

EMF (Electro Motive Force) *see* Electro Motive Force (EMF)

end stops (traveler tracks) 50

engineer's scale rules 181

English-style measurements 196–201, 196f–201f, 208

equalizers (mixing consoles) 380–381; third octave equalizers 381–382, 382f

Equity *see* Actor's Equity Association

erosion cloth 169

escape stairs 221, 221f

e-tape (vinyl) 19, 167, 357

ETC *see* Electronic Theatre Controls (ETC)

Ethernet 10, 302, 323, 378; "cat 5" cable 302f; node with Ethernet input 323f

exhaust fans 44

expanded polystyrene 143, 143f

Express-Expression light boards 317, 319, 320; console and controls 317f; fade down/up 318, 318f; softkeys 319f; submaster and fader sections 318f; *see also* Electronic Theatre Controls (ETC)

extension legs (metal framing) 271–272, 271f–272f

extruded polystyrene 143, 143f; *see also* Styrofoam

eyebolts 49f, 51, 160, 160f

eyes/thimbles (bridles) 87, 87f

F

fabrics: bobbinette 169f; canvas 168–169; cheesecloth 169–170, 170f; duvetyn/commando cloth 46, 169, 190, 208; fabric staplers 149; flame proofing 169;

jute/burlap 169; muslin *see* muslin; scenery netting 169, 169f; scrim 169, 169f; and Sobo glue 165; velour *see* velour fabric; *see also* curtains and backdrops; fire curtains; soft-covered flats

fabric staplers 149

face welds 262, 262f, 263, 263f

facing pieces (hard-covered flats) 215, 215f

factory corners 237

fade down/up (ETC boards) 318, 318f

faders/sliders: lighting control 311–312, 311f, 313f, 318, 318f (crossfaders 312, 312f); sound control 381, 381f (flying faders 380, 380f)

fanout/breakout cables 301, 302f

fasteners: basics 145f, 146; bolts *see* bolts; choosing fasteners 153; comparison chart 153f; nails *see* nails; screws *see* screws; staples *see* staples/stapling

fast squares 96

fault-finding *see* troubleshooting (electrical work)

Federal Communications Commission (FCC) 377

feedback 370; feedback frequencies 381–382; feedback loop 381

feeder cables 299

feeding lines 21

feed rate (saws) 122–123, 259

feet and inches 196–201, 196f–201f, 208

Felco cable cutters 99–100, 99f

fencing staples 149, 149f

fiberboard (medium density/MDF) 143

filaments (light bulbs) 281–282, 281f, 326–327, 326f–327f

file formats: audio files 389; *see also* Audio Interchange File Format (AIFF); computer programs; WAV (Windows Audio File)

files (metal work) 259

fillet welds 262, 262f, 263, 263f

filters *see* dichroic filters; gels

Final Cut Pro 405

final dress 23

finger-tight 152, 354–355

finish-grade lumber 138–139

finish nails 147, 147f, 148

fir: lumber 135; plywood 141–142

fire codes 41

fire curtains 42–44, 42f, 43f; *see also* flame-proofing (FP)

fire marshals 41, 44

first electrics 40, 69

first read-through 18–19

five pin XLR connectors 302; *see also* XLR connectors

fixtures, vs instruments 325

"flag the light" cue 360, 360f

flame pattern (plywood) 141

flame-proofing (FP): basic considerations 170; fabrics 169; flame retardant 170f; Iroquois Theatre fire (1903) 42; proscenium theatres 41–42; *see also* fire curtains

flanges (smoke pockets) 43, 43f
flat bars 251, 251f
flat construction: assembly process 205–210, 206f–210f; chamfering 204–205, 205f; corner blocks 203–204, 203f, 204f, 208–209, 208f–209f; covering (muslin 190, 210–213, 211f–212f; plywood 210, 210f, 213, 218); crowns 205, 207f; culling 201–202, 202f; keystones 203, 204–205, 205f, 208, 210, 210f; profile flats 195f; rails 203, 203f; safety precautions 201, 201f; stapling 209–210, 209f; stiles 201–202, 206, 206f–207f, 208; template tables 205–206, 206f, 210; toggles 207–208, 207f–208f; *see also* cut lists; door flats; hard-covered flats; soft-covered flats; window flats
flat heads (screws and bolts) 149–150, 150f
flat washers 152, 152f
flexible seating/black box theatres 32, 32f
floating fabric (curtain folding) 55
flood (Fresnel lights) 334, 361
floor/ground plans 179
floor mount lights 354, 362, 362f
floral tape 167–168
floral wire 171
flow chart (lighting cues) 316f
flush-trim bits 108, 108f, 218, 218f
flux (welding) 253, 254
fly houses/towers 30, 41, 41f
flying faders 380, 380f
flymen 8, 9, 9f, 10, 69, 78, 79–80; *see also* arena rigging; rigging; theatre rigging
foam: and band saws 130, 131; insulation 244–245; *see also* polystyrene; Styrofoam
focal points 330–331, 330f–331f, 334
focusing (lighting): hanging hardware 352–353, 352f; RFU (remote focus unit) 357, 357f, 359; techniques 359–362, 359f–362f; *see also* light hang
FOH/front-of-house lighting positions 38, 39, 353, 353f, 358–359
foldback 379
folding (curtains) 55–56, 55f, 56f
followspots 12–16, 13f, 14f, 15f, 16f, 335; *see also* ellipsoidal spotlights (Lekos); lamps/lights; light hang; lighting control; spots
footing (ladders/spot towers) 9, 10f
forced perspective 29, 29f, 30
Ford's Theatre 39
"four corner" instruction 55
FP *see* flame-proofing (FP)
fractions (woodworking calculations) 196, 196f, 208
frames: color frames (followspots) 14–15, 15f; frame parts (flats) 190–191, 190f, 191f; gel frames 351–352, 351f, 353; metal frame (definition) 264
framing (definition): flat construction 190; of a house 148; *see also* flat construction; hard-covered flats; metal framing; soft-covered flats

framing squares: definition and usage 95, 95f; step construction 229, 229f
freehand 119, 129f
frequencies: feedback frequencies 381–382; frequency agile systems 377; high/low end sounds 381; sound frequencies 369–370, 370f; wireless microphone frequencies 377
Fresnel, Augustin 332
Fresnel lights 333–334, 333f–334f, 334, 361; Fresnel lenses 332, 332f
front lights 12; *see also* followspots
front-of-house/FOH lighting positions 38, 39, 353, 353f, 358–359
front video projections 402
frost gels 343
full-body spots 14, 15f
full HD (1920x1080) 403
fullness (grand drapes) 48, 48f, 56
full-scale patterns: cutting angles 126; metal tube bends 270f, 271; odd-shaped decks 236–237
fusible links 43, 43f

G

gaff (gaffer's) tape 19, 167, 167f, 358
gain knobs (mixing consoles) 380, 381f
GAM (Great American Market) 306, 342
GamChek electrical tester 306
Garage Band 387
gas flow regulators (welders) 256, 256f
gas lights 309
gates (ellipsoidals) 331, 334
gauge system (steel tubing) 251
gelatin-based gels 340
gels: CIE color chart 341–342, 342f; color correction gels 343; color temperature scale 340, 343; complementary colors 341, 341f; diffusion gels 343; filtering effects 340–341, 340f–341f; frost gels 343; gelatin-based gels 340; gel frames 351–352, 351f, 353; gel sizes 340; gel strings 340, 340f; manufacturers 342; neutral density gels 343; swatch books 342–343, 342f
Genie lifts 356, 359f
geometrical optics 328–329, 328f–329f
ghost lights 21f, 44
Globe Theatre 31, 31f, 35
glow tape 22, 167, 167f
glue: aliphatic resin glue (carpenter's glue) 164, 209, 209f, 226, 235, 246; applying wood glue 164–165, 164f–165f; and bronzing powders 173; decking (legging construction) 241; decking (plywood) 235, 238; as "dope" component 173; Elmer's glue 164, 213; flat construction 209–210, 209f; flat coverings 210–213, 211f, 212f; glue joint strength 148, 153; hardboard (Masonite) construction 142; hard-covered flats 216, 216f; hide/animal glue 172, 210, 211f; hot melt glue (thermoplastic adhesive)

165; and paint pigments/binders 172–173; particleboard construction 142; plywood construction 140–141; polyvinyl glues 164; Sobo glue 165; Spray 77 adhesive 166, 166f; step construction 226, 227; step construction (plywood) 231; stressed-skin panels 246–247, 247f; types of glue 164–165; white glue 164–165, 172, 173, 211; yellow glue 164–165, 218; Zap (cyanoacrylate/super glue) 166; *see also* cements; construction adhesive (Liquid Nails)

gobo rotators 287, 287f, 322, 322f, 344, 345, 345f

gobos (templates/patterns) 343–346, 343f–346f, 360; mesh gobos 345, 345f

GO button: chain motors/hoists 84; light boards 318–319; playback software (audio) 395; playback software (video) 407

go cues 22

goods (drops and drapes): hanging 52–53; "stretching the goods" 53; *see also* curtains and backdrops

grain structure: grading lumber 136, 137; hardboard (Masonite) 142, 203; lauan (mahogany) 218; particleboard 142; plywood 140–141, 140f–141f

grand drapes (main drapes) 39, 48, 48f, 56

Grand Hotel, 1991 Auditorium Theatre incident 161

granny knots 65, 65f

Grapes of Wrath production, video projection 398f

Great American Market (GAM) 306, 342

Greek amphitheatres 25–27, 25f, 26f, 27f

green idea tips: battery recycling 103; CFLs (compact fluorescent lamps) 41, 328; ghost lights 44; pre-show presets 22; removable stair legs 230; re-using the Masonite 245; steel frame parts recycling 251; yellow pine and sustainable forests 142, 203; *see also* helping hints

grid method 239, 239f

grids, proscenium theatres 41

grinders *see* angle grinders (metal framing)

grips 8

grit number (sandpaper) 168, 168f

grommets 50, 52, 57, 58–59, 58f–59f, 170

ground/floor plans 179

grounding, and Ohm's laws 291, 291f

grounding clamps (welders) 253, 254

ground row lights 338

Guthrie Theatre (Minneapolis) 33, 33f

H

hair department 5

half-burger clamps 352, 352f

half-hitch bow knots 62f, 63, 66

half-hour calls 24

half-lap joints 112, 112f

Hamlet (William Shakespeare) 47

hammer drills 104, 104f

hammers and mallets: nail-driving (curved claw hammers 100, 100f; straight claw hammers 100,

100f; *see also* nails); others (ball peen hammers 101, 101f; Deadblow hammers 101; rubber mallets 101, 101f; sledgehammers 101)

hampers 55–56, 55f, 56f

hand-held electric saws: circular saws 108–109, 108f; hole saws 105, 105f; jigsaws 106–107, 106f, 107f; reciprocating (Sawzall) saws 108f, 109

hand-held microphones 375

hand-off (props) 12

hand props 12

hand tools: cabinet for 93f; clamps (c-clamps *see* c-clamps; pipe/bar clamps 101, 101f; spring clamps 102, 102f; Vise Grip clamps *see* Vise Grip clamps; wooden clamps 101, 101f); drafting tools 185, 185f; gripping/turning tools (bolt cutters 99, 99f; crimping tools 159; pliers *see* pliers; screwdrivers 98, 98f; wrenches *see* wrenches); hammers and mallets *see* hammers and mallets; marking tools *see* marking tools; measuring tools *see* measuring tools; *see also* electrical hand tools; pneumatic hand tools; woodworking tools

hanging clamps 49–50, 49f, 50f

hanging hardware: aircraft cables 77, 159, 159f; angle irons 163, 163f, 251, 251f; cane bolts 162–163, 163f; carabineers 161; casket/coffin locks 162, 162f, 233–234, 234f, 236, 236f; Cheeseborough clamps (cheeseburgers) 162, 162f, 352; corner braces 163, 163f, 190–191, 190f, 191f; D-ring plates 158, 158f; eyebolts 49f, 51, 160, 160f; hanging irons 157, 157f; quick links 77f, 160, 160f; rope thimbles 159, 159f; Rota Locks (pipe clamps) 101, 101f, 161, 161f, 235; screen door handles 162, 162f; screw eyes 160, 160f; shackles *see* shackles; S-hooks 161, 161f; snap hooks 77f, 161, 161f; swage fittings (Nicropress Sleeves) 159–160, 160f; trim chains 72, 73f, 88, 157–158, 157f; turnbuckles 158, 158f; wire rope (Crosby) clamps 72, 159, 159f; *see also* light hang

hanging irons 157, 157f

hanging schedules 184, 184f

hardboard (Masonite) 142, 142f, 203, 244, 245

hard-covered flats: bolting 213, 213f; construction 216–218 (covering 217–218, 217f; toggles 216–217, 217f; trimming and filling 218, 218f); covering 215–216, 215f, 216f; cut lists 213–214, 214f, 216f; definition 189–190, 189f, 190f; door flats 216, 216f; facing pieces 215, 215f; helping hints 218; plywood covering 210, 213, 218; practice cut lists 413f; stapling 217–218, 217f; stiles 214–215; window flats 214–216, 214f; *see also* flat construction; soft-covered flats

hard-edge spots 16f

hardware types: adhesives 164–166, 164f–166f; casters 163–164, 163f–164f; cordage 170–171, 171f; fasteners 145f, 146 (nails 146–148, 146f–148f; screws and bolts 149–153, 149f–153f;

staples 148–149, 148f–149f); flame proofing 170,
170f; hanging hardware 157–163, 157f–163f;
hinges 153–157, 153f–157f; paints/coatings
171–174, 171f–174f; sandpaper 168, 168f;
tape 167–168, 167f–168f; *see also* fabrics
hardwoods 135, 135f
head blocks 70–71, 70f
head carpenters 6
headroom (mixing console input levels) 380, 381f
heads: bolts 152–153, 152f, 153f; screws and bolts
149–150, 150f
headsets (intercom system) 10–11, 11f
head-shots (followspots) 14, 15f
hearing protectors 201f
heartwood 135
heat control knobs (welders) 255, 255f
heat distortion 260, 261f, 267, 267f
helmets, welding safety 253, 253f, 254
helping hints: cutting angles 124–126, 124f–126f;
feet and inches 201; hard-covered flats 218; legging
methods (decking) 242; soft-covered flats 213;
stairs/steps 228; *see also* green idea tips
hemp (manila) lines 170
hemp rigging system: battens 69–70, 69f, 70f;
belaying pins 71, 71f; clews and ropes 71, 71f;
dead hanging 70, 70f; depression era stagehands
68f; head blocks 70–71, 70f; hemp system rigging
69, 69f; loft blocks 70, 70f; pulleys 69, 70;
sandbags 71–72, 71f; trim setting 70; *see also* arena
rigging; counterweight rigging system; rigging;
theatre rigging
hemp ropes 60f, 61, 69, 135; purchase/operating
lines 73
Hertz (Hz) 287, 369–370, 370f, 377; feedback
frequencies 381–382; sample rates 388–389
hex bolt/screw heads 150, 152, 152f, 153
hex keys (5/16″) 233
hide/animal glue 172, 210, 211f
high-end sounds 381, 383
highest takes precedence (HTP) 318, 319
hinges: backflap hinges 155–157, 155f, 156f, 157f;
barrel hinges 153, 153f; bent nail hinge pins 146f,
147, 156; butt hinges 153–154, 154f; cabinet
hinges (self-closing/piano) 155, 155f; double action
(saloon/swinging door) hinges 154–155, 154f;
hinge parts 153, 153f; piano hinges 155, 155f;
strap hinges 154, 154f; T hinges 154; tight-pin
hinges 153
hints *see* helping hints
HMI lamps 12, 287
hog-through shape 241
Holden, Alys, *Structural Design for the Stage* (Holden
and Sammler) 252
hole saws 105, 105f
Hollywood flats 190, 190f, 210; *see also* hard-covered
flats

hooks (tape measures) 94, 94f
hookup sheets (dimmer channels) 315f, 316
Hopgood, Jeromy, *QLab 3: Show Control* 396
horn and driver loudspeakers 384f, 385
hot dogs (PAR lamps/cans) 337f, 360, 361f
hot melt glue (thermoplastic adhesive) 165
hot wires (alternating current) 289–291, 290f, 296,
297, 298
house heads 5–6
house mix positions 39
house opens 22
HPL lamp bases 327, 327f, 356
HTP (highest takes precedence) 318, 319
hubs (shackles) 87
human ear: and sound frequencies 369–370, 370f;
and sound waves 369, 369f
Hz *see* Hertz (Hz)

I

IATSE (International Alliance of Theatrical Stage
Employees) 4, 5, 6–7, 17
IGBT (insulated gate bipolar transistor) dimmers
309, 311
Image Pro (ROSCO) 343, 343f, 346, 346f
iMovie 405
"in betweens" (masking curtains) 46, 47f
induction 278, 278f, 288
inert gas 254; *see also* Metal Inert Gas (MIG)
welders
in one/in two etc. (border and leg sets) 46
in/out trims 78–79, 78f
input modules (mixing consoles) 380–381,
380f–381f
inside diameter (ID) 251
instruments, vs fixtures 325
insulated gate bipolar transistor (IGBT) dimmers 309,
311
insulated staples 149, 149f
insulation: decking 244–245, 245f; double insulation
291; electrical wires (color coding) 303–304 (SJ
insulation 303; SO insulation 303, 303f)
insulators 279, 279f
Intellabeam 320
intercom systems 10–11, 11f, 23
International Alliance of Theatrical Stage Employees
(IATSE) 4, 5, 6–7, 17
in the ear monitors 371
in trim marking 78–79, 78f
inverted chain motors/hoists 82
Ion tracking boards 318, 319–320, 320f; *see also*
Electronic Theatre Controls (ETC)
irises (lighting) 13, 13f, 14, 14f, 16, 335, 335f
iron cores (transformers) 291
Iroquois Theatre fire (1903) 42
Isadora (software) 404, 405, 406, 407–408,
407f–408f

isometric drawings 180–181, 180f
ITunes 393

J

Jablokov candles 284, 284f
jacks: ¼″ jacks 383, 383f; ⅛″ jacks 378, 378f; L-jacks 156, 156f, 269
Jaxsan 173
Jellison, Megan 9f
jigs: band saws 131; butt hinges 154; coffin/casket locks 236, 236f; corner blocks 208; notch marking 234, 235f, 236f; odd-shaped decks 237; radial arm saws 120, 121f; steel square tube construction 231, 231f; welding jigs 260–261, 261f, 264, 267, 271–272, 271f
jigsaws 106–107, 106f, 107f
jobs in theatre: artistic directors 4; assistant directors 18; assistant stage managers 10, 18, 20, 21, 22, 23; carpenters see carpenters; deckhands 8f, 9, 10, 23; designers 3, 4, 6, 18–19, 21; dressers 6f; electricians 5, 9–11, 10f, 11f, 351; flymen 8, 9, 9f, 10, 69, 78, 79–80; jobs websites 7; lighting designers see lighting designers; lighting directors 15; loaders 76; managing directors 4; production concept 3–4; projection designers 398, 404; prop guys 11–12; spot operators 12–16, 13f, 14f, 15f, 16f; stagehands see stagehands; stage managers see stage managers; technical directors 4, 183, 185; work environments 4–7, 5f
joiners 113; see also carpenters
joint compound (spackle) 173, 174f, 218
joints: butt joints 112, 112f; covered joints 113, 113f, 191; dado cuts 113, 113f; dovetail 113, 113f; half-lap joints 112, 112f; lap joints 112, 112f; mortise and tenon 113, 113f; scab joints 113, 113f
journeyman stagehands 7
jumpers 301f, 303, 306, 306f, 323, 357
jute/burlap 169

K

Kelvin color temperature scale, and gels 340, 343
kerfs: circular saw blades 115, 115f, 116; cut-off wheels 269; drawing of a kerf 115f; fall on scrap side 226; and material loss 193, 203; power miter saws 123–124; radial arm saws 121–122, 122f; table saws 116, 117, 119
key hole (decking) 234f
keys (light plots) 348, 348f
keystones: vs corner blocks 191f; flat construction 203, 204–205, 205f, 208, 210, 210f; soft-covered flats 191–192, 191f, 192f; straps 205, 210f
keystoning (video projections) 401, 401f
key to instrumentation 351, 351f
kickbacks: band saws 131; radial arm saws 123; table saws 118, 119
kicker, Zap (cyanoacrylate/super glue) 166

kicking action, jigsaws 107, 107f
kilns 137
kitchen-door hinges see saloon/swinging-door hinges
Kliegl brothers, electronical dimmer patent application 308f
Kliegl Performers 312–313, 313f, 317
knots: loose (wood) knots 138, 138f; and lumber grading 137, 138; and plywood 141, 141f; and tree growth 136
knot tying: basic terminology 62, 62f; 'good knot' criteria 60; soft-covered flats 213; types of knots (bow knots (double-overs and half-hitches) 62–63, 62f, 63f, 66; bowlines 64–65, 64f, 65f; chokes 63, 63f, 85, 85f, 311; clove hitches 64, 64f, 73f; granny knots 65, 65f; loops 62, 62f; overhand knots 61f; slip knots 63, 63f; square knots 65, 65f; trucker's hitches (snub and loop) 63, 65–66, 65f, 66f); see also ropes
knuckle busters 80, 80f

L

ladders: footing/walking up 9; light ladders 354, 354f; safety precautions 361
lag bolts 153, 153f, 266, 266f
laminates: laminated layers (stairs) 228, 230–231, 231f; positioning (with contact cement) 165, 165f
laminate trimming bits 218
lamps/lights: arc lamps 284, 327, 402–403; bite-lights 6, 6f; border lights 337–338, 338f; call lights 11; CFLs see CFLs (compact fluorescent lamps); cue lights 8, 9, 23, 79f, 79–80; cyclorama ("cyc") lights 337–338, 338f, 343; double-ended/recessed single contact (RSC) lamp bases 327, 327f; floor mount lights 354, 362, 362f; gas lights 309; ghost lights 21f, 44; ground row lights 338; HMI lamps 12, 287; HPL lamp bases 327, 327f, 356; light bulbs 281–282, 281f, 326–327, 326f–327f; Mini Strips 337–338; mogul bipost lamp bases 327, 327f; moving mirror lights 320–322, 321f; moving yoke lights 320–321, 321f; off-gassing 326; PAR lamps see PAR lamps/cans; rover lights 362f; safety 326; screw lamp bases 327; set mount lights 354; Source Four Par lamps see Source Four Par lamps; storage racks 339, 339f; strip lights 337–338, 338f; two-pin lamp bases 327, 327f; types of 326–327, 327f; wattage 44, 326, 327, 334, 338; work lights 21, 22, 41; Xenon lamps 12, 13f, 287, 402; see also ellipsoidal spotlights (Lekos); followspots; LEDs; lenses; photometrics; shutters (lighting); spots
landings 222, 222f
lap joints 112, 112f
lap splices (traveler tracks) 51, 51f
Las Vegas, commercial theatres 4
lateral stress 233, 240, 241f
latest takes precedence (LTP) 318
latex/acrylic caulk 174

latex paints 172

lauan (mahogany) plywood: bending plywood 239; characteristics 142; vs Masonite (hardboard) 203; vs plywood 218; stapling issues 148; vs yellow pine (green tip) 142

lavaliere microphones 376, 376f

lay (cordage) 170

LCD (Liquid Crystal Display) 402–403

League of Regional Theatres (LORT) 4, 17f

leaves (hinges) 153, 153f

LEDs: call lights 11; cyc lights 338–339, 338f–339f; dimmers 306, 328, 338; filters 320; ghost lights 44; video wall screen units 399, 399f; VU (Volume Units) meters 371

Lee Filters 342

leg and border sets (curtains) 46

legends (light plots) 348, 348f, 351, 351f

legs: bridles 88, 88f (practical example 88–89, 88f, 89f); curtains (drawing of 45f; folding 56, 56f; hanging 52, 52f; masking 46–47); decking, legging methods 240–243, 240f–243f; metal framing, extension legs 271–272, 271f–272f; stairs, stringer-types 230, 230f; staples 148, 148f

Lekos (ellipsoidal spotlights) 334–336, 334f–336f, 355, 359

lenses: basics 326, 326f; beam angles 333, 333f; diffusion 332–333; Fresnel lenses 332, 332f; plano-convex lenses 332, 332f; refraction/"broken straw" example 331, 331f–332f; Source Four Par lenses 332–333, 333f

lens tubes 336, 336f

leveling feet (metal framing) 268, 268f

levels/plumbs 96–97, 97f

lifts: focusing lights 359, 361; Genie lifts 356, 359f; safety precautions 361; stage electrician's skills 9; wet cells 280

light boards see Express-Expression light boards; lighting control

light bulbs 281–282, 281f, 326–327, 326f–327f; see also lamps/lights

light construction lumber 137

light hang: focusing (hanging hardware 352–353, 352f; RFU (remote focus unit) 357, 357f, 359; techniques 359–362, 359f–362f); hanging electrics 354–359, 354f–358f; lighting positions 353–354, 353f; lighting tower properties 353f; light plots 347–348, 347f–348f, 351; preparation work 351–353; see also lighting control; Vectorworks Spotlight

lighting: proscenium theatres 39–40, 39f; thrust theatres 35–36, 36f; see also dimmers; electrical theory; followspots; lamps/lights; lenses; light hang; lighting control; photometrics; power distribution

lighting control: control equipment (card-reading boards 312, 312f; crossfaders 312, 312f; Kliegl Performers 312–313, 313f, 317; presets/preset panels 311–312, 311f; two-scene preset boards 311–312, 311f); DMX 512A protocol 313–316, 314f; historical perspective (auto-transformers 309, 309f; ETC Sensor dimmers 311, 311f; gas lights 309; IGBT dimmers 309, 311; Kliegl brothers' dimmer patent application 308f; resistance dimmers 309, 309f; Silicon Controlled Rectifier (SCR) 309–310, 309f, 311; Sine Wave dimmers 310–311, 311f; Strand dimmers 311; thyristor dimmers 309); programming the board (cue flow chart 316f; cue numbers 318–319; move-fade desks 317–318, 317f–318f; move-fade vs tracking 316–317, 316f); tracking boards 319–320, 319f–320f; working with digital equipment (channels and addresses 322–323, 323f; color scrollers 322, 322f; connection with DMX 323, 323f; gobo rotators 322, 322f; moving lights 320–322, 321f); see also dimmers

lighting designers: beam angles 331; focusing lights 359; rehearsals 21; three phase power 299; Vectorworks Spotlight tools 185, 348

lighting directors 15

lighting electrics see electrics (electric lighting positions)

lighting positions: FOH/front-of-house 38, 39, 353, 353f, 358–359; light hang 353–354, 353f

lighting towers 353f, 354

light ladders 354, 354f

lightning 278–279, 278f

light plots 347–348, 347f–348f, 351, 351f

lights see lamps/lights

Lightwright 351

Li-ion batteries 103

limit (chain motors/hoists) 84

limiters (signal processing) 382

Lincoln, Abraham 39

line array speakers 384, 384f

line level inputs 380

linesets 70, 76, 77–78, 77f, 79, 79f

lineset schedules 184

line voltage/main 295

Liquid Crystal Display (LCD) 402–403

Liquid Nails (construction adhesives) 166, 166f, 235

Little Theatre 34

live end pulleys 50

live load 232

"live" rooms 370

live sounds 368

L-jacks 156, 156f, 269

loaders 76

loading doors 38

loading galleries/rails 75

load-ins/outs 6, 7

locking (lights) 359

loft blocks: hemp rigging system 70, 70f; wells (large beams) 86–87, 87f loft space 41, 41f

loge seats 39

looks (stage lighting) 311

looping (playback software) 396

loops (knots) 62, 62f

loose connections 305–306

loose knots (wood) 138, 138f

loose-pin blackflap hinges 155f, 156

LORT (League of Regional Theatres) 4, 17f

loudness: loudness war 372; measurement 371, 371f

loudspeakers: connectors 383, 383f; line array speakers 384, 384f; speaker-microphone placement 382f; types of 384–385, 384f

low-end sounds 381, 383

LTP (latest takes precedence) 318

Lucille Little Theatre (Transylvania University) 32f

lumber: defects (bows 139, 139f; checking 121, 121f; cups 139, 139f; loose knots 138, 138f; warps 139, 139f); definition 134; dimension lumber 120, 137, 142, 218, 231, 261; grading 137–139 (construction grade 138; finish grade 138–139; rough cut 138); grain structure 136, 137; running feet 139, 139f; sap 137; sizes (milled 137, 137f; nominal 136–137, 137f); sizes for drop rolling, 1x4 lumber 54, 54f; sizes for stock decking 233; SPF lumber 135; stick pricing 139; swelling 137–138, 138f; type of trees 135; see also wood and building materials

lumens 403

luminescent displays 399

M

McCandless, Stanley, *A Method for Lighting the Stage* 325, 325f

machine screws 149, 151, 152

machine threads (bolts) 149

magazines (nail guns) 109

Magic Mending (Scotch) tape 168

magic triangles (Ohm's laws) 282–283, 282f–283f, 285, 285f

magnetic squares 268

magnetism-EMF relationship 288–289, 289f

mahogany plywood (lauan) *see* lauan (mahogany) plywood

main/grand drapes 39, 48, 48f

main/line voltage 295

mallets *see* hammers and mallets

managing directors 4

manila (hemp) lines 170

marking tools: chalk lines 96, 96f; compasses 96, 96f; levels/plumbs 96–97, 97f; squares (drywall squares 96, 96f, 218, 238, 238f; framing squares 95, 95f, 229, 229f; magnetic squares 268; Speed Squares 95–96, 95f, 216, 257); trammel points 96–97, 97f, 239; see also measuring tools

marrying battens/pipes together 76–77, 77f

Martin boards 319

masking 46–47, 47f

masking flats 190, 208, 210

masking tape 167

Masonite (hardboard) 142, 142f, 203, 244, 245

master carriers 50, 50f

master electricians 351; *see also* electricians

mastic 166, 166f

MDF (medium density fiberboard) 143

measuring boards (radial arm saws) 121f

measuring tools: squares (drywall squares 96, 96f, 218, 238, 238f; fast squares 96; framing squares 95, 95f, 229, 229f; magnetic squares 268; Speed Squares 95–96, 95f, 216, 257); steel tape 95, 95f; tape measures 94–95 (blades 94, 94f; drafting method 183, 183f; electrics hanging 358f; hooks 94, 94f; markings 95f); *see also* marking tools

media servers 406

medium density fiberboard (MDF) 143

mesh gobos 345, 345f; *see also* gobos (templates/patterns)

metadata 389

metal cutting band saws 258–259, 258f, 259f, 260

metal framing: assembly 260–263, 260f–263f; bending tubing 270–271, 270f–271f; casters 270, 270f; cleaning tubing 259–260, 259f; cut lists 257, 257f; cutting/fitting parts 257–260, 257f–260f; cutting steep angles 269–270, 269f; extension legs 271–272, 271f–272f; grinding 262–263, 262f; heat distortion 260, 261f, 267, 267f; height adjustments 268, 268f; materials (aluminum vs steel 249–250; shapes and sizes 250f, 251–252, 251f–252f); odd shapes 264–268, 265f–267f; practical example 263–264, 264f; stiles 257, 260, 269; trusses 272–273, 272f–273f; welding equipment 252–256, 252f–256f; *see also* welding

Metal Inert Gas (MIG) welders 8, 252–253, 254–256, 254f–256f

method acting 34

Method for Lighting the Stage, A (Stanley McCandless) 325, 325f

metric vs American SAE (Society of Automotive Engineers) 98

Metropolitan Opera 38

mezzanines 39

mic level input 380

microphones: analog devices 372; and Audacity software 393; cables and connectors 377 (⅛″ jacks 378, 378f; audio snakes 378, 378f; RCA connectors 378, 378f; XLR connectors 377–378, 377f, 378, 378f); mic level input 380; microphone design 374–375, 375f (carbon microphones 375; cardioid microphones 375; condenser microphones

375; dynamic microphones 375; ribbon microphones 375); speaker-microphone placement 382f; use on stage (audio racks 377, 377f; diversity receivers 376–377, 376f; hand-held microphones 375; lavaliere (body) microphones 376, 376f; omnidirectional/cardioid type 375; PCC (phase-coherent-cardioid) microphones 376, 376f; Shure microphones 375–376, 375f; wireless microphone frequencies 377); *see also* mixing consoles

Midsummer Night's Dream (William Shakespeare) 113

MIG (Metal Inert Gas) welders 8, 252–253, 254–256, 254f–256f

mild steel 252, 260

milled size (lumber) 137, 137f

Mini Strips 337–338

mirror lights *see* moving mirror lights

miter boxes 123, 123f

miter cuts 112, 112f, 120; double miter cuts 120, 124, 129

miter guides 117f, 118–119, 119f

miter saws 123–124, 123f; changing angles 124, 124f; miter boxes 123, 123f; safety 124; sliding miter saws 124; usage 120

mixing consoles: analog vs digital 379–380; delay 379; flying faders 380, 380f; foldback 379; gain knobs 380, 381f; input modules 380–381, 380f, 381f; layout 379f; mono vs stereo 378–381; pad buttons 380, 381f; PFL (pre-fade listen)/solo buttons 381

module-based playback programs (video) 406

mogul bipost lamp bases 327, 327f

molding *see* crown molding

monkey/pipe wrenches 99, 99f

mono: ⅛″ jacks 378; amplifiers 383; label tracks (Audacity software) 390, 391, 391f, 392f; mixers 378

mortise and tenon technique 113, 113f

motorized winch system 40

mounting plates (casters) 270, 270f

mounts: floor mount lights 354, 362, 362f; set mount lights 354

move-fade (preset) 316–317, 316f

move-fade desks 317–318, 317f–318f

moving mirror lights 320–322, 321f

moving yoke lights 320–321, 321f

mp3 files 389

Mr. Bluebeard (play), Iroquois Theatre fire (1903) 42

muff headsets 10–11; single muff headsets 11f

multi-cables 301, 302f, 355

multi connectors 301, 302f

multiplexing 313

music, rehearsals 21

muslin: characteristics 168–169, 169f; covering flats 190, 210–213, 211f–212f; drop construction 45, 47, 56–59, 57f–59f; and synthetic casein paints 172

N

nail guns: crown molding 128; magazines 109; nails for 147–148, 148f; plywood 261; pneumatic tools 102, 109, 110; safety 109; step construction 226

nails: bent nail as hinge pin 146f, 147, 156; box nails 146; common nails 146, 146f; cut nails 146, 146f; double-headed (duplex) nails 147, 147f; finish nails 147, 147f, 148; nail boxes sizes 147, 147f; for nail guns 147–148, 148f; nail heads 147–148, 147f, 148f; nail selection 148, 148f; nail sets 147, 147f; nail sizes 146–147, 146f; spikes 146; *see also* hammers and mallets

needle-nose pliers 99, 99f

NETC (New England Theatre Conference) 7

netting 169, 169f

neutral density gels 343

neutral wires (alternating current) 289–291, 290f, 296, 297, 298

newel posts 222, 222f

New England Theatre Conference (NETC) 7

New Stagecraft movement 34

New York: IATSE Local One 6, 7; and touring shows/companies 33; *see also* Broadway theatres

nibble cuts 132

Ni-Cad batteries 103

Nicropress Sleeves (swage fittings) 159–160, 160f

no color (followspot boomerangs) 14

nodes: lighting boards 323, 323f; trusses (metal framing) 272

noise to signal ratio 382

Nominal Pipe Size (NPS) 251

nominal size lumber 136–137, 137f

non-destructive editing 390, 395f, 396, 406

non-intensity parameters 320

notch cuts: band saws 132, 132f; frame assembling (decking) 235f, 236, 236f; notch marking jigs 234, 235f, 236f; step construction 228–229; stressed-skin panels 247

not-for-profit theatres 4, 5, 34

nozzles (welders) 254

NPS (Nominal Pipe Size) 251

numerator (fractions) 196

nuts (bolts) 149

nylon ropes 60f, 61, 171

O

object lines 181

Occupational Safety & Health Administration (OSHA) 100

off-gassing lamps 326

office brads 352

off- or on-book 18, 20–21

Offstage Jobs website 7

offstage move 361

Ohm, Georg 282

ohms 282

Ohm's laws: and circuits 282–283, 282f–283f; and grounding 291, 291f; magic triangles 282–283, 282f–283f, 285, 285f; and parallel circuits 284–287, 285f–287f; practice problems 414f–415f; and series circuits 283–284, 283f–284f; see also electrical troubleshooting

oleo curtains 49, 49f

omnidirectional microphones 375

one-by (lumber) 137, 137f

O'Neill, Eugene 34

one-point perspective 29, 29f

on- or off-book 18, 20–21

onstage move 361

opaque materials 399

open circuits 283

open-end wrenches 97, 97f

opera clamps 54, 54f

operating/purchase lines 73, 76, 77–78, 79, 80

opposite/split phase hookup 296

optics see geometrical optics

orchestra (circular performance area) 26–27, 27f

orchestra pits 39

orchestra seats 39

oriented-strand board (OSB) 142, 143f

OSHA (Occupational Safety & Health Administration) 100

out/in trims 78–79, 78f

outside diameter (OD) 251

out trim marking 78–79, 78f

over and under technique 10f

overhand knots 61f

overhauling 78

overhead arm saws see radial arm saws

oxyacetylene rigs 250, 250f

P

pad buttons (mixing consoles) 380, 381f

paddle/spade bits 105, 105f

painter's tape 167

paints/coatings: coatings (Bondo 173–174; bronzing powders 173, 173f; "dope" (compound and glue) 173; elastomeric 173, 173f, 174; joint compound (spackle) 173, 174f, 218; latex/acrylic caulk 174; undercoats 172–173, 173f; water-based polyurethane 173); paints (casein paints 172, 172f, 212; latex paints 172; paint bases 172–173, 172f; paint essential elements 171–172, 171f; Universal Colorants 172, 172f)

pan: followspots 16, 16f; lighting 352, 359; sound effects 379, 391, 392

pan heads (screws and bolts) 150, 150f

parabolic reflectors 328, 328f, 329–330, 330f

parallel circuits 281, 284–287, 285f–287f

PAR lamps/cans: characteristics 336–337, 337f; diffusion 332–333; focusing 360, 361f; vs Fresnel lights 334; see also Source Four Par lamps

Parthenon 27, 27f

particleboard 142–143

PA speakers see loudspeakers

"passages"/pass doors 38

patching (dimmer-channel) 314–316, 315f, 357

patterns see full-scale patterns; gobos (templates/patterns)

PCC (phase-coherent-cardioid) microphones 376, 376f

pegboards 142, 142f

people skills, stage managing 18

Perry, Tyler 4

perspective: forced perspective 29, 29f, 30; one-point perspective 29, 29f

perspective drawings 179, 179f

PFL (pre-fade listen)/solo buttons (mixing consoles) 381

phantom power 375

phase A, B, C (three phase power) 298

phase-coherent-cardioid (PCC) microphones 376, 376f

Phillips drives 104f, 105, 150, 150f

Phillips head screwdrivers 98, 98f

photometrics: definition 325; lamps (filaments 326–327, 326f–327f; types of 326–327, 327f); lenses 326, 326f (beam angles 333, 333f; diffusion 332–333; Fresnel lenses 332, 332f; plano-convex lenses 332, 332f; refraction/"broken straw" example 331, 331f–332f); lights and color gels/media 340–343, 340f–342f; projection materials, gobos (templates/patterns) 343–346, 343f–346f; reflectors 326, 326f (ellipsoidal reflectors 328, 328f, 330–331, 330f–331f; geometrical optics 328–329, 328f–329f; parabolic reflectors 328, 328f, 329–330, 330f; spherical reflectors 328, 328f, 329, 329f; types of 328, 328f); storage racks 339, 339f; types of lights (ellipsoidal spotlights (Lekos) 334–336, 334f–336f; Fresnel lights 333–334, 333f–334f, 334; LED cyc lights 338–339, 338f–339f; PAR lamps 336–337, 337f; Source Four Par lamps 332–333, 333f, 337, 337f)

photons 328

Photoshop see Adobe Photoshop

piano hinges 155, 155f

pickles (motor controllers) 84, 84f

pick lines (cable picks) 40, 40f, 356, 356f

"pie" formula 283, 283f, 285–286, 285f, 338, 356

pigments (paint) 171–172, 171f

pigtails (lights) 301, 353, 357

pin connectors 300f, 301f, 304, 304f

pine trees 135, 135f

pink contracts 5f, 6

pink noise 382

pin rails 40, 70–71, 72

pins: hinges 153, 153f; shackles 87, 87f, 160–161, 160f

pin wire 156, 171

pipe (bar) clamps 101, 101f

pipe clamps (Rota Locks) 101, 101f, 161, 161f, 235

pipe/monkey wrenches 99, 99f

pipe pockets 53, 54, 54f, 57, 57f

pipes: bottom pipes 53, 53f, 57; and chain motors 86; and hemp rigging system 69–70; and knot tying (chokes 63; clove hitches 64); and lineset safety 76; marrying battens/pipes together 76–77, 77f; Nominal Pipe Size (NPS) 251; see also steel pipes

pipe weights 76

pitch 372

pivots (radial arm saws) 120, 120f

pixilated images 399, 399f

places call 24

plano-convex lenses 332, 332f

plans, sets of 177

plan views: carrier layout 243f; definition 178–179, 178f; entire stage 178f; light plots 348; vs lineset schedule 184; proscenium lighting 39f; proscenium theatres 37f, 38; radial arm saws 119f; rehearsal preparations 19; see also section views

plaster lines 38–39, 39, 40, 52, 181, 353

plastics: acrylic sheets 143; expanded polystyrene 143, 143f; extruded polystyrene 143, 143f

plastic welding (video projections) 400

plated casters 270, 270f

platforms: curved platforms (bending plywood 239–240, 240f; circle marking implements 239, 239f; grid method 239, 239f); vs decking 233; parallel platforms 240, 240f; see also decking

playback: audio (definition 368; digital files/programs 393–397, 394f–396f; layering sounds 392; reel-to-reel tape recorders 386–387, 386f); video (digital program types 406; Isadora 404, 405, 406, 407–408, 407f–408f; media servers 406; QLab 406–407, 406f; Watchout 405, 406, 408–410, 408f–409f)

pliers: basics 98; bolt cutters 99, 99f; diagonal pliers/dikes 99, 99f, 100; Felco cable cutters 99–100, 99f; needle-nose pliers 99, 99f; pipe (monkey) wrenches 99, 99f; slip-joint pliers 98f, 99; Vise Grip pliers 99, 99f

plugging strips 39–40, 40f, 355, 355f

plugs 287, 287f

plumbs/levels 96–97, 97f

plywood: definition 134; features (A2 cabinet-grade plywood 141; advantages 140; construction project sizes 252; fir 141–142; flame pattern 141; grading 141, 141f; grain direction and wood strength 140–141, 140f, 141f; thickness sizes 142; tree farms 142, 203); usage (circular saw cuts 108; covered joints 113; curved platforms 239–240, 240f; decking (legging) 240–243; decking (oddly shaped) 236–237; decking (stock decking) 233–235; flat construction 203–204; flat covering 210, 210f, 213, 218; floor mount lights 362; hard-covered flats 210, 213, 218; metal frame assembly 260–261; pulley bases 50; stapling 148–149, 149f; step building 223–225, 230; stressed-skin panels 246–247; sweeps (framing pieces) 195–196, 195f; table saw cuts 116, 117, 119); see also lauan (mahogany) plywood; wood and building materials

pneumatic hand tools: air compressors 102f, 109; basics 102; nail guns 102, 109, 110; safety precautions 109; staplers 109–110, 109f, 110f; see also electrical hand tools; hand tools; woodworking tools

poly brushes 212f

polyester ropes 61

polypropylene: ropes 61; webbing 57

polystyrene: and adhesives 165, 166; and band saws 131; expanded polystyrene 143, 143f; extruded polystyrene 143, 143f; see also foam; Styrofoam

polyurethane 173

polyvinyl glues 164

Pompey see Theatre of Pompey

potentiometers 311–312

power (electricity) 282; see also current; electrical theory; phantom power; power distribution

power distribution: 120/240 volt split phase system 296, 296f, 299; cables and connectors 299–302, 299f–302f; current supply and theatre business 295; electrical wires 302–304, 303f–304f; portable systems 295f; short circuits vs loose connections 305–307, 306f; three phase power and dimmers 297–299, 297f–299f; troubleshooting 304–305, 304f–305f, 306–307

power generation, and alternating current (AC) 287–291, 287f–291f

power grids 287

power loss formula 291, 292f

power miter saws see miter saws

power tools: safety 102; see also electrical hand tools; pneumatic hand tools

power transmission: mathematics of 292f; see also transformers

preamps 375

pre-fade listen (PFL)/solo buttons (mixing consoles) 381

presets: move-fade 316–317, 316f; preset panels 311–312, 311f; pre-show preset 22

preview performances 23

primary coils (transformers) 291, 292, 292f

production, definition 3–4

production books 20

production meetings 19

production stage managers see stage managers

profile flats 195f

programs (video projections) 404

projection designers 398, 404

projection materials *see* gobos (templates/patterns)

projectors: aspect ratios 403, 403f; contrast ratios 403; LCD and DLP technologies 402–403; lumens 399f, 403; resolution 403, 404; throw distance 403–404

prompt scripts 20, 20f, 22f

property department 5

props: hand-off 12; hand props 12; prop cabinets/boxes 12, 12f; prop guns 12; prop guys 11–12; prop lists 184; prop sketches 184f; rehearsal props/costumes 19–20

proscenium, origin of word 27

proscenium theatres: background (Renaissance era) 29–30; characteristics (modern times) 37 (auditorium 38–39; lighting and sound 39–40; loft area 41; motorized winch system 40; stage and fire safety 41–44; traps 40–41); illustrated features (box sets 30, 30f; cable picks 40, 40f; "in case of fire" sign 43f; chariot and pole system 30, 30f; drop boxes 40, 40f; fire curtain and smoke pocket (plan view) 43f; fire curtains 42–44, 42f, 43f; fly houses/towers 41, 41f; forced perspective 29, 29f, 30; fusible links 43, 43f; loft 41, 41f; plan view 37f, 38; plan view of lighting positions 39f; plugging strips 39–40, 40f; section view 38f; smoke doors 44, 44f; sprinkler system 42, 42f; wing and drop scenery 29, 29f)

Pro Tools 387, 387f, 388

puddled weld seams 254, 254f

pulleys: dead-end pulleys 50–51; hemp rigging system 69, 70; tension pulleys 50, 50f, 73

pulls (flymen's cues) 79–80

purchase/operating lines 73, 76, 77–78, 79, 80, 81

push sticks 118, 118f

Pythagorean Theorem 88–89, 89f

Q

QLab: audio and video cues 406–407, 406f; cue lists 393; Inspector 395f, 396, 396f; mp3 vs WAV format 389; vs SFX 394–396; sound layering 392; workspace 395f

QLab 3: Show Control (Jeromy Hopgood) 396

quartz glass 326

quick links 77f, 160, 160f

QuickTime 406

QVGA (Quarter Video Graphics Array) 404

R

rack mountable equipment 377

rack storage, lamps 339, 339f

radial arm saws: anti-kickback devices 123; checking 121, 121f; clamping mechanism 120, 120f; common usage errors 121–122; crow's foot (V mark) 121–122, 121f; description 119, 119f; double miter cuts 120; feed rate 122–123; jigs 120, 121f; measuring boards 121f; plan view 119f; saw arm pivots 120, 120f; stop blocks 122, 122f, 123f

Radio City Music Hall 49

rags 46

rails: audio racks 377; balcony rails 39, 353, 401, 404; flat construction 203, 203f; loading galleries/rails 75; pin rails 40, 70–71, 72; proscenium theatres 38; soft-covered flats 190, 190f, 191, 192, 192f; T-tracks 73, 74, 74f, 75, 75f, 78, 79

raked stage 26, 26f, 29, 30

random orbit sanders 106, 106f, 168

raster computer programs 185, 186

rays (optics) 328

RCA connectors 378, 378f

rear video projections 399–402, 399f–401f

receivers, diversity receivers 376–377, 376f

recessed single contact (RSC)/double-ended lamp bases 327, 327f

reciprocating (Sawzall) saws 108f, 109

rectangular tubing 251, 251f

rectifiers 253, 254; *see also* Silicon Controlled Rectifiers (SCRs)

reel-to-reel tape recorders 386–387, 386f

reflectors: ellipsoidal reflectors 328, 328f, 330–331, 330f–331f; geometrical optics 328–329, 328f–329f; lighting fixture component 326, 326f; parabolic reflectors 328, 328f, 329–330, 330f; spherical reflectors 328, 328f, 329, 329f

refraction 328, 331, 331f–332f

regional theatres 4, 7, 33

rehearsals: blocking rehearsals 18–19, 20, 21, 22f; character shoes 20; cue-to-cue rehearsals 21–23; dress rehearsals 23; dry tech rehearsals 21–23; final dress 23; first read through 18–19; music 21; prompt scripts 20, 20f, 22f; rehearsal phases 20–21; rehearsal preparations 19–20; rehearsal props/costumes 19–20; rehearsal skirts 20; run time 18; taping out the set 19, 19f; tech rehearsals 21–24; wet tech rehearsals 21, 23

remote focus unit (RFU) 357, 357f, 359

Renaissance, proscenium theatres 29–30

resistance: concept 281–282; copper wires 294f; Ohm's laws 282–283, 282f–283f; resistance dimmers 309, 309f; in series 283–284, 283f–284f; *see also* electrical troubleshooting

resolution (video projectors) 403, 404

reverberation 370, 372; *see also* echoes

RFU (remote focus unit) 357, 357f, 359

ribbon microphones 375

rigging: under-hung rigging 41, 41f; pay rates 7; and woodworking 112; *see also* arena rigging; flymen; theatre rigging

rigid (dumb) casters 163–164, 163f

rip cuts 112, 112f

rip fences (table saws) 116, 117, 117f
ripping blades 114
ripping wood 111f, 112
risers: decking 232f, 233; for seating (black box theatres) 32; stairs (building method 223–225, 224f–225f; construction 226–227, 226f–227f, 228, 229, 230; definition 220, 222, 222f; height 221; height calculations 222–223, 222f–223f)
RMS (Root Mean Square) 289, 310
road houses: FOH/front-of-house lighting positions 39; hemp rigging system 72; loading doors 38; proscenium houses 30; tech packages 349; see also touring shows/companies
Robertson (square) drives 105
Rockwell Scale (steel density/hardness) 115, 115f, 252
rolling (drops) 53, 54, 54f
Roman amphitheatres 26f, 27–28, 27f, 28f
Romanesque arches 27–28, 27f
Romeo and Juliet (William Shakespeare) 35
Root Mean Square (RMS) 289, 310
ropes: braided/woven vs twisted 60f, 61; breaking strength 61; cable ties 171, 171f; coiling and storage 66–67, 66f, 67f; de-rated 61, 61f; floral wire 171; hemp (manila) lines 170; hemp ropes 60f, 61, 69, 73, 135; nylon ropes 60f, 61, 171; polyester ropes 61; polypropylene 61; sash cords 61–62, 61f, 171; selection skills 60; sisal 61; steel-wire ropes 87; tie lines 59, 59f, 61–62, 62f, 171, 357, 358f; working limit 61; yarns (twisted ropes) 61; see also knot tying
rope thimbles 159, 159f
ROSCO: Image Pro 343, 343f, 346, 346f; Roscolene 342; Roscolux 342, 342f
Rosenfeld, Monroe H. (The Stage Carpenter) viii
Rota Locks (pipe clamps) 101, 101f, 161, 161f, 235
rotary cut veneers 140–141
rotators (gobo rotators) 287, 287f, 322, 322f, 344, 345, 345f
rough cut lumber 138
round bars 251, 251f
round heads (screws and bolts) 150, 150f
round-over bits 108, 108f
round tubing 251, 251f
routers 107–108, 107f, 108f, 218, 218f
rover lights 362f
RSC (recessed single contact)/double-ended lamp bases 327, 327f
rubber mallets 101, 101f
running (chain motors/hoists) 83, 83f, 86; "running the chain out" 83–84
running feet (lumber) 139, 139f
running the show: audio playback 395; stage carpenters' role 8; theatre rigging 78–80 (cue lights 79f,79– 80; cue sheets 79–80, 79f; flying a piece out 80; knuckle busters 80, 80f; marking linesets 79, 79f; marking trims 78–79, 78f)

run time (rehearsals) 18
Rutherford, Ernest 278

S

Sabbatini, Nicola 29, 31, 49, 189; page from his book 29f
SAE (Society of Automotive Engineers) vs metric 98
safety: band saws 131, 133; disconnect boxes 299; drills 102; flame proofing 41–42, 169, 170, 170f; flat construction 201; flyman work 9; ghost lights 44; Grand Hotel incident (1991) 161; grounding 291; hearing protectors 201f; lamps 326; lifts and ladders 361; linesets 76; nail guns 109; OSHA (Occupational Safety & Health Administration) 100; power miter saws 124; power tools 102; proscenium theatres 41–44; safety cables 355, 357; safety glasses 201f; stage weights 76; table saws 117, 118, 119; welding 253, 253f, 254, 256
saloon/swinging-door hinges 154–155, 154f
Sammler, Ben, Structural Design for the Stage (Holden and Sammler) 252
sampling/sample rates 372, 388–389, 389f
sandbags 71–72, 71f
sanders: belt sanders 106, 106f, 168; random orbit sanders 106, 106f, 168; steel wool 168
sanding belts 168
sandpaper 168, 168f; grit number 168, 168f
sap 137
sapwood (cambium) 135–136, 135f, 136f, 137, 140
sash cords 61–62, 61f, 171
saturation 341–342
saws: band saws see band saws; chop/cut-off saws 257–258, 257f, 258f, 269; circular saws see circular saws; feed rates 122–123, 259; hand-held electric saws see hand-held electric saws; metal cutting band saws 258–259, 258f, 259f; miter saws see miter saws; radial arm saws see radial arm saws; Sawzall (reciprocating) saws 108f, 109; sliding miter saws 124; table saws see table saws; TPI (teeth-per-inch) 129
Sawzall (reciprocating) saws 108f, 109
scab joints 113, 113f
scalability (computer programs) 186
scale rules 19, 19f, 181–183, 181f–183f
scenery construction see construction documents; cut lists; decking; flat construction; hard-covered flats; metal framing; soft-covered flats; stairs; woodworking
scenery netting 169, 169f
Scenic Art for the Theatre (Susan Crabtree) 46, 171
scenic elements lists 183, 183f
Schedule 40 steel pipes 86, 87, 161, 251
Schedule 80 steel pipes 251
schematic drawings (electrical circuits) 281, 281f, 285f
school theatres 5, 6

Schuko plugs 287, 287f
Scotch Magic Mending tape 168
screen-door handles 162, 162f
screwdrivers 98; Phillips head screwdrivers 98, 98f
screw eyes 160, 160f
screw guns/battery-powered drills 103–104, 103f; *see also* drills
screw lamp bases 327
screws: vs bolts 149, 149f; drives 150, 150f; drywall screws 150–151, 151f; head shapes 149–150, 150f; hex heads 150, 152, 152f, 153; machine screws 149, 151, 152; Phillips screws 104f, 105, 150, 150f; screw eyes 160, 160f; sizes 150; tapping screws 150, 150f; tech (self-tapping) screws 151, 151f; tightening method 152; *see also* drives
scrims: characteristics 47–48, 47f; hanging 53; scrim fabric 169, 169f; sharkstooth scrim 47, 169f; west-coasting 56, 56f
scrollers 302, 322, 322f, 340
SCRs (Silicon Controlled Rectifiers) 309–310, 309f, 311
Sculpt or Coat 172–173
SeaChanger 340
seasons, regional theatres 4
seating risers 32
secondary coils (transformers) 291, 292, 292f
Secrets of Scene Painting and Stage Effects, The (Van Dyke Browne) 367f
section views: concept 179–180, 179f; proscenium theatres 38f; stage set 180f; step construction 224, 224f; *see also* plan views
selection window (AutoCAD) 187
self-closing hinges 155, 155f
self-tapping (tech) screws 151, 151f
selvage edges 57
Sensor dimmers 311, 311f
series circuits 283–284, 283f–284f
Serlio, Sebastiano 29, 31, 189
set (blades) 114, 114f, 116
SETC (South Eastern Theatre Conference) 7
set mount lights 354
sets of plans 177
setting a trim 70
SFX (playback program) 392, 393, 394–396, 394f, 396f
shackles: arena rigging 87–88, 87f–88f, 89, 89f, 90; description/usage 160–161, 160f; marrying battens/pipes together 76–77, 77f
Shakespeare, William: *Hamlet* 47; *Midsummer Night's Dream* 113; *Romeo and Juliet* 35; *see also* Globe Theatre
sharing websites 388
sharkstooth scrim 47, 169f
Sharpie markers 79, 387
sheaves 70
shims 260

S-hooks 161, 161f
shop-built tension pulley base 50, 50f
shop carpenters 7–8; tools of the trade 8f
short circuits 305
show calls 6, 6–7
show control software 393–394
show drops 48, 48f
Shure microphones 375–376, 375f
shutters (lighting) 334, 335f, 355, 357; shutter cuts 359
side arms 361–362, 362f
sightlines: in arena/thrust theatres 31, 34; in black box theatres 32; and box seats 39; and drops 53; and followspots 13; in Greek amphitheatres 26, 26f; and leg and border sets 46, 46f; marking of 167; and masking flats 190; and tab curtains 51–52, 51f, 52f
sights (followspots) 16, 16f
signal path 374
signal processing 381–382, 382f
sign-in sheets 24
Silicon Controlled Rectifiers (SCRs) 309–310, 309f, 311
sill irons 216
sine wave: alternating current (AC) 281, 287, 289, 289f, 290–291, 290f; three phase power 297, 297f; transformers 292, 292f
Sine Wave dimmers 310–311, 311f
single-muff headsets 11, 11f
sisal 61
SJ insulation 303
skene 27, 27f
sketches: definition 178; flats 193–194, 193f–194f; Photoshop scaling 178, 178f; prop sketch 184f
Skil (circular) saws 108
sky cyc (cyclorama) 47, 48, 169, 338; *see also* cyclorama ("cyc") curtains/pipes
slag 253
sledgehammers 101
slide (followspots) 15
"slide over" cue 15
sliders *see* faders/sliders
sliding miter saws 124
slings: and bowlines 86, 86f, 89f, 90; and chokes 63, 85, 85f
slip-joint pliers 98f, 99
slip knots 63, 63f
slots 132, 132f
slotted drives 150, 150f
smart (swivel) casters 163–164, 163f
smoke doors 44, 44f
smoke inhalation 42
smoke pockets 43, 43f
snap hooks 77f, 161, 161f
Snell, Willebrord 331

snub and loop knots (trucker's hitches) 63, 65–66, 65f, 66f

Snug the Joiner (*Midsummer Night's Dream*) 113

Sobo glue 165

Socapex connectors 301, 301f

social networking sites 18

Society of Automotive Engineers (SAE) vs metric 98

sockets 327

socket wrenches 98, 98f

soft-covered flats: corner blocks 191, 191f; covering with muslin 210–213, 211f–212f; definition 189–190, 189f, 190f; door flats 193, 193f, 195, 195f; frame parts 190–191, 190f, 191f; helping hints 213; irregular shapes 195–196, 195f; keystones 191–192, 191f, 192f; masking flats 190, 208, 210; practice cut lists 412f; rails 190, 190f, 191, 192, 192f; shapes and drawings 193–196, 193f–195f; stapling 213; stiles 190, 190f, 191–192, 193, 198; sweeps (framing pieces) 195–196, 195f; thumbnail sketches 193–194, 193f–194f; toggles 190, 190f, 191, 192, 192f; window flats 193–194, 193f–194, 211; wood dimensions 192–193; *see also* flat construction; hard-covered flats

soft goods: definition 45; hanging 157; storing (hampers) 55–56, 55f, 56f; *see also* curtains and backdrops; fabrics

softkeys (light boards) 319, 319f, 320f

soft-patching 314–316, 315f

"soft side" cuts 131, 131f

software *see* computer programs

softwoods 135

SO insulation 303, 303f

solid wire 303, 303f, 305

solo/pre-fade listen buttons (mixing consoles) 381

sound: analog vs digital signals 372, 372f; decay (of a sound) 372, 390; direction 373; distance 373; dynamic range 382; high/low end sounds 381, 383; live sounds 368; loudness measurement 371, 371f; loudness war 372; pink noise 382; pitch 372; proscenium theatres 39; reverberation/echoes 370, 372, 381; sound deadening 244–245, 245f; sound frequencies 369–370, 370f; sound layering 392; sound production methods 368; sound qualities 372–373; sound waves 368–369, 368f–369f; timbre 372; underscoring 368; *see also* audio theory; digital audio files; playback; sound reinforcement

sound booths, proscenium theatres 39

sound cards 394–395

sound editing programs 387–388, 387f–388f; *see also* Audacity (sound editing software)

sound effects 368, 387, 388

Sound Forge Pro 387

sound reinforcement: amplification 382–383, 383f; cables and connectors 377 (⅛" jacks 378, 378f;

audio snakes 378, 378f; RCA connectors 378, 378f; XLR connectors 377, 377f, 378, 378f); equipment connections 374f; loudspeakers 383–385, 383f–384f; microphone design 374–375, 375f (carbon microphones 375; condenser microphones 375; dynamic microphones 375); microphone use (audio racks 377, 377f; diversity receivers 376–377, 376f; lavaliere microphones 376, 376f; omnidirectional/cardioid type 375; PCC (phase-coherent-cardioid) microphones 376, 376f; Shure microphones 375–376, 375f; wireless microphone frequencies 377); mixing consoles (analog vs digital 379–380; console layout 379f; delay 379; flying faders 380, 380f; foldback 379; gain knobs 380, 381f; input modules 380–381, 380f, 381f; layout 379f; mono vs stereo 378–381; pad buttons 380, 381f; PFL (pre-fade listen)/solo buttons 381); signal processing 381–382, 382f

soundscape 390

Source Four Par lamps 332–333, 334, 336, 337, 343, 360; lamp and "hot dog" 337f; lenses 333f; oval pattern changing 361f; *see also* PAR lamps/cans

South Eastern Theatre Conference (SETC) 7

spackle (joint compound) 173, 174f, 218

spade/paddle bits 105, 105f

Spansets 85, 85f, 86f; *see also* slings

speakers *see* loudspeakers

Speakon connectors 383, 383f

specialty curtain types: Austrian curtains 48–49, 49f; cyclorama (cyc) curtains 47, 47f; grand drape/main 48, 48f; oleo curtains 49, 49f; scrims 47–48, 47f; show drops 48, 48f

spectacle (proscenium theatres) 30

spectrum analysers 382

Speed Squares: definition and usage 95–96, 95f; hard flat construction 216; metal working 257

SPF lumber 135

spherical reflectors 328, 328f, 329, 329f

spike marks 46, 51, 51f, 167

spikes (nails) 146

spike tape 19, 167

spindles (or balusters) 222, 222f

split/opposite phase hookup 296

split ring washers 152–153, 152f

Spotlight *see* Vectorworks Spotlight

spot operators 12–16, 13f, 14f, 15f, 16f; *see also* electricians

spots: hard-edge spots 16f; sizes 14, 15f; truss spots 13f; *see also* ellipsoidal spotlights (Lekos); followspots; lamps/lights; photometrics

spot towers 9, 10f, 13, 14

Spray 77 adhesive 166, 166f

spreader plates 75, 75f

Spring Awakening (rock musical), sound reinforcement 368

spring clamps 102, 102f

sprinkler systems 42, 42f

spruce trees 135

square knots 65, 65f

squares: drywall squares 96, 96f, 218, 238, 238f; fast squares 96; framing squares 95, 95f, 229, 229f; magnetic squares 268; Speed Squares 95–96, 95f, 216, 257; T-squares 96, 118

square tubes 231, 231f, 250–251, 250f, 251f

square waves 313–314, 314f, 372

stadium seating 32, 32f

stage (proscenium theatres): fire safety 41–44; fly houses and lofts 41; traps 40–41

Stage Carpenter, The (Monroe H. Rosenfeld) viii

stage carpenters 8–9, 8f, 10, 45; see also deckhands

stage directions 18

stage doors 23f, 24

stagehands: apprentice stagehands 7; Broadway environment 5–6; clothes and equipment 6, 6f, 7f; college theatre students 7; depression era stagehands 68f; IATSE (union) 4; journeyman stagehands 7; pay rates 7; Teck Theatre (Buffalo) 3f

stage lifts see lifts

stage managers: AEA members 17, 17f; auditions 18; design meetings 18; duties 4, 6; first meeting with director 17; first read through 18–19; focusing lights 359; people skills 18; production meetings 19; rehearsal phase 20–21; rehearsals preparations 19–20; tech rehearsals 21–24

stage sets 30, 180f

stage weights, safety 76

stair gauges 229, 229f

stairs: different parts 220, 220f; escape stairs 221, 221f; planning 222–223, 222f–223f; stair terminology 222, 222f; steps (basics 220–221, 221f; building method 223–225, 223f–225f; construction 225–228, 225f–228f; cut lists 223, 223f, 224f, 225, 225f; helping hints 228; laminated layers 228, 230–231, 231f; section view 224, 224f; square tubes 231, 231f; stringer style 228–230, 228f–230f)

standard slot drives 150, 150f

standby/warn cues 22

standing parts (knots) 62, 62f

Stanislavsky, Constantine 34

staples/stapling: construction staplers 148, 209, 226; fabric staplers 149; fencing staples 149, 149f; flat construction 209–210, 209f; hard-covered flats 217–218, 217f; insulated staples 149, 149f; and plywood 148–149, 149f; pneumatic staplers 109–110, 109f, 110f; soft-covered flats 213; staple parts and sizes 148–149, 148f

static load 232

steel: carbide steel blades 115, 115f; channel steel 251, 251f; metal framing 249–252; mild steel 252, 260; recycling tip 251; Rockwell Scale (density/hardness) 115, 115f, 252; tool steel 115

steel cables: and chain motors 86, 86f, 87; steel cable eye 87f

steel pipes: aluminum vs steel 249–250; gauge system 251; Schedule 40 pipes 86, 87, 161, 251; Schedule 80 pipes 251; shapes and sizes 250f, 251–252, 251f–252f

steel tape 95, 95f

steel-wire ropes 87

steel wool 168, 168f

steep-angle cuts 269–270, 269f

stemmed casters 270, 270f

steps see stairs

stereo: ⅛″ jacks 378; amplifiers 383; label tracks (Audacity software) 390, 391, 391f, 392f; mixers 378–379

stick pricing 139

stiffeners: decking (legging) 240; flat construction 68 (backflap hinges 156, 156f)

stiles: definition 190; flat construction 201–202, 206, 206f–207f, 208; hard-covered flats 214–215; metal framing 257, 260, 269; soft-covered flats 190, 190f, 191–192, 193, 198; stock decking 233, 235, 236

stock companies 4

stock decking 233–235, 233f; coffin locks 233–234, 234f, 236, 236f; corner irons 236, 236f; frame assembling 235–236, 235f–236f; key hole 234f; notch markings 234, 235f; stiles 233, 235, 236

stock sceneries 4, 5

stop blocks 122, 122f, 123f

stops (Fresnel lights) 334

storage: curtains (folding 55–56, 55f; folding a leg 56f; hampers 55–56, 55f, 56f; west-coasting a scrim 56f); lamp racks 339, 339f

storefront theatres 3

stove bolts 152

straight claw hammers 100, 100f

strain relief 300

stranded wire 303, 303f, 305

Strand Lighting: channels and addresses 323; dimmers 311; "how to" videos 308; Lekos (ellipsoidal spotlights) 334, 343; Strand Light Palette 318, 319–320, 319f

strap hinges 154, 154f

straps (keystones) 205, 210f

Strasberg, Lee 34

Stratford Festival (Ontario) 33

stressed-skin panels 246–247, 246f–247f

stretchers (stair construction) 227, 227f

"stretching the goods" 53; see also goods (drops and drapes)

"string and pencil" method 96

stringer style stairs 228–230, 228f–230f

strip lights 337–338, 338f

Structural Design for the Stage (Holden and Sammler) 252
stud walls 243
Styrofoam 123, 143; *see also* extruded polystyrene
submasters (light boards) 317–318, 318f
subs (loudspeakers) 385
sun awning 28f
super (cyanoacrylate) glue 166
supertitles 402, 404
supplementary angles 124–125
supplies *see* hardware types
Surform (wood) rasps 143, 174
swag (hanging electrics) 356, 356f
swage fittings (Nicropress Sleeves) 159–160, 160f
swatch books (gels) 342–343, 342f
sweeps (framing pieces) 195–196, 195f
swinging/saloon door hinges 154–155, 154f
swivel (smart) casters 163–164, 163f
syndicates (theatre owners) 33

T

tab curtains 51–52, 51f, 52f
table saws: angle cuts 116, 116f; auxiliary tables 119, 119f; free handing and kickbacks 119; miter guides 117f, 118–119, 119f; push sticks 118, 118f; rip fence 116, 117, 117f; safety 117, 118, 119; table saw parts 116f
table work (rehearsals) 18
tack welds 267, 267f
tail-down lines 53–54
tails: connectors 300; knots 62, 62f
tang style blades 106, 106f, 107f
tape measures 94–95; blades 94, 94f; drafting method 183, 183f; electrics hanging 358f; hooks 94, 94f; markings 95f
tape out the set 19, 19f
tape recorders, reel-to-reel 386–387, 386f
tapes: duct tape 167, 344, 344f; electrical tape (vinyl) 19, 167, 357; floral tape 167–168; gaff (gaffer's) tape 19, 167, 167f, 358; glow tape 22, 167, 167f; Magic Mending (Scotch) tape 168; masking tape 167; painter's tape 167; spike tape 19, 167; steel tape 95, 95f; Teflon tape 167, 168f; *see also* tape measures
tapping screws 150, 150f
taps, metal frame leveling 268, 268f
tearout 114, 114f
tech (self-tapping) screws 151, 151f
technical directors 4, 183, 185
tech packages 349
tech rehearsals 21–24
tech tables 23, 357
tech week 23
Teck Theatre (Buffalo), stagehands 3f
teeth-per-inch (TPI) 129
Teflon tape 167, 168f

telegraphing (decking) 244
telescopic rifle sight 16, 16f
television: channels 314; color correction gels 343; gel color 340; hard-covered flats 190, 190f, 213; LCD technology 402; lighting 334; lighting (barn doors) 334; pixels 399; RCA connectors 378; resolution 403; sound effects 388; UHF television frequencies 377; wrap around cyclorama curtains 47
templates *see* gobos (templates/patterns)
template tables 205–206, 206f, 210
tenon and mortise technique 113, 113f
tensile strength 240, 241f
tension cable grids *see* cable grids
tension pulleys 50, 50f, 73
terminal lugs 300
terminals (circuits) 286, 287f
terminators 323
Tesla, Nikola 277–278
Textilene 169
theatre conferences 7
theatre jobs *see* jobs in theatre
Theatre of Pompey 28
theatre rigging: concept 68; counterweight system *see* counterweight rigging system; hemp system *see* hemp rigging system; running the show 78–80 (cue lights 79f, 79–80; cue sheets 79–80, 79f; flying a piece out 80; knuckle busters 80, 80f; marking linesets 79, 79f; marking trims 78–79, 78f); *see also* arena rigging; rigging
theatres in the round/arena theatres 31–32, 31f, 34
theatre syndicates (theatre owners) 33
theatre types: building types (black box theatres/flexible seating 32, 32f; Greek amphitheatres 25–27, 25f, 26f, 27f; proscenium theatres *see* proscenium theatres; Roman amphitheatres 26f, 27–28, 27f, 28f; theatres in the round/arena theatres 31–32, 31f, 34; thrust theatres *see* thrust theatres); organizational types (Broadway theatres *see* Broadway theatres; commercial theatres 4, 5, 6, 21, 24; community theatres 4; not-for-profit theatres 4, 5, 34; regional theatres 4, 7, 33; school theatres 5, 6; storefront theatres 3; university theatres 5, 351)
theatre work environments 4–7, 5f
thermoplastic adhesive (hot melt glue) 165
thimbles/eyes 87, 87f
T hinges 154
third octave equalizers 381–382, 382f
Thoroughly Modern Millie musical, supertitles 402
threaded rods 152, 152f
threads (screws and bolts) 149
threads-per-inch (TPI) 151–152, 151f
threefer cables 356f
three phase power 297–299, 297f–299f
three-quarters (followspots) 14, 15f

throw distance (video projectors) 403–404

thrust theatres: characteristics 30–31, 31f, 34–36; Dallas Theater Center 35f; Globe Theatre 31, 31f, 35; Guthrie Theatre 33, 33f; lighting 35–36; lighting positions 36f; modern interest in 33–34; "realistic interior" example 35f; vs Roman theatres 28; tension cable grids 36, 36f; unit sets 34, 34f; vomitoriums ("voms") 32, 35

thumbnail sketches see sketches

thyristor dimmers 309

tie lines: #4 black tie lines 61–62, 171, 357, 358f; grommeting 59, 59f; tie line spool 62f

TIG (tungsten inert gas) welders 250, 250f

tight-pin hinges 153

tiling (video projections) 399, 400

tilting (lights) 352, 359

timbre 372

timelines (editing programs) 387, 388f, 405–406

tinnitus 371

tips see green idea tips

tires (band saws) 130, 130f

titanium oxide 172

toggles: decking 235 (oddly shaped decking 238; stock decking 233); flats (flat construction 207–208, 207f–208f; hard-covered flats 216–217, 217f; soft-covered flats 190, 190f, 191, 192, 192f); metal framing 264

tools see electrical hand tools; hand tools; pneumatic hand tools; woodworking tools

tool steel 115

tooth washers 152–153, 152f

top hats (lighting) 334, 334f

torm booms 354

torque: battery-powered drills 103–104, 103f; torque washers 152, 152f

touring rigs (power distribution) 295f, 299

touring shows/companies: African American touring companies 4; bookings/origins from New York 33; Broadway shows and proscenium theatres 30; decks and coffin locks 236; dimmers and disconnect boxes 299–300; FOH positions/front-of-house 39; lighting packages 39–40; Socapex connectors 301; soft-covered flats and sill irons 216; theatre jobs 6; too large drops 53; towers and tab curtains 52; trailers (straps and load bars) 65; see also road houses

towers: fly towers/houses 30, 41, 41f; lighting towers 353f, 354; spot towers 9, 10f, 13, 14; and tab curtains 52

TPI (teeth-per-inch) 129

TPI (threads-per-inch) 151–152, 151f

tracking 316–317, 316f

tracking boards 319–320, 319f–320f

tracks see traveler tracks

Trackspot 320–321

trammel points 96–97, 97f, 239

transcoding 389, 406

transducers: human ear as 369f; loudspeakers 384; microphones 374

transformers 291–294, 292f–294f; alternating current 292; auto-transformers 309, 309f; center-tapped transformers 293, 293f; copper wire resistance table 294f; iron cores 291; power transmission 292f; primary/secondary coils 291, 292, 292f; schematic symbol 292f; transformer in residential area 293f; waveform effects 292f; see also power distribution

translucent vs transparent materials 399, 400f

transport controls (playback) 387

Transylvania University, Lucille Little Theatre 32f

traps (proscenium theatres) 40–41

traveler curtains 48; see also tab curtains

traveler tracks: carriers 49, 49f; channels 49; dead end pulleys 50–51; end stops 50; eyebolts 49f, 51; hanging clamps 49–50, 49f, 50f; lap splice 51, 51f; live end pulleys 50; master carriers 50, 50f; shop-built tension pulley base 50, 50f; spike marks 51, 51f; tab curtains 51–52, 51f, 52f; tension pulleys 50, 50f

traveling stage employee contracts (pink contracts) 5f, 6

treads: characteristics 220, 221, 221f, 222; stair building method 223, 223f, 224f, 225, 225f; stair construction 227–229, 230–231

trees: cambium layer 135–136, 135f, 136f, 137, 140; dead limbs 136, 136f; hardwoods vs softwoods 135; tree growth 135–136; trunk cross section 135f

trees (free-standing booms) 354

trim chains 72, 73f, 88, 157–158, 157f

trim heights 54, 95, 348, 358

trims 70, 78–79, 78f, 358, 358f

tripping 53–54, 54f

Trip to Bountiful 48

troubleshooting (electrical work) 304–305, 304f–305f, 306–307

trucker's hitches (snub and loop) 63, 65–66, 65f, 66f

trusses: box trusses 84, 84f, 352; delta trusses 84; metal framing 272–273, 272f–273f; see also slings

truss spots 13f

T-squares 96, 118

T-tracks 73, 74, 74f, 75, 75f, 78, 79

tube bending machines 270–271, 270f

tungsten carbide 115

tungsten filaments (light bulbs) 281–282, 281f

tungsten inert gas (TIG) welders 250, 250f

turnbuckles 158, 158f

TV see television

twist drill bits 105, 105f

twisted ropes 61

twist locks 301, 301f, 304

two-by (lumber) 137, 137f

twofer/threefer cables 356, 356f

two-pin lamp bases 327, 327f
two-scene preset boards 311–312, 311f

U

undercoats 172–173, 173f
under-hung rigging 41, 41f
underscoring 368
unions 4, 17; local union shops 6–7; *see also* Actor's Equity Association
United Scenic Artists (USA) 4, 17
unit sets 34, 34f
universal casters 164, 164f
Universal Colorants 172, 172f
Universal Tinting Colors 172
universes (DMX 512A protocol) 314, 314f, 322–323
university shows/theatres 5, 351; *see also* college theatre students
upstage 29
USA (United Scenic Artists) 4, 17

V

valences 48
vanishing point 29, 29f
variable-speed reversible drills 104
Vari-Light 320
Vectorworks 178
Vectorworks Spotlight: vs AutoCAD 185–186; complexity/popularity of program 348–349; key to instrumentation 351, 351f; layer options menu 349–350, 349f; lighting design template 349f; object info box 350, 350f, 351; resource browser 350, 350f; spotlight menu 350–351, 351f; workspace 349–351, 349f
vehicle (paint) 171, 171f
vela (awning system) 28
velour fabric: curtains 45, 56; qualities and usage 169; soft-covered flats 190, 210
veneers 140–141
venue 25
video projection: definition of video 402; *Grapes of Wrath* production example 398f; image creation/editing software 404–406, 404f–405f; playback (digital program types 406; Isadora 404, 405, 406, 407–408, 407f–408f; media servers 406; QLab 406–407, 406f; timelines 387; video file transcoding 389; Watchout 405, 406, 408–410, 408f–409f); projection designers 398, 404; projection methods (front projections 402; rear projections 399–402, 399f–401f; video walls 399, 399f); projector specifications (aspect ratios 403, 403f; contrast ratios 403; LCD and DLP technologies 402–403; lumens 403; resolution 403, 404; throw distance 403–404)
video walls 399, 399f
views (drafting) 178; *see also* plan views; section views
vinyl electrical tape 19, 167, 357

Vise Grip clamps 102, 102f, 122, 265, 266f
Vise Grip pliers 99, 99f
V-legs 241–242, 242f
V mark (crow's foot) 121–122, 121f
VOC (Volatile Organic Compounds) 165
voids (plywood) 141
voltage: 120/240 volt split phase system 296, 296f, 299; and amperes (amps) 281; and EMF 279, 279f; line voltage 295; Ohm's laws 282–283, 282f–283f; resistance in series 283–284, 283f–284f; voltage divider 284, 284f; voltage fluctuation (three-phase power) 297f; *see also* power distribution
VOM (volt-ohm-meters) 304–305, 305f, 306, 306f
vomitoriums ("voms") 31–32, 32f, 35
VU (Volume Units) meters 371, 371f
VW *see* Vectorworks; Vectorworks Spotlight

W

waist-shots (followspots) 14, 15f
walking up (ladders/spot towers) 9, 10f
wardrobe department 5, 6, 12, 20
warn/standby cues 22
warps (lumber) 139, 139f
washers 152–153, 152f
Watchout (software) 405, 406, 408–410, 408f–409f
water-based polyurethane 173
watts: definition 282; dimmer wattage 286, 311, 338; lamp wattage 44, 326, 327, 334, 338; Ohm's laws 282–283, 282f–283f; *see also* "pie" formula
WAV (Windows Audio File) 389, 390, 391, 392
wavelengths: audio theory 370, 370f; optics 340–343
webbing 57–58, 57f, 58f, 170
websites: sharing websites 388; social networking sites 18; theatre jobs 7
wedge monitors 379f
weights (bricks) 75–76, 75f; pipe weights 76
welding: in action 249f, 252f; face welds 262, 262f, 263, 263f; fillet welds 262, 262f, 263, 263f; puddled weld seams 254, 254f; tack welds 267, 267f; welding equipment (arc welders 252–253, 252f, 253f; Metal Inert Gas (MIG) welders 8, 252–253, 254–256, 254f–256f; oxyacetylene rigs 250, 250f; safety precautions 253, 253f, 254, 256; tungsten inert gas (TIG) welders 250, 250f; wire speed knobs 255, 256f; wire welders 254, 254f); welding jigs 260–261, 261f, 264, 267, 271–272, 271f; welding magnets 267; weld penetration 254, 255f; *see also* metal framing
wells (large beams) 86–87, 87f, 88
west-coasting 56, 56f
Westinghouse, George 278
wet cell batteries 279–280, 279f
wet tech rehearsals 21, 23
white contracts 6

white glue: as "dope" component 173; flat covering 211; as paint binder 172–173; white vs yellow glue 164–165

white pine: and c-clamps 101; curved platforms 239; defects 201; feet and inches exercise 198; soft-covered flats 192; vs yellow pine 135

Whole Hog boards 319

Wicked (musical), complementary colors 341

widescreen ratio (video projectors) 403

winches 69, 69f; motorized winch system 40

window flats 193–194, 193f–194f, 211, 214–216, 214f

Windows Audio File (WAV) 389, 390, 391, 392

Windows Media Player 393

Windows Movie Maker 405

wing and drop scenery 29, 29f, 46

wing nuts 152, 152f

wings, proscenium theatres 38

wireless microphone frequencies 377

wire rope/Crosby clamps 72, 159, 159f

wire speed knobs (welders) 255, 256f

wire welders 254, 254f

WLL (working load limit) 76–77

wood (Surform) rasps 143, 174

wood and building materials: building material unit 134f; definitions 134; lumber *see* lumber; materials sold in sheets (hardboard (Masonite) 142, 142f, 203, 244, 245; medium density fiberboard (MDF) 143; oriented-strand board (OSB) 142, 143f; particleboard 142–143); plastics (acrylic sheets 143; expanded polystyrene 143, 143f; extruded polystyrene 143, 143f); plywood *see* plywood; stick pricing 139; thickness sizes 142; trees and wood (hardwoods vs softwoods 135–136; tree growth 135, 135f, 136f); *see also* carpenters; cut lists; woodworking tools

wooden clamps 101, 101f

wood glue, application of 164–165, 164f–165f

woodworking: cuts (cross cuts 112, 112f; miter cuts 112, 112f; rip cuts 112, 112f; *see also* cut types); cutting angles 124–126, 124f–126f; cutting crown molding 126–129, 126f, 127f, 128f; feet/inches and fractions 196–201, 196f–201f, 208; joints (butt joints 112, 112f; covered joints 113, 113f; dado cuts 113, 113f; dovetail 113, 113f; half lap joints 112, 112f; lap joints 112, 112f; mortise and tenon 113, 113f; scab joints 113, 113f); ripping wood 111f, 112; *see also* carpenters; cut lists; wood and building materials; woodworking tools

woodworking tools: band saws *see* band saws; circular saws *see* circular saws; power miter saws *see* miter saws; radial arm saws *see* radial arm saws; sliding miter saws 124; table saws *see* table saws; woodworking hammers 100, 100f; *see also* carpenters; wood and building materials; woodworking

woofers 385

work (material being cut) 120

work environments 4–7, 5f

working limit (ropes) 61

working load limit (WLL) 76–77

working pieces 77, 78

work lights 21, 22, 41

woven/braided (ropes) 61

wrap 64

wrenches: box-end wrenches 98, 98f; Crescent/adjustable wrenches 10, 97, 97f, 355, 359; metric vs American SAE (Society of Automotive Engineers) 98; open-end wrenches 97, 97f; pipe (monkey) wrenches 99, 99f; socket wrenches 98, 98f

wye (Y) connections 297–298, 298f

X

Xenon lamps 12, 13f, 287, 402

XLR connectors 302, 302f, 323, 377, 377f, 378, 378f

Y

Y (wye) connections 297–298, 298f

yarns (twisted ropes) 61

yellow cards 6

yellow glue: set-in time 218; yellow vs white glues 164–165; *see also* aliphatic resin glue (carpenter's glue)

yellow pine: characteristics 135; plywood (grades 141, 141f, 203, 225; thickness sizes 142); tree farms 142, 203; *see also* plywood

yokes 352–353, 352f, 361–362; *see also* moving yoke lights

Z

Zap (cyanoacrylate/super glue) 166